REFLECTIONS
on Gifted Education

REFLECTIONS
on Gifted Education

Critical Works by
Joseph S. Renzulli
and Colleagues

Edited by Sally M. Reis, Ph.D.

PRUFROCK PRESS INC.
WACO, TEXAS

Dedication

To all of the innovative and dedicated teachers and administrators with whom we have had the opportunity to work over the decades and the many ideas they have contributed to the evolution of our work.

Library of Congress Cataloging-in-Publication Data

Renzulli, Joseph S., author.
 Reflections on gifted education : critical works by Joseph S. Renzulli and Colleagues / edited by Sally M. Reis, Ph.D.
    pages cm
  ISBN 978-1-61821-505-5 (pbk.)
 1. Gifted children--Education--United States. 2. Gifted children--United States--Identification. I. Reis, Sally M., editor. II. Title.
  LC3993.9.R459 2016
  371.95--dc23
                       2015029565

Copyright ©2016 Prufrock Press Inc.

Edited by Lacy Compton

Cover and layout design by Raquel Trevino

ISBN-13: 978-1-61821-505-5

No part of this book may be reproduced, translated, stored in a retrieval system, or transmitted, in any form or by any means, electronic, mechanical, photocopying, microfilming, recording, or otherwise, without written permission from the publisher.

Printed in the United States of America.

At the time of this book's publication, all facts and figures cited are the most current available. All telephone numbers, addresses, and websites URLs are accurate and active. All publications, organizations, websites, and other resources exist as described in the book, and all have been verified. The authors and Prufrock Press Inc. make no warranty or guarantee concerning the information and materials given out by organizations or content found at websites, and we are not responsible for any changes that occur after this book's publication. If you find an error, please contact Prufrock Press Inc.

Prufrock Press Inc.
P.O. Box 8813
Waco, TX 76714-8813
Phone: (800) 998-2208
Fax: (800) 240-0333
http://www.prufrock.com

Table of Contents

Preface — xi
An Introduction, Some Personal Stories From Some Very Special People, and a Reader's Guide
Sally M. Reis

PART I
A General Approach to the Study of Giftedness and Overview of Major Models

Chapter 1 — 3
Examining the Challenges and Caveats of Change in Gifted Education
Joseph S. Renzulli

Chapter 2 — 31
Reexamining the Role of Gifted Education and Talent Development for the 21st Century: A Four-Part Theoretical Approach
Joseph S. Renzulli

PART II
Conceptions and Identification of Giftedness

Chapter 3 — 55
The Three-Ring Conception of Giftedness: A Developmental Model for Promoting Creative Productivity
Joseph S. Renzulli

Chapter 4 — 91
Defensible and Doable: A Practical, Multiple-Criteria Gifted Program Identification System
Joseph S. Renzulli and Sally M. Reis

Chapter 5 — 129
Intelligences Outside the Normal Curve: Co-Cognitive Factors That Contribute to the Creation of Social Capital and Leadership Skills in Young People
Joseph S. Renzulli

Chapter 6 151
Assumptions Underlying the Identification of Gifted and Talented Students
Scott W. Brown, Joseph S. Renzulli, E. Jean Gubbins, Del Siegle, Wanli Zhang, and Ching-Hui Chen

PART III
Systems and Models for the Development of Giftedness and Talents

Chapter 7 173
A Theory of Blended Knowledge for the Development of Creative Productive Giftedness
Joseph S. Renzulli

Chapter 8 193
The Enrichment Triad Model: A Guide for Developing Defensible Programs for the Gifted and Talented
Joseph S. Renzulli

Chapter 9 211
The Multiple Menu Model for Developing Differentiated Curriculum
Joseph S. Renzulli

PART IV
Implementation Components and Strategies

Chapter 10 251
The Schoolwide Enrichment Model: A Focus on Student Strengths and Interests
Sally M. Reis and Joseph S. Renzulli

Chapter 11 271
Curriculum Compacting and Achievement Test Scores: What Does the Research Say?
Sally M. Reis, Karen L. Westberg, Jonna M. Kulikowich, and Jeanne H. Purcell

Chapter 12 285
A Time and a Place for Authentic Learning
Joseph S. Renzulli, Marcia Gentry, and Sally M. Reis

Chapter 13 — 295
Academies of Inquiry and Talent Development
Joseph S. Renzulli

Chapter 14 — 323
A Technology Based Program That Matches Enrichment Resources With Student Strengths
Joseph S. Renzulli and Sally M. Reis

Chapter 15 — 345
Savoring Reading Schoolwide
Sally M. Reis and Elizabeth A. Fogarty

Chapter 16 — 355
Nurturing Young Student Mathematicians
M. Katherine Gavin and Tutita M. Casa

PART V
Contemporary Issues, Challenges, and Commentary

Chapter 17 — 373
The Achievement Gap and the Educational Conspiracy Against Low-Income Children
Joseph S. Renzulli

Chapter 18 — 391
From High Potential to Gifted Performance: Encouraging Academically Talented Urban Students
Sally M. Reis and Miriam Morales-Taylor

Chapter 19 — 411
An Infusion-Based Approach to Enriching the Standards-Driven Curriculum
Joseph S. Renzulli and Nicole Waicunas

Chapter 20 — 429
Reversing Underachievement Through Enrichment
Joseph S. Renzulli, Susan M. Baum, Thomas P. Hébert, and Ken W. McCluskey

Chapter 21   443
Commentary on Contemporary Issues
Joseph S. Renzulli

Chapter 22   457
A Biographical Portrait of Joseph S. Renzulli: Scholar, Gifted Educator, and Visionary Leader
Thomas P. Hébert

About the Editor   475

PREFACE

An Introduction, Some Personal Stories From Some Very Special People, and a Reader's Guide

Sally M. Reis
University of Connecticut

If you don't know where you're going, you might wind up someplace else.
—Yogi Berra

Guiding readers through this book is both a privilege and pleasure. Organizing this volume of collected works by my husband and partner Joe Renzulli and the many colleagues whose work has been influenced by his ideas may appear, at first glance, to be an easy and even enjoyable task. However, it was more challenging than I originally thought, for Joe's work is voluminous, consisting of literally hundreds of articles, books, chapters, and research monographs. I was pretty sure that I knew his most important and wide-reaching ideas, but I did some checking of various citation indices to verify my hunches.

After reading his introductory chapter, however, I realized that although his research articles and reports are of course widely cited, the foundation that has guided his life's work has been the translation of his research findings into practical suggestions about identification and programming that work in classrooms. He constantly reminds his colleagues and graduate students that "teachers know most about what works in their classrooms." Impact points in academe are a function of citations by other researchers, but Joe has judged his own impact on the field by how many schools and teachers actually implement his many creative ideas. He often cites his proudest professional accomplishment as the pages and pages of charts, tables, statistics, and research designs that underlie his work that are widely available on the Neag Center for Gifted Education and Talented Development website (http://www.gifted.uconn.edu).

The idea behind this book has been to collect Joe's most important ideas in one place. These ideas have practical value for anyone seeking to implement what might can be described as a "brand" of gifted education and talent development that differs from traditional approaches in this field. The focus of this brand is not so much about how we group students and move them around as what we do with them in any organizational or administrative arrangement. And this brand is especially concerned with how we engage students in joyful learning rather than just what or how much we teach to them. Joe has always said that Enjoyment, Engagement, and Enthusiasm for Learning should be the goals of any special opportunities we provide to students.

One Personal Story

I met Joe soon after I moved back to my Connecticut hometown from Pittsburgh, PA. I had become interested in gifted and talented students as a result, like so many of my colleagues, of my work as an English teacher in a large public junior high school that served students in grades 7–9. I had the classic exposure to the need to know more about gifted education—an incredibly smart and turned-off student who had absolutely no interest in learning anything in my class and whose motivation was waning by the day. Reading about what to do with gifted students brought me to the work of James Gallagher and classes at the University of Pittsburgh in gifted education. Eventually, Jack Birch at the University of Pittsburgh recommended that when I returned to my home state of Connecticut, I contact a young guy at UConn named Joe Renzulli. I did just that and in 1976, Joe sent me a mimeographed copy of a two-part article he had written on the Enrichment Triad Model. This was my first exposure to his work and the ideas that would influence the rest of my professional and personal life.

As I had already taken a couple classes in this area, and had become interested in learning more, I asked him about additional classes at UConn and instead, he sent me to Southern Connecticut State University and Dr. Linda Smith who had begun teaching graduate classes there and needed more students. One of Joe's most endearing characteristics is the generosity with which

Introduction, Personal Stories, and Overview

he helps his former and current students. So rather than register for one of Joe's classes, I ended up enrolling in classes at Southern with Linda and within a year, I had talked three of my friends, all of whom were interested in gifted and talented students into joining me on my weekly trek to New Haven, CT. Peg Beecher, Mary Cianciolo, Sandy Turnquist Buckland, and I traveled together, stopping to eat well and laughing most of the way down to our classes. We were young, irreverent, and considered ourselves wildly creative teachers. It was in one of those classes that I met Joe, who was invited to give a guest lecture.

Joe and I have been best friends for a very long time. What I love most about him is his remarkable energy and passion for life—for his wife and children and family, as well as his work, ideas, cooking, love of travel, excitement in small victories, and for his constant quest to evolve. I also take pride in the joy he feels related to the outcomes of his successful work, as he loves seeing the many and diverse ways that students complete in-depth projects. He is passionate about the schools that use the Schoolwide Enrichment Model, and all of the administrators and teachers who seek a better way of engaging and enriching their students' experiences. He loves people who question authority, especially when that authority results in rigid and noncreative educational experiences for young people. Joe's ideas ignited my own—as a teacher of gifted students in my own hometown of Torrington, CT, then as a coordinator, and then as a researcher and his partner in work and life.

Joe became and remains an ardent supporter of educators who question the status quo and are not afraid to work and fight for change. He has always looked for and brought out the best in those with whom he works. His questions and quest for excellence have made my work stronger but at the end of more than three decades together, he is still my best friend and our marriage is strong and happy. What makes me proudest of him? So many things come to mind—his need to evolve and change and improve based on data and field testing; his passion for me and our family, his life, and his work, his ability to be steadfast and noble; his creativity and constant need for movement in a new direction; and perhaps, most of all, his intellectual curiosity. In this book, you will see the evolution of some of his ideas and also, some of the refinements that emerged because of his need to conduct research that became the cornerstone of his work. If his initial ideas are not practical or easy to implement by teachers, they are eventually discarded in favor of finding ones that can be more simply implemented in schools.

In the sections that follow, and as a tribute to Joe's work, you will hear from a few of our favorite collaborators and friends, including well-known scholars such as Robert Sternberg, Sandra Kaplan, and Carolyn Callahan. You will also hear from some of our colleagues at the Neag Center and former very successful graduate students (Del Siegle, Betsy McCoach, Jean Gubbins, and Sue Baum). You will also hear from one of our favorite deans of the Neag School of Education. I hope that these brief tributes, as well as a few stories about the ideas that guide Joe's work, will be a meaningful introduction to this volume, which he tells me will be his last book (but I am not sure that I really believe that). And so, to the love of my life, my greatest mentor and teacher, my wonderful, loyal, and creative husband, you are an inspiration and a source of pride and joy for me every day. After 30 years of marriage, I am still grateful to share both our personal life and work—your creativity and optimism enrich my life each day.

Some Personal Observations From Some Very Special People

Robert Sternberg, Cornell University

Joe Renzulli has had the career almost all of us academics, including myself, wish we had had. The field of gifted education has had many scholars to work in it, but how many to date truly have had *profound and lasting* impact? Really, I think there have been only two giants in the field—Lewis Terman and Joseph Renzulli. Terman's study, oddly enough, was not even well done, but it has had enormous impact on the field and countered stereotypes that gifted people are sickly, maladjusted, or just plain bizarre. In the field of the gifted, though, Terman was a one-shot deal. His main interests were elsewhere. Joseph Renzulli, in contrast, has presented us all with a career-long succession of ideas, many developed in collaboration with others and especially Sally Reis—the Three-Ring model, curriculum compacting, the Schoolwide Enrichment Model, the Houndstooth model—to name just a few. Had Joe's contributions been limited to scholarly ones, he would have been, just for those, the most eminent scholar ever in the field of gifted education. However, Joe has been unique in seeing more positive outreach and implementation of his ideas than any other scholar I can think of. His ideas combine scholarly integrity with practical applicability. Other scholars have seen their ideas implemented, but usually in limited ways and for short periods of time. And sometimes, the ideas that have been implemented were true flashes in the pan (such as the implementations of Guilford's ideas, which were based on a theory that was demonstrably false). In Joe's case, the implementations have spread because they are teachable to teachers, practical to implement, fun for students, and most of all, because they work. Had Joe's work been limited to his scholarly and outreach contributions, he would have been by far the greatest of contributors to the study of the gifted. But that's not all. His Confratute, run over three decades in collaboration with Sally Reis, has trained more skilled practitioners in the field of giftedness than any university ever has or could. So in all three domains of scholarly activity—research, outreach, and teaching—Joe has been at the top of the field. That's, well, ridiculous. Who else in any field could make that claim? I cannot wear a hat, because if I wore a hat I would have to take it off to Joe Renzulli, and it would always be off my head. Joe's contributions really are unique, in my view, in the world.

Susan Baum, Bridges Academy

It is an honor to be able to talk about the impact Joe's work has had on education and my work, specifically. I originally came to study at the University of Connecticut because of reading the Enrichment Triad Model (1977). This model talked about authentic learning where students are "practicing professionals" as they become problem solvers and creative producers. This model enabled me to understand how learning could be authentic and purposeful. Having a personal interest in students with gifts and talents who also were challenged by learning difficulties. I realized that here was a model that could allow children to learn and engage in creative productivity that aligned to their abilities instead of their being forever trapped by their disabilities. Over the years, as Joe expanded his basic idea in this seminal work to create the Schoolwide Enrichment Model and to promote the idea that schools should be about talent development rather than remediation, I have applied his ideas to make a difference in the lives of all children but especially those who we now call twice-exceptional.

Currently in my role of director of the 2e Center for Research and Development at Bridges Academy, a school for twice-exceptional students in Studio City, CA, I have been able to witness the power of talent development. We have instituted a strength-based, talent-focused program based on Joe's model. Not surprisingly, when these twice-exceptional students are engaged in talent development opportunities (TDO) such as enrichment clusters, we have found them to be more focused and productive as opposed to their behaviors during other kinds of learning. At times these TDOs are also therapeutic, especially when the students are feeling anxious and depressed due to their struggles with their learning differences. By offering them a break from their program and substituting an opportunity to explore their strengths, interests, and talents, they are able to refocus and regain their confidence. Focusing on what these exceptional students can do builds their hope and encouragement.

Interesting to me is that Joe's ongoing claim that schools should be about talent development is finally gaining recognition by forward thinking educators today. These innovators are embracing talent development and creative production. We see schools adopting "genius hour," creating makers' spaces, and advocating for authentic learning—the very same ideas that Joe has developed and promoted over the course of his career. Indeed, to me, Joe's ideas were truly visionary, paving the way for what education is becoming.

Carolyn Callahan, University of Virginia

When I first met Joe Renzulli, I was a young undergraduate student responding to a work-study posting to help analyze math test score data. Little did I know where that one interview would lead or who this man was who invited me into his world. Since taking what appeared to be a small step in my life, I have discovered over and over again that it was one of the most significant events in my career and in my personal life. I have come to appreciate and have benefitted in ways that cannot be counted from the unbounded generosity of a man who has offered me a model of what it means to be committed and passionate about education; to have a deep and abiding concern about students from every race, socioeconomic background, and gender; who respects teachers for what they do and believes in their ability to do so much more; who shares opportunities graciously and openly with students and colleagues; who is truly joyful when he can make the potential of a child come to fruition through educational experience; and who will fight tirelessly to ensure opportunity for his students, his colleagues, and most of all, for children with potential. Others will, I am sure, regale Joe for his intellectual and creative contributions. He deserves all of that praise that can come his way. But in his spirit, I hope this brief missive conveys the breadth of his personal character that makes him more just a theory developer, a researcher, or an author, but rather a distinguished educator and a truly good and noble human being.

E. Jean Gubbins, University of Connecticut

Your talent determines what you can do. Your motivation determines how much you are willing to do. Your attitude determines how well you do it.
—Lou Holtz

As a talent developer, Joe is one of a kind. I have read thousands of pages of books and articles written by Joe Renzulli. I have listened to hundreds of his presentations in venues in the United States and abroad. I have field-tested many of his ideas with students. Additionally, I have cotaught or copresented with him about his theoretical and practical systems and models that make a difference in how children and their teachers learn.

Over four decades, I have witnessed how Joe builds theories, conducts the requisite research, revises his ideas, and implements his models in schools. The typical research/practice divide does not exist as each step in creating the Enrichment Triad Model, the Revolving Door Identification Model, Schools for Talent Development, and Schoolwide Enrichment Model was a carefully thought out process in the "secret laboratory of his mind."

Joe writes and speaks about his ideas as they evolve and asks others for their perspectives. When he shares a draft about his new ideas, many of us view it as a final draft, as the words and messages are so finely tuned. Joe is the ultimate scholar, researcher, and writer. Academe has become his "playground" for designing ways to promote opportunities to learn at high levels.

Joe never settles for education as is. He always strives for what it could be. He asks the tough questions about our field of gifted education and talent development. When other researchers and scholars were "comfortable" with IQ as the way to confirm a child's designation as gifted, Joe turned to the research literature to find out what was known and not known. By raising legitimate and insightful questions, he wondered, "What Makes Giftedness?" This question opened up multiple pathways to teaching and learning.

Joe's obvious talent as a writer, his motivation to make a difference in the lives of students and their teachers, and his dedication are unstoppable. As a former graduate student and a current colleague, I can look at my bookcase containing many of his books or check my collection of articles and confirm that as a talent developer, Joe Renzulli is "one of a kind."

Del Siegle, University of Connecticut

Very few individuals produce work that challenges conventional wisdom and then changes the course of an entire field. Joe Renzulli is such an individual in gifted education. His Three-Ring Conception of Giftedness and his emphasis on the importance of talent development have left indelible marks. With his soulmate, Sally Reis, he has developed educational practices based on their Schoolwide Enrichment Model that encourage creative productivity and achievement excellence in young people.

Joe Renzulli's strengths are his creative innovation, knack for making ideas useful, and collaborative working style. Not only does Renzulli stand out for his innovative ideas, he also stands out for his ability to implement those ideas in practical ways that improve students' learning experiences. Through the entire process, he freely shares his ideas and encourages feedback from others.

My life has been enriched by his unwavering support and friendship. My work has been influenced by his resolve that students who participate in enjoyable and relevant learning experiences are more engaged and achieve more. Through our research, we have learned that students who find school meaningful are less likely to underachieve. We have also learned that making school meaningful can reverse underachievement. We have learned that the more knowledgeable and passionate teachers are, the better able they are able to share content in meaningful ways that motivate students. Others', and our work, validates what Joe Renzulli has been advocating for five decades: Enjoyment encourages engagement that results in both enthusiasm for learning and greater achievement.

Betsy McCoach, University of Connecticut

No single scholar in the last 50 years has had as profound an impact on the field of gifted education as Joe Renzulli. The Three-Ring Conception of Giftedness (1978) revolutionized the field of gifted education and ushered in an era marked by more inclusive approaches to gifted identification and services. This landmark paper also laid the groundwork for most current conceptions of talent development and differentiation. My own work (with Peters, Matthews, and McBee) on an "advanced academics" approach to service delivery rests squarely on the shoulders of Joe Renzulli (a point that I made repeatedly to my coauthors as we were writing the book). I am proud to have studied under Joe Renzulli, and I am incredibly fortunate to now be his colleague and his friend. But this familiarity with Joe does not diminish the awe that I feel for one of our field's greatest thinkers and leaders.

Sandra Kaplan, University of Southern California

There are people who ignite your own interests and abilities. There are people whose ideas provide the foundation to affirm your own ideas and give them greater credibility. There are people whose creativity serves as the fodder for your own creative expressions. There are people whose recognition of your work is the catalyst for the recognition you have received from others. The contributions of these people provide both the formal and causal encounters that significantly affect your own productivity. Joseph Renzulli has been that person for me. Whether it was at a Curriculum Council meeting in Washington, a conversation in the living room of a home in Tehran, an ideational disagreement while eating spaghetti at a conference-scheduled dinner party, or a quiet sharing of "what's next in gifted" during a brief encounter at

Confratute, these academic interactions with Joseph Renzulli have been and still remain the basis of much of my own productivity. His large and profound body of work has been and continues to be the impetus for the work of others. I, like many professionals, have been fortunate and have relished the opportunity to reap the benefits of Joseph Renzulli's profound and significant work in the field of gifted education.

Richard Schwab, Dean of the Neag School of Education

Ask any teacher of gifted and talented students in the world who the most influential scholar in their field is and most likely the name will be Joe Renzulli. In my travels around the globe—from Qatar to California—when educators find out I am from the University of Connecticut, the conversation often turns to our reputation as a world center for gifted education. The conversation centers not only on Joe's work in gifted education, but also his long-standing impact as an educational reformer. Over the course of more than 50 years of scholarship, advocacy, and program building, Joe has transformed the way we think about developing the talents and gifts of all children—not only those considered gifted.

When I met Joe 40 years ago as a graduate student, he was already established as an international scholar. Over the past four decades, his research, grant, and publication productivity have continued to grow exponentially. Joe remains a highly respected scholar and educational reformer, impacting classrooms worldwide. His enduring success stems from the fact that, in addition to being an active researcher, he is also an extremely effective leader.

Great leaders share the following attributes: First, they must have something important to say. Joe is a brilliant researcher, thinker, and prolific writer who can back what he advocates with defensible data. Second, having something to say is only as meaningful as the ability to communicate one's thinking. Joe's writing, as well as his public speaking, resonates with academics, practitioners, parents, and policymakers alike. Third, a great leader works with others to expand their thinking while helping them to grow as individuals. Joe brings a spirit of collaboration that draws out the gifts and talents of all who work with him by practicing what he preaches about how people learn and grow. Over the years, Joe and his colleagues at the Neag Center for Gifted Education and Talent Development, as well as around the globe, have not only furthered his ideas, but also created and developed their own work in this area, which is recognized worldwide. A prime example of this is the work that Sally Reis has generated over the years. Together, Joe and Sally have created and tested such transformative models of reform as the School Enrichment Model. At the same time, Sally's efforts in educating young women have established her internationally among the most recognized leading scholars in the education of girls.

And yet Joe possesses one more trait that not all great leaders share—a trait that has sustained his working relationships with eminent scholars, and educational leaders to teachers. Joe is a caring, loyal, and compassionate person who cares deeply about social justice for all.

Joe's work has thrived through multiple rounds of reform movements—from open classrooms and repeated back-to-basics movements to, more recently, the high-stakes testing and accountability era. His work persists because it is research-based, logical, and meaningful; it embodies what we would like all of our children to experience in their own education—a sense of joy in learning and creating new knowledge. Joe Renzulli will undoubtedly be renowned as one of history's most distinguished educational reformers—among the likes of John Dewey and Maria Montessori—and his influence is sure to endure well into the future.

Overview of the Book

This book is a compilation of the essential, most critical works and ideas Joe has contributed to the field of gifted education. As a result, although we sought to reprint as many articles as possible here, we have decided in a few cases to include updates or adaptations to previous works that are "classic pieces." On an editorial note, you'll find that we also made a decision to standardize the punctuation and capitalization of the various theories and models Joe has developed over his distinguished career. Additionally, where needed, we have updated reference listings to follow consistent APA style and replaced outdated links. Finally, we have removed items specific to the style of the journals or publications in which the articles were first printed, such as keyword listings, abstracts, and funding notes. We hope these small editorial changes help the reader navigate through the works with ease.

In **Chapter 1: Examining the Challenges and Caveats of Change in Gifted Education**, Joe summarizes "where he is coming from" regarding the always challenging process of educational change, how one goes about introducing new ideas to the field of gifted education, as well as dealing with the inevitable criticism that usually follows new ideas, setting the stage for chapters to follow.

A discussion of some new research in the field, as well as the changing policies and practices in both general and gifted education is presented in **Chapter 2: Reexamining the Role of Gifted Education and Talent Development for** the 21st Century: A Four-Part Theoretical Approach**. Joe also synthesizes some opportunities he has had to examine the consequences of school-based applications of his work. These opportunities always resulted in both reflection and the search for answers to questions about what can be done to improve the services to the teachers and students we serve by summarizing four subtheories developed over approximately five decades. Although Joe's early work on the Three-Ring Conception of Giftedness and the Enrichment Triad Model gained more attention than expected, he began to believe that there were still characteristics and programming opportunities that needed to be added to the overall search for factors that contribute to total talent development.

The original article on The Three-Ring Conception of Giftedness appeared in a 1978 edition of *Phi Delta Kappan*. Although it was originally rejected by all of the major journals in gifted education, this article has now become the most widely cited article in our field. Over the years, Joe has updated the article to include new research and changes in identification and programming that have taken place in the field. The original article and subsequent follow-ups have been cited more than 3,000 times in national and international journals. The most important point in the chapter is the need for differentiated provisions for both high-achieving students and the development of what Joe has described as creative productive giftedness. **Chapter 3: The Three-Ring Conception of Giftedness: A Developmental Model for Promoting Creative Productivity** reprints the most recent update of the most cited work in our field.

In **Chapter 4: Defensible and Doable: A Practical, Multiple-Criteria Gifted Program Identification System**, we discuss a number of considerations that *must* be taken into account when designing an identification system for a school, district, or state. Our step-by-step identification system is based on the Three-Ring Conception of Giftedness and designed for programs that focus on creative productive giftedness, as delineated in the Enrichment Triad Model. The identification system does, of course, provide a major pathway for all very high-achieving students but it also "opens the door" for participation by students who show potential for high performance and creative productivity using one or more nontest criteria that may not be adequately assessed by cognitive ability or achievement tests.

In the early 1970s, when Joe began work on the Three-Ring Conception of Giftedness, he embedded the rings in a houndstooth background that represented the interaction between personality and environment. In recent years, further research and theory development coupled with a growing concern in the field related to social and emotional development has led to a new dimension of his work on characteristics of the six co-cognitive factors that are discussed in **Chapter 5: Intelligences Outside the Normal Curve: Co-Cognitive**

Factors That Contribute to the Creation of Social Capital and Leadership Skills in Young People. Co-cognitive factors interact with and enhance cognitive traits that are ordinarily associated with the development of both high achievement and creative productive manifestations of giftedness. A discussion of social capital is also offered in the chapter, focusing on intangible assets that address the collective needs and problems of other individuals and our communities at large. Investments in social capital benefit our society as a whole because they help to create the values, norms, networks, and social trust that facilitate coordination and cooperation geared toward the greater public good.

Chapter 6: Assumptions Underlying the Identification of Gifted and Talented Students summarizes a research study that investigated teachers' perceptions about changes in conceptions of giftedness and the types of information that should be used in the identification process. Strong agreement was found among classroom teachers, gifted education teachers, administrators, and consultants (experts in the field and state directors) from urban, suburban, and rural districts that supported a more liberal conception of giftedness. Overall, respondents also disagreed with a test-score approach to identification of these students, supporting broader approaches to identification based on individual expression, ongoing assessment, and context information. Furthermore, they strongly agreed with the importance of using multiple criteria for the identification of gifted and talented children.

Chapter 7: A Theory of Blended Knowledge for the Development of Creative Productive Giftedness sets the stage for a better understanding of the chapters that follow in this section, pointing out that epistemology, or the study of knowledge creation, was a topic examined by ancient philosophers and continues to be reflected in modern educational templates for learning, such as Bloom's Taxonomy of Educational Objectives. Joe's quest to understand different levels of knowledge helped him to better recognize the argument he makes about the importance of focusing special programs on creative and productive giftedness. It reflects his growing fascination with the importance technology is now playing for learners of all ages and the accessibility to the wide world of knowledge that young people now have through the Internet. Joe proposes and examines three levels of knowledge in this chapter and the importance of blending them together.

The Enrichment Triad Model was developed in the mid 1970s in conjunction with the Three-Ring Conception of Giftedness discussed in Chapter 3 of this book. This model is essentially a learning theory and was primarily developed to serve as a practical guide for promoting creative productive giftedness. Both the Triad and the Three-Ring Conception of Giftedness were greeted with skepticism by the gifted education community because they challenged prevailing trends about the conception of giftedness, a focus on advanced lesson learning approaches to developing giftedness, and the belief that higher level thinking skills were the exclusive province of gifted students only. The Three-Ring and Triad models grew in popularity over the years. **Chapter 8: The Enrichment Triad Model: A Guide for Developing Defensible Programs for the Gifted and Talented** is an updated version of the original work on Triad and a compilation of the original theory plus various conceptual and practical additions that have been added over the years. The chapter serves as an overview rather than as a practical guide for implementation.

Joe designed the Multiple Menu Model, described in **Chapter 9: The Multiple Menu Model for Developing Differentiated Curriculum**, to enable teachers and students taking his curriculum development course to develop high-quality curriculum, emphasizing that it must integrate characteristics about knowledge, as well as the variety of instructional strategies with which most teachers of the gifted are familiar. The part of the Multiple Menu Model that has resonated with most curriculum developers and teachers of advanced students is the Artistic Modification Menu. This menu invites teachers to embed their own personal interests and experiences related to a selected topic into the curriculum. Most prescribed curriculum doesn't encourage teacher modifications, and this approach extends an invitation to teachers to personalize a topic, leading to more exciting and engaging experiences for their students.

Most of the work that we have completed over the last four decades has been devoted to research and development on identification practices and teaching strategies for promoting gifted behaviors. Over the years we realized that many students, in addition to those formally identified as gifted, would benefit from school experiences that are more enriching, engaging, and challenging. We also realized that in order to make changes in *entire* schools we needed to pay some attention to an organizational plan or model for the delivery of these strategies. We also learned that the professional development that was guided by our theories and research made a difference not just for gifted students but for all students—it is from this realization that the Schoolwide Enrichment Model (SEM) emerged. The SEM applies the pedagogy of gifted education to total talent development of all students. The number of SEM schools has grown over the years and **Chapter 10: The Schoolwide Enrichment Model: A Focus on Student Strengths and Interests** summarizes almost four decades of our work.

Although the focus of Joe's work has been on strategies for the development of creative productive giftedness, any plan for total talent development must also include a curriculum acceleration component that differentiates curriculum and instruction for traditionally high-achieving students. After experimenting with a few approaches, a systematic process for differentiation called *curriculum compacting*, described in **Chapter 11: Curriculum Compacting and Achievement Test Scores: What Does the Research Say?**, was developed and subsequently researched. It is now one of the most widely used and researched forms of differentiation for high-achieving and gifted and talented students.

In order to provide general enrichment opportunities for all students and simultaneously ensure that opportunities for more advanced work are available for highly able and motivated students, Joe developed a concept in the 1980s called *enrichment clusters*. This component of the Schoolwide Enrichment Model has become "the growth stock" of our implementation recommendations, and we recommend that schools begin their total talent development programs with this part of our work. Teachers who have conducted successful enrichment clusters learned to use a good deal of gifted education pedagogy and follow-up studies indicated that they were able to integrate many of the strategies used in the cluster to their regular classroom teaching. We published this work, reprinted here as **Chapter 12: A Time and a Place for Authentic Learning**, in a general education journal because our target audience for this component of our work is all schools, teachers, and students.

As the middle school "movement" began to flourish in the 1980s, several SEM schools implementing enrichment clusters asked about ways to organize their schools to capitalize on student interests and to use the pedagogy recommended in the Enrichment Triad Model. This interest resulted in the material presented in **Chapter 13: Academies of Inquiry and Talent Development**, which was originally published as a two-part series in the *Middle School Journal*. The chapter points out the ways in which a middle or high school can offer several theme-based academies within in a single school and how such academies can place a major focus on creative productivity rather than accelerated lesson learning.

One of the challenges we face in promoting the pedagogy that is based on the SEM is the almost unreasonable amount of time necessary for teachers to carry out the type of enrichment learning we advocate. **Chapter 14: A Technology-Based Program That Matches Enrichment Resources With Student Strengths** describes the program that Joe and Sally developed called the Renzulli Learning System (RLS). The system was subsequently sold by UConn to Compass Learning and is now marketed under the name of GoQuest. Renzulli Learning showed positive results in promoting improvements in student achievement and a qualitative study reported the effectiveness of the RLS as a tool for increasing achievement, engaging quality, and creating independence. Schools that do not have access to GoQuest can create profiles using print versions of our strength-based instruments and no-cost search engines that are readily available on the Internet.

The Schoolwide Enrichment Model in Reading (SEM-R) is an outgrowth of the SEM. It is a reading enrichment approach that has been shown to be effective in increasing elementary and middle school students' reading achievement and attitudes toward reading. The SEM-R provides enriched reading experiences by exposing students to books in their areas of interest, daily supported independent reading of challenging self-selected books using differentiated reading instruction, and interest-based choice opportunities in reading. In keeping with our emphasis in this book on reaching a wider range of practitioner audiences, we have selected an article that appeared in *Educational Leadership* (reprinted here as **Chapter 15: Savoring Reading Schoolwide**). Additional articles on this topic are summarized on the SEM-R website (http://www.gifted.uconn.edu/semr).

Joe's work has also influenced many of our colleagues. Kathy Gavin worked with a team of colleagues for years to develop math materials for talented students that are based on coherent and rigorous development of advanced concepts. She and her colleagues created a series of units for mathematically promising students in grades K–6 under grants sponsored by the U.S. Department of Education (Javits Grant) and the National Science Foundation, discussed here in **Chapter 16: Nurturing Young Student Mathematicians**. Based on the pedagogy set forth in the Enrichment Triad Model and the Multiple Menu Model, these materials foster in-depth understanding of advanced mathematical concepts by challenging and motivating students to discuss and solve high-level problems in a fashion similar to practicing mathematicians. They are currently being used to meet the needs of talented elementary students in all 50 states and in several other countries including Singapore and Hong Kong.

One of the biggest challenges facing the field of gifted education is the underrepresentation of low-income and minority students participating in special programs and services. **Chapter 17: The Achievement Gap and the Educational Conspiracy Against Low-Income Children** summarizes work that Joe completed over the past several years to address underrepresentation of these students in gifted programs and to make suggestions for ameliorating this problem. This chapter and the one that follows examine both the reasons for underrepresentation and one approach that has made a significant difference in the lives of high-potential/low-income students from a major urban area.

In the last decade or so, we have seen a remarkable increase in the number of schools that use the SEM as a schoolwide theme. Some of these schools are named Renzulli Academies and integrate much of the work described in this book. In **Chapter 18: From High Potential to Gifted Performance:**

Encouraging Academically Talented Urban Students, we describe an urban school called the Renzulli Academy. In the academy described in this chapter, a group of teachers who were well trained in the Schoolwide Enrichment Model, a supportive principal and central office administrators who were knowledgeable about and committed to this learning model, and a selected group of high-potential students and parents who understood the SEM helped to create an incredibly successful school!

The emergence of standards in individual states and the new Common Core State Standards, coupled with the almost overpowering influence of standardized testing, has had the effect of squeezing highly engaging enrichment activities out of the curriculum. Many teachers have become so accustomed to requirements for "teaching-the-text" and overusing worksheets to grind up standardized test scores that they no longer have the opportunity or, in some cases, the know-how to deviate from prescribed material. **Chapter 19: An Infusion-Based Approach to Enriching the Standards-Driven Curriculum** presents a strategy that teachers can use for achieving some balance between the required curriculum and a way of infusing enrichment activities into standards-driven material. Some examples of exciting ideas developed by teachers are provided to illustrate how the technique has been used to infuse enrichment in all content areas.

The vast majority of letters, phone calls, and e-mails that we collectively have received over the years at our center are made by parents of high-ability students who are underachieving. Although a great deal has been written about the underachievement dilemma, there has been surprisingly little research upon which to make recommendations about turning around underachievement. **Chapter 20: Reversing Underachievement Through Enrichment** describes one of the few intervention studies conducted on underachievement, using Renzulli's Type III enrichment, as the basis for how teachers can reduce underachievement.

Joe has written a number of short pieces for the Commentary section of *Education Week,* the nation's most widely read education newspaper, particularly by education leaders and administrators. The purpose was to promote advocacy about issues that are important to the field of gifted education by bringing them to the attention of leaders who are more likely to have decision-making power over program and service opportunities in their schools. **Chapter 21: Commentary on Contemporary Issues** includes four of my favorite commentaries.

I believe, as a lover of biographies and autobiographies, that personal narratives describing some of his life's experiences will enable the readers of this book to better understand what caused Joe to arrive at the recommendations he has contributed to the field for almost half a century. Our dear friend and former graduate student, Tom Hébert, graciously agreed to contribute **Chapter 22: A Biographical Portrait of Joseph S. Renzulli: Scholar, Gifted Education, and Visionary Leader**, based on some in-depth interviews with Joe about his related family experiences that he had previously written for another book. I thought it would be a perfect way to point out how everything that we experience in our background contributes to how what we believe and what we do make our beliefs have an impact on teachers and students—those who have always been highest on Joe's impact list.

PART I

A General Approach to the Study of Giftedness and Overview of Major Models

CHAPTER 1

Examining the Challenges and Caveats of Change in Gifted Education

Joseph S. Renzulli
University of Connecticut

Conflicts between incompatible, staunchly held, sincere beliefs make up what we may call the little wars of science, little wars which, except for size and consequences differ in pattern no whit from the big wars between nations.
—Edwin G. Boring, *History, Psychology, and Science*

Introduction From Joe

Changing beliefs, practices, and policy in any field are always a challenge. You need only look at the biographical accounts of people in all fields of human endeavor who have tried to make changes to understand how professionally risky even mild recommendations for changing the *status quo* can be. The "little wars" that Boring mentions in the above quote are necessary for our field to grow, but the value of change must go beyond conflicting papers, competing theories, and passionate seminar debates. The real payoff of any new idea is how it affects the practices that take place in the classrooms and programs that serve the young people who are the object of our work in gifted education. It is easy to criticize an idea or theory, but practical applications yield data that are subject to a wide range of evaluative criteria that go beyond unverified speculation. The proof of the pudding is in the eating, and therefore we have tried to include in this book as much practical information as is possible.

Although my collective work is best known for the systems and models for change that my colleagues and I have developed over the years, an equal and perhaps even greater focus has been devoted to how practical materials, strategies, and professional development interact with research-based findings to bring about the change processes. This chapter describes "where I'm coming from" so far as the always-challenging process of change is concerned, how one goes about introducing new ideas in the field of gifted education, and dealing with the inevitable criticism that usually accompanies new ideas, particularly those that challenge the services that traditionally have been provided in gifted education programs. This chapter hopefully will set the stage for the chapters that follow.

My former advisor and I got together over a bottle of bourbon for late-night discussions at almost every conference following the completion of my doctoral degree at the University Virginia in 1966. Dr. Virgil S. Ward was the most respected and best-known theorist in the field at the time and as the years went by and my work started to gain some attention, he would always ask, "How do you account for the *popularity* of your work?" Implicit in his inquiry was that "popularity" was not necessarily a good thing if the work was not "theoretically based" and he was fond of citing many other "trendy" educational programs that did not have what he called "a strong underlying theory."

Many others have asked the same question over the years. Although there is no easy answer to the question about popularity, an oversimplification might be that I believe practice should drive theory development rather than the other way around and that research should be a part of an ongoing process directed toward theory development. The Practice-Research-Theory Cycle depicted in Figure 1.1 is an approach that has worked for me because the ultimate consumer or end-user of my work has been the education practitioner and ultimately, students in school learning situations. When all is said and done, most of my approach to change is based on the belief that *teachers know* the most about what will work in classrooms. Like all academicians, however, there is a need to gain respect among the scholarly community and administrators who always raise the question, "Where is the research?" If my work has achieved "popularity" beyond the common sense that it makes to teachers, it is also because there are volumes of easily accessible research studies underlying the approaches I have recommended.

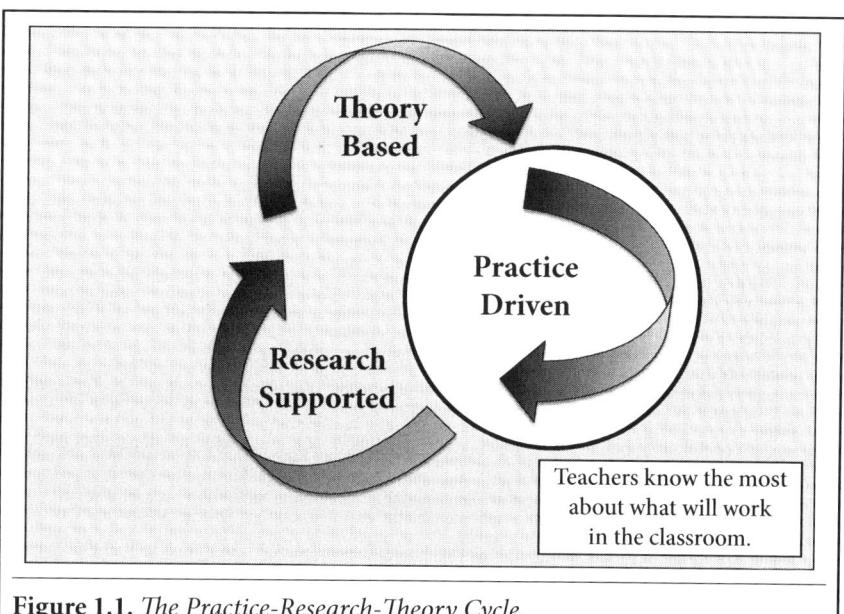

Figure 1.1. *The Practice-Research-Theory Cycle.*

However, the number of articles in refereed journals or presentations at prestigious research conferences, while important for academic respectability, are only important to me as part of the Practice-Research-Theory Cycle for making changes in schools and classrooms. Thus, for example, when I argue in the Three-Ring Conception of Giftedness theory that "task commitment" based on strong interests is an essential part of developing high-level talent, the pragmatism that is an equally important part of my way of thinking led to years of research development on a series of instruments called Interest-A-Lyzers.

Although I have contributed some major theories (or models) to the field, all of the theories had their origins in firsthand experiences from my years in the classroom and the countless brilliant teaching practices that I have observed over the years on the parts of persons with whom I have had the opportunity to work. These practices usually resulted in one or more research studies to provide the empirical support that is necessary in the evidence-base orientation so pervasive in fulfilling the criteria for academic credibility. The research enabled us to advocate or make suggestions for practice and additional research, ultimately leading to the formulation or reexamination of a theory (or model) that would both guide practice and generate further research.

If I were to come back in another life, I would like to spend a majority of my time studying the elusive process of change. How does any idea become popular, gain academic respectability and sustainability over an extended period of time, and produce verifiable results in planned learning situations?

What influences do personalities, politics, and purse strings have in the change process? How do the sights, sounds, and smells of real classrooms figure into the change process and how do teachers' ways of knowing impact their acceptance of a change initiative? And how does one respond to critics or questions about the relationship of our work with competing theories or guides for gifted student identification and program development? How should one respond to an article entitled, *Renzulli-itis—A National Disease in Gifted Education* (Jellen, 1983)? These last two questions reflect what E. G. Boring referred to in the above quote as the "little wars of science" and they have made my work interesting, challenging, and even fun. Even the severest criticism has provided an opportunity to reflect and examine the ways to make our work better. Openness to critique, criticism, and challenge undoubtedly threaten one's self-concept, but it also gives rise to the self-efficacy necessary for the courage to move forward.

The Challenges of Change

The real difficulty in changing the course of any enterprise lies not in developing new ideas but in escaping old ones.
—John Maynard Keynes, English economist (1883–1946)

The Practice-Research-Theory Cycle is all about the process of change: policy change, organizational change, and perhaps most importantly, change in the attitudes and behaviors of practitioners directly responsible for implementing a theory-driven method that differs from current practice. If policy adoption, organizational sponsorship, and practitioner support are all present, change is likely to take place more smoothly than if one element is missing. In popular parlance, both "top-down" and "bottom-up" approaches are most effective in bringing about any kind of social, political, or educational change Purely top-down change, whether or not it is theory driven or research supported, will not achieve prolonged implementation if the power elite dictating particular changes in a school or district do not win the "minds and hearts" of teachers and principals. The main strategy for winning the minds and hearts of leaders and practitioners, and for bringing about the sustained implementation of new ideas is persuasion.

Persuasion, a *prima facie* form of salesmanship, is dependent upon effective communication, which in turn is a function of the exchange of *relevant* information between and among particular constituencies. Organizations such as school districts and state departments of education are concerned with issues such as research support, tangible benefits at low costs, minimal disruption of existing routines, how the change fits in with already adopted initiatives, and political considerations related to equity, public relations, and popular support.

Practitioners (e.g., teachers, principals, school psychologists) on the other hand, are more concerned with how the proposed change will affect their day-to-day work and how much time and new knowledge will be required to implement a new initiative. Practitioners, however, also have informal "theories" and beliefs about the best ways to provide educational services, and in this regard they may be a more sophisticated and demanding audience than policy makers or organization managers. Practitioners always care about whether a proposed change makes sense in terms of what they believe, how much work will be involved, and what the best ways are to accomplish a particular objective.

These differences in the target populations for persuasive activity mean that strategies for change, and especially the genre of communication, must be carefully crafted to meet the needs of various audiences. An article or workshop for teachers, for example, should include some practical theory conveyed through clearly illustrative examples that answer questions about why they should consider a proposed change. And some information about research results, based on data from schools that resemble the workplace of teachers (rather than laboratory experiments with college sophomores), is also useful in helping them to reach conclusions about adopting a particular strategy. But the essence of persuasive communication for teachers should mainly address concerns about what is expected from them in bringing about a proposed change, how these expectations relate to their own beliefs and daily activities, and what practical materials and strategies can be provided that will make their implementation easier.

Approaches to Promoting Change

All theorists are promoters and proselytizers, but most theorists leave practical applications to others. This orientation is especially prevalent among psychologists, even if they believe that their work has applications in practical education settings: "Here is my brilliant idea —I leave its implementation to you educators" (condescension sometimes implied). Because education is my major affiliation for both theoretical and applied work, and having an impact in schools a major professional goal, one of the characteristics of my work is that it has proceeded simultaneously along both theoretical and practical lines. For better or worse, I have never been content with developing theoretical concepts without devoting equal or even greater attention to creating instruments, procedures, staff development strategies, or instructional materials for implementing the various concepts. This approach has both advantages and disadvantages! An eye toward implementation enables theory testing in practical settings—the kinds of places for which the work was intended and where the uncertainty of personalities, politics, and variations among schools and populations allow examination of impact in the so-called real world. The disadvantage is, of course, less than rigorous experimental control and thus the susceptibility to design-related criticisms.

A second advantage of pursuing a Practice-Research-Theory Cycle is that it has enabled me to stay in touch with what happens in real schools and classrooms and the practical and political challenges of people working in them. Theory in an applied field doesn't have much value if it is not compatible with real-world conditions, such as how schools work, teachers' ways of knowing, or the politics of "innovation." People or committees who haven't worked in a classroom for a long time (if ever) make far too many education policy decisions! As Dwight D. Eisenhower noted, "Farming looks mighty easy when your plow is a pencil, and you're a thousand miles from a cornfield." Our main concern has been practices that can reasonably expect to endure *beyond* the support usually accorded to pilot or experimental studies or the guiding influence of a patron saint that originated or shepherded the program in its initial implementation. Some of my greatest disappointments have been to see excellent services developed as part of a research study, but lack sustainability when the research project is concluded or to see a great program implode when a patron saint or knowledgeable and committed leader leaves the program. It is for this reason that we have built teacher leadership components into our staff development services and program monitoring devices that we call "friendly validation." The opportunity to generate research data can lend credence to the theory and point out directions where additional work needs to be done in both theory development and, perhaps even more importantly, in fitting theory-guided practices into the complexity of diverse school settings. In fact, the evolution of my work over the years is a direct result of these realities, for it is from direct experience that my ideas have taken new directions.

A third advantage of a Practice-Research-Theory approach is that it has afforded me the opportunity to collaborate with exceptionally talented practitioners, many of whom have expanded both the theoretical and practical dimensions of the ideas and suggested further needed research to enhance understanding, application, and credibility. One of the main lessons learned from my practice to theory approach is that the best ways to bridge the frequently lamented theory-into-practice gap is for the ivory tower people and the people in the trenches *to listen to one another.* And good listening means paying attention to what is not said as well as that which is spoken.

The negative side of a combined Practice-Research-Theory approach is the vulnerability of partially or poorly implemented practices. In most cases, it is the implementation rather than the theory that is the object of scrutiny. When I visit classrooms, for example, in which every student has produced cookie cutter copies of the same project while simultaneously claiming that these projects are examples of what I have defined as Type III Enrichment (i.e., individual and small-group investigations of real problems), it reminds me of the quote about the shadow that falls between the idea and the reality. Nevertheless, even negative experiences have value. Mainly, they point out that the originator of the theory has not engineered the proper conditions for implementation, communicated effectively with practitioners, provided the appropriate training and resources, overestimated what works in the real world, or all of the above! Many innovative programs work well at the experimental level because supplementary funds and highly committed research teams and patron saints support these factors. The bench chemist might be able to make a new drug work in an experimental setting, but producing millions of gallons for wholesale use is the job of chemical engineers. I view theory development that is paralleled by practical procedures for implementation as the best combination of ideas and engineering.

The result of my "engineering" has been two major theories (the Three-Ring Conception of Giftedness and the Enrichment Triad Model) that will be overviewed in Chapter 2 and covered in greater detail in Parts II and III of this book. Part IV of the book will cover related subtheories that are designed to enhance the overall talent development model that has been the theme of my work.

The Rocky Road of Educational Change: Circa the Late Sixties and Early Seventies

Obstacles related to bringing about educational change can occur on multiple levels. In the late 1960s, when I first began work on the Three-Ring Conception of Giftedness and the Enrichment Triad Model, I never dreamed: (1) that my work would become popular enough to form the basis for an invitation to prepare this book, (2) that this work would be widely used in schools throughout the world, and (3) that it would become the basis for a good deal of controversy in the field. This work was greeted by a less than enthusiastic reception from the gifted establishment of the time including rejections of my writing by all of the main journals in the field of gifted education, admonitions about my work by state directors of gifted programs to school districts seeking consultation, and rejections of papers from state and national conference organizers. My convictions about a broadened view of human potential caused me to seek an audience outside the gifted community, and in 1978, the *Kappan*, a general education journal, published my article entitled "What Makes Giftedness? Re-Examining a Definition." In the ensuing years, scholars, practitioners, and policy makers began to encounter my work, and this awareness led to an appreciation of more flexible attitudes toward the meaning of this complex phenomenon called giftedness. The 1978 *Kappan* article is now the most widely cited publication in the field. I mention this fortunate turn of events mainly to call attention to the always expectant hope that people can change their minds about a long-cherished belief and to acknowledge the courage of Robert Cole, the then *Kappan* editor, who was willing to take a chance on an unknown writer and what was, at the time, a decidedly unpopular point of view (as pointed out to him by field reviewers). Similarly, after agreeing to publish the Triad Model as a three-part series, a gifted education journal editor inexplicably decided not to publish the second or third installments. Once again, I sought audiences outside the gifted education establishment by submitting work to nongifted education publications, by establishing our summer institute at the University of Connecticut (Confratute), and by offering independent workshops around the country. If there is a strategic lesson to be learned from this scenario, it is simply that an end-run strategy is sometimes effective to go around gatekeepers and organizational power brokers (i.e., The Establishment) to bring one's message directly to the consumer. A basic principle of economics is that supply creates its own demand. When practitioners began to see value in the approaches I advocated, this bottom-up strategy resulted in gaining the sometimes-reluctant attention of the persons who select articles for publication, invite speakers to conferences, and recommend practices to schools.

A bottom-up strategy is not without its roadblocks and pitfalls. In the years since I originally published the Enrichment Triad Model (Renzulli, 1977a) and the Three-Ring Conception of Giftedness (Renzulli, 1978), a wide variety of reactions have appeared in the literature and on the professional conference circuit. These reactions have ranged from a highly positive article entitled "Renzulli Is Right" (Busse & Mansfield, 1980) to a scathing criticism that branded my work as "a national disease in gifted education" (Jellen, 1983). And my work seems to have generated enough controversy to cause some authors and speakers, regardless of the topic they are addressing, to weave into their work what Treffinger (1987) referred to as "cheap shots" about the ideas I have set forth.

To be certain, I was fully aware that the Triad Model and the Three-Ring Conception of Giftedness challenged the traditional orthodoxy that dominated the field at that time, but I never thought that state directors of gifted programs would prohibit me from speaking or consulting with school districts in their states, or that the editors of professional journals in the field would reject my articles because, as one person put it, "I disagree philosophically with your ideas." To understand the discrepancy regarding the popularity of these theories in more recent years versus the early resistance to it, it is necessary to turn back the calendar and revisit the climate in the gifted education field in the late sixties and early seventies. This was a time period prior to the landmark theories of Robert Sternberg (1984, 1985, 1999) and Howard Gardner (1985, 2000, 2006, 2008, 2011), and before the publication of influential research on talent development by Benjamin Bloom (1985), Mihaly Csikszentmihalyi (1991), Robert Albert (1975), Dean Simonton (1978, 1994), and others. Although some people were beginning to question the predominance of the single criterion, IQ score cut-off approach in the identification of students for special programs, state guidelines and regulations that were in existence or being enacted at that time still harkened back to the work of Lewis Terman and the belief that a certain level of traditionally measured intelligence was synonymous with giftedness. The only controversy within this very conservative conception of giftedness was how high to set the cut-off scores on IQ tests! Some people argued that it should be the top 1%, which was Terman's definition (see p. 180 in Renzulli, 1978), and others argued for a 3% or 5% criterion. Regardless of the cut-off level, however, there was no mistaking the absolutist belief that a person was either gifted or not gifted; and chances were that they would retain their respective designations despite evidence to the contrary, especially if that evidence was based on information other than test scores.

It is easy to understand the wide acceptance of the cut-off score approach if we also examine historically (1) the ways in which designated students were commonly served in the early days of the movement and (2) the emergence of state guidelines and especially state funding formulas. Most programs separated identified students into full-time special classes or part-time resource room arrangements for preselected students. Typical school-based programs consisted mainly of accelerated content or conglomerations of disconnected enrichment activities, frequently based on individual teachers' favored topics and units of study, the most recent trendy make-it-and-take-it workshops attended, or prescriptive curricular materials with the word "gifted" in the title. The advent of state funding, almost always based on a body count approach to reimbursement (*x* number of dollars per identified gifted student), placed additional pressure on schools to come up with tidy lists of exactly who qualified according to state-imposed guidelines. In an effort to address this very entrenched tradition regarding identification, it was necessary to raise questions about the rationale for having special programs in the first place, and to be prepared to examine the criticisms that are the inevitable weapons of the "little wars" mentioned in my opening quote by E. G. Boring.

The Purpose of Identification and Special Programs for the Development of Giftedness

The Why Question

When I came on the scene in the late 1960s and early 1970s, a number of observations helped shape what eventually became the Three-Ring Conception of Giftedness and the Enrichment Triad Model. The first observation had to do with the purpose of special programs. Implicit in any effort to define and identify a targeted group is the assumption that we will make special services available that capitalize on the characteristics that brought certain young people to our attention in the first place. In other words, the why question supersedes the who and the how questions. Little attention had been given to the why question in gifted education literature, although many people had strongly held beliefs about why special programs, funding, and services are necessary supplements to general education. The discussion that follows about two types of giftedness and status versus action information was an early attempt on my part to bring the why question into the dialogue on gifted education. When attempting to sell a theory or new idea, it is sometimes necessary to deal with these larger and, some would say, philosophical issues in order to lay the groundwork for a proposed change in orientation. Getting someone into the right frame of mind can make a theory more palatable, especially if persons have not previously thought about the larger issues.

The literature on the gifted and talented indicated that there are two generally accepted purposes for providing special education for high-potential youth. The first purpose is to provide young people with opportunities for maximum cognitive growth and self-fulfillment through the development and expression of one or a combination of performance areas where superior potential may be present. The second purpose is to increase society's reservoir of persons who will help to solve the problems of contemporary civilization by becoming producers of knowledge and art rather than mere consumers of existing information. This second purpose, sometimes referred to as the "cure-for-cancer argument," was especially useful in gaining legislative and financial support. Most people would agree that the two goals are mutually supportive of one another. In other words, the productive and creative work of scientists, authors, artists, and leaders in all walks of life provide benefits to society and also result in feelings of accomplishment, self-fulfillment, and a positive attitude about one's self. And these characteristics are, in turn, important contributors to self-efficacy (Bandura, 1977), the belief that one is capable of subsequent and usually more advanced expressions of creative productivity.

Two Types of Giftedness

General consensus about these two purposes of special education for the gifted served as a rationale for both the conception of giftedness and the programming theories. Keeping the interaction of the two purposes of gifted education in mind, it is safe to conclude that special services and supplementary expenditures of public funds should be geared primarily toward increasing society's supply of potentially creative and productive adults. This conclusion has important implications for both the who and how questions, but most importantly, it led me to propose the difference between two types of giftedness—lesson-learning or "schoolhouse" giftedness on one hand and creative productive giftedness on the other.

Schoolhouse giftedness is that which is easily measured by standardized ability tests, and therefore the type most conveniently used for selecting students for special programs. The competencies young people display on cognitive ability tests are exactly the kinds of abilities most valued in traditional school learning situations, especially those situations that focus on analytic skills rather than creative or practical skills. Research has shown a high correlation between schoolhouse giftedness and the likelihood of getting high grades in school. It is also common knowledge that for the vast majority of students, superior lesson learning and test taking remain stable over time. Schoolhouse giftedness exists in varying degrees and can easily be identified through standardized and informal assessment techniques. As a result, we should do everything in our power to make appropriate modifications for students who have the ability to cover regular curricular material at advanced rates and levels of understanding in relation to their age peers. These conclusions led me to develop one aspect of our programming model known as curriculum compacting (Renzulli, Smith, & Reis, 1982). Research on curriculum compacting (Reis et al., 1992) has shown that, with as little as 3 hours of systematic training, teachers can eliminate up to 50% of regular curricular material for high-achieving students without causing any declines in standardized achievement test scores.

Although schoolhouse giftedness is valued and accommodated in our work, mainly through curriculum modification and replacement techniques, a major focus has been on the second type of giftedness, which I have termed *creative productive giftedness*. Creative productive giftedness describes those aspects of human activity and involvement where a premium is placed on the development of original ideas, products, artistic expressions, and areas of knowledge that are purposefully designed to have an impact on one or more target audiences. Learning situations that are designed to promote creative productive giftedness emphasize the *use and application* of knowledge and thinking processes in an integrated, inductive, and real-problem-oriented manner. The role of the student is transformed from that of a learner of prescribed lessons and consumer of information (however advanced) to one in which he or she uses the *modus operandi* of the firsthand inquirer. I have written in some detail about this transformed role of the learner (Renzulli, 1982a), and will only say at this point that it serves as the main rationale for the Type III dimension of the Enrichment Triad Model.

The idea for creative productive giftedness and the Three-Ring Conception of Giftedness came from the broad range of research I reviewed on the nature of human abilities (Renzulli, 1978, 1982b, 1986), as well as numerous case studies about people of unusual accomplishment (both young people and adults) who would not have been identified or served in special programs if we relied solely on cognitive ability test scores. These observations also led me to another conclusion about the temporal and situational nature of creative productive giftedness, and especially the creativity and task commitment components of the Three-Ring Conception. Whereas lesson learning giftedness, which is mainly accounted for in the above-average ability circle of the Three-Ring Conception, tends to remain stable over time, persons do not always display maximum creativity or task commitment especially when addressing problems that do not have a single, predetermined right answer. Highly creative and productive people have peaks and valleys of high-level output. Some persons have commented that the valleys are as necessary as the peaks, because they allow for reflection, regeneration, and the accumulation of input for subsequent endeavors.

Similarly, creative productive giftedness tends to be contextual or domain specific. Although there certainly have been a small number of "Renaissance" men and women who have gained recognition for work in several fields, the overwhelming number of persons who have been recognized for their outstanding accomplishments have almost always achieved in a single field or domain. There is no focus in the Triad theory to encourage young people to "major" in a field at a very young age, although some of them do develop lifelong interests and these interests should not be discouraged. Rather, the focus is to encourage bright young people to explore interests both vertically and horizontally, and if there is an encouragement toward anything, that thing is the joy of authentic inquiry, creativity, and an emerging sense of self as a person who can be influential in his or her selected field of study.

The temporal and situational nature of creative productive giftedness has resulted in some misunderstanding and criticism about the Three-Ring Conception (Jarrell & Borland, 1990; Jellen, 1983, 1985; Kontos, Carter, Ormrod, & Cooney, 1983), and called for some effort on my part to address this phenomenon (Renzulli, 1985, 1988, 1990; Renzulli & Owen, 1983). A good deal of the misunderstanding and related controversy lies in the difficulty of defining a complex concept without creating a semantic atrocity or dwelling on rhetorical arguments such as the differences in meaning between words such as *gifted* and *talented*. In my early writing on the topic, an attempt was made to clarify the concept by adding a figural representation in the form of three intersecting circles. This Venn diagram was intended to convey figurally the dynamic properties of the concept (i.e., those properties pertaining to motion, interaction, continuous change, and energy rather than a fixed or static state). But my best efforts at both semantic and figural communication have, nevertheless, resulted in interpretations that clearly were not intended. Consider, for example, a comment by Tannenbaum (1986), in which he states: "Renzulli does not specify that giftedness requires the interplay of all three attributes in his model" (p. 31). I do indeed specify this and it was for this very reason (i.e., interaction) that I chose to present the model figurally in the form of three *overlapping* rings. The primary purpose of a Venn diagram is to portray this type of interactive relationship.

The issue of performance versus potential is probably the aspect of my work on the conception of giftedness that is most frequently discussed in the literature. As an example, let us consider a discussion of the Three-Ring Conception in a popular book for parents by Webb, Meckstroth, and Tolan (1982). But first, allow me to highlight an important phrase from the original definition (Renzulli, 1978): "Gifted and talented children are those possessing *or capable of developing* this composite set of traits and applying them to any potentially valuable area of human performance" (p. 261; italics not in the original, but perhaps should have been). My intention was to convey the message that candidates for special services need not manifest all three clusters of traits, but rather that students are identified as capable of developing these characteristics. Webb et al. seemed to have overlooked or chosen to ignore the words that have been highlighted above, because in their book they state:

Another way of stating the Renzulli model is that superior ability, itself, is not enough—there must be high motivation to use that ability, and it must be expressed in creative ways, or to an unusual degree. Because it insists on the clear *expression* of giftedness, use of the Renzulli model overlooks many gifted children who, for a variety of reasons, are unwilling to demonstrate their talents in the ways being measured. (p. 49)

Similar statements can be found in the textbook literature (e.g., Davis & Rimm, 1985, p. 12; Gallagher, 1985, p. 8; Maker, 1982, p. 232), and there is a general tendency to conclude that the Three-Ring Conception fails to take account of gifted underachievers. For example, Gagné (1985) stated, "The factor that makes Renzulli's model inapplicable to underachievers is the presence of motivation as an essential component of giftedness" (p. 105), and Davis and Rimm (1985) stated, "This model excludes underachievers" (p. 16). Similar statements focus on creativity. For example VanTassel-Baska (1998) commented, "witness Renzulli's definition of giftedness, which excludes those children who do not display evidence of creativity" (p. 384). It is precisely for this reason that general enrichment activities (Types I and II in the Triad Model) are recommended for larger groups of students, and in some cases, for all students. These types of enrichment *create* task commitment and promote creativity. They are purposefully designed to promote motivation for follow-up (Type III Enrichment) in unmotivated, bored, or underachieving students. Promoting gifted behaviors is a *developmental* process that stimulates creativity and task commitment and causes it to interact with above-average ability in one or a combination of academic areas (Reis & Renzulli, 2003).

Because, to my knowledge, none of the above commentators conducted any research on the broadened conception of giftedness or programs using the Triad Model or the Three-Ring Conception of Giftedness, I am left with the uneasy feeling that their conjecture is more journalistic than scientific. In point of fact, one of the few *intervention* studies in the research literature that shows highly favorable results for underachieving gifted students (Baum, Renzulli, & Hébert, 1995) is a study that selected participants based on the Three-Ring Conception and used the Enrichment Triad as a direct intervention for counteracting underachievement.

The major reason for the interpretations discussed above undoubtedly lies in the exploration that led me to the conclusions that are summarized in the research rationale for the Three-Ring Conception of Giftedness (Renzulli, 1978, 1986). Because this research dealt mainly with factors that contributed to the development of creative and productive behavior in adults, an obvious but not necessarily valid conclusion on the parts of some writers is that these same traits should be required of children in order to gain admission to programs for the gifted. It therefore requires only a short leap in logic to the kinds of statements quoted above, and the belief that young people, regardless of ability, will be overlooked if they do not display task commitment or creativity. Clearly, this was not what I intended, and in fact, the Three-Ring theory drew on many anecdotal experiences with young people who developed exactly the same kinds of creative productivity that can be found in the literature about accomplished adults. But to understand the rationale and the practical implications (for identification) of the Three-Ring model, we must examine another major concept underlying the theory. This concept is the important distinction between two types of information that allow us to examine and estimate human potential.

High Achieving and Creative Productiveness Giftedness

Scores on IQ tests and other measures of achievement or cognitive ability are the standards to which I refer to as high achieving giftedness. Because these measures account for a limited proportion of the common variance with school grades and other types of outstanding performance, we can be equally certain that these measures do not tell the whole story when it comes to making predictions about what I refer to as creative productive giftedness. Before defending this assertion with some research findings, let us briefly review what is meant by this second type of giftedness, the important role that it should play in programming, and the reasons we should attempt to assess it in our identification procedures, even if such assessment causes us to look below the top 3%–5% on the normal curve of IQ scores.

Creative productive giftedness describes those aspects of human activity and involvement where a premium is placed on the development of original material and products that are purposefully designed to have an impact on one or more target audiences. Learning situations that are designed to promote creative productive giftedness emphasize the use and *application* of information (content) and thinking processes in an integrated, inductive, and real-problem-oriented manner. The role of the student is transformed from that of a learner of prescribed lessons to one in which she or he uses the *modus operandi* of a firsthand inquirer. This approach is quite different from the development of lesson-learning giftedness that tends to emphasize deductive learning, structured training in the development of thinking processes, and the acquisition, storage, and retrieval of information. In other words, creative productive giftedness is simply putting one's abilities to work on problems and areas of study that have personal relevance to the student and that can be escalated to appropriately challenging levels of investigative activity. The roles that both students and teachers should play in the pursuit of these problems have been described elsewhere (Renzulli, 1982b; Renzulli & De Wet, 2010).

Why is creative productive giftedness important enough for us to question the tidy and relatively easy approach that traditionally has been used to select students on the basis of test scores? Why do some people want to rock the boat by challenging a conception of giftedness that can be numerically defined by simply giving a test? The answers to these questions are simple and yet very compelling. The research tells us that there is much more to the making of a gifted person than the abilities revealed on traditional tests of intelligence, aptitude, and achievement. Furthermore, history tells us it has been the creative and productive people of the world, the producers rather than consumers of knowledge, the reconstructionists of thought in all areas of human endeavor, who have become recognized as "truly gifted" individuals. We know the greatest creators in our world because of what they did, not because of how they scored on tests! And it is these kinds of inquirers and creators who should be the major focus of who we serve in gifted education programs. History does not remember persons who merely scored well on IQ tests or those who learned their lessons well.

Status and Action Information

Status information consists of test scores, previous grades or accomplishments, teacher ratings, and anything else we can "put down on paper" beforehand that tells us something about a person's traits and potentials. Status information is undoubtedly the best way to identify students with high levels of schoolhouse giftedness, and it can also be used to identify a Talent Pool of above-average ability students with *potential* for creativity and task commitment. But the temporal and contextual nature of creativity and task commitment in real and present problem situations require that we look for these behaviors *within* contexts where such behaviors are displayed, developed, and hopefully encouraged.

Action information, which has been described in detail elsewhere (Renzulli, Reis, & Smith, 1981), can best be defined as the type of dynamic interactions that take place when a person becomes extremely interested in or excited about a particular topic, area of study, issue, idea, or event that takes place within the school or the nonschool environment. These interactions (e.g., connections, insights, relations, discoveries, contacts) occur when students encounter or are influenced by persons, concepts, or particular pieces of knowledge.[1] They create the proverbial "Ahas" that may become triggers for subsequent involvement. It is for this reason that I included Type I Enrichment (general exploratory experiences) and Type II Enrichment (group training activities) in the Triad model. The influence of the interactions between and among the enrichment components may be relatively limited, or they may have a highly positive and extremely motivating effect on certain individuals. If the influence is strong enough and positive enough to promote further exploration and follow-up on the part of an individual or group of students with a common interest, then we may say that a dynamic interaction has taken place. These ideas, however good they may sound, must eventually be borne out in research settings, so let us now turn our attention to research about the theories and strategies for using the research in the acceptance finding process.

The Role of Research in the Change Process

No single research study can ever verify or negate a complex theory, especially a theory that has multidimensional application processes. To translate the above theories into practice, my colleagues Sally Reis and Linda Smith and I developed an identification system and service delivery model (Renzulli et al., 1981) that respects the tenants of the theories and that could be used as the bases for a variety of empirical studies. These studies have been summarized elsewhere (Reis & Renzulli, 1994). The essence of the identification system is to provide general or targeted (by ability level, domain, or interest area) "Talent Pools" of students with a broad variety of general enrichment experiences (Types I and II in the Enrichment Triad Model, as well as opportunities to follow up on regular school curricular experiences and noncurricular interests), and to use the ways in which students *respond* to these experiences to determine who and in which areas of study students should revolve into Type III Enrichment opportunities. In addition to the general enrichment provided in special program situations, we also trained classroom teachers to use a form called the Action Information Message so that they could serve as referral agents whenever students reacted in highly positive ways to regular classroom experiences.

Although this approach to identification and programming departs significantly from traditional practices, its effectiveness has been documented by a series of research studies and field tests in schools with widely varying

---

[1] In a certain sense, what I described as "action information" is not unlike the currently popular concept called *performance-based assessment*, although action information is for proactive decision making rather than program evaluation purposes.

socioeconomic levels and program organizational patterns. The most important study we conducted in the early stages of our research used a population of 1,162 students in grades 1–6 in 11 school districts (Reis & Renzulli, 1982). This study examined several variables related to the identification system based on the Three-Ring Conception of Giftedness and the effectiveness of Triad model. The Talent Pools in each participating school were designated (but not divided) into two groups. Group A consisted of students who scored in the top 5% on standardized tests of intelligence and achievement. Group B consisted of students who scored between 10 to 15 percentile points below the top 5% and/or who were rated highly by teachers using the Scales for Rating the Behavioral Characteristics of Superior Students (SRBCSS; Renzulli et al., 2013). Both groups participated equally in all program activities, and they were not aware of their group designations.

An instrument entitled the Student Product Assessment Form (SPAF; Reis & Renzulli, 1982) was used to compare the quality of products emanating from each group. This instrument provides individual ratings for eight specific characteristics of product quality and seven factors related to overall product quality. The validity and reliability of SPAF were established through a yearlong series of studies that yielded reliability coefficients as high as 0.98. A double-blind method of product coding was used so that judges did not know group membership (i.e., Group A or B) when evaluating individual products. No significant differences were found between Group A and Group B on the quality of students' products. These findings lend support to the concept that students who are above average but not necessarily superior in general ability are capable of producing high-quality products when they participate on an equal basis in a programming model that focuses on creative productivity. We concluded that there was justification for inclusion of a broader spectrum of students in this type of program than the traditional top 5% upon which traditional programs focus.

Questionnaires and interviews were used to examine several other factors related to overall program effectiveness. The data indicated that feelings about the Triad program—gathered from classroom teachers, administrators, students in the Talent Pools, and their parents—were generally positive. Many classroom teachers reported that their high level of involvement in the program had favorably influenced their teaching practices and their overall attitudes toward gifted programs in general. Parents whose children had been previously placed in traditional programs for the gifted (Group A) did not differ in their opinions about the programs' value and effectiveness from parents whose children had been identified as gifted under the expanded Three-Ring Conception criteria. And resource teachers—many of whom had been involved previously in traditional programs for the gifted—overwhelmingly preferred the expanded Talent Pool approach to traditional reliance on test scores alone. Posttreatment questionnaires and interviews indicated, among other things, that resource teachers especially appreciated working with students who showed a greater diversity of interests and creative ideas. In fact, several resource teachers in the experimental study said that they would resign or request transfers to regular classrooms if their school systems reverted to traditional identification practices (Reis, 1981).

Additional research in the early stages of theory testing (Delisle & Renzulli, 1982) examined academic self-concept and locus of control. This study established the importance of nonintellective factors in creative production and verified earlier research related to the Three-Ring Conception of Giftedness. Using a step-wise multiple regression technique to study the correlates of creative production, Gubbins (1982) found that above-average ability is a necessary but not sufficient condition for high-level productivity. The roles of task commitment and time commitment and the importance of student interests were verified. Several factors related to improved productivity were identified. A study of student, parent, and classroom teachers' attitudes toward the model (Delisle, Reis, & Gubbins, 1981) revealed support for this approach and a high degree of cooperation among all persons involved in the implementation of this type of program. These studies also showed that a more flexible approach to identification helped to minimize attitudes of elitism, and promoted a "radiation of excellence" (Ward, 1961) throughout the buildings in which the model was implemented.

The Politics of Educational Research

Knowing that yet another research study and derivative articles seldom have an impact among policy makers led us to develop a research-into-action strategy that paid off in a far shorter period of time than the usual trickle-down effect of most research. Amidst much fanfare and publicity, a meeting was organized that included superintendents who agreed to allow the above research to take place, state department of education (SDE) personnel (in the areas of both gifted education and research/evaluation), and the state commissioner of education. We agreed to have SDE personnel monitor the research and they agreed to make changes in state identification regulations if the research warranted such change. The commissioner's involvement was critical, and this research could not have gone forward without the support of a person at the highest level who was regarded as a courageous and progressive leader. The research results clearly supported a more flexible approach to identification of students for gifted programs, but when it came to changing regulations, the SDE personnel started to get a bit indecisive. But when we reminded them of the original agreement and said that *we* would send the report directly to the commissioner if they would not, quick action resulted. Within a week, a letter and executive summary of our research was sent to every superintendent and gifted program director in the state informing them that our identification system was a legally allowable alternative. In the years that followed, many schools adopted the identification system, and because the research was conducted in what many considered to be a leading state in gifted education, we were able to have an influence beyond our own state borders. Some of the influence resulted from research articles, articles written for practitioner audiences, and numerous presentations on the national and state gifted conference circuit. One thing we learned about the change process is that a little research goes a long way in influencing policy, and when well-packaged in the form of practitioner-friendly examples of effective adaptations of the model, it goes even further. And the procedural research is further enhanced when practitioners are provided with practical, inexpensive, well-researched instrument that can be used in theory driven identification and service activities. Teacher rating scales (Renzulli et al., 2013), interest (Renzulli, 1977b) and learning styles questionnaires (Renzulli, Rizza, & Smith, 1997), and expression style inventories (Kettle, Renzulli, & Rizza, 1998) that are compatible with the theories make it easier for practitioners to use recommended models, and thus serve to facilitate a Practice-Research-Theory approach. In recent years, all of these instruments have been converted to electronic formats, thus making the administration and interpretation easier and cost effective (Renzulli & Reis, 2007, 2014).

The identification system described above is the one that is most consistent with the two main theories that are the subject of this chapter, but translating theory into practice sometimes involves accommodations that take into account state and local policies that require having names on a list *before* any services are rendered. To address this political reality, a modified identification model was developed that does respect preselection requirements, but that also asks schools to leave some room in their preselected group for students who can gain entrance on the basis of nontest criteria (Renzulli & Reis, 2012). An article dealing with this identification system was published in a nongifted field journal (Renzulli & Smith, 1990) because I felt it was, once again, necessary to reach out to a larger and more responsive audience than might be found in the traditionally conservative gifted establishment.

Navigating the Rocky Road: From Frustration to Application

Although submitting the Three-Ring Conception of Giftedness article to the *Kappan* was an act born out of disappointment and frustration, it had an unexpected effect! Many persons in general education, especially school administrators, who previously had unfavorable attitudes toward programs for the gifted began to raise questions about greater flexibility in identification. Sometimes these attitudes were based on philosophic concerns about equity and fairness in the allocation of resources, especially the underrepresentation of low-income and minority students. Practical issues accounted for the unfavorable attitudes of others. Scheduling problems, pushy parents, the costs of individual testing, and conflicts between classroom teachers and teachers of the gifted led many educators to look for alternatives to traditional approaches for identification and programming. In overseas nations, especially in Western Europe and some of the Asian countries, the socialist democracies were cautious about programs that categorized students along what they perceived to be class lines. Questions were raised by gifted education professionals at local and state levels regarding the possibility of different approaches and requests for reprints of the *Kappan* article and permission to reprint it in collections of readings far exceeded my fondest expectations.

High levels of continuing interest caused me to establish an institute in the summer of 1978, and once again, enrollment far surpassed my expectations. Although the institute attracted a small number of skeptics and persons who were sent by school districts against their will, the majority of participants were liberal-minded educators who were seeking greater flexibility in identifying students and providing services; I called them "positive malcontents!" The institute, named Confratute (intended to convey the best aspects of a *confer*ence and an ins*titute*, with a measure of *fra*ternity blended within) continues today after more than 38 years, and a cumulative enrollment surpassing 30,000 participants. Although persons attending Confratute are made aware of the theoretical and research underpinnings of our work, the major focus is on *practical* strategies for implementing the theories in a variety of school settings. To this end, expert practitioners serve as the faculty for Confratute—persons with extensive experience in implementing the model, the majority of whom work in schools delivering services on a daily basis. Many Confratute faculty members were former participants in the summer program, and several have gone on to pursue graduate degrees at our university. Both participants and faculty have become, in effect, local, state, and sometimes even national emissaries for the types of services advocated in the theories underlying our work. It is not unusual to find them making presentations at conferences, conducting workshops for school districts, submitting articles to research and teacher-oriented professional journals, teaching college courses, and serving on committees that influence policy and practice in their respective states and school districts. Equally important are the unique approaches, materials, and innovations that many of these persons have contributed to practical implementation strategies. And even in this regard, communication is a critical ingredient. Through newsletters, websites, social media, and invitations to practitioners to participate in various training venues, valuable information enhances the practical application of the theories and causes dedicated professionals to feel part of a movement that is having an impact on schools and students.

Lessons Learned About Translating Theory Into Practice

As indicated earlier, translating theory into practice is all about organizational and policy change and the strategies necessary to enlist the support of practitioners who are ultimately responsible for implementing theory-driven change in an authentic fashion. Change that has its origins in the academic world usually occurs in one of two ways! A person or group has what they consider to be a big, bold, and obviously important idea, and they set the wheels in motion to slay Goliath by influencing policy makers and capturing the minds and hearts of those who they are convinced will benefit from the idea. Grand theories and systems, usually put forth by individuals from powerful institutions with high degrees of source credibility, come into the academic marketplace and become the stuff out of which great movements arise and sometimes controversy is spawned. The major change strategy is the publication of books or articles in influential journals and keynote presentations before major professional societies. This type of change begins as a behemoth and steamrolls its way to acceptance or garners much scrutiny and controversy in the academic community. Howard Gardner's (1985) book on multiple intelligences is an example, as is Herrnstein and Murray's (1994) book on the bell curve. If the work creates aspirations for change among practitioners (e.g., therapists, educators, counselors) then another level of acceptance finding must be pursued. A high degree of academic source credibility and a strong research base are decided advantages in the change process (every administrator likes to gain support for newly adopted initiatives by arguing that "research says," especially if this research is initiated at a highly prestigious university), but winning the hearts and minds of practitioners requires another level of change strategies. This level includes understanding teachers' ways of knowing, providing information that "makes sense" to practitioners, developing personal relations that show respect on the part of the researcher toward practitioners (i.e., not "talking down" to them), and being willing to make modifications based on *their* tacit knowledge about the ways schools operate. Personalities are as important to promoting effective change as are good science and elegant designs!

Persuasive communication does not ignore the importance of theory and research, but usually presents it in a practitioner friendly way (less technical jargon, tabular summaries of research, classroom examples that illustrate a theoretical concept). It is almost always targeted toward journals that teachers and other practitioners read, even though they may be less prestigious than the scholarly journals that launch new initiatives for academic audiences. But make no mistake, my bottom-up approach has reached policy makers and brought about changes in regulations at district and state levels, and it is the success stories and the practitioner satisfaction rather than the hard-core theory and research findings that has usually influenced their ultimate adoption of our approach to talent development initiatives.

What undoubtedly led to the widespread "popularity" of my work that Dr. Ward and I discussed on many late nights with good ol' Jack Daniel's always at hand is more modest in its origins than a mainly academic-oriented approach and focuses primarily on a bottom-up strategy. Because I have always believed that teachers know the most about what will work in classrooms, I have tried to view change from a practical, teacher-oriented perspective. Therefore, the main audience for persuasive communication vehicles has been teachers, gifted program coordinators, and building principals. Articles in "softer" journals such as *The Elementary Principal* and *Educational Leadership*, and presentations at practitioner rather than researcher conferences certainly call attention to the always important research base that supports the theories, but the main message is the "what" and the "how" of practices based on the theories. These articles and presentations have described and provided numerous examples about actual implementations of the theories. A recurring theme is what teachers have done to bring about various types of student involvement. It is for this reason that most of my present-day writing and speaking is liberally punctuated with the outstanding examples of theory-related practices that I receive from teachers who exhibit unparalleled creativity. The Practice-Research-Theory Cycle (Figure 1.1) begins all over again and my enthusiasm for new research and theory development is the same as it was almost half a century ago.

In the chapters that follow, I will discuss the two main theories that have been the basis for my work over the past 25 years and the strategies I have used to persuade policy makers, organizations, and educational practitioners to implement practical applications of these theories. This work has focused on (1) a human potential theory dealing with the conceptualization of giftedness and talent potential in young people, and (2) a pedagogical theory that is intended to produce a particular "brand" of learning that promotes what I refer to as gifted behaviors. Because these two theories parallel one another and are complimentary in purpose and implementation, the strategies for gaining acceptance will be discussed as a single set of entities.

References

Albert, R. S. (1975). Toward a behavioral definition of genius. *American Psychologist, 30,* 140–151.

Bandura, A. (1977). Self efficacy mechanism in human agency. *American Psychologist, 37,* 122–147.

Baum, S. M., Renzulli, J. S., & Hébert, T. P. (1995). Reversing underachievement: Creative productivity as a systematic intervention. *Gifted Child Quarterly, 39,* 224–235.

Bloom, B. (Ed). (1985). *Developing talent in young people.* New York, NY: Ballantine.

Busse, T. V., & Mansfield, R. S. (1980). Renzulli is right. *Gifted Child Quarterly, 24,* 132.

Csikszentmihalyi, M. (1991). *Flow: The psychology of optimal experience.* New York, NY: HarperCollins.

Davis, G. A., & Rimm, S. B. (1985). *Education of the gifted and talented.* Englewood Cliffs, NJ: Prentice Hall.

Delisle, J. R., & Renzulli, J. S. (1982). The Revolving Door Identification and Programming Model: Correlates of creative production. *Gifted Child Quarterly, 26,* 89–95.

Delisle, J. R., Reis, S. M., & Gubbins, E. J. (1981). The Revolving Door Identification Model and Programming Model. *Exceptional Children, 48,* 152–156.

Gagné, F. (1985). Giftedness and talent: Reexamining a reexamination of the definitions. *Gifted Child Quarterly, 29,* 103–112.

Gallagher, J. J. (1985). *Teaching the gifted child* (3rd ed.). Boston, MA: Allyn & Bacon.

Gardner, H. (1985). *Frames of mind: The theory of multiple intelligences.* New York, NY: Basic Books.

Gardner, H. (2000). *The disciplined mind: Beyond facts and standardized tests, the K–12 education that every child deserves.* New York, NY: Penguin Books.

Gardner, H. (2006). *Five minds for the future.* Boston, MA: Harvard Business School Press.

Gardner, H. (2008). *The mind's new science: A history of the cognitive revolution.* New York, NY: Basic Books.

Gardner, H. (2011). *The unschooled mind: How children think and how schools should teach.* New York, NY: Basic Books.

Gubbins, J. (1982). *Revolving Door Identification Model: Characteristics of talent pool students* (Unpublished doctoral dissertation). University of Connecticut, Storrs.

Herrnstein, R. J., & Murray, C. (1994). *The bell curve: Intelligence and class structure in American life*. New York, NY: Free Press.

Jarrell, R. H., & Borland, J. H. (1990). The research base for Renzulli's Three Ring Conception of Giftedness. *Journal for the Education of the Gifted, 13*, 288–308.

Jellen, H. G. (1983, November 14). *Renzulli-itis: A national disease in gifted education*. Paper presented at the Illinois State Conference on the Gifted, Peoria, IL.

Jellen, H. G. (1985). Renzulli's enrichment scheme for the gifted: Educational accommodation of the gifted in the American context. *Gifted Education International, 3*(1), 12–17.

Kettle, K., Renzulli, J. S., & Rizza, M. G. (1998). Products of mind: Exploring student preferences for product development using My Way . . . An Expression Style Instrument. *Gifted Child Quarterly, 42*(1), 49–60.

Kontos, S., Carter, K. R., Ormrod, J. E., & Cooney, J. B. (1983). Reversing the revolving door: A strict interpretation of Renzulli's definition of giftedness. *Roeper Review, 6*(1), 35–38.

Maker, J. (1982). *Teaching models in education of the gifted*. Rockville, MD: Aspen.

Reis, S. M. (1981). *An analysis of the productivity of gifted students participating in programs using the Revolving Door Identification Model* (Unpublished doctoral dissertation). University of Connecticut, Storrs.

Reis, S. M., & Renzulli, J. S. (1982). A research report on the Revolving Door Identification Model: A case for the broadened conception of giftedness. *Phi Delta Kappan, 63*, 619–620.

Reis, S. M., & Renzulli, J. S. (1994). Research related to the Schoolwide Enrichment Triad Model. *Gifted Child Quarterly, 38*(1), 7–20.

Reis, S, M., & Renzulli, J. S. (2003). Research related to the Schoolwide Enrichment Triad Model. *Gifted Education International, 17*(1), 15–39.

Reis, S. M., Westberg, K. L., Kulikowich, J., Caillard, F., Hébert, T. P., Purcell, J. H., . . . Plucker, J. A. (1992). *Technical report of the curriculum compacting study*. Storrs: University of Connecticut, The National Research Center on the Gifted and Talented.

Renzulli, J. S. (1977a). *The Enrichment Triad Model: A guide for developing defensible programs for the gifted and talented*. Mansfield Center, CT: Creative Learning Press.

Renzulli, J. S. (1977b). *Interest-a-lyzer*. Mansfield Center, CT: Creative Learning Press.

Renzulli, J. S. (1978). What makes giftedness? Re-examining a definition. *Phi Delta Kappan, 60*, 180–184, 261.

Renzulli, J. S. (1982a). Dear Mr. and Mrs. Copernicus: We regret to inform you . . . *Gifted Child Quarterly, 26*, 11–14.

Renzulli, J. S. (1982b). What makes a problem real: Stalking the illusive meaning of qualitative differences in gifted education. *Gifted Child Quarterly, 26*, 147–156.

Renzulli, J. S. (1985). A bull's eye on my back: The perils and pitfalls of trying to bring about educational change. *Gifted Education International, 3*(1), 18–23.

Renzulli, J. S. (1986). The Three-Ring Conception of Giftedness: A developmental model for creative productivity. In R. J. Sternberg & J. E. Davidson (Eds.), *Conceptions of giftedness* (pp. 53–92). New York, NY: Cambridge University Press.

Renzulli, J. S. (Ed.). (1988). *Technical report on research studies related to the Revolving Door Identification Model.* Storrs: University of Connecticut, Bureau of Educational Research.

Renzulli, J. S. (1990). Torturing data until they confess: An analysis of the Three-Ring Conception of Giftedness. *Journal for the Education of the Gifted, 13,* 309–331.

Renzulli, J. S., & De Wet, C. F. (2010). Developing creative productivity in young people through the pursuit of ideal acts of learning. In R. A. Beghetto & J. C. Kaufman (Eds.), *Nurturing creativity in the classroom* (pp. 24–72), New York, NY: Cambridge University Press.

Renzulli, J. S., & Owen, S. V. (1983). The Revolving Door Identification Model: If it ain't busted don't fix it, if you don't understand it don't nix it. *Roeper Review, 6*(1), 39–41.

Renzulli, J. S., & Reis, S. M. (2007). A technology based program that matches enrichment resources with student strengths. *International Journal of Emerging Technologies in Learning, 2*(3). Retrieved from http://online-journals.org/i- jet/article/viewArticle/126

Renzulli, J. S., & Reis, S. M. (2012). Defensible and doable: A practical, multiple-criteria gifted program identification system. In S. L. Hunsaker (Ed.), *Identification: The theory and practice of identifying students for gifted and talented education services* (pp. 25–56). Waco, TX: Prufrock Press.

Renzulli, J. S., & Reis, S. M. (2014). *The Schoolwide Enrichment Model: A how-to guide for talent development* (3rd ed.). Waco, TX: Prufrock Press.

Renzulli, J. S., Reis, S. M., & Smith, L. (1981). *The Revolving Door Identification Model.* Mansfield Center, CT: Creative Learning Press.

Renzulli, J. S., Rizza, M. G., & Smith, L. H. (1997). *The learning styles inventory.* Mansfield Center, CT: Creative Learning Press.

Renzulli, J. S., & Smith. L. H. (1990). A practical system for identifying gifted and talented students. *Early Child Development and Care, 63,* 9–18.

Renzulli, J. S., Smith, L. H., & Reis, S. M. (1982). Curriculum compacting: An essential strategy for working with gifted students. *The Elementary School Journal, 82,* 185–194.

Renzulli, J. S., Smith, L. H., White, A. J., Callahan, C. M., Hartman, R. K., Westberg, K. L., . . . Sytsma, R. E. (2013). *Scales for rating the behavioral characteristics of superior students* (Rev. ed.). Waco, TX: Prufrock Press.

Simonton, D. K. (1978). History and the eminent person. *Gifted Child Quarterly, 22,* 187–195.

Simonton, D. K. (1994). *Greatness: Who makes history and why.* New York, NY: Guilford Press.

Sternberg, R. J. (1984). Toward a triarchic theory of human intelligence. *Behavioral and Brain Sciences, 7,* 269–316.

Sternberg, R. J. (1985). A componential theory of intellectual giftedness. *Gifted Child Quarterly, 25,* 86–93.

Sternberg, R. J. (1999). The theory of successful intelligence. *Review of General Psychology, 3,* 292–316.

Tannenbaum, A. J. (1986). Giftedness: A psychosocial approach. In R. J. Sternberg & J. E. Davidson (Eds.), *Conceptions of giftedness* (pp. 21–52). New York, NY: Cambridge University Press.

Treffinger, D. J. (1987). [Review of the book *Critical issues in gifted education*. Maker, C. J. (Ed.)]. *Journal for the Education of the Gifted, 10,* 324–331.

VanTassel-Baska, J. (1998). *Excellence in educating gifted and talented learners.* Denver, CO: Love.

Ward, V. (1961). *Educating the gifted: An axiomatic approach.* Columbus, OH: Merrill.

Webb, J. T., Meckstroth, E. A., & Tolan, S. S. (1982). *Guiding the gifted child.* Columbus: Ohio Psychology Publishing Company.

CHAPTER 2

Reexamining the Role of Gifted Education and Talent Development for the 21st Century

A Four-Part Theoretical Approach[2]

Joseph S. Renzulli
University of Connecticut

Introduction From Joe

New research in the field, changing policies and practices in both general and gifted education, and opportunities to examine the consequences of school-based applications of one's own work are always cause for reflection and the search for answers to questions about what can be done to improve

---

2   Renzulli, J. S. (2012). Reexamining the role of gifted education and talent development for the 21st century: A four-part theoretical approach. *Gifted Child Quarterly, 56,* 150–159. Copyright 2012 National Association for Gifted Children. Reprinted with permission.

on services to the teachers and students we serve. There are probably very few theories or programming models in any field that haven't changed over time as a result of experience, critical analysis, and the emergence of new ideas and research.

This chapter provides a summation of four subtheories developed over approximately five decades. Although my early work on Subtheory I (the Three-Ring Conception of Giftedness) and Subtheory II (the Enrichment Triad Model) gained more attention than I ever expected, I began to feel that there were still characteristics and programming opportunities that needed to be added to the overall search for factors that contribute to total talent development. This concern, coupled with my own belief that programs for our most able young people should: (1) promote a sense of social justice and the use of one's gifts to make positive contributions to society, and (2) provide experiences in the development of strategies for acquiring self-regulation skills, using time and resources wisely, taking action, and managing change. And, of course, I wanted to come up with ideas that interacted with rather than replaced Three-Ring and Triad. The result was several years of research and development that led to Subtheories III and IV that are discussed in this chapter. I refer to the traits discussed in Subtheories III and IV as co-cognitive factors because they interact with and enhance the cognitive traits that are ordinarily associated with the development of human abilities. A number of researchers have suggested that constructs of this type, including social, emotional, and interpersonal intelligence, are related to each other and are at least partially independent from traditional academic measures of human abilities. I invite readers to draw their own conclusions about whether or not these four interactive subtheories promote what I describe as a fully functioning self-actualized individual.

He who loves practice without theory is like the sailor who boards a ship without a rudder and compass, and never knows where he may land.
—Leonardo da Vinci

The field of gifted education is based on the almost universally accepted reality that some learners demonstrate outstanding performance or potential for superior performance in academic, creative, leadership, or artistic domains when compared with their peers. From preschool through college and even at graduate and professional school levels, a range of learning potentials justifies an examination of differentiated opportunities and services. As the quotation above points out, if we are not guided by a unified theory when choosing options we are likely to fall for anything! Theory is, indeed, the rudder and compass that should guide us toward practices that avoid randomness in the goals we pursue.

Absence of theory in educational practice usually results in services comprising piecemeal, fragmented, and loosely related activities rather than integrated theory-driven programs characterized by internal consistency from goal setting to services and evaluation. Without sound underlying theory—and the will to stick to the charted course—what happens in classrooms is often a reaction to political or commercial interests or the whims of bureaucratic policy makers far removed from classrooms; or can be based on questionable research and scholarship or the latest fads or flavor-of-the-month "innovation" devised by gurus without credential, or well-intentioned but unapprised local sages; or a combination of the above. But theory alone will not make substantial differences unless it has generated a strong research base, is translated into logically derivative practices that are relatively easy for practitioners to understand and implement, and has the flexibility for those practices to be adapted to variations in local demographics and resources (Ambrose, Cohen, & Tannenbaum, 2003; Ambrose, VanTassel-Baska, Coleman, & Cross, 2010; Cohen, 1988; Renzulli, 2011).

Effective theories for educating gifted and talented students require two additional and related characteristics. First, the theory should exhibit a logical relationship between the theory-guided services provided to students and the conception of giftedness that serves as a rationale for the development of that theory. An acceleration-based theory that recommends the use of advanced mathematics courses, for example, should obviously be related to a conception of gifted that targets students with high aptitudes in math. Second, and particularly relevant to the enrichment-based theory presented in this article, services should be provided for both advanced cognitive development and what are referred to below to as "intelligences outside the normal curve." A rationale for this requirement and an accompanying conception of giftedness has evolved over the past three decades as a guide for the implementation of school programs designed to develop giftedness and talents in young people.

The overall theory is composed of four interrelated subtheories and is based on the belief that when one is reexamining the role of theory in gifted education we should always begin with the why question—Why should a society devote special resources to the development of giftedness in young people? Although there are two generally accepted purposes for providing special education for young people with high potential, these two purposes in combination give rise to a third purpose that is intimately related to the conception of giftedness question. The first purpose of gifted education is to provide young people with maximum opportunities for self-fulfillment through the development and expression of one or a combination of performance areas where superior potential may be present. The second purpose is to increase society's reservoir of persons who will help solve the problems of contemporary civilization by becoming producers of knowledge and art rather than mere consumers of existing information. Although there may be some arguments for and against both of the above purposes, most people would agree that goals related to self-fulfillment and/or societal contributions are generally consistent with democratic philosophies of education. What is even more important is that the two goals are highly interactive and mutually supportive of each other. In other words, self-satisfying work of scientists, artists, writers, entrepreneurs, and leaders in all walks of life has the potential to produce results that are valuable contributions to society. If, as I have argued, the purpose of gifted programs is to increase the size of society's supply of potentially creative and productive adults, then the argument for special education programs that focus on creative productivity (rather than lesson-learning giftedness) is a very simple one.

If we agree with these two goals of gifted education, and if we believe that our programs should produce the next generation of leaders, problem solvers, and persons who will make important contributions to all areas of human productivity, then the third purpose of gifted education is to show the sensibility in modeling special programs and services after the modus operandi of these persons rather than after those of good lesson learners. This view is not an argument against good lesson learning and high levels of achievement and text consumption. But good lesson learning should be the province of the best-quality general education that schooling can provide to all students according to their individual needs and aptitudes. A focus on creative productivity, however, is especially important because the most efficient lesson learners are not necessarily those persons who go on to make important contributions to knowledge. And in this day and age of exponential knowledge expansion, it would seem wise to consider a model that focuses on how our most able students access and make use of information rather than merely on how they accumulate, store, and retrieve it.

This general theory draws on the work of several researchers and scholars, and like any other theory, it is intended to synthesize accumulated knowledge and hopefully motivate further research. And, of course, the final outcome for theory in an applied field is not only an effective practice for targeted audiences, which in our field are mainly teachers and students, but also include administrators and policy makers.

A Few Words About Terminology

In both education and psychology the term *giftedness* has evolved into a theoretical construct (something to be studied). Although most writers use the word *gifted* as a noun, I have consistently used the term *gifted* as an adjective (e.g., gifted behaviors, a gifted writer) rather than a noun (e.g., referring to an individual or group as "the gifted"). And when I refer to gifted education or gifted programs, the adjective is in the context of the root meaning of the word—that which is given. Thus, I have consistently argued (e.g., Renzulli, 1998, 2005) that we should label the services necessary to develop high potentials rather than labeling the students as gifted or not gifted. Accordingly, when we identify traits or aptitudes in students, we should focus on specific behavioral manifestations (e.g., superior memory for important dates in history, ability to generate creative ideas, high task commitment in film making, advanced analytic abilities in mathematics).

I have also purposely made a distinction between two types of giftedness. The first is called high achieving or schoolhouse giftedness, referring to students who are good lesson learners in traditional school achievement. The second is creative productive giftedness, referring to the traits that inventors, designers, authors, artists, and others *apply* to selected areas of economic, cultural, and social capital. These two types of giftedness are not mutually exclusive, but the distinction is important because of the implications for the ways in which we develop gifted behaviors in educational settings. The four parts of my work that contribute to the overall theory are depicted in Figure 2.1. These subtheories, taken collectively, are designed to point out both the ways in which we can identify talent potential in young people, how we can develop both academic talent, and what I refer to as "intelligences outside the normal curve." These nonintellective traits are as important in promoting the development of fully functioning high potential individuals as are traditionally measured cognitive traits. Furthermore, the theories are based on several years of research that has been summarized by Gubbins (1995), Renzulli and Reis (1994), Reis and Renzulli (2003), and Reis et al. (2005). Also included in the development of the theories is the work of others who have conducted research related to the underlying concepts and constructs that make up the theory (Duckworth, 2009; Duckworth & Quinn, 2009; Sytsma, 2003).

Finally, the relationship between the gifted field and general education is reflected by these theories. Currently, education policy and practice focus on "21st Century Skills" (e.g., Bellanca & Brandt, 2010; Partnership for 21st Century Skills, 2011; Trilling & Fadel, 2009). Notably, these skills reflect an area that has been the centerpiece of gifted education for many years. What is most interesting about the popularization of 21st century skills is that attention is

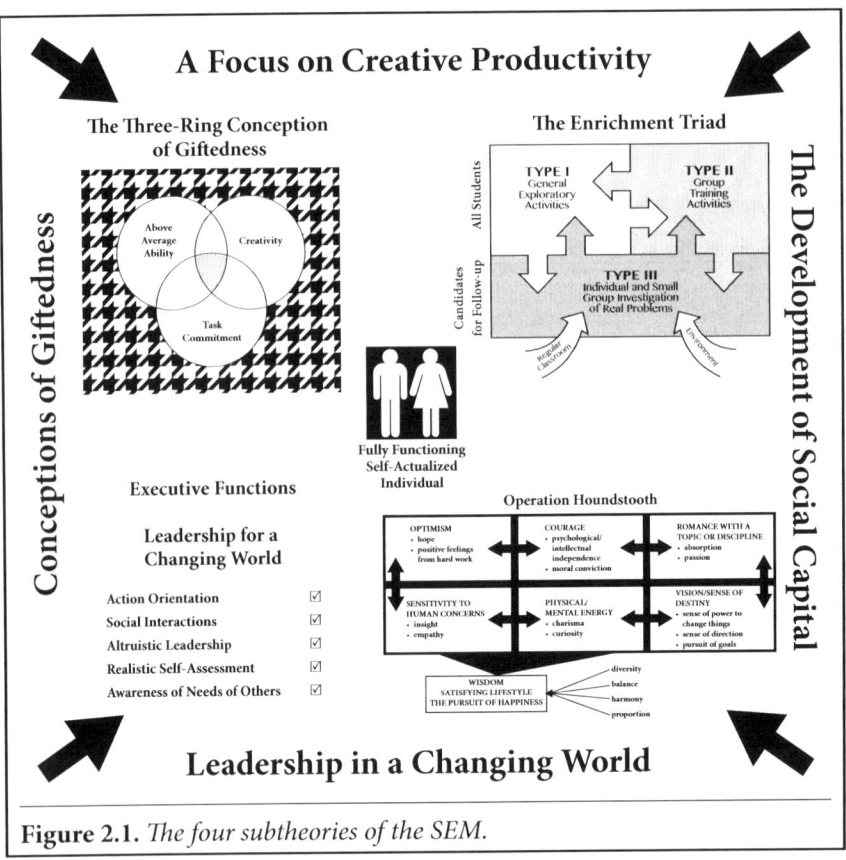

Figure 2.1. *The four subtheories of the SEM.*

now being given to noncognitive as well as strictly cognitive skills. Significant contributions in this area of research include Gardner's Good Works project, which focuses on excellence, ethics, and engagement and documents the conclusion that many young people want to work to make the world a better place (Fischman & Gardner, 2009); Sternberg's work on wisdom, which targets achieving a common good through a balance among intrapersonal, interpersonal, and extrapersonal interests (Sternberg, 1998); and Seligman's work on positive psychology, which deals with the development of character strengths and virtues (Seligman, 1998).

Hopefully, this summary and articulation of the conceptual foundations being presented will generate more research, extend dialogue among scholars in the field, and perhaps even impel more scholars to devote attention to a field that has been limited in theoretical underpinnings (Ambrose et al., 2010).

The Four-Part Theory

For over four decades I have been examining and reexamining the meaning of the age-old questions of "What makes giftedness?" and "How do we develop it in young people?" I raised the first part of this question in an article that reexamined existing conceptions of giftedness (Renzulli, 1978) and emerging research led to updates (Renzulli, 1986, 2005). I have continued to explore what causes some people to use their intellectual, motivational, and creative assets in ways that lead to outstanding manifestations of achievement and creative productivity, whereas others with similar or perhaps even greater potential fail to achieve high levels of accomplishment. I continue to wonder what causes the development of only a minuscule number of Thomas Edisons or Rachel Carsons or Langston Hughes or Isadora Duncans, whereas millions of persons with equal "equipment" and educational advantages (or disadvantages) never rise above mediocrity. Why do some people who have not enjoyed the advantages of special educational opportunities achieve high levels of accomplishment, whereas others who have benefitted from the best of educational opportunities and enriching lifestyles fade into obscurity (Dai & Renzulli, 2008; Renzulli, 1982b; Sternberg, 2005)?

Other questions have also led to attempts to frame the nature of giftedness. Is giftedness an absolute concept or a relative concept? That is, is a person either gifted or not gifted (the absolute view) or can varying kinds and degrees of gifted behaviors be displayed in certain people, at certain times, and under certain circumstances (the relative view)? Is gifted a static concept (i.e., you have it or you do not have it) or is it a dynamic concept (i.e., it varies both within persons and within learning-performance situations; Renzulli, 1986)?

This article represents a synthesis of the literature that frames my responses to the questions above in combination with the purposes of gifted education that form the rationale for recommended approaches to developing giftedness. Although I refer to this work as a general theory for the development of human potential, it is made up of four subtheories I have worked on over the years and that are presented in graphic form in Figure 2.1.

Subtheory I: The Three-Ring Conception of Giftedness

The Three-Ring Conception of Giftedness attempts to portray the main dimensions of human potential for creative productivity. The name derives from the conceptual framework of the theory—namely, three interacting clusters of traits (Above Average Ability, Task Commitment, and Creativity) and their relationship with general and specific areas of human performance.

Perhaps the most salient aspect of this theory is that it is the interaction among these clusters of traits brought to bear on a particular problem situation that creates the conditions for the creative productive process to commence. A second aspect of the theory posits that whereas abilities (especially general intelligence, specific aptitudes, and academic achievement) tend to remain relatively constant over time, creativity and task commitment are contextual, situational, and temporal. Finally, these clusters of traits emerge in certain people, at certain times, and under certain circumstances. The Enrichment Triad Model is the compatible learning theory from which I attempt to prescribe educational conditions that create the conditions for stimulating interaction between and among the three rings, described below.

Above Average Ability encompasses both general (e.g., verbal and numerical reasoning, spatial relations, memory) and specific (e.g., chemistry, ballet, musical composition, experimental design) performance areas and is the most constant of the rings. That is, any student's performance within the parameters of this ring is minimally variable, as it is linked most closely with traditional cognitive/intellectual traits. The reason that this ring makes reference to "above average ability" (as opposed to, e.g., "the top 5%" or "exceptional ability") derives from research that highlights minimal criterion validity between academic aptitude and professional accomplishments (Renzulli, 1976, 1986, 2005). In other words, research suggests that, beyond a certain level of cognitive ability, real-world achievement is less dependent on ever-increasing performance on skills assessment than on other personal and dispositional factors (e.g., task commitment and creativity). This realization highlights the limitations of intelligence tests and the innumerable aptitude and achievement tests that are used to identify candidates for "gifted programs."

Task Commitment represents a nonintellective cluster of traits found consistently in creative productive individuals (e.g., perseverance, determination, will power, positive energy). It is best summarized as a focused or refined form of motivation—energy brought to bear on a particular problem or specific performance area. The significance of this cluster of traits in any definition of giftedness derives from myriad research studies as well as autobiographical sketches of creative productive individuals. Simply stated, one of the primary ingredients for success among persons who have made important contributions to their respective performance areas is their ability to immerse themselves fully in a problem or area for an extended period of time and to persevere even in the face of obstacles that would inhibit others.

Creativity is that cluster of traits that encompasses curiosity, originality, ingenuity, and a willingness to challenge convention and tradition. For example, there have been many gifted scientists throughout history, but the scientists whose work we revere, whose names have remained recognizable in scholarly communities and among the general public, are those scientists who used their creativity to envision, analyze, and ultimately help resolve scientific questions in new, original ways.

In summary, the Three-Ring Conception of Giftedness is based on an overlap and interaction between and among the three clusters of traits that create the conditions for making giftedness. Giftedness is not viewed as an absolute or fixed state of being (i.e., you have it or you do not have it). Rather, it is viewed as a developmental set of behaviors that can be applied to problem-solving situations. Varying kinds and degrees of gifted behaviors can be developed and displayed in certain people, at certain times, and under certain circumstances. The rationale for the Three-Ring Conception of Giftedness draws on the previously mentioned anticipated social roles of persons with high potential.

Subtheory II: The Enrichment Triad Model

All learning exists on a continuum ranging from deductive, didactic, and prescriptive approaches at one end to inductive, investigative, and constructivist-based approaches at the other. This continuum exists for learners of all ages—from toddlers to doctoral students—and it exists in all areas of curricular activity. The continuum also exists for learning that takes place in the nonschool world, the kind of experiences that young people and adults pursue as they acquire new skills for their jobs or work in the kitchen, the garden, or the workshop in the basement. (There are, of course, occasions when a particular approach falls between the two ends of the continuum, but for purposes of clarifying the main features of deductive and inductive learning, I will treat the two models as polar opposites.) Both models of learning and teaching are valuable in the overall process of schooling, and a well-balanced school program must make use of both approaches as well as strategies that use a combination of these approaches.

The Deductive Model of Learning. Although many names have been used to describe the theories that define the ends of the learning continuum, I simply refer to them as the Deductive Model and the Inductive Model (Guilford, 1967). The Deductive Model is familiar to most educators, as much of the learning that takes place in classrooms and other places in which formal learning is pursued is deductive. The Inductive Model, on the other hand, represents the kind of learning that typically takes place outside formal school situations. A good way to understand the difference between these two types of learning is to compare how learning takes place in a typical classroom with how someone learns new material or skills in real-world situations. Classrooms are characterized by relatively fixed time schedules; segmented subjects or topics;

predetermined sets of information and activities, tests, and grades to determine progress; and a pattern of organization that is largely driven by the need to acquire and assimilate information and skills that are deemed important by curriculum developers, textbook publishers, and committees who prepare lists of standards. The deductive model assumes that current learning will have transfer value for some future problem, course, occupational pursuit, or life activity.

Deductive learning is based mainly on the factory model or human engineering conception of schooling. The underlying psychological theory is behaviorism, and the theorists most frequently associated with this model are Ivan Pavlov, E. L. Thorndike, and B. F. Skinner. At the center of this ideology is the ability to produce desirable responses by presenting selected stimuli. In educational settings, these theories translate into a form of structured training for purposes of knowledge and skill acquisition. A curriculum based on the Deductive Model must be examined in terms of both what and how something is taught.

The instructional effects of the Deductive Model are those directly achieved by leading the learner in prescribed directions. There is nothing inherently "wrong" with the Deductive Model; however, it is based on a limited conception of the role of the learner and fails to consider variations in interests and learning styles. Also, in this approach, students are always cast in the roles of lesson-learners and exercise-doers rather than authentic, first-hand inquirers.

The Inductive Model of Learning. The Inductive Model, on the other hand, represents the kinds of learning that ordinarily occur outside formal classrooms in places such as research laboratories, artists' studios, theaters, film and video production sets, business offices, service agencies, and within almost any extracurricular activity in which products, performances, or services are pursued. The theorists most closely associated with inductive learning are John Dewey, Maria Montessori, and Jerome Bruner. The type of learning advocated by these theorists can be summarized as knowledge and skill acquisition gained from investigative and creative activities that are characterized by three requirements (Renzulli, 1977, 1982a). First, there is a personalization of the topic or problem—students are doing the work because they want to. Second, students are using methods of investigation or creative production that approximate the modus operandi of the practicing professional, even if the methodology is at a more junior level than that used by adult researchers, film makers, or business entrepreneurs. Third, the work is always geared toward the production of a product or service intended to have an impact on a particular audience (Renzulli, 1982b).

The information (content) and the skills (process) derived in inductive learning situations are based on need-to-know and need-to-do requirements.

For example, if a group of students is interested in examining differences in attitudes toward dress codes or teenage dating between and within various groups (e.g., gender, grade, students vs. adults), they need certain background information. What have other studies on these topics revealed? Are there any national trends? Have other countries examined dress code or teenage dating issues? Where can these studies be found? Students will need to learn how to design authentic questionnaires, rating scales, and interview schedules and how to record, analyze, and report their findings in the most appropriate format (e.g., written, statistical, graphic, oral, dramatized). Finally, they will need to know how to identify potentially interested audiences, the most appropriate presentation formats (based on a particular audience's level of comprehension), and how to open doors for publication and presentation opportunities. Information used in inductive learning is based on Just-In-Time (JIT) knowledge as opposed to the To-Be-Presented knowledge that characterizes most deductive learning situations. The Internet has made JIT knowledge easily available to today's learners; and the interactive capacity of today's technology allows students to go beyond simple text consumption and worksheets-on-line.[3]

This example demonstrates how knowledge and skills become instantaneously relevant because they are necessary to prepare a high-quality product. All resources, information, schedules, and sequences of events are directed toward this goal, and evaluation (rather than grading) is a function of the quality of the product or service as viewed through the eyes of a client, consumer, or other type of audience member. Everything that results in learning in a research laboratory, for example, is for contemporaneous use. Therefore, looking up new information, conducting an experiment, analyzing results, or preparing a report or presentation is an action-oriented and investigative act of learning. We can see here the relevance of the JIT knowledge mentioned above. This kind of learning differs from deductive learning, and the skills developed in investigative learning are the better outcome for preparing young people for creative and productive futures.

In summary, the Deductive Model has dominated the ways in which most formal education is pursued, and the track record of the model has been less than impressive. One need only reflect for a moment on his or her own school experience to realize that with the exception of some basic language and mathematics skills, much of the compartmentalized material learned for some remote and ambiguous future situation is seldom used in the conduct of daily activities. The names of famous generals, geometric formulas, the periodic table, and parts of a plant learned outside an applicable, real-world situ-

---

3 For a discussion of what I refer to as "Going Beyond Gutenberg," see http://www.gifted.uconn.edu/sem/Going_Beyond_Gutenberg.html.

ation are generally quickly forgotten. This is not to say that previously learned information is unimportant, but its relevancy, meaningfulness, and endurance for future use is minimized when learned apart from situations that have personalized meaning for the learner.

The Enrichment Triad Model. The three types of enrichment in the Triad Model (see the upper right hand corner of Figure 2.1) are designed to work in harmony with one another and it is the interaction among the types of enrichment that produce the dynamic properties represented by the arrows that are as important as the individual components in achieving the goals of this inductive approach to learning. Type I Enrichment includes general, exploratory activities that expose students to problems, issues, ideas, notions, theories, skills—in sum, possibilities. Often, this type of enrichment serves as a catalyst for curiosity and internal motivation.

Type I Enrichment may be the method for externally stimulating students toward internal commitment and purpose. These activities should be made available to all students. A highlight of the model that underscores the philosophy behind the Three-Ring Conception of Giftedness is that task commitment and creativity are crucial to the development of potentially gifted students, who may "rise to the challenge" in unexpected ways or at unexpected times, given the proper environment.

Type II Enrichment involves both individual and group training in a variety of cognitive, meta-cognitive, methodological, and affective skills. This type of enrichment prepares the students to produce tangible products and/or generate resolutions to real-world problems through its emphasis on skill development and information gathering. It is not enough to be curious and moved toward action; one must also be equipped to tap and use resources in order to take action. Type I activities are intended to capture students' interests—to inspire—whereas Type II activities are intended to teach students how to move from inspiration to action. Type II activities are contingent on the students' developmental levels and, as such, should vary in complexity and sophistication with personal and academic maturity. Generally, there are five categories of Type II activities, all of which may be considered as focusing on process skills: (a) cognitive training, (b) affective training, (c) learning-how-to-learn training, (d) research and reference procedures, and (e) written, oral, and visual communication procedures. Type II Enrichment activities can also serve as points of entry into Type III involvement.

Type III activities are individual and small group investigations of real-world problems. Real-world problems are here defined as problems that evoke a personal frame of reference for students, problems with no existing or unique resolution, and problems designed to have an impact on a targeted audience. As with Type II activities, the sophistication and depth of Type III activities is contingent on students' developmental levels. Regardless of the level of influence and breadth of reach of solutions to real-world problems generated by Type III activities, all such activities encompass four objectives for students: (a) to acquire advanced-level understanding of the knowledge and methodology used within particular disciplines, artistic areas of expression, and interdisciplinary studies; (b) to develop authentic products or services that are primarily directed toward bringing about a desired impact on one or more specified audiences; (c) to develop self-directed learning skills in the areas of planning, problem finding and focusing, management, cooperativeness, decision making, and self-evaluation; and (d) to develop task commitment, self-confidence, feelings of creative accomplishment, and the ability to interact effectively with other students and adults who share common goals and interests.

Type III experiences are the culmination of natural learning, representing synthesis and an application of content, process, and personal involvement through self-motivated work. These activities serve as the vehicles within the total school experience through which everything from basic skills to advanced content and processes "come together" in the form of student-developed products and services. They may be referred to "the assembly plant of the mind." Clearly, the student's role is transformed from one of lesson-learner to first-hand investigator or creator, and the teacher's role must shift from that of instructor or disseminator of knowledge to some combination of coach, promoter, manager, mentor, agent, guide, and sometimes even colleague (Renzulli, 1982b).

Subtheory III: Operation Houndstooth—
Gifted Education and Social Capital

The rationale for this subtheory and the one that follows is based on the anticipated roles that individuals with high potential play in society. Whether we like it or not, history has shown us that highly able people assume important positions in all walks of life—government, law, science, religion, politics, business, and the arts and humanities. What kinds of leaders will these people be? What kinds of life experiences created the contrasting behaviors of Nelson Mandela and Idi Amin? This subpart of the overall theory addresses the question: "Why do some people mobilize their interpersonal, political, ethical, and moral realms of being in such ways that they place human concerns and the common good above materialism, ego enhancement, and self-indulgence?" The abundance of folk wisdom, research literature, and biographical and anecdotal accounts about creativity and giftedness are nothing short of mind boggling; and yet we are still unable to answer this fundamental question about persons who have devoted their lives to improving the human condition.

Several theorists have speculated about the necessary ingredients for giftedness and creative productivity, and their related theories have called attention to important components and conditions for high-level accomplishment. However, most of these theories have dwelt only on cognitive characteristics, and by so doing, they have failed to explain how the confluence of desirable traits result in commitments for making the lives of all people more rewarding, environmentally safe, economically viable, peaceful, and politically free.

Work related to this topic examines the scientific research that defines several categories of personal characteristics associated with an individual's commitment to the production of social capital, briefly defined here as using one's talents to improve human conditions, whether that improvement is directed toward one person or larger audiences or conditions. These characteristics include optimism, courage, romance with a topic or discipline, physical and mental energy, vision and a sense of destiny, and sense of power to change things (Renzulli, 2002). These factors and their subcomponents are portrayed in the lower right quadrant of Figure 2.1. They are represented in the Three-Ring Conception figure by the houndstooth background in which the three clusters of traits are found. I call these "Houndstooth" traits co-cognitive factors because they interact with and enhance the cognitive traits that are ordinarily associated with the development of human abilities. A number of researchers have suggested that constructs of this type, including social, emotional, and inter- or intrapersonal intelligence, are related to each other and are independent from traditional measures of ability. The two-directional arrows in this diagram point out the many interactions that take place between and among the factors.

The general goal of this work and a related intervention model is designed to infuse into the overall process of schooling experiences that promote the Houndstooth components and that ultimately give highly able young people a sense of their responsibility to society at large. It would be naïve to think that a redirection of educational goals can take place without a commitment at all levels to examine the purposes of education in a democracy. It is also naïve to think that experiences directed toward the production of social capital can, or are even intended to, replace our present-day focus on material productivity and intellectual capital. Rather, this work seeks to enhance the development of wisdom and a satisfying lifestyle that are paralleled by concerns for diversity, balance, harmony, and proportion in all the choices and decisions that young people make in the process of maturing. What people think and decide to do drives some of society's best ideas and achievements. If we want leaders who will promote ideas and achievements that take into consideration the components we have identified in Operation Houndstooth, then giftedness in the new century will have to be redefined in ways that take these co-cognitive components into account. And the strategies that are used to develop giftedness in young people will need to give as much attention to the co-cognitive conditions of development as we presently give to cognitive development.

Subtheory IV: Executive Functions—
Leadership for a Changing World

The fourth and final theory may very well be the "yeast" that enables all constructs described above to actually be used to pursue a desired goal in an efficient and effective way. I sometimes describe this final subtheory as simply "getting your act together." The most creative ideas, advanced analytic skills, and the noblest of motives may not result in positive action unless leadership skills such as organization, sequencing, and sound judgment are brought to bear on problem situations. Landmark research by Duckworth, Seligman, and others (Borghans, Duckworth, Heckman, & Weel, 2008; Duckworth, 2009; Duckworth, Peterson, Matthews, & Kelly, 2007; Duckworth & Quinn, 2009; Duckworth & Seligman, 2005) has shown that students who persist in college were not necessarily the ones who excelled on measures of aptitude, but the ones with exceptional character strengths such as optimism, persistence, and social intelligence. This research showed that measures of self-control can be more reliable predictors of students' grade-point averages than their IQ scores. Including this focus in the overall theory represents a distinctly different approach to talent development than most of the models focusing primarily on cognitive development. The research noted above documents that both IQ and self-discipline are correlated with grade-point average, but self-discipline is a much more important contributor: Those with low self-discipline have substantially lower college grades than those with low IQs, whereas high-discipline students received much better grades than high-IQ students. Even after adjusting for the students' grades during the first marking period of the year, students with higher self-discipline still had higher grades at the end of the year. The same could not be said for IQ. Furthermore, these studies found no correlation between IQ and self-discipline—these two traits varied independently.

I have focused my work in this area on what are commonly referred to in the business and human resource literature as executive functions. Executive functions are broadly defined as the ability to engage in novel situations that require planning, decision making, troubleshooting, and compassionate and ethical leadership that is not dependent on routine or well-rehearsed responses to challenging combinations of conditions. These traits also involve organizing, integrating, and managing information, emotions, and other cognitive and affective functions that lead to "doing the right thing" in situations that do not have a predetermined or formulaic driven response.

These functions are especially important to highly capable people because of the positions of power to which they typically ascend. A number of researchers have pointed out the importance of incorporating these noncognitive skills into everything from curricular experiences (Cordova & Lepper, 1996; Diamond, 2010) to educational assessments (Levin, 2011; Sedlack, 2005) and college admission considerations (Sternberg, 2005). These skills have important implications for the academic success of students, career decisions, and even the economic productivity of nations. Although not minimizing the importance of traditional cognitive ability, these authors point out that conventional assessments account for a small portion of the variance when examining long-term academic and career accomplishment, especially as it relates to the advancement of adult competencies in highly demanding professions where leadership skills and creative productivity are the criteria for success.

A good deal of the background material that led to the inclusion of executive functions in this overall talent development model comes from the field of human resources (Durlak, Weissberg, Dymnicki, Taylor, & Schellinger, 2011; Heckman & Rubenstein, 2001). These authors point out the importance of noncognitive skills in personal and social as well as academic development and—more important for this overall theory—a meta-analysis showed that these skills could be taught. Initial input was also derived from the literature on social, behavioral, and "emotional intelligence" (Goleman, 2006). Goleman argued that great leadership works through noncognitive traits such as self-awareness, self-management, motivation, empathy, and social skills. Although the research literature on these types of noncognitive traits is massive, there is general agreement that the following so-called "Big Five" personality traits (Almlund, Duckworth, Heckman, & Kautz, 2011) are the basis on which education intervention programs should focus:

1. *Openness*—Inventive and curious as opposed to consistent and cautious
2. *Conscientiousness*—Efficient and organized as opposed to easy-going and careless
3. *Extraversion*—Outgoing and energetic as opposed to solitary and reserved
4. *Agreeableness*—Friendly and compassionate as opposed to cold and unkind
5. *Neuroticism*—Secure and confident as opposed to sensitive and nervous

Our research to date on this subtheory has included the development of an instrument called *Rating the Executive Functions of Young People* (Renzulli

& Mitchell, 2011). This diagnostic instrument is designed to assist in research dealing with the types and degrees of executive function traits in young people and can be used both to identify potential leadership traits in young people and help teachers determine which curricular experiences can develop desirable leadership traits in individuals or groups. Subsequent diagnostic techniques may include simulations to determine successful performance in demanding problem-solving situations.

Themes that emerged as contributors to success from the review of research conducted in the process of instrument development included mindfulness, ethical/moral, social, motivational, and leadership traits as well as the so-called Big Five personality traits or factors mentioned. Also identified were specific traits such as being eager to learn, studious, intelligent, interested, and industrious and other variables such as positive and realistic self-appraisal, preference for long-range goals, successful leadership experience, and community service. Researchers in other domains have also identified noncognitive variables of persons who lead and make a difference. For example, in reports on the characteristics possessed by some of the most altruistic persons in American society, common traits that were demonstrated by most of these individuals included passion, determination, talent, self-discipline, and faith. Leadership, ethics, accountability, adaptability, personal productivity, personal responsibility, people skills, self-direction, and social responsibility have also been identified as critical skills in the literature dealing with 21st century skills, as were professionalism, enthusiasm, leadership, positive work ethic, values, decisiveness, teamwork, character, support, conformity, openness, self-concept, anxiety, and life-long learning.

This overwhelming list of traits that emerged from the literature review were grouped into five general categories as a result of a factor analysis of data collected from several hundred respondents using the instrument mentioned above. The first factor is Action Orientation, which includes specific characteristics that motivate an individual to succeed. The second factor is Social Interactions and it includes traits that enable someone to successfully interact with others. The third factor is Altruistic Leadership, and it includes characteristics relating to both empathy and dependability. The fourth factor, Realistic Self-Assessment, includes characteristics that demonstrate awareness of one's own abilities, realistic self-appraisal, and self-efficacy. Finally, Awareness of the Needs of Others subsumes sensitivity, approachableness, and strong communication skills. Taken collectively, all these behaviors characterize highly effective persons, but they also reflect traits that cause people who have emerged as leaders in their respective fields to "do the right thing" in the arenas and domains over which they have had an influence.

The implications for including executive functions in a theory about the study of giftedness relates to the anticipated social and leadership roles that high potential young people will play in their future endeavors. Embracing executive functions also has significance for the types of programs and experiences that should be provided to develop these skills and the roles and responsibilities of curriculum developers and service providers. The relative newness of this dimension on the parts of scholars in the field is obviously in need of more research and there are many opportunities for creative implementation practices and original research related thereto.

Summary

Gifted education, like all other specialized areas in the arts and sciences, is constantly in search of its identity. What defines a field beyond random and trendy practices are the theories and related research that delineates its parameters, promotes future research, and has an impact on defensible practice. Our field has been notably "thin" on theory development, and the work offered here is just one approach that I hope will promote discussion among scholars and practitioners, generate research on the validity of the ideas and concepts discussed here, and inspire more theoretical development on the parts of other scholars.

The most salient point to make when discussing and generalizing about theories for the study of giftedness in the 21st century is that there is an overlap and an interaction among cognitive, affective, and motivational characteristics. We cannot divorce these numerous and interactive characteristics from the ways we should go about developing gifted behaviors in young people. Developing the intelligences outside the normal curve is as important to the contributions that our field can make as have been the traditional academic markers of successful gifted programs.

A second and final consideration deals with how we should go about producing leaders for the 21st century. This consideration deals directly with how gifted education should differ qualitatively from general education. People who have gained recognition as gifted contributors in the beyond-the-school world have always done so because of something they did—an invention, a sonata, a design, and a solution to a political or economic problem. They brought myriad traits to bear on their respective challenges, and it is these types of experiences that provided such opportunities that should be the core of our efforts to educate tomorrow's people of great promise. The anticipated social roles that people of high potential will play should be the main rationale for both supporting special programs and designing learning experiences that will prepare today's students for responsible leadership roles in the future.

In my opinion, the biggest challenge in gifted education is to extend our traditional investment in the production of intellectual and creative capital to include an equal investment in social capital and the development of executive function skills (see Subotnik, Robinson, Callahan, & Gubbins, 2012). I believe that experiences designed to develop these skills should begin at early ages and focus mainly on direct involvement rather than "teaching-and-preaching" experiences. If we can have an impact on social capital and effective and empathetic leadership, then we will be preparing the kinds of leaders who are as sensitive to human, environmental, and democratic concerns as they are to the traditional materialistic markers of success in today's world. And the greatest payoff from focusing gifted education on investigative learning and using knowledge wisely will be a dramatic increase in the reservoir of people who will use their talents to create a better world.

References

Ambrose, D. C., Cohen, L., & Tannenbaum, A. J. (Eds.). (2003). *Creative intelligence: Toward theoretic integration.* New York, NY: Hampton Press.

Ambrose, D. C., VanTassel-Baska, J., Coleman, L. J., & Cross, T. L. (2010). Unified, insular, and firmly policed or fractured, porous, contested, gifted education? *Journal for the Education of the Gifted, 33,* 453–478.

Almlund, M., Duckworth, A. L., Heckman, J., & Kautz, T. (2011). *Personality psychology and economics* (IZA DP No. 5500). Retrieved from http://ftp.iza.org/dp5500.pdf

Bellanca, J., & Brandt, R. (Eds.). (2010). *21st century skills: Rethinking how students learn.* Bloomington, IN: Solution Tree.

Borghans, L., Duckworth, A. L., Heckman, J. J., & Weel, B. (2008). The economics and psychology of personality traits. *Journal of Human Resources, 43,* 972–1059.

Cohen, L. M. (1988). To get ahead, get a theory. *Roeper Review, 11,* 95–100.

Cordova, D. I., & Lepper, M. R. (1996). Intrinsic motivation and the process of learning: Beneficial effects of contextualization, personalization, and choice. *Journal of Educational Psychology, 88,* 715–730.

Dai, D. Y., & Renzulli, J. S. (2008). Snowflakes, living systems, and the mystery of giftedness. *Gifted Child Quarterly, 52,* 114–130.

Diamond, A. (2010). The evidence base for improving school outcomes by addressing the whole child and by addressing skills and attitudes, not just content. *Early Education and Development, 21,* 780–793.

Duckworth, A. L. (2009). Backtalk: Self-discipline is empowering. *Phi Delta Kappan, 90,* 536.

Duckworth, A. L., Peterson, C., Matthews, M. D., & Kelly, D. R. (2007). Grit: Perseverance and passion for long-term goals. *Journal of Personality and Social Psychology, 92,* 1087–1101.

Duckworth, A. L., & Quinn, P. D. (2009). Development and validation of the Short Grit Scale (Grit-S). *Journal of Personality Assessment, 91,* 166–174.

Duckworth, A. L., & Seligman, M. E. P. (2005). Self-discipline outdoes IQ predicting academic performance of adolescents. *Psychological Science, 16,* 939–944.

Durlak, J. A., Weissberg, R. P., Dymnicki, A. B., Taylor, R. D., & Schellinger, K. B. (2011). The impact of enhancing students' social and emotional learning: A meta-analysis of school-based universal interventions. *Child Development, 82,* 405–432.

Fischman, W., & Gardner, H. (2009). Implementing GoodWork programs: Helping students to become ethical workers. *Knowledge Quest, 37*(3), 74–79.

Goleman, D. (2006). *Emotional intelligence: Why it can matter more than IQ.* New York, NY: Bantam Press.

Gubbins, E. J. (Ed.). (1995). *Research related to the enrichment triad model* (RM95212). Storrs: University of Connecticut, The National Research Center on the Gifted and Talented.

Guilford, J. P. (1967). *The nature of human intelligence.* New York, NY: McGraw-Hill.

Heckman, J., & Rubenstein, Y. (2001). The importance of non-cognitive skills: Lessons from the GED testing program. *American Economic Review, 91,* 145–149.

Levin, H. M. (2011, May). *The utility and need for incorporating non-cognitive skills into large scale educational assessments.* Paper presented at the ETS Invitational Conference on International Large Scale Assessments, Princeton, NJ.

Partnership for 21st Century Skills. (2011). Retrieved from http://www.p21.org/

Reis, S. M., Eckert, R. D., Schreiber, F. J., Jacobs, J., Briggs, C., Gubbins, E. J., . . . Muller, L. (2005). *The Schoolwide Enrichment Model Reading Study* (RM05214). Storrs: University of Connecticut, The National Research Center on the Gifted and Talented.

Reis, S. M., & Renzulli, J. S. (2003). Research related to the Schoolwide Enrichment Triad Model. *Gifted Education International, 18,* 15–39.

Renzulli, J. S. (1976). The Enrichment Triad Model: A guide for developing defensible programs for the gifted and talented. *Gifted Child Quarterly, 20,* 303–326.

Renzulli, J. S. (1977). *The enrichment triad model: A guide for developing defensible programs for the gifted and talented.* Mansfield Center, CT: Creative Learning Press.

Renzulli, J. S. (1978). What makes giftedness? Re-examining a definition. *Phi Delta Kappan, 60,* 180–184.

Renzulli, J. S. (1982a). What makes a problem real: Stalking the illusive meaning of qualitative differences in gifted education. *Gifted Child Quarterly, 26,* 147–156.

Renzulli, J. S. (1982b). Dear Mr. and Mrs. Copernicus: We regret to inform you. *Gifted Child Quarterly, 26,* 11–14.

Renzulli, J. S. (1986). The Three-Ring Conception of Giftedness: A developmental model for creative productivity. In R. J. Sternberg & J. Davidson (Eds.), *Conceptions of giftedness* (pp. 246–279). New York, NY: Cambridge University Press.

Renzulli, J. S. (1998). A rising tide lifts all ships: Developing the gifts and talents of all students. *Phi Delta Kappan, 80,* 104–111.

Renzulli, J. S. (2002). Expanding the conception of giftedness to include co-cognitive traits and to promote social capital. *Phi Delta Kappan, 84*(1), 33–40, 57–58.

Renzulli, J. S. (2005). The Three-Ring Conception of Giftedness: A developmental model for promoting creative productivity. In R. J. Sternberg & J. Davidson (Eds.), *Conceptions of giftedness* (2nd ed., pp. 217–245). Boston, MA: Cambridge University Press.

Renzulli, J. S. (2011). Theories, actions, and change: An academic journey in search of finding and developing high potential in young people. *Gifted Child Quarterly, 55,* 305–308.

Renzulli, J. S., & Mitchell, M. S. (2011). *Rating the executive functions of young people.* Storrs: University of Connecticut, The National Research Center on the Gifted and Talented.

Renzulli, J. S., & Reis, S. M. (1994). Research related to the Schoolwide Enrichment Triad Model. *Gifted Child Quarterly, 38,* 7–20.

Seligman, M. E. P. (1998). *Learned optimism.* New York, NY: Pocket Books.

Sedlack, W. E. (2005). The case for noncognitive measures. In W. J. Camara & E. W. Kimmel (Eds.), *Choosing students: Higher education admission tools for the 21st century* (pp. 177–191). Mahwah, NJ: Lawrence Erlbaum.

Sternberg, R. J. (1998). A balance theory of wisdom. *Review of General Psychology, 2,* 347–365.

Sternberg, R. J. (2005). Augmenting the SAT through assessments of analytic, practical, and creative skills. In W. J. Camara & E. W. Kimmel (Eds.), *Choosing students: Higher education admission tools for the 21st century* (pp. 159–176). Mahwah, NJ: Earlbaum.

Subotnik, R. F., Robinson, A., Callahan, C. M., & Gubbbins, E. G. (Eds.). (2012). *Malleable minds: Translating insights from psychology and neuroscience to gifted education.* Storrs: University of Connecticut, The National Research Center on the Gifted and Talented.

Sytsma, R. E. (2003). Co-cognitive factors and socially-constructive giftedness: Distribution, abundance, and relevance among high school students. *Dissertations Collection for University of Connecticut* (Paper AAI3118971).

Trilling, B., & Fadel, C. (2009). *21st century skills: Learning for life in our times.* San Francisco, CA: Jossey-Bass.

PART II

Conceptions and Identification of Giftedness

CHAPTER 3

The Three-Ring Conception of Giftedness
A Developmental Model for Promoting Creative Productivity[4]

Joseph S. Renzulli
University of Connecticut

Introduction From Joe

The original article on The Three-Ring Conception of Giftedness appeared in a 1978 edition of the *Kappan*. Although it was originally rejected by the journals in gifted education, it has now become the most widely cited article in the field. Over the years, I have updated the article three times to include new research and changes in identification and programming that have taken place in the field over the years. The original article and subsequent follow-ups have been cited approximately 3,000 times in national and international jour-

---

[4] Renzulli, J. S. (2005). The Three-Ring Conception of Giftedness: A developmental model for promoting creative productivity. In R. J. Sternberg & J. Davidson (Eds.), *Conceptions of giftedness* (2nd ed., pp. 217–245). Boston, MA: Cambridge University Press. Copyright 2005 Cambridge University Press. Reprinted with permission.

nals. The most important point in the chapter is that our field needs to make differentiated provisions for both high-achieving students and what I have described in this chapter as creative productive giftedness. These two types of giftedness are not mutually exclusive, but it is important to recognize that creative and productive people represent the kind of giftedness found in people who have changed the world in both large and small ways. The chapter presented here is the most recent update. I am proud of the influence all of the Three-Ring articles have had because they show that a field can change its mind regarding long held beliefs about the nature of giftedness.

> Outwitted
> He drew a circle to shut us out
> Heretic, rebel, a thing to flout.
> But love and I had the wit to win
> We drew a circle that took him in.
>
> —Edwin Markham, *Quatrains*

The record of human accomplishments and the progress of civilization can, in many ways, be charted by the actions of history's most gifted and talented contributors to the arts, sciences, and all other areas of human performance. As early as 2200 B.C., the Chinese had developed an elaborate system of competitive examinations to select outstanding persons for government positions (DuBois, 1970), and down through the ages almost every culture has had a special fascination for persons who have made notable contributions to their respective areas of interest and involvement. The areas of performance in which one might be recognized as a "gifted" person are determined by the needs and values of the prevailing culture, and scholars and laypersons alike have debated (and continue to debate) the age-old issues of how certain human abilities, personalities, and environmental conditions contribute to what we call giftedness.

A fascination with persons of unusual ability and potential for extraordinary expertise in any and all fields of human performance has given rise to an area of study in psychology and education called gifted education. In a very general sense, this field focuses on two major questions:

1. What makes giftedness?
2. How can we develop giftedness in young people and adults?

These two questions are the focus of the conception of giftedness described in this chapter, which has evolved over a period of more than 30 years. Because this theory views giftedness as something we develop in certain people, at certain times, and under certain circumstances, a program development plan called the Enrichment Triad Model paralleled work on the conception of giftedness. This plan for the delivery of services describes how we can go about promoting creative productive giftedness and how various types of general enrichment for larger groups of students can serve as "identification situations" for more focused and advanced-level experiences designed to develop gifted behaviors in smaller numbers of students (Renzulli, 1977, 1982, 1992). This approach is a high-end learning example of what is popularly called performance-based or dynamic assessment. Both the conception of giftedness and program development theories have been paralleled by the creation of a wide array of practical instruments and procedures designed to implement the theories in a variety of learning environments (Reis, Burns, & Renzulli, 1992; Renzulli, 1997a, 1997b; Renzulli & Reis, 1997; Renzulli, Rizza, & Smith, 2002; Renzulli et al., 2002). I have always believed that, in an applied field of study, theory is not of much value unless it can give relatively specific direction to the persons ultimately responsible for putting the theory into practice. Most theorists leave practical applications to others; however, one of the characteristics of my work is that it has proceeded simultaneously along both theoretical and practical lines. For better or worse, I have never been content with developing theoretical concepts without devoting equal or even greater attention to creating instruments, procedures, and materials for implementing the various concepts. And theory in an applied field does not have much value if it is not compatible with practical realities, such as policies, personalities, governance, finances, how schools work, teachers' ways of knowing, and practices that can reasonably be expected to endure *beyond* the support usually accorded to pilot projects or experimental research studies. This approach has both advantages and disadvantages. An eye toward implementation allows for theory testing in practical settings and the opportunity to generate research data that can lend credence to the theory and/or point out directions where additional work needs to be done.

The research supporting the theory described in this chapter, as well as reactions to commentary by other writers, has been updated in a number of publications over the years (Renzulli, 1986, 1988, 1999). Because of space limitations, the majority of this research is referenced rather than described in detail. I do, however, refer to some of the modern theories of intelligence that have emerged since the original publication of this work because they have implications for the role that various kinds of intelligences play in the development of giftedness. In this chapter, I provide a description of the major theoretical issues underlying various conceptions of giftedness, an overview of the Three-Ring Conception of Giftedness, some of the research that led to the initial development of the theory, and a brief description of research carried out in places that have used this model. Also included are a new dimension of the overall theory that deals with co-cognitive characteristics and a brief description of a plan for identifying students for special programs and services based on this conception of giftedness.

I would like to point out at the outset that I use the G-word as an adjective rather than a noun. So rather than writing about "the gifted," my preference is to discuss the development of gifted behaviors or giftedness. This use of terminology is in no way intended to negate the existence of persons who are at the high end of a continuum in any domain—general intelligence, mathematics, swimming, piano playing—but my preference is to write about a gifted mathematician, a gifted swimmer, or a gifted piano player. I also make a distinction between potential and performance. Persons can have remarkable potentials for mathematics, swimming, or piano playing, but until that potential is manifested in some type of superior performance, I am reluctant to say they have displayed gifted behaviors. And, of course, our main challenge as educators is to create the conditions that convert potential into performance.

Issues in the Study of Conceptions of Giftedness

Relationships Among Purpose, Conceptions, and Programming

One of the first and most important issues that should be dealt with in a search for the meaning of giftedness is that there must be a purpose for defining this concept. In view of the practical applications for which a definition might be used, it is necessary to consider any definition in the larger context of overall programming for the target population we are attempting to serve. In other words, the way in which one views giftedness will be a primary factor in both constructing a plan for identification and in providing services that are relevant to the characteristics that brought certain youngsters to our attention in the first place. If, for example, one identifies giftedness as extremely high mathematical aptitude, then it would seem nothing short of common sense to use assessment procedures that readily identify potential for superior performance in this particular domain. And it would be equally reasonable to assume that a program based on this definition and identification procedure should devote major emphasis to the enhancement of performance in mathematics and related areas. Similarly, a definition that emphasizes artistic abilities should point the way toward relatively specific identification and programming practices. As long as there are differences of opinion among reasonable scholars, there will never be a single definition of giftedness, and this is probably the way that it should be. But one requirement for which all writers of definitions should be accountable is the necessity of showing a logical relationship between definitions on the one hand and recommended identification and programming practices on the other.

Implicit in any efforts to define and identify the potential for gifted behaviors in young people is the assumption that we will "do something" to provide various types of specialized learning experiences that show promise of promoting the development of characteristics implicit in the definition. In other words, the *why* question supersedes the *who* and *how* questions. Although there are two generally accepted purposes for providing special education for young people with high potential, I believe that these two purposes in combination give rise to a third purpose that is intimately related to the definition question.

The first purpose of gifted education is to provide young people with maximum opportunities for self-fulfillment through the development and expression of one or a combination of performance areas in which superior potential may be present. The second purpose is to increase society's supply of persons who will help to solve the problems of contemporary civilization by becoming producers of knowledge and art rather than mere consumers of existing information. Although there may be some arguments for and against both of these purposes, most people would agree that goals related to self-fulfillment and/or societal contributions are generally consistent with democratic philosophies of education. What is even more important is that the two goals are highly interactive and mutually supportive of each other. In other words, the self-satisfying work of scientists, artists, and leaders in all walks of life has the potential to produce results that might be valuable contributions to society. If, as Gowan (1978) has pointed out, the purpose of gifted programs is to increase the size of society's reservoir of potentially creative and productive adults, then the argument for gifted-education programs that focus on creative productivity (rather than lesson-learning giftedness) is a very simple one. If we agree with the goals of gifted education set forth earlier in the chapter, and if we believe that our programs should produce the next generation of leaders, problem solvers, and persons who will make important contributions to the arts and sciences, then does it not make good sense to model special programs and services after the *modus operandi* of these persons rather than after those of the lesson learner? This is especially true because research (as described later in the chapter) tells us that the most efficient lesson learners are not necessarily those persons who go on to make important contributions in the realm of creative productivity. And in this day and age, when knowledge is expanding at almost geometric proportions, it would seem wise to consider a model that focuses on how our most able students access and make use of information rather than merely on how they accumulate and store it.

Giftedness and Intelligence

A major issue that must be dealt with is that our present efforts to define giftedness are based on a long history of previous studies dealing with human abilities. Most of these studies focused mainly on the concept of intelligence and are briefly discussed here to establish an important point about the process of defining concepts rather than any attempt to equate intelligence with giftedness. Although a detailed review of these studies is beyond the scope of the present chapter, a few of the general conclusions from earlier research are necessary to set the stage for this analysis.[5]

The first conclusion is that intelligence is not a unitary concept but rather, there are many kinds of intelligence and therefore single definitions cannot be used to explain this complicated concept. The confusion and inconclusiveness about present theories of intelligence has led Sternberg (1984), Gardner (1983), and others to develop new models for explaining this complicated concept. After having studied the three aspects of intelligence for some years, Sternberg (1996, 2001) concluded that the answer to the question of intelligence is even more than just *the amount* of a person's analytical, creative, and practical abilities. A person may be gifted with respect to any one of these abilities or with respect to the way she or he *balances the abilities* to succeed (Sternberg & Grigorenko, 2002). "The notion of someone's being 'gifted' or not is a relic of an antiquated, test-based way of thinking" (Sternberg, 1996, p. 197). Intelligence, according to Sternberg and Grigorenko (2002), is not a fixed entity, but a flexible and dynamic one (i.e., it is a form of developing expertise). Developing expertise is "the ongoing process of the acquisition and consolidation of a set of skills needed for a high level of mastery in one or more domains of life performance" (Sternberg & Grigorenko, 2002, p. 267). Thus, someone can be gifted in one domain but not in another. Further, according to Sternberg and colleagues (Sternberg & Lubart, 1995; Sternberg & O'Hara, 1999), intelligence is just one of six forces that generate creative thought and behavior. It is the confluence of intelligence, knowledge, thinking styles, personality, motivation, and the environment that forms gifted behavior as viewed from a creative productive perspective.

---

5 Persons interested in a succinct examination of problems associated with defining intelligence are advised to review "The Concept of Intelligence" (Neisser, 1979).

Howard Gardner (1983) initially formulated a list of seven domain-specific intelligences and added an eighth one several years later. The first two intelligences—*linguistic* and *logical-mathematical*—are ones that have been typically valued in schools; *musical*, *bodily-kinesthetic*, and *spatial* are usually associated with the arts; and another two—*interpersonal* and *intrapersonal*—are what Gardner called "personal intelligences." After considering a few additional intelligences, including spiritual, moral, and existential intelligences, Gardner concluded that only the *naturalist* intelligence qualifies as intelligence in his Multiple Intelligences theory (Gardner, 1999). Linguistic intelligence, which involves sensitivity to spoken and written language, the ability to learn languages, and the capacity to use language to accomplish certain goals, is required of people such as writers, lawyers, and speakers. Scientific and mathematical thinking—required of mathematicians and physicists—on the other hand requires logical-mathematical intelligence, which includes the ability to analyze problems logically (i.e., detect patterns, reason deductively, and think logically). Musical intelligence includes the capacity to recognize and compose musical pitches, tones, and rhythms, skills necessary for performance, composition, and appreciation of musical patterns. Dancers, athletes, and mimes use their whole body or parts of the body to solve problems. Gardner calls the mental ability necessary to coordinate bodily movements bodily-kinesthetic intelligence. Spatial intelligence, the ability to represent and manipulate three-dimensional configurations, is needed by architects, engineers, sculptors, and chess players. The capacity to understand the intentions, motivations, desires, and actions of others and to act sensibly and productively based on that knowledge—interpersonal intelligence—is needed by counselors, teachers, political leaders, and evangelists. A good understanding of one's own cognitive strengths and weaknesses, thinking styles, feelings, and emotions is based on intrapersonal intelligence. Biologists need high levels of naturalist intelligence, which includes extensive knowledge of the living world and its taxonomies, and high capability in recognizing and classifying plants and animals.

In view of this recent work and numerous earlier cautions about the dangers of trying to describe intelligence through the use of single scores, it seems safe to conclude that this practice has been and always will be questionable. At the very least, attributes of intelligent behavior must be considered within the context of cultural and situational factors. Indeed, some of the most extensive examinations have concluded that "[t]he concept of intelligence *cannot* be explicitly defined, not only because of the nature of intelligence but also because of the nature of concepts" (Neisser, 1979, p. 179). Psychologists in the 1990s pointed out the existence of a wide range of contemporary conceptions of intelligence and how it should be measured. Although the psychometric approach is the oldest and best established, it is limited in its ability to explain intelligence. Multiple forms of intelligence such as Sternberg's and Gardner's theories, theories of developmental progression, and biological approaches have much to contribute to a better understanding of intelligence. Thus, some contemporary psychologists suggest that "we should be open to the possibility that our understanding of intelligence in the future will be rather different from what it is today" (Neisser et al., 1996, p. 80).

A second conclusion is that there is no ideal way to measure intelligence and therefore we must avoid the typical practice of believing that if we know a person's IQ score, we also know his or her intelligence. Even Terman warned against total reliance on tests: "We must guard against defining intelligence solely in terms of ability to pass the tests of a given intelligence scale" (Terman et al., 1926, p. 131). E. L. Thorndike echoed Terman's concern by stating, "To assume that we have measured some general power which resides in [the person being tested] and determines his ability in every variety of intellectual task in its entirety is to fly directly in the face of all that is known about the organization of the intellect" (Thorndike, 1921, p. 126).

Although to date the heritability of cognitive ability in childhood seemed to be well established (McGue, Bouchard, Iacono, & Lykken, 1993; Plomin, 1999; as cited in Turkheimer, Haley, Waldron, D'Onofrio, & Gottesman, 2003), recent research adds a new dimension to the relationship between intelligence and measured IQ. Studies among twins or adoptees and their biological and adoptive parents typically yield large genetic effects and relatively smaller effects of family environments. However, most of these studies include children from middle-class and affluent families. Turkheimer et al. (2003) conducted a study that included a substantial proportion of minority twins raised in families living near or below the poverty level. Their study showed that, in the most impoverished families, the modeled heritability of full-scale IQ was essentially zero, and shared environment accounted for almost 60 percent of the variability; whereas in the most affluent families, virtually all of the modeled variability in IQ was attributable to heritability. In other words, whereas genetic makeup explains most of the differences in IQ for children in adequate environments (middle and high socioeconomic status), *environment*—not genes—makes a bigger difference for minority children in low-income homes. The use of IQ scores as a measure of intelligence, therefore, may be even more questionable for children from impoverished families than they are for the general population. Sternberg cautioned that even if heritability is fairly high for a certain population, it does not mean that intelligence cannot be modified (Miele, 1995).

Two Kinds of Giftedness

The reason I have cited these concerns about the historical difficulty of defining and measuring intelligence is to highlight the even larger problem of isolating a unitary definition of giftedness. At the very least, we will always have several conceptions (and therefore definitions) of giftedness; but it will help in this analysis to begin by examining two broad categories that have been dealt with in the research literature. The distinction between these two categories is the foundation for the theory presented in this chapter and, in many ways, it represents the theme of my overall approach to both the identification and development of gifted behaviors. I refer to the first category as "schoolhouse giftedness" and to the second as "creative productive giftedness." Before going on to describe each type, I want to emphasize that:
1. Both types are important.
2. There is usually an interaction between the two types.
3. Special programs should make appropriate provisions for encouraging both types of giftedness as well as the numerous occasions when the two types interact with each other.

Schoolhouse giftedness. Schoolhouse giftedness might also be called test-taking or lesson-learning giftedness. It is the kind most easily measured by IQ or other cognitive ability tests and, for this reason, it is also the type most often used for selecting students for entrance into special programs. The abilities people display on IQ and aptitude tests are exactly the kinds of abilities most valued in traditional school learning situations. In other words, the games people play on ability tests are similar to games that teachers require in most lesson-learning situations. Research tells us that students who score high on IQ tests are also likely to get high grades in school. Research also has shown that these test-taking and lesson-learning abilities generally remain stable over time. The results of this research should lead us to some very obvious conclusions about schoolhouse giftedness: It exists in varying degrees, it can be identified through standardized assessment techniques, and we should therefore do everything in our power to make appropriate modifications for students who have the ability to cover regular curricular material at advanced rates and levels of understanding. Curriculum compacting (Reis, Burns, & Renzulli, 1992), a procedure used for modifying curricular content to accommodate advanced learners, and other acceleration techniques should represent an essential part of any school program that strives to respect the individual differences that are clearly evident from scores yielded by cognitive ability tests.

Although there is a generally positive correlation between IQ scores and school grades, we should not conclude that test scores are the only factors that contribute to success in school. Because IQ scores correlate only from

0.40 to 0.60 with school grades, they account for only 16 to 36 percent of the variance in these indicators of potential. Many youngsters who are moderately below the traditional 3 to 5 percent test score cut-off levels for entrance into gifted programs clearly have shown that they can do advanced-level work. Indeed, most of the students in the nation's major universities and four-year colleges come from the top 20 percent of the general population (rather than just the top 3 to 5 percent), and Jones (1982) reported that a majority of college graduates in every scientific field of study had IQs between 110 and 120. Are we "making sense" when we exclude such students from access to special services? To deny them this opportunity would be analogous to *forbidding* a youngster from trying out for the basketball team because he or she missed a predetermined "cutoff height" by a few inches! Basketball coaches are not foolish enough to establish *inflexible* cut-off heights because they know that such an arbitrary practice would cause them to overlook the talents of youngsters who may overcome slight limitations in inches with other abilities such as drive, speed, teamwork, ball-handling skills, and perhaps even the ability and motivation to outjump taller persons who are trying out for the team. As educators of gifted and talented youth, we can undoubtedly take a few lessons about flexibility from coaches!

Creative productive giftedness. If scores on IQ tests and other measures of cognitive ability only account for a limited proportion of the common variance with school grades, we can be equally certain that these measures do not tell the whole story when it comes to making predictions about creative productive giftedness. Before defending this assertion with some research findings, let us briefly review what is meant by this second type of giftedness, the important role it should play in programming, and, therefore, the reasons we should attempt to assess it in our identification procedures—even if such assessment causes us to look below the top 3 to 5 percent on the normal curve of IQ scores.

Some phenomena are called by the name "creativity" and are qualitatively different from creative productive giftedness. For purposes of clarification, I will briefly discuss Csikszentmihalyi's (1996) distinction between three phenomena. The first phenomenon refers to unusual and stimulating thoughts. People who express this kind of thinking may be referred to as *brilliant* rather than creative, unless they also contribute something of permanent significance. Second, the term *creativity* is used for people who experience the world in novel and original ways. Their perceptions are fresh and their judgments insightful. Csikszentmihalyi likes to call them *personally creative*. They may make important discoveries that are very important to themselves, but others do not know about those discoveries. Third, people who have changed our culture in some important respect can, according to Csikszentmihalyi (1996), be called *creative* without qualifications. He further emphasized:

> The difference among these three meanings is not just a matter of degree. The last kind of creativity is not simply a more developed form of the two. These are actually different ways of being creative, each to a large measure unrelated to the others. (pp. 25–26)

The development of creative productive giftedness aims to increase the chances that more students will become creative in the third way described, that is, their ideas and work will actually have an impact on others and cause change. This product-oriented view is in line with most current Western definitions of creativity. The most often mentioned features of the end product are novelty and appropriateness. Programming that addresses this kind of creativity must be qualitatively different from regular schooling. It should primarily focus on students who fall into the following two categories of talent, proposed by Tannenbaum (Sternberg & Davidson, 1986): scarcity and surplus talents. For purposes of preservation and advancement, the world needs inventive people like Jonas Salk, Martin Luther King, Jr., Marie Curie, and Sigmund Freud. Such *scarcity* talents are forever in short supply. Society also seeks beauty, which can be provided by people who possess what Tannenbaum called *surplus* talent. These people (e.g., Picasso, Mozart, and C. S. Lewis) have the rare ability to elevate people's sensibility and sensitivities to new heights through the production of great art, literature, music, and philosophy.

Psychologists who studied motivated behavior (e.g., Deci & Ryan, 1985) found that people have a desire for self-determination and competence. The need for self-determination or a sense of autonomy is satisfied when one is free to behave of one's own volition, rather than being forced to behave according to the desires of another. One also strives to feel proficient and capable of performing the task in which they choose to engage. These needs for self-determination and competence motivate people to seek and conquer optimal challenges that stretch their abilities when trying something *new* (Deci & Ryan, 1985; Deci, Vallerand, Pelletier, & Ryan, 1991). The challenge of a situation depends on the degree of match between a person's internal structures and the demands of the environment. Creative productive giftedness, therefore, describes those aspects of human activity and involvement in which a premium is placed on the development of original thought, solutions, material, and products that are purposefully designed to have an impact on one or more target audiences. Learning situations that are designed to promote creative productive giftedness emphasize the use and application of information (content) and thinking processes in an integrated, inductive, and real-problem-oriented manner, which allows students to be self-determined first hand inquirers. Creative productive giftedness also implies acting on what one knows and believes rather than merely acquiring and storing knowledge for its own sake.

The role of the student is transformed from that of a learner of prescribed lessons to one in which she or he uses the *modus operandi* of a firsthand inquirer. This approach is quite different from the development of lesson-learning giftedness, which tends to emphasize deductive learning, structured training in the development of thinking processes, and the acquisition, storage, and retrieval of information. In other words, creative productive giftedness is simply putting one's abilities to work on problems and areas of study that have personal relevance to oneself and that can be escalated to appropriately challenging levels of investigative activity. The roles that both students and teachers should play in the pursuit of these problems have been described elsewhere (Renzulli, 1982, 1983).

Why is creative productive giftedness important enough for us to question the "tidy" and relatively easy approach that traditionally has been used to select students on the basis of test scores? Why do some people want to rock the boat by challenging a conception of giftedness that can be numerically defined by simply giving a test? The answers to these questions are simple and yet very compelling. The research reviewed in the second section of this chapter tells us that there is much more to the development of gifted behaviors than the abilities revealed on traditional tests of intelligence, aptitude, and achievement. Furthermore, history tells us it has been the creative and productive people of the world, the producers rather than consumers of knowledge, the reconstructionists of thought in all areas of human endeavor, who have become recognized as "truly gifted" individuals. History does not remember persons who merely scored well on IQ tests or those who learned their lessons well but did not apply their knowledge in innovative and action-oriented ways.

It is important to mention once again that high levels of traditional achievement are necessary for all students. The breadth and depth of one's declarative knowledge base improves the foundation on which creative productive behaviors can be based and, coupled with advanced training in procedural knowledge (thinking skills, research methods, various forms of expression), combined to form the necessary ingredients for the type of giftedness described here.

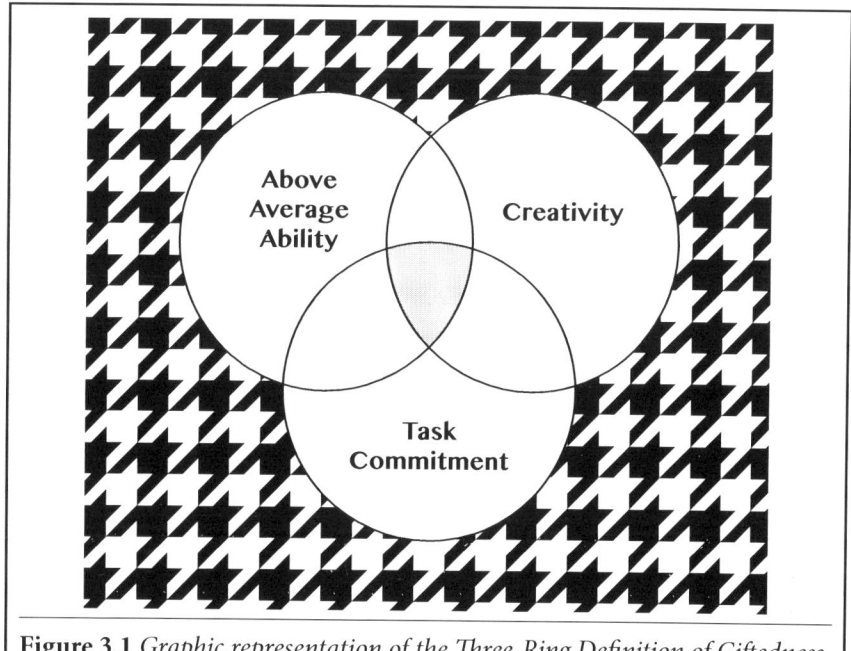

Figure 3.1 *Graphic representation of the Three-Ring Definition of Giftedness.*

The Three-Ring Conception of Giftedness

The Three-Ring Conception of Giftedness is a theory that attempts to portray the main dimensions of human potential for creative productivity. The name derives from the conceptual framework of the theory—namely, three interacting clusters of traits (above average ability, task commitment, and creativity) and their relationship with general and specific areas of human performance (see Figure 3.1). The three rings are embedded in a Houndstooth background that represents the interaction between personality and environmental factors that give rise to the three rings.

Research Underlying the Three-Ring Conception of Giftedness

One way of analyzing the research underlying conceptions of giftedness is to review existing definitions along a continuum ranging from *conservative* to *liberal*. Conservative and liberal are used here not in their political connotations, but rather according to the degree of restrictiveness that is used in determining who is eligible for special programs and services.

Restrictiveness can be expressed in two ways. First, a definition can limit the number of specific performance areas that are considered in determining eligibility for special programs. A conservative definition, for example, might limit eligibility to academic performance only and exclude other areas such as music, art, drama, leadership, public speaking, social service, and creative writing. Second, a definition can limit the degree or level of excellence that one must attain by establishing extremely high cut-off points. At the conservative end of the continuum is Terman's (1926) definition of giftedness as "the top 1 percent level in general intellectual ability as measured by the Stanford-Binet Intelligence Scale or a comparable instrument" (p. 43). In this definition, restrictiveness is present in terms of both the type of performance specified (i.e., how well one scores on an intelligence test) and the level of performance one must attain to be considered gifted (top 1 percent). At the other end of the continuum can be found more liberal definitions, such as the following one by Witty (1958):

> There are children whose outstanding potentialities in art, in writing, or in social leadership can be recognized largely by their performance. Hence, we have recommended that the definition of giftedness be expanded and that we consider any child gifted whose performance, in a potentially valuable line of human activity, is consistently remarkable. (p. 62)

Although liberal definitions have the obvious advantage of expanding the conception of giftedness, they also open up two "cans of worms" by introducing a values issue (what are the potentially valuable lines of human activity?) and the age-old problem of subjectivity in measurement. In recent years, the values issue has been largely resolved. There are very few educators who cling tenaciously to a "straight IQ" or purely academic definition of giftedness. "Multiple talent" and "multiple criteria" are almost the bywords of the present-day gifted student movement, and most persons would have little difficulty in accepting a definition that includes almost every area of human activity that manifests itself in a socially useful form of expression.

The problem of subjectivity in measurement is not as easily resolved. As the definition of giftedness is extended beyond those abilities that are clearly reflected in tests of intelligence, achievement, and academic aptitude, it becomes necessary to put less emphasis on precise estimates of performance and potential and more emphasis on the opinions of qualified human judges in making decisions about admission to special programs. The crux of the issue boils down to a simple and yet very important question: How much of a trade-off are we willing to make on the objective-subjective continuum to allow recognition of a broader spectrum of human abilities? If some degree of subjectivity cannot be tolerated, then our definition of giftedness and the resulting programs will logically be limited to abilities that can be measured only by objective tests.

Research on creative productive people has consistently shown that, although no single criterion can be used to determine giftedness, persons who have achieved recognition because of their unique accomplishments and creative contributions possess a relatively well-defined set of three interlocking clusters of traits. These clusters consist of (a) above average, although not necessarily superior ability, (b) creativity, and (c) task commitment. It is important to point out that no single cluster "makes giftedness" (in the sense of "gifted behavior" or creative productivity). Rather, it is the *interaction* among the three clusters that research has shown to be the necessary ingredient for creative productive accomplishment (Renzulli, 1978). The shaded portion of Figure 3.1 represents this interaction. It is also important to point out that each cluster plays an important role in contributing to the development of gifted behaviors. This point is emphasized because one of the major errors that continues to be made in identification procedures is to overemphasize superior abilities at the expense of the other two clusters of traits.

Amabile's (1983, 1996) Componential Theory of Creativity comprises three components that are very similar to the three clusters I proposed in the original article on the Three-Ring Conception (Renzulli, 1978). Her essential three components for creative performance are: (a) domain-relevant skills (knowledge, talents, and technical skills in the domain), (b) creativity-relevant skills (cognitive styles, working styles, and creativity heuristics), and (c) task motivation (motivational variables that determine an individual's approach to a given task). Amabile (1996) emphasized that each of the model's three components—domain-relevant skills, creativity-relevant skills, and task motivation—is necessary, and none is sufficient for creativity in and of itself. She also proposed that the level of creativity of a product or response varies as a function of the levels of each of the three components.

Well-Above-Average Ability

Well-above-average ability can be defined in two ways. *General ability* consists of traits that can be applied across all domains (e.g., general intelligence) or broad domains (e.g., general verbal ability applied to several dimensions of the language arts). These abilities consist of the capacity to process information, to integrate experiences that result in appropriate and adaptive responses to new situations, and the capacity to engage in abstract thinking. Examples of general ability are verbal and numerical reasoning, spatial relations, memory, and word fluency. These abilities are usually measured by tests of general aptitude or intelligence and are broadly applicable to a variety of traditional learning situations.

Specific abilities consist of the capacity to acquire knowledge, skill, or the ability to perform in one or more activities of a specialized kind and within a restricted range. These abilities are defined in a manner that represents the ways in which human beings express themselves in real-life (i.e., nontest) situations. Examples of specific abilities are chemistry, ballet, mathematics, musical composition, sculpture, and photography. Each specific ability can be further subdivided into even more specific areas (e.g., portrait photography, astrophotography, photojournalism). Specific abilities in certain areas such as mathematics and chemistry have a strong relationship with general ability and, therefore, some indication of potential in these areas can be determined from tests of general aptitude and intelligence. They can also be measured by achievement tests and tests of specific aptitude. Many specific abilities, however, cannot be easily measured by tests, and, therefore, areas such as the fine and applied arts, athletics, leadership, planning, and human relations skills must be evaluated through observation by skilled observers or other performance-based assessment techniques.

Within this model, the term *above average ability* is used to describe both general and specific abilities. *Above average* should also be interpreted to mean the upper range of potential within any given area. Although it is difficult to assign numerical values to many specific areas of ability, when I refer to "well above average ability," I clearly have in mind persons who are capable of performance or *possess the potential* for performance that is representative of the top 15 to 20 percent of any given area of human endeavor. One of the criticisms of this work has been that one must "perform" or produce a product to be "gifted." This is clearly not the intention, and I have responded to these criticisms in detail elsewhere (Renzulli, 1999). I also want to emphasize once again that when I refer to above average abilities that I am not restricting my use of percentages to only those things that can be measured by tests.

Although the influence of intelligence, as traditionally measured, quite obviously varies with specific areas of performance, many researchers have found that creative accomplishment is not necessarily a function of measured intelligence. In a review of several research studies dealing with the relationship between academic aptitude tests and professional achievement, Wallach (1976) has concluded that "above intermediate score levels, academic skills assessments are found to show so little criterion validity as to be a questionable basis on which to make consequential decisions about students' futures. What the academic tests do predict are the results a person will obtain on other tests of the same kind" (p. 57). Wallach goes on to point out that academic test scores at the upper ranges—precisely the score levels that are most often used for selecting persons for entrance into special programs—do not necessarily reflect the potential for creative productive accomplishment. He suggests that test scores be used to screen out persons who score in the lower ranges and that, beyond this point, decisions should be based on other indicators of potential for superior performance.

Numerous research studies support Wallach's findings that there is a limited relationship between test scores and school grades on the one hand and real-world accomplishments on the other (Bloom, 1963; Harmon, 1963; Helson & Crutchfield, 1970; Hudson, 1960; Mednick, 1963; Parloff, Datta, Kleman, & Handlon, 1968; Richards, Holland, & Lutz, 1967; Wallach & Wing, 1969). In fact, in a study dealing with the prediction of various dimensions of achievement among college students, Holland and Astin (1962) found that "getting good grades in college has little connection with more remote and more socially relevant kinds of achievement; indeed, in some colleges, the higher the student's grades, the less likely it is that he is a person with creative potential. So it seems desirable to extend our criteria of talented performance" (pp. 132–133). A study by the American College Testing Program (Munday & Davis, 1974) titled "Varieties of Accomplishment After College: Perspectives on the Meaning of Academic Talent," concluded that

> the adult accomplishments were found to be uncorrelated with academic talent, including test scores, high school grades, and college grades. However, the adult accomplishments were related to comparable high school nonacademic (extracurricular) accomplishments. This suggests that there are many kinds of talents related to later success which might be identified and nurtured by educational institutions. (p. 2)

Sternberg (1997) reported that tested differences in ability account for approximately "10% of the variation among workers in job performance" (p. 9). However, based on correlations between intelligence tests and various measures of job performance, Neisser et al. (1996) concluded that "across a wide range of occupations, intelligence test performance accounts for some 29% of the variance in job performance" (p. 83), which leaves 71 percent of variation in job performance unexplained. The pervasiveness of this general finding was demonstrated as early as 1965 by Hoyt (1965), who reviewed 46 studies dealing with the relationship between traditional indications of academic success and postcollege performance in the fields of business, teaching, engineering, medicine, scientific research, and other areas such as the ministry, journalism, government, and miscellaneous professions. From this extensive review, Hoyt concluded that traditional indications of academic success have no more than a very modest correlation with various indicators of success in the adult world and that "there is good reason to believe that academic achievement (knowledge) and other types of educational growth and development are relatively independent of each other" (p. 73).

The experimental studies conducted by Sternberg (1981) and Sternberg and Davidson (1982) have added a new dimension to our understanding about the role that intelligence tests should play in making identification decisions. After numerous investigations into the relationship between traditionally measured intelligence and other factors, such as problem solving and insightful solutions to complex problems, Sternberg (1982) concluded that

> tests only work for some of the people some of the time—not for all of the people all of the time—and that some of the assumptions we make in our use of tests are, at best, correct only for a segment of the tested population, and at worst, correct for none of it. As a result we fail to identify many gifted individuals for whom the assumptions underlying our use of tests are particularly inadequate. The problem, then, is not only that tests are of limited validity for everyone but that their validity varies across individuals. For some people, tests scores may be quite informative, for others such scores may be worse than useless. Use of test score cutoffs and formulas results in a serious problem of underidentification of gifted children. (p. 157)

These studies raise some basic questions about the use of tests as a major criterion for making selection decisions. The research reported above clearly indicates that vast numbers *and* proportions of our most productive persons are *not* those who scored at the 95th percentile or above on standardized tests of intelligence, nor were they necessarily straight-A students who discovered early how to play the lesson-learning game. In other words, more creative productive persons came from below the 95th percentile than above it, and if such cut-off scores are needed to determine entrance into special programs, we may be guilty of actually discriminating against persons who have the greatest potential for high levels of accomplishment.

The most defensible conclusion about the use of intelligence tests that can be put forward at this time is based on research findings dealing with the "threshold effect." Reviews by Chambers (1969) and Stein (1968) and research by Walberg (1969, 1971) indicate that accomplishments in various fields require minimal levels of intelligence, but that beyond these levels, degrees of attainment are weakly associated with intelligence. In studies of creativity, it is generally acknowledged that a fairly high although not exceptional level of intelligence is necessary for high degrees of creative achievement (Barron, 1969; Campbell, 1960; Guilford, 1964, 1967; McNemar, 1964; Vernon, 1967).

Research on the threshold effect indicates that different fields and subject-matter areas require varying degrees of intelligence for high-level accomplishment. In mathematics and physics, the correlation of measured intelligence with originality in problem solving tends to be positive but quite low. Correlations between intelligence and the rated quality of work by painters, sculptors, and designers is zero or slightly negative (Barron, 1968). Although it is difficult to determine exactly how much measured intelligence is necessary for high levels of creative and productive accomplishment within any given field, there is a consensus among many researchers (Barron, 1969; Bloom, 1963; Cox, 1926; Harmon, 1963; Helson & Crutchfield, 1970; MacKinnon, 1964, 1965; Oden, 1968; Roe, 1952; Terman, 1954) that once the IQ is 120 or higher, other variables become increasingly important. These variables are discussed in the following sections.

Task Commitment

A second cluster of traits that consistently has been found in creative productive persons is a refined or focused form of motivation that I have called task commitment. Whereas motivation is usually defined in terms of a general energizing process that triggers responses in organisms, task commitment represents energy brought to bear on a particular problem (task) or specific performance area. The terms that are most frequently used to describe task commitment are perseverance, endurance, hard work, dedicated practice, self-confidence, a belief in one's ability to carry out important work, and action applied to one's area(s) of interest. In addition to perceptiveness (Albert, 1975) and a better sense for identifying significant problems (Zuckerman, 1979), research on persons of unusual accomplishment has consistently shown that a special fascination for and involvement with the subject matter of one's chosen field "are the almost invariable precursors of original and distinctive work" (Barron, 1969, p. 3). This motivation to engage in an activity primarily for its own sake is often called intrinsic motivation. When one feels both self-determined and competent in pursuing a certain task, intrinsic motivation arises and leads to action. According to Deci and Ryan (1985), intrinsic motivation is innate to the human organism and is ever present as a motivator. It is a "natural ongoing state of the organism unless it is interrupted" (Deci & Ryan, 1985, p. 234) because intrinsically motivated behaviors satisfy a person's need to feel both competent and autonomous. Extrinsic motivation, often caused by factors such as money or rewards, on the other hand, can undermine one's sense of autonomy if they are perceived as externally controlling

(Amabile, Hill, Hennessey, & Tighe, 1994). The identification of these two types of motivation—intrinsic and extrinsic motivation—was, according to Collins and Amabile (1999), a breakthrough in research on the forces driving creativity. It seems, however, that any extrinsic factors that support one's sense of competence or enable one's deeper involvement with the task itself (without undermining one's sense of self-determination) may have a reinforcing effect on intrinsic motivation. This positive combination of seemingly opposite types of motivation can be called "extrinsics in service of intrinsics" (Collins & Amabile, 1999). More research on motivation and especially on the synergistic effect of extrinsic motivators on intrinsic motivation is necessary. A person's high commitment toward a task seems to be the result of this synergistic effect.

Even in young people whom Bloom and Sosniak (1981) identified as extreme cases of talent development, early evidence of task commitment was present. Bloom and Sosniak report that "after age 12 our talented individuals spent as much time on their talent field each week as their average peer spent watching television" (p. 94). The argument for including this nonintellective cluster of traits in a definition of giftedness is nothing short of overwhelming. From popular maxims and autobiographical accounts to hard-core research findings, one of the key ingredients that has characterized the work of gifted contributors is their ability to involve themselves totally in a specific problem or area for an extended period of time.

The legacy of both Sir Francis Galton and Lewis Terman clearly indicates that task commitment is an important part of the making of a gifted person. Although Galton was a strong proponent of the hereditary basis for what he called "natural ability," he nevertheless subscribed heavily to the belief that hard work was part and parcel of giftedness:

> By natural ability, I mean those qualities of intellect and disposition, which urge and qualify a man to perform acts that lead to reputation. I do not mean capacity without zeal, nor zeal without capacity, nor even a combination of both of them, without an adequate power of doing a great deal of very laborious work. But I mean a nature which, when left to itself, will, urged by an inherent stimulus, climb the path that leads to eminence and has strength to reach the summit—on which, if hindered or thwarted, will fret and strive until the hindrance is overcome, and it is again free to follow its laboring instinct (Galton, 1869, p. 33, as cited in Albert, 1975, p. 142).

The monumental studies of Lewis Terman undoubtedly represent the most widely recognized and frequently quoted research on the characteristics of gifted persons. Terman's studies, however, have unintentionally left a mixed legacy because most persons have dwelt (and continue to dwell) on "early Terman" rather than the conclusions he reached *after* several decades of intensive research. As such, it is important to consider the following conclusion that he reached as a result of 30 years of follow-up studies on his initial population:

> A detailed analysis was made of the 150 most successful and 150 least successful men among the gifted subjects in an attempt to identify some of the nonintellectual factors that affect life success.... Since the less successful subjects do not differ to any extent in intelligence as measured by tests, it is clear that notable achievement calls for more than a high order of intelligence. The results [of the follow-up] indicated that personality factors are extremely important determiners of achievement... The four traits on which [the most and least successful groups] differed most widely were *persistence in the accomplishment of ends, integration toward goals, self-confidence, and freedom from inferiority feelings*. In the total picture the greatest contrast between the two groups was in all-round emotional and social adjustment, and in *drive to achieve*. (Terman & Oden, 1959, p. 148; italics added)

Although Terman never suggested that task commitment should replace intelligence in our conception of giftedness, he did state that "intellect and achievement are far from perfectly correlated" (p. 146). Several more recent research studies support the findings of Galton and Terman and have shown that creative productive persons are far more task-oriented and involved in their work than are people in the general population. Perhaps the best known of these studies is the work of Roe (1952) and MacKinnon (1964, 1965). Roe conducted an intensive study of the characteristics of 64 eminent scientists and found that all of her subjects had a high level of commitment to their work. MacKinnon pointed out traits that were important in creative accomplishments: "It is clear that creative architects more often stress their inventiveness, independence and individuality, their *enthusiasm, determination, and industry*" (1964, p. 365; italics added).

Extensive reviews of research carried out by Nicholls (1972) and McCurdy (1960) found patterns of characteristics that were consistently similar to the findings reported by Roe and MacKinnon. Although the studies cited thus far used different research procedures and dealt with a variety of populations, there is a striking similarity in their major conclusions. First, academic ability (as traditionally measured by tests or grade-point averages) showed limited relationships to creative productive accomplishment. Second, nonintellectual factors, and especially those related to task commitment, consistently played an important part in the cluster of traits that characterized highly productive people. Although this second cluster of traits is not as easily and objectively identifiable as are general cognitive abilities, they are nevertheless a major component of giftedness and should, therefore, be reflected in our definition.

Creativity

The third cluster of traits that characterizes gifted persons consists of factors usually lumped together under the general heading of "creativity." As one reviews the literature in this area, it becomes readily apparent that the words *gifted, genius,* and *eminent creators* or *highly creative persons* are used synonymously. In many of the research projects discussed previously, the persons ultimately selected for intensive study were, in fact, recognized *because* of their creative accomplishments. In MacKinnon's (1964) study, for example, panels of qualified judges (professors of architecture and editors of major American architectural journals) were asked first to nominate and later to rate an initial pool of nominees, using the following dimensions of creativity:

1. Originality of thinking and freshness of approaches to architectural problems.
2. Constructive ingenuity.
3. Ability to set aside established conventions and procedures when appropriate.
4. A flair for devising effective and original fulfillments of the major demands of architecture, namely, technology (firmness), visual form (delight), planning (commodity), and human awareness and social purpose. (p. 360)

When discussing creativity, it is important to consider the problems researchers have encountered in establishing relationships between creativity tests and other more substantial accomplishments. A major issue that has been raised by several investigators deals with whether or not tests of divergent thinking actually measure "true" creativity. Although some validation studies have reported limited relationships between measures of divergent thinking and creative performance criteria (Dellas & Gaier, 1970; Guilford, 1967; Shapiro, 1968; Torrance, 1969), the research evidence for the predictive validity of such tests has been limited. Unfortunately, very few tests have been validated against real-life criteria of creative accomplishment; however, future longitudinal studies using these relatively new instruments might show promise of establishing higher levels of predictive validity. Thus, although divergent thinking is indeed a characteristic of highly creative persons, caution should be exercised in the use and interpretation of tests designed to measure this capacity.

Given the inherent limitations of creativity tests, a number of writers have focused attention on alternative methods for assessing creativity. Among others, Nicholls (1972) suggested that an analysis of creative products is preferable to the trait-based approach in making predictions about creative potential (p. 721), and Wallach (1976) proposes that student self reports about creative accomplishment are sufficiently accurate to provide a usable source of data.

Although few persons would argue against the importance of including creativity in a definition of giftedness, the conclusions and recommendations discussed previously raise the haunting issue of subjectivity in measurement. In view of what the research suggests about the questionable value of more objective measures of divergent thinking, perhaps the time has come for persons in all areas of endeavor to develop more careful procedures for evaluating the products of candidates for special programs.

A Definition of Gifted Behavior

Although no single statement can effectively integrate the many ramifications of the research studies I have described, the following definition of gifted behavior attempts to summarize the major conclusions and generalizations resulting from this review of research.

Gifted behavior consists of thought and action resulting from an interaction among three basic clusters of human traits, above average general and/or specific abilities, high levels of task commitment, and high levels of creativity. Children who manifest *or are capable of developing* an interaction among the three clusters require a wide variety of educational opportunities, resources, and encouragement above and beyond those ordinarily provided through regular instructional programs.

Research on the Three-Ring Conception of Giftedness

The definition of gifted behavior reported previously has served as the basis for a large number of research studies designed to examine the effectiveness of identification practices based on the Three-Ring Conception and programmatic interventions that focus on promoting creative productive giftedness. Using a population of 1,162 students in grades one through six in 11 school districts, Reis and Renzulli (1982) examined several variables related to an identification process based on the Three-Ring Conception and the

Enrichment Triad programming model. Talent Pools consisting of above average ability students in each district and at each grade level were divided into two groups. Group A consisted of students who scored in the top 5 percent on standardized tests of intelligence and achievement. Group B consisted of students who scored from 10 to 15 percentile points below the top 5 percent. Both groups participated equally in all program activities.

An instrument called the Student Product Assessment Form (SPAF) was used to compare the quality of products from each group. This instrument provides individual ratings for eight specific qualitative characteristics of products and seven factors related to overall product quality. The validity and reliability of the SPAF were established through a year-long series of studies (Reis, 1981) that yielded reliability coefficients as high as 0.98. A double-blind method of product coding was used so that the expert judges did not know group membership (i.e., A or B) when evaluating individual products. A two-way analysis of variance indicated that there were no significant differences between Group A and Group B with respect to the quality of students' products. These findings are offered as a verification of the Three-Ring Conception of Giftedness and as support for the effectiveness of the model in serving a group somewhat larger than the traditional top 5 percent. Questionnaires and interviews were used to examine several other factors related to overall program effectiveness. Data obtained from classroom and special program teachers, parents, and Talent Pool students indicated that attitudes toward this identification system were highly positive. Many classroom teachers reported that their high level of involvement in the program had favorably influenced their teaching practices and promoted more favorable attitudes toward special programs. Parents whose children had been placed previously in traditional programs for the gifted did not differ in their opinions from parents whose children had been identified as gifted under the expanded criteria. Resource teachers—many of whom had previously been involved in traditional programs for the gifted—overwhelmingly preferred the expanded identification procedure to the traditional reliance on test scores alone. In fact, several resource teachers said they would resign or request transfers to regular classrooms if their school systems did not continue to use this more flexible approach!

Additional research examined academic self-concept, locus of control, correlates of creative productivity, and administrators' attitudes toward programs based on the Three-Ring Conception of Giftedness. A summary of these and other studies about this combined identification and programming approach can be found in Renzulli and Reis (1994), and updates are included on our web site (www.gifted.uconn.edu).

New Dimensions to the Three-Ring Conception of Giftedness

In the early 1970s, when I began work on a conception of giftedness that challenged the traditional view of this concept, I embedded the rings in a Houndstooth background that represented the interaction between personality and environment. In recent years, further research and theory development has led to a new dimension of the model that calls attention to a series of six co-cognitive factors. A comprehensive review of the literature and a series of Delphi technique studies led to the development of an organizational plan for studying the 6 components and 13 subcomponents presented in Figure 3.2. I refer to these traits as co-cognitive factors be cause they interact with and enhance the cognitive traits that we ordinarily associate with the development of human abilities. Moon (2000) suggests that constructs of this type, including social, emotional, interpersonal, and intrapersonal intelligence, are related to each other and are independent from traditional measures of ability. The two-directional arrows in this diagram are intended to point out the many interactions that take place between and among the Houndstooth components.

This new initiative was prompted by a longstanding concern about the role that gifted education should play in preparing persons with high potential for ethical and responsible leadership in all walks of life and a concern for the well-documented decline of social capital in modem societies (Putnam, 1993, 1995; Portes, 1998). Social capital differs from economic and intellectual capital in that it focuses on a set of intangible assets that address the collective needs and problems of other individuals and our communities at large. Although social capital cannot be defined as precisely as corporate earnings or gross domestic product, Labonte (1999) eloquently defined it as: "something going on 'out there' in peoples' day-to-day relationships that is an important determinant to the quality of their lives, if not society's healthy functioning" (p. 430). This kind of capital generally enhances community life and the network of obligations we have to one another. Investments in social capital benefit society as a whole because they help to create the values, norms, networks, and social trust that facilitate coordination and cooperation geared toward the greater public good. Striking evidence indicates a marked decline in American social capital over the latter half of the last century. National surveys show declines over the last few decades in voter turnout and political participation and membership in service clubs, church-related groups, parent-teacher associations, unions, and fraternal groups. These declines in civic and social participation have been paralleled by an increasing tendency for young people to focus on materialism, self-indulgence, narrow professional success, and indi-

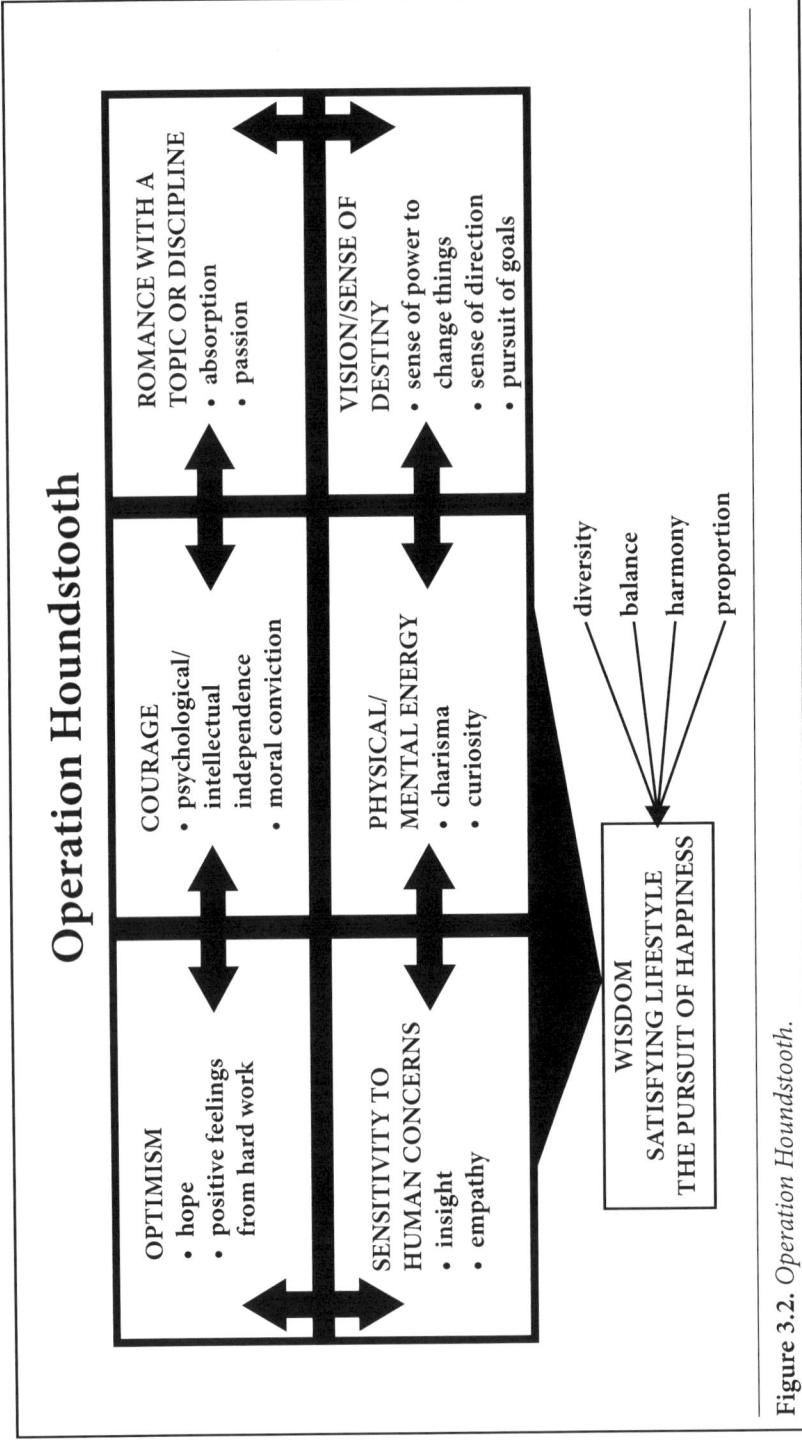

Figure 3.2. *Operation Houndstooth.*

vidual economic gain (Ahuvia, 2002; Huer, 1991; Kasser, 2002; Myers, 1993; Netemeyer, Burton, & Lichtenstein, 1995; Shrader, 1992; Tatzel, 2002).

Researchers who have studied social capital have examined it mainly in terms of its impact on communities at large, but they also point out that it is created largely by the actions of individuals. They also have reported that leadership is a necessary condition for the creation of social capital. Although numerous studies and a great deal of commentary about leadership have been discussed in the gifted education literature, no one has yet examined the relationship between the characteristics of gifted leaders and their motivation to use their gifts to advance the greater public good. A scientific examination of a more focused set of background components is necessary for us to understand the sources of gifted behaviors and, more importantly, the ways in which people transform their gifted assets into constructive action. What causes people like Martin Luther King Jr., Mother Teresa, Nelson Mandela, and Rachel Carson to devote their time and energy to socially responsible endeavors that improve the lives of so many people? And can a better understanding of people who use their gifts in socially constructive ways help us create conditions that expand the number of young people who may make commitments to the growth of social as well as economic capital? Can our gifted education programs produce future corporate leaders who are as sensitive to aesthetic and environmental concerns as they are to the corporate bottom line? Can we influence the ethics and morality of future industrial and political leaders so that they place gross national happiness on an equal or higher scale of values than gross national product? These are some of the questions we are attempting to address in an ongoing series of research studies that examine the relationship between non-cognitive personal characteristics and the role that these characteristics play in the development of giftedness.

A detailed discussion of the Houndstooth factors, the research that led to their development, and an intervention theory that promotes them is beyond the scope of this chapter; however, a description of the rationale for including them in an expanded conception of giftedness and the research that led to the identification of the factors can be found in a recent article devoted entirely to this topic (Renzulli, 2002). We are only in the early stages of examining these admittedly imprecise factors and developing strategies for promoting them, but I believe that if the gifted education community is sincere about its frequent claims of producing the next generation of leaders, our conception of giftedness and the services we provide should place some emphasis on leaders who are committed to making the world a better place. As Nelson Mandela said, "A good head and a good heart are always a formidable combination."

A Practical Plan for Identification

Translating theory into practice is always a challenging task! Although my work on a conception of giftedness has dealt with theory development, equal attention has been given to how the theory can guide practical strategies for the identification of all students who can benefit from special services. And therein lies one of the greatest challenges because a more flexible approach to identification often is at odds with traditional state or local regulations that require precision, names on lists signifying who is "gifted," and resource allocations that make sharp distinctions between the work of special program personnel and other teachers who may be able to contribute to a school's total talent development mission. These practical realities have led to an identification plan that is a compromise between a totally performance-based system and one that targets certain students while still maintaining a degree of flexibility. An overview of the plan follows, and a more detailed description titled *A Practical Plan for Identifying Gifted and Talented Students* can be found in Renzulli (1990) and on our Web site (http://www.gifted.uconn.edu).

The essence of this plan is to form a Talent Pool of students who are targeted because of strengths in particular areas that will serve as a primary (but not total) rationale for the services that the special program will provide. Before listing the steps involved in this identification system, three important considerations are discussed. First, Talent Pool size will vary in any given school depending on the general nature of the total student body. In schools with unusually large numbers of high achieving students, it is conceivable that Talent Pools will be larger than in lower-scoring schools. But even in schools where achievement levels are below national norms, there still exists an upper-level group of students who need services above and beyond those that are provided for the majority of the school population. Some of our most successful programs have been in inner-city schools that serve disadvantaged and bilingual youth; and even though these schools were below national norms, Talent Pools of approximately 15 percent of students needing supplementary services were still identified. Talent Pool size is also a function of the availability of resources (both human and material) and the extent to which the general faculty is willing to (a) make modifications in the regular curriculum for above-average-ability students, (b) participate in various kinds of enrichment and mentoring activities, and (c) work cooperatively with any and all personnel who may have special program assignments. It is very important to determine beforehand the number of students who can be served in ways that "show up" when program accountability is considered.

Because teacher nomination plays an important role in this identification system, a second consideration is the extent of orientation and training that teachers have had about both the program and procedures for nominating students. In this regard, we recommend the use of a training activity that is designed to orient teachers to the behavioral characteristics of superior students (Renzulli et al., 2002, pp. 24–28).

A third consideration is, of course, the type of program for which students are being identified. The identification system is based on models that combine both enrichment and acceleration, whether or not they are carried out in self-contained programs, inclusion programs, pull-out programs, or any other organizational arrangement. Regardless of the type of organizational model used, it is also recommended that a strong component of curriculum compacting (Reis et al., 1992) be a part of the services offered to high-achieving Talent Pool students.

Once a target number or percent of the school population is established, that number should be divided in half. In the 15 percent Talent Pool depicted in Figure 3.3, approximately half the students will be selected on the basis of test scores, thus guaranteeing that the process will not discriminate against traditionally high-scoring students. Step 2 uses a research-based teacher nomination scale (Renzulli et al., 2002) for students not included in Step 1. Again, the previously mentioned training helps to improve the reliability of ratings. With the exception of teachers who are habitually under- or overnominators, these ratings are treated on a par value with test scores. Our experience has shown that the vast majority of Talent Pool nominees result from Steps 1 and 2.

Step 3 allows for the use of other criteria (e.g., parent, peer, or self-nomination; previous product assessment) that a school may or may not want to consider but, in this case, the information is reviewed in a case-study fashion by a selection committee. Step 4 allows previous-year teachers to recommend students who were not nominated in the first three steps. This "safety valve" guards against bias or incompatibility on the part of the nominator in Step 2, and it allows for consideration of student potential that may be presently unrecognized because of personal or family issues or a turn-off to school. Step 5 provides parents with information about why their son or daughter was nominated for the Talent Pool, the goals and nature of the program as it relates to their child's strength areas, and how a program based on the Three-Ring Conception of Giftedness differs from other types of programs. Step 6 is a second safety valve. Action information nomination allows for consideration of targeted services for a young person who may show a remarkable display of creativity, task commitment, or a previously unrecognized need for highly challenging opportunities.

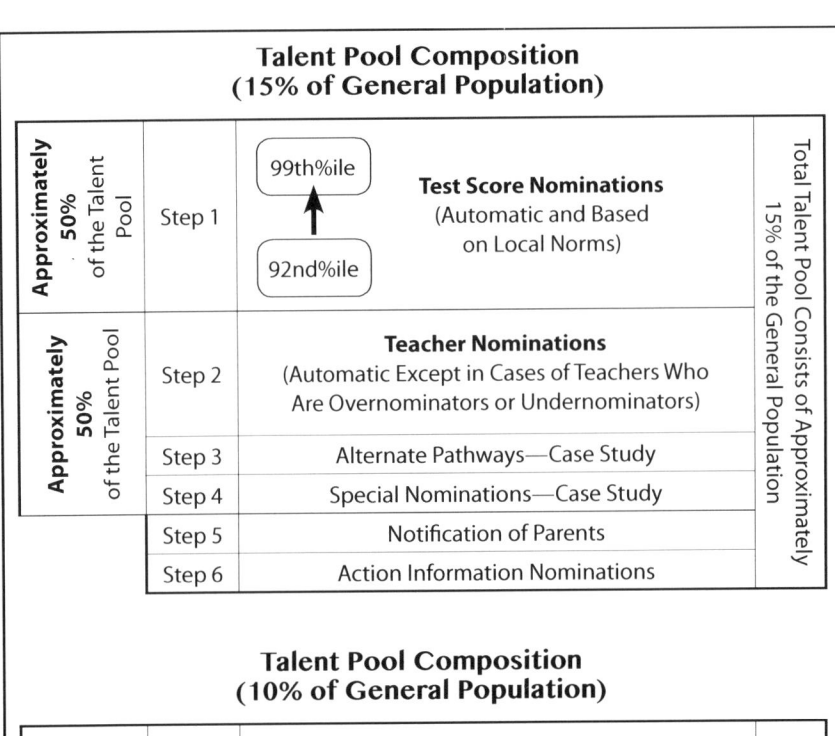
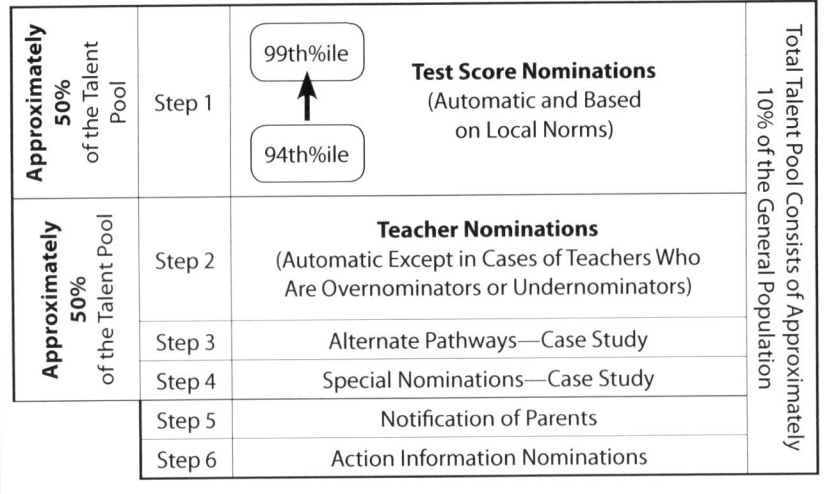

Figure 3.3. *Renzulli Identification System.*

Summary: What Makes Giftedness?

In recent years, we have seen a resurgence of interest in all aspects of the study of giftedness and related efforts to provide services for at-risk youth and young people who may show their potential in ways that are not always challenged in traditional school programs. A healthy aspect of this renewed interest has been the emergence of new and innovative theories to explain the concept and a greater variety of research studies that show promise of giving us better insights and more defensible approaches to both identification and programming. Conflicting theoretical explanations abound, and various interpretations of research findings add an element of excitement and challenge that can only result in greater understanding of the concept in the years ahead. As long as the concept itself is viewed from the vantage points of different subcultures within the general population and differing societal values, we can be assured that there will always be a wholesome variety of answers to the age-old question: What makes giftedness? These differences in interpretation are indeed a salient and positive characteristic of any field that attempts to further our understanding of the human condition.

In this chapter, I have attempted to provide a framework that draws on the best available research about creative and productive individuals. I have also referenced research in support of the validity of the Three-Ring Conception of Giftedness. The conception and definition presented in this chapter have been developed from a decidedly educational perspective because I believe that efforts to define this concept must be relevant to the people in schools who may be most influenced by this work. I also believe that conceptual explanations and definitions must point the way toward practices that are economical, realistic, and defensible in terms of an organized body of underlying research and follow-up validation studies. This kind of technical information should be presented to decision makers who raise questions about *why* particular identification and programming models are being suggested by persons who are interested in serving gifted youth.

The task of providing better services to our most promising young people cannot wait until theorists and researchers produce an unassailable ultimate truth, because such truths probably do not exist. But the needs and opportunities to improve educational services for these young people exist in countless classrooms every day of the week. The best conclusions I can reach at the present time are presented previously, although I also believe that we must continue the search for greater understanding of this concept, which is so crucial to the further advancement of civilization. In the meantime, we should follow the advice in the poem by Edward Markham at the beginning of this chapter—

we must draw our circles larger so that we do not overlook any young person who has the potential for high levels of creative productivity.

References

Ahuvia, A. C. (2002). Individualism/collectivism and cultures of happiness: A theoretical conjecture on the relationship between consumption, culture and subjective well-being at the national level. *Journal of Happiness Studies, 3,* 23–36.

Albert, R. S. (1975). Toward a behavioral definition of genius. *American Psychologist, 30,* 140–151.

Amabile, T. M. (1983). *The social psychology of creativity.* New York, NY: Springer-Verlag.

Amabile, T. M. (1996). *Creativity in context.* Boulder, CO: Westview Press.

Amabile, T. M., Hill, K. G., Hennessey, B. A., & Tighe, E. M. (1994). The work preference inventory: Assessing intrinsic and extrinsic motivational orientations. *Journal of Personality and Social Psychology, 66,* 950–967.

Barron, F. (1968). *Creativity and personal freedom.* New York, NY: Van Nostrand.

Barron, F. (1969). *Creative person and creative process.* New York, NY: Holt, Rinehart & Winston.

Bloom, B. S. (Ed.). (1956). *Taxonomy of educational objectives: Handbook 1. Cognitive domain.* New York, NY: McKay.

Bloom, B. S. (1963). Report on creativity research by the examiner's office of the University of Chicago. In C. W. Taylor & F. Barron (Eds.), *Scientific creativity: Its recognition and development* (pp. 263–315). New York, NY: Wiley.

Bloom, B. S., & Sosniak, L. A. (1981). Talent development vs. schooling. *Educational Leadership, 38,* 86–94.

Campbell, D. T. (1960). Blind variation and selective retention in creative thought as in other knowledge processes. *Psychological Review, 67,* 380–400.

Chambers, J. A. (1969). A multidimensional theory of creativity. *Psychological Reports, 25,* 779–799.

Collins, M. A., & Amabile, T. M. (1999). Motivation and creativity. In R. J. Sternberg (Ed.), *Handbook of creativity* (pp. 297–312). New York, NY: Cambridge University Press.

Cox, C. M. (1926). *Genetic studies of genius: Vol. 2. The early mental traits of three hundred geniuses.* Stanford, CA: Stanford University Press.

Csikszentmihalyi, M. (1996). *Creativity: Flow and the psychology of discovery and invention.* New York, NY: HarperCollins.

Deci, E. L., & Ryan, R. M. (1985). *Intrinsic motivation and self-determination in human behavior.* New York, NY: Plenum.

Deci, E. L., Vallerand, R. J., Pelletier, L. G., & Ryan, R. M. (1991). Motivation and education: The self-determination perspective. *Educational Psychologist, 26,* 325–346.

Dellas, M., & Gaier, E. L. (1970). Identification of creativity: The individual. *Psychological Bulletin, 73,* 55–73.

DuBois, P. H. (1970). *A history of psychological testing.* Boston, MA: Allyn & Bacon.

Gardner, H. (1983). *Frames of mind: The theory of multiple intelligences.* New York, NY: Basic Books.

Gardner, H. (1999). *Intelligence reframed: Multiple intelligences for the 21st century.* New York, NY: Basic Books.

Gowan, J. C. (1978, July 25). *New directions for gifted education.* Paper presented at the University of Connecticut, Storrs.

Guilford, J. P. (1964). Some new looks at the nature of creative processes. In M. Fredrickson & H. Gilliksen (Eds.), *Contributions to mathematical psychology* (pp. 42–66). New York, NY: Holt, Rinehart & Winston.

Guilford, J. P. (1967). *The nature of human intelligence.* New York, NY: McGraw-Hill.

Harmon, L. R. (1963). The development of a criterion of scientific competence. In C. W. Taylor & F. Barron (Eds.), *Scientific creativity: Its recognition and development* (pp. 147–165). New York, NY: Wiley.

Helson, R., & Crutchfield, R. S. (1970). Mathematicians: The creative researcher and the average Ph.D. *Journal of Consulting and Clinical Psychology, 34,* 250–257.

Holland, J. L., & Astin, A. W. (1962). The prediction of the academic, artistic, scientific and social achievement of undergraduates of superior scholastic aptitude. *Journal of Educational Psychology, 53,* 182–183.

Hoyt, D. P. (1965). *The relationship between college grades and adult achievement: A review of the literature* (Research Report No. 7). Iowa City, IA: American College Testing Program.

Hudson, L. (1960). Degree class and attainment in scientific research. *British Journal of Psychology, 51,* 67–73.

Huer, J. (1991). *The wages of sin: America's dilemma of profit against humanity.* New York, NY: Praeger.

Jones, J. (1982). The gifted student at university. *Gifted International, 1,* 49–65.

Kasser, T. (2002). *The high price of materialism.* Cambridge, MA: MIT Press.

Labonte, R. (1999). Social capital and community development: Practitioner emptor. *Australian and New Zealand Journal of Public Health, 23,* 430–433.

MacKinnon, D. W. (1962). The nature and nurture of creative talent. *American Psychologist, 17,* 484–495.

MacKinnon, D. W. (1964). The creativity of architects. In C. W. Taylor (Ed.), *Widening horizons in creativity.* New York, NY: Wiley.

MacKinnon, D. W. (1965). Personality and the realization of creative potential. *American Psychologist, 20,* 273–281.

McCurdy, H. G. (1960). The childhood pattern of genius. *Horizon, 2,* 33–38.

McGue, M., Bouchard, T. J., Jr., Iacono, W. G., & Lykken, D. T. (1993). Behavioral genetics of cognitive ability: A life-span perspective. In R. Plomin & G. E. McClearn (Eds.), *Nature, nurture and psychology* (pp. 59–76). Washington, DC: American Psychology Association.

McNemar, Q. (1964). Lost: Our intelligence? Why? *American Psychologist, 19,* 871–882.

Mednick, M. T. (1963). Research creativity in psychology graduate students. *Journal of Consulting Psychology, 27,* 265–266.

Miele, F. (1995). Interview with Robert Sternberg on *The Bell Curve. Skeptic, 3*(3), 72–80.

Moon, S. M. (2000, May). *Personal talent: What is it and how can we study it?* Paper presented at the Fifth Biennial Henry B. and Jocelyn Wallace National Research Symposium on Talent Development, Iowa City, IA.

Munday, L. A., & Davis, J. C. (1974). *Varieties of accomplishment after college: Perspectives on the meaning of academic talent* (Research Report No. 62). Iowa City, IA: American College Testing Program.

Myers, D. G. (1993). *Authentic happiness: Using the new positive psychology to realize your potential for lasting fulfillment*. New York, NY: Avon Books.

Neisser, U. (1979). The concept of intelligence. In R. J. Sternberg & D. K. Detterman (Eds.), *Human intelligence* (pp. 179–189). Norwood, NJ: Ablex.

Neisser, U., Boodoo, G., Bouchard, T. J., Jr., Boykin, A. W., Brody, N., Ceci, S. J., . . . Urbina, S. (1996). Intelligence: Knowns and unknowns. *American Psychologist, 51*, 77–101.

Netemeyer, R. G., Burton, S., & Lichtenstein, D. R. (1995). Trait aspects of vanity: Measurement and relevance to consumer behavior. *The Journal of Consumer Research, 21*, 612–626.

Nicholls, J. C. (1972). Creativity in the person who will never produce anything original and useful: The concept of creativity as a normally distributed trait. *American Psychologist, 27*, 717–727.

Oden, M. H. (1968). The fulfillment of promise: 40-year follow-up of the Terman gifted group. *Genetic Psychology Monograph, 77*, 3–93.

Parloff, M. B., Datta, L., Kleman, M., & Handlon, J. H. (1968). Personality characteristics which differentiate creative male adolescents and adults. *Journal of Personality, 36*, 528–552.

Portes, A. (1998). Social capital: Its origins and applications in modern sociology. *Annual Review of Sociology, 24*, 1–24.

Putnam, R. (1993). *Making democracy work: Civic traditions in modern Italy*. Princeton, NJ: Princeton University Press.

Putnam, R. (1995, January). Bowling alone: America's declining social capital. *Journal of Democracy, 6*, 65–78.

Reis, S. M. (1981). *An analysis of the productivity of gifted students participating in programs using the revolving door identification model* (Unpublished doctoral dissertation). University of Connecticut, Storrs.

Reis, S. M., Burns, D. E., & Renzulli, J. S. (1992). *Curriculum compacting: The complete guide to modifying the regular curriculum for high ability students*. Waco, TX: Prufrock Press.

Reis, S. M., & Renzulli, J. S. (1982). A research report on the revolving door identification model: A case for the broadened conception of giftedness. *Phi Delta Kappan, 63*, 619–620.

Renzulli, J. S. (1977). *The Enrichment Triad Model: A guide for developing defensible programs for the gifted and talented*. Mansfield Center, CT: Creative Learning Press.

Renzulli, J. S. (1978). What makes giftedness? Re-examining a definition. *Phi Delta Kappan, 60*, 180–184, 261.

Renzulli, J. S. (1982). What makes a problem real: Stalking the illusive meaning of qualitative differences in gifted education. *Gifted Child Quarterly, 26*, 148–156.

Renzulli, J. S. (1983). Guiding the gifted in the pursuit of real problems: The transformed role of the teacher. *The Journal of Creative Behavior, 17,* 49–59.

Renzulli, J. S. (1986). The Three-Ring Conception of Giftedness: A developmental model for creative productivity. In R. J. Sternberg & J. E. Davidson (Eds.), *Conceptions of giftedness* (pp. 53–92). New York, NY: Cambridge University Press.

Renzulli, J. S. (1988). A decade of dialogue on the Three-Ring Conception of Giftedness. *Roeper Review, 11,* 18–25.

Renzulli, J. S. (1990). A practical system for identifying gifted and talented students. *Early Childhood Development, 63,* 9–18.

Renzulli, J. S. (1992). A general theory for the development of creative productivity in young people. In F. J. Mönks & W. A. M. Peters (Eds.), *Talent for the future* (pp. 51–72). Assen, The Netherlands: Van Gorcum.

Renzulli, J. S. (1997a). *Interest-a-lyzer: Family of instruments. A manual for teachers.* Waco, TX: Prufrock Press.

Renzulli, J. S. (1997b). *The total talent portfolio: Looking at the best in every student.* Mansfield, CT: Creative Learning Press.

Renzulli, J. S. (1999). What is this thing called giftedness, and how do we develop it? A twenty-five year perspective. *Journal for the Education of the Gifted, 23,* 3–54.

Renzulli, J. S. (2002). Expanding the conception of giftedness to include co-cognitive traits and to promote social capital. *Phi Delta Kappan, 84,* 33–40, 57–58.

Renzulli, J. S., & Reis, S. M. (1994). Research related to the Schoolwide Enrichment Triad Model. *Gifted Child Quarterly, 38*(1), 7–20.

Renzulli, J. S., & Reis, S. M. (1997). *The Schoolwide Enrichment Model: A how-to guide for educational excellence* (2nd ed.). Waco, TX: Prufrock Press.

Renzulli, J. S., Rizza, M. G., & Smith, L. H. (2002). *Learning styles inventory–version III: A measure of student preferences for instructional techniques. Technical and administration manual.* Mansfield Center, CT: Creative Learning Press.

Renzulli, J. S., Smith, L. H., White, A. J., Callahan, C. M., Hartman, R. K., & Westberg, K L. (2002). *Scales for rating the behavioral characteristics of superior students—revised edition.* Mansfield Center, CT: Creative Learning Press.

Richards, J. M, Jr., Holland, J. L., & Lutz, S. W. (1967). Prediction of student accomplishment in college. *Journal of Educational Psychology, 58,* 343–355.

Roe, A. (1952). *The making of a scientist.* New York, NY: Dodd, Mead.

Shapiro, R. J. (1968). Creative research scientists. Psychologia Africana. Monograph supplement 4.

Shrader, W. K. (1992). *Media blight and the dehumanizing of America.* New York, NY: Praeger.

Stein, M. I. (1968). Creativity. In E. Borgalta & W. W. Lambert (Eds.), *Handbook of personality theory and research.* Chicago: Rand McNally.

Sternberg, R. J. (1981). Intelligence and nonentrenchment. *Journal of Educational Psychology, 73,* 1–16.

Sternberg, R. J. (1982). Lies we live by: Misapplication of tests in identifying the gifted. *Gifted Child Quarterly, 26,* 157–161.

Sternberg, R. J. (1984). Toward a triarchic theory of human intelligence. *Behavioral and Brain Sciences, 7,* 269–316.

Sternberg, R. J. (1996). *Successful intelligence: How practical and creative intelligence determine success in life.* New York, NY: Simon & Schuster.

Sternberg, R. J. (1997). *Thinking styles.* New York, NY: Cambridge University Press.

Sternberg, R. J. (1998). A balance theory of wisdom. *Review of General Psychology, 2,* 347–365.

Sternberg, R. J. (2001, November). *The theory of wisdom.* Presented at the 48th annual conference of the National Association for Gifted Children, Cincinnati, OH.

Sternberg, R. J., & Davidson, J. E. (Eds.). (1986). *Conceptions of giftedness.* New York, NY: Cambridge University Press.

Sternberg, R. J., & Grigorenko, E. L. (2002). The theory of successful intelligence as a basis for gifted education. *Gifted Child Quarterly, 46,* 265–277.

Sternberg, R. J., & Lubart, T. I. (1995). An investment perspective on creative insight. In R. J. Sternberg & J. E. Davidson (Eds.), *The nature of insight* (pp. 535–558). Cambridge, MA: Bradford.

Sternberg, R. J., & O'Hara, L. A. (1999). Creativity and intelligence. In R. J. Sternberg (Ed.), *Handbook of creativity* (pp. 251–272). New York, NY: Cambridge University Press.

Tatzel, M. (2002). "Money worlds" and well-being: An integration of money dispositions, materialism and price-related behavior. *Journal of Economic Psychology, 23,* 103–126.

Terman, L. M. (1954). The discovery and encouragement of exceptional talent. *American Psychologist, 9,* 221–230.

Terman, L. M., Baldwin, B. T., Bronson, E., DeVoss, J. C., Fuller, F., Goodenough, F. L., Kelley, T. L., et al. (1926). *Genetic studies of genius: Mental and physical traits of a thousand gifted children* (2nd ed.). Stanford, CA: Stanford University Press.

Terman, L. M., & Oden, M. H. (1959). *Genetic studies of genius: The gifted group at midlife.* Stanford, CA: Stanford University Press.

Thorndike, E. L. (1921). Intelligence and its measurement. *Journal of Educational Psychology, 12,* 124–127.

Torrance, E. P. (1969). Prediction of adult creative achievement among high school seniors. *Gifted Child Quarterly, 13,* 223–229.

Turkheimer, E., Haley, A., Waldron, M., D'Onofrio, B., & Gottesman, I. I. (2003). Socioeconomic status modifies heritability of IQ in young children. *Psychological Science, 14,* 623–628.

Vernon, P. E. (1967). Psychological studies of creativity. *Journal of Child Psychology and Psychiatry, 8,* 153–164.

Walberg, H. J. (1969). A portrait of the artist and scientist as young men. *Exceptional Children, 35,* 5–12.

Walberg, H. J. (1971). Varieties of adolescent creativity and the high school environment. *Exceptional Children, 38,* 111–116.

Wallach, M. A. (1976). Tests tell us little about talent. *American Scientist, 64,* 57–63.

Wallach, M. A., & Wing, C. W., Jr. (1969). *The talented students: A validation of the creativity-intelligence distinction.* New York, NY: Holt, Rinehart & Winston.

Witty, P. A. (1958). Who are the gifted? In N. B. Henry (Ed.), *Education of the gifted. Fifty-seventh Yearbook of the National Society for the Study of Education, Part 2* (pp. 41–63). Chicago: University of Chicago Press.

Zuckerman, H. (1979). The scientific elite: Nobel laureates' mutual influences. In R. S. Albert (Ed.), *Genius and eminence* (pp. 241–252). Elmsford, NY: Pergamon.

CHAPTER 4

Defensible and Doable

A Practical, Multiple-Criteria Gifted Program Identification System[6]

Joseph S. Renzulli and Sally M. Reis
University of Connecticut

Introduction From Joe

In an applied field such as education we have always maintained that a theory doesn't have much value (beyond generating research proposals) unless it can ultimately guide practice, and hopefully policy. We also maintain that there is no such thing as a "perfect" identification system and any system is always a series of compromises that must take into account state rules and regulations, political realities (e.g., parent pressures, underrepresentation of low-income and minority groups), practical issues (e.g., time and costs of testing), and of course the conception(s) of giftedness and the programming model(s) that guide the services for which students are being identified.

---

6 Renzulli, J. S., & Reis, S. M. (2012). Defensible and doable: A practical, multiple-criteria gifted program identification system. In S. L. Hunsaker (Ed.), *Identification: The theory and practice of identifying students for gifted and talented education services* (pp. 25–56). Waco, TX: Prufrock Press. Copyright 2012 Prufrock Press. Adapted with permission.

In this chapter, we first discuss a number of considerations that *must* be taken into account when designing an identification system for a school, district, or even a state. The step-by-step system that is described here is an attempt to address as many of these considerations as possible, but we must also state up front that the system presented in this chapter is based on the Three-Ring Conception of Giftedness. Further, it is designed for programs that focus mainly on creative productive giftedness as delineated in the Enrichment Triad Model. The system does, of course, provide a major pathway for the highest achieving students but it also "opens the door" for participation by students who show potential for high performance through one or more nontest criteria that may not be adequately assessed by cognitive ability or achievement tests.

Introduction

In his classic work, *Diffusion of Innovations*, Everett Rogers (1962) detailed how new ideas and technologies come to be adopted within an organization or social system. In the first two stages, a decision maker gains initial awareness of an innovation and then is persuaded to actively seek more information about the innovation. In the third stage, the decision maker chooses to accept or reject the innovation. If the decision maker accepts the innovation, she proceeds to the fourth stage—implementation. Once the innovation has been implemented, the decision maker can observe the outcomes and determine whether she will continue or discontinue using the innovation (see Figure 4.1).

This chapter provides decision makers with knowledge that will facilitate the implementation of a multiple-criteria identification system for gifted programs and poses two key questions:

1. Why is a multiple-criteria identification system preferable to a traditional test-score based identification system?
2. How can my school system implement a multiple-criteria identification system in a practical, efficient, and feasible manner?

Answers to the first question endeavor to persuade decision makers that the current state of research on human potential requires a transition in the systems we use to identify children and adolescents for special programming in schools. After choosing to accept this innovation, decision makers can use the answers to the second question as a roadmap for both a practical and efficient implementation of multiple-criteria identification systems.

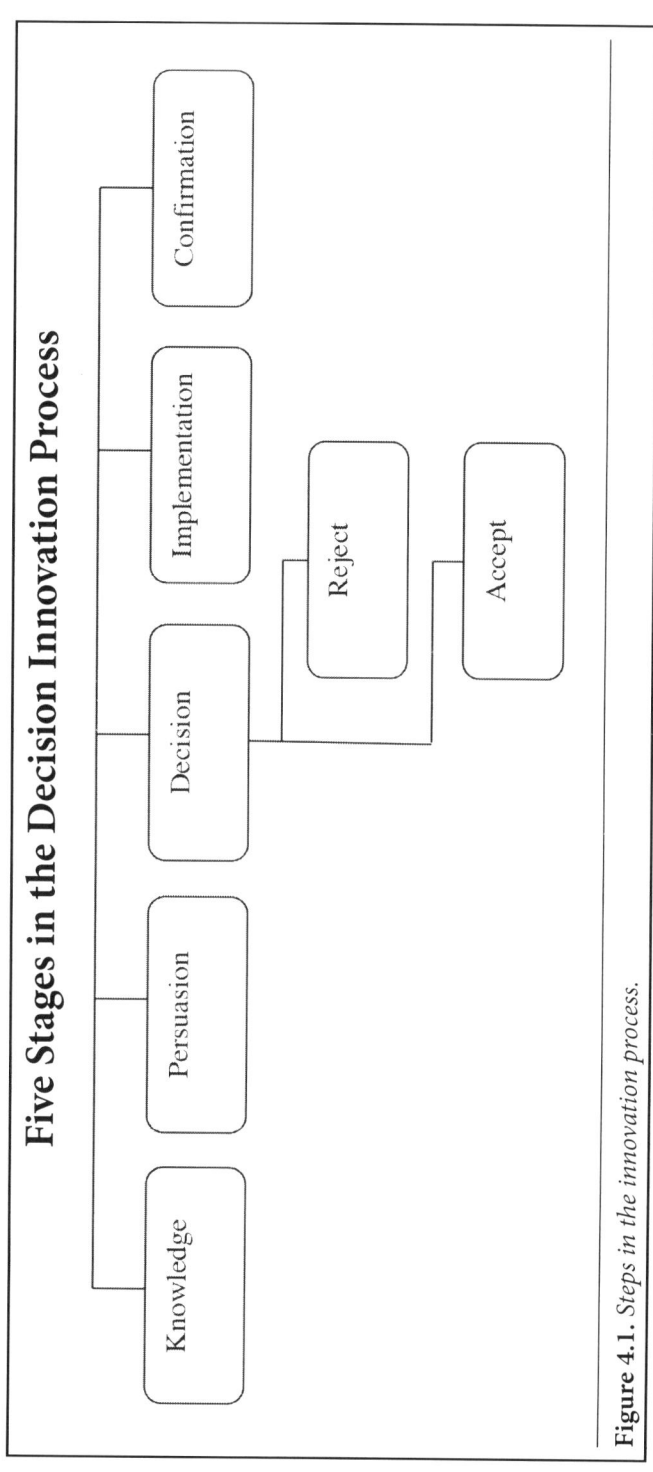

Figure 4.1. Steps in the innovation process.

This chapter presents an identification system that addresses issues of excellence, equity, and economy in gifted education programs. It is supported by decades of thorough research concerning its underlying theories (Reis & Renzulli, 2004; Renzulli & Reis, 1994). It is designed to be economical in terms of the time and paperwork required for identification, to provide access to special services for both traditionally high-scoring students and those students whose potential may only be recognized through the use of a more flexible range of identification criteria. It is versatile enough to accommodate talent potentials in different domains, and it respects regulations made by district policy makers and state departments of education (especially important since these entities often provide much needed financial assistance).

The first order of business for any particular school or school system wishing to identify and serve high-potential youngsters is to decide on a conception or definition of giftedness. The identification system described in this chapter is based on the Three-Ring Conception of Giftedness, a definition developed from research that identifies three interlocking clusters of ability that characterize highly creative and productive people, as seen in Figure 4.2. These three clusters are (1) well-above-average (not necessarily superior) ability, (2) task commitment, and (3) creativity. These clusters of ability are brought to bear on specific performance areas. The Three-Ring Conception additionally posits that there are two kinds of giftedness: academic giftedness and creative productive giftedness. Both of these types of giftedness are important and often interact, and both should be encouraged in special programs.

Further, this identification system is firmly based on the assumption that there should be congruence between the criteria used in the identification process and the program goals and types of services that constitute the day-to-day gifted program's activities in which students will be involved. It is therefore also linked to a broad range of services and teaching practices that are specifically designed to develop a variety of talents in young people.

Another critical consideration that went into developing this identification system is our firm belief that we should label the services rather than the student. Instead of labeling a student as "gifted" or "not gifted," this identification system enables teachers to document specific strengths and use this information to make decisions about the types of activities and the levels of challenge that should be made available to the student. This system identifies students who would benefit from services that recognize both academic as well as creative productive giftedness and provides opportunities to develop talents through an integrated continuum of special services.

A key feature of this identification system is the formation of a Talent Pool that includes students who have been identified by both test and nontest criteria. The system includes students who earn high scores on traditional mea-

A Practical Gifted Identification System

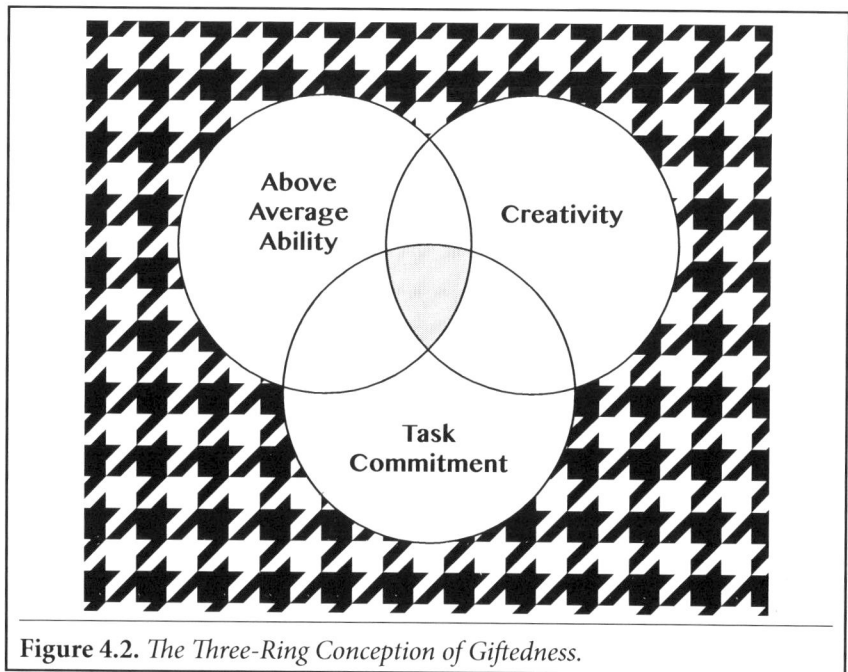

Figure 4.2. *The Three-Ring Conception of Giftedness.*

sures, but also leaves room for students who show their potentials in other ways or who have high academic potential, but underachieve in school.

In districts where this system has been implemented, students, parents, teachers, and administrators have expressed high degrees of satisfaction with this approach. By eliminating many of the problems usually associated with identifying gifted students, we gain support from teachers and administrators, and by expanding services to students below the top few percentile levels usually admitted into special programs, we eliminate the sometimes justifiable criticism that we are denying entrance to students who are in need of special opportunities, resources, and encouragement. This identification system is not as tidy as using cut-off scores, but it is a more flexible approach to identifying and serving young people with great potential, and one that can be completed in much less time than more traditional approaches.

Persuasion: Why Multiple Criteria?

As scientific study advances our understanding of how human potential develops over the course of a lifetime, the systems created to enhance that potential (i.e., the education system) should also change to reflect contemporary theories. In the field of gifted education during the past three decades, research has supported a broadened, expanded conception of giftedness (Gardner, 1983; Renzulli, 1978; Sternberg, 1985). A thorough review of this research is beyond the scope of this chapter (see, for example, Dai, 2010; Sternberg & Davidson, 2005), but to simplify a complex and active debate, very few researchers and theorists continue to accept an isolated IQ or achievement test score as a valid measure of a child's capacity for producing notable accomplishments over the course of the lifetime. It does not mean that IQ or achievement scores should not be included as one of a number of criteria, only that they should not form the entire basis for decision making and identification for gifted and enrichment programs. Despite these developments, the administrative tidiness of using a single IQ or achievement score in the identification process has persisted in America's schools.

Considerations in Developing Identification Systems

Districts just starting to develop gifted and talented programs and those with programs already in place both benefit from considering (or reconsidering) how to analyze the appropriateness of identification systems designed to select students for participation in those programs. The following questions constitute a starting point for reflection on the practical, political, and psychometric complexities of the issue:

1. Will this identification system be applicable to diverse school populations and groups of students that have been traditionally underrepresented in programs for the gifted?
2. How will we "label" students identified for these programs?
3. How much individual testing by school psychology staff will be required?
4. Will the system be economical in terms of the personnel time, group and individual testing costs, and other resources necessary to identify students?
5. Will the system be flexible enough to accommodate talent potentials across different domains such as music, art, drama, technology, and other nonverbal or mathematical talent areas?
6. Will it be flexible enough to make changes if student performance warrants a reexamination of selection or rejection decisions?
7. How will the system fit in with regulations of state departments of education (especially in those cases where some level of financial reimbursement is provided by state agencies for each identified gifted student)?

8. How will the system help avoid parental dissatisfaction or legal challenges?

In any plan to identify gifted and talented students, the following six important considerations should be kept in mind. Any number of identification approaches exist in the field, including some based on theories and research about the development of human potential and others based on beliefs and school district traditions and policies about the types of educational services that develop high levels of performance. An examination of these considerations can guide how decision makers respond to the aforementioned recurring and problematic questions.

Consideration 1: There is no such thing as a perfect identification system. There is no perfect way to identify who is or is not gifted, just as there is no single best way to develop giftedness and/or talent potentials in special program candidates. Every identification system is a trade-off between the instruments and criteria selected, the ways we make decisions about any and all types of information we collect, and how much weight we give each type of information in the decision-making process. Because so many different conceptions of giftedness can be found in the theoretical and research literature, the first and most important decision we should make regarding practical procedures for identification is about the conception or definition of giftedness adopted by the school or school system. In some cases where state reimbursement is provided, state regulations mandate the definitions that guide identification and the number or proportion of students that can be served. There are programs, however, where additional students with high potential may be served if supported by local funds; and in such cases, this group may be designated by a label that is different from the state-certified group designated as "the gifted" (e.g., Talent Pool, Advanced Learners, High Potential). Local circumstances notwithstanding, the conception or definition issue should be consistent with the types of services for which students are being identified, as discussed in Consideration 6.

A number of excellent resources exist to help decision makers reach agreement on a conception/definition decision. Appendix 4.A (at the end of the chapter) presents a selected bibliography of the best resources to guide this decision-making process, and we recommend that decision makers examine and discuss these references to reach consensus before selecting or designing an identification system.

Consideration 2: The objective versus subjective trade-off. Tests of cognitive ability and/or academic achievement are the most frequently used type of identification information. These types of tests are considered objective because they rely on student performance rather than the judgment of others.

Some people question the objectivity of these tests because the decision to use them is, in and of itself, a subjective act (e.g., imagine using an IQ test to select students for an advanced music or drama program). Another concern focuses on whether or not a one-hour "glimpse" into a young person's overall potential can be considered an objective appraisal of a student's total capacity for high-level performance.

Almost all other criteria (e.g., teacher, parent, peer, or self ratings; portfolio or writing-sample assessments; or grades earned in school subjects) are considered to be subjective, as their use implies personal judgments that may be open to personal bias, an idiosyncratic view of giftedness, or inconsistent grading standards. Many argue that these types of criteria enable us to see other signs of potential such as motivation, creativity, leadership and executive functions (initiation, execution, and completion of tasks), and intense interest in a topic that is not reflected in more objective cognitive ability tests. If we view some of these noncognitive skills as important, then we need to examine the degree to which we are willing to make trade-offs between objective and subjective information.

Consideration 3: People, not instruments, make decisions. Regardless of the number or types of instruments used in a multicriteria identification system, instruments only provide selected sources of information; they do not make decisions! Therefore, it is important to specify reasons for selecting the members (e.g., teachers, program coordinators, school psychologists, district liaisons) who will be involved in the information-processing and decision-making team. In addition, we must provide these team members with the level of orientation and training they need to become well-informed evaluators. Members from different areas of the school community may need different levels of training. Protocols for resolving the differences of opinion that will invariably emerge should be structured in advance, reducing the need for ad hoc solutions to team member disagreements.

How much "weight" will be given to the various instruments or decision-making criteria should also be determined before implementing the identification system. For example, if a decision is made to use two or three cognitive ability measures (e.g., aptitude test, achievement test, and course grades[7]) and only one measure of creativity (e.g., a creativity test or a teacher rating), there will be triple weighting of cognitive ability and single weighting of the creativity criterion. The relative emphasis on different sources of information should be aligned with the overall intent of the program. This consideration is important in both the design of the identification system and

---

[7] Course grades are not as precise as test scores, but they are reflections of cognitive ability so far as school performance is concerned. One should, however, be cautious of varying grading standards displayed by different teachers.

the interpretation of the information provided to the committee who will review students' records and subsequently make decisions.

Consideration 4: Avoid the multiple-criteria smokescreen. Most identification systems use a traditional nomination/screening/selection approach, and at least part of a multiple-criteria screening process is usually based on nontest information (e.g., teacher nominations and/or ratings). A problem arises, however, if the nomination or screening process only determines which students will be eligible to take an individual IQ test or a more advanced cognitive ability test. In such cases, the test still remains the ultimate "gatekeeper" for which students enter or do not enter the program. Unselected students are often those who were nominated for screening on the basis of one or more nontest criteria, but who did not make the cut after taking a cognitive ability test. In other words, a teacher nomination or high ratings is only used as a "ticket" to take an individual or a group ability test, but in most cases, the test score is the deciding factor. Any highly positive attributes that might have been the basis for a teacher nomination, or favorable information discovered in the screening process, are ignored when it comes to the final selection decision. The danger here is, of course, that we may be systematically excluding high-potential students from culturally diverse backgrounds or students who have shown signs of high potential in areas other than the high verbal, mathematical, or analytic skills measured by standardized tests. What appears to be a multiple-criteria approach ends up being a smokescreen for a more traditional cut-off score approach.

The multiple-criteria smokescreen has other unintended side effects. Often, attempts to give the impression of a more flexible approach result in so much paperwork that it becomes inordinately time consuming, expensive, and unwieldy. In other cases, the smokescreen could be used to give the appearance of concerns for equity when such concerns don't really exist.

Consideration 5: What will we call selected students? A fifth consideration emerges from the discussion above and relates to the degree of specificity we are attempting to achieve in the identification process. The tradition has been to label all selected students as "the gifted," thereby relegating all others to a nongifted category. In recent years, however, a large body of research has argued very forcefully against such a broad stroke labeling process (Frasier & Passow, 1995; Gardner, 1983; Renzulli & Reis, 1997; Sternberg, 1985; Winner, 1996), and in some cases recommendations have been made to do away with any labeling altogether (Borland, 2004). A more current trend is to document specific student strengths by preparing an electronic multiple-criteria profile (Field, 2009; Renzulli & Reis, 1997). We can use this strength-based profile to make more personalized decisions about the types of resources and activities recommended for talent development.

It would be nice to think that we can do away with any kind of labeling, but the reality is that we can't make accommodations for students if we don't recognize individual strength areas. Experience has shown that far too many teachers claiming to differentiate for all students have, in reality, provided minimal or no advanced-level opportunities for high-potential students. Behavioral definitions (i.e., those targeting specific strengths) are important because, if we know and can document particular strengths, there is a greater likelihood that schools will attempt to cultivate these strengths in targeted students. This approach also helps to introduce an element of accountability into programming, and it gives direction to efforts that schools should take in evaluating their programs (Delcourt, Dewey, & Goldberg, 2007)

In recent years, an approach that has gained in popularity is to label the service rather than the student (Renzulli & Reis, 1994, 1997). For example, in a school using the Schoolwide Enrichment Model, a special service offered to all students called an "enrichment cluster" enabled any interested students to participate in a class, "Statistical Techniques for Young Researchers." This class was specifically designed for upper elementary students with strong aptitudes and interests in mathematics. Without needing to be labeled, students benefited from material that was much more advanced than the math being covered in their sixth-, seventh-, and eighth-grade math classes.

Another example of a labeled service is curriculum compacting (Reis & Purcell, 1993; Reis & Renzulli, 2005; Reis, Westberg, Kulikowich, & Purcell, 1998). Teachers use curriculum compacting in the regular classroom with students who have already mastered the concepts and skills in a given unit of instruction and/or who are capable of covering the regular material at a faster pace and higher level of comprehension than their classmates. The process involves specific procedures for identifying particular strength areas, documenting these competencies in a systematic fashion, and providing advanced-level enrichment and/or acceleration opportunities with the time gained from eliminating already mastered material. Students are identified for the service, but there is no need to label them.

Consideration 6: The relationship between identification and programming. Our final consideration addresses the congruence between the criteria used in the identification process and the goals and types of services that constitute the daily activities of students in a special program. Congruence between identification and programming is so important that it might be viewed as "the golden rule" of gifted education! For example, identification for advanced courses in a content area such as math is best accomplished through math testing, examination of previous math grades, teacher recommendations or ratings on mathematical skills, and perhaps even estimates of a student's motivation to work hard in math.

A problem arises, however, when we expect an "all purpose" gifted program to develop strengths that are unique to each child. If a general gifted program has a curriculum, or if individual teachers in the program choose most of the activities (e.g., the teacher's favorite rainforest unit or play production), then little room exists for variations in students' interests, learning styles, or preferred modes of expression. In other words, the materials covered in the general gifted program may be different from the regular curriculum, but the prescriptive nature of what is to be learned uses essentially the same approach to teaching used in regular classrooms. Therefore, a related decision in developing an identification system is the selection of a pedagogical programming model that will be used to guide direct and indirect services to students regardless of how they are grouped or organized for special program services. In this case, we are not discussing organizational models, but rather what the teaching/learning process looks like within any predetermined organizational arrangement.

Again, there are numerous programming models recommended for serving this population, and these programming models can be divided into two categories. Organizational or administrative models address how we group students and move them from one activity to another (e.g., full-time classes, pull-out programs, centers where students go for a given period of time each week, regular class inclusion approaches). Theoretical or pedagogical models focus on the kind and quality of learning experiences that are offered within any grouping or organizational arrangement. The Enrichment Triad Model (Renzulli, 1977), the Autonomous Learner Model (Betts & Kercher, 2009), and a variety of acceleration, problem-based learning, and Socratic-reasoning approaches are examples of theoretical or pedagogical models. The importance of this consideration in guiding the identification process suggests that program planners review the continuum of learning theories from which all pedagogy is derived, as seen in Figure 4.3. (An excellent resource for examining the range of programming options can be *found in Systems and Models for Developing Programs for the Gifted and Talented* [Renzulli, Gubbins, McMillen, Eckhart, & Little, 2009].)

By way of summary, the six considerations discussed above point out the "landscape" surrounding the always complicated and frequently controversial topic of identifying gifted and talented students for services in special programs. This discussion of the issues will not provide ready-made answers to the many challenges of identification system design, but it does provide an understanding of some historically encountered problems and may be helpful in avoiding the pitfalls encountered by so many persons who have set out on the journey of creating an efficient, effective, and equitable plan for identification.

Continuum of Learning Theories

Pedagogy	
Deductive Didactic & Prescriptive Knowledge Acquisition. Storage and Retrieval	Inductive, Investigative & Inquiry Oriented Knowledge Application, High Engagement, Motivation And Enjoyment

Outcomes	
Basic Skill Acquisition Text Consumption	21st Century Thinking Skills Creative Productivity

Major Theorists	
Behaviorists •Pavlov •Thorndike •Skinner	Constructivists •Pestalozzi •Montessori •Piaget & Bruner •Dewey

National Goals	
Increased Academic Achievement Higher Test Scores Technically Proficient Professional and Skilled Workers	Inventors Creative Designers in Sciences, Arts, & Technology Innovative Leaders Entrepreneurs People Who Make a Difference

Figure 4.3. *The continuum of learning theories.*

Implementation: The Nuts and Bolts of the Renzulli Identification System for Gifted Program Services (RIS/GPS)

Now that we have reviewed the research, presented the evidence, and introduced the key considerations, we hope that you agree that a multiple-criteria identification system is preferable to a traditional system. What next? The following section outlines a pragmatic approach to implementing such an identification system. The diagram in Figure 4.4 forms the basis for the step-by-step process to selecting students for services based on multiple sources. After following the steps in the Renzulli Identification System, identification team members can assemble a Talent Pool comprised of the students who have been identified through multiple ability/achievement scores, teacher ratings, parent ratings, peer ratings, and self-nominations.

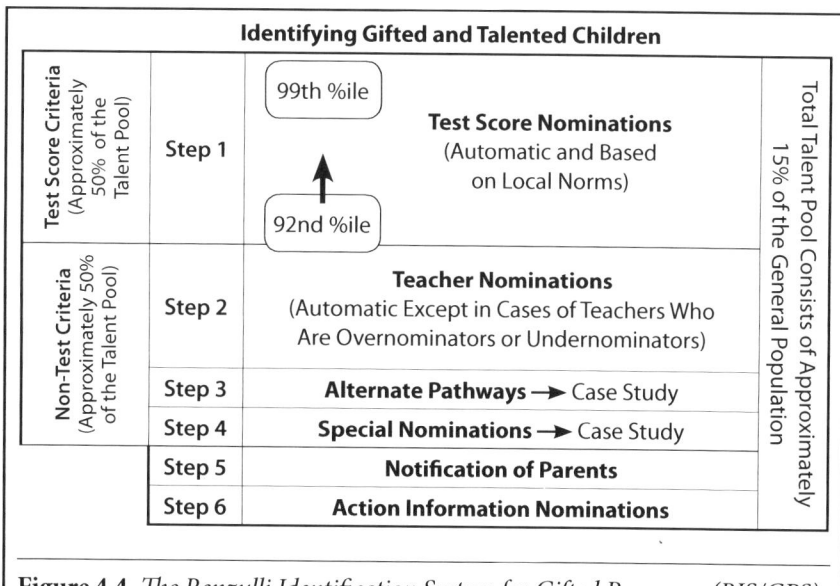

Figure 4.4. *The Renzulli Identification System for Gifted Programs (RIS/GPS).*

Decisions About Talent Pool Size

The size of the Talent Pool is a function of two major decisions. The first is the number of special program personnel assigned to the program and the number of students that these personnel can provide adequate services to each week in such a manner that it makes a difference in the accomplishment of program goals. The second decision is the nature of and extent to which an expanded range of services can be made available to targeted students by classroom teachers (e.g., curriculum compacting, enrichment clusters, mentorship programs for advanced students). Services such as robotics club; history day competition; math league; music, art, and drama clubs; or any other organized, interest-based grouping that focuses on a specific talent area falls within the scope of most special program goals. These types of opportunities reflect a total school talent development perspective, and they are especially valuable for a student or small group that has a high degree of potential, but only in a particular area of interest. It is important to convey to parents that this expanded range of services is, in fact, part of the special program opportunities that fall under the purview of the gifted program.

This second decision about an expanded range of services also has implications for special program administrative personnel. If we expect classroom teachers to participate in the services mentioned above, and if we hope to offer a robust range of extracurricular activities geared toward talent development, it is essential to have a program coordinator who plans and "grows" such services, monitors the effectiveness of the services, maintains student records, and communicates talent development progress with parents. All teachers involved in the expanded range of services should believe they are an integral part of the program rather than a random provider of an extracurricular activity. They should be aware of the program mission and goals, participate in staff development that focuses on talent development, and attend "gifted program" meetings. Their accomplishments should be described in program brochures, reported in program announcements and newsletters, and recognized in special events about program activities. The program coordinator helps to create an expanded range of services that are an essential part of a Total Talent Development program.

The RIS/GPS respects and includes students who earn high scores on traditional measures of cognitive ability, but a major variation from traditional identification practices is that this system leaves room in the Talent Pool for students who show their potentials in other ways. The percentage of total students in the Talent Pool and the corresponding proportions of students identified through test and nontest criteria can and should be modified based on the resources and goals of the individual program involved.

Steps in Forming the Talent Pool

A team of school personnel, including teacher(s) of the gifted, classroom teachers, administrators, and pupil personnel specialists (e.g., counselor, school psychologist, social worker), should be responsible for managing the Talent Pool selection process. This group can be thought of as the Review and Selection Team. Any and all information related to the selection process should be made available to all members of the team and a case study approach should be used to review each set of student records. On some occasions, it will be necessary to seek supplementary information about a student and to request that nonteam members meet with the team to provide additional information. It is important for all persons on the team (and parents and the general faculty as well) to understand that *instruments provide information, but people make decisions*! A multiple-criteria approach means that simply setting arbitrary cut-off points or adding up points from various instruments cannot make decisions. Informed human judgment is crucial for an identification system that (1) seeks to develop diverse talent potentials in diverse segments of the school population and (2) is geared toward services that place a premium on developing creative productivity rather than mere advanced lesson learning.

Step 1: Academic performance and test score nominations. Academic performance based on end-of-year grades for the past 2 years and the most recent total verbal and total numerical scores from districtwide achievement tests are the first two criteria used in forming the Talent Pool. In a 15% Talent Pool example, students who score at or above the 92nd percentile on either verbal or numerical sections of the achievement test should automatically be placed in the Talent Pool. In schools that serve diverse populations, it is also recommended that a nonverbal cognitive ability test be used in addition to standard achievement tests or aptitude tests. A very big caution, however, is in order here: There is a good deal of controversy about the effectiveness of nonverbal tests for increasing the proportion of minority students in programs for the gifted (Lohman, 2005; Naglieri & Ford, 2003, 2005). Until more definitive studies are conducted, we should treat nonverbal test scores as another piece of information in the overall decision-making process rather than a substitute for regular cognitive ability tests and school performance. Lohman has argued forcefully that

> (1) admission to programs for the gifted should be guided by evidence of aptitude for the particular types of advanced instruction that can be offered by schools; (2) the primary aptitudes for development of academic competence are current knowledge and skill in a domain, the ability to reason in the symbol systems used to communicate new knowledge in the domain, interest in the domain, and persistence; (3) inferences about aptitude are most defensible when made by comparing a student's behavior to the behavior of other students who have had similar opportunities to acquire the skills measured by the aptitude tests; however, (4) educational programming and placement should be based primarily on evidence of current accomplishment. (Lohman, 2005)

Lohman further argued that comparisons should only be made between students who share similar learning opportunities or background characteristics. It is for this reason that this identification system recommends the use of local norms (i.e., calculated by school and grade level). Our goal is to identify the most promising students in each school and at each grade level who are the best candidates for supplementary services. Because we are not admitting students from other school districts or states, it does not make sense to engage in national comparisons. The use of national norms invariably results in the underrepresentation of minorities and students whose potentials may be manifested in nontraditional ways.

Students who score below the 92nd percentile, but who have demonstrated "straight A" academic performance in their end-of-year grades should also be considered eligible for gifted program services unless the selection team notes unusual discrepancies between test scores and grades. Or there may be cases in which high-scoring students do not have high grades due to underachievement or personal or social issues. In such cases, before determining which services are appropriate, additional individual assessment and record review should be carried out to determine if factors such as underachievement, a learning disability, personal or family problems, or difficulty with timed group tests are giving an inaccurate picture of the student's potential. Individual intelligence tests administered by a qualified examiner are needed when discrepancy information is found in the types of assessment mentioned above. This approach will help to control the expensive and time-consuming use of individualized testing, thereby meeting the economy goal of this identification system.

Scores from the most recent regularly administered standardized achievement or aptitude test can be used for this purpose; however, we recommend that admission to the Talent Pool be granted on the basis of either a high verbal or a high mathematics score. This approach will enable students who are high in verbal or mathematical ability (but not necessarily both) to gain admission. Programs that focus on special talent areas such as music, art, drama, or leadership should use nontest criteria (see Step 2) as major indicators of above-average ability in a particular talent area. In a similar fashion, whenever test scores are not available or there is some question as to their validity, the nontest criteria recommended in the following steps should be used. This approach is especially important when considering primary age students, disadvantaged populations, or culturally and linguistically different groups.

The conclusion of Step 1 should be the creation of a list of names with an approximately equivalent number of students selected from each grade level. Through team discussions and negotiations, this list should represent approximately one-half of the predetermined number of "slots" in the Talent Pool.

Step 2: Teacher nominations. If we were using nothing but test scores to identify a 15% Talent Pool, the task would be ever so simple. Any child who scores above the 85th percentile (using local norms) would be placed in the Talent Pool. In this identification system, however, we have made a commitment to "leave some room" for students whose potentials may not be reflected in standardized tests. This approach guarantees that all traditionally bright youngsters will automatically be selected, and they will account for approximately 50% of the Talent Pool. This process also guarantees admission to bright underachievers.

In order to minimize paperwork on the parts of classroom teachers, the first activity in Step 2 is to provide classroom teachers with a list of the names of students from their class who have already been selected for the Talent Pool in Step 1. After being provided with a brief training activity on the use of teacher rating forms (see Appendix 4.B at the end of the chapter), teachers are asked to complete ratings on other students (i.e., other than those already selected in Step 1) whom they might consider for admission to the Talent Pool. In other words, teachers should be informed about all students who have gained entrance through test score nominations so that they will not have to complete ratings for students who have already been admitted. Step 2 allows teachers to nominate students who display characteristics that are not easily determined by tests (e.g., high levels of creativity, task commitment, unusual interests, talents, or special areas of superior performance or potential).

The instrument recommended for teacher ratings is the Scales for Rating the Behavioral Characteristics of Superior Students (SRBCSS; Renzulli et al., 2013). These scales are the most thoroughly researched and widely used teacher-rating instrument in the world (Renzulli, Reis, Gavin, & Sytsma Reed, 2009). The scales are now available in an online version, (http://www.prufrock.com/Scales-for-Rating-the-Behavioral-Characteristics-of-Superior-Students-Online-Version-50-Seats-P2217.aspx) which allows for ease of rating, and, more importantly (because this system recommends the use of local norms[8]), the online version automatically calculates local norms as well as individual student profiles. Local norms should be calculated on a broad achievement range of students across the grade levels targeted to be identified before the scales are used to nominate high-potential and gifted students.

Most schools use the three scales that correspond to the Three-Ring Conception of Giftedness (Learning, Motivation, and Creativity); however, employing one or a combination of the other scales (Leadership, Reading, Mathematics, Science, Technology, Music, Art, Drama, Communication: Precision, Communication: Expression, and Planning) may be appropriate for programs focusing on special areas of talent or for categorical programs such as Future Problem Solving, WebQuest, or MathCounts. Table 4.1 includes examples of how these rating scales may be used to nominate students for special topic programs by matching program goals and targeted skills to relevant rating scales. Once again, local norms based on school and grade-level ratings are used rather than state, regional, or national norms, and each scale is considered a categorical data point. *In other words, scores from the scales should never be added together or averaged.*

With the exception of teachers who are overnominators or undernominators, nominations from *teachers who have received training in this process*

---

[8] National norms for SRBCSS are not offered because we do not believe that national information is meaningful or appropriate since student populations differ from school district to school district and even between and among schools in the same district. Accordingly, we believe that local norms should be calculated for a broad achievement range of students across the grade levels targeted to be identified. The step-by-step procedure for calculating local norms (percentile ranks) is outlined in Appendix E of the manual for SRBCSS (Renzulli et al., 2013) or, if you are using the online version of the Scales, it is calculated for you.

Table 4.1
Matching SRBCSS Scales to Program Goals

Program	Program Goals	Rating Scales to Use
Future Problem Solving (FPS)	<ul><li>Increase creative thinking abilities</li><li>Improve analytical thinking skills</li><li>Stimulate an interactive interest in the future</li><li>Extend perceptions of the real world</li><li>Explore complex societal issues</li><li>Refine communication skills—written, verbal, and technical</li><li>Promote research</li><li>Integrate problem-solving into the curriculum</li><li>Encourage cooperative, responsible group membership</li><li>Offer authentic assessment</li></ul>	<ul><li>Creativity</li><li>Motivation</li><li>Leadership</li></ul>
WebQuest	To develop the following skills:<ul><li>Comparing</li><li>Classifying</li><li>Inducing</li><li>Deducing</li><li>Analyzing errors</li><li>Constructing support</li><li>Abstraction</li><li>Analyzing perspectives</li></ul>	<ul><li>Technology</li><li>Planning</li><li>Learning</li><li>Reading</li></ul>
MathCounts	<ul><li>Challenge students' math skills</li><li>Develop their self-confidence</li><li>Reward them for their achievements</li></ul>	<ul><li>Mathematics</li><li>Motivation</li><li>Communication: Precision</li></ul>
National History Day	<ul><li>Engage students in the process of discovery and interpretation of historical topics</li><li>Combine creativity and scholarship</li></ul>	<ul><li>Learning</li><li>Motivation</li><li>Creativity</li><li>Planning</li><li>Communication: Precision</li><li>Communication: Expressive</li></ul>

are accepted into the Talent Pool on a par value with test score nominations. We do not refer to students nominated by test scores as the "truly gifted" and the students nominated by teachers as the moderately or potentially gifted. Nor do we make any distinctions in the opportunities, resources, or services provided other than the normal individualization that should be a part of any program that attempts to meet unique needs and potentials. Thus, for example, if a student gains entrance on the basis of teacher nomination because he or she has shown advanced potential for creative writing, we would not expect this student to compete on an equal basis in an advanced math class with a student who scored at or above the 92nd percentile on a math test. Nor should we arrange program experiences that would place the student with talents in creative writing in an advanced math cluster group. *Special programs should first and foremost respect and reflect the individual characteristics that brought students to our attention in the first place.*

In cases of teachers who are overnominators, the selection team can and should request that teachers rank order their nominations for review (i.e., place the scales in a pile from high to low) and return them to the selection team. Procedures for dealing with undernominators or nonnominators will be described in Step 4.

Step 3: Alternate pathways. Most schools using this identification system make use of test scores and teacher nominations, and in most cases, the majority of the Talent Pool will come from these two criteria.

Alternate pathways are optional, locally determined by individual schools, and pursued in varying degrees by individual school districts. Alternate pathways generally include parent nominations, peer nominations, self-nominations, specialized tests (e.g., creative writing, spatial or mechanical ability), product evaluations, or virtually any other procedure that might lead to *initial* consideration by a selection team. A large number of instruments for gathering alternate pathway information are available in the identification literature. (A good source for information about traditional testing instruments can be found in *Assessment of Children: Cognitive Applications* [Sattler, 2001] and reviews of instruments specifically related to gifted programs can be found in *Instruments Used in the Identification of Gifted and Talented Students* [Callahan, Hunsaker, Adams, Moore, & Bland, 2005].) A few examples of instruments that can be used for parent, peer, and product evaluation are included in Appendix 4.C at the end of the chapter. The language of the cover letter for "Things My Child Likes to Do" is written in a way that seeks parent input about particular strength areas, but it does not place the parent in the awkward position of favoring or jeopardizing their child's designation as a "gifted" student. It is, of course, important and ethically responsible for teachers to put the results from the use of this instrument (described in the cover letter) to use, whether or not the child is placed in the Talent Pool. This information should always be shared with classroom teachers and periodically monitored to determine if appropriate attention is given to information about special interests or activities.

Sensitive issues need to be addressed whenever we open the door to parent input. Objectivity is always a concern when parents are asked to rate their own child, and it is for this reason that the parent rating scale mentioned above is not characterized as a "gifted instrument." Examples of representative behaviors associated with each scale item are included so that we can avoid, at least to some extent, the surplus interpretation that parents may bring to the ratings.

There are even more important issues related to parent input, primarily school districts that allow scores obtained through private testing to be submitted for consideration in the identification process. Assuming that reputable psychologists are administering the tests,[9] there is the issue of parents who are wealthy enough to afford private testing, and even in cases where private testing may be underwritten by the school district, there is the issue of parent savvy—simply knowing that the service is available and making the arrangements to have one's child tested. Because private testing is frequently a function of program history that has become accepted tradition, or even school board policy, the only way we can guard against unfair advantage is to make certain that (1) all parents are made aware of and have access to equivalent testing offered by or supported by the school, (2) inferences about test results are only made by comparing a student's behavior to the behavior of other students who have had similar opportunities to acquire the skills measured by the test, and (3) no single piece of identification information be used as the sole gatekeeper for admission decisions. The major difference between alternate pathways on the one hand (Step 3) and test score and teacher nomination on the other (Steps 1 and 2) is that alternate pathways are not automatic. In other words, students nominated through one or more alternate pathways will become the subjects of a case study by the Review and Selection Team, after which a selection decision will be made. In most cases, the team carries out a case study that includes examination of all previous school records; interviews with students, teachers, and parents; and the administration of individual assessments (as needed) that may be recommended by the team. In some cases, students recommended on the basis of one or more alternate pathways can be placed in the Talent Pool on a trial basis.

---

9 We are reminded of a newspaper article that made reference to a local psychologist who was popularly known as "Dr. 130!" For the right fee, he would automatically make a child gifted by giving him or her an IQ of 130 or higher.

A local planning committee or the Review and Selection Team should make decisions about which alternative pathways might be used. Some consideration should also be given to variations in grade level. For example, self-nomination is more appropriate for students who may be considering advanced classes at the secondary level. Peer nomination is particularly useful for program services that focus on particular talent areas such as technology, music, or drama, and students themselves are sometimes better at revealing which students have natural or "street smart" leadership potential.

Step 4: Special nominations (Safety valve no. 1). Special nominations represent the first of two "safety valves" in this identification system. This procedure involves preparing grade-level lists of all students who have been nominated through one of the procedures in Steps 1 through 3 and circulating these lists to all previous year teachers. The directions sent with the lists are as follows:

> These lists contain the names of all students who have been nominated for the Talent Pool for the forthcoming year. Will you please review the lists and send us the names of any students you have previously taught who are not on the lists, but who you think should be considered for Talent Pool membership?

Teachers should not be required to give a reason for their special nominations at this time. Busy schedules may discourage teachers from preparing justifications "on the spot." A later meeting or request that teachers complete a set of rating scales can also help to ensure that invitations for special nominations are not ignored by busy teachers.

This procedure allows previous year teachers to nominate students who have not been recommended by their present teacher, and it also allows gifted education teachers to make recommendations based on their own previous experience with students who have already been in the Talent Pool or students they may have encountered as part of enrichment experiences that have been offered in regular classrooms. This process also allows special topic teachers (e.g., music, art, physical education) or teachers who have had responsibilities for special programs (e.g., Future Problem Solving, National History Day) to have opportunities for input into the nomination process. These teachers often observe students in nontraditional learning environments, and, therefore, they are excellent talent scouts for a variety of creative, practical, and motivational strengths. Faculty orientation about such opportunities is, of course, very important for gaining such input.

The Special Nomination step allows for a final review of the total school population and is designed to circumvent the opinions of present-year teachers who may not have an appreciation for the abilities, styles, or even the personality of a particular student. This one last "sweep" through the population also helps to pick up students who may have "turned off" to school or developed patterns of underachievement as a result of personal or family problems. This step also helps to overcome the general biases of any given teacher who is an undernominator or a nonnominator. As with the case of alternate pathways, special nominations are not automatic. Rather, a case study is carried out, and the final decision rests with the selection team.

Step 5: Notification and orientation of parents. A letter of notification and a comprehensive description of the program should be forwarded to the parents of all Talent Pool students indicating that their youngster has been placed in the Talent Pool for the year. The letter does not indicate that a child has been certified as "gifted," but rather explains the nature of the program and extends an invitation to parents to an orientation meeting. At this meeting, a description of the Three-Ring Conception of Giftedness should be provided, as well as an explanation of the differences between "high achieving giftedness" and "creative productive giftedness." It is important to emphasize that both types of giftedness are important and will be addressed in the program. What should also be emphasized is that creative productive giftedness is the type that represents the way that the larger society has recognized persons of significant accomplishment (Treffinger & Renzulli, 1986).

The meeting with parents should also provide an explanation of all program policies, procedures, and activities. Parents should learn about how admission to the Talent Pool is determined, that selection is carried out on an annual basis, and that changes in Talent Pool membership might take place during the year as a result of evaluations of student participation and progress. Parents are also invited to make individual appointments whenever they feel additional information about the program in general, or their own child, is required. A similar orientation session should be provided for students, with emphasis once again being placed on the services and activities being provided. Parents are *not* told that their children are "the gifted," but through a discussion of the Three-Ring Conception and the procedures for developing general and specific potentials, they should come to understand that the development of gifted behaviors is a program goal as well as part of their own responsibility.

Step 6: Action information nominations (Safety valve no. 2). In spite of our best efforts, this system will occasionally overlook highly creative students or students talented in a specific area, who, for one reason or another, are not selected (but should have been) for Talent Pool membership. To help overcome this problem, a process called Action Information Nomination is used, and all teachers are provided with an orientation related to spotting unusually favorable high-interest topics in the regular curriculum.

Action information can best be defined as the dynamic interactions that occur when a student becomes extremely interested in or excited about a particular topic, area of study, issue, idea, or event that takes place in school or the nonschool environment. It is derived from the concept of performance-based assessment, and it serves as the second safety valve in this identification system. The transmission of an Action Information Message (see Appendix 4.D) does not mean that a student will automatically be placed in the Talent Pool. It does, however, serve as the basis for a careful review of the situation to determine if any types of special services are warranted. Action Information Messages are also used within Talent Pool settings (i.e., pull-out groups, advanced classes, cluster groups) to make determinations about the pursuit of individual or small-group investigations (Type III Enrichment in the Triad Model). In order for the Special Nomination process to work effectively, all school personnel should be provided with an orientation to "talent spotting" situations where the initiation and transmission of an Action Information Message may be warranted. Transmission to the Review and Selection Team or to someone in the school and/or community who might provide guidance, serve as a mentor, or help the student to follow up in his or her area of interest are obligations that accompany the use of Action Information Messages in the effort to leave no stone unturned in helping young people develop their potential talents. In programs based on the Schoolwide Enrichment Model (Renzulli & Reis, 1997, 2014), we also provide a wide variety of in-class enrichment experiences that might result in recommendations for special services through the Action Information process. This process is facilitated through the use of a teacher training activity that can be used to orient teachers in the use of the Action Information Message (Renzulli & Reis, 1997, 2014).

Processing Identification Information: Keeping It Organized and Communication-Friendly

Despite our initial admonitions against emphasizing administrative "tidiness" at the expense of multiple sources of data identifying young people's talents, it is nonetheless important to keep all sources organized in a coherent manner that enhances communication among stakeholders. We recommend placing a summary sheet, such as the one presented in Figure 4.5, at the very top of each student's file. This allows a concise condensation of the multiple measures used in the identification process that is clearly visible to anyone who accesses the information.

Another possible way to summarize multiple criteria into a meaningful format for decision making is to use the following steps, developed by Lohman and Renzulli (see also Chapter 12). This process incorporates verbal, quantitative, and nonverbal CogAT scores, math and reading achievement scores, and SRBCSS Learning Ability, Creativity, and Motivation scales in the review and selection process.

Seven Step Identification System (Lohman & Renzulli, 2007)
1. Enter percentile ranks (PRs) from the three CogAT batteries (Verbal, Quantitative, and Nonverbal) in the first column of the worksheet in Figure 4.6.
2. Convert Percentile Ranks (PRs) to points (Standard Age Scores) following Table 4.2. Enter these points into the worksheet.
3. Average the points for the Quantitative and Nonverbal batteries. Enter this value on the worksheet in the QN Avg space.
4. Sum the points for CogAT Verbal and Reading Total and enter this value in the **V-RT Sum** space on the worksheet.
5. Sum the points for the CogAT Quant-Nonverbal Composite (from Step 3) and Mathematics Total and enter this value in the **QN-M Sum** space on the worksheet.
6. Take the **higher value** of **V-RT** and **QN-M** and enter it on the **Max** space of the worksheet.
7. Enter ratings for the three SRBCSS scales.
8. Compute the average teacher rating on each of the three SRBCSS scale for the group of students who were nominated for the program.

The point totals for the composite verbal/reading total and the composite quant/nonverbal/mathematics total can now be used to identify students. Figure 4.7 assumes that cut points are set at the 80th and 96th PRs.

Category I: Superior reasoning and achievement. Rated as highly capable, motivated, or creative by their teachers

Category II: Superior reasoning and achievement. Not rated as highly by their teachers on any one of the three major scales of the SRBCSS

Category III: Somewhat lower but strong reasoning abilities (between 80th and 96th PR) on one of the ability-achievement composites. Rated as highly capable, motivated, or creative by their teachers

Category IV: Good but not exceptional abilities (between 80th and 96th PR). Not rated as unusually capable, motivated, or creative by their teachers

Renzulli Identification System: Information Summary Form

Name: _____ Date: _____

School: _____ Grade: _____

I. Academic Performance

A. Achievement Test Scores (Most Recent Achievement Test Scores)

	Test	Date	Raw Score	Grade Equiv.	Local %ile
Verbal					
Numerical					
Non-verbal					

B. End of Year Grades for Past 2 Years

Subject	Year 1	Year 2	Subject	Year 1	Year 2
Reading			Music		
Mathematics			Art		
Language Arts/English			Foreign Language		
Social Studies			Other:		
Science			Other:		

II. Teacher Ratings [Scales for Rating the Behavior Characteristics of Superior Students (SRBCSS)]

Scale	Score	Group Mean	Scale	Score	Group Mean
Learning			Technology		
Motivation			Artistic		
Creativity			Musical		
Leadership			Dramatic		
Reading			Communication I		
Mathematics			Communication II		
Science			Planning		

III. Alternative Pathways

	Scale	Summary of Strengths
Parenting Rating		
Peer Rating		
Product Rating		

IV. Special Nominations

Figure 4.5. *Summary information sheet for review and selection process.*

For a more detailed description of this system of multiple-criteria identification and appropriate educational services for children who fall under the four categories mentioned above, see Chapter 10.

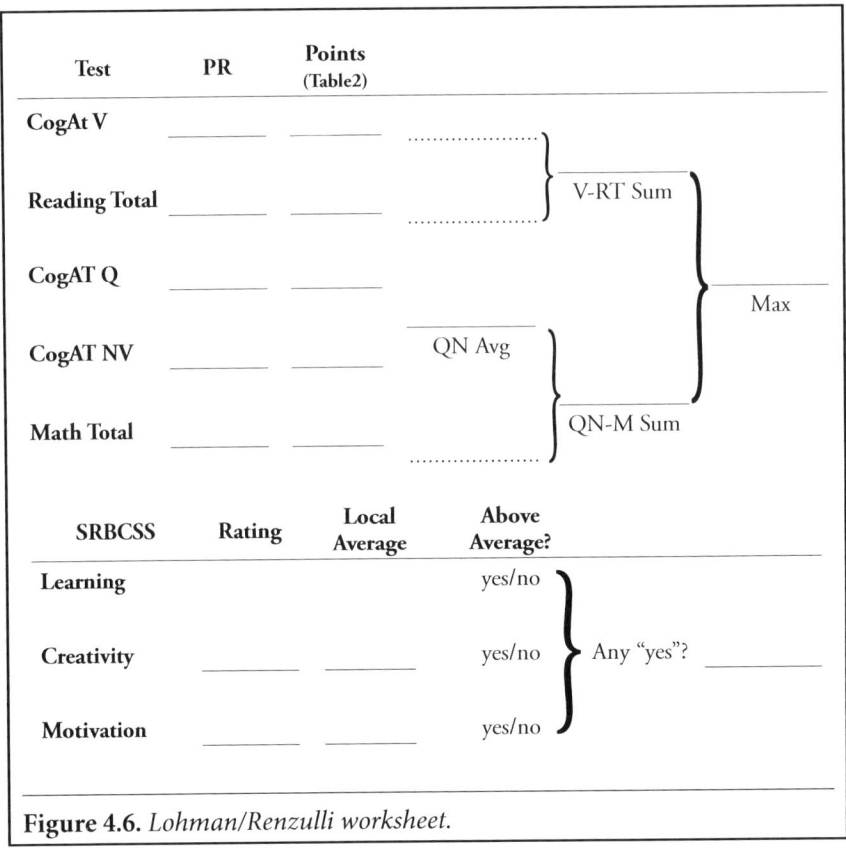

Figure 4.6. Lohman/Renzulli worksheet.

Table 4.2
Conversion Chart for CogAT Scores

Use to convert PR from any test or CogAT SAS scores to points

Points	PR	SAS
1	80-83	113-115
2	84-88	116-119
3	89-92	120-123
4	93-95	124-127
5	96-97	128-131
6	98	132-135
7	99	136-139
8	99+	140+

		Teacher Rating on Learning, Motivation, or Creativity	
		Below Average Teacher Ratings	Above Average Teacher Ratings
CogAT Verbal + Reading T. OR CogAT QN + Math T.	8 or more points (≥96th PR)	II	I
	2 – 7 points (80th – 95th PR)	IV	III

Figure 4.7. *Using CogAT, achievement test scores, and teacher ratings.*

Closing Thoughts

The most important factor that should be addressed when considering any identification system is the consistency that should exist between and among (1) the conception/definition of giftedness selected by a school or district, (2) the congruence between the conception/definition and the criteria used in the identification process, and (3) the goals and types of services that constitute the day-to-day activities that students will pursue in a special program. This consistency or "flow" between conception, identification, and programming is so important that it might be viewed as "the golden rule" of gifted education! The material covered in any special program should reflect the purposes or mission of gifted education and the characteristics that brought particular students to our attention through a systematic identification process. Intimately related to the development of an identification system is the selection of one or more organizational models that determine how we group students and move them around a pedagogical model that will guide instructional practices regardless of how students are grouped or organized for special program services.

Finally, we would like to close by again pointing out that simplistic single-score identification systems cannot provide us with the rich information necessary in making decisions on how to best provide services to develop children's unique talents and gifts. Choosing to implement a multiple-criteria identification system harnesses the best theoretical evidence about talent development across the lifespan. It also provides avenues for traditionally underrepresented student populations to participate in special programming, thus enhancing social equity. The chapter details how implementing such a system is not only desirable, but practically feasible as well. As educators move to the implementation stage of any decision-making innovation process, we hope this chapter has provided a practical roadmap as well as resources to guide a successful implementation of a flexible and fair identification system. We believe that the focus of tradition and expediency that has characterized gifted program identification must give way to expanded conceptions and innovative approaches to identification. These expanded approaches may not be as "tidy" or expedient as past practices, but they will help our field fulfill its promise of developing outstanding talent in more young people and increasing society's reservoir of creative and productive adults.

References

Betts, G., & Kercher, J. J. (2009). The Autonomous Learner Model for the gifted & talented. In J. S. Renzulli, E. J. Gubbins, K. S. McMillen, R. D. Eckert, & C. A. Little (Eds.), *Systems and models for developing programs for the gifted and talented* (2nd ed., pp. 49–102). Waco, TX: Prufrock Press.

Borland, J. (2004). *Issues and practices in the identification and education of gifted students from under-represented groups* (RM04186). Storrs: University of Connecticut, The National Research Center of the Gifted and Talented.

Callahan, C., Hunsaker, S., Adams, C., Moore, S., & Bland, L. (2005). *Instruments used in the identification of gifted and talented students* (RM95130). Storrs: University of Connecticut, The National Research Center of the Gifted and Talented.

Dai, D. Y. (2010). *The nature and nurture of giftedness: A new framework for understanding gifted education.* New York, NY: Teachers College Press.

Delcourt, M., Dewey, C., & Goldberg, M. (2007). Cognitive and affective learning outcomes of gifted elementary school students. *Gifted Child Quarterly, 51,* 359–381.

Field, G. B. (2009). The effects of using Renzulli Learning on student achievement: An investigation of Internet technology on reading fluency, comprehension, and social studies. *International Journal of Emerging Technology, 4,* 29–39.

Frasier, M. M., & Passow, A. H. (1995). *A review of assessment issues in gifted education and their implications for identifying gifted minority students* (RM95204). Storrs: University of Connecticut, The National Research Center of the Gifted and Talented.

Gardner, H. (1983). *Frames of mind.* New York, NY: Basic Books.

Lohman, D. F. (2005). Review of Naglieri and Ford (2003): Does the Naglieri Nonverbal Ability Test identify equal proportions of high-scoring White, Black, and Hispanic students. *Gifted Child Quarterly, 49,* 19–28.

Lohman, D. F., & Renzulli, J. S. (2007). *A simple procedure for combining ability test scores, achievement test scores, and teacher ratings to identify academically talented children.* Retrieved from http://faculty.education.uiowa.edu/dlohman

Naglieri, J., & Ford, D. (2003). Addressing underrepresentation of gifted minority students using the Naglieri Nonverbal Ability Test (NNAT). *Gifted Child Quarterly, 47,* 155–161.

Naglieri, J., & Ford, D. (2005). Increasing minority children's participation in gifted classes using the NNAT: A response to Lohman. *Gifted Child Quarterly, 49,* 29–36.

Reis, S. M., & Purcell, J. H. (1993). An analysis of content elimination and strategies used by elementary classroom teachers in the curriculum compacting process. *Journal for the Education of the Gifted, 16,* 147–170.

Reis, S. M., & Renzulli, J. S. (2004). Current research on the social and emotional development of gifted and talented students: Good news and future possibilities. *Psychology in the Schools, 41,* 119–130.

Reis, S. M., & Renzulli, J. S. (2005). *Curriculum compacting: An easy start to differentiating for high potential students.* Waco, TX: Prufrock Press.

Reis, S. M., Westberg, K. L., Kulikowich, J. M., & Purcell, J. H. (1998). Curriculum compacting and achievement test scores: What does the research say? *Gifted Child Quarterly, 42,* 123–129.

Renzulli, J. (1977). *The Enrichment Triad Model: A guide for developing defensible programs for the gifted and talented.* Mansfield Center, CT: Creative Learning Press.

Renzulli, J. (1978). What makes giftedness? Re-examining a definition. *Phi Delta Kappan, 60,* 180–184.

Renzulli, J., Gubbins, E. J., McMillen, K., Eckhart, R., & Little, C. (Eds.). (2009). *Systems and models for developing programs for the gifted and talented* (2nd ed.). Waco, TX: Prufrock Press.

Renzulli, J., & Reis, S. (1994). Research related to the Schoolwide Enrichment Triad model. *Gifted Child Quarterly, 38,* 7–20.

Renzulli, J., & Reis, S. (1997). *The Schoolwide Enrichment Model: A how-to guide for educational excellence* (2nd ed.). Waco, TX: Prufrock Press.

Renzulli, J. S., & Reis, S. M. (2014). *The Schoolwide Enrichment Model: A how-to guide for educational excellence* (3rd ed.). Waco, TX: Prufrock Press.

Renzulli, J. S., Reis, S. M., Gavin, M. K., & Sytsma Reed, R. E. (2009). An investigation of the reliability and factor structure of four new scales for rating the behavioral characteristics of superior students. *Journal of Advanced Academics, 22*(1), 84–108

Renzulli, J., Smith, L., White, A., Callahan, C., Hartman, R., Westberg, K., . . . Sytsma Reed, R. (2013). *Scales for rating the behavioral characteristics of superior students. Technical and administration manual* (3rd ed.). Waco, TX: Prufrock Press.

Rogers, E. (1962). *Diffusion of innovations.* New York, NY: Free Press.

Sattler, J. (2001). *Assessment of children: Cognitive applications* (4th ed.). Austin, TX: Jerome M. Sattler.

Sternberg, R. (1985). *Beyond IQ: A triarchic theory of human intelligence.* Cambridge, England: Cambridge University Press.

Sternberg, R., & Davidson, J. (Eds.). (2005). *Conceptions of giftedness* (2nd ed.). New York, NY: Cambridge University Press.

Treffinger, D., & Renzulli, J. (1986). Giftedness as potential for creative productivity: Transcending IQ scores. *Roeper Review, 8,* 150–154.

Winner, E. (1996). *Gifted children: Myths and realities.* New York, NY: Basic Books.

Appendix 4.A
A Bibliography of Resources for Conceptions and Definition of Giftedness and Talent Development

Borland, J. H. (2005). Gifted education without gifted children: The case for no conception of giftedness. In R. J. Sternberg & J. E. Davidson (Eds.), *Conceptions of giftedness* (2nd ed., pp. 1–19). New York, NY: Cambridge University Press.

Brody, L. E., & Stanley, J. C. (2005). Youths who reason exceptionally well mathematically and/or verbally: Using the MVT:D4 model to develop their talents. In R. J. Sternberg & J. E. Davidson (Eds.), *Conceptions of giftedness* (2nd ed., pp. 20–37). New York, NY: Cambridge University Press.

Feldman, D. H., & Benjamin, A. C. (1986). Giftedness as the developmentalist sees it. In R. J. Sternberg & J. E. Davidson (Eds.), *Conceptions of giftedness* (pp. 285–305). New York, NY: Cambridge University Press.

Field, G. B. (2009). The effects of the use of Renzulli Learning on student achievement in reading comprehension, reading fluency, social studies, and science. *International Journal of Emerging Technologies in Learning, 4*(1), 23–28.

Gagné, F. (2005). From gifts to talents: The DMGT as a developmental model. In R. J. Sternberg & J. E. Davidson (Eds.), *Conceptions of giftedness* (2nd ed., pp. 98–119). New York, NY: Cambridge University Press.

Renzulli, J. S. (2005). The Three-Ring Conception of Giftedness: A developmental model for promoting creative productivity. In R. J. Sternberg & J. E. Davidson (Eds.), *Conceptions of giftedness* (2nd ed., pp. 246–279). New York, NY: Cambridge University Press.

Renzulli, J. S., & Delcourt, M. A. B. (1986). The legacy and logic of research on the identification of gifted persons. *Gifted Child Quarterly, 30,* 20–23.

Robinson, N. M. (2005). In defense of a psychometric approach to the definition of academic giftedness. In R. J. Sternberg & J. E. Davidson (Eds.), *Conceptions of giftedness* (2nd ed., pp. 280–294). New York, NY: Cambridge University Press.

Stanley, J. C., & Benbow, C. P. (1986). Youths who reason exceptionally well mathematically. In R. J. Sternberg & J. E. Davidson (Eds.), *Conceptions of giftedness* (pp. 361–387). New York, NY: Cambridge University Press.

Sternberg, R. J. (1986). A triarchic theory of intellectual giftedness. In R. J. Sternberg & J. E. Davidson (Eds.), *Conceptions of giftedness* (pp. 223–243). New York, NY: Cambridge University Press.

Tannenbaum, A. J. (1986). Giftedness: A psychosocial approach. In R. J. Sternberg & J. E. Davidson (Eds.), *Conceptions of giftedness* (pp. 21–52). New York, NY: Cambridge University Press.

Walters, J., & Gardner, H. (1986). The crystallizing experience: Discovering an intellectual gift. In R. J. Sternberg & J. E. Davidson (Eds.), *Conceptions of giftedness* (pp. 306–331). New York, NY: Cambridge University Press.

Appendix 4.B
SRBCSS Training Activity for Teachers: Mathematics Characteristics

TASK No. 1: Individually, select the letter of a key concept that you believe most closely matches each item.

TASK No. 2: In a small group, discuss specific examples of when you have observed each behavior in a student.

Key Concepts		
A. Multiple illustrations	E. Mental manipulation	H. Readily absorbs
B. Finds challenge pleasurable	F. Diverges from the ordinary	I. Strives to understand
C. Organizer	G. Variety of methods	J. Seeks solutions
D. Numeracy		

The student . . .	
1. is eager to solve challenging math problems. (A problem is defined as a task for which the solution is not known in advance.)	
2. organizes data and information to discover mathematical patterns.	
3. enjoys challenging math puzzles, games, and logic problems.	
4. understands new math concepts and processes more easily than other students.	
5. has creative (unusual and divergent) ways of solving math problems.	
6. displays a strong number sense (e.g., makes sense of large and small numbers, estimates easily and appropriately).	
7. frequently solves math problems abstractly, without the need for manipulatives or concrete materials.	
8. has an interest in analyzing the mathematical structure of a problem.	
9. when solving a math problem, can switch strategies easily, if appropriate or necessary.	
10. regularly uses a variety of representations to explain math concepts (written explanations, pictorial, graphic, equations, etc.).	

Answer Key
1. J   4. H   7. E   10. A
2. C   5. F   8. I
3. B   6. D   9. G

Note. Adapted from *Scales for rating the behavioral characteristics of superior students. Technical and administration manual* (3rd ed.) by J. S. Renzulli, L. Smith, A. White, C. Callahan, R. Hartman, K. Westberg, K., . . . R. Sytsma Reed, 2013, Waco, TX: Prufrock Press. Copyright 2013 Prufrock Press. Adapted with permission.

Appendix 4.C
Examples of Special Nomination Forms to Use for Multiple Criteria Identification

Things My Child Likes to Do
Cover Letter

TO: Parents of All Students
FROM: Carol Moran, Enrichment Specialist
DATE: April 16, 2014

One of the major goals of our Schoolwide Enrichment Program is to provide each student with an opportunity to develop his or her strengths and talents. We would also like to supplement our basic curriculum to offer your child experiences that are challenging, enjoyable, and of personal interest.

Although the work your child does in school provides a lot of information on his or her strengths and interests, activities your child pursues at home will help us develop ways to further enrich his or her school program. For this reason, we are asking you to complete the attached questionnaire.

Each of the items on the questionnaire deals with a general type of interest or activity you may or may not have seen in your child. These might be the result of school assignments, extracurricular activities such as Girl Scouts or 4-H projects, or home activities. To help clarify the items, we have included an example. You should rate your child on the general item, not on the example. If possible, also include specific examples of your child's interests or activities.

If you have any questions, please feel free to contact me. I appreciate your help in providing the best possible educational program for your child.

Sincerely,

Carol Moran

Appendix 4.C, continued

Things My Child Likes to Do

Your Name _____ Your Child's Name _____

_____ Child's School _____ Today's Date _____

Child's Age _____

	Seldom or Never	Sometimes	Quite Often*	Almost Always*	Examples From Your Own Child's Life
1. My child will spend more time and energy than his or her agemates on a topic of his or her interest. (For example: Joan is learning to sew and spends every free minute designing new dress patterns and trying to sew them herself.)					
2. My child is a "self-starter" who works well alone, needing few directions and little supervision. (For example: After watching a film about musical instruments, Gary began to make his own guitar from materials he found around the garage.)					
3. My child sets high personal goals and expects to see results from his or her work. (For example: Marcy insisted on building a robot from spare machine parts even though she knew nothing about engines or construction.)					
4. My child gets so involved with a project that he or she gives up other pleasures in order to work on it. (For example: Don is writing a book about his town's history and spends each night examining historical records and documents—even when he knows he's missing his favorite TV show.)					

Appendix 4.C, continued

	Seldom or Never	Sometimes	Quite Often*	Almost Always*	Examples From Your Own Child's Life
5. My child continues to work on a project even when faced with temporary defeats and slow results. (For example: After building a model rocket, Sally continued to try to launch it, despite several failures and "crash landings.")					
6. While working on a project (and when it's finished) my child knows which parts are good and which parts need improvement. (For example: After building a scale model of a lunar city, Kenny realized that there weren't enough solar collectors to heat all the homes he had built.)					
7. My child is a "doer" who begins a project and shows finished products of his or her work. (For example: Mary began working on a puppet show 4 months ago, and has since built a stage and puppets and has written a script. Tomorrow she's presenting her play to the PTA!)					
8. My child suggests imaginative ways of doing things, even if the suggestions are sometimes impractical. (For example: "If you really want to clean the refrigerator, why don't we move it outside and I'll hose it down—that will defrost it, too.")					

A Practical Gifted Identification System

Appendix 4.C, *continued*

	Seldom or Never	Sometimes	Quite Often*	Almost Always*	Examples From Your Own Child's Life
9. When my child tells about something that is very unusual, he or she expresses him/herself by elaborate gestures, pictures, or words. (For example: "The only way I can show you how the ballet dancer spun around is if I stand on my tiptoes on the record player and put the speed up to 78.")					
10. My child uses common materials in ways not typically expected. (For example: "I'll bring a deck of cards when we go camping. If it rains, we can use them to start a fire and if it's dry, we can play Go Fish around the campfire.")					
11. My child avoids typical ways of doing things, choosing instead to find new ways to approach a problem or topic. (For example: "I had trouble moving this box to the other side of the garage so I used these four broom handles as rollers and just pushed it along.")					
12. My child likes to "play with ideas," often making up situations which probably will not occur. (For example: "I wonder what would happen if a scientist found a way to kill all insects, then went ahead and did it.")					
13. My child often finds humor in situations or events that are not obviously funny to most children his/her age. (For example: "It was really funny that after our coach showed us a movie on playground safety, he sprained his ankle while lining us up to go back to class.")					

Appendix 4.C, continued

	Seldom or Never	Sometimes	Quite Often*	Almost Always*	Examples From Your Own Child's Life
14. My child prefers working or playing alone rather than doing something "just to go along with the gang." (For example: "I always misspell the first word in a spelling bee; then I get to sit down and do something I like.")					

* If your child scores in either of these two columns, it would be helpful if you would write a specific example in the last column, using the reverse side of this page if necessary.

Note. From *The Schoolwide Enrichment Model: A how-to guide for educational excellence* (3rd ed., pp. 72–75), by J. S. Renzulli & S. M. Reis, 2014, Waco, TX: Prufrock Press. Copyright 2014 by Prufrock Press. Reprinted with permission.

Appendix 4.C, *continued*

Peer Referral Form

Teacher's Name:_____

    I'm going to ask you to think of your classmates in a different way than you usually do. Read the questions below and try to think of which child in your class fits best each question. Think of the boys and girls, quiet kids and noisy kids, best friends and those with whom you don't usually play. You may only put down one name for each question. You may leave a space blank. You can use the same name for more than one question. You may not use your teacher's name or names of other adults. Please use first and last name. You do not have to put your name down on this form, so you can be completely honest.

What boy OR girl learns quickly, but doesn't speak up in class very often?
_____

What girl OR boy will get interested in a project and spend extra time and take pride in his or her work? _____

What boy OR girl is smart in school, but doesn't show off about it?
_____

What girl OR boy is really good at making up dances?
_____

What boy OR girl is really good at making up games?
_____

What girl OR boy is really good at making up music?
_____

What boy OR girl is really good at making up stories?
_____

What girl OR boy is really good at making up pictures?
_____

What boy OR girl would you ask first if you needed any kind of help at school?_____

What girl OR boy would you ask to come to your house to help you work on a project? (Pretend that there would be someone to drive that person to your house.)_____

Anne Udall, Vice President for Professional Development,
Northwest Evaluation Association, Copyright Pending

Appendix 4.D
Action Information Message Form

ACTION INFORMATION MESSAGE

General Curriculum Area
_____

Activity or Topic
_____

In the space below, provide a brief description of the incident or situation in which you observed high levels of interest, task commitment, or creativity on the part of a student or small group of students. Indicate any areas you may have for advanced-level follow-up activities, suggested resources, or ways to focus the interest into a firsthand investigative experience.

_____

To: _____
From: _____
Date: _____

☐ PLEASE CONTACT ME
☐ I WILL CONTACT YOU TO ARRANGE A MEETING

Date Received: _____ Date of Interview With Child: _____
Date When Services Were Implemented: _____

Note. From *The Schoolwide Enrichment Model: A how-to guide for educational excellence* (3rd ed., p. 81), by J. S. Renzulli & S. M. Reis, 2014, Waco, TX: Prufrock Press. Copyright 2014 by Prufrock Press. Reprinted with permission.

CHAPTER 5

Intelligences Outside the Normal Curve

Co-Cognitive Factors That Contribute to the Creation of Social Capital and Leadership Skills in Young People[10]

Joseph S. Renzulli
University of Connecticut

A good head and a good heart are always a formidable combination.
—Nelson Mandela

Introduction From Joe

In the early 1970s when I began work on the Three-Ring Conception of Giftedness, I embedded the rings in a houndstooth background that represented

---

10 Renzulli, J. S. (2002). *Intelligences outside the normal curve: Co-cognitive factors that contribute to the creation of social capital and leadership skills in young people.* Storrs: University of Connecticut, The National Research Center on the Gifted and Talented. Adapted with permission.

the interaction between personality and environment. In recent years, further research and theory development coupled with a growing concern in the field related to social and emotional development has led to a new dimension of my work on characteristics that calls attention to a series of six co-cognitive factors that are discussed in this chapter. A comprehensive review of the literature and a series of Delphi technique studies led to the development of an organizational plan for studying these six components and 13 subcomponents. Factor analysis identified these clusters of discrete but interrelated traits. I refer to these as co-cognitive factors because they interact with and enhance the cognitive traits that we ordinarily associate with the development of both high achievement and creative productive manifestations of giftedness. This new initiative was prompted by a longstanding concern about the role that gifted education should play in preparing persons with high potential for ethical and responsible leadership in all walks of life. Investments in this type of social capital benefit society as a whole because they help to create the values, norms, networks, and social trust that facilitate coordination and cooperation geared toward the greater public good. Striking evidence indicates a marked decline in American social capital over the latter half of the century just ending. National surveys show declines over the last few decades in voter turnout and political participation, membership in service clubs, church-related groups, parent-teacher associations, unions, and fraternal groups. These declines in civic and social participation have been paralleled by an increasing tendency for young people to focus on materialism, self-indulgence, narrow professional success, and individual economic gain (Ahuvia, 2002; Huer, 1991; Kasser, 2002; Myers, 1993; Netemeyer, Burton, & Lichtenstein, 1995; Shrader, 1992; Tatzel, 2002).

Background Underlying the Study of Co-Cognitive Traits

The field of gifted education has had a longstanding interest in examining noncognitive characteristics such as social and emotional development, self-concept, self-efficacy, and issues related to leadership, self-regulated learning, and character development. Research in these areas has taken many forms ranging from studies dealing with maladaptive behaviors faced by gifted children and adults to a more recent concentration on "positive psychology" approaches, which focus on providing young people with the opportunities, resources, and encouragement to support matters that touch their social consciousness and other noncognitive skills. We believe that all people have a "social intelligence" (Goleman, 2006) and that leadership styles play an important part in the evolution of people who have made a difference in their chosen areas of societal contributions. We further believe that one of the challenges faced by our field is to devote resources to the development of noncognitive behaviors just as we have for so long focused on cognitive development.

This chapter focuses on the latter two parts of a four-part theory summarized in Figure 5.1. The first two parts of this general theory, the Three-Ring Conception of Giftedness and the Enrichment Triad Model, address questions about conceptions of giftedness and how we develop creative productivity in young people. Concurrently, the latter two sub-theories, Operation Houndstooth Co-Cognitive Factors and Executive Functions Leadership Development, address questions about how we can promote an orientation toward using one's gifts for the promotion of social capital, and how we can provide executive function experiences that create effective and compassionate leadership in the population of young people with exceptionally high potential. We refer to these two areas of focus as "co-cognitive" characteristics or "intelligences outside the normal curve" because they interact with and give rise to cognitive development, while also playing a role in the formation of beliefs, attitudes, values, and the development of an action orientation for following through on one's beliefs and values.

This work is based on the assumption that people with the highest potential will assume positions of leadership and policy-making in all walks of life including religion, politics, business, government, science, the arts and humanities, and other domains that define a society and a culture. What kinds of leadership will these people display? Will they use their gifts and talents to make the world a better place? We need only contrast a Nelson Mandela with an Idi Amin or a Bill Gates with a Bernard Madoff to realize that life's experiences can take people in directions that benefit or hinder the public good.

Relatively rare among programs that serve gifted and talented youth are concerted efforts to provide experiences that will develop the kinds of moral, ethical, and compassionate leadership characteristic that encourage using one's gifts and talents in positive ways. While the development of academic talent is and will continue to be the centerpiece of gifted education programs, this chapter presents an intervention theory for co-cognitive development that is designed to promote a much-needed *supplement* to the traditional focus only on academic development in special programs that serve gifted youth. The intervention theory discussed later in this chapter was developed to guide activities that promote the social capital and leadership objectives implicit in the two subtheories at the bottom of Figure 5.1.

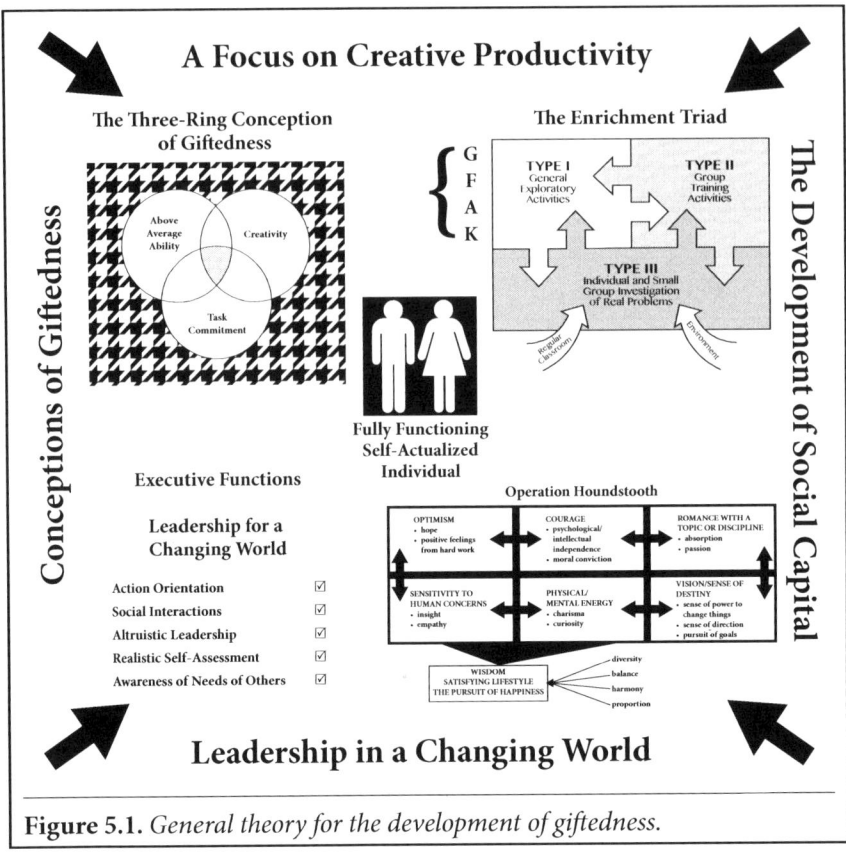

Figure 5.1. *General theory for the development of giftedness.*

Summary of Underlying Subtheories

The first two subtheories in Figure 5.1, the Three-Ring Conception of Giftedness and the Enrichment Triad Model, have been dealt with extensively in the literature and information about them can be found in referenced material. As discussed in previous publications, it is our belief that gifted behavior occurs when three dimensions of human potential (above-average academic ability, creativity, and task commitment) interact and are brought to bear on a domain of interest (Renzulli, 1977, 1978, 1986, 2005). The three rings of potential are embedded on a houndstooth background to represent the interaction between personality and environment with giftedness. Recent research has given rise to the addition of another aspect to the original Three-Ring theory: the components of Operation Houndstooth and intelligences outside the normal curve, which we will address in detail in sections that follow (Renzulli, 2002; Renzulli, Koehler, & Fogarty, 2006). It is our belief that gifted education need not be limited to academic components, but can also include preparation for a life-long pursuit of the common good and ethical and responsible leadership (Renzulli, 2002, 2005)

As referenced in previous works (Renzulli, 1977, 1978, 1986, 2005) it is our belief that there are two types of giftedness: high-achieving giftedness—the more traditional presentation of gifted behaviors in school-related learning activities—and creative productive giftedness, where gifted behaviors are applied to product creation in nonformulaic original experiences. In an attempt to maximize creative productive giftedness, we created the Enrichment Triad Model (Renzulli & Reis, 1997). The Enrichment Triad Model depicts three different types of activities that, when combined, we believe inspire students to think in creative ways and search out inspiration. The first type of activity is Type I Enrichment: General Exploratory Activities. These activities are designed to expose students to a wide variety of topics, disciplines, people, places, events, and cultures that they would not generally have the opportunity to explore. Type II Enrichment: Group Training Activities are meant to promote the development of thinking and feeling processes and a concern for making contributions to the creation of social capital. Finally, Type III Enrichment: Individual and Small Group Investigations of Real Problems hinge on student passion and romance with a topic. The enrichment activities are based on the student's advanced interest and place the student in the role of a firsthand inquirer. The activities used in teaching students about Type III Enrichment encourage them to practice problem solving, complex thinking and higher order executive functioning tasks, while simultaneously exposing the students to a complex, changing and challenging world that gives rise to self-reflection on diversity, human concerns, altruism, and ethics.

Developments in more recent research have led to an expansion in this thinking, resulting in the conceptualization of the latter two subtheories, Operation Houndstooth and Executive Functions Leadership Development. Sternberg (1998, 2005) greatly contributed to the existing body of theory and research with his argument that wisdom in combination with intelligence and creativity promotes gifted behavior. Sternberg asserted that wisdom is present when individuals pursue the common good and that without wisdom, an individual may be a good contributor to society, but will never be a great contributor. He further stated that intelligent individuals who use their unique gifts for evil or selfish ends or those who ignore the well-being of others may be smart but they are also foolish. Sternberg's statements echo our beliefs that there are intelligences beyond what standardized tests can measure and that those with high ability may become a Bill Gates, but they may also become a Bernard Madoff if social capital and social responsibility are not pursued. In a similar fashion, Gardner (Fischman & Gardner, 2009; Gardner, 1993; Gardner,

Csikszentmihalyi, & Damon, 2001) has developed a subtheory that relates to Sternberg's and our ideas with his idea of good work, which combines the factors of excellence, ethics, and engagement.

Recently, Operation Houndstooth research has focused on examining co-cognitive factors (Sytsma, 2003) and the effects of various types of activities for promoting social capital and leadership skills (Sands, 2012). Additionally, Reilly (2009) recently examined the connection between goal orientations (specifically, a contribution orientation and a challenge orientation) and the components of Operation Houndstooth. These studies will be discussed in greater detail in the sections that follow. Currently, our research focus is creating an implementation plan for Direct Involvement I and II activities as well as assessing the effect of these activities on leadership potential and the development of a social capital orientation on the parts of young people. The following sections will provide a brief overview of the theories that guide the development of social capital and executive function experiences and that form the rational for the Co-Cognitive Factors Intervention Theory discussed below.

Overview of Subtheory on Gifted Education and Social Capital (Operation Houndstooth)

The rationale for this subtheory and the one that follows is based on the anticipated roles that high potential young people will play in society. This subpart of the overall theory addresses the question: "Why do some people mobilize their interpersonal, political, ethical, and moral realms of being in such ways that they place human concerns and the common good above materialism, ego enhancement, and self-indulgence?" The abundance of folk wisdom, research literature, and biographical and anecdotal accounts about creativity and giftedness are nothing short of mind boggling, and yet, we are still unable to answer this fundamental question about persons who have devoted their lives to improving the human condition. Several theorists have speculated about the necessary ingredients for giftedness and creative productivity, and their related theories have called attention to important components and conditions for high-level accomplishment. However, most of these theories have dwelt only on cognitive characteristics, and by so doing, they have failed to explain how the confluence of desirable traits result in commitments for making the lives of all people more rewarding, environmentally safe, economically viable, peaceful, and politically free.

Work related to this topic examines the scientific research that defines several categories of personal characteristics associated with an individual's commitment to the production of social capital, briefly defined here as using one's talents to improve human conditions, whether that improvement is directed toward one person or larger audiences or conditions. These characteristics include: Optimism, Courage, Romance with a Topic or Discipline, Physical and Mental Energy, Vision and a Sense of Destiny, and Sense of Power to Change Things (Renzulli, 2002). These factors and their subcomponents are portrayed in the lower right quadrant of Figure 5.1 and comprise the mosaic of Operation Houndstooth. They are represented in the Three-Ring Conception of Giftedness in Figure 5.1 by the houndstooth background in which the three clusters of traits are embedded. We call these constructs co-cognitive factors because they interact with and enhance the cognitive traits that are ordinarily associated with the development of human abilities. A number of researchers have suggested that constructs of this type, including social, emotional, and inter- or intrapersonal intelligence (Gardner, 1993; Gardner et al., 2001; Goleman, 2006) are related to each other and are relatively independent from traditional measures of cognitive ability. The two-directional arrows seen in the Operation Houndstooth subtheory diagram in Figure 5.1 point out the many interactions that take place between and among the factors.

The general goal of this work and the Co-Cognitive Factors Intervention Theory discussed below is to infuse activities that promote the Houndstooth components and Executive Functions Leadership attributes into students' overall daily school experience in order to ultimately assist high-ability young people in developing a sense of their responsibility to society at large. It would be naïve to think that a redirection of educational goals can take place without a commitment at all levels to examine the purposes of education in a democracy. It is also naïve to think that experiences directed toward the production of social capital can, or are even intended to, replace our present day focus on material productivity and intellectual capital. Rather, this work seeks to enhance the development of wisdom and a satisfying lifestyle that are paralleled by concerns for diversity, balance, harmony, and proportion in all of the choices and decisions that young people make in the process of maturing. What people think and decide to do drives some of society's best ideas and achievements. If we want leaders who will promote ideas and achievements that take into consideration the components we have identified in Operation Houndstooth, then the development of giftedness in the new century will have to be redefined in ways that take these co-cognitive components into account. Thus, the strategies that are used to develop giftedness in young people will need to give as much attention to the co-cognitive conditions of development as we presently give to cognitive development.

Overview of Subtheory on Gifted Education and Executive Functions—Leadership for a Changing World

This subtheory may very well be the "yeast" that enables all constructs described above to actually be used to pursue a desired goal in an efficient and effective way. We sometimes describe this final subtheory as simply "getting your act together." The most creative ideas, advanced analytic skills, and the noblest of motives may not result in positive action unless leadership skills such as organization, sequencing, and sound judgment are brought to bear on problem situations. Landmark research by Duckworth, Seligman, and others (Borghans, Duckworth, Heckman, & Weel, 2008; Duckworth, 2009; Duckworth, Peterson, Matthews, & Kelly, 2007; Duckworth & Quinn, 2009; Duckworth & Seligman, 2005) has shown that students who persist in college were not necessarily the ones who excelled on measures of aptitude, but the ones with exceptional character strengths such as optimism, persistence, and social intelligence. This research showed that measures of self-control can be more reliable predictors of students' grade-point averages than their IQ scores. Including this focus in the overall theory represents a distinctly different approach to talent development than most of the models focusing primarily on cognitive development. The research noted above documents that both IQ and self-discipline are correlated with GPA, but self-discipline is a much more important contributor. Those with low self-discipline have substantially lower college grades than those with low IQs, while high-discipline students received much better grades than high-IQ students. Even after adjusting for the student's grades during the first marking period of the year, students with higher self-discipline still had higher grades at the end of the year. The same could not be said for IQ. Further, these studies found no correlation between IQ and self-discipline—these two traits varied independently.

This subtheory dealing with leadership development focuses on what are commonly referred to in the business and human resource literature as executive functions. These functions are broadly defined as the ability to engage in *novel* situations that require planning, decision making, troubleshooting, and compassionate and ethical leadership that is not dependent on routine or well-rehearsed responses to challenging combinations of conditions. These traits also involve organizing, integrating, and managing information, emotions, and other cognitive and affective functions that lead to "doing the right thing" in situations that do not have a predetermined or formulaic response. These functions are especially important to highly capable people because of the positions of power to which they typically ascend.

A number of researchers have pointed out the importance of incorporating these noncognitive skills, such as those described in the latter two subtheories, into everything from curricular experiences (Diamond, 2010) to educational assessments (Levin, 2011; Sedlack, 2005) and college admission considerations (Sternberg, 2005). These skills have important implications for the academic success of students, career decisions, and even the economic productivity of nations. While not minimizing the importance of traditional cognitive ability, these authors point out that conventional assessments account for a small portion of the variance when examining long-term academic and career accomplishment, especially as it relates to the advancement of adult competencies in highly demanding professions where leadership skills and creative productivity are the criteria for success.

A good deal of the background material that led to the inclusion of executive functions in this overall talent development model comes from the field of human resources (Durlak, Weissberg, Dymnicki, Taylor, & Schellinger, 2011; Heckman & Rubenstein, 2001). These authors point out the importance of noncognitive skills in personal and social, as well as academic development and—more importantly for this overall theory—a meta-analysis showed that these skills can be taught. Initial input was also derived from the literature on social, behavioral, and "emotional intelligence" (Goleman, 2006). Goleman argued that great leadership works through noncognitive traits such as Self-Awareness, Self-Management, Motivation, Empathy, and Social Skills. Although the research literature on these types of noncognitive traits is massive, there is general agreement that the following so-called "Big Five" personality traits (Almlund, Duckworth, Heckman, & Kautz, 2011) are the basis on which education intervention programs should focus:

1. *Openness*—inventive and curious as opposed to consistent and cautious.
2. *Conscientiousness*—efficient and organized as opposed to easy-going and careless.
3. *Extraversion*—outgoing and energetic as opposed to solitary and reserved.
4. *Agreeableness*—friendly and compassionate as opposed to cold and unkind.
5. *Self-Assured*—secure and confident as opposed to neurotic and nervous.

Our research to date on this subtheory has included the development of an instrument called Rating the Executive Functions of Young People (Renzulli & Mitchell, 2011). This diagnostic instrument is designed to assist in research dealing with the types and degrees of executive function traits in young people and can be used both to identify potential leadership traits in young people and help teachers determine which curricular experiences can develop desirable leadership traits in individuals or groups. Subsequent diagnostic techniques may include simulations to determine successful performance in demanding problem-solving situations.

A review of research conducted in the process of instrument development revealed several constructs including mindfulness, ethical/moral, social, motivational, and leadership traits as well as the so-called Big Five personality traits or factors mentioned above as contributors to success (Renzulli & Mitchell, 2011). Also identified were specific traits such as being eager to learn, studious, intelligent, interested, and industrious and other variables such as positive and realistic self-appraisal, preference for long-range goals, successful leadership experience, and community service. Researchers in other domains have also identified noncognitive variables of persons who lead and make a difference (Durlak et al., 2011; Goleman, 2006; Heckman & Rubenstein, 2001). For example, in reports on the characteristics possessed by some of the most altruistic persons in American society, common traits that were demonstrated by most of these individuals included passion, determination, talent, self-discipline, and faith (Goleman, 2006). Leadership, ethics, accountability, adaptability, personal productivity, personal responsibility, people skills, self-direction, and social responsibility have also been identified as critical skills in the literature dealing with 21st-century skills, as were professionalism, enthusiasm, leadership, positive work ethic, values, decisiveness, teamwork, character, support, conformity, openness, self-concept, anxiety, and lifelong learning (Goleman, 2006).

This overwhelming list of traits that emerged from the literature review has been grouped into five general categories as a result of a factor analysis of data collected from several hundred respondents using the instrument mentioned above. The first factor is Action Orientation, which includes specific characteristics that motivate an individual to succeed. The second factor is Social Interactions and it includes traits that enable someone to successfully interact with others. The third factor is Altruistic Leadership, and it includes characteristics relating to both empathy and dependability. The fourth factor is called Realistic Self-Assessment and it includes characteristics that demonstrate awareness of one's own abilities, realistic self-appraisal, and self-efficacy. The fifth factor, Awareness of the Needs of Others, subsumes sensitivity, approachableness, and strong communication skills. Taken collectively, all of these behaviors reflect not only the characteristics of highly effective persons, but also include traits that cause people who have emerged as leaders in their respective fields to "do the right thing" in the arenas and domains over which they have had an influence.

The implications for including executive functions in a theory about the study of giftedness relates to the anticipated social and leadership roles that high-potential young people will play in their future endeavors. Embracing executive functions also has significance for the types of programs and experiences that should be provided to develop these skills and the roles and responsibilities of curriculum developers and service providers. The relative newness of this dimension on the parts of scholars in the field is obviously in need of more research and there are many opportunities for creative implementation practices and original research related thereto.

Co-Cognitive Factors Intervention Theory

If we agree with the arguments put forth above about the need to include concerns that deal with enhancing the development of social capital and executive functions leadership skills within the services provided to high-potential students, then the next challenge is to devise a theory or paradigm about how to organize, select, and deliver such services. The Co-Cognitive Factors Intervention Theory (see Figure 5.2) evolved from research studies summarized below and is based on procedures that have been used to create learning experiences directed toward various aspects of co-cognitive development. Our research has shown that as experiences proceed from the bottom to the top of the six listed interventions, we observe a higher degree of internalization of the attitudes, beliefs, and values that have been identified in the two subtheories of Operation Houndstooth and Executive Functions Leadership Development discussed above. Although all of the activities offer valuable information for a chain of events leading from lower to higher levels displayed on the chart, the Vicarious Experience and Direct Involvement I and II show that these higher levels are the most productive in the pursuit of goals related to the two subtheories. Following is a brief description of each of the six components of the intervention theory:

1. *Rally-Round-the-Flag.* This approach is sometimes referred to as the cheerleading method. It involves visual displays promoting certain values, slogans, or examples of desired virtuous behavior (Renzulli et al., 2006).
2. *The Gold Star Approach.* This approach is very similar to the traditional ways we have rewarded students for good behavior in the past. This level of intervention provides positive reinforcement through the form of prizes, tokens, and gold stars (Renzulli et al., 2006).
3. *The Teaching-and-Preaching Approach.* This is one of the most frequently utilized methods to convey attitudes and behaviors related to character development and social capital. This approach involves the

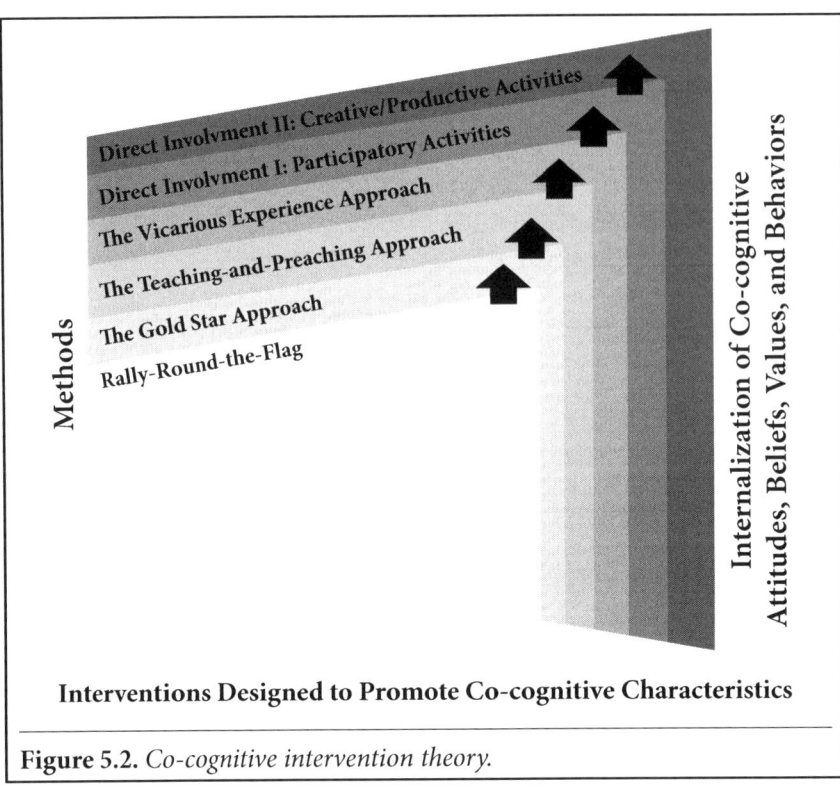

Figure 5.2. *Co-cognitive intervention theory.*

teaching of character development and leadership skills through dialogue, discussion, films, or books (Renzulli et al., 2006).

4. *The Vicarious Experience Approach.* This level of intervention involves placing the student in situations where he or she is expected to learn the value of a certain character trait, practice a leadership skill, or reach a noncognitive learning objective. This intervention is frequently done through role-playing, dramatization, and simulations that force the student to think critically and use executive functioning (Renzulli et al., 2006).

5. *Direct Involvement I: Participatory Activities.* Activities in this category are what we believe to be one of the most persuasive and valuable levels of intervention for character development. In these activities, students internalize noncognitive skills through direct contact with situations and events that result in affective behaviors and the use of executive functioning. Volunteering and service learning action projects are frequently used examples of activities that expose the student to new situations, raise new questions, and ignite new curiosities (Renzulli et al., 2006).

6. *Direct Involvement II: Creative Productive Activities.* Activities in this category have a large impact on the development of social capital. These activities consist of situations where students actively utilize executive functions through true leadership roles with the goal of bringing about positive social, educational, environmental, or political change (Renzulli et al., 2006).

Several aspects of the Intervention Theory are supported by empirical studies conducted by other researchers. Research done by McNally, Brown, and Jackson (2012) studied the veracity of the social intelligence hypothesis, a theory that states social interactions provide the pressures necessary for the evolution of advanced cognitive abilities. McNally, Brown, and Jackson constructed computer models of artificial organisms with artificial brains and had the brains interact in a social manner and use decision-making skills. It was found that brains evolved and became more complex as they encountered more social interactions and led to the utilization of cooperation and decision-making skills. The findings of McNally, Brown, and Jackson lend support to the idea that social interactions are key to the evolution of intelligence. These findings support our argument that character development and leadership development activities that require the active use of executive functioning skills, including decision making and social interaction, can yield benefits for students with high leadership potential.

Research on moral development and leadership potential in talented students further supports our assertion that these students are equipped for executive functioning challenges and complex thinking. Lee and Olszewski-Kubilius (2006) used three psychometric scales, the BarOn Emotional Quotient Inventory: Youth Version, Short Form (Bar-On & Parker, 2000), the Defining Issues Test-2 (Rest, Narvaez, Thoma, & Bebeau, 1999), and the Roets Rating Scale for Leadership (Roets, 1997), to examine gifted students' levels of emotional intelligence, moral judgment, and leadership. It was found that academically gifted students possessed higher degrees of moral reasoning, and greater leadership potential than the comparison group. Both male and female academically gifted students scored higher on adaptability. These findings support our assertion that talented and precocious children have extraordinary leadership potential and a keen ability to use higher level moral reasoning when presented with real-life situations requiring executive functioning and decision making. Lee and Olszewski-Kubilius stated, "while academically gifted students appear to have some propensity for reaching higher levels of moral development and demonstrating leadership, specific programs and interventions are also needed to optimize the development of these attributes"(p. 60). Our research has shown that the interventions specified in

Operation Houndstooth Intervention Theory are effective methods to maximize leadership potential and utilize elevated levels of moral reasoning skills.

A study done by Manning (2005) found that valuable benefits can be derived when social interaction experiences are made available to young people. Manning looked at a model that brought together disadvantaged kindergarten students and gifted second-grade students from disadvantaged backgrounds. The gifted second-grade children acted as mentors and models of social behaviors for the kindergartners, and Manning observed that not only did the kindergartners improve their leadership skills, but the leadership skills of the second graders were improved as well. Manning's findings support the assertion by Berkowitz and Hoppe (2009) that "allowing gifted children to teach, care for, and even design and run a character education curriculum for younger children can be both effective character education for both age groups but also an outlet for the desire to lead and assert manifested by gifted children" (p. 138). Another benefit of Manning's mentoring intervention is that it allows students to utilize their decision-making skills, social interaction skills, and other executive functioning processes.

A study done by Chan (2000) looked at the benefits of the Saturday Creative Leadership Training Program for School Prefects, a leadership training program in Hong Kong that focuses on three aspects of leadership skills: characteristics of leadership, teaching of leadership skills, and activities that encourage the student to actively utilize leadership skills. Students self-assessed their leadership skills before and after the program. Chan found that the students reported higher ratings of leadership skills after the program, as well as significant increases in the students' reported levels of self-confidence, self-assertiveness, accepting challenges, persistence, creativeness, courage, directing ability, and expressiveness. Chan's findings that show a relationship between certain personal characteristics and leadership skills support the research done by Scarf and Mayseless (2009). Scarf and Mayseless examined what characteristics were most represented in students with high levels of social leadership. Social leadership skills were most exhibited by students who displayed positive perceptions in various domains, low social anxiety, and secure orientation to peers.

Depending on the circumstances, service learning under Operation Houndstooth Interventions can be either a Direct Involvement I or a Direct Involvement II activity. The distinction hinges on whether or not students have an opportunity to be creative in their positions while volunteering. For example, a student can volunteer at a homeless shelter and reap skills that contribute to both skills identified in Operational Houndstooth and executive functioning goals. Students may, for example, have a different and possibly more enriching experience if they perceive a problem and then find and implement a creative solution for the problem. Koliba, Campbell, and Shapiro (2006) investigated the distinction between service learning and more traditional forms of community service. It was found that service learning typically has six key features:

1. A clearly articulated community partner.
2. The existence of a service to be rendered.
3. The existence of learning objectives that accompany the service-learning experience.
4. The existence of a reflective component used to facilitate the learning objectives.
5. An appropriate duration dependent on the type of project.
6. The grade level of participating students. (Koliba, Campbell, & Shapiro, 2006, p. 685–686)

As previously discussed, there is value in traditional forms of volunteer service (Koliba et al., 2006); however, the emphasis on reflection with service learning activities yields a greater utilization of Co-Cognitive Factors and executive functioning processes.

Terry (2000) studied three high-level service learning programs, which she termed Community Action Programs, with gifted adolescents and found that students who participated in service learning programs were empowered and engaged in social issues. These students also gained benefits with regard to their academic skills, problem-solving skills, self-confidence levels, teamwork, cooperation, and ability to recognize real-life problems in their community. The students involved in the study found that "working cooperatively and using creative problem-solving methods and reflective activities, as well as the cognitive apprenticeship framework supported the development of the other four areas [attitudes, personal and social development, commitment, and empowerment]" (Terry, 2000). This finding supports Berkowitz, Battistich, and Bier's (2008) assertion that the most effective programs for promoting student character development utilize multiple strategies rather than a single approach, including: "adult modeling, promotion of character, opportunities for student service, the promotion of a caring community and positive relationships, and a safe and clean environment" (p. 429). A key for successful implementation of our proposed interventions is flexibility and allowing the needs of the students to shape the interventions with a multifaceted approach.

The Civic Leadership Institute (CLI) is a service-learning program for gifted adolescents that helps students explore complex social issues that are faced by today's society (Lee, Olszewski-Kubilius, Donahue, & Weimholt, 2007). The students in the CLI program participate in a combination of rigorous academic coursework, community service, meetings with top community leaders, seminars on specific topics of interest, and rich residential and recreational experiences. Many of these activities, particularly the community service and meetings with community leaders, exemplify leadership behavior and thus help develop executive functioning processes and the important goals of the Operation Houndstooth Intervention Theory. The CLI conducted a study to assess civic attitudes, civic behaviors, and leadership over time in two groups: one group that received a service learning program, and one group that received an accelerated academic program. It was found that the level of civic responsibility of the service learning students both going into and following the program was significantly greater than the level of civic responsibility of the accelerated academic students, reinforcing our argument about the greater impact of Direct Involvement I and Direct Involvement II interventions on social capital development. It was also found that the service learning students indicated a "stronger personal attachment to the community . . . and a greater belief in making a difference in the community" (Lee et al., 2007, p. 187). Additionally, the researchers examined within-group differences and found positive changes within the service learning group with regard to the "students' attachment to their communities; awareness of political, social, and civic issues; and responsibility to help improve the community" (p. 188).

The CLI conducted an additional study to examine the benefits of the program and found that the students reported that they benefited from the field activities and meetings with community leaders (Lee, Olszewski-Kubilius, Donahue, & Weimholt, 2008). Both of these activities are prime examples of students developing and utilizing skills such as intellectual curiosity, self-directed learning, and investigations of real-world problems. The researchers also found that the combination of hands-on experiences and academic coursework impacted the students' level of awareness of civic issues and the level of motivation to engage in social issues. It was also found that many students reported that their leadership skills were enhanced and many reported that they gained a "new respect and understanding for difference and diversity" (Lee et al., 2008, p. 302).

Although Operation Houndstooth is a relatively new addition to the body of research, there have been several studies that have examined components of Operation Houndstooth (Reilly, 2009; Sytsma, 2003) and explored the effectiveness of its interventions (Sands, 2012). Reilly (2009) studied the connections between the two goal orientations—contribution orientation and challenge orientation,[11] and the components of Operation Houndstooth. Reilly conducted in-depth interviews with two gifted adolescents who were

---

11 *Contribution orientation* is defined here as an orientation where goals span beyond self-based outcomes. *Challenge orientation* is defined here as an orientation where difficult goals are set that benefit the individual but have little or no concern about larger impacts.

strong examples of the two goal orientations. Reilly found that the contribution orientation integrates well with the components of Operation Houndstooth. Specifically, the Houndstooth components of courage, optimism, sensitivity to human concerns, physical and mental energy, and romance with a topic integrate well with the contribution orientation. Whereas challenge orientation exhibits the physical and mental energy component of Operation Houndstooth, it is largely lacking in the moral and ethical characteristics upon which the theory focuses. Reilly's work helps demonstrate that the co-cognitive factors of Operation Houndstooth are interrelated with goal orientation. Young gifted learners have the potential to change the world for the better and thus it would be beneficial for all of these individuals to exhibit not only academic excellence but also altruism and ethical conduct.

Sands (2012) examined the effects of different Operation Houndstooth Inventions by examining three different groups: a peer leadership program that met the description of a Direct Involvement II activity, a volunteer organization where students had the opportunity to participate in Direct Involvement I activities, and a comparison group that did not receive any Direct Involvement activities. Sands found that students who participated in the peer leadership program and received Direct Involvement II activities had higher levels of mental/physical energy after the intervention than the comparison groups. Previous research done by Sytsma (2003) theorized that increased levels of mental/physical energy are most likely the result of students' perceptions of their effort's efficacy in achieving their goals. Sands also found that students who participated at a volunteer organization and received Direct Involvement I experiences scored higher on *sensitivity to human concerns* than the comparison group and the peer leadership program group. We contend that Direct Involvement I experiences, such as service learning programs, allow students to develop valuable skills such as empathy and sensitivity through their close associations with various populations in society (Renzulli et al., 2006). We also believe that a combination of Direct Involvement I and Direct Involvement II activities greatly benefits students and results in the achievement of the co-cognitive factor goals of the Operation Houndstooth Intervention Theory.

Summary

In the preceding section, we gave a brief overview of the current research on development of leadership skills, leadership potential, and social capital factors, as well as our rationale for the importance of implementing the interventions described in Operation Houndstooth. It is our belief that classrooms contain great potential in the form of the next Marie Curie, Carl Sagan, or Leonardo Da Vinci. We acknowledge that we are hardly the first to attempt to answer the question of how to produce young thinkers who care about care improving the world, but we believe we are offering an effective and feasible model to promote such development through the interventions based on Operation Houndstooth and the Executive Functions Leadership Development subtheories. Gifted education, like all other specialized areas in the arts and sciences, is constantly in search of its identity. What defines a field beyond random and trendy practices are the theories and related research that delineates its parameters, promotes future research, and has an impact on *defensible* practice. Our field has been notably "thin" on theory development, and the work offered here is just one approach that we hope will promote discussion among scholars and practitioners, generate research on the validity of the ideas and concepts discussed here, and inspire more theoretical development on the parts of other scholars.

The most salient point to make when discussing and generalizing about theories for the study of giftedness in the 21st century is that there is an overlap and an interaction among cognitive, affective, and motivational characteristics. We cannot divorce these numerous and interactive characteristics from the ways we should go about developing gifted behaviors in young people.

A second and final consideration deals with how we should go about producing leaders for the 21st century. This consideration deals directly with how gifted education should differ *qualitatively* from general education. People who have gained recognition as gifted contributors in the beyond-the-school world have always done so because of something they did—an invention, a sonata, a design, a solution to a political or economic problem. They brought a myriad of traits, including their own co-cognitive constructs, to bear on their respective challenges, and it is these types of experiences that provided such opportunities that should be the core of our efforts to educate tomorrow's people of great promise. We propose that the creation of an extraordinary/revolutionary solution or product is enhanced by the integration of healthy and robust co-cognitive factors that propel the individual toward social capital that is both compassionate and globally focused. The anticipated social roles that people of high potential will play should be the main rationale for both supporting special programs and designing learning experiences that will prepare today's students for responsible leadership roles in the future.

In our opinion, the biggest challenge in gifted education is to extend our traditional investment in the production of intellectual and creative capital to include an equal investment in social capital and the development of executive function skills (Renzulli, 2012). We believe that experiences designed to develop these skills should begin at early ages and focus mainly on direct involvement rather than "teaching-and-preaching" experiences. If we can have an impact on social capital and effective and empathetic leadership, then we will be preparing the kinds of leaders who are as sensitive to human, environmental, and democratic concerns as they are to the traditional materialistic markers of success in today's world. And the greatest payoff from focusing gifted education on investigative learning and using knowledge wisely will be a dramatic increase in the reservoir of people who will use their talents to create a better world.

References

Ahuvia, A. C. (2002). Individualism/collectivism and cultures of happiness: A theoretical conjecture on the relationship between consumption, culture and subjective well-being at the national level. *Journal of Happiness Studies, 3,* 23–36.

Almlund, M., Duckworth, A. L., Heckman, J. & Kautz, T. (2011). *Personality psychology and economics* (IZA DP No. 5500). Retrieved from http://ftp.iza.org/dp5500.pdf

Bar-On, R., & Parker, J. D. A. (2000). *BarOn Emotional Quotient Inventory: Youth version (BarOn EQ-i:YV).* North Tonawanda, NY: Multi-Health Systems.

Berkowitz, M., Battistich, V. A., & Bier, M. C. (2008). What works in character education: What is known and what needs to be known. In L. Nucci & D. Narvaez (Eds.), *Handbook of moral and character education* (pp. 414–431). New York, NY: Routledge.

Berkowitz, M., & Hoppe, M. (2009). Character education and gifted children. *High Ability Studies, 20,* 131–142.

Borghans, L., Duckworth, A. L., Heckman, J. J., & Weel, B. (2008). The economics and psychology of personality traits. *Journal of Human Resources, 43,* 972–1059.

Chan, D. (2000). Developing the creative leadership training program for gifted and talented students in Hong Kong. *Roeper Review, 22,* 94–97.

Diamond, A. (2010). The evidence base for improving school outcomes by addressing the whole child and by addressing skills and attitudes, not just content. *Early Education and Development, 21,* 780–793.

Duckworth, A. L. (2009). Backtalk: Self-discipline is empowering. *Phi Delta Kappan, 90,* 536.

Duckworth, A. L., Peterson, C., Matthews, M. D., & Kelly, D. R. (2007). Grit: Perseverance and passion for long-term goals. *Journal of Personality and Social Psychology, 92,* 1087–1101.

Duckworth, A. L., & Quinn, P. D. (2009). Development and validation of the Short Grit Scale (Grit-S). *Journal of Personality Assessment, 91,* 166–174.

Duckworth, A. L., & Seligman, M. E. P. (2005). Self-discipline outdoes IQ predicting academic performance of adolescents. *Psychological Science, 16,* 939–944.

Durlak, J. A., Weissberg, R. P., Dymnicki, A. B., Taylor, R. D., & Schellinger, K. B. (2011). The impact of enhancing students' social and emotional learning: A meta-analysis of school-based universal interventions. *Child Development, 82,* 405–432.

Fischman, W., & Gardner, H. (2009). Implementing GoodWork programs: Helping students to become ethical workers. *Knowledge Quest, 37,* 74–79.

Gardner, H. (1993). *Frames of mind: the theory of multiple intelligences.* New York, NY: Basic Books.

Gardner, H., Csikszentmihalyi, M., & Damon, W. (2001). *Good work: When excellence and ethics meet.* New York: Basic Books.

Goleman, D. (2006). *Emotional intelligence: Why it can matter more than IQ.* New York, NY: Bantam Press.

Heckman, J., & Rubenstein, Y. (2001). The importance of non-cognitive skills: Lessons from the GED testing program. *American Economic Review, 91,* 145–149.

Huer, J. (1991). *The wages of sin: America's dilemma of profit against humanity.* New York, NY: Praeger.

Koliba, C., Campbell, E., & Shapiro, C. (2006). The practice of service learning in local school community contexts. *Educational Policy, 20,* 683–717.

Kasser, T. (2002). *The high price of materialism.* Cambridge, MA: MIT Press.

Lee, S., & Olszewski-Kubilius, P. (2006). The emotional intelligence, moral judgment, and leadership of academically gifted adolescents. *Journal for the Education of the Gifted, 30,* 29–67.

Lee, S., Olszewski-Kubilius, P., Donahue, R., & Weimbolt, K. (2007). The effects of a service learning program on the development of civic attitudes and behaviors among academically talented adolescents. *Journal for the Education of the Gifted, 31,* 165–197.

Lee, S., Olszewski-Kubilius, P., Donahue, R., & Weimbolt, K. (2008). The civic leadership institute: A service learning program for academically gifted youth. *Journal of Advanced Academics, 19,* 272–308.

Levin, H. M. (2011). *The utility and need for incorporating non-cognitive skills into large scale educational assessments.* ETS Invitational Conference on International Large Scale Assessments.

Manning, S. (2005). Young leaders growing through mentoring. *Gifted Child Today, 28*(1), 14–21.

McNally, L., Brown, S., & Jackson, A. (2012). Cooperation and the evolution of intelligence. *Proceedings of the Royal Society B,* 1–8. doi:10.1098/rspb.2012.0206

Myers, D. G. (1993). *Authentic happiness: Using the new positive psychology to realize your potential for lasting fulfillment.* New York, NY: Avon.

Netemeyer, R. G., Burton, S., & Lichtenstein, D. R. (1995). Trait aspects of vanity: Measurement and relevance to consumer behavior. *The Journal of Consumer Research, 21,* 612–626.

Putnam, R. (1995, January). Bowling alone: America's declining social capital. *Journal of Democracy, 6,* 65–78.

Reilly, T. (2009). Talent, purpose, and goal orientations: Case studies of talented adolescents. *High Ability Students, 20,* 161–172.

Renzulli, J. S. (1977). *The Enrichment Triad Model: A guide for developing defensible programs for the gifted and talented.* Mansfield Center, CT: Creative Learning Press.

Renzulli, J. S. (1978). What makes giftedness? Re-examining a definition. *Phi Delta Kappan, 60,* 180–184.

Renzulli, J. S. (1986). The Three-Ring Conception of Giftedness: A developmental model for creative productivity. In R. J. Sternberg & J. Davidson (Eds.), *Conceptions of giftedness* (pp. 246–279). New York, NY: Cambridge University Press.

Renzulli, J. S. (2002). Expanding the conception of giftedness to include co-cognitive traits and to promote social capital. *Phi Delta Kappan, 84*, 33–40, 57–58.

Renzulli, J. S. (2005). The Three-Ring Conception of Giftedness: A developmental model for promoting creative productivity. In R. J. Sternberg & J. Davidson (Eds.), *Conceptions of giftedness* (2nd ed.). New York, NY: Cambridge University Press.

Renzulli, J. S. (2012). A theory of giftedness based on the anticipated social roles of high potential youth. In R. Subotnik, A. Robinson, C. M. Callahan & E. J. Gubbins (Eds.). *Malleable minds: Translating insights from psychology and neuroscience to gifted education.* Storrs: University of Connecticut, The National Research Center on the Gifted and Talented.

Renzulli, J., Koehler, J., & Fogarty, E. (2006). Operation houndstooth intervention theory: Social capital in today's schools. *Gifted Child Today, 29*(1), 15–24.

Renzulli, J. S., & Mitchell, M. S. (2011). *Rating the executive functions of young people.* Storrs: University of Connecticut, The National Research Center on the Gifted and Talented.

Renzulli, J. S., & Reis, S. M. (1997). *The Schoolwide Enrichment Model: A how-to guide for educational excellence* (2nd ed.). Waco, TX: Prufrock Press.

Rest, J., Narvaez, D., Thoma, S. J., & Bebeau, M. J. (1999). DIT-2: Devising and testing a new instrument of moral judgement. *Journal of Educational Psychology, 91*, 644–659.

Roets, L. F. (1997). *Leadership: Skills training programs for ages 8–18* (8th ed.). Des Moines, IA: Leadership.

Sands, M. (2012). *The impact of a peer leadership program on high school students' social capital, as measured by co-cognitive factors of the Renzulli Houndstooth Theory* (Unpublished doctoral dissertation). Western Connecticut State University, Connecticut.

Scarf, M., & Mayseless, O. (2009). Socioemotional characteristics of elementary school children identified as exhibiting social leadership qualities. *The Journal of Genetic Psychology, 170*(1), 73–94.

Shrader, W. K. (1992). *Media blight and the dehumanizing of America.* New York, NY: Praeger.

Sedlack, W. E. (2005). The case for noncognitive measures. In W. J. Camara & E. W. Kimmel (Eds.), *Choosing students: Higher education admission tools for the 21st century* (pp. 177–191). Mahwah, NJ: Lawrence Earlbaum.

Sternberg, R. J. (1998). A balance theory of wisdom. *Review of General Psychology, 2*, 347–365.

Sternberg, R. J. (2005). Augmenting the SAT through assessments of analytic, practical, and creative skills. In W. J. Camara & E. W. Kimmel (Eds.), *Choosing students: Higher education admission tools for the 21st century* (pp. 159–176). Mahwah, NJ: Lawrence Erlbaum.

Sytsma, R. E. (2003). *Co-cognitive factors and socially-constructive giftedness: Distribution, abundance, and relevance among high school students* (Unpublished doctoral dissertation). University of Connecticut, Storrs.

Tatzel, M. (2002). "Money worlds" and well-being: An integration of money dispositions, materialism and price-related behavior. *Journal of Economic Psychology, 23,* 103–126.

Terry, A. (2000), An early glimpse: Service learning from an adolescent perspective. *Journal of Secondary Gifted Education, 11,* 115–136.

CHAPTER 6

Assumptions Underlying the Identification of Gifted and Talented Students[12]

Scott W. Brown, Joseph S. Renzulli,
E. Jean Gubbins, Del Siegle, Wanli Zhang,
University of Connecticut,

and Ching-Hui Chen
Ming Chuan University

Introduction From Joe

This chapter is based on a research project that produced some "hard data" to support the assertion made earlier stating that the field has changed its mind about the conception of giftedness and the types of information that should be used in the identification process. Strong agreement was found among classroom teachers, gifted education teachers, administrators, and

---

12 Brown, S. W., Renzulli, J. S., Gubbins, E. J., Siegle, D., Zhang, W., & Chen, C. H. (2005). Assumptions underlying the identification of gifted and talented students. *Gifted Child Quarterly, 49,* 68–79. Copyright 2005 National Association for Gifted Children. Reprinted with permission.

consultants (experts in the field and state directors) from urban, suburban, and rural districts. Overall, respondents disagreed with a totally test-score approach and supported approaches that used individual expression, ongoing assessment, and context-bound identification procedures. Furthermore, they strongly agreed with the importance of using multiple criteria for the identification of gifted and talented children. This study has important implications about the need for change in both policy and identification practice and its most valuable use to the field is that it should be brought to the attention of policy makers responsible for developing state and district guidelines.

Its better to have imprecise answers to the right questions than precise answers to the wrong questions. —Donald Campbell

Procedures for identifying gifted and talented students are probably the most discussed and written about topic in our field. For the better part of the previous century, test scores dominated the identification process. Even with the advent of new theories of intelligence (e.g., Gardner, 1983; Sternberg, 1985) and broadened conceptions of giftedness (e.g., Gagné, 1999; Renzulli, 1978, 1988; Simonton, 1997), actual practices specified in state and district guidelines continue to be dominated by cognitive ability test scores. Recognition of the need for a broader base of identification criteria has progressed from theoretical and research-based advances to generally accepted recommendations included in standard textbooks in the field (Colangelo & Davis, 1997; Coleman & Cross, 2001; Davis & Rimm, 1998, 2004; Gallagher & Gallagher, 1994; Maker & Nielson, 1996; VanTassel-Baska, 1998). The quest for objectivity has undoubtedly perpetuated the comfort that "numbers" and the tidiness that cutoff scores have provided for those who design identification systems. However, people closest to direct services (classroom teachers and teachers of the gifted) often challenge the validity of purely objective approaches. Frequently commented upon are examples of high levels of performance and creativity among nonselected students and the lack of program-sponsored opportunities, resources, and encouragement for students who would clearly benefit from such services.

What is interesting about differences between recent developments in theory and teachers' reactions to identification decisions is that no one has empirically examined the attitudes of people most affected by identification systems and people who frequently make policy decisions or advise decision makers. The beliefs of practitioners and policymakers are important because, in the final analysis, these are the people who must carry out their responsibilities harmoniously and ensure that there is integrity between guidelines and regulations on one hand and the implementation of program practices on the other. Therefore, the overall question for this research is "What are the assumptions of educators underlying the identification of gifted and talented students?"

Background of the Study

Historically, the identification of gifted and talented students has been inextricably linked to intelligence tests. During the early part of the 20th century, Terman (1916, 1925) focused on developing and administering the Stanford-Binet Intelligence Scale, based on the earlier work in France by Binet. Terman offered his well-known premise, which essentially stated that gifted and talented individuals are those who scored at the top 1% of the population on the Stanford-Binet. In the minds of many, the phrase "gifted and talented" equaled an intelligence test score of at least 135. Students responded to items, their answers were compared to others, and the results were calculated. The resulting IQ score seemed precise, and the measurement approach carried with it a bit of mystery for those who may not be totally familiar with test construction and the interpretation of data. Some may have wondered what the number meant for the students' future or their ability to navigate the requirements of school successfully, while others had a measure of comfort with the notion that the student scored higher than 99% of others who took the test. Intelligence became synonymous with what the test measured. A child was labeled as gifted and talented by a cutoff score on an intelligence test, which promoted an absolutist view of giftedness. All other children who did not achieve the cutoff score were viewed as "not gifted."

Intelligence and achievement tests continue to be developed and modified to inform teachers, administrators, psychologists, parents, and the general public about the characteristics of children and adults. Their influence on people's views of children's abilities remained strong throughout the 20th century.

Exploring the expressed and applied abilities of young people is a complex process. Assessment tools are administered to establish an objective profile of students' intellectual abilities. Terman's longitudinal study of "geniuses" also revealed the difficulties in predicting what a person accomplishes in life. Terman's research team (Oden, 1968) analyzed the accomplishments of the single generation of 1,528 geniuses over time and found that early intelligence test score was not necessarily the main determinant of adult accomplishments.

Tannenbaum (1991) reflected on the contributions of Terman and associates and stated, "In the last analysis, high IQ is a boon or a bust in the configuration of factors that make up giftedness, depending on how much confidence is invested in it" (p. 31). The complexities of understanding one's current and future abilities and accomplishments are somewhat daunting. Tannenbaum offered a five-factor conception of giftedness if a person is to "achieve excellence in any publicly valued area of activity" (p. 29). He stated that these "five factors have to interweave most elegantly: (1) superior general intellect, (2) distinctive special aptitudes, (3) supportive array of nonintellective traits, (4) a challenging and facilitative environment, and (5) the smile of good fortune at crucial periods of life" (p. 29). The final factor adds levity to the heady topic of intellectual ability, but it is also poignant because of the insistence that one measure cannot begin to define or explain giftedness fully. General intellectual ability and specific aptitudes are revealed by tests, but there is more to understanding giftedness. Breaking away from a reliance on tests to determine abilities is not easy. Some people may think that using an achievement test, rather than an intelligence test, makes a difference. However, several researchers, including Sternberg (1985) and Sattler (2001), believe that intelligence and achievement tests are so similar that a quest to broaden conceptions of giftedness by including achievement is halted.

In 1950, Guilford proposed a theoretical model of intelligence that included an emphasis on creative thinking and problem solving. The multiplicity of more than 150, and eventually more than 220, abilities caught people's attention, as did views of other psychologists and researchers who proposed multiple abilities. Later, Renzulli (1978, 1988) reexamined the definition of giftedness by reviewing the research findings of several notable researchers and psychologists (Bloom, 1985; MacKinnon, 1965; Sternberg, 1985; Terman, 1925; Torrance, 1969) and looking for the substantiation of factors beyond ability that played critical roles in actualizing potential. Essentially, he wanted to know the characteristics of creative, productive adults that defined gifted behaviors. His review led to the following definition:

> Giftedness consists of an interaction among three basic clusters of human traits—these clusters being above-average general abilities, high levels of task commitment, and high levels of creativity. Gifted and talented children are those possessing or capable of developing this composite set of traits and applying them to any potentially valuable area of human performance. Children who manifest or are capable of developing an interaction among the three clusters require a wide variety of educational opportunities and services that are not ordinarily provided through regular instructional programs. (p. 261)

In later years, Gardner (1983) proposed the theory of multiple intelligences. Seven intelligences (linguistic, logical-mathematical, spatial, musical, bodily-kinesthetic, interpersonal, and intrapersonal) were initially identified, and one more (naturalist) has been added recently. One or more of these intelligences could be the focus of an identification procedure.

While Gardner (1983) posited a domain approach to intelligences, Sternberg (1985) developed his triarchic theory of intelligence, cogently arguing against the reliance on IQ as the sole determinant of giftedness. His triarchic theory looked at analytical, synthetic/creative, and practical intelligences as singular and multiple forms of abilities. Both Gardner and Sternberg's theoretical approaches are carefully defined and researched. These theorists have also experimented with various formal and informal measurement techniques, but neither theoretical model limits the assessments of children's gifts and talents to paper-and-pencil, timed tests that yield a single or multiple scores.

As more current theoretical perspectives on abilities and talents embrace intellective and nonintellective characteristics, identification procedures have to reflect such changes. One way to check the status of definitions of gifted and talented students and related assessment approaches is to review summary data from *State of the States: Gifted and Talented Education Report* (Council of State Directors of Programs for the Gifted, 1999). The state directors produce the results of a biennial survey on the status of identification and programming at the state level and in the territories. Questions focus on the existence of legislative mandates that guide the direction of screening and identification procedures, the requirements of programming, or both. Definitions of gifted and talented are provided by states. For example,

> Idaho Definition: "Gifted and talented children" means those students who are identified as possessing demonstrated or potential abilities that give evidence of high performing capabilities in intellectual, creative, specific academic or leadership areas, or ability in the performing or visual arts and who require services or activities not ordinarily provided by the school in order to fully develop such capabilities. (Council of State Directors of Programs for the Gifted, 1999, p. 18)

> Georgia Definition: Gifted Student—a student who demonstrates a high degree of intellectual and/or creative ability(ies), exhibits an exceptionally high degree of motivation, and/or excels in specific academic fields, and who need special instruction and/or special ancillary services to achieve at levels commensurate with his or her abilities. (Council of State Directors of Programs for the Gifted, 1999, p. 17)

Many state definitions have similar language (although the specificity varies) to a definition developed by a team of people in response to a governmental request of the then Commissioner of Education, Sidney Marland. The 1972 Marland definition stated:

> Gifted and talented are those identified by professionally qualified persons who by virtue of outstanding abilities are capable of high performance. These are children who require differentiated educational programs and services beyond those normally provided by the regular school program in order to realize their contributions to self and society.
>
> Children capable of high performance include those with demonstrated achievement and/or potential in any of the following areas:
> 1. General intellectual ability
> 2. Specific academic aptitude
> 3. Creative or productive thinking
> 4. Leadership ability
> 5. Visual and performing arts
> 6. Psychomotor ability (p. 10)

Over the years, the Marland definition changed (e.g., psychomotor ability was eliminated), but many elements were retained, maintaining a broader perspective on demonstrated and potential abilities. In 1993, the U.S. Department of Education released *National Excellence: A Case for Developing America's Talent*, a report whose definition of gifted and talented maintains some phrasing that was also in the earlier definition from the 1970s:

> Children and youth with outstanding talent perform or show the potential for performing at remarkably high levels of accomplishment when compared with others of their age, experience, or environment.
>
> These children and youth exhibit high performance capability in intellectual, creative, and/or artistic areas, possess an unusual leadership capacity, or excel in specific academic fields. They require services or activities not ordinarily provided by the schools.
>
> Outstanding talents are present in children and youth from all cultural groups, across all economic strata, and in all areas of human endeavor. (p. 26)

As the understanding of human abilities expanded, the notion of using multiple methods to examine the gifts and talents of young people was embraced. One of the earliest sets of guidelines for a comprehensive identification system was presented in an unpublished paper presented by Marshall Sanborn and reported in a book on identification by Renzulli, Reis, and Smith (1981). Based on his work with a broad range of diverse students at the University of Wisconsin, Sanborn argued for a broad-based comprehensive identification system using the following guidelines:

- apply multiple techniques over a long period of time;
- understand the individual, the cultural-experiential context, and the fields of activity in which the student performs;
- employ both self-chosen and required performances;
- reassess the adequacy of the identification program on a continuous basis; and
- use the identification data as the primary basis for programming experiences.

These guidelines also reflect the researchers and practitioners' experiences of Colangelo and Davis (1997), Coleman and Cross (2001), Davis and Rimm (2004), Feldhusen (1993), Gagné (1999), Gallagher and Gallagher (1994), and Tannenbaum (1997). Callahan, Tomlinson, and Pizzat (n.d.) studied noteworthy practices in identification of gifted students based on what was learned from various Javits Grants awarded by the U.S. Department of Education's Office of Educational Research and Improvement during the early 1990s. The commonalities and themes emerging from the model projects and their innovative practices included the following:

- acceptance of intelligence as multifaceted;
- recognition of the multiple manifestations of giftedness;
- emphasis on authentic tools and assessment over time;
- expanding sources of evidence;
- development of a philosophy of inclusiveness;
- strong links between the identification process and instruction;
- collaborative efforts;
- use of identification to enhance understanding; and
- early and ongoing plans and procedures to evaluate the process (pp. v–vii).

To understand current beliefs and practices related to identifying gifted and talented students, teachers, administrators, and consultants throughout the country were asked to share their assumptions in response to a 20-item survey.

Methods

Procedure

Sanborn's guidelines were studied, along with a review of the literature, to create an item pool that would become the basis for a national survey, The Assumptions Underlying the Identification of Gifted and Talented Students. These guidelines were selected because they reflect an amalgamation of the collective wisdom of the major theorists, researchers, and textbook writers in the field when broader conceptions of giftedness began to emerge. Twenty items were generated, field-tested, revised, and field-tested again with content area experts (professors and doctoral students majoring in gifted and talented education) and participants at gifted and talented conferences. The 20 revised items were ultimately retained and the survey was disseminated to potential respondents.

Sample

A total of 6,000 surveys were mailed or distributed to university professors, educational leaders in gifted education, gifted and talented specialists, administrators, and classroom teachers. Educators attending two national conferences on the gifted and talented and several workshops conducted by staff from The National Research Center on the Gifted and Talented received surveys. Although a systematic geographic distribution was not sought, each region of the country was represented. The respondents returned approximately half of the surveys ($N = 2,918$). Since a 50% response rate is considered adequate for survey research, follow-up mailings were not conducted.

All types of communities were represented, including those with diverse demographic, ethnic, and socioeconomic characteristics. Teachers at all grade levels and administrators with various building- and district-level responsibilities were included in the sample. School setting, educator classification, and respondents' professional level subdivided the sample. Respondents classified their schools as urban ($n = 579$), suburban ($n = 1,323$), or rural ($n = 1,016$). Within the educator classification, there were 489 teachers of the gifted; 1,099 regular classroom teachers; 253 professors and consultants; 912 administrators; and 165 individuals who did not indicate an educator classification. The respondents' professional level indicated 1,033 in elementary education; 1,467 in secondary education; 171 in postsecondary education; and 247 who did not indicate a professional level.

Instrument

The survey featured 20 items, each with a 5-point scale (1 = strongly agree, 2 = agree, 3 = uncertain, 4 = disagree, and 5 = strongly disagree). Respondents were asked to indicate the degree to which they agreed or disagreed with each item. Sample items included statements such as the following:

- Identification should be based primarily on an intelligence or achievement test.
- Teacher judgment and other subjective criteria should not be used in identification.
- Identification should take into consideration the cultural and experiential background of the student.
- Giftedness in some students may develop at certain ages and in specific areas of interest.
- Regular, periodic reviews should be carried out on both identified and nonidentified students.

Given the number of items, the most effective way to interpret the results was to distill the data using an exploratory factor analysis. This type of analysis searches the data set for correlations and determines the number of underlying factors in the instrument. The Kaiser- Meyer-Olkin (KMO) index was used to test the appropriateness of conducting a factor analysis of the assumptions survey. The KMO is an index for comparing the magnitudes of the observed correlation coefficients to the magnitudes of partial correlation coefficients (Norusis, 1990). Small values for the KMO measure indicate that a factor analysis of the variables may not be advisable since correlations between pairs of variables cannot be explained by the other variables. Kaiser (1974) characterized measures in the 0.90s as marvelous and in the 0.80s as meritorious. The value of the overall KMO statistic for the current sample study was 0.87. Since it was between 0.8 and 0.9, it met the Kaiser criteria for conducting a factor analysis.

Since the squared multiple correlations (SMC) of each variable with all other variables of this study ranged from 0.10 to 0.33 (mean = 0.21), 0.30 was used as a critical value for the eigenvalues of the correlation matrix after the substitution of communality estimates at final iteration to specify the number of factors. Principal Axis Factoring (PAF) with a varimax rotation extracted 6 factors from the 20 items. These 6 factors (see Table 6.1) explained 51.6% of the variance in the initial correlation matrix and 31.9% in the final matrix.

To test the reliability of each factor, Cronbach's alphas were conducted. The resulting reliability estimates were 0.61, 0.67, 0.51, 0.54, 0.65, and 0.36, respectively. The sixth factor had a very low alpha and consisted of only two items. Four outside experts in gifted education believed that the items of the

Table 6.1

Item Means, Standard Deviations, and Factor Loadings for the 20-Item Survey

Item	M	SD	Loading
Factor I: Restricted Assessment, M = 3.96, SD = .60, Alpha = .63			
4. Achievement/IQ	3.86	1.03	.58
8. Precise cutoff score	3.58	1.08	.69
11. No teacher judgment/subjective criteria	4.13	.84	.59
14. Restricted percentage	4.13	.84	.65
15. Services for identified students only	3.95	1.00	.60
Factor II: Individual Expression, M = 1.71, SD = .48, Alpha = .67			
6. Case study data	1.67	.63	.47
7. Assess student-selected tasks	2.11	.80	.71
10. Multiple formats for expressing talent	1.44	.58	.58
19. Non-intellectual factors	1.64	.69	.64
Factor III: Ongoing Assessment, M = 1.85, SD = .41, Alpha = .51			
9. Identification information lead to programming	1.81	.60	.51
13. Judgment by best qualified person	1.91	.62	.59
17. Alternative identification criteria	1.85	.70	.55
18. Regular periodic reviews	1.84	.63	.54
Factor IV: Multiple Criteria, M = 1.32, SD = .37, Alpha = .55			
1. Multiple expression of abilities	1.18	.41	.76
2. Developmental perspective and interest	1.54	.65	.67
3. Multiple types of information	1.26	.48	.62
Factor V: Context-Bound, M = 2.13, SD = .55, Alpha = .65			
5. Cultural/experiential background	1.99	.90	.85
16. Knowledge of student's cultural/environmental background	1.99	.75	.74
Factor VI: Unnamed, Alpha = .37 (Alpha = .53 when combined with Factor V)			
12. Locally developed methods and criteria	2.27	.84	.67
20. Reflect services and activities provided	2.30	.99	.75

fifth and sixth factor were conceptually connected and these two factors could be collapsed. The revised factor analysis with a 5-factor solution accounted for 47.1% of the total variance. The new factor (a combination of factors 5 and 6) included items 5, 16, 12, and 20 and had an alpha = 0.52. The final 5 factors were: Restricted Assessment, Individual Expression, Ongoing Assessment, Multiple Criteria, and Context-Bound. Restricted Assessment involved the sole use of test data with precise cutoff scores. Individual Expression emphasized case study data with multiple formats for students to express their talents. Ongoing Assessment advocated periodic review using alternative criteria. Multiple Criteria involved selection based on multiple types of information. Context-Bound considered student's cultural, environmental, and experiential background. Factor scale scores were created for each of the 5 factors by summing the values associated with each item of each factor and dividing by the number of items for each respondent in the sample. The item means, standard deviations, and factor loadings are shown in Table 6.1.

Data Analysis

To check for potential outliers in the data set, the Mahalanobis' distance for centroids procedure was conducted. The Bonferroni adjustment based on the number of the subjects showed that there were 16 outliers in this sample. These outliers were eliminated from further analyses since they might adversely affect further statistical analyses. Once removed, the sample was considered free of outliers.

Since the 5 factors appeared to be related and the correlations among the factor scale scores ranged from .22 to .45, a multivariate analysis of variance procedure (MANOVA) was appropriate to examine differences in responses according to demographic information. The dependent variables were the 5 factor scale scores and the independent variables were School Setting (urban, suburban, and rural), Educator Role (gifted, regular, consultant, and administrator), and respondent's Professional Level (elementary, secondary, and postsecondary).

Two of the three MANOVA main effects were found to be statistically significant: School Setting (Wilks lambda = .989; F = 3.56; p < .001) and Educator Role (Wilks lambda = .98; F = 4.82; p < .001). Professional Level (Wilks lambda = .99; F = 1.807; [ns]) was not statistically significant. None of the interaction effects were statistically significant. As a follow-up, univariate analyses of variances (ANOVAs) were conducted on the two significant main effects. Because there were multiple ANOVAs, a modified Bonferroni-type adjustment (Tabachnick & Fidell, 1996) was made for inflated Type I error. The alpha level for each analysis was set at $p \leq .01$. There were significant differences among School Settings on the Multiple Criteria and Context-Bound factors. Data analyses revealed significant differences among Educator's Roles on all but the Individual Assessment factor (see Table 6.2).

Table 6.2
ANOVA Results for School Setting and Educator's Role

Factor	F	df	p
School setting			
Restricted Assessment	0.82	2, 2584	.442
Individual Expression	1.22	2, 2584	.296
Ongoing Assessment	1.18	2, 2584	.308
Multiple Criteria	7.35	2, 2584	.001
Context-Bound	4.53	2, 2584	.01
Educator's Role			
Restricted Assessment	4.30	3, 2584	.005
Individual Assessment	1.57	3, 2584	.195
Ongoing Assessment	16.45	3, 2584	.001
Multiple Criteria	22.14	3, 2584	.001
Context-Bound	21.95	3, 2584	.001

The univariate approach requires certain assumptions about the data used (Tabachnick & Fidell, 1996). Since cells in this study were not equal by the grouping characteristics, the main assumption required for using the univariate results is that the variances of all the "transformed variables" for each effect be equal and that their covariances be 0 (Norusis, 1990). Mauchly's test of sphericity is appropriate for testing the hypothesis that the covariance matrix of the transformed variables has a constant variance on the diagonal and zeroes off the diagonal. This was used to test this assumption. It should be noted that, for large sample sizes, Mauchly's test may be significant even when the impact of the departure on the analysis of variance results may be small (Norusis, 1990). The sample size in this study was very large and the hypothesis of sphericity was rejected. Since the sphericity assumption appeared to be violated, modifications to the univariate results were conducted.

Based on the results of univariate variance analysis, follow-up tests were conducted. Scheffé's procedure was used because of unequal cell sizes. These analyses utilized an alpha of 0.05. The results of the Scheffé statistical tests for School Setting indicated that, for Multiple Criteria (Cohen's $d = .29$) and Context-Bound (Cohen's $d = .22$), rural respondents were found to have statistically higher means than the urban respondents ($p < .05$). Since the factor scores are on the same scale of measurement as the original items, lower means indicate greater levels of agreement (1 = strongly agree and 5 = strongly disagree). Additionally, the results indicated that rural respondents had a higher mean on the Multiple Criteria factor than the suburban respondents ($p < .05$,

Table 6.3

Means and Standard Deviations by School Setting for Each Factor

Setting	Factors				
	Restricted Assumption	Individual Expression	Ongoing	Multiple Criteria*	Context-Bound
Urban	3.96 (.61)	1.67 (.47)	1.82 (.42)	1.27 (.35)	2.04 (.57)
Suburban	3.95 (.58)	1.71 (.48)	1.85 (.40)	1.29 (.35)	2.15 (.55)
Rural	3.91 (.60)	1.74 (.47)	1.87 (.40)	1.38 (.40)	2.16 (.54)

Note. * Significant univariate results that warranted Scheffé post hoc.

Cohen's $d = .24$), but there was no significant difference between the means for the urban and suburban respondents. In contrast, the Context-Bound factor was found to have a significantly higher mean for suburban respondents than urban respondents ($p < .05$, Cohen's $d = .20$), but no significant difference between the suburban and rural respondents. The means and standard deviations for School Setting are presented in Table 6.3.

The Scheffé results for the Educator Role and factors revealed that teachers of the gifted ($p < .05$, Cohen's $d = .15$) and consultants ($p < .05$, Cohen's $d = .14$) had significantly higher means (greater disagreement) on the Restricted Assessment factor than classroom teachers. There were no other significant differences among the educator roles on the Restricted Assessment factor.

The Ongoing Assessment factor mean was highest (strongest disagreement) for the classroom teachers and lowest for the teachers of the gifted. The mean for the gifted teachers was significantly lower than any of the other three educator groups (classroom teachers: $p < .05$, Cohen's $d = .43$; administrators: $p < .05$, Cohen's $d = .29$; consultants: $p < .05$, Cohen's $d = .18$), indicating the greatest level of support for the Ongoing Assessment factor by this group of teachers. There were no significant differences among the means of the other three educator groups.

The results for the Multiple Criteria factor indicated that the mean responses of the teachers of the gifted were significantly lower than the responses from the classroom teachers ($p < .05$, Cohen's $d = .46$) and administrators ($p < .05$, Cohen's $d = .27$), but were not significantly different from the consultants. Additionally, the administrators' mean response was significantly lower than the classroom teachers' mean ($p < .05$, Cohen's $d = .18$) for this factor.

The mean response for the teachers of the gifted on the Context-Bound factor was found to be significantly lower than each of the other three educator groups (classroom teachers: $p < .05$, Cohen's $d = .51$; administrators: $p < .05$, Cohen's $d = .37$; consultants: $p < .05$, Cohen's $d = .29$). There were no signif-

Table 6.4

Means and Standard Deviations by Educator's Role for Each Factor

Educator's Role	Factors				
	Restricted Assessment*	Individual Expression	Ongoing*	Multiple Criteria*	Context-Bound*
Gifted	3.99 (.60)	1.67 (.50)	1.73 (.41)	1.22 (.30)	1.93 (.52)
Regular	3.90 (.57)	1.67 (.50)	1.90 (.39)	1.38 (.40)	2.18 (.53)
Administrator	3.97 (.61)	1.72 (.44)	1.85 (.41)	1.31 (.37)	2.11 (.56)
Consultant	3.98 (.61)	1.68 (.48)	1.81 (.44)	1.26 (.33)	2.08 (.59)

Note. * Significant univariate results that warranted Scheffé post hoc.

icant differences among the means for the classroom teachers, consultants, and administrators. The means and standard deviations for Educator's Role are presented in Table 6.4

Discussion and Conclusions

The group differences as reported in effect sizes were small. These small differences are a positive finding; educators in various roles and from a variety of school settings appear to be in general agreement about the need for more flexible identification systems.

For decades, the "metric of giftedness" has been test scores, more specifically, IQ scores. The tradition of relying on IQ scores to define one's ability curried favor with psychologists and educators as the technology of measurement took hold. Numbers became the determinant of what students could accomplish in school. Using an objective approach to assessing abilities was comfortable. That level of comfort, however, was often challenged when there were dramatic differences between students' academic accomplishments and what the numbers had predicted. The realization was that the prophecy of the numbers was really just for future numbers on the same or similar tests. Assumptions about identification techniques definitely influence the process and strategies one uses to screen and identify gifted and talented students.

The survey results present an interesting picture of the assumptions underlying identification practices. Respondents disagreed with a Restricted Approach and supported Individual Expression, Ongoing Assessment, and Context-Bound procedures. Furthermore, they strongly agreed with the importance of using Multiple Criteria for the identification of gifted and talented children. This does not sound too unusual, as these assumptions are part of the litany of responses to the question "How do you identify gifted and talented students?"

Overall, gifted teachers were in favor of expanded views of giftedness and were certain that there were many identification techniques that would be most appropriate in studying the obvious and emergent talent potential of students. Perhaps their responses to the survey paint a slightly different picture because of firsthand experience with screening and identification systems that they designed or implemented based on an agreed-upon system developed in conjunction with state regulations. Administrators, consultants, and classroom teachers may have played more indirect roles in reviewing or monitoring an existing identification system. Therefore, their convictions about the various assumptions were not as strong.

What is unusual and somewhat perplexing about the assumptions underlying the identification of gifted and talented students is the discrepancy between the assumptions expressed by educators and (a) subsequent practices documented by other researchers in recent times and (b) the degree to which many states and school districts continue to use restricted approaches in their identification procedures.

The *1998–1999 State of the States Gifted and Talented Education Report* (Council of State Directors, 1999) reported on the status of identification requirements by state. Each state director was asked to respond to the following survey question:

> If identification is mandated, which of the following are required as identification measures in your state?
> 1. Intelligence/ability/aptitude assessment
> 2. Academic achievement/performance assessment
> 3. Teacher/parent/student/peer nomination
> 4. Characteristics or behavioral checklists/observations
> 5. Grades/anecdotal records/student interest inventories/assessment of student motivation
> 6. Other

Of the 16 state directors who selected the numbered identification measures above, 94% indicated that an intelligence/ability/aptitude assessment was mandated; 75% indicated that an academic achievement/performance assessment was mandated; 44%, a teacher/parent/student/peer nomination; 44%, characteristics of behavioral checklists/observations; 38%, grades/anecdotal records/student interest inventories/assessment of student motivation; and 63%, other. These percentages indicate, once again, that more objective measures such as intelligence and achievement tests are more frequently mandated than subjective measures that require personal judgments of students' work, behaviors, or characteristics.

In The National Research Center on the Gifted and Talented Classroom Practices Study of more than 3,000 3rd- or 4th-grade teachers, Archambault et al. (1993) found that most of the public schools surveyed used achievement tests (79%), followed by IQ tests (72%), and teacher nomination (70%) as their main sources of data collection. The data sources were similar, but the order was different in the findings by Cox, Daniel, and Boston (1985), who indicated that teacher nomination (91%), achievement tests (90%), and IQ tests (82%) were used most often. In an earlier study, Alvino, McDonnel, and Richert (1981) also found that most identification procedures included intelligence tests, teacher nominations, and achievement tests. These procedures of using tests or teacher recommendations do not reflect the findings of this study on The Assumptions Underlying the Identification of Gifted and Talented Students.

Understanding that assumptions and practices may not be in full agreement is a first step in reviewing the appropriateness of existing or future identification policies and the specific identification practices that should be guided by state and local policy. Two simple, but recurring questions must be discussed at length: Who are the gifted and talented? How do we find them? Responses to these questions should influence future beliefs and research-based practices that are more congruent with the assumptions revealed in the present study. The challenge, then, is to bring beliefs and practices together and to include other techniques, such as biographical and autobiographical data; product or portfolio review; performance assessment; and self-, peer, or parent nominations in the development of a flexible and defensible identification system that is responsive to students' educational needs.

Most of the confusion and controversy surrounding the identification of giftedness can be placed into proper perspective by examining a few key questions. Is giftedness an absolute or relative concept? That is, is a person either gifted or not gifted (the absolute view) or can varying degrees of gifted behaviors be developed in certain people at certain times under certain circumstances (the relative view)? Is gifted a static concept (you have it or you don't have it) or is it a dynamic concept (it varies within the individual and learning/performance situations)?

These questions have led to a fundamental change in the ways in which the concept of giftedness is viewed. Except for certain functional purposes related mainly to professional focal points (i.e., research, training, legislation) and to ease of expression, the absolutist view of "the gifted" is not supported by current theory, research, and the assumptions of the various groups represented in this study. This research, plus the contributions of Bloom (1985), Gardner

(1983), Renzulli (1978, 1988), and others, suggests a shift in the emphasis from the traditional concept of "being gifted" (or not being gifted) to a concern about the development of giftedness or gifted behaviors in those youngsters who have the highest potential for benefiting from special educational services. This slight shift in terminology might appear to be an exercise in heuristic hair splitting, but it has significant implications for the concept of giftedness and subsequent identification and programming endeavors. Identification procedures that result in a total preselection of certain students and the concomitant implication that these young people are and always will be "the gifted" must be reexamined. This absolute approach, coupled with the almost total reliance upon test scores, is inconsistent with current research.

The alternative to such an absolutist view is to forego the tidy and comfortable tradition of knowing on the first day of school who is gifted and who is not. The research in favor of a more flexible approach is so overwhelming that it no longer needs to be argued (see, for example, Sternberg & Davidson, 1986). Therefore, it is time to examine identification guidelines and practical procedures (Renzulli, 1990) that are more consistent with present-day research on human abilities.

Fortunately, some states have made changes in existing guidelines and others have allowed greater access to services for underrepresented groups by allowing more flexibility in the interpretation of present regulations and guidelines. To be sure, there will be less tidiness in the identification process, but the trade-off for tidiness and administrative expediency is a much more equitable approach to both identification and programming and a system that not only shows greater respect for the research reported here, but is more acceptable to educators represented in this study.

Limitations

The small differences among groups found in this study may be an artifact of the low reliability estimates of the 5 factors. The survey developed for this study was purposefully kept short and was designed to include a wide variety of identification practices. Future researchers may wish to develop a longer survey with more tightly aligned items. This should increase the reliability estimates of the factors.

Most of the educators who responded to the survey were attendees at gifted conferences. Their attendance at these conferences is probably indicative of an interest in gifted education. They possibly were also more aware of concerns about bias in the identification of gifted and talented students.

For these reasons, these results may not generalize to classroom teachers and administrators with less exposure to gifted education. While the results are likely to generalize to the gifted specialists and consultants who regularly attend such events, caution is warranted since this was a convenience sample.

References

Alvino, J., McDonnel, R. C., & Richert, S. (1981). National survey of identification practices in gifted and talented education. *Exceptional Children, 48,* 124–132.

Archambault, F. X., Jr., Westberg, K. L., Brown, S. W., Hallmark, B. W., Emmons, C. L., & Zhang, W. (1993). Classroom practices used with gifted third and fourth grade students. *Journal for the Education of the Gifted, 16,* 103–119.

Bloom, B. (Ed.). (1985). *Developing talent in young people.* New York, NY: Ballantine.

Callahan, C. M., Tomlinson, C. A., & Pizzat, P. M. (Eds.). (n.d.). *Contexts for promise: Noteworthy practices and innovations in the identification of gifted students.* Charlottesville: University of Virginia, National Research Center on the Gifted and Talented.

Colangelo, N., & Davis, G.A. (Eds.). (1997). *Handbook of gifted education* (2nd ed.). Boston, MA: Allyn & Bacon.

Coleman, L. J., & Cross, T. L. (2001). *Being gifted in school: An introduction to development, guidance, and teaching.* Waco, TX: Prufrock Press.

Council of State Directors of Programs for the Gifted. (1999). *The 1998–99 state of the states gifted and talented report.* Longmont, CO: Author.

Cox, J., Daniel, N., & Boston, B. A. (1985). *Educating able learners: Programs and promising practices.* Austin: University of Texas Press.

Davis, G. A., & Rimm, S. B. (1998). *Education of the gifted and talented* (4th ed.). Boston, MA: Allyn & Bacon.

Davis, G. A., & Rimm, S. B. (2004). *Education of the gifted and talented* (5th ed.). Boston, MA: Allyn & Bacon.

Feldhusen, J. (1993). Talent development as an alternative to gifted education. *Journal of Secondary Education, 5,* 5–9.

Gagné, F. (1999). My convictions about the nature of abilities, gifts, and talents. *Journal for the Education of the Gifted, 22,* 109–136.

Gallagher, J. J., & Gallagher, S. A. (1994). *Teaching the gifted* (4th ed.). Boston, MA: Allyn & Bacon.

Gardner, H. (1983). *Frames of mind: The theory of multiple intelligences.* New York, NY: Basic.

Guilford, J. P. (1950). Creativity. *American Psychologist, 5,* 444–454.

Kaiser, H. F. (1974). An index of factorial simplicity. *Psychometrika, 39,* 31–36.

MacKinnon, D. W. (1965). Personality and the realization of creative potential. *American Psychologist, 20,* 273–281.

Maker, C. J., & Nielson, A. B. (1996). *Curriculum development and teaching strategies for gifted learners* (2nd ed.). Austin, TX: PRO-ED.

Marland, S. P., Jr. (1972). *Education of the gifted and talented, Volume 1: Report to the Congress of the United States by the Commissioner of Education.* Washington, DC: U.S. Government Printing Office.

Norusis, M. J. (1990). *SPSS/PC+ Statistics 4.0.* Chicago: SPSS.

Oden, M. H. (1968). The fulfillment of promise: 40 year follow-up of the Terman gifted group. *Genetic Psychology Monographs, 77,* 3–93.

Renzulli, J. S. (1978). What makes giftedness? Re-examining a definition. *Phi Delta Kappan, 60,* 180–184, 261.

Renzulli, J. S. (1988). A decade of dialogue on the Three-Ring Conception of Giftedness. *Roeper Review, 11,* 18–25.

Renzulli, J. S. (1990). A practical system for identifying gifted and talented students. *Early Child Development and Care, 63,* 9–18.

Renzulli, J. S., Reis, S. M., & Smith, L. H. (1981). *The Revolving Door Identification Model.* Mansfield Center, CT: Creative Learning Press.

Sattler, J. M. (2001). *Assessment of children: Cognitive applications* (4th ed.). San Diego, CA: Sattler.

Simonton, D. K. (1997). When giftedness becomes genius: How does talent achieve eminence? In N. Colangelo & G. A. Davis (Eds.), *Handbook of gifted education* (2nd ed., pp. 335–340). Boston, MA: Allyn & Bacon.

Sternberg, R. J. (1985). *Beyond IQ: A triarchic theory of human intelligence.* New York, NY: Cambridge University Press.

Sternberg, R. J., & Davidson, J. (Eds.). (1986). *Conceptions of giftedness.* New York, NY: Cambridge University Press.

Tabachnick, B., & Fidell, L. S. (1996). *Using multivariate statistics* (3rd. ed.). New York, NY: HarperCollins.

Tannenbaum, A. (1991). The social psychology of giftedness. In N. Colangelo & G. A. Davis (Eds.), *Handbook of gifted education* (pp. 27–44). Boston, MA: Allyn & Bacon.

Tannenbaum, A. (1997). The meaning and making of giftedness. In N. Colangelo & G. A. Davis (Eds.), *Handbook of gifted education* (2nd ed., pp. 165–169). Boston, MA: Allyn & Bacon.

Terman, L. M. (1916). *The measurement of intelligence.* Boston, MA: Houghton Mifflin.

Terman, L. M. (1925). *Genetic studies of genius: Vol. 1. Mental and physical traits of a thousand gifted children.* Stanford, CA: Stanford University Press.

Torrance, E. P. (1969). Prediction of adult creative achievements among high school seniors. *Gifted Child Quarterly, 13,* 223–229.

U.S. Department of Education, Office of Educational Research and Improvement. (1993). *National excellence: A case for developing America's talent.* Washington, DC: U.S. Government Printing Office.

VanTassel-Baska, J. (1998). *Excellence in educating gifted & talented learners* (3rd ed.). Denver, CO: Love.

PART III

Systems and Models for the Development of Giftedness and Talents

CHAPTER 7

A Theory of Blended Knowledge for the Development of Creative Productive Giftedness

Joseph S. Renzulli
University of Connecticut

Introduction From Joe

Information is not knowledge. —Albert Einstein
Knowledge is love and light and wisdom. —Helen Keller

This recently written chapter is designed to set the stage for a better understanding of the chapters that follow in this section of the book. As will be pointed out, epistemology, the study of knowledge creation and use, was a topic examined by ancient philosophers and is reflected in modern educational templates for learning such as Bloom's Taxonomy of Educational Objectives. I was surprised that no articles in the gifted literature had addressed this topic. It wasn't until recent years that I realized different types of knowledge are the "grist for the mill of mind." Understanding different levels of knowledge helped me to better recognize the argument made in the following chapter about the importance of focusing special programs on creative and productive giftedness. This work also reflects my growing fascination with the importance that technology is now playing for learners of all ages and the easy accessibility to the wide world of knowledge that young people now have through the Internet. An examination of the three levels of knowledge discussed in this chapter and the importance of blending them together will strike some readers as "common sense," and this is exactly what I intended.

Any new theory is first attacked as absurd; then it is admitted to be true, but obvious and insignificant; finally it seems to be important—so important that its adversaries claim that they have discovered it themselves.
—William James

Our history and culture can be charted to a large extent by the creative contributions of the world's most gifted and talented individuals. What causes some people to use their intellectual, motivational, and creative assets in such a way that it leads to outstanding manifestations of creative productivity, while others with similar or perhaps even greater assets fail to achieve at expected levels of accomplishment? The sheer amount of folk wisdom, portrayals in popular media, and biographical and anecdotal accounts about creativity and giftedness are nothing short of mindboggling. Some clarity, however, can be found by carefully examining the creativity literature.

Creativity researchers, for instance, tend to agree that creativity is the combination of originality and task appropriateness as defined in a particular context (Plucker, Beghetto, & Dow, 2004). Moreover, researchers have differentiated among different levels of creativity, ranging from the more subjective (mini-c) to the everyday (little-c) experiences of creativity to professional (Pro-c) and finally, eminent (Big-C) levels of creativity (Beghetto & Kaufman, 2007; Kaufman & Beghetto, 2009). Along these same lines, creativity researchers have also argued that although creativity can be experienced across multiple domains at lower levels of performance, high levels of creative production tend to be domain specific (Kaufman, Beghetto, Baer, & Ivcevic, 2010).

Even with these insights from creativity research, we are still unable to answer the fundamental question of how and why some individuals develop their talents and perform at superior levels in analytic, investigative, and creative ways. Although it would be tempting to present a yet another "combination-of-ingredients theory" (based on the characteristics of giftedness) to explain why some people achieve at high levels, the theory described in detail this chapter addresses how three interrelated levels of knowledge fit into the structure and quality of one's formal learning experiences. These levels are Received Knowledge, Analyzed Knowledge, and Applied and Created Knowledge. The theory is based on the role that knowledge plays in developing an investigative mindset and creative productivity, and how the integrated use of three levels of knowledge contribute to a major goal of gifted education: to increase the world's reservoir of creative and productive individuals. This work is purposefully different from theories about the characteristics of giftedness because it deals with the organization and structure of knowledge and has implications for both curriculum development and teaching strategies that can be implemented in programs for gifted and talented students. These services represent a central focus of the literature in our field and what we actually do in programs that serve gifted students.

The field of gifted education is replete with systems and models for identification, curriculum development, program development, and program evaluation (Dai & Chen, 2014; Hunsaker, 2012; Renzulli, Gubbins, McMillen, Eckert, & Little, 2009; VanTassel-Baska & Brown, 2007) but little attention has been given to an underlying theory that focuses on the role of knowledge in the development of characteristics that bring high-potential students to our attention. Just as flour, water, salt, and yeast are the main ingredients for making bread, so also are knowledge and the creative construction and application of knowledge the main "ingredients" for developing highly creative and productive bright young minds.

Epistemology

Theories of knowledge are the focus of the study of epistemology, that branch of philosophy that investigates the origin, nature, methods, construction, and diffusion of human knowledge. In the Western world, epistemology had its origin in the work of Plato and Aristotle, as explained in this elegant quotation.

> For Plato, sense data were at best a distraction from knowledge, which was the province of unaided reason. For Aristotle, knowledge consisted of generalizations, but these were derived in the first instance from information gathered from the outside world. These two models of human thinking, termed rationalism and empiricism, respectively,

formed the major intellectual legacy of the West down to Descartes and Bacon, who represented, in the seventeenth century, the twin poles of epistemology (Berman, 1981, p. 46).

Bacon's approach to knowledge and learning became the standard for the development of the scientific method and for all subsequent taxonomic systems for organizing knowledge such as Bloom's Taxonomy of Educational Objectives (Anderson & Krathwohl, 2001; Bloom, 1954). Bacon's taxonomic scheme set forth the paradigm for what has become the major guide for the pursuit of intellectual knowledge.

Bacon's theory states that knowledge comes primarily from sensory experience and evidence, especially through experimentation guided by six steps: (1) state the problem, (2) gather information/research, (3) formulate a hypothesis, (4) do the experiment, (5) analyze results, (6) draw conclusions (Fitch, 1981; Machlup, 1980). Thus, Bacon's ideas on what has now become universally recognized as the scientific method have had serious implications for the basic ingredients of what we should be examining as an epistemological framework for developing giftedness in young people.

An interesting historical footnote about the theory discussed here is that the ancient Greeks never believed that certain types of knowledge were more useful than others! Rather, they argued that the advancement of understanding occurred when different types of knowledge worked together to enhance learning and wisdom. The advent of formal curriculum that emerged over the centuries resulted in content and process being treated as separate pedagogical entities by subsequent education theorists. And when testing for content acquisition became the major criterion for measuring school success, we moved away from the original concept of blended knowledge embodied in the Aristotelian and Platonic concepts of knowledge (Fitch, 1981). In a certain sense, the theory presented in this article serves as "connective tissue" between the ways in which the ancient thinkers viewed knowledge and the changes that have taken place in formal education. These changes have forced a distinction in learning theories among the three levels of knowledge around which the theory is structured. Modern-day theorists in cognition and instruction (e.g., Bereiter, 2002; Bransford, Brown, & Cocking, 2000) have pointed to the changes that have taken place in learning theory as a result of the advent of the "knowledge age," and this is the reason that a brief consideration of the *sources* of knowledge, as well as the levels of knowledge, have been integrated into account in the rationale of this theory.

The theory presented here simply intends to portray the ways that different kinds of knowledge interact with one another to produce the "blended knowledge" at the center of Figure 7.1. Learners receive information, but as

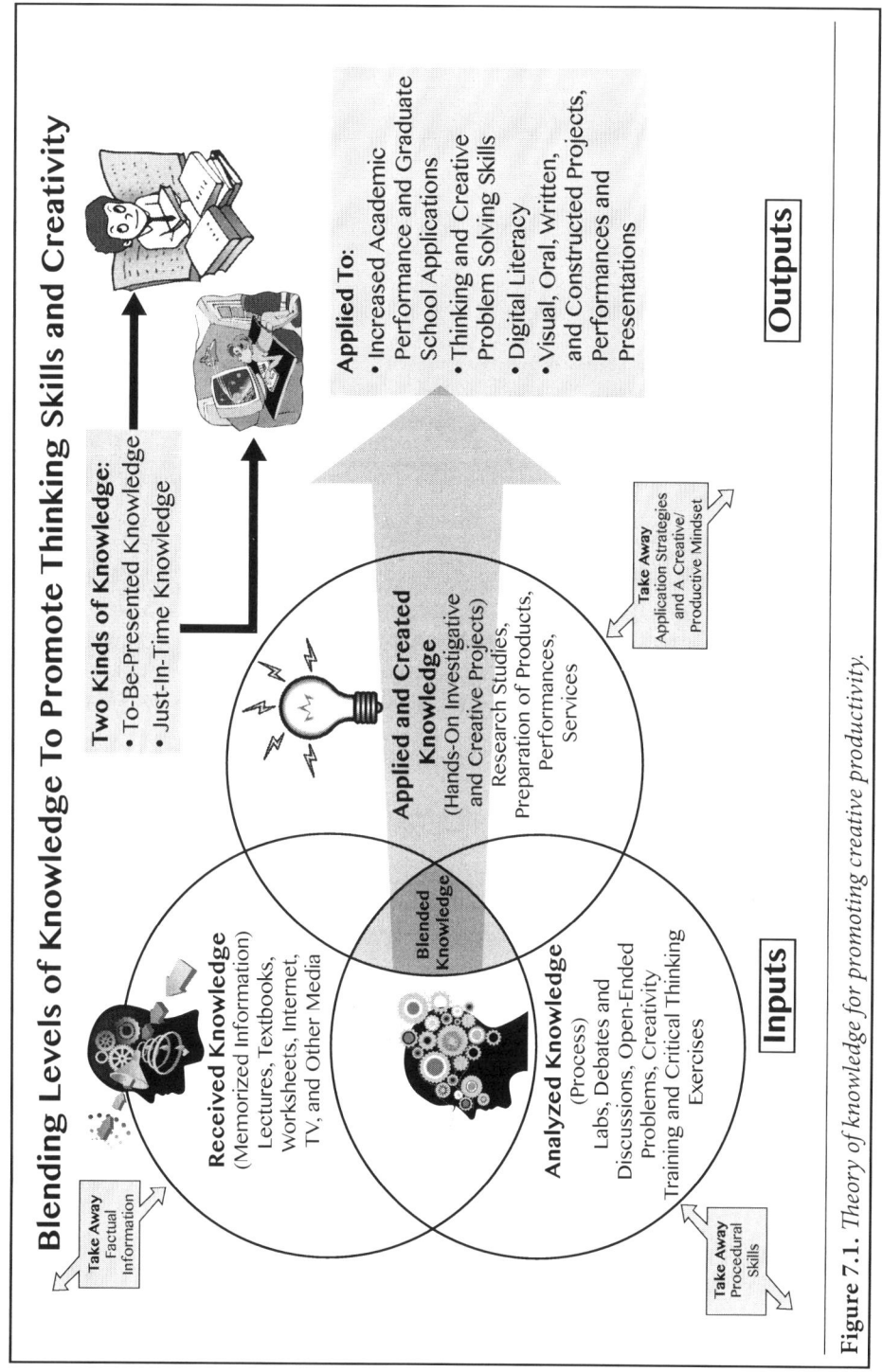

Figure 7.1. *Theory of knowledge for promoting creative productivity.*

they begin to analyze this information they may find it necessary to "go back" and gather more material to carry out an analysis. Similarly, when they reach the applied and creative stage, they may also need to return to the received and applied levels, and "return trips" to these levels are usually based on just-in-time rather than presented information. And in those cases when new knowledge, innovative contributions to a field, or even new ways of analyzing data (Big-C contributions) are made at the applied and creative level, the innovative person may be contributing content that becomes part of received knowledge. Although this process is the natural way that learning takes place, an overly standardized test-prep curriculum may severely emphasize received knowledge and in a certain sense "discriminate" against both the analyzed and applied/creative levels of learning. It is for this reason that the theory has relevance to the pedagogy advocated in special programs and the ways in which we train teachers to work with gifted students. The reason that gifted education advocates were among the educators who latched on early to Bloom's theory of cognitive development was that it called attention to the higher mental processes important to high levels of development.

Bloom's work, however, has usually been interpreted as a lineal sequence to the pursuit of higher levels of thinking (not necessarily his intention). The Theory of Blended Knowledge presented in this article views knowledge acquisition and usage as an interactive and cyclical process and thus is presented in the form of a Venn diagram in an effort to portray this interaction (see Figure 7.1).

Before describing the Theory of Blended Knowledge that is the focus of this article, it is important first to discuss two related issues that are part of the rationale underlying this theory. These issues are important because the production and diffusion of knowledge is central to the advancement of our civilization and an important part of the rationale for establishing and supporting programs for young people with exceptionally high potential.

The Purpose of Gifted Education

The first issue is the justification for providing special services to the targeted group of young people served in special programs for the gifted. "Why," many people have asked, "should a school, state, or nation provide supplementary funds, specially trained teachers and teacher training programs, conferences, professional journals, and other resources for a group of students that are already endowed with superior potentials?" Although we often respond to this question by talking about the "needs" of these students that are sometimes met but more often not addressed, it seems apparent to state that all students in our schools have needs that should be respected and accommodated. Or we run down a list of our usual maxims (e.g., the need for creative thinking, critical thinking, problem solving, decision making, etc.), but leaders of a recent report entitled *21st Century Skills, Education & Competitiveness: A Resource and Policy Guide* (Partnership for 21st Century Skills, 2008) have argued emphatically that:

> Public education has traditionally thought of higher level thinking as the purview of talented and gifted programs, while the teaching of basic skills was geared toward those on a trade track in high schools. Now, the focus must be on making sure all students have a broad array of these skills in addition to strong grounding in core subjects. (p. 27)

When asked the question addressed above about why we need special services for gifted and talented students, I have always stated unequivocally that the purpose of providing supplementary resources for the development of giftedness is to increase the world's reservoir of highly creative and productive individuals. Simply explained, we need more scientists, artists, writers, statesmen, political leaders, entrepreneurs, and designers in all fields of human endeavor who will address the problems of our modern society and improve the health, economy, quality of life, human freedoms, aesthetics, arts, and preservation of the Earth's resources. Although this response may sound abstract and idealistic, it bears a direct relationship to the kinds of contributions that we admire in such gifted individuals as Jonas Salk, Ludwig Beethoven, Margaret Sanger, Pablo Picasso, Martin Luther King, Jr., Rachel Carson, Steve Jobs, Marion Anderson, and others who have left their stamp on making the world a better place.

Sources of Information and Knowledge

The second issue related to this theory has to do with the *sources* of information and knowledge for learners of all ages. Who and what are the providers of information and knowledge in formal learning situations? When it comes to schooling there are essentially two major sources of knowledge. I define the first source as To-Be-Presented (T-B-P) knowledge, the type usually transmitted to students through lectures, textbooks, and other forms of print, visual, or auditory media. Committees that develop curricular standards and textbook writers almost universally determine what T-B-P knowledge is used in today's schools, and it is also highly influenced by persons who develop standardized tests. Most traditional learning is based on this source of knowledge.

I call the second source of knowledge Just-In-Time (J-I-T) Knowledge. This type of knowledge is described as the one that people only "go and get" because it is necessary to address a particular problem or to learn more about something assigned or that is of personal interest to the individual. The advent of technology and the Internet has now made access to J-I-T Knowledge ubiquitous to most teachers and students. Technology has also provided us with software that can personalize learning in a way never before available; and it can personalize learning beyond merely modifying the amount and level of content provided to students. Programs such as Study Island (http://www.studyisland.com), Compass Learning (https://compasslearning.com), and Naviance (http://www.naviance.com), and a program formerly called Renzulli Learning System (now known as GoQuest; http://www.renzullilearning.com) developed at the University of Connecticut (Field, 2009; Renzulli & Reis, 2007) enable teachers to personalize and differentiate learning experiences for their students. For example, the Renzulli Learning System creates an individual profile for each student based on his or her interests, learning styles, and preferred modes of expressions, and a unique search engine matches each profile to high engagement resources according to the ways students have responded to the questionnaire that generates the profile. Teachers can also use this software to review, select, and infuse high-engagement enrichment activities into selected curricular topics or units of study being pursued by individuals, small groups, or entire classrooms. True personalization of learning is now possible through the use of today's technology, and teachers now have at their disposal the tools that allow them to blend together the three types of knowledge described below.

Adults in most practical, work-related, and problem-solving situations use J-I-T Knowledge routinely and the advent of easy-to-use digital age technology has now made J-I-T Knowledge readily accessible to most school-age learners. For example, a middle school student investigating the reasons for the collapse of a large building used National Weather Bureau data to obtain the snow accumulations and temperature records for his region of the country over a 50-year period. He also obtained building code regulations and hypothesized that weight-bearing regulations written decades earlier were insufficient to accommodate present-day large roof building designs. Imagine how dreadfully boring and irrelevant it would be if all students were required to learn or even memorize 50 years of weather data? The student conducting this study, however, needed the information and therefore it became instantaneously relevant.

Today's students are growing up in a world where their access to and familiarity with mobile devices provides them with instant entrée to the wider world of knowledge. The Center for Applied Special Technology (see http://www.cast.org/our-work/publications for a variety of reports) has gathered compelling research and evaluation findings about the influences that technology is having on achievement, higher order thinking skills, and workforce preparation, and the CEO Forum (2001) has argued that technology has had a significant impact on all areas of the curriculum. The warp-speed technological changes taking place in schools today have become one of the most pervasive occurrences having a significant impact on the education system, so much so that technology is actually influencing learning theory itself. Consequently, technology has provided the necessary impetus to reassess more traditional methods and techniques that we use to bring knowledge into the classroom and guide students in its use.

The Content and Methodology of a Discipline

Received Knowledge (Content) and Analyzed Knowledge (Process) form the basis of all disciplines and their role and interaction have been widely discussed by learning and curriculum theorists. Phenix (1964) recommended that a focus on representative concepts and ideas is the best way to capture the essence of a discipline. Representative ideas or concepts consist of themes, patterns, main features, sequences, organizing principles and structures, and the logic that defines a discipline and distinguishes it from other disciplines. Representative ideas and concepts can also be used as the bases for interdisciplinary or multidisciplinary studies. When we select content, the level of advancement, or complexity of material, we must first and foremost take into consideration the age and ability, maturity, previous study, and experiential background of the students. Beyond these considerations, three principles of content selection are recommended (Bransford et al., 2000):

1. Curricular material should escalate along a hierarchy of the following dimensions of knowledge: facts, conventions, trends and sequences, classifications and categories, criteria, principles and generalizations, and theories and structures.
2. Movement toward the highest level, theories and structures, should involve continuous recycling to lower levels so that facts, trends, and sequences, and so on can be understood in relation to a more integrated whole rather than isolated bits of irrelevant information.

3. The cluster of diverse procedures that surround the acquisition of knowledge—that dimension of learning commonly referred to as "process" or thinking skills—should themselves be viewed as a form of content. It is these more enduring skills that form the cognitive structures and problem-solving strategies that have the greatest transfer value.

When we view process as content, we avoid the artificial dichotomy and the endless arguments about whether content or process should be the primary goal of learning. Combining content and process leads to a goal that is larger than the sum of the respective parts. Simply stated, this goal is the acquisition of a scheme for acquiring, managing, and producing information in an organized and systematic fashion. A focus on methodology is the most direct way to prepare young people for their roles as contributors in future fields of professional involvement. A focus on methodology also means more than just teaching students about methods of inquiry. Rather, it is designed to promote an understanding of and appreciation for the *application* of both content and methods to the kinds of problems that are the essence of particular fields of knowledge. The goal of a focus on methodology is, therefore, to cast the young person in the role of a firsthand inquirer rather than mere learners-of-lessons, and to create a mindset that prepares young students for confrontations with knowledge that are the starting point of their own applied and created knowledge.

A Theory of Blended Knowledge

Although philosophers and epistemologists have written for centuries about the general nature of knowledge, the theory presented here is restricted to the acquisition, application, and creation of knowledge in formal (schoolhouse) learning. Thus, the main "ingredients" for developing young minds mentioned above (information, knowledge, and the creative application of knowledge) can be categorized into three general levels of knowledge depicted in Figure 7.1. Before describing each of these three levels, it should be emphasized that while they are hierarchical in level of complexity so far as the powers of mind are concerned (c.f., Bloom's hierarchy), it is the *interaction* between and among all three levels that creates the blended knowledge, which is represented in the center of the three concentric circles in Figure 7.1. And, as indicated above, the investigative learner returns to various levels and sources of knowledge as particular learning situations dictate. This cyclical pursuit and application of knowledge is depicted in Figure 7.2.

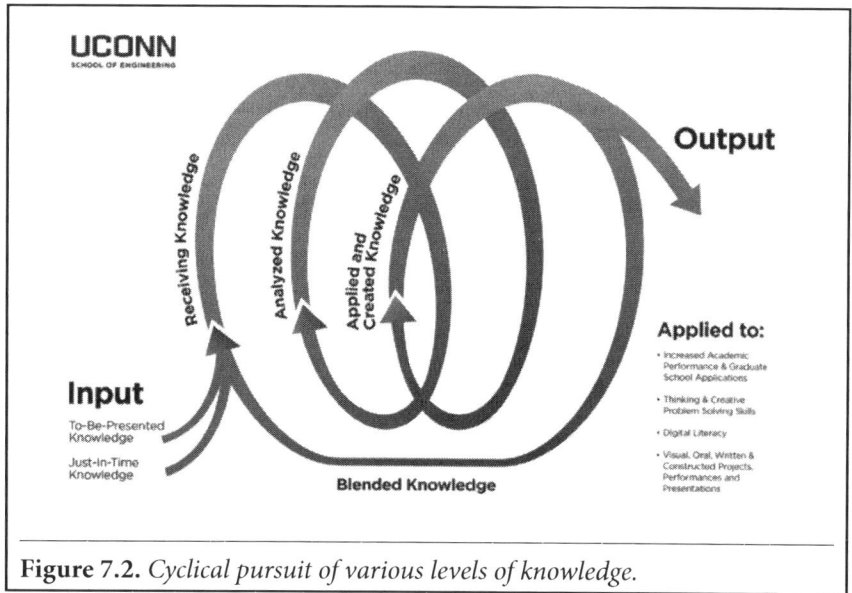

Figure 7.2. *Cyclical pursuit of various levels of knowledge.*

Received Knowledge

The first level of knowledge is Received Knowledge, and this is the type of material most often associated with what traditional schooling is all about. At this level, information and knowledge are frequently used synonymously; however, leading knowledge scholars define small differences (Machlup, 1980). Information captures data at a single point and refers to material that has been given some meaning by way of a relational connection (e.g., Boston and Atlanta are state capital cities). This type of knowledge is the concise and appropriate collection of information but has value only when it is made useful in situations that are relevant to the learner. It refers to a deterministic process where patterns within a given set of information are ascertained (e.g., capital cities are seats of government); what Whitehead (1929) called "inert knowledge" and described as "knowledge that students can exhibit when it is specifically called for (on an examination for instance), but that otherwise plays no roles in their lives" (Bereiter, 2002, p. 309).

Received Knowledge such as facts, data, vocabulary, numeracy, names, dates, and other types of information are typically conveyed to students through lectures, textbooks, worksheets, and various types of digital media. It is the type of information that is usually assessed through standardized achievement tests or "right answer" tests constructed by teachers. Received Knowledge is the foundation for all learning and thus an essential component of the blended knowledge concept that makes up the center of Figure 7.1. The left side of this figure represents the major inputs to the learning process and the right side represents the outputs or what we "take away" from a learning process that blends together three levels of knowledge. Although memorization, note-taking skills, and recall are the main mental processes developed for the acquisition of Received Knowledge, teachers have used attractive materials, the media, and a variety of classroom organization and management techniques to convert "raw" information into meaningful knowledge; and creative teachers have devised ways to make this level of knowledge more interesting and useful to students.

Analyzed Knowledge

The second level of knowledge and the type that has frequently been associated with programs for the gifted is Analyzed Knowledge. This level of knowledge has grown in popularity in recent years due to the focus on 21st-century thinking skills, the process standards included in the Common Core State Standards (National Governors Association Center for Best Practices & Council of Chief State School Officers, 2010), and the Next Generation Science Standards developed by The National Research Council, the National Science Teachers Association, and the American Association for the Advancement of Science (NGSS Lead States, 2013). Kaplan (2009) discussed how this level of knowledge contributes to the depth and complexity that should be a hallmark of curriculum for gifted students. Analyzed Knowledge develops thinking skills such as: interpreting, extrapolating, recognizing attributes, discriminating between same and different, comparing and contrasting, categorizing, classifying, determining criteria, ranking, prioritizing, sequencing, seeing relationships, determining cause and effect, pattern finding, and making analogies. These skills are typically associated with Bloom's higher level thinking categories of analysis, synthesis, and evaluation (Bloom, 1954).

Classroom practices that promote Analyzed Knowledge are much more advanced than merely receiving, storing, and retrieving information. Discussions, debates, simulations, role-playing, critiquing, and questioning that focus on attitudes, values, conclusions, and why, how, and cause-and-effect are typically the ways in which analysis skills are developed. Analyzed Knowledge obviously draws upon Received Knowledge but it also interacts with Received Knowledge in a cyclical manner. When students are working at the analysis level, they may find the need to acquire ("go back") and obtain additional factual information to further examine or scrutinize an argument, point of view, or interpretation of a problem they are addressing. If Received Knowledge is "grist for the mill of the mind," then Analyzed Knowledge is the "relentless grinding" of information that uses Received Knowledge to develop more complex levels of thinking and understanding.

Applied and Created Knowledge

These first two levels of knowledge are both priorities for all of our students. The ability to solve problems evolves from retrieving facts, data, and information and manipulating this material in ways that create meaning for the individual and improve the powers of mind. More advanced levels of problem solving and the construction of knowledge, however, require curiosity, creativity, and the task commitment (Renzulli, 1982) to pursue problems that go beyond acquisition, prescribed problems, and even teacher-assigned problem-based learning activities. These traits should be the focus of programs for developing giftedness and they should constitute the mission of gifted education mentioned above—increasing the world's reservoir of highly creative and productive individuals. It is this broader set of skills that develops the investigative, creative, and entrepreneurial mindsets that are exactly the characteristics that we most admire in people who have made important contributions to their respective fields of endeavor—indeed, the creative and productive people that the larger world ultimately refers to as "gifted."

The best way to promote the use of Applied and Created Knowledge is to ensure that special programs place a major focus on providing opportunities to pursue real problems in investigative and creative ways (Delcourt, 1994; Hébert, 1993; Renzulli, 1982; Westberg, 2010). Real problems differ from other types of assigned problem-solving activities in four basic ways. First, students select the specific problem they want to pursue. This selection may be restricted to an assigned topic or course (e.g., The Civil War in a history course), but within any general or specific topic area opportunities for personalization of interest creates internal motivation because students have choices based on their own interests. For example, within the general topic area of the Civil War, students might choose to study the music, uniforms or women's clothing fashions, fiction, photography, weaponry, human rights, biographies of famous individuals or persons from their hometowns, sea battles, the Underground Railroad, the role of women, or any other issue that holds a particular fascination for the individual or group. A series of general exploratory experiences such as a speaker or virtual field trips to Civil War sites or battlefields can be used to give students ideas about the choice of a problem in which they might develop a sustained interest (see, for example, Type I Enrichment in the Enrichment Triad Model, Renzulli, 1977).

Second, students are guided in procedures for formulating a hypothesis or research question and the use of authentic investigative methodology such as how practicing historians go about investigating a particular area of study. Developing a hypothesis or research question, selecting a topic for creative writing, or designing an artistic or community service project ensures that students extend beyond just "looking stuff up" and reporting it! It is at this point that teachers need to be able to assist students in tracking down how-to books and web resources that guide them in finding and focusing on investigable problems. For example, in a book entitled *Understanding History: A Primer of Historical Method*, Gottschalk (1969) wrote briefly about how practicing historians choose subjects and find information about them:

> The beginner, with or without aid, can easily discover a subject that interests him or her and that will be worthy of investigation—at least at an introductory level. They need only to ask four sets of questions:
> 1. The first set of questions is geographical. They center around the interrogative: "Where?" What area of the world do I wish to investigate? The Far East? Brazil? My country? My city? My neighborhood?
> 2. The second set of questions is biographical. They center around the interrogative: "Who?" What persons am I interested in? The Chinese? The Greeks? My ancestors? My neighbors? A famous individual?
> 3. The third set of questions is chronological. They center around the interrogative: "When?" What period of the past do I wish to study? From the beginnings till now? The fifth century B. C.? The Middle Ages? The 1780's? Last year?
> 4. The fourth set of questions is functional or occupational. They center around the interrogative: "What?" What spheres of human interest concern me most? What kinds of human activity? Economics? Literature? Athletics? Sex? Politics? (pp. 62–63)

The third guideline for investigating a real problem is that there is no single predetermined or "correct answer" or prescribed way for conducting a study. There may be some general procedural standards that apply to research in general, but the creativity literature clearly shows us that people who have taken the road less traveled are often the ones who make innovative breakthroughs in their fields of study (Barron, Montuori, & Barron, 1997; Kaufman & Sternberg, 2006; Sternberg, 1988, 2007).[13] The problems that students pursue should also be "fuzzy" or open-ended ones, and they should be structured in

---

13 John Gurdon, the 2013 winner for the Nobel Prize in medicine was criticized and given low marks by a high school teacher because: "he will not listen and will insist in doing his work in his own way."

such a way that they have the potential to change actions, attitudes, or beliefs. Teacher flexibility and a willingness to entertain and respect learning style differences are important conditions at this stage for promoting creativity and the self-efficacy that Bandura (1977) argued are important contributors to independent growth. The teacher or mentor must truly serve as "the-guide-on-the-side" by giving feedback, making suggestions, recommending and helping students secure resources, and providing general support and encouragement. The skills mentioned above for facilitating Analyzed Knowledge activities can be applied here as well. In many ways, the teacher's role at this stage is similar to a college professor's role when guiding a student through a master's or doctoral thesis. This guidance may refer back to both analysis skills and the need to carry out further searches of the Received Knowledge level described above.

The *raison d'être* of the creative productive person in all societies is to have an impact and create change for one or more intended audiences. That is the reason why writers write, artists paint, builders build, and scientists and engineers produce new products to improve existing work and to make it more effective, efficient, and/or aesthetic. *The main goal of creative producers is to make a difference.*

The final guideline for helping students at the Applied and Creative Knowledge level is to assist young people in exploring potential outlets and audiences for their work. This exploration should begin early in the investigative and creative process because it provides motivation to complete and disseminate students' best work. An exploration of outlets and audiences allow students to become familiar with the formats and genres of the areas and disciplines in which they are working. These opportunities enable students to submit work for publication or display, both in and especially outside the school, to make presentations and performances to special interest groups, and to enter their work into the almost unlimited number of special talent and academic contests and competitions that exist in practically all areas of knowledge. These highly motivating opportunities to publish, present, and perform create real-world experiences to teach students about self-regulation, time management, meeting deadlines, and other executive function skills. One need only examine the legendary success of programs such as the Future Problem Solving Program, National History Day, Intel International Science and Engineering Fair, Invention Convention, and a host of other competitions to understand the role that outlets and audiences play in the creative and productive process.

Summary

This Theory of Blended Knowledge has the most critical relevance for what and how we teach high-potential young people, as it focuses on opportunities for creative productivity within standard curriculum practices, and on how we train teachers of gifted and highly creative students. If one of the goals of gifted education is to increase the world's reservoir of highly creative and productive individuals, we must devote as much attention to Analyzed and Applied and Created Knowledge as we do to requiring students to simply acquire larger and larger amounts of information. One student described her Advanced Placement courses as "test-prep on steroids," and said that she learned more about creativity, joyful learning, and "thinking hard" through working on the school yearbook, participating in the debate club, and preparing for a National History Day competition. *Using and blending* knowledge, both T-B-P and J-I-T, create a different brand of learning, and this brand should be the focus of work with high-potential young people.

This theory simply portrays the ways that different kinds of knowledge interact with one another to produce "blended knowledge" as depicted at the center of Figure 7.1. Learners receive information, but when they begin to analyze this information they may find a need to "go back" and gather additional material for a more advanced analysis. Similarly, when they reach the applied and creative stage, it is often necessary for them to return to the received and applied levels, and "return trips" to these levels are usually based on just-in-time rather than presented information. And in cases when new knowledge, innovative contributions to a field, or even new ways of analyzing data (e.g., Big-C contributions such as Rubin's Causal Model in statistics) are made at the applied and creative level, the innovative person will then have added content that will become part of received knowledge in other learning venues. Although this process is a natural way that learning takes place, an overly standardized test-prep curriculum that severely emphasizes received knowledge can and will "discriminate" against both the analyzed and applied/creative levels of learning. Although this theory ideally can be applied to learning situations for all students, the inclusion of the applied and creative level of knowledge is most associated with the goals that should be allied with programs for gifted and talented students. It is for this reason that the theory presented here has special relevance to the pedagogy advocated in talent development programs. The ways in which we develop curriculum and instructional techniques and train teachers to work with gifted students strives to build an identity that is qualitatively different from general educational theories.

Like any other conceptual formulation, this theory is designed, first and foremost, to generate research testable hypotheses. Are accelerated courses that only provide advanced coverage of received knowledge producing desired results? Does adding analyzed knowledge result in different outcomes? What happens when we add all three levels to produce truly blended knowledge? These questions strike at the heart of the age-old dichotomy in our field between acceleration and enrichment. The Theory of Blended Knowledge described in this article can and should be tested as it asserts that *both* acceleration and enrichment should be important components of gifted and talented programs.

The righthand side of Figure 7.1 represents the outputs of a blended knowledge approach to learning and creative productivity. Increased academic achievement in the traditional sense is mentioned first because, whether we like it or not, any theory that does not include advanced content and the benefits of acceleration is logically flawed and will be rejected out of hand by policy makers and administrators. But a focus on 21st-century skills has caused some reform-minded policy makers to embrace the importance of including Analyzed Knowledge in the goals of general education. It may also be reasonable to assume that these persons will see the value of considering the importance of blending all three levels of knowledge discussed here to further enhance creative productivity in our high potential students. Finally, it may even be reasonable to hope that they may see some logic in giving students at all levels opportunities to engage in some of the activities that promote Applied and Created Knowledge as well as Received and Analyzed Knowledge. The enjoyment, engagement, and enthusiasm for learning that results from blending all three levels of knowledge in the learning process could reduce the achievement gap and the boredom factor that continues to plague so many students in our schools, especially in schools serving low-income students. This challenge may be one of the first research questions that this theory could promote. A blended knowledge theory is particularly relevant to our highest achieving students (regardless of income level) because it represents the *modus operandi* of gifted contributors in the larger world of knowledge construction, usage, and dissemination.

The Theory of Blended Knowledge draws upon the wisdom of intellectual founders in the field of epistemology, takes into account the overstandardization of formal schooling that has taken place over the past several decades, and recognizes the dramatic changes in learning that are now possible through the use of technology. The theory also has special relevance to gifted education because knowledge creation, utilization, and diffusion is what creative and productive people do. The type of learning advocated by this theory is the way that the pursuit of knowledge naturally occurs in "real-world" places. Scientists in research laboratories, writers working on a book or play, and social scientists gathering data to analyze various human behaviors do exactly what this theory specifies. If we want our most able young people to think, feel, and do like practicing professionals, we must include in their overall school experiences these kinds of opportunities to pursue and act on existing knowledge as it is done outside of formal schooling. Although learning in this "natural way" should occur for all students and at all grade levels, mass education and the textbook/testing industrial complex have kidnapped the process by overprescription, a test-prep driven curriculum, and a linear/sequential interpretation of learning hierarchies.

The current focus on deductive, didactic, and prescriptive approaches to "canned curriculum" have resulted in limited opportunities for inductive, investigative, and inquiry approaches to learning. This emphasis has been especially detrimental to our most able students by turning them into efficient lesson learners and consumers of knowledge, but limiting their opportunities for developing high levels of creative productivity and an *investigative learning* mindset. The young people who have the potential to make significant contributions to the arts, sciences, and all other areas that result in economic, social, and culture growth cannot change the world if educators do not integrate applied and created knowledge with advanced content. Like any other theory, I hope this blended knowledge theory will generate research on the parts of interested scholars, and will serve a practical purpose of causing us to reexamine our mission, goals, practices, and especially the ways in which we train teachers who will work with gifted students. An important part of the research that this theory might generate should focus on longitudinal studies of highly creative and productive adults whose work has made a difference in their chosen fields of endeavor and even changed the world. If we want special programs and services for high-potential young people to gain the recognition and support we advocate, the best "data" we can put forward is testimony that demonstrates their gifted programs made a difference beyond merely enabling them to earn good grades, high test scores, and advanced degrees. It must demonstrate that these programs have, indeed, contributed to expanding the reservoir of the world's highly creative and productive individuals.

References

Anderson, L. W., & Krathwohl, D. R. (2001). *A taxonomy for learning, teaching, and assessing: A revision of Bloom's taxonomy*. New York, NY: Longman Publishing.

Bandura, A. (1977). Self-efficacy: Toward a unifying theory of behavioral change. *Psychological Review, 84*, 191–215.

Barron, F., Montuori, A., & Barron, A. (Eds.). (1997). *Creators on creating: Awakening and cultivating the imaginative mind*. New York, NY: Putman.

Beghetto, R. A., & Kaufman, J. C. (2007). Toward a broader conception of creativity: A case for mini-c creativity. *Psychology of Aesthetics, Creativity, and the Arts, 1,* 73–79.

Bereiter, C. (2002). *Education and mind in the knowledge age.* Mahwah, NJ: Lawrence Erlbaum.

Berman, M. (1981). *The reenchantment of the world.* New York, NY: Cornell University Press.

Bloom, B. S. (Ed.). (1954). Bloom's taxonomy of educational objectives, Book 1: Cognitive domain. New York, NY: Longman.

Bransford, J. D., Brown, A. L., & Cocking, R. R. (2000). *How people learn: Brain, mind, experience, and school.* Washington, DC: National Academy Press.

The CEO Forum on Education and Technology. (2001). *Education technology must be included in comprehensive education legislation.* Washington, DC: Author. Retrieved from http://www.hscdsb.on.ca/pdf/publications/5/55/CEO%20Forum%202001%20Policy%20Paper.pdf

Dai, D. Y., & Chen, F. (2014). *Paradigms of gifted education.* Waco, TX: Prufrock Press.

Delcourt, M. A. B. (1994). Characteristics of high level creative productivity: A longitudinal study of students identified by Renzulli's Three-Ring Conception of Giftedness. In R. F. Subotnik & K. D. Arnold (Eds.), *Beyond Terman* (pp. 401–436). Norwood, NJ: Ablex.

Field, G. B. (2009). The effects of the use of Renzulli Learning on student achievement in reading comprehension, reading fluency, social studies, and science. *International Journal of Emerging Technologies in Learning, 4,* 23–28.

Fitch, R. E. (1981). *The knowledge cycle.* Beverly, CA: SAGE.

Gottschalk, L. (1969). *Understanding history: A primer of historical method.* New York, NY: Alfred A. Knopf.

Hébert, T. P. (1993). A developmental examination of young creative producers. *Roeper Review, 16,* 22–28.

Hunsaker, S. L. (Ed.). (2012). *Identification: The theory and practice of identifying students for gifted and talented education services.* Waco, TX: Prufrock Press.

Kaplan, S. N. (2009). The grid: A model to construct differentiated curriculum for the gifted. In J. S. Renzulli, E. J. Gubbins, K. S. McMillen, R. D. Eckert, & C. A. Little (Eds.), *Systems and models for developing programs for the gifted and talented* (2nd ed., pp. 235–252). Waco, TX: Prufrock Press.

Kaufman, J. C., & Beghetto, R. A. (2009). Beyond big and little: The Four C Model of creativity, *Review of General Psychology, 13,* 1–12.

Kaufman, J. C., Beghetto, R. A., Baer, J., & Ivcevic, Z. (2010). Creative polymathy: What Benjamin Franklin can teach your kindergartener. *Learning & Individual Difference, 20,* 380–387.

Kaufman, J. C., & Sternberg, R. J. (2006). *International handbook of creativity.* Cambridge, England: Cambridge University Press.

Machlup, F. (1980). *Knowledge: Its creation, distribution, and economic significance* (Vol. 1: Knowledge and knowledge production). Princeton, NJ: Princeton University Press.

National Governors Association Center for Best Practices, & Council of Chief State School Officers. (2010). *Common Core State Standards.* Washington, DC: Authors.

NGSS Lead States. (2013). *Next generation science standards: For states, by states.* Washington, DC: The National Academies Press. Retrieved from http://www.nextgenscience.org/next-generation-science-standards

Partnership for 21st Century Skills. (2008). *21st century skills, education & competitiveness: A resource and policy guide.* Retrieved from http://www.p21.org/storage/documents/21st_century_skills_education_and_competitiveness_guide.pdf

Phenix, P. H. (1964). *Realms of meaning.* New York, NY: McGraw-Hill.

Plucker, J. A., Beghetto, R. A., & Dow, G. T. (2004). Why isn't creativity more important to educational psychologists? Potential, pitfalls, and future directions in creativity research. *Educational Psychologist, 39,* 83–97.

Renzulli, J. S. (1977). *The Enrichment Triad Model: A guide for developing defensible programs for the gifted and talented.* Mansfield Center, CT: Creative Learning Press.

Renzulli, J. S. (1982). What makes a problem real: Stalking the elusive meaning of qualitative differences in gifted education. *Gifted Child Quarterly, 26,* 147–156.

Renzulli, J. S., Gubbins, E. J., McMillen, K. S., Eckert, R. D., & Little, C. A. (2009). *Systems and models for developing programs for the gifted and talented* (2nd ed.). Waco, TX: Prufrock Press.

Renzulli, J. S., & Reis, S. M. (2007). A technology based program that matches enrichment resources with student strengths. *International Journal of Emerging Technologies in Learning, 2*(3), 1–8.

Sternberg, R. J. (Ed.). (1988). *The nature of creativity—Contemporary psychological perspectives.* Cambridge, England: Cambridge University Press.

Sternberg, R. J. (2007). *Wisdom, intelligence, and creativity synthesized.* New York, NY: Cambridge University Press.

VanTassel-Baska, J., & Brown, E. F. (2007). Toward best practice: An analysis of the efficacy of curriculum models in gifted education. *Gifted Child Quarterly, 51,* 342–358.

Westberg, K. L. (2010). Young creative producers: Twenty-five years later. *Gifted Education International, 26,* 261–270. doi:10.1177/02614294100260031

Whitehead, A. N. (1929). *The aims of education.* New York, NY: Macmillan.

CHAPTER 8

The Enrichment Triad Model
A Guide for Developing Defensible Programs for the Gifted and Talented

Joseph S. Renzulli
University of Connecticut

The whole process of education should thus be conceived as the process of learning to think through the solution of real problems.
—John Dewey, 1938

Introduction From Joe

The Enrichment Triad Model was developed in conjunction with the Three-Ring Conception of Giftedness discussed in Chapter 3 of this book. This model, which is essentially a learning theory, is primarily designed to serve as a practical guide for promoting what I referred to in Chapter 3 as creative productive giftedness. It was originally published as articles in a two-part series (Renzulli, 1976, 1977b) and subsequently a short book (Renzulli, 1977a). Both of these models were greeted with a fair amount of skepticism in the gifted education community because they disagreed with prevailing trends about the conception of giftedness, a focus on advanced lesson-learning approaches to developing giftedness, and the belief that higher level thinking skills were the exclusive province of gifted students only. The Three-Ring and Triad models, however, "got legs," and as they grew in popularity over the years, I gained new insights about issues related to practical strategies for implementing the three types of enrichment around which the Triad Model is organized.

This chapter is an updated version of the original work on Triad and a compilation of the original theory plus various conceptual and practical additions that have been added over the years. The chapter serves as an overview rather than as a practical guide for implementation. Readers interested in the nuts and bolts of implementing the Triad Model are referred to a much more detailed guide that can be found in Chapters 5–7 of our book, *The Schoolwide Enrichment Model: A How-To Guide for Talent Development* (Renzulli & Reis, 2014).

Background

During the course of my involvement in the gifted education movement, I have observed a never-ending quest to define those things uniquely or *qualitatively* different about the types of curricular experiences that should be recommended for gifted and talented students. Indeed, the term *qualitative differentiation* has emerged as one of the field's major contemporary clichés. With the possible exception of the age-old concern about *who* are the gifted, more attention has been given to this search for our identity than any other issue in the theoretical literature. Like searches for the fountain of youth and the pot of gold at the end of the rainbow, this quest for the meaning of qualitative differentiation has largely eluded us. This has resulted in a great deal of controversy and confusion about one of the major issues that could very well determine whether our field will gain the financial and political support necessary to grow and prosper.

My own attempt to deal with the issue of qualitative differences in learning was largely put forth in my book on the Enrichment Triad Model (Renzulli, 1977a). In the intervening years, I have given a considerable amount of thought as to whether or not Triad had the "power" to stand up to the very criticisms described in the early chapters of that book. A good deal of that thought was stimulated by two main influences. First and foremost have been the experiences I have gained as a result of the many Triad-based programs that have developed over the years. It has been my good fortune to have become directly or indirectly involved in many of these programs. Through them I have learned a great deal about "what works," and also what we are capable of delivering in view of our own teacher training services, program planning activities, and resource utilization. These experiences have enabled me to reflect further upon the Triad Model, as well as other models that have been proposed to guide programming for gifted students. As I stated in the original writing about Triad, if we are going to survive and prosper as a specialized field of knowledge, we must become as adept at defining those things for which we stand as we have been in dealing with educational practices to which we are opposed.

The best way to justify the services to students recommended in Triad is to first say a few words about the purpose of gifted education and how we can defend supplementary funds, resources, teacher training, and separate legislative acts, school district and university departments, academic majors and certificate programs, and research endeavors and publications. We can't do this by simply listing all of our traditional clichés (e.g., creative thinking, critical thinking, problem solving, etc.) because education leaders and policy makers have argued in recent years that these higher level thinking skills should be part of the curriculum for all students. And we can't talk about helping these students "achieve their potential" because critics have said that this rationale is a legitimate argument for improving the education of all students.

I have maintained that, in addition to the "achievement-of-potential" argument, *the major purpose of gifted education is to increase the world's reservoir of creative and productive people* —the people who will become the inventors, authors, scientists, artists, entrepreneurs, and the business, political, religious, social, and economic leaders of the future. These are the individuals that philosopher Harold Rudd called "force people," and hopefully, if we create in these people a sense of social responsibility (see Chapter 5), then our field will be producing individuals who will make the world a better place. This purpose of gifted education should not be interpreted as an expectation that we should focus our efforts on potential Nobel Prize winners, best-selling authors, designers, or composers, or other people who have achieved national or world eminence. People can use their creativity and task commitment to make changes that have an impact on local target audiences or even single individuals. And many people progress through levels of impact such as those delineated in Kaufman and Beghetto's (2009) Four C Model of Creativity, which ranges from small-scale contributions (Mini-c) to the everyday (Little-c) experiences of creativity to professional contributions (Pro-c) and finally, eminent (Big-C) levels of creativity.

This standpoint on the purpose of gifted education leads to the types of learning experiences built into the Triad model and the ways in which I define qualitative differentiation. If we want to improve the world's supply of creative productive people, then it is necessary to provide learning experiences for young people to develop an investigative and creative mindset. This is not an argument against curriculum acceleration or advanced lesson learning of received knowledge (see Chapter 7), but it does argue for experiences that emphasize the three types of enrichment that are described in the remainder of this chapter. I believe that acceleration and enrichment are complementary rather than competitive approaches for developing gifted behaviors, but without a balance between these two approaches we are likely to produce smart people who will not make the kinds of contributions that will change the world in little and big ways.

The Enrichment Triad Model

The Triad model is designed to encourage creative productivity on the part of young people by: (1) exposing them to various topics, areas of interest, and fields of study; (2) teaching them how to integrate advanced content, thinking skills, and investigative and creative problem solving methodology to self-selected areas of interest; and (3) providing them with the opportunities, resources, and encouragement to apply these skills to self-selected problems and areas of interest. Accordingly, three types of enrichment are included in the Enrichment Triad Model (See Figure 8.1).

The Triad model is based on the ways in which people learn in a natural environment rather than the artificially structured environment that characterizes most classroom learning conditions. External stimulation, internal curiosity, necessity, or combinations of these three starting points cause people to develop an interest in a topic, problem, or area of study. Children are by nature curious, problem-solving beings, but in order for them to act upon a problem or interest with some degree of commitment and enthusiasm, the interest must be a sincere one and one in which they see a personal reason for taking action. The Enrichment Triad Model is designed to promote the *interaction* between and among the three types of enrichment depicted in Figure 8.1. The arrows in Figure 8.1 are as important as the individual cells because they give the model dynamic properties that cannot be achieved if the three types of enrichment are pursued independently or sequentially. A Type I exposure experience may, for example, have value in and of itself, but it achieves maximum payoff if it leads to Type II or III experiences for one or more students. And the backward arrows in Figure 8.1 are intended to convey paths through which the Type III productions of some students can serve as both Type I and Type II training for other students. In other words, these two types of general enrichment serve to fulfill both awareness and instructional purposes, and they produce maximum pay-off when they also stimulate potential

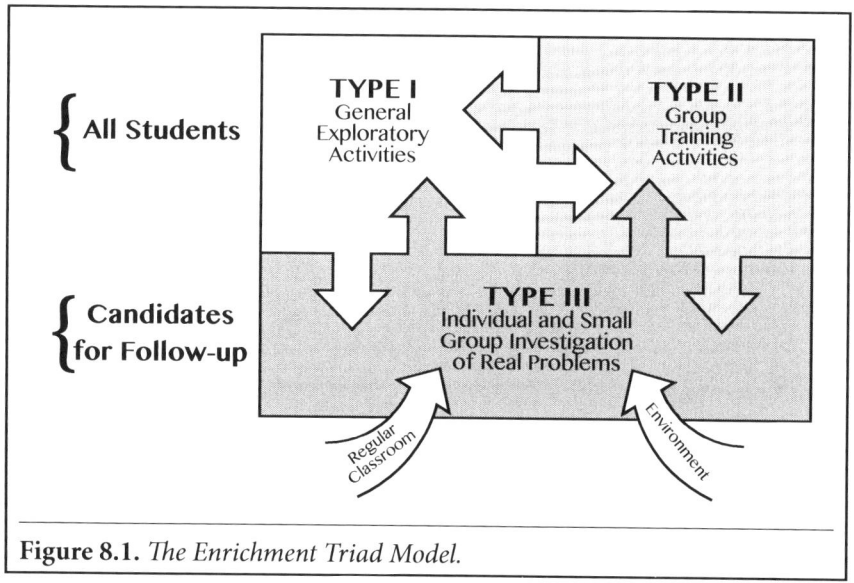

Figure 8.1. *The Enrichment Triad Model.*

new interests on the parts of other students. For example, in one school, a group of students carried out a comprehensive study on lunchroom waste and then presented their work to other groups both within their school and at other schools and community groups.

A major change has taken place in our work over the years and has resulted from our concern about providing a practical organizational model to expand and enhance the delivery of the pedagogical services specified by Triad. In the Schoolwide Enrichment Model (see Chapter 10), we are now recommending that Types I and II Enrichment be provided to larger groups of students than those formally identified as gifted. In some cases, this enrichment can be provided to all students and in other cases, it might be for targeted groups (e.g., advanced math groups, students with a special interest in creative writing). The reason for this change is because formal identification obviously helps us select students with high cognitive and/or achievement levels; however, we may miss students who have great potentials for higher level performance because of high interest and motivation, task commitment, and creativity: traits that are frequently overlooked in formal test-based identification procedures. This change is especially important if we want to examine the potentials of underachieving students, twice-exceptional students, and low-income and minority-group students who typically do not do as well on standardized tests as middle class students. In this regard, it is a good idea to view Types I and II enrichment as *identification situations*[14] that may lead to Type III experiences, which are the most advanced type of enrichment in the model.

The Enrichment Triad Model is the pedagogical core for the organizational structure of our work described in the chapter dealing with The Schoolwide Enrichment Model. The Triad has also been used in a variety of gifted programs, regular classroom curriculum enrichment approaches, and as charter and magnet school themes. The Triad has been adapted and adopted in diverse suburban, rural, and urban schools throughout the country and it is widely used in schools around the world. A special issue of *Gifted Education International* (Renzulli & Reis, 2010) was devoted to worldwide adoptions of this model.

Type I Enrichment: General Exploratory Experiences

Type I Enrichment is designed to expose students to a wide variety of disciplines, topics, occupations, hobbies, persons, places, and events that would not ordinarily be covered in the regular curriculum. In schools using this model, an enrichment team of parents, teachers, and students often organizes and plans Type I experiences by contacting speakers, arranging mini-courses, demonstrations, or performances, or by ordering and distributing films, DVDs, videotapes, or other print or nonprint media. Type I experiences are designed to motivate students to such an extent that they will act on their interests in creative and productive ways. The major purpose of Type I Enrichment is to include, within the overall school program, selected experiences that are purposefully developed to be motivational. This type of enrichment can also expose students to a wide variety of disciplines, topics, ideas, and concepts. Typical Type I methods of delivery include bringing in a guest speaker, creating an interest center, showing videos, directing students to web sites, or hosting a debate.

Type I Enrichment experiences can be based on regular curricular topics or innovative outgrowths of prescribed topics, or stand-alone topics in which teachers think students will have an interest. But in order to qualify as a bona fide Type I experience, any and all planned activities in this category must be designed to stimulate new or present interests that may lead to more intensive follow-up on the parts of individuals or small groups of students. In Type I experiences, students are aware that the activity is an *invitation* to various kinds and levels of follow-up. The most successful Type I experiences

---

14 This concept has gained a good deal of popularity in recent years under the designation of "performance-based assessment."

are dynamic in nature, include some hands-on activities rather than a "straight lecture" approach, and demonstrate investigative and creative opportunities in the topic area. A systematic debriefing of the experience will enable students to envision further involvement and the ways that follow-up might be pursued. Some sample debriefing questions include:

- What did you find interesting about the presentation (field trip, demonstration, website, etc.) and did it make you think of anything else about the topic?
- Which part of the presentation caught your attention?
- Did this presentation raise any questions in your mind?
- What else would you like to know?
- Can you think of another person, place, or thing that would enable us to gain more information about this topic?
- Who would like to conduct a brainstorming session, based on what we have seen today?
- Take a few minutes and write down ideas, thoughts, and emotions that you have, based on what you have seen, heard, and experienced after watching today's presentation. Then let's share what we have discovered.
- Can you think of someone who wasn't here today to see the presentation who would have really enjoyed it?
- What skills do you have that would make this presentation something you would like to pursue further?
- Where could we find more information about this topic?
- Are there any careers that this presentation makes you think of?
- What good ideas can you share about projects, research studies, creative writing, etc. that might be used to learn more about this topic?
- Would anyone like to meet with me individually to explore possible follow-ups to this Type I?

An experience is clearly not a Type I if every student is required to follow up on an activity in the same or similar way. Required follow-up is a regular curricular practice, and although prescribed follow-up certainly has a genuine role in general education, it almost always fails to capitalize on differences in students' interest and learning styles. To make Type I experiences exciting to students, visiting speakers, for example, should be selected for both their expertise and passion about a particular area *and* their ability to energize and capture the imagination of students. Persons presenting Type I experiences should be provided with enough orientation about the model to understand the objectives described previously and the need to help students explore the realms and ranges of opportunity for further involvement that are available within various age and grade considerations. Without such an orientation, these kinds of experiences may not be viewed as exciting opportunities with potential for follow-up.

It is important to incorporate Type I activities into the regular classroom curriculum because these activities need to be seen as rooted in classroom instruction. Following any Type I activity, an assessment of the levels of interest of all students can be conducted and advanced Type I activities that pursue the material in greater depth might be planned for highly interested students. In this case, there is an interest-based rationale for a special grouping or field trip that is different from offering Type I experiences only to high-ability students. A general or introductory Type I should, of course, include all students at given grade levels.

The Type I dimension of the Enrichment Triad Model can be an extremely exciting aspect of overall schooling because it creates a legitimate slot within the curriculum for bringing the vast world of knowledge and ideas that are above and beyond the regular curriculum. It is also an excellent vehicle for teams of teachers, students, and parents to plan and work together on a relatively easy-to-implement component of the model. Type I Enrichment is also an excellent vehicle for getting started in an enrichment cluster.

Type II Enrichment: Group Training Activities

Most educators agree about the need to blend into the curriculum more training in the development of higher order thinking skills. In this section, we discuss a systematic approach for organizing a process skills component, which we refer to as Type II training. Type II Enrichment includes materials and methods designed to promote the development of thinking and feeling processes. Some Type II Enrichment is general, consisting of training in areas such as creative thinking and problem solving, learning how-to-learn skills such as classifying and analyzing data, and advanced research, reference, and communication skills. And some Type II training is very specific because it focuses on a particular discipline or projects upon which students may be working. Type II training is usually carried out both in classrooms and in enrichment programs and includes the development of skills outlined in the following chart:

Taxonomy of Cognitive and Affective Processes

I. Cognitive Thinking Skills
   a. Creative thinking skills
   b. Critical problem-solving and decision making
   c. Critical and logical thinking

II. Character Development and Affective Process Skills
   a. Character development
   b. Interpersonal skills
   c. Intrapersonal skills

III. Learning How-to-Learn Skills
   a. Listening, observing, and perceiving
   b. Reading, note taking, and outlining
   c. Interviewing and surveying
   d. Analyzing and organizing data

IV. Using Advanced Research Skills and Reference Materials
   a. Preparing for research and investigative projects
   b. Library and electronic references
   c. Finding and using community resources

V. Written, Oral, and Visual Communication Skills
   a. Written communication skills
   b. Oral communication skills
   c. Visual communication skills
   d. The acquisition and appropriate application of digital literacy skills and Just-In-Time Knowledge

Type II Enrichment skills are now receiving more attention in general education as a result of the Common Core State Standards (National Governors Association Center for Best Practices & Council of Chief State School Officers, 2010) and the Next Generation Science Standards developed by The National Research Council, the National Science Teachers Association, and the American Association for the Advancement of Science (NGSS Lead States, 2013). There are also a large variety of commercial materials that have been developed to teach specific thinking skills, and we have found that an almost unlimited number of "how-to" books are particularly useful in developing the skills listed in the above chart.

Specific implementation of Type II Enrichment cannot be planned in advance and usually involves advanced instruction in an interest area selected by the student. For example, students who became interested in botany after taking part in a Type I hosted by a local florist pursued advanced training in this area by doing additional reading in botany. These students compiled, planned, and carried out plant experiments while learning about hydroponic research methods from how-to books that they found on the Internet. When we refer to these strategies, we use the term *process skills*, and include examples of specific skills within each of the five general categories listed above. Type II Enrichment also serves a motivational purpose similar to that discussed in connection with Type I activities.

In general, Type II training provides students with various learning opportunities designed to improve their independent learning skills as well as the quality of their personal assignments, projects, and research. Type II Enrichment also includes a broad range of affective training activities designed to improve social and emotional development, interpersonal and intrapersonal skills, and to promote greater degrees of cooperation and mutual respect among students. By placing this instruction within the framework of the regular curriculum, enrichment clusters, and any other special groupings of students, teachers can offer these valuable training activities without the risk of having the training be viewed as an end in and of itself. This category of enrichment has generally been well received by students because it usually involves more hands-on activities and students can begin to see the relevance of these skills for projects that they may want to pursue.

Developing a schoolwide "scope-and-sequence" of Type II resources should be a major responsibility of the Schoolwide Enrichment Team but the entire faculty should always be on the lookout for materials and resources that they believe would be worthwhile additions to the scope-and-sequence.[15] And teachers who become proficient in the use of any particular set of process skills should be asked to share their expertise with other members of the faculty. Material selection and use should be considered a long-term and ongoing undertaking. Specific resources should be classified by the taxonomy listed above and cross-referenced by grade levels and students' developmental levels. Almost all process skills can be introduced at early grade levels and reinforced with more advanced-level resources as students progress through the grades. Teacher and student feedback should be used to determine the effectiveness of

---

15 An example of a scope-and-sequence chart can be found on pages 143–144 of our book on the Schoolwide Enrichment Model (Renzulli & Reis, 2014).

Type II training and replacements should be sought when selected materials are not doing the job well.

Type III Enrichment: Individual and Small-Group Investigations of Real Problems

Works of theorists such as Jean Piaget (1976), Jerome Bruner (1960, 1973), Leta Hollingworth, (1926), and John Dewey (1909) provided a part of the rationale for the original Enrichment Triad Model (Renzulli, 1976), but the ways that people learn in the outside-of-school world was what fascinated me and subsequently led to the guidelines for Type III Enrichment. The model was fashioned into a series of creative instructional methods and curricular practices that found their way into programs for high-ability students looking for ideas to offer opportunities in addition to merely accelerating the regular curriculum. Essentially, Triad was developed to motivate and engage students by exposing them to various topics and areas of interest, offering instruction in thinking skills, creative problem solving, and investigative methodology, and providing them with the opportunities, resources, and encouragement to apply these content and process skills to selected areas of interest. The biggest "payoff" of the Triad model is having students engage in the kinds of Type III Enrichment that will be described in this section of the chapter. In many ways, Type III Enrichment is based on the ways in which people learn in a natural environment rather than the artificially structured classroom and prescribed curriculum environments that characterize most school learning situations. Type III Enrichment incorporates investigative activities and the development of creative products in which students assume roles as firsthand investigators, writers, artists, or other types of practicing professionals. Although students pursue these kinds of involvement at a more junior level than adult professionals, the overriding purpose of Type III Enrichment is to create situations in which young people are thinking, feeling, and doing what practicing professionals do, even if at a less sophisticated level than adult researchers, writers, or entrepreneurs. Bona fide Type III experiences incorporate the following four characteristics of what makes a problem real:

1. Personalization of interest
2. Use of authentic methodology
3. No existing solution or "right" answer
4. Designed to have an impact on an audience other than or in addition to the teacher

Type III Enrichment is the vehicle through which everything from basic skills to advanced content and process skills blend together into student-developed products and services. In much the same way that all of the separate but interrelated parts of an automobile come together at an assembly plant, this form of enrichment serves as "the assembly plant of mind." This kind of learning represents a synthesis and an application of content, process, and personal involvement. The student's role is transformed from one of lesson-learner to firsthand inquirer, and the role of the teacher changes from an instructor and disseminator of knowledge to a combination of coach, resource procurer, mentor, and "guide-on-the-side."

When teachers work with students to reach this highest level of enrichment, they create in students the most rigorous kind of learning because students pursue a study or project of their own selection that is either related to a unit being studied or a topic that is of extreme interest to a student. The goals of Type III Enrichment are summarized in Figure 8.2.

A Few Examples of Type III Enrichment Projects

The best way to understand what Type III Enrichment is all about is to look at a few examples that point out roles that teachers, students, and even parents play in the Type III process.

- A parent drove her child and other students to architecturally significant buildings in their community so they could photograph them and subsequently design and build scale models. They researched the buildings' histories and presented their findings, models, photos, and the "talking biographies" of each building at a town shopping mall.
- A math teacher who is passionate about origami conducted a Type I demonstration about how to make different origami figures and followed up by serving as a mentor to a student who wanted to pursue a more in-depth Type III project and enter her work in an origami competition. This teacher also helped a second-grade student use origami to create Japanese paper cranes, which were subsequently suspended from the ceiling of the school library.
- An advanced first-grade student wrote and illustrated an ABC book about the animals in Africa and used it to teach her classmates about the alphabet and African geography.
- A third-grade student created and illustrated a dictionary and audio recording identifying items in architecture in two languages. He used his work to teach other students about this topic.

	Type III Enrichment Summary Sheet
Definition	Investigative activities and artistic productions in which the learner assumes the role of a firsthand inquirer; the student is thinking, feeling, and acting like a practicing professional.
Target Audiences	Individuals and small groups of students who demonstrate sincere interests in particular topics or problems and who show a willingness to pursue these topics at advanced levels of involvement.
Objectives	1. To provide opportunities in which students can apply their interests, knowledge, creative ideas, and task commitment to a self-selected problem or area of study. 2. To acquire advanced level understanding of the knowledge (content) and methodology (process) that are used within particular disciplines, artistic areas of expression, and inter-disciplinary studies. 3. To develop authentic products that are primarily directed toward bringing about a desired impact upon a specified audience. 4. To develop self-directed learning skills in the areas of planning, organization, resource utilization, time management, decision making, and self-evaluation. 5. To develop task commitment, self-confidence, feelings of creative accomplishment, and the ability to interact effectively with other students, teachers, and persons with advanced levels of interest and expertise in a common area of involvement.
Key Concepts	• Personalized learning by doing. • Real purpose applied to the production of a real product for a real audience. • Student's role is transformed from lesson learner to firsthand inquirer. • A synthesis and application of content, process, and personal involvement.
Action Forms	• Action Information Message* • Management Plan for Individual and Small-Group Investigations* • Type III Mentor Matrix* *In chapter and online

Figure 8.2. *Summary of Type III Enrichment.*

- A fifth-grade student studied bullfighting and moderated a debate on ethical issues related to this sport for a group of students in his classroom.
- A middle school student wrote a historical fiction novel on her family's immigration chronicle and prepared illustrated copies for several family members.
- A group of secondary students wrote, produced, and were the actors in an original play for a drama competition.
- A student interviewed his neighbor, who was a Brooklyn Dodger baseball player with Jackie Robinson, the first African American to play professional baseball. He wrote an article that was published in a local newspaper.
- A student learned to cook with her mother and grandfather. Neither her mother nor grandfather measured any ingredients nor were the recipes written down. Fearful that the great food they produced would one day be lost, she made working recipes that she and her siblings could replicate. She created a family cookbook that included photographs and short segments about memories of each dish and subsequently shared the cookbook with family members and other interested persons.
- A student interviewed his family members about their memories of 9/11. Although it is a current event for adults, 9/11 is history for our students. His uncle was in the military and provided a unique perspective. His mother, father, and grandfather all provided their memories, and the student compiled them in a book.

A good way to "test" whether or not student products are bona fide Type IIIs is to reflect upon them using the questions in Figure 8.3. If the "answers" are the same as those indicated in the following box, then we can be assured that students' work meets the criteria we are seeking for high-level applications of this concept.

Each Type III topic and product idea is almost inevitably germinated by an enrichment experience about something that happens to trigger the interest, either in or out of school. Many excellent resources are available to help students consider their interests and the potential Type III Enrichment projects they might like to pursue. Thanks to the Internet and the types of electronic resources such as the one described in Chapter 14 of this book, young students in almost any part of the world can have access to a wealth of resources that were previously available to only a very small group of scholars and adults. In excellent Type III studies, students select both the topics and the products they wish to pursue. And in a certain sense, the teacher builds the curriculum

Criteria For Type III Enrichment		
	Yes	No
1. Did every student do it?		X
2. Should every student do it?		X
3. Could every student do it?		X
4. Would every student want to do it?		X
5. Did the student do it willingly and enthusiastically?	X	
6. Did the student use appropriate resources and methodology?	X	
7. Was the work directed toward having an impact upon an audience other than or in addition to the teacher?	X	

Figure 8.3. *Criteria for Type III Enrichment.*

around the child as depicted in Figure 8.4. Rather than define each product and determine the content and outcomes prearranged in typically prescribed curriculum, teachers help guide and facilitate the learning process of individuals and small groups. Teachers provide support and guidance for planning, organization, decision making, resource procurement, audience finding, and editorial assistance to bring product quality to its highest level. The experience becomes a dynamic learning environment where a students' gifts and talents emerge in creative and investigative ways, but the student (not the teacher) is in charge of his or her own learning. Each student's unique blend of interests are developed and celebrated. The management plan in Figure 8.5 is designed to guide students toward focusing on problem finding and focusing, exploring various product formats and possible outlets and audiences, and procuring the resources necessary to carry out their work in a professional way.

Follow-up studies with numerous young adults who participated in Triad-based programs (Delcourt, 1993; Hébert, 1993; Starko, 1988; Westberg, 2000) have almost always revealed that one or more of their Type III experiences have been determining factors in making decisions about college majors and career choices. And many respondents to follow-up inquiries point out how their own professional contributions can be traced back to work carried out in Triad programs.

The *most important things* students have "taken away" from their Type III Enrichment projects are obviously a greater interest in and expertise for

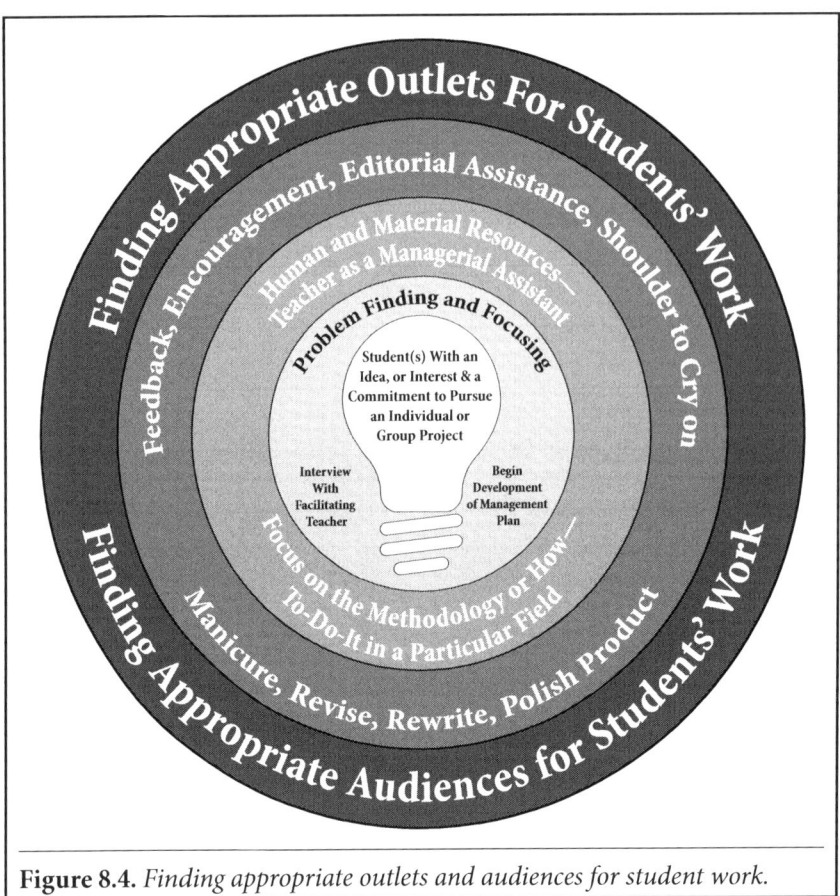

Figure 8.4. *Finding appropriate outlets and audiences for student work.*

examining a topic of their own choosing in a rigorous and highly professional way. They also developed a set of advanced-level thinking skills and a creative and investigative mindset that is transferable to a much broader range of competencies essential for future work and careers that place a premium on creative productivity. These skills include increased self-efficacy—a belief that they can do something that was bigger, more robust, and more challenging than what they have previously done in school. They also developed important executive function skills such as organizational and time management skills, self-regulation, task commitment, goal orientation, a strong work ethic, the ability to work cooperatively with others, and the communication skills that allowed them to share their work with target audiences. Mostly, they learn that this "assembly plant of the mind" can make the learning process itself a more joyful experience than simply acquiring and storing information. It is for

Management Plan for Individual and Small-Group Investigations

Name: _____ Grade: _____ Estimated Beginning Date: _____ Ending Date: _____
Teacher: _____ School: _____ Progress Reports Due on Following Dates: _____

General Area(s) of Study (Check all that apply)
☐ Language Arts/Humanities ☐ Science ☐ Personal and Social Development
☐ Social Studies ☐ Music ☐ Other (Specify) _____
☐ Mathematics ☐ Art ☐ Other (Specify) _____

Specify Area of Study
Write a brief description of the problem that you plan to investigate. What are the objectives of your investigation? What do you hope to find out?

Intended Audiences
Which individuals or groups would be most interested in the findings? List the organized groups (clubs, societies, teams) at the local, regional, state, and national levels. What are the names and addresses of contact persons in these groups? When and where do they meet?

1. _____
2. _____
3. _____
4. _____
5. _____

Intended Product(s) and Outlets
What form(s) will the final product take? How, when, and where will you communicate the results of your investigation to an appropriate audience(s)? What outlet vehicles (journals, conferences, art shows, etc.) are typically used by professionals in this field?

Methodological Resources and Activities
List the names and addresses of persons who might provide assistance in attacking this problem. List the how-to books that are available in this area of study. List other resources (films, collections, exhibits, etc.) and special equipment (e.g., camera, tape recorder, questionnaire, etc.). Keep continuous record of all activities that are part of this investigation.

Getting Started
What are the first steps you should take to begin this investigation? What types of information or data will be needed to solve the problem? If "raw data," how can it be gathered, classified, and presented? If you plan to use already categorized information or data, where is it located and how can you obtain what you need?

Figure 8.5. *Management plan for individual and small-group investigations.*

these reasons that I continue to advocate for the Triad model as an essential approach for talent development in young people.

References

Bruner, J. S. (1960). *The process of education*. New York, NY: Random House.
Bruner, J. S. (1973). *Beyond the information given: Studies in the psychology of knowing*. New York, NY: Norton.
Delcourt, M. A. B. (1993). Creative productivity among secondary school students: Combining energy, interest, and imagination. *Gifted Child Quarterly, 37,* 23–31.
Dewey, J. (1909). *How we think*. New York, NY: D.C. Heath.
Hébert, T. P. (1993). Reflections at graduation: The long-term impact of elementary school experiences in creative. *Roeper Review, 16,* 22–38. doi:10.1080/02783199309553529
Hollingworth, L. S. (1926). *Gifted children: Their nature and nurture*. New York, NY: Macmillan.
Kaufman, J. C., & Beghetto, R. A. (2009). Beyond big and little: The Four C Model of creativity, *Review of General Psychology, 13,* 1–12.
National Governors Association Center for Best Practices, & Council of Chief State School Officers. (2010). *Common Core State Standards*. Washington, DC: Authors.
NGSS Lead States. (2013). *Next generation science standards: For states, by states*. Washington, DC: The National Academies Press. Retrieved from http://www.nextgenscience.org/next-generation-science-standards
Piaget, J. (1959). *Language and thought of the child*. East Sussex, UK: Psychology Press.
Renzulli, J. S. (1976). The Enrichment Triad Model: A guide for developing defensible programs for the gifted and talented. *Gifted Child Quarterly, 20,* 303–326.
Renzulli, J. S. (1977a). *The Enrichment Triad Model: A guide for developing defensible programs for the gifted and talented*. Mansfield Center, CT: Creative Learning Press.
Renzulli, J. S. (1977b). The enrichment triad model: A guide for developing defensible programs for the gifted and talented: Part II. *Gifted Child Quarterly, 21,* 237–243.
Renzulli, J. S., & Reis, S. M. (2010). The Schoolwide Enrichment Model: A focus on student strengths and interests. *Gifted Education International, 26,* 140–156.
Renzulli, J. S., & Reis, S. M. (2014). *The Schoolwide Enrichment Model: A how-to guide for talent development* (3rd ed.). Waco, TX: Prufrock Press.
Starko, A. J. (1988). The effects of the revolving door identification model on creative productivity and self-efficacy. *Gifted Child Quarterly, 32,* 291–297.
Westberg, K. L. (2010). Young creative producers: Twenty-five years later. *Gifted Education International, 26,* 261–270. doi:10.1177/02614294100260031

CHAPTER 9

The Multiple Menu Model for Developing Differentiated Curriculum[16]

Joseph S. Renzulli
University of Connecticut

Introduction From Joe

Some of the best curriculum I have ever seen has been developed by teachers of the gifted, and I have admired these contributions because they have blended together the best aspects of acceleration and enrichment activities. I designed the Multiple Menu Model for my curriculum development course and emphasized that high-quality curriculum must take into account characteristics about knowledge (e.g., the Structure of Knowledge, Basic Principals and Functional Concepts, the Methodology of Disciplines, and Applications of Knowledge) as well as the variety of instructional strategies with which most teachers of the gifted are familiar. The part of the model I like best is called the

---

[16] Renzulli, J. S. (2009). The Multiple Menu Model for developing differentiated curriculum. In J. S. Renzulli, E. J. Gubbins, K. S. McMillen, R. D. Eckert, & C. A. Little (Eds.), *Systems and models for developing programs for the gifted and talented* (2nd ed., pp. 353–382). Waco, TX: Prufrock Press. Copyright 2009 Prufrock Press. Adapted with permission.

Artistic Modification Menu because it invites teachers to put their own personal interests and experiences related to a selected topic into the curriculum. Most prescribed curriculum doesn't encourage teacher modifications. The invitation to teachers to personalize a topic invariably leads to more exciting and engaging experiences on the parts of their students.

Thinking ability is not a substitute for knowledge; nor is knowledge a substitute for thinking ability. Both are essential. Knowledge and thinking are two sides of the same coin. —R. S. Nickerson

Anyone who sets out to develop curriculum will come face to face with two unavoidable realizations. First, developing curriculum is a difficult and demanding process. It involves far more thought and work than "slapping together" a bunch of information and activities, no matter how exciting these activities may be. An extraordinary amount of effort is necessary to produce material that reflects established curricular principles and creates authentic, relevant, and personally meaningful instructional activities.

A second realization is that present-day curriculum writers generally agree about underlying principles for developing curriculum. Most of these principles, invariably phrased as "should" statements, point out the need for curricular experiences that focus on identifying the curriculum standards to be addressed in the unit of instruction, focusing instruction on abstract concepts, selecting the content and process skills that will be introduced to the students and used to develop student activities, and determining the assessment devices to judge student performance and acquisition of knowledge. These same "should" lists typically include principles that call for cooperative efforts between content scholars and teachers or instructional specialists in designing the curriculum. However, these principles are far too general to provide the kinds of specific guidance necessary for the practical job of writing curricular units of instruction. Knowing, for example, that a curricular unit should focus on higher level thinking skills and advanced content is valuable, but this knowledge does not tell curriculum writers how to identify appropriate content or skills, how to examine various instructional sequences and activity options, or how to prepare a blueprint for fitting together the pieces that will allow content and process to work together in a harmonious and effective fashion. The Multiple Menu Model attempts to address these issues by providing a management plan that allows curriculum developers to select content and strategies from a number of options or "menus" that draw upon theories of knowledge, instruction, and curricular design.

Understanding the Rationale of the Multiple Menu Model

In order to design effective curriculum, the curriculum writer must first understand how knowledge within a discipline is constructed. Disciplines have evolved as discrete entities over centuries as the result of the different kinds of questions researchers have asked and the different research methodologies they have developed to answer them. The Multiple Menu Model was created to help curriculum designers use the information on how knowledge develops to create interesting and more authentic units of instruction. When the designer understands how knowledge develops, choices about which content and which instructional approaches to use in the unit become explicit.

A Brief Theory of Knowledge

The theory of knowledge underlying the Multiple Menu Model is based on the three levels of knowing first suggested by the American psychologist and philosopher, William James (1885). These levels include knowledge-of, knowledge-about (also referred to as knowledge-that), and knowledge-how.

Knowledge-of

This entry level of knowing might best be described as an awareness level. Knowledge-of consists of being acquainted with, rather than familiar with a topic. James (1885) referred to this level as "knowledge by acquaintance" to distinguish it from more advanced levels, which he referred to as "knowledge by systematic study and reflection." For example, a layperson may be knowledgeable of a field of study called astrophysics and might even know something about what astrophysicists study; however, it would be inaccurate to say that this person is knowledgeable about astrophysics in any way other than on a very superficial awareness level.

Knowledge-of involves remembering (storage of knowledge), recollecting (retrieval of knowledge), and recognizing, but this level does not ordinarily include more advanced processes of the mind. Most curriculum development efforts begin with the knowledge-of level, but proceed quickly to the knowledge-about level because this level represents the systematic study and reflection that James used to distinguish between lower and higher levels of knowing.

Knowledge-About

Knowledge-about represents a more advanced level of understanding than merely remembering or recalling information. Knowledge-about builds upon remembering and recalling, but it also includes more advanced elements of knowing such as distinguishing, translating, interpreting, and being able to explain a given fact, concept, theory, or principle. Being able to explain a given fact, concept, theory, or principle may involve the ability to demonstrate it through physical or artistic performance (e.g., demonstrating a particular dance movement) or through a combination of verbal and manipulative activities (e.g., demonstrating how a piece of scientific apparatus works).

Among the most important decisions a curriculum developer makes is to determine how much knowledge-about to include in a unit, lesson, or lesson segment and the depth or complexity of coverage. It is at this knowledge-about level that learners must begin to deal with the underpinnings of the discipline. In order to move from acquaintance with facts to mental facility and practical use of content in a field, students will need to understand key concepts that organize the discipline, essential principles that govern the concepts, and ways in which practicing professionals in the field do their work. Teachers who do not have an extensive background in the knowledge area in which they plan to develop curricular units will need to acquire the knowledge. They could take formal courses, study the topic independently, or team up with content specialists in the area in which they plan to develop curricular units. A carefully selected introductory college textbook in a content field is usually the most economical way to begin acquiring the knowledge base necessary for curriculum development in a given field.

Knowledge-How

This level of knowing represents types of knowledge that enable individuals to construct their own meanings and make new contributions to their respective fields of study. In the knowledge-how level, a person applies investigative methodology in order to generate knowledge-about aspects of a given field of study. Most knowledge experts consider the appropriate use of methodology to be the highest level of competence in a content field. It represents the kind of work that is pursued by researchers, writers, and artists who are making new contributions to the sciences, humanities, and the arts. It is this level of knowledge that is typically missing from curricular units of instruction, yet it is this level of knowledge that seems to yield the most excitement from students who are placed in the role of "firsthand inquirers" by using the methodological skills of the practicing professional.

These three levels, especially the second and third levels, also exist on a continuum from the simple to the complex. The curriculum developer is responsible for determining the degree of complexity appropriate for a given age or ability group. In the final analysis, it is the curriculum developer's understanding of the content field and instructional techniques plus an understanding of cognitive and developmental psychology that will determine the level of knowledge and content that is appropriate for a particular age group. Much of this understanding comes as a result of experience working with students of varying ages and instructional levels.

In the Multiple Menu Model, the theory of knowledge represented by James's three levels is used in harmony with Alfred North Whitehead's (1929) concepts of romance, technical proficiency, and generalization. For example, according to Whitehead, a young person might develop a romance with (or interest in) the field of medicine while still at the knowledge-of level. This person might pursue the romance (interest) to the point of technical proficiency and become a practitioner in one of the medical professions. Most professionals within a field reach their maximum involvement at the level of technical proficiency, however a few go on to the generalization level. It is these persons who say, in effect, "I want to add new information and contribute new knowledge to the field of medicine." This third level is, in many respects, consistent with one of the major goals of special programming for high-ability students.

Changes in Curriculum Theory

Curriculum theory has taken a major turn in a different direction with the advent of easy access to the Internet by most learners, teachers, and curriculum developers. No longer are teachers and textbooks the "gatekeepers" of knowledge; now any student, teacher, or curriculum developer can draw upon knowledge that was previously restricted to scholars who had the skills, the time, and the resources to examine the millions of documents collected in the archives of past and present civilizations. At the same time, certain basic principles of curriculum development remain constant, but can be integrated with the remarkable advances in instructional communication technology to produce high-quality curriculum and to make the work of the curriculum developer easier. Figure 9.1 represents an attempt to convey to the curriculum developer the relationship between basic principles of curriculum development and a theory of knowledge that provides a perspective for the underpinnings of the Multiple Menu Model.

The section at the top of the diagram represents all knowledge (obviously broadly categorized) and the sources of information that curriculum developers draw upon in constructing learning experiences for young people. What knowledge will be drawn from this almost unlimited reservoir of information is, in part, a function of the ways in which the curriculum developer understands how knowledge is organized in the general categories listed on the face of the cube. We have indicated above the importance of certain organizational categories such as principles, generalizations, and concepts, which form the "backbone" of any particular area of study, but the curriculum developer might want to illustrate a concept or broad interdisciplinary theme such as freedom by finding a landmark event, supportive set of statistics, or a highly illustrative trend that exemplifies a basic principle or concept. And here is where the characteristics of the learner mentioned above can also be taken into account. Younger students might gain insight into the concept of freedom by reading and discussing one or more stories from *Classic Fairy Tales* (Foreman, 2005), whereas older students might explore the topic by reading selected parts of *Aunt Harriet's Underground Railroad in the Sky* (Ringgold, 1995). Using the Internet, the curriculum developer can easily locate materials such as these books that will enhance discussions about the concept of freedom. In the Theory of Knowledge depicted in Figure 9.1 (Renzulli, 2004), this type of search represents the use of what is referred to on the righthand side of the model as "Just-In-Time" knowledge—knowledge that one locates because it fulfills a particular need. Information about the facts, principles, or concepts, on the other hand, is classified as "To-Be-Presented" knowledge—basic information around which the study of freedom is organized.

The face of the cube in Figure 9.1 represents the ways in which knowledge is organized. The curriculum developer should view this organizational pattern as a "menu" from which various levels and categories of knowledge will be included in a unit of study. An understanding of the differences between and among these categories provides guidance for introducing balance into the curriculum and guarding against producing curricular materials that may be overloaded at the factual level. Each category is important in this theory of knowledge; however, deeper levels of understanding result when the more complex and abstract categories such as theories and structures become the focus of student activities. And at the upper end of student participation in any curricular unit of study, what William James called "knowledge how," we find a category called *investigative methods*. This is the dimension of curriculum development

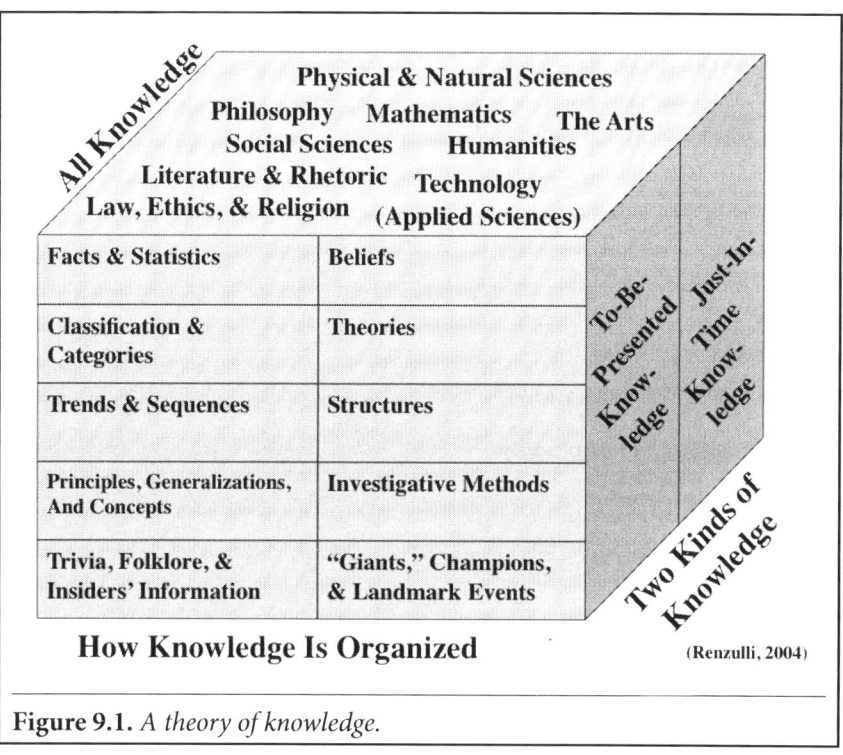

Figure 9.1. *A theory of knowledge.*

in which the student is guided toward becoming a firsthand inquirer in a particular domain. In other words, the student's role changes from one of being a consumer of knowledge and thinking skills to that of being a producer of knowledge.

Selected Concepts From Theories of Curriculum and Instruction

The rationale underlying this model draws upon the work of several other theorists who have made important contributions to curricular and instructional theory, Jerome Bruner and Philip Phenix. Bruner (1960, 1966) believed that inductive instruction should be the focus of teaching and that content could be taught to any student at any level of development, "that any subject can be taught to any child in some honest form" (Bruner, 1971, p. 71). A major responsibility of the teacher, according to Bruner, is to help the student understand the structure of the subject. This task requires that students learn the fundamental ideas of a subject and how they relate to each other, and he suggested that teachers employ a spiral curriculum to accomplish this goal. In a spiral curriculum, the teacher presents the material at the child's level in an interesting manner. Then as the student moves through the educational process, the teacher presents the same ideas in greater depth and in more complex ways.

Philip Phenix's contributions to curriculum development can be found throughout the Multiple Menu Model. In his work, "Realms of Meaning" (1964), he addressed the problem of curriculum in light of the "knowledge explosion" and provided four criteria for selecting appropriate content. First, he suggested that content for instruction should be drawn from organized scholarly disciplines or fields of inquiry. It becomes the role of the teacher to mediate the knowledge from these scholarly disciplines so that the knowledge has relevance and meaning for students. Second, Phenix (1964) argued that material should be typical and characteristic of the discipline from which it was taken. By selecting content material in this manner, the representative ideas "stand for" large quantities of material, allowing the curriculum developer to be economical in the amount of material selected. The third criterion requires that materials be selected to "exemplify the methods of inquiry in the disciplines" (p. 333). The methods of inquiry or the manner in which practicing professionals in the disciplines create new knowledge defines the discipline. Knowledge and curriculum content are always changing, but the basic means of inquiry change very little. This type of learning leads to a better understanding of the discipline or field of study and also encourages active student participation. Phenix's (1964) fourth criterion demands that material be "selected so as to appeal to the imagination of the students" (p. 342). This criterion addresses student motivation and interest. Because students learn best when they want to know, student imagination is the means to make the educational experience meaningful. Thus it becomes important for the curriculum writer to select material and design activities that tap into the interests of the students.

The Multiple Menu Model is also based on the ideas of a group of theorists and researchers including Ausubel (1968), Bandura (1977), Bloom (1954), Gagné and Briggs (1979), Kaplan (1986), Passow (1982), Tomlinson (1999), and Ward (1960). The work of these persons, coupled with our own ideas about the process of learning, has given rise to this approach to writing curriculum. Although these writers have influenced the development of the Multiple Menu Model, some of them might disagree with the applications of their work. For example, the Multiple Menu Model relies heavily on Bloom's taxonomy for major sections of the Knowledge and Instructional Objectives Menus, but changes the placement of certain segments in the taxonomy. The largest change deals with the category of Application (Bloom's Level 3), which for the purposes of curriculum development and the Multiple Menu Model will be considered a product or outcome of all of the other processes listed in the taxonomy.

Applying Theory to the Construction of the Multiple Menu Model

The Multiple Menu Model was developed as a way for educators to design curricular units that place a premium on both the organization and pursuit of knowledge and the application of investigative methodologies as they pertain to a particular discipline or field of study. It requires teachers to identify a discipline's principles and concepts and to carefully reflect on how they can share the meaning of these ideas with the young people with whom they work. It encourages the curriculum writer to offer students opportunities to apply the research methodologies that practicing professionals use in their fields of study. The curriculum writer needs to consider all of these elements because it helps students develop deep understandings of the subject matter, grounds students' learning in meaningful and authentic contexts, and equips students with the skills used by practicing professionals so they can apply them in learning new information. This type of curricular planning helps students pursue the depth and complexity of a discipline and its content, rather than learning surface-level content knowledge.

Because of the accelerated rate at which knowledge is expanding today, we have organized The Multiple Menu Model to address the selection of content and the selection of procedures in a way that maximizes the transfer of learning to new situations. The model concentrates on the various structural elements of a discipline and focuses instruction on the basic principles, functional concepts (Ward, 1960), and methodologies within that discipline. Teachers should view principles and concepts as tools that help the learner understand any and all of the selected topics of a content field. Information of this type is referred to as "enduring knowledge," as opposed to time-sensitive topics or transitory information. For example, understanding the concept of reliability is central to the study of psychological testing; reliability, therefore, may be considered an enduring element of that field. The specific reliability of any given test, however, is more timely or transitory in nature because it changes over time (and from test to test). It is the type of information that learners can always "look up" and understand if they have a basic comprehension of the more enduring concept of reliability.

In a similar fashion, the Multiple Menu Model deals with content selection by focusing on what Phenix (1964) called representative topics. These topics consist of any and all of the content in a field that the curriculum developer might choose as the focus of a unit, lesson, or lesson segment. For example, a teacher might choose *The Merchant of Venice* as a representative literary selection to illustrate the key concept of a tragic hero. He or she may also integrate other selections that employ this key concept into the unit of study, and a second or third selection might be necessary if an instructional objective is to compare and contrast tragic heroes. It is not necessary to cover an extensive list of selections if one or a few representative literary selections can convey the concept. Similarly, a teacher can cover the biological topic of tropism by selecting phototropism as the major focus of a unit and then making reference to other tropisms (geo-, hydro-, chemo-, and thigmo-) that are based on the same general principle. Students should, of course, have the opportunity to follow up on related topics if they develop an advanced interest.

The Multiple Menu Model emphasizes process objectives that have broader transfer value such as application, appreciation, self-actualization, and improved cognitive structures. In other words, this model views representative topics as *vehicles* for process development, not ends in and of themselves. The structural dimensions and key concepts mentioned above provide the learner with tools for examining any topic in a given discipline. This model views the learner as one who is developing, practicing, applying, and gaining an appreciation of a particular segment of knowledge by studying a representative topic. The student may then use the same strategies to examine other topics.

This model also emphasizes appropriate use of methodology within content fields. All content fields can be defined, in part, by the research methods and investigative techniques that are used to add new knowledge to that field, and most knowledge experts consider the appropriate use of methodology to be the highest level of competence in a content field. Indeed, research scientists, composers, authors, and academicians who are making new contributions to their fields typically operate at this level. Although this level requires an advanced understanding of a field and sometimes requires the use of sophisticated equipment, young students can successfully learn and apply some of the entry-level methodologies that are associated with most fields of knowledge (Bruner, 1960). A focus on the acquisition and application of methodology encourages more active learning and an active involvement with a content field.

The Structure of the Knowledge Menu

The Multiple Menu Model provides curriculum developers with a set of practical planning guides or menus to help them in the process of combining authentic knowledge with instructional technique. Just as software programs such as Microsoft® Word present menus to help users create documents, each menu in this model offers a range of options from which the curriculum developer can choose. Each menu represents the knowledge segments that will form the basis for a curricular unit, lesson, or lesson segment and the various instructional techniques that will enable the knowledge to be taught in an interesting and effective manner.

Using the Knowledge Menu

The Multiple Menu Model focuses on inquiry, asking curriculum developers to select the most important concepts and ideas to share with learners. The Knowledge Menu requires educators to examine a discipline from four perspectives: its location and organization within the larger context of knowledge, its underlying principles and concepts, its methodology, and its most representative topics and contributions to the universe of knowledge and wisdom.

These perspectives become the components of the instructional unit. The first three sections or perspectives of the Knowledge Menu are considered "tools." The final section represents the topics within any field to which the tools may be applied as one goes about the process of "studying" a topic.

Section I—Structure of Knowledge: Helping Students Understand the Location, Definition, and Organization of a Field of Knowledge

Teachers designing curriculum units based on the Multiple Menu Model must first locate the targeted discipline in the larger domain of knowledge in order to provide students with an overview of the unique perspectives each discipline or field of study offers in understanding complex phenomena. Next, teachers should examine with their students the characteristics of the discipline and subdivisions to learn why people study a particular area of knowledge and what they hope to contribute to human understanding. This first dimension of the Knowledge Menu helps students examine questions such as "What is sociology?" "What do sociologists study and why?" "How is sociology similar to and different from other disciplines (e.g., psychology and anthropology)?" "What, then, is social psychology or social anthropology?" and "How does each fit into the larger picture and purpose of social sciences?" These questions about the structure of the discipline help students gain an understanding of not only where the discipline is located, but also the discipline's connectedness with other disciplines.

Relationships within a discipline and between disciplines can be best illustrated by using teacher and student graphic organizers, or Knowledge Trees such as the example provided in Figure 9.2. Curriculum writers can also organize a series of instructional activities that provide an overview and address introductory questions about the specific field of study such as the following:

1. How is this field of study defined?
2. What is the overall purpose or mission of this field of study?
3. What are the major areas of concentration of each subdivision?
4. What kinds of questions are asked in the subdivisions?
5. What are the major sources of data in each subdivision?
6. How is knowledge organized and classified in this field or subdivision?
7. What are the basic reference books in the field or subdivision?
8. What are the major professional journals?
9. What are the major databases? How can we gain access to them?
10. Is there a history or chronology of events that will lead to a better understanding of the field or subdivision?
11. Are there any major events, persons, places, or beliefs that are predominant concerns of the field, or best-case examples of what the field is all about?
12. What are some selected examples of "insiders' knowledge" such as field-specific humor, trivia, abbreviations and acronyms, "meccas," scandals, hidden realities, or unspoken beliefs?

Introductory activities should motivate students to study a particular field and help them develop an interest. For example, in a high school psychology course, an instructor we observed always began the course by showing slides of Sigmund Freud and other early leaders and telling students a few anecdotes related to Freud's most famous cases. This introduction piqued students' interest, and they began to ask inquisitive questions about the information. Similarly, we watched a fourth-grade teacher effectively introduce her students to the study of anthropology by bringing in pictures, artifacts, and stories from another culture. She showed a video of a group of cultural anthropologists researching the ways members of a culture view their world. Through the

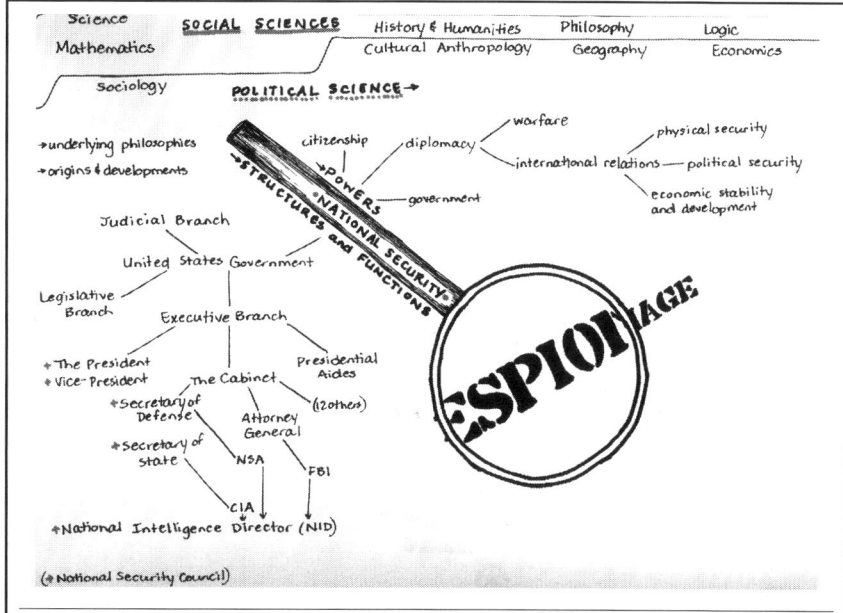

Figure 9.2. *Knowledge tree from unit on espionage. From* Real Patriot Games *by Ann Murdock, 2006. Copyright 2006 Prufrock Press. Reprinted with permission.*

video, she was able to begin exploring the following questions, escalating the level of interest in anthropology and setting the stage for future learning:

- What is human about human beings, and how do we get those qualities?
- What are the common characteristics of different cultures?
- How does the culture change to accommodate different ideas and beliefs?
- What is valued in a culture?

She asked her students to look through the artifacts and speculate on the stories they might tell about a culture and how their own culture tells something about their beliefs, values, and traditions. Eventually, she wanted the students to use the skills of an anthropologist to study a culture and to consider their own culture and how the culture helps define who they are.

The outcome of this particular segment of the Knowledge Menu should lead students into an examination of the questions listed above, in each case with regard to a specific field or subdivision of the field around which a curricular unit is being developed. Not every question needs to be explored, nor should this section of the Knowledge Menu necessarily be considered a major focus of the unit of study. Rather, the purpose is to help learners see the "big picture" and the interrelationships that might exist between a field in general and its various subdivisions. This section of the Knowledge Menu is also designed to provide an overview of the field of study. A teacher might deal with the third question (What are the major areas of concentration of each subdivision?) in a relatively superficial way during the early stages of a unit, but when he or she reaches the last section of the Knowledge Menu (Representative Topics), this topic may become a major area of concentration in the study of a particular subdivision.

Section II—Identifying the Basic Principles and Functional Concepts: Helping Students Get the Big Idea

The second dimension of the instructional unit focuses on identifying and selecting the most important ideas in a particular field of study that need to be explored by the students. Every field of knowledge is built on a set of basic principles and key concepts, and they help facilitate comprehension, information processing, and communication of information that is representative of the essence of the field. These principles and concepts consist of themes, patterns, main features, sequences, and structures that define an area of study. Some of these principles and concepts are applicable to several subdivisions within a given field, but ordinarily the subdivisions have a few concepts that are unique to that branch of knowledge. Indeed, subdivisions of major fields of knowledge probably come into being because of unique concepts (as well as other factors) that result in the establishment of a field's individual identity or a particular subdivision of that field.

Basic principles are generally agreed upon truths that have been arrived at through rigorous study and research. Principles are often stated as relationships among concepts, they concisely summarize a great deal of information, and they have the potential to provide information that applies to diverse situations. While these principles can be viewed as "enduring truths," they may need to be modified in the future in light of new evidence. Principles may be factual and concrete (e.g., in order to survive, a civilization must be able to answer the basic biological needs of its members: food, drink, shelter, and medical care) or abstract and open to various interpretations (e.g., each culture views the physical environment in a unique way, prizing aspects of it that may be different from those prized by others). When carefully worded, teachers can use these statements as the organizational framework of a curricular unit. Principles help learners probe the "big ideas" of a discipline and help teachers get to the heart of the content. We have found that when teachers carefully consider these principles as the central organizers of the unit, they are better equipped to explain to students the relevance of the content to their lives.

Functional concepts (Ward, 1960) are the intellectual instruments or tools with which a subject area specialist works. In many ways, these concepts serve as the vocabulary of a field and the vehicles by which scholars communicate precisely with one another. Concepts are powerful organizers of meaning that help label and make sense of large quantities of information within a field of knowledge. Unlike facts, which are limited to specific situations, concepts are broad enough to apply to many sets of conditions. A good way to identify the functional concepts of a field is to examine the glossary from a basic textbook in that field or highlighted words in a teacher's instructional manual. Like principles, there is usually a high degree of general agreement among scholars in a particular field about the meaning of functional concepts. Using principles and concepts as the focus of curricular studies is particularly useful because of the potential they hold for organizing large quantities of information together in some meaningful manner, generating student inquiries which in turn can lead to enhanced understanding and student involvement, and illustrating the interconnections between and among various disciplines.

In looking at concepts as organizing frames of reference, Brandwein (1987) suggested that when curriculum is developed it should create a plan or a structure for seeking, recognizing, and valuing experience. If constructed correctly, a curriculum helps learners select what is meaningful and useful in their lives. He further explained that the structure of a particular curriculum has at least three characteristics:

1. It has a body of concepts, and these concepts will be useful for recognizing the elements and details of the subject matter.
2. The concepts will control the procedures (or modes) chosen for inquiry.
3. The concepts (and modes) lead to other concepts and modes as learning proceeds.

Theoretically, this process is never-ending. Brandwein (1987) provided an explanation of how using concepts and principles as the unit's conceptual framework allows for variety, for comparison and contrast, and for exploration and discovery:

> Knowledge is, in a sense, organic: it grows. In the social sciences, for example, there are such major concepts (often called "conceptual themes") as interaction between social groups, market choices in an economy, and resolution of international conflict. Subsidiary and lesser concepts exist, of course. In social interaction, there are subsumed the concepts of group, family, community, leadership, cit-

izenship, and the like. In market economics there is a range of subsidiary concepts, such as gross national product, balance of trade, the cost of production of goods and services and currency. These concepts can be thought of as a shorthand of conceptual language: they are the sentences of conceptual grammar. Thus the concepts of price, goods, and services are linked in the concept-statement: "The price of goods and services in an otherwise unregulated market depends on supply and demand." Such a statement is for common purposes generally "true." In the sciences there are major concepts (or conceptual themes): life, matter, energy, interdependence, and continuity. In the humanities there are truth, beauty, justice, love and faith. These are stated in terms that the teacher grasps immediately. But the child's comprehension and language are, of course, different. (p. 36)

He further explained the difference between constructing curriculum that focuses on topics and those that are designed around conceptual ideas:

A concept opens up a variety of experience, of intelligible content. It leads to analysis and synthesis. It is not concepts but encyclopedic "topics" that tend to be rigid and confined in sequence. A topic can be "lectured." A concept is "sought" and perhaps "caught" in good time. One can "finish" a topic; a concept grows. In fact, in teaching say history or economics, a topical sequence is extremely rigid, for it states inflexibly the body of knowledge that is meant to be "covered." A conceptual sequence, on the contrary, allows for variety, for comparison, and contrast, for exploration and discovery. It depends on problem-posing that varies within the idiosyncratic modes of inquiry. (p. 36)

In this section of the Knowledge Menu, curriculum writers determine which basic principles and functional concepts will become the focus of the instructional unit. Teachers must ask themselves important questions as they begin the curriculum planning process: "What is it that I am trying to teach an understanding of? What is it about cultures (for example) that I want my students to understand?" After selecting these principles and concepts, the curriculum writer can then begin to create a series of learning experiences that will help students uncover the meaning behind these conceptual ideas. The learning experiences should motivate students to explore, discover, examine, question, and scrutinize the principles and concepts so that they render meaning for the students; they should not simply mention or cover the concepts in some artificial manner. Developing a unit that has students construct an understanding of a discipline's principles and concepts helps students apply and transfer their understanding to other topics and to other disciplines.

Section III—Knowledge About Methodology: Helping Students Act Like Practicing Professionals

The third section of the instructional unit focuses on designing instructional activities that engage students in exploring research-based inquiries that are common to a particular field of study (e.g., in a study of plants, activities that lead students to use methods and procedures used by a botanist). There are two types of methodologies: general and specific. The first type deals with the research method used by practitioners in a field to seek answers to their questions and to make contributions to a discipline. Although these methods may vary across disciplines, they generally involve the following series of investigative procedures:

1. Identify a problem within a content field.
2. Find and focus a problem within an area of study.
3. State hypotheses of research questions.
4. Identify sources of data.
5. Locate and construct appropriate data-gathering instruments.
6. Classify and categorize data.
7. Summarize and analyze data.
8. Draw conclusions and state generalizations.
9. Report findings.

Although general college-level textbooks can be a useful and economical source of information for locating knowledge about the other sections of the Knowledge Menu, we found that information about the research methodologies used in various fields is seldom included in these sources. As a result, we suggest that teachers begin to gather a comprehensive collection of methodological resource books, sometimes called how-to books (e.g., how to conduct a science experiment, how to conduct oral history interviews) that can be used to teach students the skills necessary for acquiring knowledge about a specific field's methodology. Other useful sources of information are laboratory manuals that frequently accompany college-level textbooks.

The second type of how-to methodology is more domain specific and assists the researcher in completing the more comprehensive tasks outlined above. For example, a student might learn how to conduct a survey in order to locate and construct appropriate data-gathering instruments needed for a research study. This section of the Knowledge Menu is especially important for curriculum development because it affects the more active kinds of instructional techniques a teacher can select to use in his or her unit. By providing students with the know-how of investigative methodology, teachers increase the probability of more inductive or "hands-on" learning experiences. Once students have learned basic information about a field or topic and the procedures for doing some kind of research related to that topic, they can proceed to the application level—the level considered by many to be the highest level of involvement in a field of study. Student investigations may be limited in scope and complexity, and they frequently may follow prescribed scenarios such as the ones typically found in laboratory manuals or how-to books. Nonetheless, including even junior-level investigative activities in curricular materials forces teachers to go beyond the omnipresent didactic mode of instruction that has been the subject of so much criticism of education (Goodlad, 1984).

What is asked of teachers in this section is to design learning experiences that will engage students in the methodologies of the discipline being studied. Teachers who write their instructional units using this model will explain, illustrate, and involve students in the process of research as defined by the methodology dimension of the Knowledge Menu (e.g., identify a problem area in the study of archaeology, focus the problem, state a hypothesis, locate resources, classify and organize data, draw conclusions, report findings) and/or create situations for students to apply the domain-specific methodologies to acquire new information. These clusters of diverse methodological procedures that surround the acquisition of knowledge—that dimension of learning commonly referred to as "process" or thinking skills—should themselves be viewed as a form of content. It is these more enduring skills that form the cognitive structures and problem-solving strategies that have the greatest transfer value. When teachers view process as content, they avoid the artificial dichotomy and the endless arguments about whether content or process should be the primary goal of learning. Combining content and process leads to a goal that is larger than the sum of the respective parts. The goal is to place students in situations in which they acquire, manage, and produce information in an organized and systematic fashion by applying the thinking and research processes that are used to create this knowledge in the first place. We believe that when students are armed with the tools learned in the Knowledge Menu and have acquired a more mature understanding of the methodology of the field, they are no longer passive recipients of information; they are able to begin the process of gaining and then generating knowledge within the field.

Section IV—Knowledge About Specifics (Representative Topics): Helping Students Apply Basic Principles and Concepts

The fourth section of the unit focuses on the last dimension of the Knowledge Menu and encompasses the main body of knowledge that makes up the content of any given field. In this section, teachers will help students apply the "tools" from Sections I, II, and III to selected representative topics in order to acquire an understanding of a specific discipline's content. Unlike traditional instruction, which asks teachers to cover an entire text by the end of the year or semester, the Multiple Menu Model asks teachers to winnow out from all of the possible topics in a field the few that truly represent the field's principles and concepts. By narrowing the scope of information to be taught and selecting representative topics, a teacher can focus on finding interesting and dynamic issues that maximize student interest, motivation, and enthusiasm about a particular field of study. For example, there are thousands of studies in psychology that deal with principles of animal learning, but an unusually interesting study (e.g., Skinner's famous experiments on classical conditioning with pigeons) might have more motivational power than less dramatic studies, especially if presented through an engaging film or demonstration. Examples of representative topics from five fields of knowledge are listed in Table 9.1.

Knowledge About Specifics provides a vast warehouse of information from which selected aspects of content may be drawn and to which the "tools" can be applied. The subcategories listed under "Knowledge About Specifics" in Figure 9.3 are based on the first level of Bloom's (1954) taxonomy. This analysis of the various ways in which knowledge is organized is helpful in identifying organized components of a particular field. When examining a content area for curriculum development, it may not always be easy to classify a topic according to the subcategories listed in Figure 9.3. For this reason, curriculum developers should consider selecting content based on the ways in which topics are organized in standard (college-level) text and reference books. After a teacher has developed a unit, he or she should review the material in an effort to identify facts, conventions, trends, and sequences. The teacher should call these subcategories to the attention of students, either through direct instruction or by asking them to analyze material according to the ways in which "Knowledge About Specifics" are classified.

The following example illustrates how a teacher used this dimension of the Multiple Menu Model in a literature course. This teacher explored a concept in literature—tragic heroes—through intensive examination of three prototypical examples (e.g., *The Merchant of Venice*, Joan of Arc, and *The Autobiography of Malcolm X*). Selecting more than a single exemplar of the concept allowed for both in-depth analysis and opportunities for students to compare and contrast authors' styles; historical perspectives; ethnic, gender, and cultural differences;

Table 9.1
Examples of Representative Topics

Field	Representative Topics
Botany	Applying the principles of botany in understanding the problems of deforestation in the rain forests.
Geography	Applying the concept of regionalization to world geography or world history. In history, students can apply the concept of regionalization in analyzing the South, or students can apply the concept of regionalization and its effect on voting behavior in a particular area.
Mythology	Exploring how various myths (from various cultures) and descriptions of their main characters reveal cultural belief systems of the past that were largely mysterious.
Cytology	Applying knowledge of the principles and concepts of cells to engage in debates on genetic testing, closing, mutations, etc.
Microbiology	Examining the relationship between the dumping of animal waste and the health of a stream.

and a host of other comparative factors that single selections would prohibit. The aim of the instruction in the beginning stages of the unit was to assist students in understanding the concept of tragic heroes and why it was being studied. One of the main purposes of the first three sections of the Multiple Menu Model is to learn *how* to study tragic heroes; therefore *who* should be studied (i.e., which tragic hero) was less important as long as the hero was representative of the concept. An emphasis on *how* rather than *who* also legitimized a role for students. The payoff as far as transfer was concerned was to follow up the in-depth coverage with more advanced learning that focused on factors that define the concept of tragic heroes (e.g., characteristics, themes, patterns, etc.).

To continue to build this cognitive understanding of the tragic hero and to apply literary analysis skills, students formed small interest groups to compile categorical lists and biographical summaries of tragic heroes in sports, politics, science, civil rights, religion, the women's movement, arts and entertainment, and other areas in which students expressed special interest. It is in these small groups that students began to understand the concept in literature known as the tragic hero.

Once students have learned how to analyze a particular concept and after they have explored categorical representatives of the concept, students may show an interest in exploring this area in greater detail (e.g., investigating the lives or exploits of tragic heroes and heroines). The beauty of this approach is that students first gain the "tools" for studying a topic; they can then apply those tools to their own interest area.

A. Knowledge about Facts
This category includes knowledge about dates, events, persons, research findings, and terminology. Information such as time periods in history or ages in paleontology would also be included in this category. Knowledge about Facts might include single circumscribed bits of information (e.g., the date of the battle of Lexington and Concord) or entire chains of events (e.g., the chronology of the battles of the Revolutionary war). Also included in this category is knowledge about sources of information, particular books, data tables, and compilations of facts associated with various fields of study.

B. Knowledge about Conventions
This category includes rules, formulas, common symbols and representational devices (e.g., the symbols used on a weather map), and the forms that are commonly used to represent work in a particular field (e.g. verse, narrative, story boarding, scientific papers). The rules of grammar, usage, punctuation, and spelling for written and spoken language are a good example of Knowledge about Conventions.

C. Knowledge about Trends and Sequences
This category represents interrelationships between and among specific pieces of information in a field. The relationships may be temporal or chronological (e.g., the sequence of events in a plant's reproduction cycle), but in almost every case knowledge about trends and sequences involves some types of causal relationship. Thus, for example, plant reproduction, stock market increases, or a decline in the infant mortality rate can usually be studied from a cause and effect perspective. Some trends and sequences might be based on direct, obvious, and factual relationships, or they might be complex, subtle, and open to many different interpretations.

D. Knowledge about Classifications and Categories
This category deals with grouping information according to various elements of commonality. In many cases, these categories serve as the basis or organizational theme through which a topic can be studied in a systematic matter. Types of literature, forms of government, and classes of plants or animals are all examples of how information is classified for more organized study and ease of understanding. Classifications and categories are extremely useful tools in helping students manage large amounts of information, and they also help facilitate meaningfulness between and among individual pieces of information by calling attention to common characteristics, themes, or structures.

E. Knowledge about Criteria
This category deals with the quantitative and qualitative standards by which information, objects, or events are judged. Quantitative (i.e., numerical) standards are usually easier to learn than qualitative criteria. Thus, it is far easier to teach students to judge a poet by the number of publications than by the quality of an individual work. Qualitative analysis represents extremely mature levels of development in any field. Curriculum developers should devote some attention to providing students with knowledge about criteria (both quantitative and qualitative) even if they do not expect entry level students to engage in sophisticated judgments. For example,

Figure 9.3. *Knowledge about specifics.*

> younger students might be made aware of various criteria by which literary material is accepted for publication, even if their present level of development does not allow them to make sophisticated judgments. Knowledge about criteria is always the beginning point for more sophisticated applications that take place at a later point.
>
> **F. Knowledge about Principles and Generalizations**
> This category deals with the major ideas and broad abstractions that help to summarize and organize large quantities of information about a given discipline. Typically, they include abstract statements that help to explain, describe, predict, or determine the most appropriate and relevant action or direction to be taken. Principles and generalizations become the organizational structures under which specific facts and events can be placed and assist students in seeing the "whole picture" of a particular phenomena. For example, in geography, there are many principles and concepts that geographers consider important (i.e., the location of an area in relation to other places helps to explain its pattern of development; the character of a place is not constant—it reflects the place's past, present use, and future prospects). The challenge to the teacher is to identify the principles and concepts that become the foundation for the curricular units they are writing. This foundation helps set the stage for determining how they will assist their students in uncovering what is meant by these statements of relationship among concepts.
>
> **G. Knowledge about Theories and Structures**
> This category deals with the interrelationships between a body of principles and generalizations which are interrelated to form a theory or structure. When teachers ask students to explain the structure and organization of Congress or even the local city government, they are asking students to explain how various governmental systems interact, what their main purpose is, and how these systems help citizens accomplish a particular goal. The explanation of the structure requires that students reach a level of sophistication in organizing this information to illustrate a complete understanding of this concept called government. Knowledge of theories and structures is the most abstract category, because of the abstract thinking required to generate and understand these types of interrelationships.

Figure 9.3. *Continued*

The Instructional Techniques Menus

Engaging students in the act of learning requires much consideration by the curriculum writer. Planning a unit involves a number of instructional decisions that are critical and must be made consciously and purposefully. Viewed broadly, the Instructional Techniques menus require educators to carefully consider how learning will take place as students interact with the content. The types of decisions that teachers make regarding which instructional techniques they will use to assist young people in the acquisition and application of knowledge become as important in the curriculum planning process as selecting the content for the instructional unit. The deeper the pool of strategies from which a teacher can select, the more variety he or she can offer students as they set about making meaning from these organized learning experiences.

The next menus from the model focus on pedagogy, organization, and the sequence of lessons. Specifically, these menus provide curriculum developers with a range of options related to how they will engage students in the process of "uncovering" the authentic content of the Knowledge Menu.

The Instructional Objectives and Student Activities Menu

This combined menu of instructional objectives and student activities (see Figure 9.4) is designed to provide the curriculum developer with a taxonomy of processes and behaviors that are used by learners as they construct knowledge about a discipline. This menu reminds the curriculum designer that in a well-balanced curriculum, activities must address both content and process objectives. The balance provides learners with practice in the spectrum of encoding and recoding activities associated with learning new information. By clarifying the process skills and sharing the objectives of the activities, students learn to identify and control their own thinking patterns and behaviors.

The first category of the menu (Assimilation and Retention) deals with information input or pickup processes. At this level, teachers need to decide how the students will acquire information about a particular event, topic, or concept: Will students take notes as they read a particular book? Will students need to make observations of a particular event and record the information on a chart? The second category (Information Analysis) focuses on a broad range of thinking skills that describe the ways in which information can be processed in order to achieve greater levels of understanding. At this level, teachers consider how their students will interact with the information: Will students be asked to compare and contrast pieces of information, tabulate data they have gathered, make predictions based on data they have collected, or summarize information? The third category (Information Synthesis and Application) deals with the output or products of the thinking process. At this level, teachers will make decisions to suggest avenues in which students can create new ways of using the information they have gathered or analyzed: Will students use the information to create a new model or explanation, produce a book, make a presentation, or develop a new theory? The final category (Evaluation) is also an output process, but in this case the focus is on the review and judg-

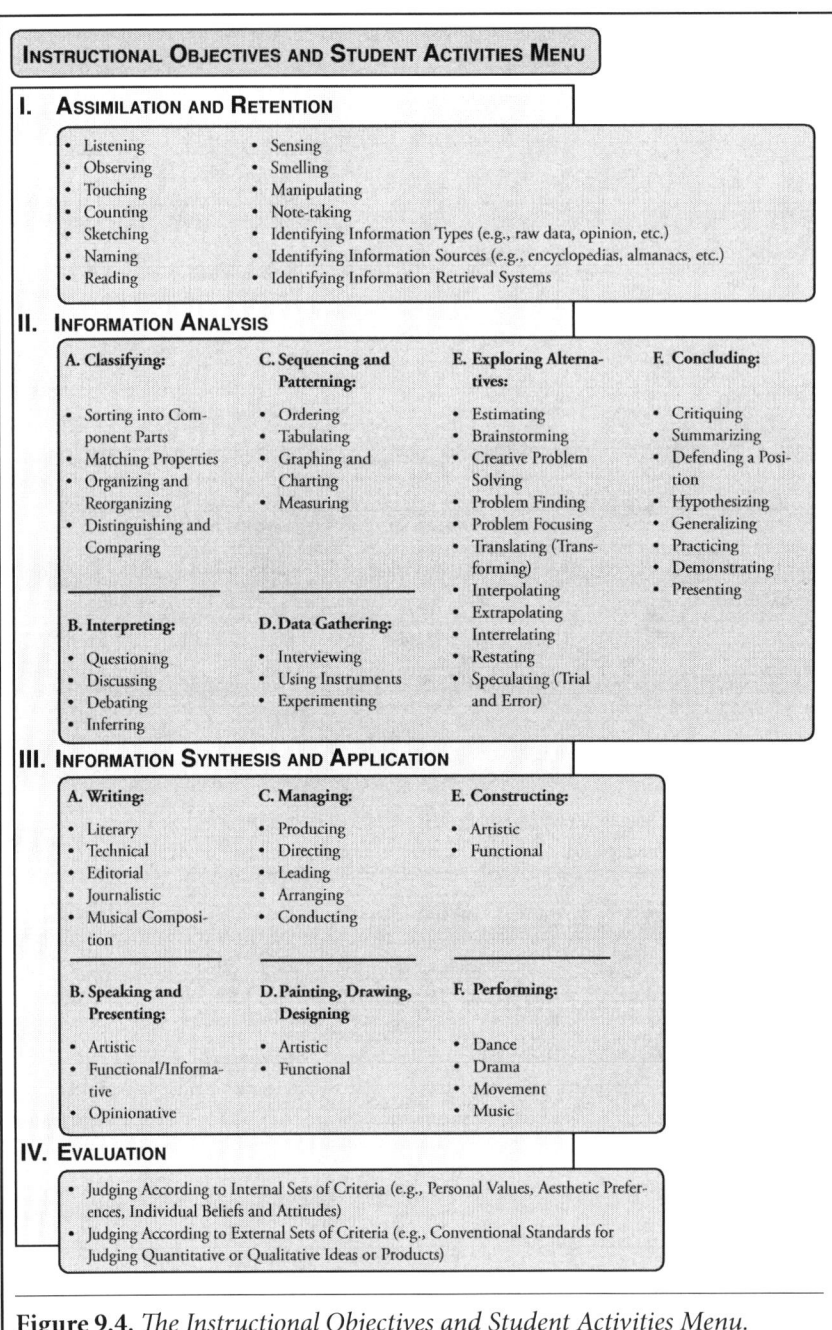

Figure 9.4. *The Instructional Objectives and Student Activities Menu.*

ment of information in terms of aesthetic, ethical, and functional qualities. Teachers engaging students at this level might generate activities that help students judge the quality of a solution or determine whether something is worthy of receiving merit.

There are three important considerations the curriculum developer should keep in mind when using this menu. First, the four categories on this menu are not intended to be followed in a linear and sequential fashion. In the real world of thinking and problem solving, one must often cycle back to lower levels of information input and analysis activities in order to improve the scope and quality of the products and judgments. The overall process, therefore, must be viewed as a cyclical or spiraling sequence of interrelated activities rather than a linear chain of events.

The second consideration relates to the general goal of achieving both specificity and comprehensiveness in the overall process of curriculum development. Each unit and lesson should be developed in such a way that the curriculum writer is as certain about the process objective as he or she is about the content to be taught. Over a given period of time, the teacher should attempt to achieve comprehensiveness in process development by selecting a diverse range of objectives and student activities. In this regard, the curriculum developer should use this menu and the other instructional techniques menus as checklists that will help achieve balance as well as a catalog of processes from which selections can be made.

Finally, we have designed the objectives and activities in this menu to embrace the full range of affective processes. We have assumed that processes such as attending, receiving, and valuing take place in an integrated fashion when students pursue activities set forth in this menu and when such activities are combined with certain topics (knowledge) that enhance the development of affective processes. For this reason, we did not include a separate affective menu in the model.

Instructional Strategies Menu

The next menu, the Instructional Strategies Menu, provides a broad range of teaching strategies (e.g., discussion, dramatization, independent study) that represent the ways in which teachers organize learning situations. A variety of carefully selected instructional strategies from this menu provides students with multiple ways to be engaged with knowledge and to employ the full range of their intellectual abilities and learning styles. The strategies range from highly structured teaching methods to those in which greater degrees of self-directedness are placed upon the learner. Many of the strategies are used in combination with one another.

As is the case with the menus discussed earlier, teachers should make an effort to achieve a balance in the use of these strategies. They should also work to develop curricular experiences for students that favor the less structured end of the instructional strategies continuum. This recommendation is consistent with the emphasis that educators place on both self-directed learning and creative productivity. Finally, teachers should attempt to match certain strategies with particular types of knowledge. Thus, for example, the simulation or role-playing strategy might fit more appropriately with content dealing with a controversial issue, and the programmed instruction strategy would work well with content designed to teach computer operation skills.

Figure 9.5 lists various instructional strategies teachers use to engage young people in the act of learning. This list does not represent every instructional strategy, but it provides the curriculum writer with numerous options to consider when designing curricular activities.

Instructional Sequences Menu

The Instructional Sequences Menu (Figure 9.6) is based on the work of major learning theorists such as Gagné and Briggs (1979) and Ausubel (1968). Ausubel placed considerable stress on meaningful learning, which involves relating the content of the lesson to the student's knowledge base, experiential background, and capacity to learn. He argued that "the most important single factor influencing learning is what the learner already knows. Ascertain this and teach him accordingly" (Ausubel, Novak, & Hanesian, 1978). The specific aspects of their work that are reflected in this menu deal with the organization and sequence of events that help maximize the outcomes of a preplanned learning activity. This menu differs from the others in that the items are likely to be followed in a sequential fashion. It is important to point out that, since the menu is intended to be a helpful framework rather than a rigid prescription, the sequence may be "recycled" several times in a single unit or even a given lesson.

According to Gagné and Briggs (1979), an important consideration in sequencing instruction is to organize material in such a way that the learner has mastered necessary prerequisites. Prerequisites are broadly interpreted to include a favorable attitude toward the material to be learned as well as essential terminology, functional concepts, and basic factual information. It is for this reason that the Instructional Sequences Menu begins with an item that

INSTRUCTIONAL STRATEGIES MENU

- Recitation and Drill
- Peer Tutoring/Teaching
- Programmed Instruction
- Lecture
- Discussion
- Guided or Unguided Independent Studies or Explorations
- Simulations
- Learning or Interest Center Activities
- Dramatization
- Role Playing
- Guided Fantasy
- Replicative Reports or Projects
- Investigative Reports or Projects
- Apprenticeships, Internships, and Mentorships
- Audiovisual Presentation
- Literature Circles
- Problem-based Learning
- Technology-supported Learning
- Grouping Strategies
    - Flexible Grouping
    - Interest Grouping
    - Skills Grouping
    - Cooperative Learning
    - Cluster Grouping
    - Content Grouping
- Storytelling
- Socratic Inquiry
- Advance Organizers
- Concept Mapping
- Oral Reading
- Interactive Video
- Shared Inquiries
- Experimentation
- Brainstorming
- Demonstration
- Field Trips
- Guest Speakers
- Group Debate
- Virtual Field Trips
- Internet/Computer Simulations
- "Ask an Expert" Inquiries

Figure 9.5. *The Instructional Strategies Menu.*

Instructional Sequences Menu

I. Gain Attention, Develop Interest, and Motivation
- Tell a story about an event that is related to the lesson.
- Read a story that is related to the information.
- Begin a lesson with a discrepant event—an event that is contrary to what one might expect.
- Provide a brief demonstration that generates interest.
- Ask students to brainstorm what they already know about a concept and to share their thoughts.

II. Inform Students about the Purpose/Objective of a Lesson or Lesson Segment and Provide Advance Organizers
- Provide a graphic or narrative organizer that will assist students in organizing ideas. For example, Gail started her unit by explaining to her students that humanity leaves evidence of their common culture in their artifacts. She then continued by stating to the students, "As you watch this video, I want you to identify the types of artifacts archeologists have located to help them understand this particular culture." By using an advance organizer, Gail has provided her students with a way to structure the ideas and facts in this learning experience.
- Use the principles and concepts of a discipline as advance organizers and then relate the lessons back to these ideas.
- Relate how the purpose of the lesson will help students accomplish a specific goal or answer a particular set of questions.
- Help students connect the objective of the lesson to other disciplines or with real life.

III. Relate Topic to Relevant Previously Learned Material
- Ask students to recall what they have already learned and address how this new information relates to their prior learning experience. "Do you remember yesterday when ..."
- As students are in the process of learning something new, have them explain their strategies to their peers or have them explain how they arrived at a particular understanding. Have students talk out loud about what they have learned and how it is related to previous learning.

IV. Present Material Through a Combination of Instructional Strategies and Student Activities
- Choose a variety of instructional strategies and design student activities that will engage students in the act of learning.
- Focus on strategies that will require students to interact with the content (e.g., look for examples or evidence, apply a concept to related disciplines or experiences, arrive at a solution to a problem, etc.).
- Monitor and coach students as they perform a task. Escalate student thinking as they work individually or in small groups.

V. Provide Options/Suggestions for Advanced Level Follow-Up Activities on an Individual or Group Basis
- Listen carefully to student-generated questions and record these questions on a chart for future investigations.
- Generate a list of interesting projects related to the topic that may appeal to students.
- Ask students to consider what they don't know about a topic studied, but would like to know.
- Pose ill-structured problems that are relevant to students' lives and related to the topic or subtopic.

VI. Assess Performance and Provide Feedback
- Embed assessment strategies throughout lessons:
  - Oral assessments
  - Essay assessments
  - Attitudinal assessment
  - Portfolio assessment
  - Anecdotal assessment
  - Performance-based assessment (specific tasks, presentations, product)
  - Student self-evaluation
  - Metacognitive coaching
  - Student observation/interview
  - Journaling
  - Debriefing/Questioning
  - Checklists

VII. Provide Advance Organizers for Related Future Topics
- Explain how concepts and principles are related to other disciplines. For example, how are the concepts of homeostasis in biology similar to or different from the concepts of disequilibrium, assimilation, or accommodation in a culture?

VIII. Point Out Transfer Opportunities and Potential Applications
- Arrange for students to take information they know and apply it to novel problems or a related topic.

Figure 9.6. *The Instructional Sequences Menu.*

highlights the need for gaining attention and developing motivation. Gagné and Briggs also emphasized the value of relating present topics to relevant previously learned material and, whenever possible, integrating present topics into a larger framework that will add greater meaning to the topic at hand. This concern is dealt with, in part, through the strategies recommended in the first section of the Knowledge Menu, Locating the Discipline. Finally, Gagné and Briggs recommended that transfer not be left to chance; instead, curriculum developers provide links between information learned and other situations in which such information may be applied. In a similar fashion, Ausubel's (1968) theory of meaningful learning maintains that learning is enhanced when students are provided with a preview or overview of the material to be taught and the ways in which the material is organized. These "advance organizers" can be most easily dealt with by making students aware of content and process objectives at the beginning of an instructional sequence and by connecting specific information back to the concepts and principles selected as the organizing frameworks for the unit.

The Artistic Modification Menu

Most teachers have had, at one time or another, the experience of teaching a lesson that was so successful and satisfying that at its conclusion they might have signed it (figuratively speaking) in much the same way that an artist signs a painting. This kind of personal involvement and excitement is more likely to occur when teachers use materials that they have developed themselves or in which they have a special personal interest. When teachers routinely use material prepared by others, some of the excitement and effervescence of good teaching is likely to be lost. Teachers can take steps to recapture the potential for excitement inherent in almost any curricular topic by applying a concept called artistic modification. This concept is an *invitation* to teachers to inject something of their own choosing and of personal relevance into curricular material that has been prepared by others.

Rationale and Description

A major part of the rationale underlying the concept of artistic modification is derived from the work of Philip Phenix (1987). He pointed out that instructional material can be either alive or dead, depending on the way it is used or misused in the teaching-learning process. According to Phenix, material is most appropriately used when it serves as an instrument for dialogue and active engagement. When material is imported from sources other than the teacher's own experience, it may assume an alien quality when not mediated by the teacher. Phenix pointed out that prepared curricular material is misused when taken literally and uncritically and when it is considered in only a theoretical and abstract context without constant concern for concrete application and practical outcomes.

Texts and other prepared curricular materials may not encourage the type of engagement and dialogue discussed above because they are often viewed as objective and authoritative presentations of information and reality. Such a view often discourages teachers from "tampering" with textbook content, thus minimizing opportunities for the kinds of dialogue that will make material personally meaningful for students. Phenix (1987) believed that if teachers are to make significant changes in student attitudes and conduct, they must reexamine the ways in which they adapt curricular material. Teachers can properly adapt materials by personalizing, interpreting, criticizing, and dissecting curricular material in ways that bring life and meaning to content. The problem, of course, is how teachers go about doing this type of adaptation. In cases in which teachers' guides are overly prescriptive, curriculum developers do not view adaptation as a legitimate part of teachers' roles. In addition, many teachers simply lack training and practice in bringing their own modifications to the curricular material they are using. The concept is also difficult to convey to teachers because the overuse of prescribed material prepared by others frequently results in an attitude that curricular content can come only from the "content experts." Such an attitude may cause some teachers to perceive themselves as not having the content background necessary to add material of their own to already prepared curriculum. Contrary to this perception, artistic modification does not require an extremely high level of content expertise because it is essentially a personalization process. Each teacher is the best expert of his or her own experience, and artistic modification is simply a process of inviting teachers to put this personalized experience into the material they are using.

In using the Artistic Modification Menu, teachers make their own creative contributions to previously developed materials. These modifications include criticizing and interpreting curricular content, examining content in relation to the teacher's own values and experiences, and adding content of the teacher's own choosing, even if additional material is in conflict with the prescribed content of a particular unit of study. Figure 9.7 presents eight categories and examples.

From a practical standpoint, we designed these categories and examples to help teachers analyze and understand the different ways in which artistic mod-

> **ARTISTIC MODIFICATION MENU**
>
> I. Share with students a personal experience that is directly or indirectly related to the content. (During a unit on Shakespeare, show personal slides of the rebuilt Globe Theater, Stratford-on-Avon, Anne Hathaway's cottage, and other sites related to the Elizabethan era.)
>
> II. Share personal knowledge or insider information about a person, place, event, or topic. (While pursuing a unit on anthropology, point out a *Time* or *Newsweek* magazine article on the controversy surrounding the authenticity of Margaret Mead's research, or draw attention to biases reflected in news reporting about events in science or history.)
>
> III. Share personal interests, hobbies, independent research, or significant involvements in personal activities. (Show students a family tree and/or immigration documents and share interesting family stories and archives while studying genealogy.)
>
> IV. Share personal values, beliefs, and reflective experiences. (While working on a unit on American history, describe events related to personal participation in a civil rights demonstration, women's equality activities, or positions related to events or critical historical issues.)
>
> V. Share personal collections, family documents, or memorabilia. (While studying the Civil War and the assassination of Abraham Lincoln, bring to class a collection of newspapers, magazines, etc. that describe the events surrounding the death of John F. Kennedy.)
>
> VI. Interpret and share personal enthusiasm about a book, film, television program, or artistic performance. (Tell a "spy story" from a book such as *The Man Called Intrepid* while covering a unit on World War II.)
>
> VII. Point out controversies, biases, or restrictions that might be placed on books, newspapers, or other sources of information. (Point out that magazines that depend heavily on advertising by tobacco and liquor corporations might tend to avoid publishing articles on the dangers of tobacco and alcohol.)
>
> VIII. Other ... There is no limit to the variety of personal touches that can make learning more engaging and relevant to students.

Figure 9.7. *Artistic Modification Menu.*

ifications can be made. Suggestions for modifications can be both general and specific, but they must always be personal rather than prescribed by textbooks or curriculum guides. The goal of this process is to encourage teachers to put themselves into the curriculum rather than drawing totally on the knowledge and experience of the person(s) who developed the material. A related goal is to create excitement and involvement within teachers so that they can, in turn, arouse interest, curiosity, and motivation on the parts of their students.

Designing Artistic Modifications

The Artistic Modification Template (Figure 9.8) is one strategy for generating artistic modification topics. The template is divided into three types of personal experiences: Direct, Indirect (or Vicarious), and Creative. Each type is further subdivided into categories that represent logical components of the three general types of experiences. Generating a list of artistic modifica-

Artistic Modification Template

Topic: _____

Direct Experience: Work Related | Travel | Personal Acquaintances | Group Affiliations | Realia / Memorabilia | Personally Significant Event

Indirect (Vicarious) Experience: Fiction | Nonfiction | Film, Audio, Video Experiences | Fantasy or Simulation

Creative Modification (Output): Written | Visual | Oral/Performed | Constructed | Leadership Oriented | Film, Video, Computer Program

Figure 9.8. *Artistic Modification Template.*

tion topics based on personal interest and enthusiasm for a topic, book, film, personal experience, or event helps teachers energize themselves and thus increases the potential of energizing and engaging students.

Teachers can also begin generating topics for artistic modification by working with others in a small-group brainstorming situation. Group interaction often prompts a related idea that may evolve into a good teaching idea/activity. However, in order for a subsequent idea or activity to qualify as a personal artistic modification, it must be something that is relevant to the teacher and a product of his or her own experience. It is also a good idea for teachers to pursue this activity individually as a new unit of study or topic is being developed. Artistic modification should always be approached experimentally—that is, teachers should try various approaches with groups of students, and modify them according to students' reactions.

Reflecting upon material before teaching it, even if it has been taught many times before, is as important to the teaching process as warm-up activities are for creating physical readiness and a positive mental attitude for the athlete. The interaction between prepared curricular material and the personal involvement of teachers will result in a "spontaneous combustion" that helps bring the material to life. In some cases, teachers may already be prepared to inject their own personal involvement into prepared material, but others may need to do some background reading or other types of preparation. Supplementary books on a particular topic may contain unusual insights, controversies, little-known facts, or insider's information usually not included in the regular material prepared for students.

Instructional Products Menu

The Instructional Products Menu deals with the outcomes of learning experiences that the teacher presents. Two kinds of outcomes are likely to emerge during the learning process and are directly planned: concrete products and abstract products. Concrete products are the physical constructions young people create as they investigate the representative topics and interact with the principles, concepts, and methodology of the discipline. These physical constructions may include products such as essays, videos, dramatizations, and experiments. Abstract products include observed behaviors such as increased self-confidence and leadership characteristics in addition to less obvious but equally important products such as problem-solving strategies and appreciation of the structures and functions of knowledge. It is important to note that the two kinds of products are mutually reinforcing. As students produce new kinds of concrete products, they will also demonstrate new abstract products, such as methodological skills and self-assurance. Likewise, as self-confidence and leadership opportunities increase, it is likely that students will create additional physical products as well.

Curriculum writers can use the lists presented in Figure 9.9 to generate a variety of concrete and abstract products that will help the learner demonstrate the type of learning that has occurred.

Curriculum by Design: Putting It All Together

As was mentioned at the outset of this chapter, developing high-quality curriculum is a very challenging task and one that must be guided by a strong theoretical background if the final product is going to be more than a hodgepodge of activities and a jumble of factual information. But curriculum developers are, by definition, pragmatists—they must come up with tangible, practical outcomes. The Multiple Menu Model represents an attempt to use the major underlying theories of knowledge and instruction in a way that creates "templates" that help us respect good theory, but at the same time provides guidance for the practical tasks of selecting and sequencing content and deciding upon objectives, activities, and outcomes. It even provides a vehicle for encouraging teachers to "paint" themselves into the curriculum they are developing through a technique called artistic modification.

The goal of the Multiple Menu Model is to achieve balance and coordination between knowledge and instructional technique and to proceed from the abstract to the practical in the process of curriculum development. The complexity of the task defies simplification, but a certain amount of efficiency can be introduced into curriculum development by specifying the options that are available with regard to content and process and by pointing out procedures that can be used for blending together several factors that need to be considered simultaneously when developing curriculum.

Although the several options that represent the structure of this model are presented in the respective menus, two other conditions are necessary for the effective use of this or any other planning guide. First, the curriculum developer must understand the concepts presented in the menus. The appropriate use of an instructional activity such as extrapolating or an instructional strategy such as simulation will elude us if we do not have a practical understanding of both the concepts and how we can put them to work in a learning situation.

The second condition for successful use of this model involves some kind of plan or guide for synthesizing the respective menus at the practical

The Multiple Menu Model

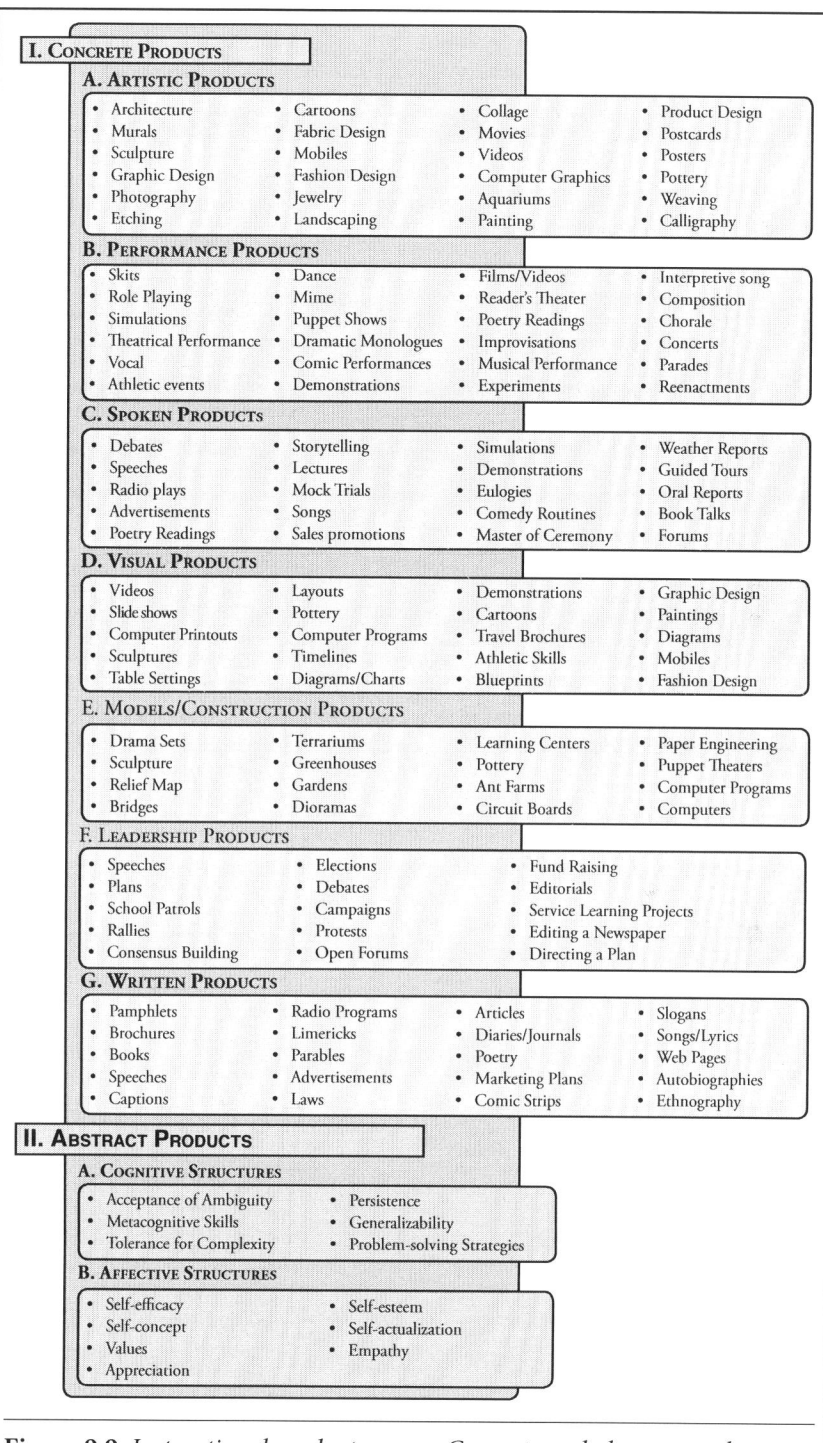

Figure 9.9. *Instructional products menu: Concrete and abstract products.*

or output level (i.e., actually writing curricular material). Although there is still some controversy about whether knowledge (content) or instructional technique (process) should be the focus of curriculum planning, this model has chosen to place knowledge at the center for the planning process. At the same time, however, the planning guides built into the model have been structured in a way that encourages curriculum developers to consider each of the instructional techniques menus in conjunction with the preparation of content. Taken collectively, the several menus and planning guides direct us to consider a broad range of options and to interrelate the many factors that must be considered when attempting to achieve balance and comprehensiveness in curriculum development.

References

Ausubel, D. P. (1968). *Educational psychology: A cognitive view.* New York, NY: Holt, Rinehart and Winston.
Ausubel, D. P., Novak, J. D., & Hanesian, H. (1978). *Educational psychology: A cognitive view* (2nd ed.). New York, NY: Holt, Rinehart & Winston.
Bandura, A. (1977). Self-efficacy: Toward a unifying theory of behavioral change. *Psychological Review, 84,* 191–215.
Bloom, B. S. (Ed.). (1954). *Taxonomy of educational objectives. Handbook I: Cognitive domain.* New York, NY: Longman.
Brandwein, P. (1987). On avenues to kindling wide interests in elementary school: Knowledges and values. *Roeper Review, 10,* 32–40.
Bruner, J. S. (1960). *The process of education.* Cambridge, MA: Harvard University Press.
Bruner, J. S. (1966). *Toward a theory of instruction.* Cambridge, MA: Harvard University Press.
Bruner, J. S. (1971). The process of education, revisited. *Phi Delta Kappan, 53,* 18–21.
Foreman, M. (2005). *Classic fairy tales.* New York, NY: Sterling.
Gagné, R. M., & Briggs, L. J. (1979). *Principles of instructional design* (2nd ed.). New York, NY: Holt, Rinehart and Winston.
Goodlad, J. I. (1984). *A place called school: Prospects for the future.* New York, NY: McGraw-Hill.
James, W. (1885). On the functions of cognition. *Mind, 10,* 27–44.
Kaplan, S. N. (1986). The grid: A model to construct differentiated curriculum for the gifted. In J. S. Renzulli (Ed.). *Systems and models for developing programs for the gifted and talented* (pp. 180–193). Mansfield Center, CT: Creative Learning Press.
Passow, A. H. (1982). *Differentiated curricula for the gifted/talented.* Ventura, CA: Leadership Training Institute on the Gifted and Talented.
Phenix, P. H. (1964). *Realms of meaning.* New York, NY: McGraw-Hill.

Phenix, P. H. (1987). *Views on the use, misuse, and abuse of instructional materials.* Paper presented at the Annual Meeting of the Leadership Training Institute on the Gifted and Talented, Houston, TX.

Renzulli, J. S. (Ed.). (2004). *Identification of students for gifted and talented programs.* Thousand Oaks, CA: Corwin Press.

Ringgold, F. (1995). *Aunt Harriet's Underground Railroad in the sky.* New York, NY: Crown.

Tomlinson, C. A. (1999). *The differentiated classroom: Responding to the needs of all learners.* Alexandria, VA: Association for Supervision and Curriculum Development.

Ward, V. S. (1960). Systematic intensification and extensification of the school curriculum. *Exceptional Children, 28,* 67–71, 77.

Whitehead, A. N. (1929). The rhythm of education. In A. N. Whitehead (Ed.), *The aims of education.* New York, NY: Macmillan.

PART IV

Implementation Components and Strategies

CHAPTER 10

The Schoolwide Enrichment Model

A Focus on Student Strengths and Interests[17]

Sally M. Reis and Joseph S. Renzulli
University of Connecticut

Introduction From Joe

Most of our work has been devoted to research and development on identification practices and teaching strategies for promoting gifted behaviors. Over the years we realized that many students, in addition to those formally identified as gifted, could benefit from school experiences that are more enriching, engaging, and challenging. We also realized that in order to make changes in *entire* schools we needed to pay some attention to an organizational plan or model for the delivery of these strategies and the professional develop-

---

17 Reis, S. M., & Renzulli, J. S. (2009). The Schoolwide Enrichment Model: A focus on student strengths and interests. In J. S. Renzulli, E. J. Gubbins, K. S. McMillen, R. D. Eckert, & C. A. Little (Eds.), *Systems and models for developing programs for the gifted and talented* (2nd ed., pp. 323–352). Waco, TX: Prufrock Press. Copyright 2009 Prufrock Press. Adapted with permission.

ment that is guided by our theories and research. We believe that a Total Talent Development model must look at the mission, culture, and commitment of entire schools in addition to what goes on in special programs. This approach to applying the pedagogy of gifted education to total talent development is a departure from most traditional approaches that focus only on identified gifted students. Although there has been some criticism from persons representing more conservative positions in the field, national interests in both promoting 21st-century skills for all students and the need to recognize talent potentials in underrepresented groups (see Chapter 17) have resulted in a growing number of adoptions of the programming model presented in this chapter. The Schoolwide Enrichment Model is, in essence, a plan for total school change that incorporates many of the conceptual ideas presented in earlier chapters of this book. The chapters that follow cover major components of the model in greater detail. Because this is an overview of the SEM, we are updating content from the most recently published version of the book.

In this chapter, we provide an overview of the Schoolwide Enrichment Model and recommend that interested readers find our text on the topic (Renzulli & Reis, 2014) for detailed information about implementing the model. This book contains several instruments and planning guides that can be reproduced with permission for individual use.

What's a Model?

Before providing this overview of the Schoolwide Enrichment Model (SEM), it might be worthwhile to reflect for a moment about the meaning and purpose of this or any other plan that is designed to bring about selected changes in a school and the ways in which educators serve young people. The first consideration in answering the above question is the distinction between two categories of educational models. We will refer to the first category as administrative models and the second as theoretical models.

Administrative models consist of patterns of school organization and procedures for dealing with such issues as how educators group students, develop schedules, and allocate time, money, and human resources. Administrative models focus mainly on how educators group students and "move around" and how they *arrange* for the delivery of services. Issues dealt with in administrative models might include homogeneous versus heterogeneous grouping, length of the school day or year, inclusion of special education students in regular classrooms, and whether or not educators should use a resource room or within-the-classroom program for the gifted.

Theoretical models, on the other hand, focus on the ways that educators provide the actual services to students, regardless of the manner in which they organize their schools or school schedules. Theoretical models consist of principles that guide the learning process and give direction to the content of the curriculum, the assessment and instructional strategies that teachers use, and ways in which educators evaluate the extent and quality of what their students have learned. Theoretical models focus on the actual outcomes of learning experiences that might take place within any given administrative pattern of organization. Theoretical models are influential in determining the *quality* of school experiences, whereas administrative models are more concerned with the efficiency and "smoothness" of the school's operation.

Although the SEM has certain implications for organizational patterns, we consider it a theoretically based model because it is guided by the Enrichment Triad discussed in Chapter 8 and based on: (1) a series of assumptions about individual differences in learners, (2) research-based principles of learning, and (3) recommended practices that logically follow from these assumptions and principles. A crucial consideration in selecting this or any other model is whether or not there is a consensus of agreement among teachers, parents, and administrators about the assumptions, principles, and recommended practices. We have found that when such a consensus exists, the relatively small organizational or administrative changes necessary for implementing the model are easily accomplished by most schools. Our experience has also shown that a theoretical model that infuses instructional practices into existing administrative patterns of organization has a higher probability of success than an approach that tries to completely reorganize the school.

A Brief History of the SEM

How can we develop the potentials of all children? What services should be provided to students who are identified for gifted and talented programs and *how can we* provide some enrichment services to all students who can benefit from more engaging and challenging school experiences? Can enrichment programs for all students help to increase academic achievement scores? Can creative productivity be enhanced when students participate in enrichment or gifted programs? How can we help children learn to think creatively and value opportunities for creative, self-selected work?

The Schoolwide Enrichment Model (SEM) was developed to encourage and develop creative productivity in young people. In this chapter, a description of the model is followed by an explanation of a new SEM service delivery resource that uses a computer-generated profile of each student's academic strengths, interests, learning styles, and preferred modes of expression (see Chapter 14). After this strength-based profile is completed, a highly sophisticated search engine matches carefully selected Internet resources with each student's profile. This breakthrough in technology enables teachers to provide true differentiated instruction and enrichment and saves thousands of hours of teachers' time in implementing the SEM.

The SEM promotes engagement for all students through the use of three types of enrichment experiences that are enjoyable, challenging, and interest-based. Separate studies on the SEM have demonstrated its effectiveness in schools with widely differing socioeconomic levels and program organization patterns (Olenchak, 1988; Olenchak & Renzulli, 1989). The SEM was developed using the Enrichment Triad (Renzulli, 1977; Renzulli & Reis, 1985, 1997) as a core and other components such as enrichment clusters and curriculum compacting, which will be described in detail in Chapter 11. It has been implemented in more than 2,000 schools across the country (Burns, 1998) and interest in this approach has continued to expand internationally. The effectiveness of the SEM has been studied in more than 30 years of research and field-tests, suggesting that the model is effective at serving high-ability students and providing enrichment in a variety of educational settings, including schools serving culturally diverse and low-socioeconomic populations.

The original Enrichment Triad Model (Renzulli, 1976), the curriculum core of the SEM, was developed in the mid-1970s and initially implemented as a gifted and talented programming model in many diverse school districts throughout the country. The model, initially field-tested in several districts, proved to be quite popular, and requests were received from all over the country for visitations to schools using the model as well as for information about how to implement the model increased. A book about the Enrichment Triad Model (Renzulli, 1977) was published, and increasing numbers of districts began implementing this approach. It was, at this point, that a clear need was established for research regarding the effectiveness of the model as well as for other vehicles that could provide technical assistance for interested educators to help develop programs in their schools. Different types of programs based on the Enrichment Triad were designed and implemented by classroom, gifted education, and enrichment teachers. In some of these programs, the focus was on many different types of introductory enrichment, such as speakers, presentations, films, and other Type I exposure opportunities. In others, the process was on Type II process skills, such as problem solving and critical and creative problem solving. In some Triad programs, high levels of student creative productivity occurred, while in others, *few* students engaged in this type of work. In some programs, enrichment opportunities were offered to students not formally identified for the enrichment program, while in others, only identified "gifted" students had any access to enrichment experiences. Some teachers and coordinators were extremely successful in implementing the model, while others were not. Certain professional development opportunities and resources proved to be extremely helpful in enabling some teachers to better implement the program, and we wondered how we could make these opportunities more readily available to larger numbers of teachers and students. And, of course, we became increasingly interested as to why the model was working and how we could further expand the research base of this approach. Thus began almost 30 years of field-testing, research, and dissemination.

The Dual Goal of Developing Academic Giftedness and Creative Productivity

Present efforts to develop giftedness are based on a long history of previous theoretical or research studies dealing with human abilities (Gardner, 1983, 2008, 2011; Sternberg, 1984, 1988, 1990; Sternberg & Davidson, 1986; Thorndike, 1921) and a few general conclusions from the most current research on giftedness (Sternberg & Davidson, 2005), which provide critical background for this discussion of the SEM. The first essential understanding is that giftedness is not a unitary concept, but rather, that students possess many manifestations of gifts and talents and therefore single definitions cannot adequately explain this multifaceted phenomenon. The confusion about present theories of giftedness has led many researchers to develop new models for explaining this complicated concept, but most agree that giftedness is developed over time and that culture, abilities, environment, gender, opportunities, and chance contribute to the development of gifts and talents (Sternberg & Davidson, 2005).

The SEM focuses on the development of both academic and creative productive giftedness. Creative productive giftedness describes those aspects of human activity and involvement where a premium is placed on the development of original material and products that are purposefully designed to have an impact on one or more target audiences. Learning situations designed to promote creative productive giftedness emphasize the use and application of information (content) and thinking skills in an integrated, inductive, and real-problem-oriented manner. In the SEM, traditional academic gifts are developed using curriculum compacting, acceleration, differentiated instruction, and various forms of academic enrichment. Our focus on creative productivity complements our efforts to increase academic challenge when we attempt to transform the role of the student from that of a learner of lessons to one of a firsthand inquirer who can experience the joys and frustrations of creative productivity (Renzulli, 1977). This approach is quite different from the development of giftedness that tends to emphasize deductive learning, advanced content and problem solving, and the acquisition, storage, and retrieval of information. In other words, creative productive giftedness enables children to work on issues and areas of study that have personal relevance to the student and can be escalated to appropriately challenging levels of investigative activity.

Why is creative productive giftedness important enough to question the traditional approach that has been used to select students for gifted programs on the basis of test scores? Why do some people want to rock the boat by challenging a conception of giftedness that can be numerically defined by simply giving a test? The answers to these questions are simple and yet compelling. A review of research literature (Neisser, 1979; Reis & Renzulli, 1982; Renzulli, 1978, 1986, 2005) tells us that there is much more to identifying human potential than the abilities revealed on traditional tests of intelligence, aptitude, and achievement. Furthermore, history tells us it has been the creative and productive people of the world, the producers rather than consumers of knowledge who have been recognized in history as "truly gifted" individuals. Accordingly, the SEM integrates both opportunities for academic giftedness, as well as creative productive giftedness.

The major theories underlying the SEM have been presented in Parts II and III of this book and implementation of specific service delivery components will be described in detail in the chapters that follow in this section. In this overview, we will discuss issues that should be considered for persons interested in implementing the model.

Understanding the Overall Concept of Schoolwide Enrichment

In addition to a working knowledge of the underlying theories presented in earlier chapters, understanding the relationship between the various components presented in Figure 10.1 is necessary for implementation.

The three major service delivery components on the face of the cube in Figure 10.1 are designed to be brought to bear on the three school structures at the top of the diagram. The comprehensive strength assessment is achieved by

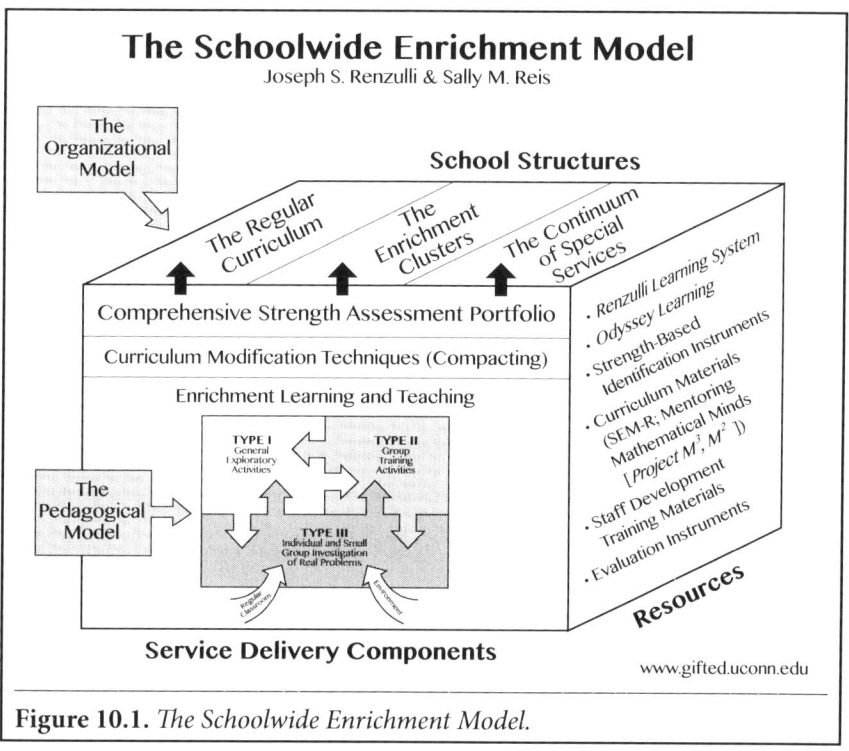

Figure 10.1. *The Schoolwide Enrichment Model.*

compiling a Total Talent Portfolio for each student that includes information from achievement tests, teacher ratings of potential for creativity and task commitment (Renzulli, Hartman, & Callahan, 1971), as well as self-ratings that students complete about their interests, learning styles (Renzulli & Sullivan, 2009), and preferred modes of expression (Kettle, Renzulli, & Rizza, 1998). Interest questionnaires cover the full range of academic areas as well as questions about topics in which students may have interests that are outside traditional academic areas. Learning style preferences include: projects, independent study, teaching games, simulations, peer teaching, computer-assisted instruction, lecture, drill and recitation, and discussion; expression style preferences include preferences for production in the following areas: computer, service, drama, artistic, audio/visual, written, commercial, oral, manipulative, and musical. We recommend that a Total Talent Portfolio that focuses on student strengths rather than deficits be completed for all students.

The other two service delivery components (curriculum modification techniques and enrichment learning and teaching) are covered respectively in other chapters in this book and a separate chapter is devoted to the school structure that we call enrichment clusters (see Chapter 12). Chapter 14 describes an electronic system for creating Total Talent Portfolios for each student and an Internet-based system for matching enrichment resources with student profiles. This system can also be used by teachers to locate enrichment resources for selected curricular topics.

The continuum of special services mentioned in Figure 10.1 represents a broad range of opportunities and grouping arrangements that a school might provide to meet individual needs. Clubs, service organizations, and extracurricular activities fall into this category. Finally, the resources listed in the righthand side of the cube are examples of items that we have developed over the years to make implementation of the SEM easier for teachers and administrators.

Common Goals and Unique Means

Far too many school improvement models have become so structured and prescriptive that they seldom achieve sustainability. In schools using highly structured approaches, teachers often feel that their professionalism has been taken away from them, that they must essentially follow someone else's "script," and therefore they cannot make creative contributions to what goes on in their own classrooms. Long lists of state-dictated standards, highly structured fill-in-the-blank forms for lesson planning, and endless teacher evaluation rubrics have resulted in a generally disheartened profession and teachers who feel as though they lack any form of ownership in what goes on in their own schools. We have avoided these kinds of structures by establishing three general goals for schools implementing the Schoolwide Enrichment Model in which most educators would agree with the theory, thereby allowing teachers a wide degree of laterality for achieving these goals (see Figure 10.2). The first goal is *enjoyment*. Anything that we enjoy doing we generally do better and we tend to grow and try to improve in the process. Enjoyment leads to *engagement*: a commitment to become intrinsically involved in and energetic about what one is learning or doing. Research has shown that higher engagement results in higher achievement (Dotterer & Lowe, 2011; Greenwood, 1991; Reyes, Brackett, Rivers, White, & Salovey, 2012; Wang & Holcombe, 2010). And engagement leads to *enthusiasm* for the act of learning itself. We also recommend that the following list of high-end learning objectives be used as a guide for planning all enrichment activities:

- plan a task and consider alternatives;
- monitor one's understanding and the need for additional information;
- identify patterns, relationships, and discrepancies in information;
- generate *reasonable* arguments, explanations, hypotheses, and ideas using appropriate vocabulary and concepts;
- draw comparisons and analogies to other problems;

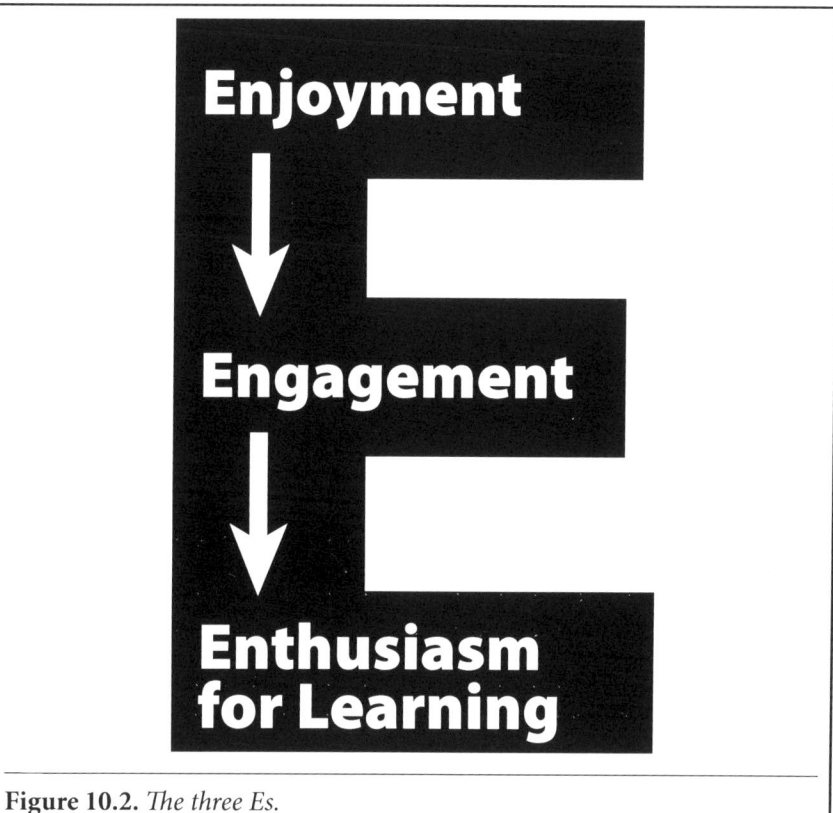

Figure 10.2. *The three Es.*

- formulate meaningful questions;
- transform factual information into usable knowledge;
- rapidly and efficiently access Just-In-Time information and selectively extract meaning from that information;
- extend one's thinking beyond the information given;
- detect bias, make comparisons, draw conclusions, and predict outcomes;
- apportion time, money, and resources;
- apply knowledge and problem-solving strategies to real-world problems;
- work effectively with others;
- communicate effectively in different genres and formats;
- derive enjoyment from active engagement in the act of learning; and
- creatively solve problems and produce new ideas.

These are the learner-centered skills that grow young minds, promote genuine student engagement, and increase achievement. Although focusing on these outcomes may be counterintuitive[18] to the "more-practice-is-better" pedagogy, we need only look at the track record of compensatory learning models to realize we have been banging our collective heads against walls and following an endless parade of reforms being forced through the schoolhouse door with no results. We need to be courageous enough to explore bolder and more innovative alternatives that will provide all students with a more highly enriched diet—the kind of diet that characterizes learning in the nation's best public and private schools. This is not to say that we should abandon a strong, standards-based curriculum that focuses on basic competencies, nor should we forget to demand accountability data to evaluate returns on investment in alternate approaches to addressing the problem.

But we also need to infuse into the curriculum a series of motivationally rich experiences that promote student engagement, enjoyment, and a genuine enthusiasm for learning. Common sense and our own experience tell us that we always do a better job when we are working on something in which we are personally engaged—something that we are really "into," and that we truly enjoy doing. Take, for example, the demonstrated benefits in performance that result from extracurricular activities that are based on a pedagogy that is the opposite of the pedagogy of drill and practice. How many *un*engaged students have you seen on the school newspaper staff, the basketball team, the chess club, the debate team, or the concert choir? Their engagement occurs because these students have some choice in the area in which they will participate, and they interact in a goal-oriented environment with other likeminded students interested in developing expertise in their chosen area. They use authentic problem solving, interpersonal, and creative strategies in order to produce a product, service, or performance and their work is brought to bear on one or more intended audiences other than, or, at least, in addition to the teacher. The engagement that results from these kinds of experiences exemplifies the best way to approach learning, one that differs completely from the behaviorist theory that guides so much of prescriptive and remedial education.

All learning, from diapers to doctorate, exists on a continuum ranging from deductive, didactic, and prescriptive on one hand to inductive, investigative, and inquiry oriented on the other. Students who have not achieved a certain, predetermined score are subjected to endless amounts of repetitious practice material guided by the didactic model. Then, when scores do

---

18 I have referred to the argument made here as a counterintuitive approach because almost every bone in most policy maker's bodies sees a certain logic in the more-practice-is-better approach to closing the achievement gap—it just seems to "make sense." The fact that this approach simply has not worked is the best evidence for coming at the problem from a different direction—this conclusion also makes sense!

not improve, we often think that the obvious solution is to simply redouble our efforts with what has been popularly called a "drill and kill" approach to learning; an approach that has turned many of our schools into joyless places that promote mind numbing boredom, lack of genuine student and teacher engagement, absenteeism, increased dropout rates, and the other byproducts of overdependence on mechanized learning. Proponents of popular but extremely prescriptive reading programs may boast slightly higher test scores, however the endless drill and practice only prepares students for more test taking rather than actually *learning to read*, enjoying reading, and making reading an important part of their lives.

All Roads Lead To Rome

With these three common goals and the above list of objectives in mind, we encourage schools to make their own decisions about how the goals will be achieved. The metaphor that we sometimes use is that "all roads lead to Rome" (in this case, the 3Es). However, there are many ways to get to Rome. We believe that the unique means for "getting to Rome" is based on the selection and use of a program development model that has two essential requirements. First, a model should consist of a shared mission and set of objectives. Everyone (or at the very least, almost everyone) involved in the selection and implementation of a model should agree that the mission and objectives represent a "destination" that they would like to reach. If an agreed-upon goal is "to get to Rome," then there is no ambiguity, vagueness, or misunderstandings about where everyone is going.

This first requirement of a model means that a great deal of front end time should be spent exploring alternative models, discussing and debating the advantages and disadvantages of various approaches, and examining related factors such as underlying research, implementation in other schools, and the availability of supportive resources. Reaching consensus *before* embarking upon a journey will help ensure that everyone involved will get to Rome rather than to Venice or Moscow!

Although we advocate that programs based on the Schoolwide Enrichment Model should strive to accomplish an agreed-upon mission and set of objectives, we also believe that any plan for program development must allow for a great deal of flexibility in the achievement of its objectives. This flexibility is necessary because no written plan or set of procedures can take into account the variations that exist at the local school level. Differences in school populations, financial resources, the availability of persons from the community at large, and a host of other local variables must be considered in the implementation of this or any other approach to school improvement. A model that does not allow for such flexibility could easily become a straightjacket that simply will not work when one or more of the local considerations are not taken into account. Some schools will have supplementary resource teachers for advanced-level students and others will not. Some school districts will have an abundance of community resources readily available, and others, perhaps more geographically isolated, will have limited access to museums, planetariums, colleges and universities, etc. Some schools may serve larger proportions of culturally diverse students than others and certain highly selective schools may have such a large number of high-achieving students that they have been designated as a school for the gifted.

Another reason why we believe that a model for program development must maintain a large degree of flexibility is that educators tend to quickly lose interest in "canned" programs and models that do not allow for local initiative, creativity, and teacher input. New and better ways to provide enrichment experiences to students will be discouraged if program development does not encourage local adaptation and innovation to occur. The SEM does provide a certain amount of general direction in both the development of program objectives and in the procedures for pursuing these objectives. At the same time, however, the specific types of activities that educators select and develop for their programs, and the ways in which they make these activities available to various populations of students will actually result in the creation of their own programming model. Educators will, in effect, be writing their own resource guide based on the activities that they select and develop. We have found that if the three general goals of the Schoolwide Enrichment Model and the objectives listed above are maintained, even if in a slightly modified form, a school's program will achieve the integrity that is sought in this total system approach. In this regard, the program that educators develop will attempt to achieve the best of two worlds! First, their program will benefit from the theoretical and research developments and the many years of field testing and practical application that have led to this particular approach for total talent development. Second, the ideas, resources, innovations, and adaptations that emerge from local situations will contribute to the uniqueness and practicality of programs that are developed to meet local needs. And we have found over the years that many teachers and leaders from excellent SEM schools have contributed to the profession by sharing their work at conferences, workshops, and in various publications. We view this type of sharing as a best-case example of teacher leadership and the extended professionalization of the work of teachers who have achieved the best of both worlds.

In all of our work, we have consistently recommended that educators should make whatever modifications and adaptations are necessary to the particular procedures recommended for accomplishing various program tasks.

We believe that there are many pathways and alternatives to reaching desired program outcomes. Once everyone in a school has agreed upon a destination, the uniqueness and excitement of the journey should involve the creation of an individualized plan for getting there. If all roads lead to Rome, what an unimaginative, and indeed, even boring world it would be if there was only one way to get there! Each school develops its *own* ownership of the SEM by the ways in which it selectively adopts, adapts, and creates the methods, materials, and organizational components that will make the school and program an *original* application of the Schoolwide Enrichment Model.

Research Related to SEM

A collective body of research on the SEM (Gubbins, 1995; Renzulli & Reis, 1994) summarized at http://www.gifted.uconn.edu/sem/semresearch.html suggests that the model is effective at serving high-ability students in a variety of educational settings and in schools serving diverse ethnic and socio-economic populations. These studies also suggest that the pedagogy of the SEM can be applied to various content areas, implemented in a wide variety of settings, and used with diverse populations of students including high-ability students with learning disabilities and those who underachieve. This research suggests that implementation of the SEM results in more use of advanced reasoning skills and thinking skills. This research has also demonstrated that students who are involved in SEM activities achieve at higher levels in traditional achievement tests than students who continue to use regular curricular or remedial activities.

Non-Negotiables in Implementing the SEM

The many changes taking place in general education have resulted in some unusual reactions to the SEM that might best be described as the good news/bad news phenomenon. The good news is that many schools are expanding their conception of giftedness and they are more willing than ever to extend a broader continuum of services to larger proportions of the school population. The bad news is that the motivation for these changes is often based on mistaken beliefs (a) that we can adequately serve high-potential students without some forms of grouping, (b) that we don't need special program teachers, or

(c) that special program teachers are best utilized by going from classroom to classroom with a "shopping cart" of thinking skill lessons and activities.

Non-Negotiable #1

The first non-negotiable is that anyone who tries to implement an SEM reads our book entitled *The Schoolwide Enrichment Model: A How-to Guide for Talent Development* (3rd ed.; Renzulli & Reis, 2014). A thorough knowledge of the goals and components is essential.

Non-Negotiable #2

Although we have advocated a larger Talent Pool than traditionally has been the practice in gifted education, a Talent Pool that includes students who gain entrance on both test and nontest criteria (Renzulli, 1988), we firmly maintain that the concentration of services necessary for the development of high-level potentials cannot take place without identifying and documenting individual student abilities. Targeting and documenting does not mean that we will simply play the same old game of classifying students as "gifted" or "not gifted," and let it go at that. Rather, targeting and documenting are part of an ongoing process that produces a comprehensive and always evolving "Total Talent Portfolio" about student abilities, interests, and learning styles (Dunn, Dunn, & Price, 1977). The most important thing to keep in mind about this approach is that all information should be used to make individual programming decisions about present and future activities, and about ways in which we can enhance and build upon documented strengths. Documented information will enable us (a) to recommend enrollment in advanced courses or special programs (e.g., summer programs, college courses), and (b) it will provide direction in taking extraordinary steps to develop specific interests and resulting projects within topics or subject matter areas of advanced learning potential.

Non-Negotiable #3

Enrichment specialists (a.k.a. gifted education teachers) must devote a majority of their time to working directly with Talent Pool students, and this time should mainly be devoted to facilitating individual and small-group investigations (i.e., Type IIIs). Some of their time with Talent Pool students can be devoted to stimulating interest in potential Type IIIs through advanced

Type I experiences and advanced Type II training that focuses on learning research skills necessary to carry out investigations in various disciplines. To do this, we must encourage more classroom teachers to become involved in talent development through both enrichment opportunities and in curriculum modification and differentiation within their classrooms. We must also encourage more classroom teachers to participate in enrichment teams who work together to provide talent development opportunities for all students in the school, enabling the enrichment specialists to work with more advanced students.

Non-Negotiable #4

SEM programs must have specialized, trained personnel who work directly with Talent Pool students to teach advanced courses and to coordinate enrichment services in cooperation with a Schoolwide Enrichment Team. The old cliché, "Something that is the responsibility of everyone ends up being the responsibility of no one," has never been more applicable than when it comes to enrichment or gifted education specialists. The demands made upon general education classroom teachers, especially during these times of mainstreaming and heterogeneous grouping, leave precious little time to challenge our most able learners and to accommodate interests that clearly are above and beyond the regular curriculum. In a study completed by The National Research Center on the Gifted and Talented (Westberg, 1991), it was found that in 84% of general education classroom activities, no differentiation was provided for identified high-ability students. Accordingly, time spent in enrichment programs with specialized teachers is even more important for high-potential students.

Related to this non-negotiable are the issues of teacher selection and training, and the scheduling of special program teachers. Providing unusually high levels of challenge requires advanced training in the discipline(s) that one is teaching, in the application of process skills, and in the management and facilitation of individual and small-group investigations. It is these characteristics of enrichment specialists rather than the mere grouping of students that have resulted in achievement gains and high levels of creative productivity on the parts of special program students.

Every profession is defined, in part, by its identifiable specializations, according to the task(s) to be accomplished. But specialization means more than the acquisition of particular skills. It also means affiliation with others who share common goals, the promotion of one's field, participation in professional activities, organizations, and research, and contributions to the advancement of the field. It also means the kinds of continued study and growth that make a difference between a job and a career. Now, more than ever, it is essential to fight for the special program positions that are falling prey to budget cuts. All professionals in the field should work for the establishment of standards and specialized certification for enrichment specialists. They should also help parents organize a task force that will be ready at a moment's notice to call in the support of every parent (past as well as present) whose child has been served in a special program.

Conclusion

There may never have been a time when so much debate about what should be taught has existed in American schools. The current emphasis on testing as connected to federal legislation, the standardization of curriculum, and the drive to increase achievement scores has produced major changes in education during the last two decades. Yet at the same time, our society continues to need to develop creativity in our students. As overpopulation, disease, war, pollution, and starvation increase both here and throughout the rest of the world, the need for creative solutions to these and other problems is clear. The absence of opportunities to develop creativity in all young people, and especially in talented students, is troubling. In the SEM, students are encouraged to become partners in their own education and develop a passion and joy for learning. As students pursue creative enrichment opportunities, they learn to acquire communication skills and to enjoy creative challenges. The SEM provides the opportunity for students to develop their gifts and talents and to begin the process of lifelong learning, culminating, we hope, in creative productive work that they choose.

Enrichment programs have been the true laboratories of our nation's schools because they have presented ideal opportunities for testing new ideas and experimenting with potential solutions to long-standing educational problems. Programs for high-potential students have been an especially fertile place for experimentation because such programs are usually not encumbered by prescribed curriculum guides or traditional methods of instruction. The SEM provides a repertoire of services that can be integrated in such a way so as to create "a rising tide lifts all ships" approach. The model includes a continuum of services, enrichment opportunities and three distinct services: curriculum modification and differentiation, enrichment opportunities of various types, and opportunities for the development of individual portfolios including interests, learning styles, product styles, and other information about student strengths. Not only has this model been successful in addressing the problem of high-potential students who have been underchallenged, it also provides additional important learning paths for creative students who achieve academic success in more traditional learning environments but long for opportunities for innovation in school.

The absence of opportunities to develop creativity in all young people, and especially in talented students, is troubling. In the SEM, students are encouraged to become responsible partners in their own education and to develop a passion and joy for learning. As students pursue creative enrichment opportunities, they learn to acquire communication skills and enjoy creative challenges. The SEM provides the opportunity for students to develop their gifts and talents and to begin the process of lifelong learning, culminating, we hope, in higher levels of creative and innovative work in their areas of interest and passion as adults.

When all is said and done, we hope you will agree with a school superintendent who said, "the Schoolwide Enrichment Model is nothing more than organized common sense."

References

Burns, D. E. (1998). *SEM network directory.* Storrs: University of Connecticut, Neag Center for Gifted Education and Talent Development.

Dotterer, A. M., & Lowe, K. (2011). Classroom context, school engagement, and academic achievement in early adolescence. *Journal of Youth and Adolescence, 40,* 1649–1660.

Dunn, R., Dunn, K., & Price, G. E. (1977). Diagnosing learning styles: Avoiding malpractice suits against school systems. *Phi Delta Kappan, 58,* 418–420.

Gardner, H. (1983). *Frames of mind: The theory of multiple intelligences.* New York, NY: Basic Books.

Gardner, H. (2008). *The mind's new science: A history of the cognitive revolution.* New York, NY: Basic Books.

Gardner, H. (2011). *The unschooled mind: How children think and how schools should teach.* New York, NY: Basic Books.

Greenwood, C. R. (1991). Longitudinal analysis of time, engagement, and achievement in at-risk versus non-risk students. *Exceptional Children, 57,* 521–535.

Gubbins, E. J. (Ed.). (1995). *Research related to the enrichment triad model* (RM 95212). Storrs: University of Connecticut, The National Research Center on the Gifted and Talented.

Kettle, K. E., Renzulli, J. S., & Rizza, M. G. (1998). Exploring student preferences for product development: My Way . . . An Expression Style Instrument. *Gifted Child Quarterly, 42*(1), 49–60.

Neisser, U. (1979). The concept of intelligence. In R. J. Sternberg & D. K. Detterman (Eds.), *Human intelligence* (pp. 179–189). Norwood, NJ: Ablex.

Olenchak, F. R. (1988). The Schoolwide Enrichment Model in the elementary schools: A study of implementation stages and effects on educational excellence. In J. S. Renzulli (Ed.), *Technical report on research studies relating to the revolving door identification model* (2nd ed., pp. 201–247). Storrs: University of Connecticut, Bureau of Educational Research.

Olenchak, F. R., & Renzulli, J. S. (1989). The effectiveness of the Schoolwide Enrichment Model on selected aspects of elementary school change. *Gifted Child Quarterly, 32*, 44–57.

Reis, S. M., & Renzulli, J. S. (1982). A case for the broadened conception of giftedness. *Phi Delta Kappan, 64*, 619–620.

Renzulli, J. S. (1976). The Enrichment Triad Model: A guide for developing defensible programs for the gifted and talented. *Gifted Child Quarterly, 20*, 303–326.

Renzulli, J. S. (1977). *The Enrichment Triad Model: A guide for developing defensible programs for the gifted and talented*. Mansfield Center, CT: Creative Learning Press.

Renzulli, J. S. (1978). What makes giftedness? Re-examining a definition. *Phi Delta Kappan, 60*, 180–184, 261.

Renzulli, J. S. (1986). The Three Ring Conception of Giftedness: A developmental model for creative productivity. In R. J. Sternberg & J. E. Davidson (Eds.), *Conceptions of giftedness* (pp. 53–92). New York, NY: Cambridge University Press.

Renzulli, J. S. (Ed.). (1988). *Technical report of research studies related to the enrichment triad/revolving door model* (3rd ed.). Storrs: University of Connecticut, Teaching the Talented Program.

Renzulli, J. S. (2005). The Three-Ring Conception of Giftedness. In R. J. Sternberg & J. E. Davidson (Eds.), *Conceptions of giftedness* (2nd ed., pp. 246–279). New York, NY: Cambridge University Press.

Renzulli, J. S., Hartman, R. K., & Callahan, C. M. (1971). Teacher identification of superior students. *Exceptional Children, 38*, 211–214.

Renzulli, J. S., & Reis, S. M. (1985). *The Schoolwide Enrichment Model: A comprehensive plan for educational excellence*. Mansfield Center, CT: Creative Learning Press.

Renzulli, J. S., & Reis, S. M. (1994). Research related to the Schoolwide Enrichment Model. *Gifted Child Quarterly, 38*, 2–14.

Renzulli, J. S., & Reis, S. M. (1997). *The Schoolwide Enrichment Model: A how-to guide for educational excellence* (2nd ed.). Waco, TX: Prufrock Press.

Renzulli, J. S., & Reis, S. M. (2014). *The Schoolwide Enrichment Model: A how-to guide for talent development* (3rd ed.). Waco, TX: Prufrock Press.

Renzulli, J. S., & Sullivan, E. E. (2009). Learning styles applied: Harnessing students' instructional style preferences. In L. Zhang & R. J. Sternberg (Eds.), *Perspectives on the nature of intellectual styles* (pp. 209–232). New York, NY: Springer Publishing.

Reyes, M. R., Brackett, M. A., Rivers, S. E., White, M., & Salovey, P. (2012). Classroom emotional climate, student engagement, and academic achievement. *Journal of Educational Psychology, 104*, 700–710.

Sternberg, R. J. (1984). Toward a triarchic theory of human intelligence. *Behavioral and Brain Sciences, 7*, 269–287.

Sternberg, R. J. (1988). Three facet model of creativity. In R. J. Sternberg (Ed.), *The nature of creativity* (pp. 125–147). Boston, MA: Cambridge University Press.

Sternberg, R. J. (1990). Thinking styles: Keys to understanding student performance. *Phi Delta Kappan, 71,* 366–371.

Sternberg, R. J., & Davidson, J. E. (Eds.). (1986). *Conceptions of giftedness.* New York, NY: Cambridge University Press.

Sternberg, R. J., & Davidson, J. E. (Eds.). (2005). *Conceptions of giftedness* (2nd ed.). New York, NY: Cambridge University Press.

Thorndike, E. L. (1921). Intelligence and its measurement. *Journal of Educational Psychology, 12,* 124–127.

Wang, M. T., & Holcombe, R. (2010). Adolescents' perceptions of school environment, engagement, and academic achievement in middle school. *American Educational Research Journal, 47,* 633–662.

Westberg, K. L. (1991). *The effects of instruction in the inventing process on students' development of inventions* (Unpublished doctoral dissertation). University of Connecticut, Storrs.

CHAPTER 11

Curriculum Compacting and Achievement Test Scores

What Does the Research Say?[19]

Sally M. Reis, Karen L. Westberg,
Jonna M. Kulikowich, and Jeanne H. Purcell
University of Connecticut

Introduction From Joe

Although the Enrichment Triad Model has been the centerpiece of my recommendations for developing creative and productive giftedness, it is also necessary to have within any comprehensive model for talent development a systematic component to accommodate those students who are capable of covering the regular curriculum at a faster pace than average and lower achieving students. To accomplish this goal, I developed a process in the 1970s called *curriculum compacting*.

---

19 Reis, S. M., Westberg, K. L., Kulikowich, J. M., & Purcell, J. H. (1998). Curriculum compacting and achievement test scores: What does the research say? *Gifted Child Quarterly, 42,* 123–129. Copyright 1998 National Association for Gifted Children. Reprinted with permission.

Curriculum compacting is an instructional technique designed to make appropriate curricular adjustments for students in any curricular area and at any grade level. Essentially, the procedure involves (1) defining the goals and outcomes of a particular unit or segment of instruction, (2) determining and documenting which students have already mastered most or all of a specified set of learning outcomes, and (3) providing replacement strategies for material already mastered through the use of instructional options that enable a more challenging and productive use of the student's time.

Staff development for compacting should be provided to all classroom teachers, and we further recommend that gifted education specialists work with classroom teachers to discuss the various acceleration and enrichment options that may be used for the time that students accrue as a result of demonstrating comprehension of regular curriculum material. In this article, Sally and her colleagues describe the results of a large national study that used advanced research methodology. This research demonstrates that most teachers could eliminate approximately 40%–50% of curriculum for academically talented students in their classrooms. It also showed that the students whose regular curriculum work was compacted because they had already mastered it did as well or better on standardized achievement tests than a control group of similarly high-potential students.

Recent research seems to indicate that increasing numbers of high ability and high achieving students spend large proportions of their time in regular classrooms and that few curricular modifications are made for high ability students in regular classrooms (Archambault et al., 1993; Purcell, 1993; Renzulli & Reis, 1991; U.S. Department of Education, 1993; Westberg, Archambault, Dobyns, & Salvin, 1993). The minimal use of differentiation strategies persists even though a variety of instructional strategies are recommended to better meet the academic needs of high ability and high achieving students.

Several strategies can be used to differentiate curricula and instruction for high ability students including the use of advanced content, higher level questioning skills, curriculum compacting, independent study, tiered assignments, flexible grouping, and others. Little empirical research has examined the use of these strategies and this study of curriculum compacting was an attempt to address this area. Curriculum compacting (Reis, Burns, & Renzulli, 1992; Renzulli & Reis, 1985; Renzulli & Smith, 1978) is an instructional strategy that has been used to streamline the learning activities for students who demonstrate proficiency on curricular objectives prior to teaching. It has been widely recognized and suggested by educational experts as a method to address the needs of high ability and high achieving students (Barbour & Kiernan, 1994; George, 1995; Winebrenner, 1992). The curriculum compacting process uses a document called The Compactor (Renzulli & Smith), which enables record-keeping. The Compactor form includes three columns which parallel the steps of the curriculum compacting process. In the first column, teachers document what a student knows prior to beginning a curricular unit or area of study. The second column provides space for teachers to indicate the concepts or material a student has yet to master, and in the third column, teachers list appropriate replacement activities which are usually enrichment or acceleration options for a student whose curriculum has been compacted. The following case study provides an example of the use of curriculum compacting.

Shanoah is a 9-year-old attending fourth grade in a large, urban setting. Within the first two weeks of the school year, her teacher noted that she was a voracious reader. He subsequently checked the scores she received on state-wide mastery tests and discovered that she scored above the 90th percentile in all subtests related to reading and writing. Shanoah scored 100% in literal understanding and inference making and at the 90th percentile on evaluation skills. With respect to writing, she had mastered 100% of the skills required at her grade level.

Shanoah appeared restless in class, frequently asked for more challenging assignments, and, on occasion, began to disturb other students around her. It was clear that her classroom work in reading and writing needed to be compacted. Her teacher eliminated the workbook assignments related to the reading skills she had mastered, as well as basic writing assignments. To extend Shanoah's understanding in reading and writing, he substituted advanced-level reading in a subject of Shanoah's choice and provided her with choices for creative writing assignments. Through the time that was gained with compacting, he and Shanoah pursued several enrichment options. She had choices including: reading for pleasure, working on monthly reading projects of her choice, pursuing her interest in African American history, and working as co-editor on the school newspaper. Shanoah chose to work on all of these enrichment options during fourth grade.

Research about curriculum compacting has indicated that high achieving students may already know between 40%–50% of their lessons before they are taught (Reis et al., 1993). This research and other studies about curriculum compacting also indicated that teachers discuss several reasons when asked why curriculum compacting is not widely adopted, including: lack of sufficient teacher preparation to initiate preassessment and differentiation, limited time during the school day and year to prepare supplemental lessons, and financial exigencies that preclude the purchase of enrichment material necessary for replacement learning activities (Imbeau, 1991; Westberg, Archambault, & Brown, 1997). One of the reasons frequently cited by teachers is their fear that students whose curriculum is compacted may not score as well on state mastery tests and other standardized measures of achievement. Many teachers indicate that their administrators do not want teachers to eliminate any skills, even for high ability students, for fear of lower standardized achievement tests or state mastery scores.

Little empirical research exists to address teachers' questions related to the effect of compacting on elementary students' academic achievement. Schultz (1991) conducted one study in which she examined the effect of curriculum compacting on the mathematics achievement of fourth grade mathematics students in a midwestern school district. One hundred and thirty-two students participated in Schultz' research, in which achievement was measured in both October and May of one school year using the Mathematics Concepts, Mathematics Problem Solving, and Mathematics Computation subtests of the *Iowa Tests of Basic Skills*. Schultz reported no significant differences between control and treatment groups with respect to scores on any of the mathematics subtests; students whose curriculum was compacted achieved equally as well as their agemates whose curriculum had not been compacted.

This article describes the results of a national research study that examined the academic achievement of elementary students whose curriculum was compacted. Three research questions guided the study.

1. Do students whose curriculum was compacted in one or more content areas perform differently on measures of achievement than students whose curriculum was not compacted?
2. Do students whose curriculum was compacted in mathematics perform differently than their control counterparts on measures of achievement?
3. Do students whose curriculum was compacted in language arts perform differently than their control counterparts on measures of achievement?

The findings related to these research questions can be used to address questions related to the academic achievement of students who have sections of curriculum eliminated from their curricula, and the diverse replacement strategies employed by their classroom teachers.

The Curriculum Compacting Study

Sample

A sample of 27 school districts and 436 second through sixth grade classroom teachers throughout the country from collaborative school districts that are a part of The National Research Center on the Gifted and Talented (NRC/GT) was selected for this study. The achievement data of 336 students are reported here. These data represent complete sets of pretest and posttest scores on all subscales of the *Iowa Tests of Basic Skills*. To participate, districts had to meet two criteria: no previous training or implementation of curriculum compacting and a willingness to accept random assignment to one of three treatment groups or a control group. Efforts were made to recruit districts with widely varying demographics including elementary school populations that included economically disadvantaged, limited English proficient, and students with disabilities. The districts participating in the study represented elementary schools from across the country, ranging from a small rural school in Wyoming to a magnet school for Hispanic students in California. Districts were randomly assigned to a control group or to one of three treatment groups in which teachers received increasing amounts of inservice about curriculum compacting.

After receiving staff development about curriculum compacting and the characteristics of students who need their curricula modified, the teachers selected one or two students from their classrooms. These students had either been identified as gifted and talented and participated in a district's program or had demonstrated high achievement in a content area which indicated that they would benefit from curriculum compacting. Students were used as the unit of analysis because the treatment, curriculum compacting, was provided to individual students rather than to the class as a whole.

Several out-of-level (one grade higher) *Iowa Tests of Basic Skills* subtests were given to the students in the fall (pre-achievement test), and again at the end of May or beginning of June (post-achievement test). The median percentile for all students on the out-of-grade-level reading and math concepts subtests was 93. The median percentile in the out-of-level math computation subtest was 90. These data indicate that teachers selected students for whom compacting was appropriate.

Procedure

Three treatment groups of teachers who received increasing levels of staff development were used to examine the most efficient but effective method for training teachers to modify curricula. All treatment group teachers received the first staff development session which provided two half-hour videotapes and a book about the compacting process. After receiving the first staff inservice session in October, teachers were asked to select one or two qualified students from their classroom. Teachers in Treatment Group 2 received the videotape training and book, as well as approximately two hours of group compacting simulations (Starko, 1986) conducted by the local gifted and talented resource teacher or consultant. The simulations developed by Starko have been a standard resource in this type of training. Treatment Group 3 received the same training as Treatment Group 2, with the addition of local peer coaching or consultant services. Local consultants provided informal peer coaching throughout the year and provided 6–10 hours of organized peer coaching between March and June. All treatment group teachers completed the Compacter form detailing the amount of content eliminated or compacted, as well as replacement strategies used.

Instrumentation

Three instruments were used to address the research questions stated earlier in this article: the Classroom Practices Questionnaire, the Compactor, and the *Iowa Tests of Basic Skills*.

The Classroom Practices Questionnaire and the Compactor form were used to assess classroom teachers' practices related to the curriculum compacting procedure. At the end of the treatment period, teachers were asked to indicate the content areas in which curriculum compacting had been completed and to estimate the percentage of curricula that had been eliminated for each selected student. The Compactor was used to identify the amount of content eliminated or streamlined as well as the type of replacement strategies used by classroom teachers. Teachers in all treatment groups provided curriculum compacting most frequently in mathematics in which 39%–49% of content was eliminated. The next most frequently compacted content area was language arts in which 36%–54% of the content was eliminated. Research about these replacement strategies indicated that many diverse strategies were used and that teachers who had higher levels of professional development (Treatment Group 3) used more enrichment strategies within content areas than did the other treatment groups (Reis & Purcell, 1993). Replacement strategies included: independent study, projects, alternative assignments, advanced content, interdisciplinary units and studies, learning games, self-selected study topics, technology opportunities, and a variety of other choices. Replacement strategies were not necessarily provided in the same content area as the one in which curriculum compacting occurred.

Pre and post student achievement was assessed by the *Iowa Tests of Basic Skills* (ITBS), which was administered to students in the control and experimental groups. The reading, mathematical concepts, mathematical computation, science, social studies, and spelling subscales of Form J of the ITBS were administered. Tests designed for students one grade level above each student's current grade level were administered to guard against potential ceiling effects.

Validity and reliability information on the ITBS is well documented as is additional technical support. Detailed information is reported in *The Tenth Mental Measurement Yearbook* in which Willson (1989) concludes, "the ITBS is not a perfect battery, but it represents the best that modern educational measurement can produce" (p. 398). The reliability coefficients for the various subscales range from .85 to .95 (see *Iowa Tests of Basic Skills*, Form J, 1990).

Data Analysis

Multivariate analysis of covariance procedures were conducted to address the research questions in this study. For these analyses, all subscale scores of the *Iowa Tests of Basic Skills* (i.e., reading, spelling, mathematical concepts, mathematical computation, social studies, and science) which were administered at posttest measures were the dependent variable. All subscale pretest measures were covariates, and treatment (i.e., three treatment levels and control) was the independent variable. Multivariate analysis of covariance was selected for the analysis because we anticipated strong correlations among the set of dependent variables and the multivariate covariate vector (Stevens, 1986). The results of these analyses follow.

Results

Question 1: Do students whose curriculum was compacted in one or more content areas perform differently on measures of achievement than students whose curriculum was not compacted?

To address research question one, the complete data sets of 336 students were submitted to a multivariate analysis of covariance procedure. The results demonstrated that all covariates were significant. Wilks' Lambda (Λ) values, corresponding F-ratios, and levels of significance were as follows: a) Reading Pretest, ($\Lambda = .73$, $F[6, 321] = 20.12$, $p < .0001$); b) Spelling Pretest, ($\Lambda = .50$, $F[6, 321] = 54.50$, $p < .0001$); c) Mathematical Concepts Pretest, ($\Lambda = .72$, $F[6,$

321] = 21.15, $p < .0001$); d) Mathematical Computation Pretest, ($\Lambda = .67$, $F[6, 321] = 26.90$, $p < .0001$); e) Social Studies Pretest, ($\Lambda = .87$, $F[6, 321] = 8.35$, $p < .0001$); and f) Science Pretest, ($\Lambda = .79$, $F[6, 321] = 14.06$, $p < .0001$). The main effect for treatment was also significant, ($\Lambda = .85$, $F[18, 908.41] = 2.98$, $p < .0001$).

Table 11.1 displays the overall means and standard deviations for the dependent variables and covariates. Means, standard deviations, and adjusted means are reported by treatment groups.

Interpretations of the adjusted means at the univariate level should be made with care as the significant main effect for treatment is a multivariate effect. Upon examination of the adjusted posttest means, descriptively, Treatment Group 2 had the highest means for three of the six subscales (i.e., reading, mathematical concepts, and social studies). Treatment Group 1 had the highest adjusted mean for science. In spelling and mathematical computations, the control group outperformed all curriculum compacting groups. While these mean comparisons should be made with care, we determined that for Treatment Group 2, 86% of the students in the group had curriculum that was compacted in language arts, mathematics, or both areas simultaneously. By comparison, we determined that 71% of the students assigned to Treatment Group 1 had their curriculum compacted in language arts, mathematics, or both areas. Finally, the lower results observed for Treatment Group 3 may be in part due to the fact that only 67% of the students' curriculum was compacted in the areas of language arts, mathematics, or a combination of both content areas.

Question 2: Do students whose curriculum was compacted in mathematics perform differently than their control counterparts on measures of achievement?

Question 3: Do students whose curriculum was compacted in language arts perform differently than their control counterparts on measures of achievement?

To address the effects of the content areas (i.e., mathematics or language arts) in which one's curriculum was compacted on achievement scores, two multivariate analyses of covariance (MANCOVAs) were performed on two randomly selected subsamples of the students' data. The random selection of subsamples was considered necessary in order to examine the effects of content area curriculum compacting given specific subscales of the ITBS instead

Table 11.1
ITBS Means, Adjusted Means, and Standard Deviations by Levels of Treatment

	Pretests							Posttests					
	Read M (SD)	Spell M (SD)	MathC M (SD)	Comp M (SD)	SS M (SD)	Science M (SD)		Read Adj.M (SD)	Spell Adj.M (SD)	MathC Adj.M (SD)	Comp Adj.M (SD)	SS Adj.M (SD)	Science Adj.M (SD)
Treatment Group 1 (n=72)	139.17 (25.16)	135.60 (28.98)	132.68 (21.80)	125.88 (22.88)	136.44 (30.02)	147.26 (28.74)		141.64 (25.71)	135.02 (28.96)	137.26 (24.97)	130.75 (23.95)	140.44 (32.70)	153.28 (27.22)
Treatment Group 2 (n=57)	135.98 (24.11)	129.14 (27.66)	128.07 (24.78)	119.07 (17.78)	134.18 (27.18)	146.91 (25.16)		144.45 (22.65)	136.92 (25.45)	137.42 (23.87)	127.70 (19.87)	144.63 (30.10)	151.12 (23.68)
Treatment Group 3 (n=66)	139.73 (24.47)	131.36 (27.92)	132.97 (24.48)	127.70 (19.79)	135.08 (27.73)	147.71 (26.40)		142.05 (24.45)	133.90 (24.63)	134.08 (24.32)	127.28 (21.25)	136.40 (26.03)	146.08 (27.36)
Control (n=141)	131.61 (25.21)	127.09 (28.36)	123.41 (21.88)	117.86 (20.37)	127.01 (34.93)	135.08 (30.36)		143.59 (24.68)	138.85 (27.49)	136.67 (23.33)	132.03 (21.44)	141.18 (30.77)	149.15 (28.13)
Total (n=336)	135.57 (25.20)	130.09 (28.36)	128.06 (23.20)	121.71 (20.77)	131.83 (31.48)	142.18 (28.68)		143.01 (24.62)	136.73 (26.88)	136.42 (24.21)	130.09 (21.86)	140.67 (30.37)	149.76 (27.53)

of the full battery of scores. Because the full battery of subscales is highly correlated, we anticipated that the random subsample selections would eliminate some of the problems associated with the variance inflation attributable to the strong intercorrelations among dependent variables and covariates.

For research question two, two levels of curriculum compacting (i.e., those students in Treatment Groups 1, 2, or 3 whose curriculum was compacted specifically in mathematics versus control) made up the independent variable. The dependent variables were scores on the ITBS mathematics concepts and computation subscales. Pretest scores for these two measures served as covariates. While covariates were significant ($\Lambda s > .66$, $Fs > 47.57$, $ps < .0001$), there were no significant differences between treatment levels.

For research question three, a parallel analysis to the one described above was performed for language arts. A random subsample was selected to examine the effects of curriculum compacting in language arts on achievement scores. For this analysis, reading scores, spelling scores, and social science scores of the posttests were the dependent variable and the pretest scores of these scales were covariates. As with the analysis for mathematics curriculum compacting, treatment had two levels: students in any of the three treatment groups with curriculum compacting in language arts and the control group. Results were similar to those observed for the mathematics analysis. While all covariates were significant ($\Lambda s > .45$, $Fs > 16.51$, $ps < .0001$), there was no main effect for treatment.

A discriminant function analysis was run as a follow-up procedure to the MANCOVA. This analysis was conducted to identify whether partial correlations among the subscales would have discriminated among the groups. The discriminant function coefficients were comparable across groups, which indicates that each treatment group made similar pretest to posttest gains.

Discussion

Three research questions were addressed in this study: Do students whose curriculum was compacted in one or more content areas perform differently on measures of achievement than students whose curriculum was not compacted? Do students whose curriculum was compacted in mathematics perform differently than their control counterparts on measures of achievement? Do students whose curriculum was compacted in language arts perform differently than their control counterparts on measures of achievement? To answer these three questions, students' achievement test scores were examined by three multivariate analyses of covariance. Results of these multivariate analyses supported that there were no significant differences in favor of the control group over the treatment groups.

The findings related to these questions provide empirical support for concerned practitioners who want to 1) provide alternative learning activities for high achieving students in heterogeneous classrooms, and 2) ensure that highly able students continue to score well on standardized tests. Three findings from this research are particularly salient. First, as mentioned above, the achievement test scores of gifted students whose curriculum was compacted did not differ significantly from gifted students whose curriculum was not compacted. Even when as much as 40%–50% of content was eliminated for some students, they still scored as well as their counterparts who did not have their curricula eliminated or streamlined. These results are based on out-of-level tests scores which were used to increase the sensitivity to gains and declines at the upper end of the scale. The median percentile performance on all post subscales of the ITBS was greater than 90. Using one year beyond grade level tests may still not have been sufficient to prevent ceiling effects, however. If ceiling effects had an impact, a Type II error occurred; namely gains in post scores, not declines, would have been masked.

Second, the descriptive findings, as shown in Table 11.1, suggest that students in some of the treatment groups performed better than the control group on some of the subscales. For example, students in Treatment Group 1 had higher adjusted posttest scores in science than all other groups. Similarly for Treatment Group 2, students had higher adjusted posttest social studies scores than the other groups. We did note two trends which suggested that students in the control group performed slightly better than students in the treatment groups in mathematical computation and spelling. This probably reflects that they experienced more drill practice in these areas. All differences are minimal, however, and should not be interpreted as having practical significance.

Third, the findings in the Compacting Research Study support the beliefs of many classroom teachers who maintain that high ability and high achieving students need curriculum differentiation. The median pretest achievement test scores of students selected by teachers for curriculum compacting were high; selected children scored above the 90th percentile on one year above grade level tests in reading and mathematics. This clearly indicated classroom teachers' ability to identify high achieving students who would benefit from curriculum compacting. The scores of these children support the opinions of teachers and underscore the critical need for practitioners to identify advanced students and provide appropriate instruction for young people who know a great deal of the curriculum before it is taught.

Finally, the findings prompt questions related to the use of curriculum compacting over long periods of time and at the secondary level. Specifically, what are the effects of compacting students' curricula over several years? Would the continuous use of this instructional strategy be associated with long-term achievement and attitudinal gains? In addition, new research should focus on eliminating basic skill instruction for gifted students in favor of complex, faster paced, problem-based learning and the effects of this change on future achievement test scores. Empirical research must also examine the achievement effects of compacting at the secondary level. Can substantial portions of secondary students' curriculum be eliminated without affecting students' scores on standardized achievement tests? Answers to these research questions will provide classroom practitioners with the additional empirical data necessary to make well-grounded decisions about students' learning opportunities at all grade levels.

Conclusion

Our research began with a question that teachers have wrestled with for some time: What effect will compacting elementary school students' curricula have on standardized measures of academic achievement? As demands for accountability grow, the question is a critical one for professionals who want students to perform at high levels on standardized achievement tests. The results of this study may provide support for elementary teachers who seek empirical evidence for eliminating content which students have already mastered. Curriculum compacting provides documentation of students' knowledge of the regular curriculum covered in class, and it enables teachers to provide many types of differentiated replacement learning opportunities. The research presented in this article suggest that elementary teachers can preassess students' prior knowledge of content, eliminate portions of the curriculum that students already know, replace those portions with various types of interdisciplinary learning activities, and remain reasonably confident that students' achievement test scores will not decline. Furthermore, it should be noted that students' scores did not decline, even when the replacement material is not within the same content area, rather in students' interest areas.

References

Archambault, F. X., Jr., Westberg, K. L., Brown, S., Hallmark, B. W., Zhang, W., & Emmons, C. (1993). Classroom practices used with gifted third and fourth grade students. *Journal for the Education of the Gifted, 16,* 103–119.

Barbour, C. M. (Director & Writer) & Kiernan, L. J. (Writer). (1994). *Challenging the gifted in the regular classroom* [Videotape]. (Available from Association for Supervision and Curriculum Development, Alexandria, VA)

George, P. S. (1995). Talent development and grouping in the middle grade: Challenging the brightest without sacrificing the rest. *Middle School Journal, 26*(4), 12–17.

Imbeau, M. B. (1991). *Teachers' attitudes toward curriculum compacting: A comparison of different inservice strategies* (Unpublished doctoral dissertation). University of Connecticut, Storrs.

Iowa Tests of Basic Skills. (1990). *Manual for school administrators supplement.* Chicago, IL: Riverside.

Purcell, J. H. (1993). The effects of the elimination of gifted and talented programs on participating students and their parents. *Gifted Child Quarterly, 37,* 177–187.

Reis, S. M., Burns, D. E., & Renzulli, J. S. (1992). *Curriculum compacting: The complete guide to modifying the curriculum for high ability students.* Waco, TX: Prufrock Press.

Reis, S. M., & Purcell, J. H. (1993). An analysis of content elimination and strategies used by elementary classroom teachers in the curriculum compacting process. *Journal for the Education of the Gifted, 16,* 149–170.

Reis, S. M., Westberg, K. L., Kulikowich, J., Caillard, F., Hébert, T., Plucker, J., . . . Smist, J. M. (1993). *Why not let high ability students start school in January? The curriculum compacting study* (RM93106). Storrs: University of Connecticut, The National Research Center on the Gifted and Talented.

Renzulli, J. S., & Reis, S. M. (1985). *The Schoolwide Enrichment Model: A comprehensive plan for educational excellence.* Mansfield Center, CT: Creative Learning Press.

Renzulli, J. S., & Reis, S. M. (1991). The reform movement and the quiet crisis in gifted education. *Gifted Child Quarterly, 35,* 26–35.

Renzulli, J. S., & Smith, L. H. (1978). *A guidebook for developing individualized educational programs for gifted and talented students.* Mansfield Center, CT: Creative Learning Press.

Schultz, C. B. (1991). *The effects of curriculum compacting upon student achievement in fourth grade mathematics* (Unpublished master's thesis). University of Northern Iowa, Cedar Falls.

Starko, A. J. (1986). *It's about time: Inservice strategies for curriculum compacting.* Mansfield Center, CT: Creative Learning Press.

Stevens, J. (1986). *Applied multivariate statistics for the social sciences.* Hillsdale, NJ: Lawrence Erlbaum.

U.S. Department of Education. (1993). *National excellence: A case for developing America's talent.* Washington, DC: Author.

Westberg, K. L., Archambault, F. X. Jr., & Brown, S. W. (1997). A survey of classroom practices with third and fourth grade students in the United States. *Gifted Education International, 12,* 29–33.

Westberg, K. L., Archambault, F. X. Jr., Dobyns, S. M., & Salvin, T. J. (1993). The classroom practices observation study. *Journal for the Education of the Gifted, 16,* 120–146.

Willson, V. L. (1989). Review of the Iowa Tests of Basic Skills, forms G & H. In J. C. Conoley & J. J. Kramer (Eds.), *The tenth mental measurement yearbook* (pp. 395–398). Lincoln, NE: Buros Institute of Mental Measurements.

Winebrenner, S. (1992). *Teaching gifted kids in the regular classroom: Strategies and techniques every teacher can use to meet the academic needs of the gifted and talented.* Minneapolis, MN: Free Spirit.

CHAPTER 12

A Time and a Place for Authentic Learning[20]

Joseph S. Renzulli,
University of Connecticut,

Marcia Gentry,
Purdue University,

and Sally M. Reis
University of Connecticut

Introduction From Joe

In order to provide general enrichment opportunities for all students and, at the same time, to ensure that opportunities for more advanced work are available for highly able and motivated students, I developed a concept in the 1980s called *enrichment clusters*. This component of the Schoolwide Enrichment Model has become "the growth stock" of our implementation

---

20 Renzulli, J. S., Gentry, M., & Reis, S. M. (2004). A time and a place for authentic learning. *Educational Leadership, 62*(1), 73–77. Copyright 2004 Association for Supervision and Curriculum Development. Reprinted with permission.

recommendations, and we recommend that schools begin their Total Talent Development programs with this part of our work. Teachers who have conducted successful enrichment clusters learned to use a good deal of gifted education pedagogy and follow-up studies indicated that they were able to carry over many of the strategies used in the cluster to their regular classroom teaching. In a certain sense, they became their own best professional development expert.

As is the case with the article on curriculum compacting, we published this work in a general education journal because our target audience for this component of our work is all schools, teachers, and students. Persons interested in examining the research on enrichment clusters can find it at the following website: http://www.gifted.uconn.edu/nrcgt/reports/rm95118/rm95118.pdf.

Each week, all the students at the Bret Harte Middle School in Oakland, California, leave their classrooms to participate in interest-based enrichment clusters. Under a teacher's guidance, one group of students is identifying, archiving, and preserving documents from the 1800s that were found in a suitcase belonging to the first pharmacist in Deadwood, South Dakota. Another group with strong interests in media, technology, and graphic art is converting the archives into digital format and making the students' research available on a web site.

These cross grade clusters are scheduled on a rotating basis during the fall months. They usually last for eight weeks, generally meeting weekly for a double-period time block, with a new series scheduled in the spring. A medium-sized school might typically offer 15 to 20 clusters. The number of students in each cluster varies depending on student interest in the topic and teacher requirements for effective student participation. Teachers develop the clusters around their own strengths and interests, sometimes working in teams that include parents and community members.

Numerous schools across the United States have developed the enrichment cluster concept to deal with what many education leaders believe is a crisis in our schools. The focus on test preparation has squeezed more authentic kinds of learning out of the curriculum, thereby minimizing the one aspect of U.S. education that contributes to the innovativeness and creative productivity of the nation's culture, economy, and leadership role in the world. Improved test scores are important, but it's the *application* of knowledge in authentic learning situations—not perpetual memorization and testing—that characterizes a progressive education system.

What Is Authentic Learning?

All learning exists on a continuum that ranges from deductive and prescriptive leaning on one end to inductive, self-selected, and investigative learning on the other. The essence of inductive or high-end learning is applying relevant knowledge and skills to solving real problems. Such learning involves finding and focusing on a problem; identifying relevant information; categorizing, critically analyzing, and synthesizing that information; and effectively communicating the results.

Real-life problems share four criteria. First, a real-life problem has a personal frame of reference. In other words, the problem must involve an emotional or internal commitment on the part of those involved in addition to a cognitive interest. Second, no agreed-on solutions or prescribed strategies for solving the problem exist. If they do, the process would more appropriately be classified as a training exercise because its main purpose would be to teach predetermined content or thinking skills.

Third, real-life problems motivate people to find solutions that change actions, attitudes, or beliefs. A group of students might gather, analyze, and report on data about the community's television-watching habits, causing people in that community to think critically about the television-viewing habits of young people. Last, real-life problems target a real audience. For example, students working on a local oral history project—a biographical study of Connecticut residents who died in Vietnam—initially presented their findings to their classmates, mainly to rehearse presentation skills. Their authentic audience consisted of members of a local historical society, members of veterans groups, family members of servicemen and servicewomen, attendees at a local commemoration of Vietnam veterans, and community members who had read about the research in the local newspaper.

Enrichment clusters are *not* mini-courses. There are no predetermined content or process objectives. The nature of the problem guides students toward using Just-In-Time knowledge, appropriate investigative techniques or creative production skills, and professional methods for communicating results. In this type of learning, students assume roles as investigators, writers, artists, or other types of practicing professionals.

Authentic learning is the vehicle through which everything from basic skills to advanced content and processes come together in the form of student-developed products and services. The student's role changes from lesson-learner to firsthand inquirer, and the role of the teacher changes from instructor and disseminator of knowledge to coach, resource procurer, and mentor. Although products play an important role in creating authentic learning, students learn principally from the cognitive, affective, and motivational processes involved.

A Different Approach

Developing an authentic enrichment cluster draws on skills that most teachers already possess, especially if they have been involved in clubs or other extracurricular activities. As you begin the process of developing your own cluster, keep in mind the following:

- *Reverse the teaching equation.* Your role in planning and facilitating an enrichment cluster differs from the teacher's traditional role. Too much preplanning on your part may push the cluster toward deductive rather than inductive teaching and learning. Enrichment clusters develop Just-In-Time knowledge that has immediate relevance in resolving the problem. Students typically move to higher levels of knowledge than grade-level textbooks support.

- *Reverse the role of students.* Young people working on an original piece of historical research, creative writing, or play production become young historians, authors, scenery designers, and stage managers. Instead of teaching lessons, you will begin to think about how to help a young poet get work published, how to get the shopping mall manager to provide space for a display of models of historically significant town buildings, and how to engineer a presentation by young environmentalists to the state wildlife commission.

- *Create a unique enrichment cluster.* As long as you follow the guidelines for inductive teaching, there is no wrong way to plan and facilitate an enrichment cluster. Differences in interests, personalities, and styles among cluster facilitators contribute to the uniqueness of this type of learning. Experience in an inductive learning environment will help you hone the skills that will become a natural part of your teaching repertoire both in clusters and in your classroom.

- *When in doubt, look outward.* To mirror real-world situations, examine conditions outside the classroom for models of planning, teaching, and organizing. Athletic coaches, advisors for the drama club or the school newspaper, and 4-H Club leaders make excellent enrichment cluster facilitators. Similarly, tasks and organizational patterns should resemble the activities that take place in a small business, a social service agency, a theater production company, or a laboratory.

Guidelines for Developing an Enrichment Cluster

Select a Topic

Base enrichment clusters on topics in which you have a strong interest. Make a list of topics that fascinate you. Reflect on your choices, discuss your list with colleagues—there may be possibilities for collaboration—and prioritize the topics to help you decide on the focus of your first enrichment cluster.

Focus on Key Questions

Develop enrichment clusters around the following six key questions:
- What do people with an interest in this topic or area of study do?
- What products do they create, and what services do they provide?
- What methods do they use to carry out their work?
- What resources and materials are needed to produce high-quality products and services?
- How and with whom do they communicate the results of their work?
- What steps do cluster participants need to take to have an impact on an intended audience?

These questions do not need to be answered immediately, sequentially, or comprehensively at this stage. As your cluster develops, have students discuss the questions and allow them to reach their own conclusions about the activities, resources, and products that professionals pursue in particular areas of study. If you have all the answers ready before the cluster begins, the excitement of pure inquiry will be lost.

Explore the Topic

The most obvious way to learn about the work of a professional is to discuss the key questions with someone working in the field. A cartoonist, landscape architect, or fashion designer will give you the lay of the land and offer some recommended resources. When talking with professionals, keep in mind that you want to learn what they routinely do in their jobs, how they do it, and what they produce. This background material will help you plan the cluster, but students should also pursue the same questions with professionals after the cluster commences. Such interaction dramatically increases motivation and engagement.

Almost all professionals belong to professional associations. A quick Internet search turns up approximately 3,500 professional organizations. To learn about the work that genealogists do, one teacher went to the Association of Professional Genealogists Web site (www.apgen.org) and found a treasure trove of resources on careers in the field, conferences, publications, places where family records can be found, and local chapters. She also located a directory of members by state. Association membership lists can suggest speakers, mentors, or enrichment cluster co-facilitators. By clicking on *Connecticut*, the teacher found the names, addresses, and phone numbers of 13 professional genealogists in the state, one of whom lived in close proximity to the school.

Another way to explore the key questions as you develop cluster content is to obtain resource books on the methodology of a particular field. A visit to the Genealogical Publishing Company Web site yielded an extensive list of potential resources: 423 titles, to be exact. Librarians and college bookstores can also help locate methodological resource books.

In the real world, almost all work is intended to have an impact on at least one targeted audience. In finding target audiences, you will be serving as a referral agent, promoter, or marketing manager of student work. In school, fellow students and parents are obvious audiences for whom students can practice and perfect performances and presentations, but young people will begin to view themselves in a much more professional role when you help them seek audiences outside the school. The students themselves should make the contacts and be prepared to answer questions.

Local newspapers, city or state magazines, and literary reviews—especially those that target young authors—are excellent places to submit written work. Public buildings and business offices are often receptive to requests to display student artwork. Local or state organizations—such as historical societies, writers clubs, civic groups, environmental preservation originations and advocacy groups—also provide opportunities for young entrepreneurs to present their work. Young dramatists can take their performances on the road to senior citizen centers, day-care centers, religious groups, or professional organizations. One group of students who wrote and produced a legal thriller presented a synopsis of the plot at a county bar association meeting.

Contests and competitions are also great outlets. Most teachers are familiar with science fairs, National History Day, and Math League, but thousands of other competitions take place in such areas as photography, fashion design, inventions, drama, and Web design. Searching for outlets and audiences; writing query letters and submitting work for possible publication, presentation, or display; and receiving replies—both positive and negative—are all part of the creative process and motivate aspiring writers, scientists, and artists.

Write Your Enrichment Cluster Description

The enrichment cluster description should convey, in no more than 100 words, the essence of the experience. Use verbs that emphasize the explorative nature of the cluster by conveying action and illustrating tasks. For example, in a cluster that involves building and marketing compost bins, you might use verbs such as *design, field-test, construct, advertise, market, contact, display,* and *sell*.

You might pose questions about potential student interests and possible types of involvement. Do you like to express your feelings by writing poetry and short stories? Are you concerned about finding better ways to protect wildlife? Would you like to try your hand at designing fashions for teens? Each of these questions relates to a topic around which a cluster might be developed, yet they are all open-ended enough to encompass a broad range of activities in specific interest areas.

Launch Your Enrichment Cluster

Although students who have signed up for your cluster have expressed an interest in the topic, it may take them some time to understand the cluster's approach to learning. Displaying products or tools that professionals in your topic area typically use is always a good way to begin. In a cluster on archaeology, entitled *The Trash Heaps of Mankind*, the facilitator showed slides of famous and local archaeological discoveries. She opened a Mystery Box in the front of the room to reveal a trowel, a sieve, a pair of gloves, a dust brush, pegs and string, a marking pen, and a camera. She pointed out that these were the main tools of the archaeologist and that an examination of material found in garbage dumps was one of the ways in which archaeologists analyzed past and present cultures. A short videotape of a dig in the students' own state heightened student interest in the work of practicing archaeologists.

Escalate Content and Process

One of the problems we encountered in our research on enrichment clusters was a failure on the part of some facilitators to escalate the level of content and methodology pursued within a cluster. Indeed, critics may point out that clusters are nothing more than fun and games or that students carry out their work using existing skills rather than acquiring more advanced ones. You can guard against these criticisms by examining each cluster with an eye toward providing authentic and rigorous content within the topic area.

In a cluster on research about political opinion, for example, students evaluated archived news articles and editorials from the World War II and Vietnam War eras to analyze and compare public support for these wars. Students in an ecology and evolutionary biology cluster studied the survival prospects of tropical plants grown in the school's greenhouse and conducted experiments to explore optimal conditions for propagation. Content and process objectives evolve as a result of the investigations that students conduct, and this is one factor that highly differentiates the clusters from regular instruction.

Gathering Original Data

During many years of working with students in authentic learning situations, we have discovered that there is a certain magic associated with gathering original data and using that information to create new knowledge. This knowledge may not be new for all humankind, but it may be original to students and their local audiences. A group of elementary students spent an entire school year gathering and analyzing samples of rainwater for sulfur and nitrogen oxide emissions, the main pollutants responsible for acid rain. The students then prepared a report concerning the extent of acid rainfall in their region of the country. Their teacher helped them obtain a standard rain gauge and a kit for testing acidity.

Additional resources enabled these students to prepare statistical and graphic summaries of their data; compare their findings with data from national and regional reports that were easily accessed on the Internet; and design maps showing acid rain trends over time and across geographic regions. The data provided participants with the excitement and motivation to study environmental and health problems associated with various types of pollution. The students found receptive audiences for their work among state environmental protection groups, the U.S. Environmental Protection Agency, and the National Weather Bureau.

Putting It All Together

Most teachers have had a vision, at one time or another, about what they thought teaching would entail. They pictured themselves in classrooms with interested and excited students dramatizing dangerous midnight journeys on the Underground Railroad, conducting science experiments to find out how things work, or experiencing the exhilaration that occurs when a student-developed board game unlocks the relationships between a set of numbers and everyday experiences.

Many teachers, however, experience a disconnect between their vision of a challenging and rewarding career and the day-to-day grind of test preparation. What is most ironic about the separation between the ideal and the reality of today's classrooms is that most teachers actually have the skills and motivation to do the kinds of teaching they dream of. Unfortunately, lists, regulations, and other people's requirements have resulted in both a prescriptive approach to teaching and a barrier to creating a challenging and exciting classroom. Overprescribing the work of teachers has, in some cases, lobotomized good teachers and denied them the creative teaching opportunities that attracted them to the profession in the first place.

Freedom to teach still exists, as does the possibility of making learning enjoyable, engaging, and enriching. You can find both in enrichment clusters, where authentic learning is in the driver's seat.

CHAPTER 13

Academies of Inquiry and Talent Development[21]

Joseph S. Renzulli
University of Connecticut

Introduction From Joe

Most of our work in program development has been at the elementary level. Attempts to influence middle and especially high school programs for gifted students have been somewhat more challenging. Typically, inquiries to high schools about services to gifted students are responded to by comments about offerings such as AP, honors, and IB courses. These courses are obviously valuable to high achieving students, but in most cases they have limited opportunities for creative productivity. One student described her AP courses as "test prep on steroids!"

As the middle school "movement" began to flourish in the 1980s, several schools that were using versions of our enrichment clusters model asked

---

21 Renzulli, J. S. (2000). Academies of inquiry and talent development: Part I: Organizing exploratory curriculum. *Middle School Journal, 32*(2), 5–14. Copyright 2000 Association for Middle Level Education. Reprinted with permission.
  Renzulli, J. S. (2001). Academies of inquiry and talent development: Part II: How does an AITD program get started? *Middle School Journal, 32*(3), 7–14. Copyright 2001 Association for Middle Level Education. Reprinted with permission.

about ways of organizing their schools to capitalize on student interests and to use the pedagogy recommended in the Enrichment Triad Model. This interest resulted in the material presented in this chapter, which was originally published as a two-part series in the *Middle School Journal*. What is interesting to note about this academy concept is that in recent years many districts in the U.S. have started offering whole school theme-based academies at both middle and high school levels. The organizational model described in this chapter is a little different from the whole school academy model. It points out the ways in which a middle or high school can offer several theme-based academies within in a single school and how such academies can place a major focus on creative productivity rather than accelerated lesson learning.

Part I: One Way to Organize Exploratory Curriculum

Nothing happens unless first a dream. —Carl Sandburg

One afternoon a week all of the students and teachers at Johnson Middle School depart from their regular schedule to participate in a different "brand" of learning. This learning experience is designed to provide high levels of challenge and to capitalize on special areas of student and teacher interest. On this special afternoon, all students from across all grade levels are enrolled in a self-selected Academy of Inquiry and Talent Development (AITD). Students enter one of six or seven AITDs (e.g., physical and life sciences, applied mathematics, fine and performing arts) upon entering their middle school years, and usually remain in the same AITD for the duration of their years in the middle school. Similarly, teachers from across grade levels organize themselves into the faculties of the AITDs. They usually remain with the same group of students for a three- or four-year period. New students enter each year as other students move on to the high school. Although a majority of teachers choose an AITD in their regular academic area, an analysis of their own special interests occasionally leads some teachers to work in AITDs that are outside the area in which they normally teach. The AITDs also provide a vehicle for the involvement of community members who have expertise in the fields of knowledge around which the AITDs are organized. A graphic representation of the structure for each academy is presented in Figure 13.1.

The time devoted to the AITDs is selectively "borrowed" from the regular schedule and the advisement periods. Although the AITDs are organized

	Students	
6th	7th	8th
	Faculty	
6th	7th	8th
Special subject teachers for art, family and consumer sciences, foreign language, guidance, music, technology, etc.		**Community resource persons**
Possible academies would include literature, language arts and humanities; applied mathematics; social sciences; fine and performing arts; sport and leisure studies; computer sciences and technology; and physical and life sciences.		

Figure 13.1. *Academies of inquiry and talent development.*

around the traditional fields of knowledge, the work done within any given "academy" often naturally evolves into interdisciplinary endeavors.

The idea for AITDs grew out of several years of research and field testing the application of learning strategies that were originally developed in programs for the gifted to educational opportunities for all students. In the sections that follow, a rationale for this "type" of learning will be discussed, and specific examples of the activities pursued in the AITDs will be described. In the next section, suggestions will be provided for organizing and implementing a program that emphasizes high levels of challenge within selected areas of student and teacher interest.

Background and Rationale

Middle school educators are committed to providing a challenging and enjoyable academic experience while, at the same time, maintaining strong support for the social and personal goals of middle level education set forth by the National Middle School Association (1995) and other organizations that have laid the foundation for middle school programming (Carnegie Council on Adolescent Development, 1989).

In addition to the academic and social/personal outcomes, the AITD plan enables each student to develop a close, meaningful, multi-year relationship with one teacher or a small group of teachers. Sustained relationships with adults is one of the goals of most middle school advisor/advisee (A/A) programs. Although this plan is not intended to replace present efforts directed toward helping middle school students understand and value self, others, and life experiences, many of the goals of A/A programs can be accomplished within this plan as a result of the common bonds that develop between people who share common interests. In this regard, the plan seeks to promote communities of learning and mutual support that are not unlike the relationships that develop over multi-year periods between students and athletic coaches, band and chorus directors, or club advisors.

The AITD plan also respects the strong emphasis that middle schools place on teaming. In this case, however, teams of adults and students are organized across grade levels according to common areas of student and teacher interests. The teams can also involve other adults in the community who have specialized areas of interest and expertise. Once again, this approach is not intended to disrupt traditional, grade-level teams. Rather, it creates another kind of interest-based team that resembles the way in which people organize themselves in real-world, problem-solving situations.

The idea for Academies of Inquiry and Talent Development grew out of research and development dealing with a component of the Schoolwide Enrichment Model (SEM) called enrichment clusters (George, Renzulli, Reis, & Erb, 1997; Reis, Gentry, & Park, 1995; Renzulli, 1994; Renzulli & Reis, 1997). Enrichment clusters are multi-grade groups of students and adults with common interests who come together on a regular basis to pursue the development of products or services using the methodologies of practicing professionals. No predetermined lesson or unit plans are used (Renzulli, 1997b), and even the products and services are decided upon collaboratively by the respective groups and subgroups within a given cluster. In this regard, what takes place within an enrichment cluster is more analogous to the workings of a real-world entity, such as a film studio, research laboratory, publishing company, or historical society, rather than what typically takes place in a traditional classroom. All learning takes place within the context of developing authentic products or services for real-world audiences. Divisions of labor are encouraged to ensure that maximum respect is given to each student's interests, learning styles, and preferred modes of expression. This type of learning is what John Dewey called collateral learning and what is popularly referred to today as constructivist learning theory.

Although enrichment clusters are usually planned on a semester or annual basis, our experience with middle level students has shown that they frequently express an eagerness to remain together for additional, and usually more challenging, involvement in their respective areas of interest. Strong associations develop between and among both students and adults, due to their common interests and collaborative approach to product or service development that is the hallmark of the cluster concept. It is for this reason that we have developed this plan, not unlike the practice of "looping," to keep the same group of students and adults together during designated time blocks for the duration of their middle school years. There will, obviously, be times when individual student interests change, and accordingly, changes in student placement should occur. Similarly, adults may also want to "try something new" after a given number of years within an AITD, and that opportunity should also be provided.

The Objectives of Academies of Inquiry and Talent Development

The objectives of AITDs are based on two fundamental concepts around which all learning activities within the AITDs are organized. These concepts are authentic learning and real-life problems. Because of the central role these concepts play in this model, a brief definition is provided in the following paragraphs.

Authentic learning and real-life problems defined. Authentic learning consists of applying relevant knowledge, thinking skills, and interpersonal skills to the solution of real problems. Real-life problems share four criteria. First, a real problem requires a personal frame of reference for the individual or group pursuing the problem. In other words, the problem must involve an emotional or internal commitment in addition to a cognitive or scholarly interest. For example, stating that global warming and urban crime are "real problems" does not make them real for individuals or groups unless they decide to do something to address the problem.

A second characteristic of real problems is that they do not have existing or unique solutions for persons addressing the problem. If an agreed-upon solution or prescribed strategies for solving the problem exist, then it is more appropriately classified as a "training exercise." Even simulations based on approximations of real-world events are considered training exercises if their main purpose is to teach predetermined content, thinking skills, or problem-solving strategies.

The third characteristic of a real problem is best described in terms of why people pursue these problems. The main reason is they want to create new products or services that will change levels of understanding, appreciations, actions, attitudes, or beliefs on the part of a targeted audience. For example, a group of young people who gathered, analyzed, and reported on data about television watching habits in their community were contributing information that was new, at least in a relative way, and that would cause people to think critically about the television viewing actions of young people. In the realm of service-oriented activities, several motivated and mathematically advanced girls organized a group at their middle school called the Female Mathematics Support Team. They provided mentoring services and emotional support to other girls who were struggling with general math and the transition to algebra.

The final characteristic of real problems is that they are directed toward a real audience. Real audiences consist of persons who voluntarily attend to information, events, services, or objects. A good way to understand the difference between a real and a contrived audience is to reflect on what one group of students did with the results of their local, oral history project. Although they presented their findings to classmates, they did so mainly to rehearse presentation skills. Their authentic audience consisted of members of a local historical society and persons who chose to read about their research in the feature section of a local newspaper.

To understand the essence of authentic learning is to compare how learning takes place in a traditional classroom with how someone might learn new material or skills in real-world situations. Classrooms are characterized by relatively fixed time schedules, segmented subjects or topics, predetermined information and activities, tests and grades to determine progress, and an organizational pattern largely driven by the need to acquire and assimilate information and skills imposed from outside the classroom.

Contrast this type of learning with the more natural chain of events that takes place in real-world situations, including research laboratories, business offices, or film studios. In these situations, the goal is to produce a product or service. All resources, information, schedules, and events are directed toward this goal, and evaluation (rather than grading) is a function of the quality of the product or service as viewed through the eyes of a client or consumer. Looking up new information, conducting experiments, analyzing results, or preparing a report is focused primarily on present action rather than storing it for possible future use. Interestingly enough, material learned through authentic pursuits has the greatest amount of transfer value for future use. When content and processes are learned in authentic, contextual situations, they result in more meaningful uses of information and problem-solving strategies than the learning that takes place in overly structured, prescribed classroom situations. If persons involved in authentic learning experiences are given some choice of the domains and activities in which they are engaged, and if present experience is directed toward realistic, personalized goals, this type of learning creates its own relevancy and meaning.

The objectives of the AITDs. Authentic learning consists of investigative activities and the development of creative products in which students assume roles as firsthand investigators, writers, artists, or other types of practicing professionals. Although students pursue these kinds of involvement at a more junior level than adult professionals, the overriding purpose is to create situations in which young people are thinking, feeling, and doing what practicing professionals do in the delivery of products and services. These experiences should be viewed as vehicles through which the following five objectives of AITDs can be achieved:

1. To provide students with opportunities, resources, and encouragement to apply their interests, knowledge, thinking skills, creative ideas, and task commitment to self-selected problems or areas of study
2. To acquire advanced-level understanding of the knowledge and methodology used within particular disciplines, artistic areas of expression, and interdisciplinary studies
3. To develop authentic products or services that are directed primarily toward bringing about a desired impact on one or more specified audiences
4. To develop self-directed learning skills in the areas of planning, problem finding and focusing, organization, resource utilization, time management, cooperation, decision making, and self-evaluation
5. To develop task commitment, self-confidence, feelings of creative accomplishment, and the ability to interact effectively with other students and adults who share common goals and interests

Authentic learning should be viewed as the vehicle through which everything from basic skills to advanced content and processes comes together in the form of student-developed products and services. In much the same way that all the separate but interrelated parts of an automobile come together at an assembly plant, so also do we consider this form of learning as the assembly plant of the mind. This kind of learning represents a synthesis and an application of content, process, and personal involvement. The student's role is transformed from one of lesson learner to firsthand inquirer, and the role of the teacher changes from an instructor and disseminator of knowledge to a combination of coach, resource procurer, mentor, and, at times, partner or colleague. Although products play an important role in creating authentic learning situations, a major concern is the development and application of a wide range of cognitive, affective, and motivational processes.

In many ways our view of authentic learning compliments the guidelines Beane (1993a, 1993b) proposed for middle school curriculum. He stated one guideline as follows: "The central purpose of the middle school curriculum should be helping early adolescents explore self and social meanings at this time in their lives" (1993a, p. 18). We believe that self-selected, authentic investigations create an important "space" for middle school students to find points of personal engagement. Beane also stated that "the middle school curriculum should be firmly grounded in democracy" (1993a, p. 19). He believes that democratic curriculum can only be conceived when all people, both adults and students, collaborate to determine the curriculum. Like Beane, we firmly believe that authentic, investigative experiences, mutually determined by students and teachers, will provide the most powerful and meaningful learning experiences.

How Are Academies of Inquiry and Talent Development Organized?

Student and teacher interest assessment. Prior to or upon entrance into middle school, all students are assessed for their major strengths and interest areas. Using a simple interest inventory (Renzulli, 1997a) and a data gathering format called the Total Talent Portfolio (Purcell & Renzulli, 1998), this assessment process compiles information about previous successful to exemplary performance in academic subjects, extracurricular pursuits, and collected works that reflect high levels of interest and creativity. The portfolio also includes responses to interest assessment instruments, learning and expression styles assessments, and various goal setting statements. Teachers simultaneously complete an adult interest assessment questionnaire, such as "Targeting My Ideal Teaching and Learning Situation" (Gentry & Renzulli, 1995), and use the results to explore the AITD in which they might like to participate. Teachers are encouraged to consider special areas of interest outside of their major teaching assignment as well as special topical interests within the subjects they regularly teach (Reis, Gentry, & Park, 1995).

The results of student assessment lead to "enrollment" in one of the following Academies of Inquiry and Talent Development, and the results of teacher interest assessment lead to joining the "faculty" of one of these academies (see Figure 13.1). Other academies may also be formed as a result of specialized interests, and academies can be subdivided into specialized areas within a general area of knowledge (e.g., physical sciences, biological sciences, environmental studies). Typically, however, these subdivisions will take place through the variety of enrichment clusters formed within each of the general academies.

What Takes Place in an Academy of Inquiry and Talent Development?

All activity within the AITDs is directed toward the acquisition and application of advanced levels of knowledge and investigative methodology within the respective fields of study subsumed under each academy. The theory of learning that guides inquiry in this plan is called the Enrichment Triad Model (Renzulli, 1977; Renzulli & Reis, 1997). This model consists of three interrelated types of enrichment (see Figure 13.2) that are focused toward the development of interests, the skills of inquiry, and the production of creative and authentic products. Ideally, involvement in the first two types of enrichment should lead to problem finding and focusing that will become the focal point of the third type of enrichment.

Type I Enrichment: General exploratory experiences. Type I Enrichment consists of experiences and activities that are purposefully designed to expose students to a wide variety of disciplines, topics, occupations, issues, hobbies, persons, places, and events that are not normally covered in the regular curriculum. A major objective of this type of enrichment is to stimulate new interests that may lead to more intensive follow-up on the parts of individuals or small groups. Type I Enrichment is typically carried out by exposure to visiting speakers, the use of visual and print media or interest development centers, attendance at performances or demonstrations, or visitations to places where persons are engaged in scientific, artistic, or other kinds of professional activities. Through a series of recommended debriefing, discussion, and brainstorming activities, students examine each experience to see if they would like to learn more about the topic and perhaps initiate an investigative or creative endeavor within the topic area. Thus, for example, a subgroup of students who attended a large-group presentation on environmental engineering in the Academy of Physical and Life Sciences decided that they would like to learn more about how park landscapes and pathway designs are developed. They formed an enrichment cluster on landscape architecture; and with the help of one of their teachers—a local landscape architect who recommended books, materials, and information obtained from the Internet—they developed several designs for schools, parks, and public buildings in their city. This example shows the progression from Type I (the speaker on environmental engineering), to Type II (studying the methodology of landscape architecture), to Type III (actually applying authentic methods of inquiry to develop their own designs). One of the designs for a school playground was approved by their local board of education for actual construction.

Type II Enrichment: Group training activities. Type II Enrichment activities are designed to develop (a) general thinking skills, (b) affective processes related to better understanding of self and others, (c) learning-how-to-learn

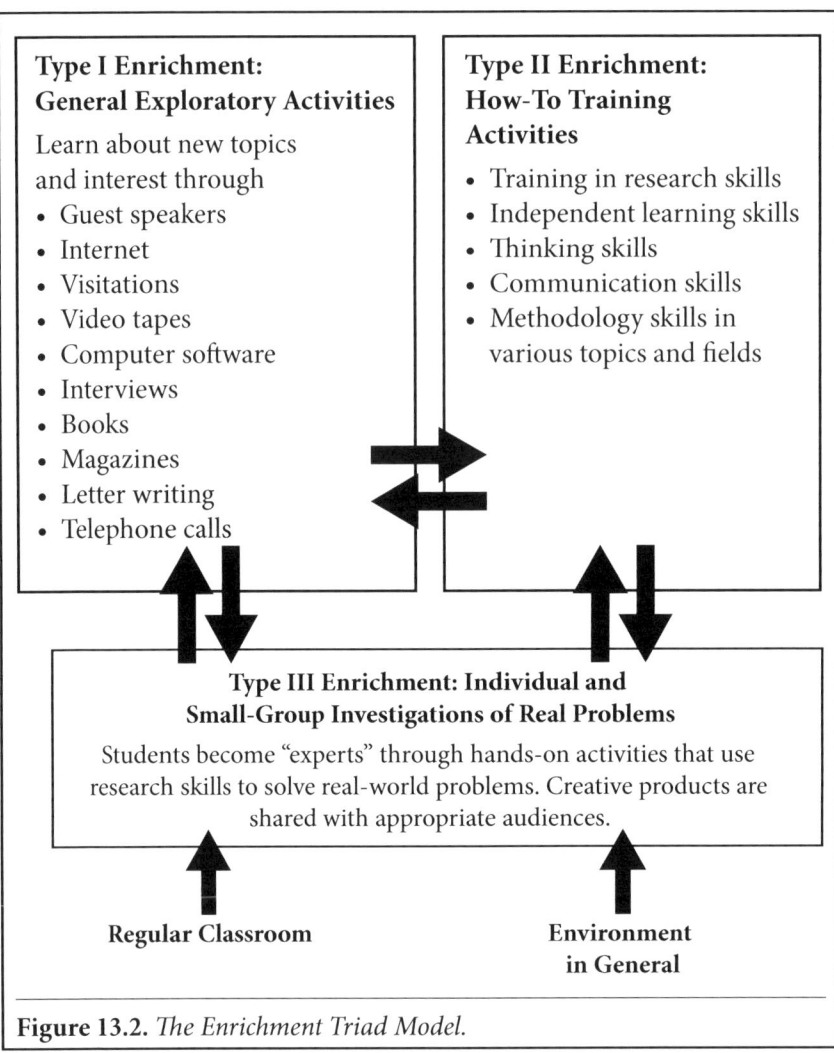

Figure 13.2. *The Enrichment Triad Model.*

skills, (d) methodological (i.e., research and reference) skills, and (e) skills designed to enhance various modes of communication. Type II Enrichment is typically carried out through planned lessons that focus on one or more of the five skill areas mentioned in the previous sentence. In some cases, the topics for these lessons cannot be selected in advance because the interests might emerge (as in the above example) from a Type I experience. Although all of the skill areas mentioned above are important, numbers 4 and 5 are especially relevant to the goals of the Academies for Inquiry and Talent Development. In order for young people to carry out authentic investigations, it is necessary for them to understand and apply the methods of inquiry in a particular field and to communicate effectively the findings of their research or the products resulting from their creative endeavors. All fields of knowledge have a fairly substantial sub-set of books and materials that focus on the methodology or how-to knowledge of the field. For example, a book entitled *A Student's Guide to Conducting Social Science Research* (Bunker, Pearlson, & Schultz, 1999) is a wonderful resource for students who are interested in pursuing a research project. *Research Comes Alive: Guidebook for Conducting Original Research for Middle and High School Students* (Schack & Starko, 1998) is another example of a reference book that addresses the methodological skills. These materials can serve as excellent resources for Type II training; however, it is important to keep in mind that this type of learning should be viewed as preparation for investigative (Type III) activities rather than as an end in itself.

Summary: Types I and II Enrichment. Within the Academies of Inquiry and Talent Development, Types I and II Enrichment are designed to play a very special role. This role is to help students find and focus problems that will lead to Type III Enrichment, either in the formation of group investigation teams called enrichment clusters, or individual projects of a creative or investigative nature carried out by a single person. Accordingly, all Type I and II activities should be geared toward answering the following critical questions:

1. What do people with an interest in this area do?
2. What products do they create and/or what services do they provide?
3. What methods do they use to carry out their work?
4. What resources and materials are needed to produce high quality products and services?
5. How, and with whom, do they communicate the results of their work?
6. What steps need to be taken to have an impact on intended audiences?

Type I Enrichment can be carried out in a large-group setting for all students within an AITD, or it can take place within smaller groups that have already expressed an interest in a particular topic or subdivision of knowledge included in a general field. For example, a Type I in cartoon art would be more meaningful for students interested in the visual arts, whereas a Type I in mime or set design might be more appropriate for students with an interest in the dramatic arts. Since one of the goals of this model is to provide opportunities for students to reach out in new directions and develop new interests, all Type I activities should be widely advertised and open to all students within the AITD who want to attend.

Whereas both Types I and II Enrichment focus on the first two critical questions listed above, questions three through six are more relevant to persons who have already made a decision to further pursue a topic or area of study. Accordingly, most Type II Enrichment activities take place in smaller groups (i.e., enrichment clusters) after students have focused on a particular area in which they would like to carry out investigative work. For example, a group of students with a general interest in the social sciences developed a more specific concern about the attitudes of students and parents toward the adoption of a school uniforms policy that was being considered by several communities in their region of the state. They formed an enrichment cluster called "The Attitude Data Detectives." With resources provided by their teacher and information they obtained from the Internet, they learned the skills necessary for designing a very professional questionnaire and survey instrument. Additional methodological skills included how to tabulate and statistically analyze data and how to report findings in written, oral, and graphic formats. Examples of how Type I and Type II Enrichment in the area of social studies are planned around the six questions listed above are shown in Figure 13.3.

Type III Enrichment: Individual and small-group investigations of real problems. The real "pay off" in terms of high-level learning in the Enrichment Triad Model is Type III Enrichment. This type of enrichment includes investigative activities, creative productions, and artistic performances in which the learner assumes the role of a firsthand inquirer—the student thinking, feeling, and doing like the practicing professional, even if the work is at a more junior level than that pursued by adult scientists, writers, and other professionals. Type III Enrichment is typically carried out by providing students with opportunities, resources, and encouragement to apply their interests, knowledge, creative ideas, and task commitment to a self-selected problem or area of study.

By developing authentic products that are intended to have an impact on targeted audiences, students acquire, in a natural and relevant way, advanced levels of knowledge and investigative methodology in their areas of interest. They also learn how to develop self-directed learning skills, organizational skills, the appropriate use of advanced level reference materials, and time management skills. When Type III Enrichment takes place in a group, students also learn how to interact as an effective member of a team, how to work cooperatively with others, and how to participate in activities where success is based on divisions of labor and mutual interdependence.

At the middle school level, Type III investigations are carried out in small-group arrangements called enrichment clusters or by an individual student who has identified an area of study that has personalized interest for him or her. Most Type III investigations begin when students have a general area of interest (e.g., film making, environmental concerns, robotics, dramatics, creative writing), but in order to avoid the typical give-a-report approach to learning, it is essential that general interests be refined and focused into researchable, investigable problems or creative challenges. The transition from a general area of interest to a specific problem that requires investigative

Potential Areas of Study Experiences	Type I Enrichment General Exploratory Experiences	Type II Enrichment Group Training Activities	Type III Enrichment Individual and Small-Group Investigations of Real Problems (Enrichment Clusters)	Outlets/Products/Audiences For Type III Enrichment
History Geography Political Science Sociology Psychology Economics Anthropology Archaeology	• Presentations by persons in each of the disciplines • Visitations to sites where these people work • Brainstorming sessions about topics that might be interesting to study • Reading biographies • Debate • Panel discussion • Visitation to historical sites • Brainstorming sessions about "hot topics" in the news	• Developing a survey instrument • Conducting an oral history interview • Examination and discussion of interesting documents and products from the discipline • Methods historians use to find and focus a research problem • Socratic method • Comparison/contrast • Primary/secondary sources • Multicultural Sensitivity Training • Interpreting data • Descriptive statistics • Graphs/charts	• The Oral History Research Team • The Creative Cartographers Guild • The Animal Learning Laboratory • The Local Survey Research Team • Investors, Inc. • The Political Action Society • Shipwreck Explorers Lab • Students for Social Action • The Social Behavior Lab • Where Your History Book Leaves Off • The Psychology of Dreams	• Presentations to local or state historical societies • Maps of local historical sites, recreation areas • Articles in school and city newspapers and magazines • CT Geographic Olympiad • Displays at public buildings, shopping malls, senior centers • National Geography Bee • Letter to congressman/senator • Lobbying effort • PAC • History Day • USA Today Stock Market Game

Figure 13.3. *Academies of inquiry and talent development: The academy of social sciences.*

Potential Areas of Study Experiences	Type I Enrichment General Exploratory Experiences	Type II Enrichment Group Training Activities	Type III Enrichment Individual and Small-Group Investigations of Real Problems (Enrichment Clusters)	Outlets/Products/ Audiences For Type III Enrichment
		▪ Recognizing and detecting bias and stereotypes ▪ Forecasting and predicting	▪ The Native American Heritage Society ▪ The Hispanic-American Cultural Group ▪ The Asian-American Heritage Society ▪ The African-American Literature Institute ▪ The Women's History Society ▪ Society in Conflict ▪ The 21st Century Historical Society ▪ The Business Researchers' Team	▪ Archaeological dig ▪ "Mansfield Monopoly" to Chamber of Commerce ▪ Petition to state and local officials ▪ Cultural presentations to primary students ▪ Presentations to UConn Psychology Department ▪ History text for kids ▪ Web page ▪ Debate/public panel ▪ Presentation to Chamber of Commerce ▪ Editorial in school or local newspaper

Figure 13.3. *Continued.*

methodology is, once again, dependent on applying the methods used by professionals to find and focus a problem. Guidance by professionals and the use of how-to books can help students learn how to develop testable hypotheses and raise research questions. Group discussions and brainstorming sessions lead eventually to specific problems that are viable for this investigative type of learning. Sometimes the products of enrichment clusters represent ongoing services of a creative nature. Thus, for example, one group of middle school students who formed a television production company established an enrichment cluster that lasted over a six-year period. They presented their work on a weekly cable access television program in their city. New students joined the cluster as other students went on to high school, and the more experienced students served as mentors to the beginning students.

In some cases, advanced level competitions are ideal situations for participation in existing programs that require high levels of scholarship, involvement, and creativity. The Math Olympiad for Middle Schools and the National History Day Competitions are examples of programs that might be the focus of enrichment clusters or individual Type III pursuits. Opportunities for student publications at the school, local, state, and national levels are virtually unlimited, and other vehicles, such as science fairs and artistic productions, provide numerous opportunities for students to bring their work to bear on a variety of target audiences. Our experience has shown that the audience requirement for Type III Enrichment has a remarkably positive effect on students' motivation, the relevance and realness of their work, and their willingness to pursue advanced levels of understanding, scholarship, and creativity.

Part II

Being consistent with both the academic goals and the emphasis middle schools place on personal and social development, Academies of Inquiry and Talent Development promote academic rigor through instructional differentiation.

How Does an AITD Program Get Started?

1. General orientation for students and parents. Prior to students entering the middle school, a booklet describing the AITD program is sent home to them and their parents. The booklet contains information about the mission, goals, and structure of the program, and a brief description of the general

Academies of Inquiry and Talent Development around which the program is organized. In addition to the main focus of the respective academies, a few examples of potential clusters and cluster activities should be described. Initial year examples can be borrowed from other successful middle school cluster programs. In subsequent years, local examples should be described, and students who have been involved in clusters should be asked to present examples of their work at the orientation sessions.

Emphasis should be given to the diversity of options that will be available over the three or four years of middle school enrollment. If students have been in an elementary school that uses the Total Talent Portfolio, the booklet should provide directions about analyzing their portfolio with their parents and teachers in order to make a decision about which AITD they would like to join. If students have not experienced a portfolio assessment at the elementary level, an interest assessment instrument can be sent home with the booklet, and students can be asked to spend some time analyzing their interests and making plans for the AITD they would like to join upon entering middle school.

In addition to the orientation booklet, an assembly for students and an orientation night for parents should be provided at the beginning of each year. After the first year of the program, students who have previously participated in clusters should be asked to make brief presentations about some of their cluster activities at the orientation sessions. The outstanding products of students should also be displayed throughout the building or in an "academic trophy case."

2. Teacher planning. Although many teachers have well-defined interests associated frequently (but not always) with their teaching assignment, we were surprised to find in our research on enrichment clusters that many teachers also had interests in a wide variety of other areas. Regardless of present levels of interest, we recommend that teachers begin by completing an interest assessment instrument entitled *Inspiration: Targeting My Ideal Teaching Situation* (Gentry & Renzulli, 1995). An analysis of the responses to this instrument, and perhaps some discussion with friends and colleagues, will help teachers identify the AITD with which they would like to be associated. Teachers can, of course, make changes over time, and it is not unreasonable for some teachers to be associated with more than one of the AITDs.

Following this introspective process, teachers organize themselves into AITDs around the general areas of knowledge (mathematics, science, art, etc.). They have informal meetings to develop a compatible philosophy, working relationship, and plan for team governance. They brainstorm some of the activities they would like to consider for short-term and long-term offerings using a planning format that is consistent with the mission and goals of the

Students		
6th	7th	8th
Faculty		
6th	7th	8th
Special subject teachers for art, family and consumer sciences, foreign language, guidance, music, technology, etc.		Community resource persons
Possible academies would include literature, language arts and humanities; applied mathematics; social sciences; fine and performing arts; sport and leisure studies; computer sciences and technology; and physical and life sciences.		

Figure 13.4. *Academies of Inquiry and Talented Development: The academy of social sciences.*

program and the pedagogical rationale underlying the three types of enrichment described in the first part of this article (Renzulli, 2000). It is essential at this point to emphasize that this program does not involve another preparation in the traditional way that teachers prepare to teach a new course. There are no prescribed lesson plans or unit plans. Various start-up activities have been suggested in descriptive material about this approach to teaching and learning, but it is also important for each AITD faculty to create its own *modus operandi* within the overall goals of their area of study. Figure 13.4 illustrates an example of an AITD devoted to the social sciences.

During the first year of the program, the early part of the school year should be devoted to Type I experiences that are designed to answer the six critical questions listed in Part I, especially questions 1 and 2. Students should continuously be reminded that Type Is and IIs are invitations to various opportunities for individual or small group follow-up; and a debriefing guide (Renzulli & Reis, 1997, p. 150) should be used following each Type I and II experience in order to assess follow-up possibilities. Debriefing sessions result in clarifications of student interests, which in turn lead to the natural formation of groups that may eventually become enrichment clusters. Whether or not a group with a common interest becomes an ongoing cluster is dependent upon group consensus regarding a specific problem they want to investigate, a product or performance they want to produce, or a service they want to provide.

Keeping the focus on creative productivity is absolutely crucial! One of the major problems we have encountered in the enrichment cluster concept is a tendency on the part of some facilitators to turn the clusters into mini-courses. Mini-courses are designed to teach a prescribed set of content or thinking skills to students. The topic(s) may differ from regular instructional units in that they deal with material not ordinarily covered in the regular curriculum, and they may use teaching strategies that are different from traditional recitation, drill, and testing practices. But the ultimate purpose of a mini-course is to "put into the heads of students" a pre-selected set of content and/or process objectives. While this is not an unworthy goal (indeed, such is the make-up of most school learning experiences), we have something different in mind when it comes to the central purposes of an enrichment cluster.

An enrichment cluster is a learning situation that is purposefully designed to produce a product or service that will have an impact on an intended audience. All learning that takes place within a cluster, whether that learning is new content, new or improved thinking processes, or new interpersonal skills is learned within the context of a real and present problem. We purposefully avoid pre-specifying content or process objectives because we want students to follow the investigative methodology used by practicing professionals in the real world. If we approached clusters by pre-specifying what and how students are going to learn, we would be returning to a traditional instructional model rather than a model that places primary responsibility for learning on the students.

Planning an enrichment cluster is, in many ways, an easier and more natural process than planning for traditional teaching. We need only determine (through discussions with students) a product or service and an intended audience, and then go about acquiring the resources and know-how needed to produce the product or deliver the service. Whatever information, materials, problem solving skills, or assistance is needed to solve the problem automatically becomes relevant because these things are required to produce the product or deliver the service. Imagine for a moment all of the things about arithmetic, geometry, geography, architecture, purchasing, aesthetics, computer graphics, advertising, photography, accounting, cooperativeness, leadership, and ornithology that a group of middle school students learned simply by deciding that they wanted to design, construct, and market "environmentally friendly" bird houses and feeders. And notice how this topic became naturally interdisciplinary, rather than having to artificially look for ways to involve related disciplines.

Although enrichment clusters are modeled after natural learning situations, most of our teacher training has taught us that we must begin by "first stating our objectives and learning outcomes," and then "designing lessons to achieve these objectives." This traditional approach to pedagogy is a difficult habit to break. But it is essential that we move to an inductive approach to pedagogy rather than the prescribed/presented approach that typifies most traditional curriculum and mini-course activities. The teacher's role at this juncture is crucial. Rather than serving as lecturer or disseminator of knowledge, the teacher assumes the role of facilitator and coordinator of inquiry. Through the use of a planning guide called the Management Plan for Individual and Small Group Investigations (Renzulli & Reis, 1997, p. 223), the teacher assists students in framing investigative questions, locating resources, and identifying potential outlets and audiences.

The enrichment cluster titles listed under Type III Enrichment in Figure 13.5 are examples of various offerings that have been developed over the years within the general domain of literature, language arts, and the humanities. The number and type of specific clusters that any given AITD might want to develop should be decided upon collectively by the AITD faculty and students. These decisions should represent a blend of information based on (a) the strengths of teachers and their interests within the general area of knowledge around which the AITD will be organized, and (b) a general sense of the strengths and interests of students as expressed in their Total Talent Portfolios or interest assessments.

Using a brainstorming/webbing technique (Renzulli, 1994, p. 232), teachers can start to "flush out" what might be some of the specific areas of opportunity for creative productivity within the general cluster theme. Thus, for example, a group of teachers and students in an AITD that they chose to call the "Academy of Literature, Languages and Humanities" came up with ideas for possible sub-groups and product outlets related to six different groups of literature that can be categorized as: personal writing, imaginative writing, informative writing, drama, popular forms, and media composition. This brainstorming activity can be carried out with other subdivisions within the AITD (e.g., languages and humanities).

3. Maintaining high academic standards. A second problem we encountered in our research on enrichment clusters is a failure on the part of some facilitators to escalate the level of knowledge pursued within a cluster. We have observed many exciting, fun-filled activities, and this kind of enjoyment of learning is unquestionably one of the most desirable features of a good cluster. At the same time, some critics have said that certain clusters are nothing more than "fun-and-games," and others have said that the clusters are "soft on content," that they do not represent "real school." We can guard against

Potential Areas of Study	Type I Enrichment General Exploratory Experiences	Type II Enrichment Group Training Activities	Type III Enrichment Individual and Small-Group Investigations of Real Problems (Enrichment Clusters)	Outlets/Products/ Audiences for Type III Enrichment
Personal Writing Journals, diaries, autobiography, monologue, writer's notebook	Presentations by people in each discipline	Interviewing techniques	The future language inventors	Family folklore festival
	Writer-in-residence	Observation	The worldwide language guild	Anthology of student writing
	Speakers whose careers depend on language	Data collection		School/community newspaper
		Primary research skills	The "other worlds"	
Imaginative Writing Fiction, fantasy, adventure, science fiction, poetry, short story, songs, dialogues, plays	Communication with authors through letters, videos, guest presentations	Analysis	Communication research team	Literary magazine
		Listening skills		Writing contests for kids
		How to get published	The "teen talk" investigators	Poster campaigns
	Writers' symposium	Writing skills		Poetry reading events
		Speaking skills	The professional terminology collectors	Storytelling troupe (cross-age)
Informative/ Persuasive Writing Essay, letter, report, editorial, news story	Internet communication with various regions/ dialects	Keeping a writer's notebook	The ancient writings	Lexicon of "teen talk"
	Exploring ideas	Brainstorming strategies	Discoveries	The language of professionals handbook
Drama/Oral English Storytelling, debate, mime, discussion, choral readings, interviews, conversation	Stories told/read by school personnel, community leaders, parents	How to make recordings	The script/play writers group	Feature articles in local newspaper
		Guidelines on how to invite guest speakers/ presenters	The journalists team	
	Listening to excellent recordings of poetry/prose		The reference preference	Word origins quiz bowl

Figure 13.5. *The academy of language, literature, and the humanities (Prepared by Nancy Bickley).*

Potential Areas of Study	Type I Enrichment General Exploratory Experiences	Type II Enrichment Group Training Activities	Type III Enrichment Individual and Small-Group Investigations of Real Problems (Enrichment Clusters)	Outlets/Products/Audiences for Type III Enrichment
Popular Forms Posters, propaganda, reviews, criticism, ads, satire **Media Composition** TV scripts, radio programming, tapings, recordings, commercials, storyboard, bulletin boards	Discussing books that all have read	Decision making Defining purpose and audience	Searchers (collecting quotable quotes expressly for kids, selected by kids) The rewriters society The diary detectives The story recorders The movie critics The consumer and school resource guide compilers The advertising team Portmanteau word inventors The speech writers society The songwriters guild The "great books" club for kids The language game creators The folklore collectors	Cable TV news broadcast Public address communique Literary fair "Talking books" production Play production Bulletin board displays Book of quotations for kids A guide to local emporia Adopt a senior citizen pen pal Story calendars Portmanteau olympics Pop-up books

Figure 13.5. Continued.

these criticisms by examining each cluster with an eye toward what constitutes authentic and rigorous content within the field or fields of study around which clusters are organized. For example, in the cluster on bird houses and feeders mentioned earlier, the teacher/facilitator began by helping the students obtain some books on ornithology, marketing, and advertising as well as how-to books on birdhouse and feeder construction. The students studied maps to learn about birds indigenous to their area of the country and their migratory habits; they learned about anatomy in order to determine the sizes of bird houses and openings; and they studied different kinds of preferred diets, colors, mating habits, and optimal locations. Display boards with attractive drawings and photographs were prepared to help market their products, and printed material (produced with the aid of desktop publishing software) accompanied each bird house and feeder that was sold. The students became specialists in the various subtopics, the tasks required to develop high quality products, and the procedures for researching, constructing, and marketing their products.

The teacher/facilitator's role is crucial in escalating the content level of a cluster. Although it is not necessary for the teacher/facilitator to be thoroughly familiar with the content area(s) beforehand, it is necessary (a) to have an interest in the topic and a "feel" for content escalation, (b) to know how to find the resources that will advance the level of study, (c) to organize cluster activities so that knowledge escalation is pursued as part and parcel of the hands-on activities, and (d) to document the extent and level of the advanced resources used and the advanced content that was pursued in the cluster.

Left to their own devices, the students in the bird house cluster might have skipped the underlying research in ornithology and marketing in favor of the sawing, hammering, and painting that was involved in the bird house construction. If such were the case, the cluster experience would have prevented students from having opportunities for higher levels of learning. Indeed, it could have easily fallen prey to the "fun-and-games" criticism that a casual observer might have made.

Guidelines for planning enrichment clusters (Reis, Gentry, & Park, 1995; Renzulli & Reis, 1997) offer suggestions for raising questions and obtaining resources that will assist teacher/facilitators in the process of content escalation. This process is obviously more demanding than merely guiding the hands-on aspects of a cluster, but it is also an opportunity for offering creative suggestions about the direction that the work of a cluster can take and for guaranteeing that powerful learning is the hallmark of any cluster.

4. Finding time for AITDs. The assassin of most new ideas for school improvement seldom has anything to do with the ideas themselves. The literature on strategic innovation has identified the major barriers to successful change: structural and cultural inertia, internal politics, complacency, weak or unimaginative leadership, fear of cannibalizing pet projects, satisfaction with the status quo, and a general lack of incentive to abandon a comfortable present for an uncertain future. However, the biggest problem we have encountered in implementing the ideas discussed above is time. In spite of almost universal acceptance of the objectives and the potential benefits of a comprehensive enrichment model, there is frequently an unwillingness on the part of many educators to "mess around with the schedule." We have, however, seen some very innovative ways for dealing with the time issue. At a middle school in North Carolina, for example, a double period per week is set aside for the enrichment program by eliminating the home room/advisement period on what students called "cluster day" and shaving nine minutes per period from each of the other classes on that day. At a school in Connecticut, the principal "tightened up" the Friday schedule so that Friday afternoons were free for the enrichment program. She said that Friday afternoons "were formerly a down time, you know, TGIF; but the enrichment program turned that attitude around, and everyone left school on a high for the weekend!" Some schools have allocated time for the program through block scheduling arrangements, and still other schools have dropped one class meeting of each major subject area per month to yield a double time block once a week. Some schools have used their activity block for the program, others have carried out the program after school, and a few schools have made the "enrichment class" a part of the regular daily schedule. Other schools have devoted two half-days per month to the enrichment program, rotating the time blocks so that the same classes will not be missed.

There is no right or wrong way to schedule any program that requires a variation from the status quo. What is needed is a willingness to experiment with various scheduling options, a sincere belief that the experiences gained through an enrichment program are as valuable as what is being "missed" from the regular program, and an openness to the collective creativity of all persons who are willing to share their ideas about scheduling options. Scheduling options should always be pursued on an experimental basis, and input should be obtained from all persons involved (including students) following the conclusion of a trial period.

Getting Started and Creating Your Own Unique AITD Program

All roads lead to Rome! There is no right or wrong way to implement a program based on the ideas and suggestions discussed above; however, the selection and use of a program development model must meet two essential requirements. The first requirement is consensus about objectives on the part of persons who will implement the model. Everyone (or at the very least, almost everyone) involved in the selection and implementation of a model should agree that the mission and objectives represent a "destination" that they would like to reach. If an agreed upon goal is "to get to Rome," then there is no ambiguity, vagueness, or misunderstandings about where everyone wants to go.

This first requirement of a model means that a great deal of front-end time should be spent exploring alternative models, discussing and debating the advantages and disadvantages of various approaches, and examining related factors such as underlying research, implementation in other schools, and the availability of supportive resources. Reaching consensus before embarking upon a journey will help ensure that everyone involved gets to Rome rather than to Venice or Moscow!

There are many ways to get to Rome. A second requirement of a program development model is unique means for implementation. Although I believe that programs based on the AITD model should strive to accomplish an agreed upon mission and set of objectives, I also believe that any plan for program development must allow for a great deal of innovation and flexibility in the achievement of these objectives. This flexibility is necessary because no written plan or set of procedures can take into account the variations that exist at the local school level. Differences in school populations, administrative leadership, faculty motivation, financial resources, the availability of persons from the community at large, and a host of other local variables must be considered in the implementation of this or any other approach to school improvement. A model that does not allow for such flexibility could easily become a straightjacket that simply will not work when one or more of the local considerations is not taken into account. Some schools will have supplementary resource teachers for advanced level students and others will not. Some school districts will have an abundance of community resources readily available and others, perhaps more geographically isolated, will have limited access to museums, planetariums, colleges, and universities. Some schools may serve larger proportions of culturally diverse students than others, and certain schools may already be embarking on major school improvement initiatives.

Another reason I believe that a model for program development must maintain a large degree of flexibility is that educators tend to quickly lose interest in "canned" programs and models that do not allow for local initiative, creativity, and teacher input. New and better ways to provide enrichment experiences to students will be discouraged if program development does not encourage local adaptation and innovation to occur. The AITD plan provides a certain amount of general direction in both the development of program objectives and in the procedures for pursuing these objectives. At the same time, however, the specific types of activities that educators select and develop for their programs, and the ways in which they make these activities available to various populations of students will actually result in the creation of their own unique programming model. Educators will, in effect, be writing their own resource guide, because the actual content of the enrichment experiences will be developed locally by their own school personnel. I believe that if the AITD objectives are maintained, even in a slightly modified form, a school will achieve the integrity that is sought in this approach to increased levels of challenge within the context of the middle school philosophy. In this regard, the AITD model that educators develop locally will attempt to achieve the best of two worlds! First, programs will benefit from the theoretical and research developments and the many years of field testing and practical application that have led to this type of enrichment model. Second, the ideas, resources, innovations, and adaptations that emerge from local situations will contribute to the uniqueness and practicality of programs that are developed to meet local needs.

Making change at the top of your game. John Maynard Keynes, the noted economist said, "The real difficulty in changing the course of any enterprise lies not in developing new ideas but in escaping old ones." Studies of strategic planning and innovation among the world's most successful companies (Markides, 1998) provide excellent guidance for the timing of innovative changes in schools. Most organizations wait until there is a crisis before they strike out in new directions; and in many cases, they are too late to overcome the disruption caused by the crisis. The result is usually a takeover by external forces and a devaluing of the people in the organization. Educators are all too familiar with this routine. Any shortcomings in our schools or education system, whether real or perceived, are usually met with external, top-down pressure that has little regard for the opinions of the persons who carry out the day-to-day operation of a school. Witness the almost endless proliferation of guidelines, standards, state regulations, and test-driven curriculum that are imposed on teachers and schools because somebody in the policy hierarchy thought we were not doing a good job! Trying to change in the middle of a crisis is the worst time to do so. It is much better to think about introducing innovative practices in a proactive, long-term way when times are good and the majority of our constituents think we are doing a good job.

The small but growing lack-of-challenge criticism directed at middle schools has not yet reached epidemic proportions, but professional publications and the popular press are already beginning to raise questions that we need to take seriously. A recent article in a major education newspaper (Bradley, 1998) entitled "Muddle in the Middle" extols readers to consider how middle schools are "supplanting academic rigor with a focus on students' social, emotional, and physical needs" (p. 38). An earlier article in the same publication entitled "A Crack in the Middle" (Killion & Hirsh, 1998) reports that "recent national and international student test results [for the middle grades] reveal the depth of academic problems and the decline between 4th and 8th grade" (p. 44). Unless we are creative and proactive in the ways in which we respond to these criticisms, the external forces mentioned above will undoubtedly put pressure on middle schools to substitute our concerns about a conceptually challenging and enjoyable learning environment with simplistic solutions such as hosing kids down with vast amounts of factual material in the hope that it will improve test scores.

The most successful and innovative companies did not wait for a crisis or a state of "blissful stability" to occur before venturing out into new directions. They were not afraid to introduce changes into a smooth running machine, or to "shake things up a little" in order to revitalize their organizations and inspire their personnel. They made changes when their companies were the most successful, at the top of their game, so to speak, and these changes inevitably paid off in a big way. This is not to say that the leaders of these companies did not perceive early warning signs that trouble was brewing. In some cases these warnings were simply a recognition of complacency and an acceptance of the status quo on the parts of company personnel. In other cases the threats were external to the organization.

Although the middle school movement is currently enjoying a high degree of success and popularity, there are some early warnings that should cause us to sit up and take notice. The majority of these warnings relate to the lack of challenge issue and the use of a one-size-fits-all curriculum. Some schools have responded to this issue by reexamining their curriculum, and others have reverted to homogeneous grouping, especially in the areas of math and reading. But the overall success that most middle schools are experiencing is the best reason to experiment with new initiatives at this time. Like the successful companies mentioned above, a big challenge for middle schools is to develop the commitment, the know-how, the mind-set, and the underlying environment to continually examine current success while promoting continual experimentation. The AITD plan is consistent with both the academic goals and the emphasis middle schools place on personal and social development. The plan does not make unreasonable new demands on teachers or administrators; and with the exception of small changes in the ways we schedule school time, there is minimal disruption in the way schools operate, and virtually no changes in present day middle school philosophy. Someone once said, "You will never discover new lands if you don't venture outside the safety of the harbor." The strong foundation on which the current middle school movement rests is the best reason to venture outside the harbor and to search for new ways of serving our unique population of young people.

References

Beane, J. A. (1993a). *A middle school curriculum: From rhetoric to reality* (2nd ed.). Columbus, OH: National Middle School Association.

Beane, J. A. (1993b). The middle school: Natural home of integrated curriculum. *Educational Leadership, 49,* 9–13.

Bradley, A. (1998, April 15). Muddle in the middle. *Education Week, 17*(31), 38–42.

Bunker, B. B., Pearlson, H. B., & Schultz, J. W. (1999). *A student's guide to conducting social science research.* Mansfield Center, CT: Creative Learning Press.

Carnegie Council on Adolescent Development. (1989). *Tuning points: Preparing American youth for the 21st century.* New York, NY: The Carnegie Corporation.

Gentry, M., & Renzulli, J. S. (1995). *Inspiration: Targeting my ideal teaching situation.* Storrs: University of Connecticut, The National Research Center on the Gifted and Talented.

George, P. S., Renzulli, J. S., Reis, S. M., & Erb, T. O (Ed.). (1997). *Dilemmas in talent development in the middle grades: Two views.* Columbus, OH: National Middle School Association.

Killion, J., & Hirsh, S. (1998, March 18). A crack in the middle. *Education Week, 17*(27), 44–48.

Markides, C. (1998). Strategic innovation in established companies. *Sloan Management Review, 39,* 31–42.

National Middle School Association. (1995). *This we believe: Developmentally responsive middle level schools.* Columbus, OH: Author.

Purcell, J. H., & Renzulli, J. S. (1998). *The total talent portfolio: A systematic plan to identify and nurture gifts and talents.* Mansfield Center, CT: Creative Learning Press.

Reis, S. M., Gentry, M., & Park, S. (1995). *Extending the pedagogy of gifted education to all students.* Storrs: University of Connecticut, The National Research Center on the Gifted and Talented.

Renzulli, J. S. (1977). *The Enrichment Triad Model: A guide for developing defensible programs for the gifted and talented.* Mansfield Center, CT: Creative Learning Press.

Renzulli, J. S. (1994). *Schools for talent development: A practical plan for total school improvement.* Waco, TX: Prufrock Press.

Renzulli, J. S. (1997a). *Interest-a-lyzer family of instruments: A manual for teachers.* Waco, TX: Prufrock Press.

Renzulli, J. S. (1997b). *How to develop an authentic enrichment cluster.* Storrs: University of Connecticut, The National Research Center on the Gifted and Talented.

Renzulli, J. S. (2000). Part I, One way to organize exploratory curriculum: Academies of inquiry and talent development. *Middle School Journal, 32*(2), 5–14.

Renzulli, J. S., & Reis, S. M. (1997). *The Schoolwide Enrichment Model: A how-to guide for educational excellence* (2nd. ed.). Waco, TX: Prufrock Press.

Schack, G., & Starko, A. (1998). *Research comes alive: Guidebook for conducting original research for middle and high school students.* Mansfield Center, CT: Creative Learning Press.

CHAPTER 14

A Technology Based Program That Matches Enrichment Resources With Student Strengths[22]

Joseph S. Renzulli and Sally M. Reis
University of Connecticut

Introduction From Joe

One of the challenges we faced in promoting the pedagogy that is based on the systems and models described in Part 3 of this book is the almost unreasonable amount of time necessary for teachers to carry out the type of learning we advocate. We addressed this challenge with what was for us a bold new adventure into the worlds of both technology and entrepreneurism. With the help of the UConn Research and Development Corporation, we raised a

---

22 Renzulli, J. S., & Reis, S. M. (2007). A technology based program that matches enrichment resources with student strengths. *International Journal of Emerging Technologies in Learning, 2*(3), 1–13. Copyright 2007 *International Journal of Emerging Technologies in Learning.* License available at http://creativecommons.org/licenses/by/3.0/at/legalcode. Reprinted with permission.

million dollars in venture capital to develop an Internet-based system that is designed to create an online strength-based learning profile for each student and a search engine that matches highly engaging enrichment resources with student profiles. Teachers can use the system to find and infuse enrichment activities into any and all areas of the curriculum.

This chapter describes the program that was originally marketed by UConn R and D under the title "the Renzulli Learning System (RLS)." The system was subsequently sold by UConn to Compass Learning Corporation and is now marketed under the name of GoQuest. A "gold standard" research study (Field, 2009) showed positive results in promoting improvements in student achievement and a qualitative study (Swicord, Chancey, & Bruce-Davis, 2013) reported the effectiveness of the RLS as a tool for school success, its engaging quality, and selective independence. Schools that do not have access to GoQuest can still create profiles using print versions of our strength-based instruments and no cost search engines that are readily available in the Internet.

One hesitates using the word revolutionary in this day of technological advancements by the hour, but the word did occur to me as I reviewed the Renzulli Learning System. It provides a new level of differentiation and engagement. —John Lounsbury National Middle School Association Georgia College & State University

Every teacher has had the satisfaction of seeing a child "turn on" to a topic or school experience that demonstrates the true joy and excitement of both learning and teaching. We have sometimes wondered how and why these high points in teaching occur, why they don't occur more frequently, and why more students are not engaged in highly positive learning experiences. Teachers are also painfully aware of the boredom and lack of interest that so many of our young people express about so much of the work they do in school. Highly prescriptive curriculum guides, endless lists of standards to be covered, and relentless pressure to increase achievement test scores have often prevented us from doing the kind of teaching that results in those joyous but rare times when we have seen truly remarkable engagement in learning.

One teacher we interviewed as part of a research project dealing with high engagement in learning said, "I could easily improve student enthusiasm, enjoyment, and engagement if I had about a dozen teaching assistants in my classroom!" It was comments like this plus the almost infinite resources that are now available through the Internet that inspired the development of the Renzulli Learning System (RLS) at the University of Connecticut's Neag School of Education. The program is sponsored by the University of Connecticut Research and Development Corporation, with income from subscriptions used to support further research.

The use of instructional technology, and especially the Internet, has evolved rapidly over the past decade. First "generation" use of technology consisted mainly of what might be called worksheets-on-line, with the added advantage of providing students with immediate feedback about correct responses and subroutines for remediating incorrect answers. This generation was not unlike the teaching machines of the 1950s. The next generation consisted mainly of courses-on-line, and although this innovation enabled students to have access to teachers and professors with expertise beyond what might be available locally, it usually followed the same pedagogy to traditional courses (i.e., read the chapter, answer questions, take a test). The third generation was a great leap forward because of the advent of hypertext. Students could now click on highlighted items in on-line text to pursue additional, more advanced information, and the kinds of scaffolding that consumes more time that most teachers can devote to individualized learning.

The Renzulli Learning System might best be viewed as the next generation of applying instructional technology to the learning process. This program is not a variation of earlier generations of popular e-learning programs or web-surfing devices being offered by numerous software companies. It is a totally unique use of the Internet that combines computer based strength assessment with search engine technology, thus allowing true differentiation in the matching of thousands of carefully selected resources to individual strengths. The RLS also has what might best be called theoretical integrity. It is based on a high-end learning theory called the Enrichment Triad Model (Renzulli, 1977) and numerous research studies dealing with model implementation (Renzulli & Reis, 1994). The Triad Model focuses on the kinds of creative productivity that develops higher-level thinking and investigative skills, and it places a premium on the application of knowledge to learning situations that approximate the *modus operandi* of the practicing professional. With minimal skills in the use of the Internet, and only a small amount of the teacher's time, all schools can easily make use of a system that will give teachers the equivalent of "a dozen assistants" in their classrooms. The Renzulli Learning System is a four-step procedure that is based on more than thirty years of research and development dealing with the diagnosis and promotion of advanced level thinking skills, motivation, creativity, and engagement in learning.

Step 1: Strength Assessment Using the Electronic Learning Profile

The first step consists of a computer-based diagnostic assessment that creates a profile of each student's academic strengths, interests, learning styles, and preferred modes of expression. The on-line assessment, which takes about thirty minutes, results in a personalized profile that highlights individual student strengths and sets the stage for step two of the RLS. The profile acts like a compass for the second step, which is a differentiation search engine that examines thousands of resources that relate specifically to each student's profile. Student profiles can also be used to form groups of students who share common interests. A project management tool guides students and teachers to use specifically selected resources for assigned curricular activities, independent or small group investigative projects, and a wide variety of challenging enrichment experiences. Another management tool enables teachers to form instructional groups and enrichment clusters based on interests and learning style preferences. Teachers have instant access to student profiles, all sites visited on the web, and the amount of time spent in each activity. Parents may also access their own child's profile and web activities. In order to promote parent involvement, we suggest that students actually work on some of their favorite activities with their parents.

Step 2: Enrichment Differentiation Databases

In step two the differentiation search engine matches student strengths and interests to an enrichment database of 10,000 enrichment activities, materials, resources, and opportunities for further study that are grouped into the following categories:
- Virtual Field Trips
- Real Field Trips
- Creativity Training
- Critical Thinking
- Projects and Independent Study
- Contests and Competitions
- Websites
- Fiction Books
- Non-Fiction Books
- How-To Books

- Summer Programs
- On-Line Classes and Activities
- Research Skills
- Videos and DVDs

These resources are not merely intended to inform students about new information or to occupy time surfing around the web. Rather, they are used as vehicles for helping students find and focus a problem or creative exploration of personal interest that they might like to pursue in greater depth. Many of the resources provide the methods of inquiry, advanced level thinking and creative problem solving skills, and investigative approaches that approximate the *modus operandi* of the practicing professional. Students are guided toward the *application of knowledge* to the development of original research studies, creative projects, and action-oriented undertakings that put knowledge to work in personally meaningful areas of interest. The resources also provide students with suggestions for outlets and audiences for their creative products. A set of learning maps for teachers is provided for each of the fourteen enrichment resource databases and for the many other resources available for teachers. Teachers can also download numerous curricular activities for use in their classrooms. Management tools classify and cross reference activities by subject area, thinking skill, and subject matter standards.

Our goal in this approach to learning is to promote high levels of engagement by providing a vehicle where students can engage in *thinking, feeling, and doing like the practicing professional*, even if they are operating at a more junior level than adult scientists, artists, writers, engineers, or other adults who pursue knowledge in professional ways.

Research on the role of student engagement is clear and unequivocal—high engagement results in higher achievement, improved self-concept and self-efficacy, and more favorable attitudes toward school and learning. There is a strong body of research that points out the crucial difference between time-spent and time-engaged in school achievement. In the recently published international PISA study, the single criterion that distinguished between nations with the highest and lowest levels of student achievement was the degree to which students were engaged in their studies. This finding took into account demographic factors such as ethnicity and the socioeconomic differences among the groups studied. In a longitudinal study comparing time-spent vs. time-engaged on the achievement of at-risk students, Greenwood (1991) found that conventional instructional practices were responsible for the students' increased risk of academic delay. And a study by Ainley (1991) reported that there were important differences in achievement outcomes favoring engaged over disengaged students of similar ability.

The resources available in step two also provide students with places where they can pursue advanced level training in their strength areas and areas of personal interest. On-line courses and summer programs that focus on specific academic strengths and creative talents are ways that any school or parent can direct highly able and motivated students to resources that may not be available in the regular school program.

Step 3: The Wizard Project Maker

A special feature of Renzulli Learning is a project organization and management plan for students and teachers called The Wizard Project Maker. This guide (see p. 341) allows teachers to help students use their web-based explorations for original research, investigative projects, and the development of a wide variety of creative undertakings. The sophisticated software used in this tool automatically locates potentially relevant web-based resources that can be used in connection with the student's investigative activity. This management device is designed to fulfill the requirements of a Type III Enrichment experience, which is the highest level of enrichment described below in the discussion of the Enrichment Triad Model. Specifically, the Project Maker provides students with the metacognitive skills to: Define a project and set a goal; Identify and evaluate both the resources to which they have access and the resources they need (e.g. time, Internet sites, teacher or mentor assistance); Prioritize and refine goals; Balance the resources needed to meet multiple goals; Learn from past actions, projecting future outcomes; and Monitor progress, making necessary adjustments as a project unfolds.

The Wizard Project Maker helps students make the best use of web resources, it helps to focus their interests as they pursue advanced level work, and it is a built in safeguard against using Renzulli Learning merely to surf around the web. It also establishes a creative and viable responsibility for teachers in their role as "the guide on the side." By helping students pursue advanced levels of challenge and engagement through the use of the Wizard Project Maker, students see teachers as mentors rather than task masters or disseminators of knowledge. The Wizard Project Maker also has a metacognitive effect on students (i.e., they have a better understanding about what investigative learning is all about). As one teacher recently said, "The Wizard Project Maker helps my students understand 'the why' of using the Internet." A Wizard Project Maker template is attached to this article and Wizard Software is built into the System to help students acquire resources for the various sections of this planning device.

Step 4: The Total Talent Portfolio

The final step in the Renzulli Learning System is an automatic compilation and storage of all student activity from steps one, two, and three into an on-going student record called the Total Talent Portfolio. A management tool allows students to evaluate each site visited and resource used, students can complete a self-assessment of what they derived from the resource, and if they choose they can store favorite activities and resources in their portfolio. This feature allows easy-return-access to on-going work. The portfolio can be reviewed at any time by teachers and parents through the use of an access code, which allows teachers to give feedback and guidance to individual students and provides parents with information about students' work and opportunities for parental involvement. The portfolio can also be used for:

- Providing points of reference for future teachers
- Making decisions about possible class project extra credit options
- Selecting subsequent enrichment preferences
- Designing future projects and creative activities
- Exploring on-line courses and competitions
- Participating in extra-curricular activities
- Deciding on electives in Middle and High School
- Guiding college selection and career exploration alternatives

The Total Talent Portfolio "travels" with students throughout their educational career. It can serve as a reminder of previous activities and creative accomplishments that they might want to include in college applications and it is an ongoing record that can help students, teachers, guidance counselors, and parents make decisions about future educational and vocational plans.

The Theory and Research Underlying the Renzulli Learning System

The RLS is based on a learning theory called the Enrichment Triad Model, which was developed in 1977 and implemented in thousands of schools in the United States and several overseas nations (see Figure 14.1). A wide range of programs based on the Enrichment Triad Model were developed by classroom teachers and gifted education specialists in different school districts across the country that serve diverse populations of students at all grade levels. Many

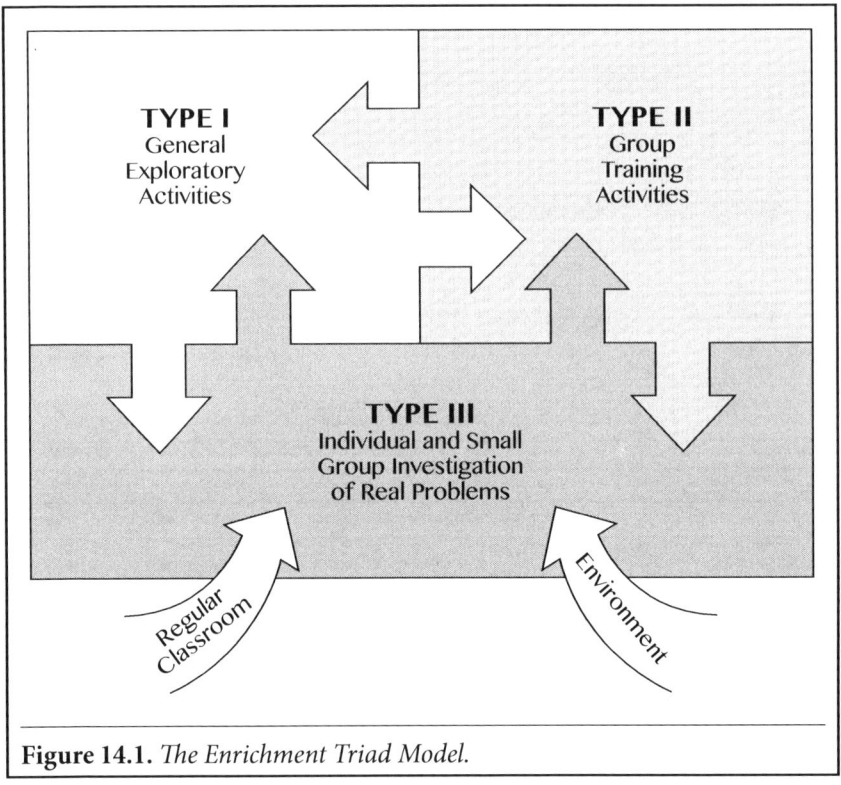

Figure 14.1. *The Enrichment Triad Model.*

examples of creative student work were completed as part of the enrichment opportunities built around the Triad Model.

Teachers using the model worked very hard to access resources to provide enrichment for students, but the many responsibilities of classroom teachers and the amount of time required to track down resources made this a daunting task. In the Renzulli Learning System, thousands of resources and enrichment materials are provided for teachers and students with the click of a mouse. And what makes this system unique is that these resources are individually tailored to students' abilities, interests, and learning styles. The resources can be accessed in school, during after-school programs, or even at home when students want to pursue enriched learning opportunities on their own.

The Enrichment Triad Model was designed to encourage advanced level learning and creative productivity by: (1) exposing students to various topics, areas of interest, and fields of study in which they have an interest or might develop an interest, (2) providing students with the skills and resources necessary to acquire advanced level content and thinking skills, and (3) creating opportunities for students to **apply** their skills to self-selected areas of interest and problems that they want to pursue.

Type I Enrichment is designed to expose students to a wide variety of disciplines, topics, occupations, hobbies, persons, places, and events that would not ordinarily be covered in the regular curriculum or that are extensions of regular curriculum topics. In the Renzulli Learning System, Type I Enrichment includes virtual field trips, on-line activities that challenge student thinking, exciting web sites, books, videos, and DVDs related to areas of special interest, and other exposure activities that are associated with independent projects and other components of the system. Type I experiences might be viewed as the motivational "hook" that causes individual students to become turned-on to a particular topic or area of study that they will subsequently pursue in greater depth.

Type II Enrichment consists of materials and activities designed to develop a broad range of higher level thinking processes and advanced inquiry skills. Some Type II training is general, including the development of: (1) creative thinking and problem solving, critical thinking, and affective processes; (2) a wide variety of specific learning how-to-learn skills; (3) skills in the appropriate use of advanced-level research methods and reference materials; and (4) written, oral, and visual communication skills. Teachers can use general Type II Enrichment activities (e.g., a lesson in creative thinking) that are available on-line for whole group or small group instruction, or an on-line activity can be recommended for individuals or small groups to pursue on their own.

Type II Enrichment consists of materials and activities designed to develop a broad range of higher level thinking processes and advanced inquiry skills. Some Type II training is general, including the development of: (1) creative thinking and problem solving, critical thinking, and affective processes; (2) a wide variety of specific learning how-to-learn skills; (3) skills in the appropriate use of advanced-level research methods and reference materials; and (4) written, oral, and visual communication skills. Teachers can use general Type II Enrichment activities (e.g., a lesson in creative thinking) that are available on-line for whole group or small group instruction, or an on-line activity can be recommended for individuals or small groups to pursue on their own.

Other forms of Type II Enrichment are specific to a particular project that a student might be pursuing. It cannot be planned in advance and usually involves advanced research skills in an interest area selected by the student. For example, a small group of students became interested in mechanical engineering after a Virtual Field Trip that dealt with some of the world's most imaginative bridges. They located resources on the Internet that provided instruction for designing, planning, and building a model of a bridge. They also found a number of model bridge competitions to which they subsequently submitted their designs.

In the Renzulli Learning System, Type II training is embedded across many of the Enrichment Activities listed above. A quick tour of the various categories will help you become familiar with the vast array of resources that can be used for all three types of enrichment in the Triad Model. If several students are using the Renzulli Learning System it will be fun and informative to take a "tour" through their Enrichment Activities with them.

Our experience in using the Enrichment Triad Model over the years has shown that Types I and II enrichment and/or interests gained in the regular curriculum or out-of-school activities will motivate many students to pursue self-selected topics in greater depth. We call these advanced types of involvement Type III Enrichment, which is defined as individual or small group investigations of real problems. When students choose to become involved in Type III Enrichment, they usually are interested enough in a topic to pursue a self-selected area of study in great depth. They also are willing to commit the time necessary for advanced content acquisition and process training in which they assume the role of a first-hand inquirer. The goals of Type III Enrichment are:

- to provide opportunities for applying interests, knowledge, creative ideas and task commitment to a self-selected problem or area of study,
- to acquire advanced level understanding of the knowledge (content) and methodology (process) that are used within particular disciplines, artistic areas of expression and interdisciplinary studies,
- to develop authentic products that are primarily directed toward bringing about a desired impact upon a specified audience,
- to learn self-directed learning skills in the areas of planning, organization, resource utilization, time management, decision making, and self-evaluation,
- to further develop task commitment, self-confidence, and feelings of creative accomplishment.

In the Renzulli Learning System, the Type III component can emerge from almost any of the options that students choose to pursue. They can, for example, get an idea for what they might like to learn more about by becoming involved in a virtual field trip, or a real field trip. They might find an idea from a creativity training exercise or critical thinking activity. The most logical way for students to become involved in a Type III project is by pursuing an independent study or by becoming involved in a contest or a competition. We have also found that students may become interested in doing in-depth research by using any of the other components of the RLS such as special topic websites, Fiction, Non-Fiction, and How-to books, Summer Programs, On-Line Activities and Research Skills. There are also numerous options in Renzulli

Learning for students to pursue Type III studies in specialized areas (e.g., Math League, Invention Convention, National History Day Competition, to mention only a few of the hundreds of available options).

Type III Enrichment is different from the types of projects and reports that students typically do in connection with their regular schoolwork. The best way to describe this difference is to list the three things that make a problem "real" to a student. First, real problems are based on a sincere interest of the student rather than one assigned by the teacher. It is something the student *wants* to do rather than something he or she is assigned to do. You may discuss and provide guidance in helping a student find and focus a problem, and the problem might be within the general curriculum area you are covering, but the subject or theme on which a student chooses to work must represent a personalization of the topic for him or for her.

The second distinguishing feature of working on a real problem is that the student will use the methods of investigation of the practicing professional. They're going to do what the real geologist, scenery designer, or community activist does, even if it is at a more junior level than an adult professional working in one of these fields. This focus will help to distinguish a *bona fide* Type III project from the ritualistic reports that students typically complete by merely gathering and summarizing information from reference books or Internet sites. The most powerful tools for giving students the know-how of authentic methodology, such as *How-To Books for Conducting Research and Creative Projects*, can be found in the Enrichment Database under the category How-To Books. Take a quick tour of this enrichment category to get a "feel" of the many exciting books that provide the skills for helping students become practicing professionals. And think about using some of the material in these books for whole-class and small group lessons on teaching research and investigative skills. We have found that teaching young people a practical data gathering technique such as questionnaire design, for example, will motivate them to identify a problem that allows them to use their new skill on a problem in which they have a personal interest.

The third characteristic of a real problem is that it is always geared toward an audience other than or in addition to the teacher. In the adult world, practicing professionals carry out their work because they want to have an impact on one or more relevant audiences—others who voluntarily attend a performance, read a newsletter, or go to a science fair. Presenting to classmates occasionally may qualify as a real audience but such presentations should be viewed more as practice sessions for more real world settings such as a presentation to the local historical society, submission of one's writing to a magazine that publishes poetry or short stories, or entering an invention contest. The enrichment category entitled *Contests and Competitions* will give you and your students many ideas about opportunities for audiences in all areas of student interest. And the *Websites* category includes many organizations and professional societies that produce journals and newsletters where high quality student products might be included. These organizations are also excellent sources for resources in specialized areas of study, and some of them even provide on-line mentoring services for students.

The goal of Type III Enrichment is to transform the role of the student from a person who merely acquires information to a role in which she or he is thinking, feeling, and doing like the practicing professional by actually engaging in *authentic* activities. In reflecting on the characteristics of authentic activities described by researchers, ten broad design characteristics that relate to on-line learning have been identified by Reeves, Herrington, and Oliver (2002). These characteristics are:

- Authentic activities have real-world relevance: Activities match as nearly as possible the real-world tasks of professionals in practice rather than decontextualized or classroom-based tasks.
- Authentic activities are ill-defined, requiring students to define the tasks and sub-tasks needed to complete the activity: Problems inherent in the activities are ill defined and open to multiple interpretations rather than easily solved by the application of existing algorithms. Learners must identify their own unique tasks and sub-tasks in order to complete the major task.
- Authentic activities comprise complex tasks to be investigated by students over a sustained period of time: Activities are completed in days, weeks and months rather than minutes or hours. They require significant investment of time and intellectual resources.
- Authentic activities provide the opportunity for students to examine the task from different perspectives, using a variety of resources: The task affords learners the opportunity to examine the problem from a variety of theoretical and practical perspectives, rather than allowing a single perspective that learners must imitate to be successful. The use of a variety of resources rather than a limited number of pre-selected references requires students to detect relevant from irrelevant information.
- Authentic activities provide the opportunity to collaborate: Collaboration is integral to the task, both within the course and the real world, rather than achievable by an individual learner.
- Authentic activities provide the opportunity to reflect: Activities need to enable learners to make choices and reflect on their learning both individually and socially.

- Authentic activities can be integrated and applied across different subject areas and lead beyond domain-specific outcomes: Activities encourage interdisciplinary perspectives and enable students to play diverse roles thus building robust expertise rather than knowledge limited to a single well-defined field or domain.
- Authentic activities are seamlessly integrated with assessment: Assessment of activities is seamlessly integrated with the major task in a manner that reflects real world assessment, rather than separate artificial assessment removed from the nature of the task.
- Authentic activities create polished products valuable in their own right rather than as preparation for something else: Activities culminate in the creation of a whole product rather than an exercise or substep in preparation for something else.
- Authentic activities allow competing solutions and diversity of outcome: Activities allow a range and diversity of outcomes open to multiple solutions of an original nature, rather than a single correct response obtained by the application of rules and procedures (p. 565).

To help students understand the difference between an authentic Type III and the more traditional kinds of reports that they typically do in school, we have developed The Wizard Project Maker, a completed sample of which is attached. This form also highlights the specific ways in which teachers can provide guidance in helping students find and focus a problem, examine potential outlets and audiences, and obtain the necessary resources to carry out their investigative activities. Blank copies of this form can be downloaded at the RLS web site. The teacher's role in this type of enrichment becomes more like a coach and guide-on-the-side rather than a disseminator of knowledge. The teacher's role is an active one, but requires minimal time because it does not require large amounts of face-to-face instruction. You can learn more about the role that teachers play in facilitating Type III Enrichment by reviewing the short article on this topic in the **Teacher Resource** section of this web site.

One of the questions that teachers frequently ask is, "Where will students find the time to do Type III projects?" All students can use the Renzulli Learning System, but we have found that above average ability students—those who can master the regular curriculum at a faster pace than others—can "buy" some time for enrichment activities through a sub-component of the RLS called curriculum compacting. Essentially, compacting is a process through which the teacher uses formal and informal assessment at the *beginning* of a unit of study to determine which students have already mastered basic skills, and therefore do not need the same amount of practice material as others. Indeed, it is sometimes this excessive practice of skills already mastered that causes many of our more able students to become bored with school! And in subjects such as science and social studies, students may not know the material to be covered, but are eager to select an option that allows them to cover it at an accelerated pace. Many students are especially eager to select this option if they know that it will "buy" them the time to work on Type III Enrichment as well as other options in the RLS. We have provided a brief article on the steps teachers use in curriculum compacting in the **Teacher Resource** section of this web site.

The Value Added Benefits of Learning *With* Technology

The conditions of learning have changed dramatically for young people going to school today. Don Leu and his team of New Literacies researchers at the University of Connecticut (2004) have pointed out that the Internet is this generation's defining technology for literacy and learning; and that profound changes have already taken place in higher education, adult learning and the workplace, all situations for which we are preparing the young students who are in our classrooms today. There was a time when teachers and textbooks were the gatekeepers of knowledge, but today virtually all of the world's knowledge is accessible to any student who can turn on a computer and log into the Internet. One of the dangers of a content abundant resource such as the Internet, however, is that we might be tempted to simply use it to cram more information into students' heads! But by applying a learner-centered pedagogy rather than a traditional drill-and-practice approach, we can harness the power of the Internet in a way that respects principles of high-level learning developed by the Task Force on Psychology of the American Psychological Association (1997). A crucial question, therefore, is will we use this information wisely? Or will we simply turn the powerful resources available through the Internet into electronic work sheets, test-prep tutorials, and on-line courses that adhere to the same prescriptive model for learning that almost all reform initiatives have followed thus far—a model that has indeed left so many young people bored, disengaged and behind? Or will the new technologies be the workhorse that can finally allow teachers to truly differentiate learning experiences for all students? These technologies now make it possible to apply to all students the pedagogy typically used with high achieving students. In an article entitled "A Rising Tide Lifts All Ships" (1998), I pointed out how a "gifted education approach" can improve engagement and achievement for all students.

With almost unlimited access to the world's knowledge, a critical issue for educators is selecting the software and providing the training that will help young people use this access safely, efficiently, effectively, and wisely. Leu and his colleagues define the five major skill sets of the new literacies as follows:
1. Identifying Important Questions
2. Locating Relevant Information
3. Critically Evaluating Information
4. Synthesizing Information
5. Communicating Effectively

In addition to improved academic achievement and opportunities for creative productivity, which are the major goals of the Renzulli Learning System, there are a series of metacognitive tools that result from computer based learning environments. Metacognition is generally defined as the monitoring and control of one's own thinking processes. Metacognitive tools are skills that help students organize and self-regulate their learning so that they can make the most efficient use of time, resources, and the cognitive skills that contribute to higher levels of thinking. Metacognition involves problem-solving skills such as exploring alternative options and strategies in open-ended problem situations; and applying critical thinking skills such as examining the sources of evidence, the logic of arguments, and how to find and use reliable information. Training and experiences in metacognitive skills may be the single biggest difference between the education provided in high and low achieving schools!

Several researchers studying constructivist models of learning and metacognition have developed or modified traditional theories of learning to explain the role of computer environments in mediating the interactions between and among the cognitive, metacognitive, affective, and social processes that are involved in learning complex material (Bandura, 1986; Corno & Mandinach, 1983; Pintrich, 2000; Schunk, 2001). Promising results have emerged from these new developments in theory and research on the ways in which computer learning environments facilitate metacognitive skill development.

The Internet can also be a good educational tool for hard-to-reach populations. Researchers from Michigan State University examined the positive effects of home Internet access on the academic performance of low-income, mostly African American children and teenagers involved in a home Internet project. In this research, 140 children aged 10–18 years old (83% African American and 58% male) living in single-parent households (75%) with a $15,000 or less median income were followed for a two-year period to see whether home Internet use would influence academic achievement.

The children who participated in the project were online for an average of 30 minutes a day. Findings indicate that children who used the Internet more had higher standardized test scores in reading and higher grade point averages (GPAs) at one year and at 16 months after the project began compared to children who used the Internet less, said lead author Linda Jackson, Ph.D. Internet use had no effect on standardized test scores in math.

"Improvements in reading achievement may be attributable to the fact that spending more time online typically means spending more time reading," said Dr. Jackson. "GPAs may improve because GPAs are heavily dependent on reading skills," she added.

An even more promising trend is emerging as computer use evolves from traditional e-learning (i.e., taking an on-line course or developing basic skills through computer assisted instruction) to inquiry based software that focuses on the application of knowledge to creative productivity and investigative research projects that promote high levels of student engagement. Students learn the basic difference between to-be-presented information that characterizes traditional instruction and just-in-time information, which is the hallmark of problem-based learning. Skills such as: problem finding and focusing; stating research questions; task understanding and planning; identifying appropriate investigative methodologies; searching, skimming, selecting, and interpreting appropriate resource material; identifying appropriate outlets, products, and audiences; and preparing effective communication vehicles are all value added benefits when the learning theory that underlies the Enrichment Triad Model is combined with the vastness of resources available through the internet.

The Renzulli Learning System—Summing It All Up

The Renzulli Learning System is designed to be an aid to busy teachers who seek the tools for effective differentiation as they go about the process of dealing with a broad range of individual differences, diverse student needs, and increased pressures to improve student achievement. Through the use of technology and an approach to learning that is the opposite of highly prescriptive instruction, the RLS provides teachers with the "dozen teaching assistants" that every teacher would like to have in his or her classroom. The main goal of the RLS is to simultaneously increase achievement and enjoyment of learning by making available an inexpensive, easy-to-use, research-based system that promotes student engagement. Although student engagement has been defined in many ways, we view it as the infectious enthusiasm that students display when working on something that is of personal interest and that challenges them to "stretch" for the use of materials and resources that are above their current comfort level of learning. Research on the role of student engagement is clear and unequivocal—high engagement results in higher achievement, improved self-concept and self-efficacy, and more favorable attitudes toward school and learning. Numerous students involved in our field tests of the RLS summed it up with one word—"Awesome!"

References

Ainley, M. D. (1991). Styles of engagement with learning: Multidimensional assessment of their relationship with strategy use and school achievement. *Journal of Educational Psychology, 85,* 395–405.

APA Work Group of the Board of Educational Affairs. (1997). *Learner-centered psychological principles: A framework for school reform and redesign.* Washington, DC: American Psychological Association.

Bandura, A. (1986). *Social foundation of thought and action: A social cognitive theory.* Englewood Cliffs, NJ: Prentice Hall.

Corno, L., & Mandinach, E. (1983). The role of cognitive engagement in classroom learning and motivation. *Educational Psychologist, 18,* 88–109.

Field, G. B. (2009). The effects of the use of Renzulli Learning on student achievement in reading comprehension, reading fluency, social studies, and science. *International Journal of Emerging Technologies in Learning, 4*(1), 23–28.

Greenwood, C. R. (1991). Longitudinal analysis of time, engagement, and achievement in at-risk versus non-risk students. *Exceptional Children, 57,* 521–536.

Leu, D. J., Jr., Kinzer, C. K., Coiro, J., & Cammack, D. (2004). Toward a theory of new literacies emerging from the Internet and other information and communication technologies. In R. B. Ruddell & N. Unrau (Eds.), *Theoretical models and processes of reading* (5th ed., pp. 1568–1611). Newark, DE: International Reading Association.

Pintrich, P. R. (2000). The role of goal orientation is self-regulated learning. In M. Boekaerts, P. Pintrich, & M. Zeidner (Eds.), *Handbook of self-regulation* (pp. 452–502). New York, NY: Academic.

Reeves, T. C., Herrington, J., & Oliver, R. (2002). Authentic activities and on-line learning. In A. Goody, J. Harrington, & M. Northcote (Eds.), *Quality conversations: Research and development in higher education* (Vol. 25, pp. 562–567). Jamison, ACT: HERDSA.

Renzulli, J. S. (1977). The Enrichment Triad Model: A guide for developing defensible programs for the gifted and talented: Part II. *Gifted Child Quarterly, 21,* 237–243.

Renzulli, J. S. (1998). A rising tide lifts all ships: Developing the gifts and talents of all students. *Phi Delta Kappan, 80,* 105–111.

Renzulli, J. S., & Reis, S. M. (1994). Research related to the Schoolwide Enrichment Triad Model. *Gifted Child Quarterly, 38,* 7–20.

Schunk, D. (2001). Social cognitive theory of self-regulated learning. In B. Zimmerman & D. Schunk (Eds.), *Self-regulated learning and academic achievement: Theoretical perspectives* (pp. 125–152). Mahwah, NJ: Lawrence Erlbaum Associates.

Swicord, B., Chancey, J. M., & Bruce-Davis, M. N. (2013). "Just what I need": Gifted students' perceptions of an online learning system. *Sage Open, 3,* 1–14. doi:10.1177/2158244013484914

A Technology Based Program That Matches Enrichment Resources With Student Strengths

 Renzulli learning	The Wizard Project Maker™ for Individual and Small Group Work
Name(s): Liza Teacher: Ms. Latino School: Southeast School	Start Date: Completion Date: January 15, 2006 June 15, 2006 **Dates for Progress Meetings with My Teacher:** 2/21/06 3/11/06 4/2/06 5/13/06
Project Description: Write a brief description of the project, problem, topic, or interest area that you want to learn about and study. What do you hope to find out or learn? I love theater and want to try to direct and produce a play starring some of my friends and classmates. I will have to find some of the following kinds of information. 1. What is a good play for elementary students to perform? 2. What types of tasks will I have to do to successfully direct a play for kids? 3. What type of play will I select? Will I have to pay for it? What other tasks are involved in directing and producing a play?	Intended Project(s): What form or format will the final project take? How, when, and where will you share and communicate the results of your project with other people? In what ways will you share your work (competition, on-line magazine, art show, performance, science fair, etc.) 1. Direct and produce a play for my class and if it goes well, the school and even the community. 2. Design and build a set for the play; learn about lighting! 3. Design and produce a program for the play.
Interest Areas for this Project -------------- **Check All That Apply**---------------- ○Architecture ●Arts (drawing & painting) ○ Athletics/Sports/Fitness ○Business/Management ○Building Things (robots, models) ○Creative Writing ●Computers/Technology/Gaming ●Drama/Performing ●Graphic Design/Animation ○ Foreign Languages ○ Geography ○Helping in the Community ●History ●Journalism ○ Mathematics ○ Music	**What Format Will Your Project Take?** ----------------**Check All That Apply**--------------- ● Artistic ● Audio/video/DVD ○ Display ● Drama/Performance ○ Musical ● Photographic ● Written ○Service/Leadership ● Technology/Computer ○ Oral/Discussion (speech, teach, presentation) ○ Using my hands to make/build something ○Other:

Copyright © 2005 Renzulli Learning Systems, LLC. All Rights Reserved

Reflections on Gifted Education

A Technology Based Program That Matches Enrichment Resources With Student Strengths

> Getting Started: What are the first steps you should take to begin your work? What types of information do you need to find in order to do your work? Where will you get the information you need? What questions do you have that you need answered in order to start your work? What help do you need from your teacher or parents? List that information here.
>
> 1. Learn how to direct a play and how to produce one.
> 2. Conduct research about children's plays and drama and find specific information about which plays might be good for my class and for me
> 3. Locate information on how to create sets and produce a play.

> Project Skills, Resources and Materials I Will Need: List the Renzulli Learning™ resources here along with other resources (people, organizations, businesses, etc.) you have located that will help you with your work. Include websites, contact names, addresses and phone numbers, lists of the materials you will need, etc.
>
> **Drama Map**
> This site helps you to organize your search for plays and other dramatic material. You can choose to organize your knowledge by character, setting, conflict, or resolution. This will help you keep information neat and organized.
>
> http://www.readwritethink.org/materials/dramamap/
>
> **The American Century Theater**
> The American Century Theater
> P.O. Box 6313
> Arlington, VA 22206
> 703-553-8782
> Dedicated to Great, Important & Neglected American Plays and Playwrights of the 20th Century! Ten years ago, a group of us started The American Century Theater because we felt that great Twentieth Century American plays and playwrights were getting short shrift in this area. Thanks to the indispensable assistance and support of Arlington County, we were provided with the opportunity to discover if enough other theater-lovers felt the same way.
>
> http://americancentury.org/index.htm
>
> At the site below, I will be able to consider directing and producing Snow White with my friends and classmates. I will need to also find out how I might earn the money to be able to buy the rights to stage this show. Maybe I can charge a minimum amount for tickets? I can also do some more searching for plays in the school library.
>
> http://www.childrenstheatreplays.com/sw.htm
>
> We can also look at other plays that will be available at this site. I will have to check with my teacher as some of these will require a small fee that I can make from ticket sales.
>
> http://playsandmusicalsnewsletter.pioneerdrama.com/public/blog/100616

Copyright © 2005 Renzulli Learning Systems, LLC. All Rights Reserved

A Technology Based Program That Matches Enrichment Resources With Student Strengths

I can also take an online journey through Shakespeare's life to learn about his writing and access some of it online. After all, he was the greatest playwright who ever lived.

http://www.tramline.com/tours/lit/shake/_tourlaunch1.htm

Try Out These Theater Games
If you are interested in drama this is the activity for you. Practice your acting skills by playing these games in a group. Learn the art of being a mime or act out roles that you draw from a pile.

http://library.thinkquest.org/5291/games.html

How-to books:

Acting and Theatre
Author: Cheryl Evans and Lucy Smith
Copyright 1992
64 pages
ISBN: 0-7460-0699-3
Grade Level: 4-12

Introduce students to every aspect of the theatrical world! This book illustrates and explains some of the ways actors train and rehearse, as well as the practical arts of set, prop, and costume design and the technical basics of lighting and sound.

Break a Leg!: The Kid's Guide to Acting and Stagecraft by Lise Friedman and Mary Dowdle (Workman Publishing Company, 2002) ISBN: 0761122087
A complete drama course for kids in a book. BREAK A LEG! teaches budding thespians everything they need to know about stagecraft and the production of performances, in home or out. There are sections on body preparation, including warm-ups, stretches, and breathing exercises. Theater games, improv, miming, and other fun ways to develop technique. Important acting skills, such as voice projection, crying on command, learning accents, and staging falls and fights without getting hurt. The performance: analyzing scripts, building a character, what to expect from rehearsals, and overcoming stagefright. A backstage look at blocking, lighting, and other technical aspects of theater production. And for the fun of costumes and make-up, a 16-page color insert. In addition, it covers legends and lore (Why is Macbeth cursed? Why do we say "break a leg"?) and offers dozens of must-see movie recommendations. Plus, for the ambitious, talented, and just plain curious, there's advice on how to make a career of it all, with tips on agents and auditions and getting jobs in theater, film, TV, and radio.

Copyright © 2005 Renzulli Learning Systems, LLC. All Rights Reserved

A Technology Based Program That Matches Enrichment Resources With Student Strengths

Intended Audience(s): Who would be most interested in your work or project? Consider organized groups (clubs, organizations, societies, teams) at the local, state, regional and national levels, and list them here. Also consider contests, places where your work might be displayed or published, and web sites that include work done in your area of study. Include contact names, phone numbers, addresses and email, along with meeting times and locations.

1. Class project
2. School Play
3. Town Play (open to public)
4. If I decide to write my own play, I can submit it to the following using Renzulli Learning:

http://www.edta.org/rehearsal_hall/thespian_playworks.asp

Create a Play for Thespian Playworks
Thespian Playworks
2343 Auburn Avenue
Cincinnati, OH 45219
Activity Type: Writing a play

Bring out the writer and director inside of you by entering this contest. Write a short (thirty minutes or less) play and send it in for review. If the judges select your work for the Thespian Festival, you will join them during the workshops that bring your play to life. In order to be eligible you must be enrolled in a high school and a member of the Thespian Society.

For Completion By Teacher *(Optional)*
List of state standards addressed with this project:

Copyright © 2005 Renzulli Learning Systems, LLC. All Rights Reserved

CHAPTER 15

Savoring Reading Schoolwide[23]

Sally M. Reis
University of Connecticut

and Elizabeth A. Fogarty
East Carolina University

Introduction From Joe

The Schoolwide Enrichment Model in Reading (SEM-R) is a reading enrichment approach that has been shown to be effective in increasing elementary and middle school students' reading achievement and attitudes toward reading. The SEM-R provides enriched reading experiences by exposing students to books in their areas of interest, daily supported independent reading of challenging self-selected books using differentiated reading instruction, and interest-based choice opportunities in reading. In keeping with our emphasis in this book on reaching a wider range of practitioner audiences, we have selected an article that appeared in *Educational Leadership* rather than

---

23   Reis, S. M., & Fogerty, E. A. (2006). Savoring reading schoolwide. *Educational Leadership, 64*(2), 32–36. Copyright 2006 by Association for Supervision and Curriculum Development. Reprinted with permission.

the many articles that have been published in research journals. In one study (Reis et al., 2007), researchers found that when they eliminated 5 hours of regular grouped reading instruction and replaced it with short conferences and enriched reading based on interests, significant differences were found, favoring the SEM-R group, in reading fluency and attitudes toward reading.

In another related study on the SEM-R (Reis, McCoach, Little, Muller, & Kaniskan, 2011), a randomized design investigated the effects of this enriched reading program on urban elementary students' reading comprehension, reading fluency, and attitude toward reading. Results indicate that students in the SEM-R treatment group scored statistically significantly higher or at least as well as students in the control group in both reading achievement and fluency, as well as in attitudes toward reading.

Imagine 3rd and 4th grade classrooms in which silent reading is interrupted only by rapidly turning pages and the occasional chuckle. Imagine a group of boisterous boys reading with intense focus for 30 minutes in a corner of a classroom. During the last four years, with a team of teachers and researchers from the University of Connecticut, we have helped bring about such scenarios daily in high-poverty schools through an alternative approach to reading instruction: the Schoolwide Enrichment Model in Reading (SEM-R; Reis et al., 2003). This enrichment-based approach, which evolved from the Schoolwide Enrichment Model (Renzulli, 1977, Renzulli & Reis, 1997), focuses on engaging students in challenging reading accompanied by instruction in higher-order thinking and strategy skills. Teachers differentiate both instruction and student reading materials and guide students in continually regulating and challenging themselves as readers.

Why Enrichment Is Not Optional

Standardized reading achievement scores show that many students are unprepared for success in college or jobs, especially minority students and children living in poverty. Results of the 2005 American College Testing program's college admission and placement exam indicate that 79 percent of Black students, 67 percent of Latino students, and 33 percent of students from families with annual incomes below $30,000 were not prepared for college-level reading (ACT, 2006). Reading and literacy contribute to academic success (Burns,

Griffin, & Snow, 1999; National Reading Panel, 2000), and strong reading comprehension predicts performance on achievement tests (Allington, 2002).

Because reading is a salient ingredient in life success, it is imperative that schools try alternative methods of teaching reading that promote enjoyment. Our research team has implemented the SEM-R in urban high-poverty schools under rigorous research conditions, with successful results in every study (Reis et al., 2005). In schools in which we have used this approach, students' reading fluency scores have increased significantly compared with a control group, and in some schools comprehension scores have increased for students receiving SEM-R instruction as well. Results were so promising that in 2005, federal funds through the Jacob K. Javits Act enabled us to "gear up"; our team is currently implementing the model for an entire academic year in three Title I elementary schools in West Palm Beach, Florida, and two in Manchester, Connecticut.

How the Model Works

The SEM-R includes three categories of reading instruction: (1) broad exposure to appropriate texts and areas of possible interest, (2) higher-order thinking skills training and methods instruction, and (3) opportunities to pursue self-selected activities. It was developed as an outgrowth of a model widely used in gifted education programs; pedagogy geared toward gifted students can be used to enrich learning for all students. The model has been applied by schools not involved in our study that have become informed about SEM-R or taken our training.

This instructional program focuses on increasing student readers' enjoyment of the learning process through planned enrichment experiences. In some schools in which we worked, the SEM-R was integrated into regular reading instruction; in others, it was offered as an additional literacy block. In our study, teachers were randomly assigned to either a treatment group that received some form of supplementary reading instruction using SEM-R's methods or a control group that used the school's traditional form of literacy instruction. We provided teachers in the treatment group with a day of training and a manual that described all aspects of the approach; research team members frequently observed in classrooms and guided implementation. As we trained teachers in the three phases of SEM-R, we encouraged them to continue using their own teaching styles and to adapt the strategies rather than feel tied to a mechanical routine. Through working with teachers as they implemented the SEM-R, we observed how instruction in each phase helped individual students become motivated readers.

Phase 1: Hooking Kids on Literature

The key to enriching students' reading skills is providing them with challenging books they are eager to read. In Phase 1 of the SEM-R, teachers read out loud to students from diverse texts. After talking with teachers and reviewing the literacy assessments of students in each class, our team selected a set of high-interest books for each grade level and augmented this selection with books geared to each class's interests, reading levels, and background cultures. For example, if a class had several less-skilled readers who were interested in sports, we ordered a set of biographies of sports heroes. Each teacher received approximately 125 books and a gift certificate to choose and purchase more books for particular students.

In 10–20 minute "book hook" sessions, teachers used book excerpts to hook students on reading, interspersing readings with higher-order questioning. We gave teachers laminated bookmarks printed with cognitively challenging questions to help students become accustomed to answering questions connected to higher-level thinking and reading skills. Similar bookmarks were later provided to students to spur deeper questioning (see Figure 15.1). Teachers asked significantly more high-level questions in the SEM-R Phase 1 read-aloud than they did in control classrooms not using this approach (Fogarty, 2006).

During the book hook sessions, students jotted in their reading logs the titles of books that they wanted to read fully on their own.

Phase 2: Supported Independent Reading With Conferences

At this stage, teachers encourage students to select high-interest books slightly above their current reading level, and in regular conferences they assess whether the books readers have picked are an appropriate match. In our studies, the majority of students initially selected books that were easy for them. Teachers told them to take these easier books home to read because at

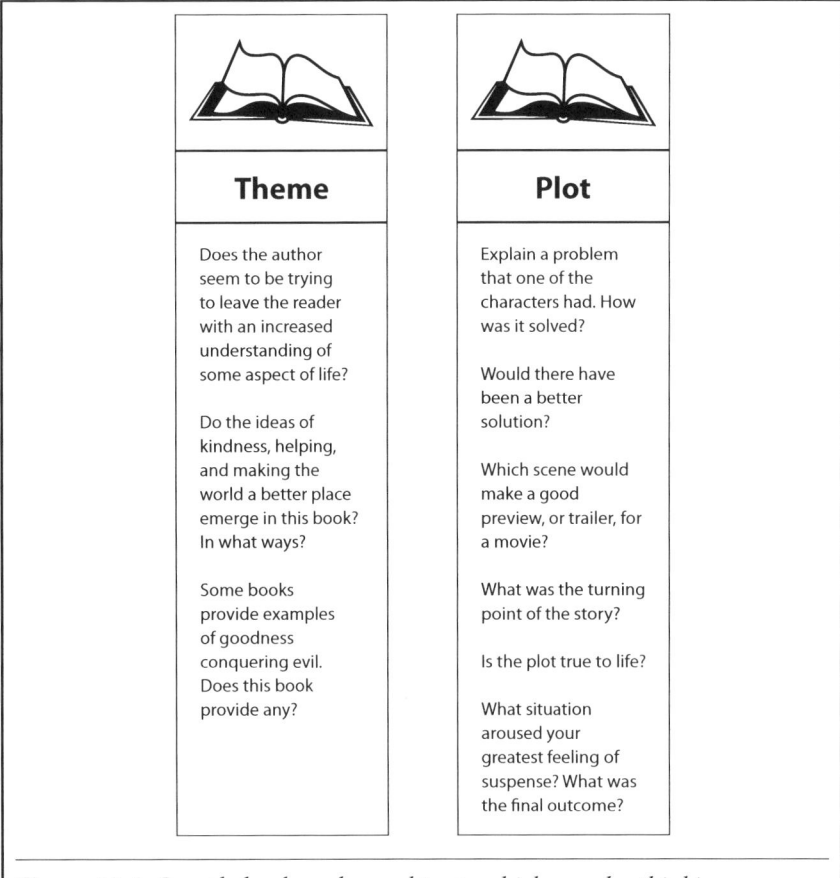

Figure 15.1. *Sample bookmarks used to spur higher-order thinking.*

school it was their job to select books with some words and ideas that were new to them.

Many teachers we worked with showed creativity in encouraging reading, and students responded. At North Grade Elementary School in Palm Beach County, Florida, Ms. Duke created a weekly "Beach Day," filling a corner with buckets of sand, blankets, and beach chairs for atmosphere. She reminded her students that spending a day at the beach means you can just flop down and read. "This is awesome; we actually get to sit and read in reading class!" one boy said.

Initially, many students read their chosen books with concentration for only 5–10 minutes a day. Teachers added a minute or two of reading time each day, eventually extending the time students read on their own to 30–45 minutes daily. We coached teachers in ground rules for silent reading and in strategies to help students gradually increase sustained reading, including

- Talking openly about the need to develop the habit of focused reading for success in life, especially in higher education.
- Telling students to pretend their brain is a television and that reading is only on one channel. If they let their attention "channel surf," they're not maintaining an appropriate focus on reading.
- Letting each student choose a comfortable spot in class in which to read. We found that students who moved around and chose where to sit read quietly for longer periods of time.

During in-class reading time, teachers circulated around the room conducting 5- to 10-minute conferences to provide individualized support and differentiated instruction. Teachers reviewed book selections, listened to each student read, and helped readers practice reading and questioning strategies. The challenge for most teachers was to provide individualized strategies and critical thinking instruction when there was a huge range of reading levels among students. A teacher might need to coach one 3rd grader on fluency strategy—for example, breaking free from using his finger as he reads—then help a more advanced 3rd grader explore how setting can influence plot. During training, we taught teachers how to differentiate instruction and modeled how to use a conference to meet a student's individual needs. The SEM-R materials include a series of lessons on how to increase self-regulation in reading.

Phase 3: Options for Individual Interests

In Phase 3 of SEM-R, teachers encourage students to participate about one hour each week in literacyrelated activities that give them considerable choice and match their interests. The teachers we worked with either set aside 15 minutes each day as "Interest and Choice" time or devoted one period of language arts each week to this phase of SEM-R. Teachers gave students several different options:
- Exploring the Internet and reading materials online.
- Creative or expository writing.
- Visiting learning centers on topics in which they show interest.
- Interest-based projects.
- Reading aloud with a friend.
- Book chats in literature circles.
- Studies in a particular literary genre.
- Listening to books on tape.

These experiences enable students to explore personal interests and apply creative- and critical-thinking skills to self-selected work. This component of the SEM-R pushes students to read critically and to find enjoyable and challenging literature beyond the texts that the teacher provided.

A free-choice period we observed in Ms. White's 5th grade classroom in Jupiter Elementary School in Palm Beach County, Florida, shows a snapshot of typical Phase 3 instruction. A group of three students were engrossed in listening to a Harry Potter book on tape while reading from the book. In another section of the room, a girl read a book online. Two students were reading a novel to each other, and three others were working on a readers theater activity. At a bank of computers, five students had logged on to an online enrichment program, Renzulli Learning, through which students complete a questionnaire about their interests and learning styles and then receive hundreds of individually selected enrichment opportunities in their specific areas of interest.

Results in Urban Schools

Results from schools where we have used the SEM-R approach indicate that students taught through this method had more positive attitudes toward reading, higher reading fluency and comprehension scores, and increased confidence in answering higher-order thinking questions, when compared with students in control groups in these schools.

In 2002, our research team implemented the SEM-R in two urban schools in Hartford, Connecticut—Batchelder Elementary and Kinsella Elementary. Each school has a population of over 90 percent minority students, and most of the students receive free or reduced-price lunch. All students in these schools participated in a direct-instruction reading block in the morning. Students in the treatment group had an additional one-hour afternoon literacy block featuring the SEM-R program, whereas control group students received remedial instruction and preparation for the statewide mastery test. In both schools, students who participated in the SEM-R instruction had significantly higher oral reading fluency scores and reading achievement scores on the Iowa Test of Basic Skills than did students in the control group. Students who received the reading enrichment also had significantly more positive attitudes toward reading than did students in the control group.

In the 2003–2004 school year, we implemented SEM-R as half of a regular two-hour basal language arts program in two other Connecticut schools for 12 weeks. One school had a majority population of culturally diverse students, most of whom spoke Spanish as their first language. The other school, a suburban school, had a more affluent, nonminority student body. Students in the SEM-R group at the more diverse school had significantly higher reading fluency and comprehension scores than did students who participated only in the basal language arts program. Interestingly, readers in the suburban school also benefited from the program, with significant differences evident in measures of reading ability between the SEM-R and control groups.

The positive changes that we saw in schools using SEM-R extended beyond increases in test scores. We saw students who could not wait to begin to read and who groaned when it was time to put their books down. Students who rarely read before the intervention devoured an entire book series. Teachers consistently reported positive changes in their teaching practices and excitement about reading and higher-order thinking skills instruction. They also found students participated in more advanced conversations about what they were reading.

As a teacher in Palm Beach County, Florida, explained, "My Phase 2 SEM-R conferences with kids expanded from one-word answers at the beginning of the year to long, thoughtful conversations about literature and themes. I actually had to cut them off for lack of time." When students are able to have these kinds of conversations with teachers about their reading, they are clearly taking charge of their own reading—and their own literature-related thinking.

References

ACT. (2006). *Reading between the lines.* Retrieved from www.act.org/path/policty/reports/reading.html

Allington, R. L. (Ed.). (2002). *Big brother and the national reading curriculum: How ideology trumped evidence.* Portsmouth, NH: Heinemann.

Burns, S. M., Griffin, P., & Snow, C. E. (Eds.). (1999). *Starting out right: A guide to promoting children's reading success.* Washington, DC: National Academy Press.

Fogarty, E. A. (2006). *Teachers' use of differentiated reading strategy instruction for talented, average, and struggling readers in regular and SEM-R classrooms.* Storrs: University of Connecticut, The National Research Center on the Gifted and Talented.

National Reading Panel. (2000). *Teaching children to read: An evidence-based assessment of the scientific research literature on reading and its implications for reading instruction.* Washington, DC: Author.

Reis, S. M., Gubbins, E. G., Briggs, C., Schreiber, F. J., Richards, S., Jacobs, J., . . . Alexander, M. (2003). *Reading instruction for talented readers: Case studies documenting few opportunities for continuous progress* (RM03184). Storrs: University of Connecticut, The National Research Center on the Gifted and Talented.

Reis, S. M., Eckert, R. D., Schreiber, F. J., Jacobs, J. K., Briggs, C., Gubbins, E. J., . . . Muller, L. (2005). *The Schoolwide Enrichment Reading Model: Technical report* (RM05214). Storrs: University of Connecticut, The National Research Center on the Gifted and Talented.

Reis, S. M., McCoach, D. B., Coyne, M., Schreiber, F. J., Eckert, R. D., & Gubbins, E. J. (2007). Using planned enrichment strategies with direct instruction to improve reading fluency, comprehension, and attitude toward reading: An evidence-based study. *The Elementary School Journal, 108*(1), 3–24.

Reis, S. M., McCoach, D. B., Little, C. A., Muller, L. M., & Kaniskan, R. B. (2011). The effects of differentiated instruction and enrichment pedagogy on reading achievement in five elementary schools. *American Educational Research Journal, 48*, 462–501.

Renzulli, J. S. (1977). *The Enrichment Triad Model.* Mansfield Center, CT: Creative Learning Press.

Renzulli, J. S., & Reis, S. M. (1997). *The Schoolwide Enrichment Model.* Mansfield Center, CT: Creative Learning Press.

CHAPTER 16

Nurturing Young Student Mathematicians[24]

M. Katherine Gavin and Tutita M. Casa
University of Connecticut

Introduction From Joe

Many math materials for talented students focus on a variety of logic problems, mind benders, and enrichment worksheets. In order to provide mathematics curriculum materials that promote a coherent and rigorous development of advanced concepts, we created a series of units for mathematically promising students in grades K–6 under grants sponsored by the U.S. Department of Education (Javits Grant) and the National Science Foundation. Based on the pedagogy set forth in the Enrichment Triad Model, these materials foster in-depth understanding of advanced mathematical concepts by challenging and motivating students to discuss and solve high-level problems in a fashion similar to practicing mathematicians. They are currently being used to meet the needs of talented elementary students in all 50 states and in several other countries including Singapore and Hong Kong. For further information

---

[24] Gavin, M. K., & Casa, T. M. (2012). Nurturing young student mathematicians. *Gifted Education International, 29*, 140–153. Copyright 2012 SAGE Publications. Reprinted with permission of SAGE Publications.

on our curriculum, visit http://www.gifted.uconn.edu/projectm3 and http://www.projectm2.uconn.edu.

In keeping with our emphasis in this book on reaching a wider range of practitioner audiences, we have selected an article that appeared in *Gifted Education International* rather than the many articles that have been published in research journals. The curricula have undergone national field tests with proven research results showing significant achievement gains for students studying the curricula over a comparison group of like-ability students. Persons interested in examining the research results can reference the following articles:

Gavin, M. K., Casa, T. M., Adelson, J. L., & Firmender, J. M. (2013). The impact of advanced geometry and measurement units on the achievement of grade 2 students. *Journal for Research in Mathematics Education, 44*, 478–510.

Gavin, M. K., Casa, T. M., Firmender, J. M., & Carroll, S. R. (2013). The impact of advanced geometry and measurement units on the mathematics achievement of first-grade students. *Gifted Child Quarterly, 57*, 71–84.

Gavin, M. K., Casa, T. M., Adelson, J. L., Carroll, S. R., & Sheffield, L. J. (2009). The impact of advanced curriculum on the achievement of mathematically promising elementary students. *Gifted Child Quarterly, 53*, 188–202.

Outstanding mathematical ability is a precious societal resource, sorely needed to maintain leadership in a technological world.—(NCTM, 1980: 18)

The following question was posed to a group of Project M³ students:

Miranda thinks all squares are rectangles. Do you agree or disagree with her thinking? Explain your thinking.

Jacinta wrote: [sic]

I agree to Miranda's theory. I agree because a square has all the attributes of a rectangle. Those attributes are: 4 sides, 4 90° angles, and 2 *sets* of opposite parallel and congruent lines. A square fits all those attributes but it also has 1 extra attribute. That all its sides are congruent. A square also has many other names. Those are: rectangle, parallelogram, rhombus, and quadrilateral. But its clearest name is square.—(Gavin et al., 2007a: 20)

Reading this at first glance, you may be impressed with the quality and thoroughness of the justification. The abundant and appropriate use of mathematical terms may also have stood out. It might have surprised you how the student was able to express her thinking in writing. It is certainly evident that this student understands that geometric shapes can be classified hierarchically (e.g., squares have one more defining property than rectangles—mainly, the sides of a square are all congruent). Many students do not understand that individual shapes, much less the relationships among shapes, are categorized by their properties until their high school years (ages 13–16) (Clements, 2003). So, what may be even more impressive about this response is that a fourth-grade 9-year-old student was the author.

This student was participating in Project M^3: Mentoring Mathematical Minds, a United States Department of Education research grant program in which curriculum units for mathematically talented students in grades 3–5 were developed. This curriculum was written to challenge and motivate young students by engaging them in the types of thinking, discussing, and writing done by practicing mathematicians. The exemplar response above is a concrete representation of the mathematical reasoning developed across 4 years of field-testing in 61 classrooms in diverse urban and suburban schools. Talented students studying the Project M^3 units significantly outperformed their peers of like ability on open-response questions taken from released items on the Trends in International Math and Science Study (TIMSS, 1994) and the National Assessment of Educational Progress (NAEP; National Center for Education Statistics, 1996). These items were designed to assess in-depth understanding of algebra, data, geometry, measurement, number and probability concepts. (Results show highly significant differences favoring the Project M^3 students with a consistent p-value of < 0.001 for two cohorts of students participating over 3 years. Effect sizes ranged from 0.69 to 1.78. For further description of the research study and results see Gavin et al., 2009.)

The Project M^3 curriculum units foster rich mathematical thinking. This type of thinking, along with the underlying philosophy of encouraging students to think and act like practicing mathematicians, is the basis for a second advanced curriculum project for primary students in kindergarten, first and second grades being developed under the auspices of a National Science Foundation grant, Project M^2 (Gavin et al., 2013). It is noteworthy that we are finding promising results in terms of achievement gains similar to Project M^3. The aim of both projects is to have elementary students think in depth about challenging mathematical concepts, as mathematicians do, and to make their thinking more public and accessible to the entire class with the use of verbal and written communication. The results are a classroom transformed into a true mathematical community of sharing that result in written responses such as Jacinta's.

This article describes ways in which both curriculum projects help teachers develop an innovative and unique learning environment for elementary students where students are challenged to think and act like young mathematicians. We next present some of the literature that informed the development of the units followed by a description of the instructional strategies and learning environment that emerged as part of the curriculum projects.

Background

George Polya, a well-respected mathematician, believed that the only difference between the work of a professional mathematician and a talented student of mathematics was in the degree of sophistication they use (as cited in Sriraman, 2008). Polya believed that students are capable of mathematical creativity just as mathematicians are, with each operating at their own level of understanding. The philosophy of both Project M^3 and Project M^2 builds on this and is grounded in gifted education pedagogy that focuses on students working and learning in the same way that practicing professionals in the field do. In particular, our underlying philosophy of student as practicing mathematician was based on the Multiple Menu Model for curriculum design developed by Joseph Renzulli (Renzulli et al., 2000). This model promotes the creation of instructional activities that engage students in exploring key ideas that are akin to a particular field of study. Students are encouraged to use the same investigative methods that practitioners in the field do to seek answers to their questions and make contributions to their field. The Curriculum of Practice from the *Parallel Curriculum Model: A Design to Develop High Potential and Challenge High-Ability Learners* (Tomlinson et al., 2009) was also embedded in the units. The Parallel Curriculum Model was written by leading experts in the field of gifted education to guide curriculum developers in their quest to produce high-quality, challenging materials for gifted students. The Curriculum of Practice is one of four types of curricula outlined in the Parallel Curriculum Model. Using the Multiple Menu Model as its foundation, the Curriculum of Practice delineates two functions for the student mathematician as learner. First, as a scholar, the young mathematician uses similar knowledge, problem-solving strategies, and mathematical tools that a mathematician would use to develop a deeper understanding of the mathematics being explored. Second, as an expert practitioner, the student uses the same methods to produce new knowledge, that is, create something original.

In order to help students acquire the skills of the practicing professional, the materials with which they work must be rich with problems and situations similar to what a practitioner would encounter, albeit at the appropriate student level. Thus, the curriculum content for Projects M^3 and M^2 has as its basis the Core Curriculum, another of the curricula in the Parallel Curriculum Model (Tomlinson et al., 2009). According to this model, the Core Curriculum "is the foundational curriculum that should establish a rich framework of knowledge, understanding, and skills most relevant to the discipline." This curriculum should cause students to "grapple with ideas and questions, using both critical and creative thinking" and should be "mentally and affectively engaging and satisfying to learners" (p. 21). Using the design structure of the Core Curriculum model, the authors based their curriculum on the essential mathematical concepts and processes outlined in the National Council of Teachers of Mathematics (NCTM) *Principles and Standards for School Mathematics* (2000) and the *Curriculum Focal Points for Prekindergarten Through Grade 8 Mathematics: A Quest for Coherence* (2006). In doing so, the curriculum aligns with the new Common Core State Standards (CCSS) for Mathematics (Council of Chief State School Officers & National Governors Association, 2010). The CCSS have recently been adopted at the mathematics framework for grades K–12 curriculum by 46 of the 50 states in the U.S.

From Theory to Practice: A Classroom of Young Student Mathematicians

Before we explore what a classroom of student mathematicians following these tenets might look like, we begin by taking a look at typical elementary U.S. mathematics instruction today. It is actually easier to compare typical classrooms with what mathematicians do not do than with how they actually practice. So what don't mathematicians do? Mathematicians do not start with a problem to which they already know the answer, or even one that they immediately know how to solve. These are simply not interesting. They do not have someone at the front of the room telling them how to solve a problem and then engage in doing 20 more of the same kind of problem. Again, this is not interesting to them. Yet, most elementary mathematics curricula are designed in this fashion and/or delivered in this manner. Rarely does one find a long discussion involving the entire class centered on agreeing and disagreeing with conceptual thinking. Rarely does one find students tested with challenging problems that interest them so much so that the problem-solving experience goes beyond a class period without a solution being found or told. This is so different from the real work of practicing mathematicians.

What do mathematicians do? They love to grapple with problems in which they may have no idea of even where to start. They just dig in and start trying some strategies. They are not afraid to change strategies and direct their thinking elsewhere when a solution is not forthcoming. They try to find connections between the problem and other areas of mathematics and/or real-life situations. Unlike the stereotypical picture of the solitary mathematician working behind closed doors, they talk to each other. In doing so, they come up with new, "outside of the box" ideas to try. They persist in solving a problem until that "a-ha" moment arrives. It could take days, months, even years! But when it does arrive, it is infinitely satisfying. Then, they usually write about how they solved the problem and focus on making the explanation clear to themselves and, in so doing, clear to others. They call this an "elegant" solution.

This is what our young mathematicians should do, too. Student mathematicians need to enjoy problems that are challenging; ones in which they might not know where to begin. Student mathematicians need to struggle with a problem, try out a variety of strategies, talk to fellow classmates and their teacher in trying to solve it, and find new ways to solve it. Student mathematicians need to, and want to, persist in problem solving until that wonderful "a-ha" moment arrives. Student mathematicians need to talk about their reasoning and listen to others' explanations. In doing so, a deeper understanding of the mathematics emerges. Student mathematicians need to write about their reasoning to convince themselves and to convince others. Student mathematicians need to discover the joy in creating new problems to solve and the ultimate joy in solving those problems. Most of all, student mathematicians need to love doing mathematics. So, upon entering a Project M^3 or M^2 classroom, one will encounter an environment that promotes this type of learning and love of mathematics. Students are engaged with the mathematics. They struggle to solve problems as they talk and listen to each other's ideas. And they love what they are doing.

Supporting the Participation of Students as Mathematicians

In order to develop a community of student mathematicians mimicking the thinking of professional mathematicians, Projects M^3 and M^2 provide teachers with tools to support students to speak, listen, and write mathematically. We present features across the two projects, including the classroom environment, the verbal model, the nature of the writing tasks, and an instructional tool that helps students connect verbal ideas with their writing.

Classroom Environment

Early on, we recognized the need to set up a nurturing environment where all student mathematicians' ideas are considered important. Furthermore, we wanted students to make sense of those ideas and incorporate them into their own thought processes. If you were to visit a Project M^3 or M^2 class, you would not see students raising their hands wildly while someone else was speaking or looking out the window lost in thought, even if those thoughts are mathematical in nature. What you would see is a respectful environment that promotes a community of thinkers and problem solvers. In order to establish such classroom norms, we provided students with guidelines about how to participate in classroom discussions.

The Rights and Obligations incorporated into the Project M^3 units (Gavin et al., 2007b) helped define learning expectations in terms of what was valued in the environment and establish a supportive culture in which students were encouraged to take risks, try new strategies, and ask questions when uncertain. Teachers took note of how the Rights and Obligations prompted students to take greater responsibility for their own learning and to respect all students and their ideas. Students were encouraged to focus on the conversation and ideas being shared rather than the person sharing the ideas. In this way disagreements never got personal but were honored as a way to better understand the mathematics.

Kristen, a fifth-grade teacher, reflected on how the Rights and Obligations impacted her instruction: "As a group, students view themselves as a community of mathematicians. I think this sense of community has been especially powerful." Jack, a fourth-grade teacher described how the learning environment positively impacted one of his students: "The most important success that he has had this year . . . is that he has become more comfortable discussing mathematical ideas. He has realized that his ideas have meaning and that others are interested in what he has to say."

To acknowledge the need to be more explicit with younger students in kindergarten, first and second grades, the Project M^2 units represented these Rights and Obligations as ways in which students should behave as both speakers and listeners (Gavin et al., 2010a). All of these roles give credence to students' ideas. The *speaker roles* ensure that students:

- speak loudly enough to be heard;
- relay their thoughts to the class, not just the teacher;
- explain their ideas so others will understand them; and
- agree and disagree with others' ideas rather than with the person.

Not only is it important to contribute to class discussions, listening to what fellow student mathematicians say is equally important. Strong listening skills are actually more difficult for students to develop. They are generally more eager to share their own ideas rather than hear what others have to say. We found this is especially true with talented, creative students who have many new ideas that they wish to contribute. However, listening to others' ideas helps them evaluate their own idea and will benefit them greatly in collaborative problem solving as members of the workforce. The listener roles encourage students to:

- ask the speaker to speak up, if necessary;
- demonstrate that they are listening (i.e., their bodies are positioned in a way to show they are listening) and making sense of ideas; and
- ask questions when needed to clarify thoughts.

The speaker and listener roles go hand in hand and help support an environment that nurtures students as mathematicians. Our best indicator of success in nurturing this environment was the frequent comment from students after listening and making sense of others' ideas: "I now disagree with myself!"

Verbal Communication

Facilitating discussions. For two decades, the NCTM has been calling for teachers to move away from talk that is more didactic (where the teacher acts as the knowledge bearer and students as repositories of this knowledge) towards one that positions students as part of a sense-making community. This has major implications for the nature of discussions, also commonly referred to as discourse. Discussions should center "on mathematical reasoning and evidence as the basis for the discourse. In order for students to develop the ability to formulate problems, to explore, conjecture, and reason logically, to evaluate whether something makes sense, classroom discourse must be founded on mathematical evidence" (NCTM, 1991: 34). Students in these classrooms engage with fellow peers to make sense of the mathematics, with the teacher acting as a facilitator of such interactions (NCTM, 1991). Our vision of student mathematicians incorporates such exchanges. Nevertheless, orchestrating this discussion can be challenging, and, in fact, one of the reasons for NCTM's

2000 publication, *Principles and Standards for School Mathematics*, was that discourse was not being implemented as intended (NCTM, 2000).

Teachers are expected to facilitate discussion so that students:
- "organize and consolidate their thinking through communication;
- communicate their mathematical thinking coherently and clearly to peers, teachers, and others;
- analyze and evaluate the mathematical thinking and strategies of others;
- use the language of mathematics to express mathematical ideas precisely"—(NCTM, 2000: 60)

Although teachers may agree with these expectations and understand *what* the talk should look like, we felt it necessary to incorporate tools that would guide teachers as to *how* to implement such discussions. This is especially important when the content is advanced and the goal is to foster high-end learning in order to nurture talent. As a result, we adapted Chapin et al.'s (2009) "talk moves." Although at first glance they may appear to be simplistic, these talk moves provide teachers with the tools to orchestrate discussions that help ensure that all students understand the questions being posed, allow them to grapple with and make sense of the mathematics, and come to mathematically valid conclusions. All the while, teachers encourage students to interact with others' ideas, much like professional mathematicians do. The talk moves (Gavin et al., 2010b) include:
- repeat and check;
- agree/disagree and why;
- partner talk;
- add on; and
- think time.

Repeat and check has students or the teacher repeat an idea shared by a student. Then the teacher confirms that the repeated idea was heard accurately. For example, a teacher can ask, "Joshua, can you repeat what Emma said? . . . Joshua, is that what you meant to say?" This talk move serves to set students' ideas as the center for discussion, help students clarify their thinking, and allow others more time to consider an idea. Once the topic of the discussion has been established and the teacher feels students have had sufficient time to digest it, she can move on to *agree/disagree and why* where students reason mathematically about the given idea: "Do you agree or disagree with Tristan's idea? Tell us why." This talk move places the onus of defending the mathematical validity of answers on students—in a similar vein as professional mathematicians—rather than the teacher. *Partner talk* is a talk move designed to give students an immediate audience to grapple with their ideas and make their thoughts more cohesive and clear. *Add on* prompts students for further participation, which serves to open up the discussion and elaborate on others' ideas. Lastly, *think time* can be used throughout the discussion to allow students to formulate their thoughts before and after they are called on to share their ideas with the group. It demonstrates that student reasoning is valued and encourages all students to participate. The following sample dialogue connected to the question posed to students at the beginning of this article incorporates the talk moves to help student mathematicians reason about whether or not all squares are rectangles.

Teacher: So do you agree with Miranda? Is a square a rectangle, too? Why or why not? Jackie.

Jackie: I think she is wrong. A square looks different than a rectangle. The two rectangle sides are long, but the square ones are not.

Teacher: Did you say that a square is not a rectangle because the sides of a rectangle are long and the sides of a square are not?

Jackie: Yes. Squares look more like a box.

Teacher: Who agrees or disagrees with Jackie's idea and can tell us why? Scott?

Scott: I think I disagree with her idea because squares have things that are the same as rectangles.

Teacher: Leena, can you add on to what Scott just said?

Leena: I know that squares and rectangles both have four sides.

Teacher: Who can repeat what Leena just said? Edya?

Edya: I think she said that squares are rectangles. They both have four sides.

Teacher: Turn to your partner and talk about what else might be the same about squares and rectangles. [Partners discuss for about 2 minutes.] Lenny, what did you and your partner talk about?

Lenny: We said that both squares and rectangles have square corners.

Teacher: Who can add on to this idea? Maxie?

Maxie: I think that they mean they both have all 90° angles.

Teacher: So I hear you saying that the squares and rectangles both have four sides and have all 90° angles. Richard?

Richard: Tommy and I said that the square sides have to be the same.

Teacher: Do you mean the sides of the square are the same length? Do you have a math vocabulary word that could be used here?

Richard: Yeah. They are not long, just the same. Congruent.

Teacher: Now talk to your partner about these ideas. Is a shape with four sides that are the same length and has four 90° angles a rectangle? [Students talk for about 3 minutes.] Henry, what do you and Isabella think, and why?

Henry: We think so because a rectangle has to have four sides and four 90° angles—a square has all of this! It just has one more thing. Cause, well, it's special. It has, um, the sides are all the same.

Teacher: Can someone repeat what Henry said? Gina?

Gina: Henry said that a square has to be a rectangle because it fits what a rectangle means. It's just that a square has an extra thing about it—the sides are congruent.

Developing mathematical vocabulary. As the previous dialogue indicates, it is essential for students to incorporate mathematical vocabulary into their reasoning so that other student mathematicians can better understand the message: "It is important to give students experiences that help them appreciate the power and precision of mathematical language" (NCTM, 2000: 63). The Project M³ and M² units provide additional support in this area, including providing teachers with a mathematical language section in each lesson, a teacher and student glossary of terms, and a word wall. The mathematical language section within each lesson includes the list and definitions of vocabulary that teachers can anticipate students will use during the lesson, making note that students are not expected to regurgitate a formal definition.

In the Project M² units, we have designed the student glossary (Gavin et al., 2010a) to be interactive in nature for these younger students. This glossary in the back of their Student Mathematician's Journal contains several pictorial representations of important vocabulary words. When the teacher introduces the vocabulary term, the student finds the pictures that match the term and writes the word in the blank space next to the term. The word wall mimics the student glossary. Each term includes one card with the name and another card with several representations. Teachers are encouraged to post the word walls in a prominent location and use them during instruction. They might ask students to repeat or add on to someone's idea using a word from the word wall. Students also can interact with the word wall by playing matching and sorting games. Thus, our student mathematicians are actively engaged in developing meaning for mathematical vocabulary and using it appropriately in their discussions and writing.

Talk Frame

The talk frame was infused into the units to serve as a vehicle that connects verbal and written communication. It is a graphic organizer used on the board that captures student ideas about a significant and high-level mathematical question as it unfolds during a discussion (Gavin et al., 2010b; Williams & Casa, 2011/2012). Casa (2012) explains that the talk frame (Figure 16.1) begins with the "Think" section that has students reword the question to ensure that they understand what is being asked of them. The teacher paraphrases all ideas shared by students under multiple "Talk Ideas," and these include correct mathematical ideas as well as underdeveloped ones and misconceptions. This feature forces students to rely on their reasoning rather than the teacher's affirmation to determine the mathematical validity of ideas—similar to how professional mathematicians work to solve problems. An impetus of the talk frame was to capture student ideas to give them more permanence than just the spoken word. This allows peers to revisit previously shared thoughts and build upon them. Finally, when the class reaches a mathematically valid conclusion, the teacher records students' summaries of their understanding in the "We Understand" section. Figure 16.1 presents a sample of a talk frame that would capture the discussion presented in the previous dialogue. Note that students would have discussed what was being asked of them. This rewording of the question is just one example of how this could be done, as are the contributions made by students and how a teacher records them. Regardless, the "We Understand" summary would represent the same valid mathematical conclusion.

Written Communication

Although NCTM notes that "written communication should be nurtured" (2000: 62), there is little guidance about how to go about this. In the Project M^3 and M^2 units, the talk moves and talk frame serve to provide a model to help

Nurturing Young Student Mathematicians

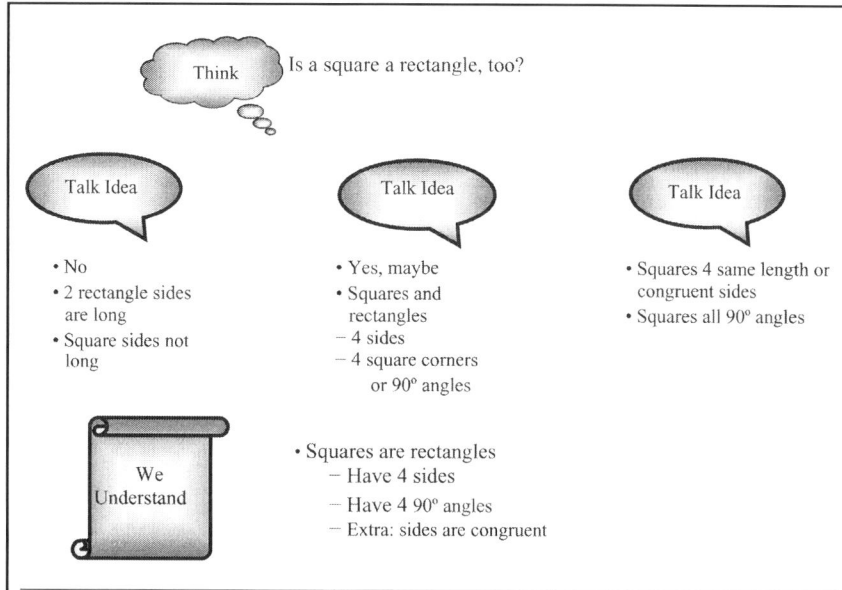

Figure 16.1. *Sample talk frame representing a discussion about whether or not squares are rectangles. General talk frame © 2010 Tutita M. Casa.*

develop quality written responses to "Think Deeply" questions. These high-level questions, posed at the end of each lesson, typically take 3 days to resolve and are focused on a significant mathematical idea from the lesson, such as the Think Deeply question offered at the beginning of the paper. In fact, we consider the Think Deeply question the heart and soul of the lesson.

As a collection, the Think Deeply questions encourage students to reason about "sound and significant mathematics" (NCTM, 1991: 25). To help them learn the conventions of quality mathematical writing, we approached this in a similar fashion as students learning to write in any other genre (NCTM, 2000), and considered what professional mathematicians would require of one another. We developed writer's roles that include:

- thinking about the question;
- talking about the answer; and
- telling all ideas, the answer, and why.

We also encourage teachers to scaffold the introduction of mathematical writing into their teaching. To begin, students complete the initial Think Deeply question as a class while discussing the characteristics of the writing. Then partners write some responses together for the next couple of Think Deeply questions. Finally, individuals compose their own response for the remainder of the Think Deeply questions in the unit. Throughout, students share their work to give peers the opportunity to see that "writing" can include not only words, phrases, and sentences, but also other representations to support those ideas, such as drawings. In a similar fashion to verbal exchanges, students see a reason to use mathematically precise vocabulary in an effort to more effectively communicate their ideas (NCTM, 2000).

Conclusion

We have found that with a mathematical learning community established using the structure, instructional strategies, and curriculum described above, students have made great gains in terms of deep mathematical understandings of advanced concepts, as evidenced in our research results. Just as rewarding, we have found that students truly love mathematics and describe math class as "being in heaven." When asked what he wanted to be when he grew up, one first grader wrote that he wants to grow up to be a "Mathematician Texan!" We believe that encouraging this passion for and understanding of mathematics at a young age is an essential component in developing future career mathematicians. We must nurture the talents of our budding mathematicians in order to create a global society where the workforce is capable of innovative mathematical problem solving. And we can never begin this process too early.

References

Casa, T. M. (2012). Capturing thinking on the talk frame. *Teaching Children Mathematics, 19,* 184.

Chapin, S. H., O'Connor, C., & Anderson, N. C. (2009). *Classroom discussions: Using math talk to help students learn, Grades 1–6* (2nd ed.). Sausalito, CA: Math Solutions Publications.

Clements, D. (2003) Teaching and learning geometry. In J. Kilpatrick, W. G. Martin, & D. Schifter (Eds.), *A research companion to principles and standards for school mathematics* (pp. 151–178). Reston, VA: National Council of Teachers of Mathematics.

Council of Chief State School Officers, & National Governors Association. (2010). *Common Core State Standards for Mathematics.* Retrieved from http://www.corestandards.org/assets/CCSI_Math%20Standards.pdf

Gavin, M. K., Dailey, J., Chapin, S. H., & Sheffield, L. J. (2007a). *Getting into shapes.* Dubuque, IA: Kendall/Hunt.

Gavin, M. K., Dailey, J., Chapin, S. H., & Sheffield, L. J. (2007b). *Getting into shapes, Student mathematician's journal.* Dubuque, IA: Kendall/Hunt.

Gavin, M. K., Casa, T. M., Adelson, J. L., Carroll, S. R., & Sheffield, L. J. (2009). The impact of advanced curriculum on the achievement of mathematically promising elementary students. *Gifted Child Quarterly, 53,* 188–202.

Gavin, M. K., Casa, T. M., Adelson, J. L., & Firmender, J. M. (2013). The impact of advanced geometry and measurement units on the achievement of grade 2 students. *Journal for Research in Mathematics Education, 44,* 478–510.

Gavin, M. K., Casa, T. M., Chapin, S. H., & Sheffield, L. J. (2010a). *Designing a shape gallery: Geometry with the meerkats, Student mathematician's journal.* Dubuque, IA: Kendall/Hunt.

Gavin, M. K., Casa, T. M., Chapin, S. H., & Sheffield, L. J. (2010b). *Designing a shape gallery: Geometry with the meerkats.* Dubuque, IA: Kendall/Hunt.

Gavin, M. K., Casa, T. M., Firmender, J. M., & Carroll, S. R. (2013). The impact of advanced geometry and measurement units on the mathematics achievement of first-grade students. *Gifted Child Quarterly, 57,* 71–84.

National Center for Education Statistics. (1996). National Assessment of Educational Progress (NAEP). NAEP mathematics grade 4. Washington, DC: Author.

National Council of Teachers of Mathematics. (1980). *An agenda for action: Recommendations for school mathematics for the 1980s.* Reston, VA: Author.

National Council of Teachers of Mathematics. (1989). *Curriculum and evaluation standards for school mathematics.* Reston, VA: Author.

National Council of Teachers of Mathematics. (1991). *Professional standards for teaching mathematics.* Reston, VA: Author.

National Council of Teachers of Mathematics. (2000). *Principles and standards for school mathematics.* Reston, VA: Author.

National Council of Teachers of Mathematics. (2006). Curriculum focal points for prekindergarten through grade 8 mathematics: A quest for coherence. Reston, VA: Author.

Renzulli, J. S., Leppien, J. H., & Hays, T. S. (2000). *The Multiple Menu Model: A practical guide for developing differentiated curriculum.* Mansfield Center, CT: Creative Learning Press.

Sriraman, B. (2008). Are mathematical giftedness and mathematical creativity synonyms? A theoretical analysis of constructs. In B. Sriraman (Ed.), *Creativity, giftedness, and talent development in mathematics* (pp. 85–112). Charlotte, NC: Information Age.

Trends in International Math and Science Study. (1994). *Mathematics items; Population 1 item pool grades 3 & 4.* The Hague: IEA, Trends in International Math and Science Study.

Tomlinson, C. A., Kaplan, S. N., Renzulli, J. S., Purcell, J., Leppien, J., & Burns, D. (2009). *The parallel curriculum: A design to develop high potential and challenge high-ability learners* (2nd ed.). Thousand Oaks, CA: Corwin Press.

Williams, M. M., & Casa, T. M. (2011/2012). Connecting class talk with individual student writing. *Teaching Children Mathematics, 18,* 314–321.

PART V

Contemporary Issues, Challenges, and Commentary

CHAPTER 17

The Achievement Gap and the Education Conspiracy Against Low-Income Children[25]

Joseph S. Renzulli
University of Connecticut

Introduction From Joe

One of the biggest challenges facing the field of gifted education is the underrepresentation of low-income and minority students participating in special programs and services. The lack of appropriate services for high-potential low-income students has had a significant effect on the achievement gap in America. It has also contributed to the loss of human capital from young people who have the potential to go on to 4-year colleges, graduate and professional schools, and careers that will enhance the economic, cultural, and

---

25 Renzulli, J. S. (2013). The achievement gap and the educational conspiracy against low income children. *International Journal for Talent Development and Creativity, 1,* 45–55. Copyright 2013 *International Journal for Talent Development and Creativity.* Reprinted with permission.

social development of our country. A focus of our work over the past several years at the National Research Center on the Gifted and Talented has been to address underrepresentation and to make suggestions for ameliorating this problem. This chapter and the one that follows examine both the reasons for underrepresentation and one approach that has made a significant difference in the lives of high-potential, low-income students from a major urban area.

Nobody believes in action anymore, so words have become a substitute for action, all the way to the top, a substitute for the truth nobody wants to hear because they can change it, or they'll lose their jobs if they change it, or maybe they simply don't know how to change it.
—John Le Carré, *The Russia House*

While a major challenge facing today's schools is the achievement gap that exists between advantaged and low income students, the ways we have addressed this problem have also produced flatline academic growth among our most able students, rampant boredom among students at all levels, and public dissatisfaction with an education system that is immune to anything but the superficial trappings of change. The National Assessment of Educational Progress (NAEP) reports in *The Nation's Report Card* in 2005 that half of all immigrant, minority, and low-income children never graduate from high school, and in many of our cities more than 30 percent of low-income students score at the lowest percentiles on national reading and math tests. We have addressed this achievement problem inadequately; indeed, the "collateral damage" has seriously undermined effective teaching and learning, in even our best schools. Many of our teachers are being deskilled, and outside of essential math, science, and reading courses, there is an erosion of creative curricula that include art, music, and drama. Experiential learning and a holistic vision of education have been undermined. Data juggling, test result falsification, making state tests easier, and outright lying on the parts of desperate administrators who will do almost anything to avoid being branded leaders of "failing schools" are outcomes of this short-sighted and narrow specialization. Even when we do see reports of test improvements, they sometimes mask other types of collateral damage such as increased dropout rates, de-emphasis of the arts, sciences, and social studies, and diminished matriculation to post high school education.

The Three Trillion Dollar Misunderstanding

How did we get into this mess? Why has the estimated three trillion dollars spent on school reform since the 1960s not made more of an impact (Miami-Dade County Public Schools, 2008)? We have tried just about everything—smaller schools, year-round schools, longer-school days, single-sex classes, after school mentoring, school uniforms, vouchers, charter schools, school-business partnerships, merit pay for teachers, paying students (and even parents) for higher scores, private management companies and for-profit schools, takeovers by mayors and state departments of education, distributive leadership, site-based management, data-based decision making, and just about every scheme imaginable into which someone can insert the words, "standards-based," "accountability," or "brain-based." Every buzz word in a profession that already thrives on too much jargon eventually creeps into the repertoire of policy-makers, shifting the focus off student needs and appropriate pedagogy for meeting these needs and on to inflexible bureaucratic solutions that ignore individual learning needs. All of these suggested solutions, usually launched with much fanfare, endless and usually mind-numbing workshops for teachers, and little if any research or track record for success have been offered as "silver bullets" that can "save" our schools and raise the test scores of our lowest-achieving students. The sad fact is these schemes simply have not worked.

What do all of these reform initiatives have in common? Most are built on structural changes, designed by well-intentioned policy-makers or agencies (usually far removed from the classroom), and calculated to have an impact on entire school districts, states, or even the entire nation. More importantly, however, is that these structural changes have drawn mainly upon (and even forced) a low level pedagogy that is highly prescriptive and didactic, approaches to learning that emphasize the accumulation, storage, and retrieval of information that will show up on the next round of standardized tests. We have become so obsessed with content standards and test scores that assess mainly memory, that we have lost sight of the most important outcomes of schooling: thinking; reasoning; creativity; and problem solving skills that allow young people to *use* the information driven by content standards in interesting and engaging ways.

Are There Reasonable and Practical Alternatives?

Over the past decade the mainstream diet for the majority of low income and struggling learners has been dominated by a remedial and compensatory pedagogy that has not diminished the achievement gap, but, as research has shown, has actually contributed to its perpetuation (American Educational Research Association [AERA], 2004; Ford, Howard, Harris & Tyson, 2000). Many of these programs are designed to find out what a child cannot do, does not like to do, and sees no reason for doing, and then teachers are told to spend the majority of classroom time making sure the child concentrates on these programs to the point of boredom. This pedagogy of prescription and practice simply has not worked!

Documentation of this failure is plainly evident in one national report after another (National Assessment of Educational Progress [NAEP], 2005; Center for Education Policy [CEP], 2008), and yet we continue our search for yet another quick-fix through structural rearrangements of schools, rather than alternative pedagogical modifications that deal directly with the enjoyment, engagement, and enthusiasm that results from a more inductive and investigative brand of learning. The solutions offered by whatever new names we give them (e.g., Competency-Based, Outcomes-Based, Standards-Based) are always reiterations of the same pedagogy—the same drill-and-practice model for learning that simply has not worked. The universal criterion for accountability always remains the same, again with new names given to the same old achievement tests that mainly measure memorized factual information. It is the singular reliance on these tests for accountability, at the exclusion of other important performance-based outcomes that forces the pedagogy of prescription, a pedagogy that drives good teachers from the profession, and that prevents those teachers who remain from teaching creatively. Is it any wonder that some of our very best teachers are fleeing urban schools where prescription has become the almost universally practiced pedagogy?

Learning Theory 101: The Short Course

All learning experiences exist on a continuum ranging from deductive, didactic, and prescriptive on one hand to inductive, investigative, and inquiry-oriented on the other. Students who have not achieved are subjected to endless amounts of repetitive practice material guided by the didactic model. Then, when scores do not improve, we often think that the obvious solution is to simply redouble our efforts with what has been popularly called a "drill and kill" approach to learning; an approach that has turned many of our schools into joyless places that promote mind-numbing boredom, lack of genuine student and teacher engagement, absenteeism, increased dropout rates, and other byproducts of over-dependence on mechanized learning. Proponents of popular but highly prescriptive reading programs frequently boast about test score gains, but the endless "drill and practice" only prepare students for taking tests correlated to the worksheets *rather than actually learning to read*, let alone enjoying reading, and making reading an important part of their lives (Reis et al., 2004). Many students subjected to over-prescription never pick up a book on their own. This is a sad commentary on how we have messed up the teaching of reading by turning the teaching of reading into the teaching of taking tests.

With this kind of track record should we not be smart enough to blend the benefits of an inductive and investigative pedagogy into a system that has mainly failed our at-risk populations? Should we not also be smart enough to note the rising dissatisfaction of middle class parents whose children are also becoming subjected to the same drill-oriented, test-prep curriculum? One high school student recently described her Advanced Placement (AP) courses as ". . . nothing more than *high-speed* test prep." Two Ohio students from an affluent school district wrote in a letter to their governor, "Schools once renowned for their unique learning programs are becoming nothing more than soulless factories that churn out those that can excel at standardized tests while discarding those who can't." Is it any wonder that a parent from a high status community speculated that there was indeed a sinister conspiracy afoot to close the achievement gap, and the conspiracy consisted of dragging down the scores of high-achieving students?

Research on the role of student engagement is clear and unequivocal. High engagement results in higher achievement, improved self-concept and self-efficacy, and more favorable attitudes toward school and learning (Ainley, 1993; Herrington, Oliver, & Reeves, 2002). There is a strong body of research that points out the crucial difference between time-spent and time-engaged in school activities. In the recently published Program for International Student Assessment (PISA) study (Organization for Economic Cooperation and Development [OECD], 2007), the single criterion that distinguished between nations with the highest and lowest levels of student achievement was the degree to which students were engaged in their studies. This finding took into account demographic factors such as ethnicity and the socioeconomic differences among the groups studied.

The Most Important Outcomes of Education

The pedagogy of prescription has perhaps unintentionally, but clearly in terms of demonstrated results, withheld from low-income children the exact kinds of thinking skills that are necessary for successful participation in today's higher education and our growing global economy. The word, "perhaps" is used because I do not think there is a clandestine conspiracy on the parts of policy makers and the textbook/testing cartel to keep low-income children poorly educated thereby limiting access to economic mobility. However, make no mistake, neglect, mismanagement, and a lack of courage to challenge unsuccessful practices is the equivalent of a *bona fide* conspiracy.

If failed approaches have continued to produce dismal results, perhaps it is time to examine a counter-intuitive approach based on a pedagogy that is the polar opposite of the pedagogy that Pavlov used to train his dogs. Accountability for the truly-educated mind in today's knowledge-driven economy should first and foremost attend to students' ability to:

- plan a task and consider alternatives;
- monitor one's understanding and the need for additional information;
- identify patterns, relationships, and discrepancies in information;
- generate *reasonable* arguments, explanations, hypotheses, and ideas using appropriate information sources, vocabulary, and concepts;
- draw comparisons and analogies to other problems;
- formulate meaningful questions;
- apply and transform factual information into usable knowledge;
- rapidly and efficiently access just-in-time information and selectively extract meaning from that information;
- extend one's thinking beyond the information given;
- detect bias, make comparisons, draw conclusions, and predict outcomes;
- apportion time, schedules, and resources;
- apply knowledge and problem solving strategies to real-world problems;
- work effectively with others;
- communicate effectively in different genres, languages, and formats;
- derive enjoyment from active engagement in the act of learning; and
- creatively solve problems and produce new ideas.

These are the student engagement-oriented skills that grow young minds, promote genuine enthusiasm for learning, and, as our research has shown, increase achievement (Renzulli & Reis, 1985). Although student engagement has been defined in many ways, I view it as the infectious enthusiasm that students display when working on something that is of personal interest and that is pursued in an inductive and investigative approach to learning. It takes into account student-learning styles and preferred modes of expression as well as interests and levels of knowledge in an area of study. It is through these highly engaging approaches that students are motivated to improve basic skills and bring their work to higher levels of perfection. True engagement results from learning activities that challenge young people to "stretch" above their current comfort level, activities that are based on resources and methods of inquiry that are qualitatively different from excessive practice. Our research has shown that teaching students to think critically, analytically, and creatively actually improves plain old-fashioned achievement (Renzulli & Reis, 1997; Renzulli, 2008). Our guiding principle in this kind of learning is simply: *No Child Left Bored!*

Moreover, the key role of engagement cannot be overemphasized for students whose achievement has been hampered by limited experiences, resources, or supports. In a longitudinal study comparing time-spent versus time-engaged on the achievement of at-risk students, conventional-instructional practices were found to be responsible for the students' increased risk of academic delay (Greenwood, 1991). Another study reported important differences in achievement outcomes favoring engaged over disengaged students of similar ability (Greenwood, 1991). Hours of drilling on ACT test questions in Chicago high schools may be hurting, not helping, students' scores on the college-admission exam, according to a study released recently by a university-based research organization (Samuels, 2008). The Consortium on Chicago School Research (2008), based at the University of Chicago, found in their 2005 report that teachers in the 409,000-student district would spend about one month of instructional time on ACT test practice in the core classes offered during junior year. However, the ACT test scores were lower in schools where 11th grade teachers reported spending 40 percent of their time on test preparation, compared with schools where teachers devoted less than 20 percent of their class time to the ACT. The boredom factor was cited as an explanation for this seemingly counterintuitive finding.

Although focusing on the engagement-oriented outcomes listed above may be counterintuitive to the "more-practice-is-better" pedagogy; we need only look at the track record of compensatory learning models to realize we have been banging our collective heads against the wall and following an endless parade of failed reforms being forced through the schoolhouse door by people far removed from classrooms, schools, and local level decision-makers.

How did we allow committees of bureaucrats to write endless lists of content standards without equal or even greater attention to standards for good thinking and the kinds of authentic assessment that shows how good thinking is demonstrated? How did we allow textbook companies to "stuff" their books with more and more mind-numbing practice materials that prescribe and dictate what teachers must do every minute of the school day? How did we give the test publishers the gun that is held against the collective heads of every superintendent, principal, teacher, and student in the nation? Even state-education commissioners and their agencies, some of which are responsible for buying into various silver-bullet solutions, are now being "held accountable" for low scores in their states.

If we are going to break the stranglehold that the perpetrators of failed practices have had on our schools and the lives of children, we need some leaders at all levels (federal, state, and local) courageous enough to explore bolder and more innovative alternatives that will provide all students with a more highly enriched diet—the kind of diet that characterizes learning in the nation's very best public and private schools. This is not to say that we should abandon a strong curriculum that focuses on basic competencies, nor should we forget to demand accountability data to evaluate returns on investment for alternate approaches to addressing the problem. We need to move the focus away from memorizing content and toward the kinds of thinking skills listed above. We need to develop accountability procedures (not just tests) that show us how well students are learning to *apply* their thinking to authentic problem-solving situations. This kind of accountability may not put the bubble sheet companies out of business, but it will help force the issue of building a richer school pedagogy.

We also need to infuse into the curriculum a series of motivationally-rich experiences that promote student engagement, enjoyment, and a genuine enthusiasm for learning. Common sense and our own experiences tell us that we always do a better job when we are working on something in which we are personally engaged, something that we are really "into," and that we truly enjoy doing. For instance, the demonstrated benefits in performance that result from extra-curricular activities are based on a pedagogy that is the polar opposite of the pedagogy of "drill and practice" (Kaufman & Gabler, 2004). How many *un*engaged students have you seen on the school newspaper staff, the basketball team, the chess club, the debate team, or the concert choir? Their engagement occurs because these students have some choice in the area in which they will participate; they interact in a real-world goal oriented environment with other likeminded students interested in developing expertise in their chosen area; they use authentic problem solving, interpersonal, and creative strategies; they produce a product, service, or performance that is evidence of the level and quality of their work; and their work is brought to bear on one or more intended audiences other than, or at least in addition to, the teacher (Renzulli & Reis, 1985). The engagement that results from these kinds of experiences exemplifies the best way to approach joyful and engaging learning; one that differs completely from the prescriptive and remedial education that are the main approaches to learning in low-income classrooms.

Is There a Way to Make Real Change Rather Than the Appearance of Change?

Recognition of the achievement gap problem and the effect that failed solutions have had on schools that serve *all* of our young people have resulted in some very predictable activity. The usual national commissions and new rounds of federal, state, and foundation reports calling for "bolder and broader approaches" have at least recognized the existence of the crisis facing our schools; but we must be cautious of looking for approaches that emphasize the same structural solutions without primary consideration to the pedagogy which is at the core of any substantive changes in learning. We must also be cautious about seeking solutions from the same people and practices that caused these problems in the first place! Requiring all students to take x number of courses, raising passionate calls for more teacher and administrator training, rigorous standards-based curriculum, extending the regular school day and year, providing tutoring, homework helpers and summer school will not bring about substantive change unless we change *how* the required courses, tutoring, or summer school are taught. Let us take as an example the tutoring issue and the $595 million spent on this service in 2006–07. Findings on tutoring from three cities presented before the American Educational Research Association (AERA) (2008) support previous research about the effectiveness of tutoring (Arnott, Hastings, & Allbritton, 2008). In Milwaukee, however, researchers found no improvements in the scores of students receiving tutoring. "One reason," says Patricia Burch of the University of Wisconsin-Madison, "is that, in many sessions, tutors used uninspired practices, such as handing out worksheets. Researchers in L.A. found similar results." This example points out the disconnect between a perfectly good (indeed, ancient, and honorable) educational practice (tutoring) and the pedagogical way in which it was carried out.

Two approaches that have been used to make changes that serve challenged as well as traditionally high-achieving students are a pedagogical approach called The Enrichment Triad Model and an approach that guided research on underachieving students called The Prism Metaphor. The Enrichment Triad Model (see Figure 17.1) set out to transform high-ability students from lesson learners or consumers of facts to producers of new knowledge (Renzulli, 1977; Renzulli & Reis, 1997).

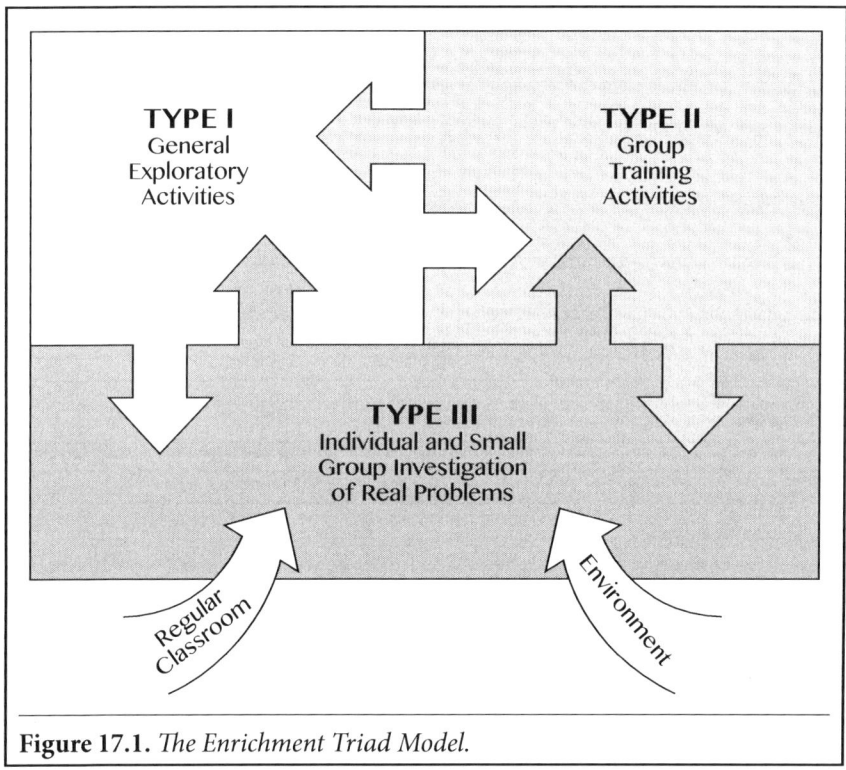

Figure 17.1. *The Enrichment Triad Model.*

The model laid out three categories of experience: *Type I Enrichment* consisting of general exploratory activities to expose students to new, exciting material not covered in the basic curriculum; *Type II Enrichment* involving group-training activities to develop creative and cognitive skills and research, communication, learning-how-to-learn, and affective skills and; and *Type III Enrichment* featuring the application of these skills to self-selected investigative and creative projects. More specifically, at the Type III level, children become actual investigators of real-world problems and target their work for real-life audiences. They produce creative products through the collection of raw data, the use of advanced problem-solving techniques, and the application of research strategies or artistic innovations that are employed by front-line people in various fields, albeit at a more junior level than adult investigators.

Baum, Renzulli, and Hébert (1995) built upon this foundation to propose another highly original way to view and motivate reluctant children and youth. Specifically, their Prism Metaphor—presented schematically in Figure 17.2—highlights the potential impact enrichment can have on underachievement. According to this visual metaphor, underachieving students are overwhelmed by learning and emotional problems, social/behavioral issues, and inappropri-

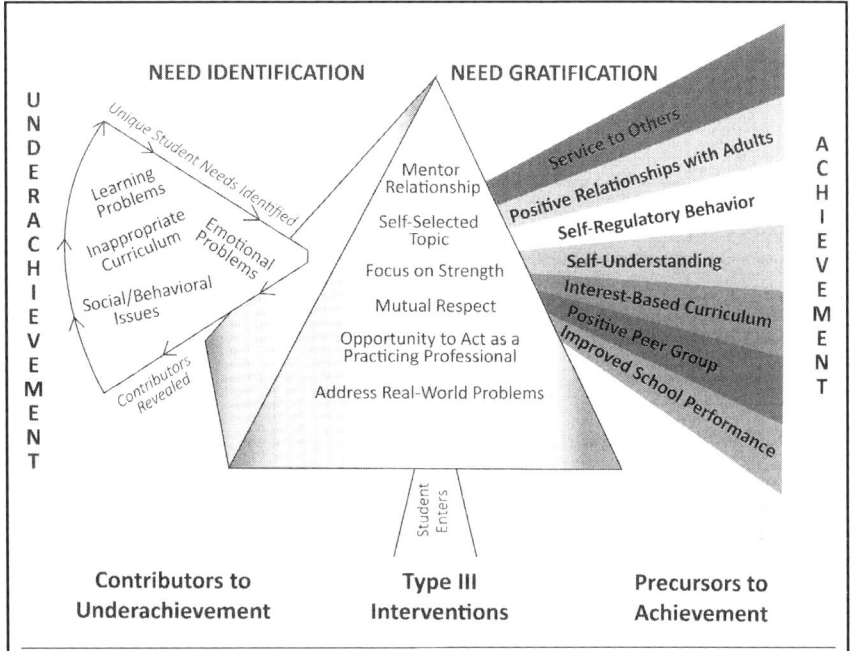

Figure 17.2. *The Prism Metaphor for reversing underachievement (Baum, Renzulli, and Hébert, 1995). Used with permission of the National Research Center on the Gifted and Talented, The University of Connecticut.*

ate curriculum. They are not moving forward, likely because interventions to date have used the wrong lens (i.e., traditional teacher-directed approaches) to focus the problem. However, once relevant Type III Enrichment activities, involving mentoring, real-world problem solving, and self-selected topics, are put in place, things change for the better. Indeed, just as a prism somehow converts nondescript white light into a magical array of colors, so can Type III Enrichment inspire and lead underperforming gifted students toward positive outcomes and productivity. Although somewhat speculative, the optimistic undercurrent of this framework is uplifting.

Renzulli and his team went on to demonstrate the value of the Prism Metaphor in a tangible fashion by exploring the possibility of using Type III Enrichment activities to reverse underachievement in talented children (Baum, Renzulli, & Hébert, 1995). In their study, twelve teachers, all trained in The Enrichment Triad approach, selected seventeen identified gifted students who were performing below potential in school.

The children, five girls and twelve boys, ranged in age from eight to thirteen. Each was guided through a Type III experience by the referring teacher, who took on the role of researcher. Rather than assume control of the learning process, the teachers became facilitators—helping students to focus problems, to secure necessary materials, to review and revise their work, and to overcome obstacles within the context of pursuing a topic that had great personal meaning. The teachers also assumed the roles of mentor and confidant to the students and, as such, discovered much about the personal lives, frustrations, interests, and dreams of their young students. In their extended role as educators-researchers, the teachers also acted as participant observers, recording their observations systematically, reflecting upon their entries, and documenting effective strategies.

Three Things We Can Do to Create a 21st Century Pedagogy

Before describing three things we can do to change the pedagogy, a word is in order about the role of technology in the modern world. To a large degree, we have become what our technology has made us. We began communicating more effectively because of inventions such as the telegraph, the telephone, and the Internet; and travel became faster and more efficient with the inventions of the steam engine, the airplane, and jet engines. In his book, *The Power Makers: Steam, Electricity and the Men Who Invented Modern America* (2008), Klein documents the well-known economic principle that supply creates its own demand. Education changed dramatically when the technology evolved from books that families and the schoolmaster had at hand to textbooks from which all students could learn simultaneously. When schools gained the technology of copy machines, easily-reproducible workbooks and practice materials became a mainstay of the learning process. This technology has driven both what and how young people have learned for most of the past and present century. Students memorize factual material and engage in endless practice simply because such material is available. Supply creates its own demand!

Almost every area of modern life has made imaginative uses of technology, while in education we have settled for electronic applications of the same old technology that did not differ pedagogically from standard "drill and practice" forms of teaching (i.e., worksheets-on-line). These early generations of educational technology may have given teachers some extra "helpers," but because they were based on a knowledge-acquisition pedagogy the skills that students need for success in the 21st century are still only by-products of present-day models of teaching and learning.

How can we bring about the changes in the engagement-oriented pedagogy necessary to turn things around? Although I will not argue that technology without planned teacher involvement and technology-savvy teachers is the answer to our prayers, we now have the next generation of education technology that can give teachers the tools to do several important things to promote a high-engagement pedagogy. However, we must be careful not to use this technology to recreate electronic forms of the same old pedagogy we are trying to improve upon. This technology goes beyond the online, electronic encyclopedias, and courses-on-line worksheets that were the earliest applications of technology to classroom use. These applications did not differ pedagogically from the standard "drill and practice" forms of teaching.

Although it may sound clichéd, the advent of the Internet and easy access to most of the world's knowledge by young people is literally changing the time-honored learning theories that have guided curriculum and instruction for several centuries. Teachers and textbooks are no longer the gatekeepers of knowledge and the old curriculum paradigm that consisted mainly of To-Be-Presented knowledge is giving way to what I call Just-In-Time (JIT) knowledge. It is the kind of knowledge that students seek out when it is necessary to solve a problem, whether posed by the teacher or self-selected by a student (or small group) because of personal interest. Students will obviously need to learn the basic skills of the three Rs, but they will also need to learn the following technology skills of inquiry in order to make efficient use of JIT knowledge:

- the ability to identify trustworthy and useful information;
- the ability to selectively manage overabundant information;
- the ability to organize, classify, and evaluate information;
- the ability to conduct self-assessments of web-based information;
- the ability to use relevant information to advance the quality of one's work; and
- the ability to communicate information effectively in various genres and modes of expression.

This use of JIT knowledge, once the method of inquiry employed exclusively by scholars, researchers, and creative producers, is the paradigm that is now available to all young people and the paradigm that will create the motivation and engagement that has largely been lost when most of the learning followed a "to-be-presented" curriculum and a brand of learning that minimized the sheer joy of finding-out things on one's own. So let us now look at three things we can do to apply this new generation of education technology to modem-day learning.

1. Assessment of student strengths. The first innovative use of this next-generation technology is that teachers can now get a comprehensive look at *all* the major characteristics of their students, characteristics that go beyond simply knowing a student's standardized achievement test standings compared to a norm-based reference group. Using a computer-generated student profile developed at the University of Connecticut, we are able to quickly and easily provide information about student interests, learning styles, and preferred modes of expression as well as how students perceive their strengths in the traditional academic subject areas (Reis & Renzulli, 2008). The simple assumption underlying the use of this technology-generated profile is that the more teachers know about all of these dimensions of the learner, the better able they will be to make decisions about what materials and activities have the highest potential for engaging that learner.

2. Matching resources to student profiles. Although "differentiation" is an important contemporary goal of much of today's efforts to make learning more meaningful for young people, the sad fact is that most teachers simply do not have the time to seek out the resources that can accommodate the varied learning needs of a increasingly diverse school population. The second way technology can affect pedagogy is by giving teachers easy access to the wealth of enrichment and engagement-oriented material that is available through the Internet and through materials and activities that have been purposefully selected and placed into easily accessible databases. Now let us look at a little of the "magic" of combining these two uses of technology and why we consider this work to be a new generation of education technology. Through advanced programming techniques, a search engine can examine thousands of multiple classified (e.g., subject areas, reading level, state standards, interests, learning styles, and expression styles) high-engagement resources and match these resources to information about learner characteristics revealed in student profiles. This tool provides teachers with the kind of tool that allows for true differentiation based on individual student profiles, and the computer has done the heavy lifting. In view of the number and diversity of young people that teachers must deal with every day, it would be impossible to achieve this kind of personalized learning without the use of technology. What is even more important is that the easy availability of highly-engaging resources and the matching capability of the technology "forces" the kind of engagement-oriented pedagogy we are trying to infuse into the curriculum.

3. Teacher training. The third thing we can do is re-examine the ways that we train teachers, especially already employed teachers who have not had access to the technology courses now routinely available in most undergraduate teacher-training programs. The research shows that most school-based professional development has had little or no effect on teachers' classroom behaviors. Most teachers can tell their own horror stories about sitting through endless hours of irrelevant workshops. Endless lists of glittering generalities, flashy slide shows, flavor-of-the-month "innovations," and strategies with absolutely no research support are delivered by entertaining, motivational speakers. I have no argument with a certain amount of professional development in general and content-specific-teaching strategies, and all teachers should be constantly improving their subject-matter competency, but the focus of professional development in a technology-driven pedagogy should be on the skills that allow teachers to help young people master the technology skills of inquiry listed above. The acquisition and application of these skills will turn our teachers into the proverbial "guides-on-the-side" rather than simply traditional disseminators of information which have characterized so much of our education system in pre-technology approaches to learning. This transformed role of teachers and approaches to instruction will bring about the sought-after differentiation and changes in engagement and motivation that have eluded us in reform efforts thus far.

Many national education leaders and politicians are describing the current challenges facing our schools as a crisis in the American education system. It will not be easy to turn around a school system whose leaders have made massive financial and policy investments in one particular brand of learning, nor will it be easy to circumvent the powerful influence of the textbook and test-publishing industries that have thrived on a prescriptive curriculum and standardized test-driven approaches to accountability. But a gentle and evolutionary rather than revolutionary approach to school reform is possible if we begin to take advantage of the remarkable advances that have taken place in the information technologies, advances that have brought within reach the equivalent of a dozen teaching assistants in every classroom, all day, every day. These technologies now make it possible to quickly and easily assess students' interests, learning styles, and preferred modes of expressing themselves. What formerly took teachers weeks or even months to learn about student strengths can now be assessed in less than an hour through computer-generated profiles, and powerful search engines can examine thousands of high-end learning resources that *match* these resources to individual student profiles. True differentiation, much talked about but seldom achieved, can take place if we can let the technology do the hard work of finding and matching resources that are engagement-oriented rather than practice-oriented.

Dr. Leon Lederman, the Nobel Prize winning physicist (1988), recently said, *"Once upon a time, America sheltered an Einstein, went to the Moon, and gave the world the laser, electronic computer, nylon stockings, television, and the cure for polio. Today we are in the process, albeit unwittingly, of abandoning this leadership role."* Every school and classroom in this country has in it young people who are capable of continuing this remarkable tradition. However, the tradition will not survive without a national resolve and bold action on the parts of policy makers at all levels to change the pedagogy that drives instruction in classrooms that serve *all* of our young people. You do not produce future scientists and inventors such as Jonas Salk, George Washington Carver, Thomas Edison, Sally Ride, or Marie Curie by forcing them to learn in a one-size-fits-all "drill and practice" curriculum or by spending hundreds of hours preparing for state achievement tests. You do not develop the potential of thousands of Leonard Bernsteins, Aretha Franklins, or Miles Davises without providing them with highly engaging opportunities in music that typically are only available in out-of-school opportunities and mainly to the children of the well-to-do. You do not develop world leaders such as Martin Luther King, Golda Meir, Eleanor Roosevelt, and Mahatma Gandhi by having them memorize endless lists of facts that today's technology-savvy young people can find *when they need them* using a few clicks on the web. You do not produce the next generation of talented writers such as Rachel Carson, Langston Hughes, and Tennessee Williams by having them spend endless hours completing mindless worksheets in preparation for the next round of state-mastery tests. It is only through expanding our pedagogy, engaging *all* students, and making imaginative uses of technology that America's schools will be able to truly engage our children and develop their creative potential, as well as their love of learning.

References

Ainley, M. (1993). Styles of engagement with learning: Multidimensional assessment of their relationship with strategy use and school achievement. *Journal of Educational Psychology, 85,* 395.

American Educational Research Association. (2004, Fall). Closing the gap: High achievement for students of color. *Research Points: Essential Information for Education Policy, 2*(3). Washington, DC: Edmund W. Gordon.

Amott, E., Hastings, P., & Allbritton, D. (2008, August). Research Methods Tutor: Evaluation of a dialoguebased tutoring system in the classroom. *Behavior Research Methods, 40,* 694–698.

Baum, S. M., Renzulli, J. S., & Hébert, T. (1995). *The prism metaphor: A new paradigm for reversing achievement.* Storrs: The University of Connecticut, The National Research Center on the Gifted and Talented.

Center for Education Policy. (2008, Fall). *A call to restructure restructuring: Lessons from the No Child Left Behind Act in Five States.* Washington, DC: Caitlin Scott.

Consortium on Chicago School Research. (2008). *From high school to the future: Too much, too late.* Chicago, IL: Elaine Allensworth, Macarena Correa, and Steve Ponisciak.

Ford, D. Y., Howard, T. C., Harris, J. J., & Tyson, C. A. (2000). Creating culturally responsive classrooms for gifted African American students. *Journal for the Education of the Gifted, 23,* 397–427.

Greenwood, C. R. (1991). Longitudinal analysis of time, engagement, and achievement in at-risk versus nonrisk students (at risk of low academic achievement). *Exceptional Children, 57,* 521–535.

Herrington, J., Oliver, R., & Reeves, T. (2002). *Patterns of engagement in authentic online learning environments.* Lismore, NSW: Southern Cross University Press.

Kaufman, J., & Gabler, J. (2004, April). Cultural capital and the extracurricular activities of girls and boys in the college attainment process. *Poetics, 32,* 145.

Klein, M. (2008). *The power makers: Steam, electricity and the men who invented modern America.* London: Bloomsbury Press.

Miami-Dade County Public Schools. (2008). *Regal plan: Revamping education for the gifted and all learners.* Retrieved from http://advancedacademicprograms.dadeschools.net/regalPlan/GiftedTaskForceReport.pdf

National Assessment of Educational Progress. (2005). *The nation's report card: Reading 2005.* Washington, DC: The National Center for Education Statistics.

Organization for Economic Cooperation and Development. (2007). *Assessing scientific, reading and mathematical literacy: A framework for Program for International Student Assessment (PISA).* Paris, France: Author.

Reis, S. M., Eckert, R. D., Jacobs, J. K., Coyne, M. D., Richards, S., Briggs, C. J., Schreiber, F.J., Gubbins, E. J. (2004). *Schoolwide enrichment model reading framework.* Storrs: The University of Connecticut, The National Research Center on the Gifted and Talented.

Reis, S., & Renzulli, J. (2008, June). Differentiation and enrichment. *District Administration, 44*(7), 22–23.

Renzulli, J. S. (1977). *The Enrichment Triad Model: A guide for developing defensible programs for the gifted.* Mansfield Center, CT: Creative Learning Press.

Renzulli, J. S., & Reis, S.M. (1985). *The Schoolwide Enrichment Model: A comprehensive plan for educational excellence.* Mansfield Center, CT: Creative Learning Press.

Renzulli, J. S., Reis, S. M. (1997). *The Schoolwide Enrichment Model: A how-to guide for educational excellence* (2nd ed.). Waco, TX: Prufrock Press.

Renzulli, J. S. (2008). Engagement is the answer. *Education Week, 27*(43), 30–31.

Samuels, C. (2008, June 4). ACT test-prep backfiring in Chicago, Study warns. *Education Week, 27*(39), 6–7.

CHAPTER 18

From High Potential to Gifted Performance

Encouraging Academically Talented Urban Students[26]

Sally M. Reis
University of Connecticut

and Miriam Morales-Taylor
Hartford Public Schools

Introduction From Joe

Although it would be desirable to make talent development opportunities a priority in all schools, the complexity of large urban school district politics and the massive challenge of training huge numbers of teachers and administrators have made it difficult to bring about significant progress in provid-

---

26 Reis, S. M., & Morales-Taylor, M. (2010). From high potential to gifted performance: Encouraging academically talented urban students. *Gifted Child Today, 33*(4), 28–38. Copyright 2010 SAGE Publications. Reprinted with permission from SAGE Publications.

ing services for high-potential low-income students. In this chapter, Sally and Miriam describe an urban school that is based on a concept we borrowed from chemistry called "critical mass." Critical mass simply means gathering and concentrating the necessary number of relevant resources to cause a particular result. This concept is not unlike what has been done in thousands of gifted programs that serve students in more affluent schools and districts across the country.

In the urban school described in this chapter, the critical mass assembled included a group of teachers who were highly trained in the Schoolwide Enrichment Model, a supportive principal and central office administrators who were knowledgeable about and committed to this learning model, and a selected group of high-potential students and their parents who understood beforehand what this school would be all about.

Academically talented students in many urban areas in our Northeastern corner of the country have little access to gifted and talented programs due to lack of funding and attention focused on students who are achieving well below grade level. In the city of Hartford, for example, no gifted program has been available for more than a decade, and teachers and administrators acknowledge that the needs of many high-potential and gifted students often are not met in classrooms. In fact, the Renzulli Academy emerged from an initiative of the Assistant Superintendent with the full support of the Superintendent, Dr. Steven Adamowski. The creation of the Renzulli Academy is the result of this awareness and the collaborative effort between Assistant Superintendent Miriam Morales-Taylor and Sally Reis, professor and researcher in gifted education and talent development at the Neag School of Education, University of Connecticut. It was Miriam Morales-Taylor's vision that created the impetus for the academy. Having worked closely with the Institute for Learning (IFL) at the University of Pittsburgh, Mrs. Morales-Taylor recognized that the principles of learning, particularly academic rigor, clear expectations, and socializing intelligence, should play an important role in the development of the Renzulli Academy.

Over the course of several months, a preliminary plan was developed about the curriculum and instruction that would guide the program, as well as its organization. Our plan was simple: to identify and serve gifted students from across many of the 25 elementary schools in the district. A decision was made to serve these students by creating a school within a school characterized by differentiated curriculum and instruction across all core content areas.

In addition, students would be offered opportunities for enrichment according to the Schoolwide Enrichment Model, as these types of resources and opportunities for enrichment were considered to be critical needs for these children. An additional part of the Renzulli Academy was the opportunity for independent study and mentoring services during the students' time in the program. This article briefly describes the academy, its philosophy and model, social and emotional adjustment of the students, curriculum and instructional programming, strategies that worked, and changes and modifications.

Introduction to the Renzulli Academy

The Renzulli Academy at Simpson Waverly School was created for 60 identified gifted/high-potential Hartford public students in grades 4, 5, and 6 in September of 2009 and is currently at full capacity in a high-poverty school that also houses another 350 students. Three teachers with master's degrees in gifted education, a commitment to work with urban students of poverty, and strong content knowledge were hired to engage and challenge the students who had been selected and housed in one wing of the school. In this section, we briefly describe the philosophy of the academy, the curricula used to challenge these advanced learners, the strategies that have worked, and subsequent changes and modifications. All students at the academy are from high-poverty families and most (more than 95%) are from culturally and linguistically diverse backgrounds.

Philosophy and Model

The philosophy of the Renzulli Academy is based on the Schoolwide Enrichment Model (SEM; Renzulli & Reis, 1985, 1997), a product of more than three decades of research and field-testing that combines the previously developed Enrichment Triad and Revolving Door Identification Models. The SEM has been implemented in school districts worldwide, and extensive evaluations and research studies indicate the effectiveness of the model, which Van Tassel-Baska and Brown (2007) called one of the mega-models in the field (Reis & Renzulli, 2003; Renzulli & Reis, 1994). Prior research suggests that the model is effective at serving high-ability students in a variety of educational settings and works well in schools that serve diverse ethnic and socioeconomic populations, exactly the population targeted by this school (Reis & Renzulli, 2003; Renzulli & Reis, 1994).

The Hartford Public Schools' Department of Assessment identified students in grades 4, 5, and 6 who scored at the highest levels on the recent Connecticut Mastery Tests. The parents/guardians of those students were invited to attend an informational session regarding the implementation of the Renzulli Academy. With this information at hand, they were able to make an informed decision whether to apply for admittance to the academy. Other school records also were used to make final decisions about admissions.

The Schoolwide Enrichment Model (SEM)

The Schoolwide Enrichment Model (SEM) has evolved over time after three decades of research and field-testing by both educators and researchers (Reis & Renzulli, 2003; Renzulli & Reis, 1994). It combines the previously developed Enrichment Triad Model (Renzulli, 1977) with a more flexible approach to identifying high-potential students (Renzulli & Reis, 1997). Research on the SEM has been conducted in schools with widely differing socioeconomic levels and program organizational patterns and has shown consistently positive results (Reis & Renzulli, 2003; Renzulli & Reis, 1994).

In the SEM, a Talent Pool of 15%–20% of above-average ability/high-potential students is identified through a variety of measures, including achievement tests, teacher nominations, assessment of potential for creativity, and task commitment, as well as alternative pathways of entrance (e.g., self-nomination, parent nomination). These measures were used in the academy, with the highest levels of performance on achievement tests documenting the basis for identification in this school.

In the SEM, students receive several kinds of services, also delivered in the Renzulli Academy. First, interest, learning styles, and product style assessments are conducted with Talent Pool students using the Renzulli Learning System (http://www.renzullilearning.com). Each student has created a profile that identifies his or her unique strengths and talents and teachers can identify patterns of a student's interests, products, and learning styles across the three classes. These methods are being used in the academy to both identify and create students' interests and to encourage students to develop and pursue these interests in various ways. Learning style preferences assessed include projects, independent study, teaching games, simulations, peer teaching, programmed instruction, lecture, drill and recitation, and discussion. Product style preferences include the kinds of products students like to do, such as those that are written, oral, hands-on, artistic, displays, dramatization, service, and multimedia.

Curriculum Compacting

To maximize instructional time, we incorporated rigor into the compacted curriculum. Compacting is used to document the content areas that have been compacted and the alternative work that has been substituted. This approach requires academic rigor, which includes commitment to a knowledge core, high thinking demands, and active use of knowledge (Resnick & Hall, 2005). Resnick and Hall (2005) challenged educators to integrate rigorous content with high-level thinking and active use of knowledge. Research on compacting has shown that it eliminates and streamlines curriculum, enabling high-potential students to avoid repetition of previously mastered work and guaranteed mastery while simultaneously finding time for more appropriately challenging activities (Reis & Purcell, 1993; Reis, Westberg, Kulikowich, & Purcell, 1998).

Curriculum compacting was provided to all eligible students, as the teachers modified the general education curriculum by eliminating portions of previously mastered content when students showed strengths in these areas (Reis, Burns, & Renzulli, 1992).

Enrichment

The Enrichment Triad Model was used as the basis for all enrichment in the academy, based on previous research about its success with all students including those in urban areas (Reis & Renzulli, 2003; Renzulli & Reis, 1994). For example, it was integrated into all content areas and was the basis for the reading program, the enrichment clusters, the social studies and science projects, and the regular exposure and training across all other content areas.

Type I Enrichment consists of general exploratory experiences such as guest speakers, field trips, demonstrations, interest centers, and the use of audiovisual materials and technology (such as webinars), which are designed to expose students to new and exciting topics, ideas, and fields of knowledge not ordinarily covered in the regular curriculum. Type II Enrichment includes instructional methods and materials purposefully designed to promote the development of thinking, feeling, research, communication, and methodological processes. Type II training, usually carried out both in classrooms and in enrichment programs, includes the development of creative thinking and problem solving, critical thinking, and affective processes; a variety of specific learning-how-to-learn skills; skills in the appropriate use of advanced-level reference materials; and written, oral, and visual communication skills.

Type III Enrichment is the most advanced level in the Enrichment Triad Model. Although Types I and II Enrichment and curriculum compacting should be provided on a regular basis to Talent Pool students, the ability to revolve into Type III Enrichment depends on an individual's interests, motivation, and desire to pursue advanced level study. Type III Enrichment is defined as investigative activities and artistic productions in which the learner assumes the role of a first-hand inquirer, thinking, feeling, and acting like a practicing professional, with involvement pursued at as advanced or professional level as possible given the student's level of development and age. The most important feature of the model is the "flow" or connection among the experiences. Each type of enrichment is viewed as a component part of a holistic process that blends present or newly developed interests (Type I) and advanced-level thinking and research skills (Type II) with application situations based on the modus operandi of the first-hand inquirer (Type III).

Renzulli Learning

Students in the Academy also have had access to the Renzulli Learning System (RLS), another research-based component of the SEM (Field, 2009). Field (2009) studied the use of the RLS, an innovative online enrichment program based on the Enrichment Triad Model, for students in both an urban and suburban school. In this 16-week experimental study, both gifted and nongifted students who participated in this enrichment program and used Renzulli Learning for 2–3 hours each week demonstrated significantly higher growth in reading comprehension than control group students who did not participate in the program. Students also demonstrated significantly higher growth in oral reading fluency and in social studies achievement than those students who did not participate (Field, 2009). Four steps enabled students in the academy to have access to enrichment during the day as well as after school and at home if the technology was available in their homes.

Step 1. The first step consisted of a computer-based diagnostic assessment that created a profile of each student's academic strengths, interests, learning styles, and preferred modes of expression. The online assessment, which took about 30 minutes, resulted in a personalized profile that highlighted individual student strengths and set the stage for Step 2 of the RLS.

Step 2. The profile served as a compass for the second step, which was a differentiation search engine that examined thousands of resources that related specifically to each student's profile. Student profiles also could be used to form groups of students who shared common interests. A project management tool guided students and teachers to use specifically selected resources for assigned curricular activities, independent or small-group investigative projects, and a wide variety of challenging enrichment experiences. Another management tool enabled teachers to form instructional groups and enrichment clusters based on interests and learning style preferences. Teachers had instant access to student profiles, all sites visited on the web, and the amount of time spent in each activity. Parents also had access to their own child's profile and web activities. In order to promote parent involvement, we suggested that students work on some of their favorite activities with their parents. Next, the differentiation search engine matched student strengths and interests to an enrichment database of 40,000 enrichment activities, materials, resources, and opportunities for further study that were grouped into the following categories: virtual field trips, real field trips, creativity training, critical thinking, projects and independent study, contests and competitions, websites, fiction and nonfiction books, summer programs, online activities, research skills, and high-interest videos and DVDs. These resources were not merely intended to inform students about new information or to occupy time surfing around the web. Rather, they were used as vehicles to help students find and focus on a problem or creative exploration of personal interest to pursue in greater depth. Many of the resources provided the methods of inquiry, advanced-level thinking and creative problem-solving skills, and investigative approaches. Students were guided toward the application of knowledge to the development of original research studies, creative projects, and action-oriented undertakings that put knowledge to work in personally meaningful areas of interest, and provided students with suggestions for outlets and audiences for their creative products. The resources available in Step 2 also provided students with opportunities to pursue advanced-level training in their strength areas and areas of personal interest.

Step 3. The third part of the RLS for students was a project organization and management plan called The Wizard Project Maker. Using this project planner, teachers could help students target their web-based explorations to undertake original research, investigative projects, and the development of a wide variety of creative undertakings. The sophisticated software used in this tool automatically located potentially relevant web-based resources that could be used in connection with the student's investigative activity. This management device was designed to fulfill the requirements of a Type III Enrichment experience, which is the highest level of enrichment described in our discussion of the Enrichment Triad Model. Specifically, the Wizard Project Maker provided students with the metacognitive skills to define a project and set a goal; identify and evaluate both the resources to which they had access and the resources they needed (e.g., time, Internet sites, teacher or mentor assistance); prioritize and refine goals; balance the resources needed to meet multiple goals; learn from past actions and project future outcomes; and monitor progress, making necessary adjustments as a project unfolded. The Wizard Project Maker helped students make the best use of web resources, helped to focus their interests as they pursued advanced-level work, and established a creative and viable responsibility for teachers in their role as "the guide on the side." By helping students pursue advanced levels of challenge and engagement through the use of the Wizard Project Maker, we hoped students would begin to regard their teachers as mentors rather than just as disseminators of knowledge.

Step 4. The final step in the RLS was an automatic compilation and storage of all student activity from Steps 1, 2, and 3 into an ongoing student record called the Total Talent Portfolio. A management tool allowed students to evaluate each site visited and resource used, students completed a self-assessment of what they derived from the resource, and, if they chose, they stored favorite activities and resources in their portfolio. This feature allowed easy-return access to ongoing work. The portfolio could be reviewed at any time by teachers and parents through the use of an access code, which allowed teachers to give feedback and guidance to individual students and provided parents with information about students' work and opportunities for parental involvement. The Total Talent Portfolio will travel with students throughout their years at the academy to serve as a reminder of previous activities and creative accomplishments that they might want to include in college applications and as an ongoing record that can help students, teachers, guidance counselors, and parents make decisions about future educational and vocational plans.

Teacher resources in the RLS enabled teachers to differentiate assignments and send tiered and compacted assignments to students by placing them in their electronic talent portfolio. Teachers also have used the RLS to group students based on their interests, learning, and expression or product styles.

Social-Emotional Adjustment of These Urban Academically Talented Students

A comprehensive review of research (Neihart, Reis, Robinson, & Moon, 2001) found that high-ability students are generally at least as well adjusted as any other group of youngsters, suggesting that most talented students do not face any more social and emotional problems than do other students. One exception to this statement is creatively gifted adolescents, such as those talented in writing or the visual arts, who have been found to manifest significantly higher or lower rates or severity of depression than those for the general population (Neihart et al., 2001). This review also found that gifted and talented students faced a number of situations that, while not unique to them, constituted sources of risk to their social and emotional development if their needs were not met (Neihart et al., 2001). One example of these risks is underachievement, widely regarded as one of the most pervasive problems affecting this population (Reis & McCoach, 2000). In the city in which the academy is housed, underachievement of gifted students at the high school level was found to be approximately 50% (Hébert & Reis, 1999) and findings from this study suggested that early lack of challenge contributed to the underachievement of these students (Reis, Hébert, Díaz, Maxfield, & Ratley, 1995). However, our experiences with students in this academy identified other social and emotional challenges in addition to lack of exposure to effort and an inability to deal with challenging content. These alone could contribute to underachievement, but in addition to these, students at the academy were from high-poverty environments and some had encountered very challenging situations in their early lives. We also found, for some of the students, difficulties in controlling impulses and aggression to others.

Findings from earlier research about academically talented high school students who underachieved in the same city suggested that certain factors can positively influence the self-regulation of high-ability students (Reis & Colbert, 2005) such as a strong belief in self and ways to cope with the negative aspects of their school and urban environment. Other protective factors included supportive adults, friendships with other achieving students, opportunity to take honors and advanced classes, and participation in multiple extracurricular activities both after school and during the summer. The Renzulli Academy has been created to provide these types of support, with students interacting with all three teachers on a regular basis.

Almost half of students at the Renzulli Academy have demonstrated signs that they are at risk for underachievement, most likely due to the fact that they have been in underchallenging classrooms and schools, have faced peer pressure to conform to patterns of minimal effort, and in some cases have faced social isolation in their neighborhood schools because they are so smart. Some have also faced family tragedies as they have lost siblings to deaths from gunshots and parents to drugs, crime, and prison. Unfortunately, the pattern of underachievement is difficult to reverse and can persist into adulthood without intervention (Reis & McCoach, 2000). Therefore, attempts to reverse negative patterns have been both proactive and immediate. These students may also encounter barriers to racial identity development if they believe they must choose between academic success and social acceptance, and so grouping them together at the academy has given them peer models for high achievement (Ford & Harris, 2002; Neihart et al., 2001). The pervasive problems students have experienced at the academy relate to their absence of self-regulation manifested in an inability to extend effort when faced with challenge, to focus for any extended periods of time, and to learn how to garner their own resources to avoid following social impulses related to aggression.

Self-Regulation

Current research indicates that some gifted students possess better self-regulated learning strategies than their peers; however, some gifted students may have done very well in school without using good self-regulation strategies because of a combination of their high abilities and/or an unchallenging curriculum (Zimmerman, 1989, 1990). If learning is relatively easy for someone, less effort, organization, and other self-regulated activities are expended. Social conditions or personal issues may prevent students from developing self-regulated learning strategies. For some students who already have some of these strategies, social or personal issues may prevent them from using them regularly, and thus, they need to be helped and encouraged to do so. Some talented students with high potential may find it difficult to learn self-regulation when it is not taught, modeled, or rewarded by the adults in their home and family. Even if students interact regularly with adults who demonstrate self-regulation, they may fail to use these skills themselves due to peer pressure or refuse to use the strategies their parents or teachers regularly employ at home or school.

Compared with low-achieving students, high achievers set more specific learning goals, use a variety of learning strategies, self-monitor more often, and adapt their efforts more systematically (Zimmerman, 1989). The quality and quantity of self-regulation processes is crucial. We must recognize that one self-regulation strategy will not work for all students, and that the use of only a few strategies will not work optimally for a person on all tasks or occasions. It is important that students learn to use multiple self-regulatory learning skills rather than single strategies, and so, at the academy, students are reminded continually that both their goals and their use of self-regulation strategies will have to be adjusted over time. Our hope in this school is that we will be able to continue to work with students who will learn to persist when they are challenged, which is especially critical for talented students who have seldom experienced high levels of challenge. We have continued to integrate self-regulation strategies across all content areas in the Renzulli Academy.

Self-regulation is an integrated learning process, consisting of the development of a set of constructive behaviors that affect one's learning. These processes are planned and adapted to support the pursuit of personal goals in changing learning environments. According to Zimmerman (1989), self-regulated learning involves the regulation of three general aspects of academic learning. First, self-regulation of behavior involves the active control of the various resources students have available to them, such as their time, their study environment (e.g., the place in which they study), and their use of others such as peers and faculty members to help them (Garcia & Pintrich, 1994; Pintrich & De Groot, 1990). Second, self-regulation of motivation and affect involves controlling and changing motivational beliefs such as self-efficacy and goal orientation, so that students can adapt to the demands of a course. In addition, students can learn how to control their emotions and affect (such as anxiety) in ways that improve their learning. Third and finally, self-regulation of cognition involves the control of various cognitive strategies for learning, such as the use of deep processing strategies that result in better learning and performance than students showed previously (Garcia & Pintrich, 1994). Within days of school starting, as we had expected, we found that many of these talented students lacked all three aspects of self-regulation, and so our goals have been to help them acquire specific strategies that work for them and enable them to increase their control over their own behavior and patterns of study. This has been a major goal at the academy, as it has meant that students learn to decrease negative behaviors across all three aspects of self-regulation and increase positive behaviors. Progress has been made with almost all students in this regard, and we anticipate that this progress will continue, enabling students to succeed personally as well as academically.

Curriculum and Instructional Programming

It is critical for teachers to have clear expectations and to effectively communicate them to the students. Clear expectations include: standards and objectives posted and discussed, models of student work displayed, students judging their own and others' work, intermediate expectations specified, and communication with family and community (Resnick & Hall, 2005).

The curriculum and instructional program adopted for the academy combined the philosophy and work of Renzulli and Reis (1997) and Sandra Kaplan's (2009) grid approach to adding depth and complexity for gifted and high potential students. The SEM was infused across all content areas as both enrichment and opportunities for independent and small-group study were used to enrich and extend the regular content curriculum across the content areas. Each content area curriculum combined the depth and complexity advocated by Kaplan with the ideas included in the Multiple Menu Model (Renzulli, Leppien, & Hayes, 2000). Research on the SEM has documented its benefits for students in urban areas and the use of engagement and interest-based opportunities for gifted and high-potential students (Reis & Renzulli, 2003; Renzulli & Reis, 1994).

Mathematics

Students in the Renzulli Academy participate in an advanced mathematics curriculum called Project M^3, Mentoring Mathematical Minds (Gavin, Casa, Adelson, Carroll, & Sheffield, 2009; Gavin et al., 2007). This program emerged as a result of a collaborative research effort coordinated by Dr. Katherine Gavin, a faculty member at the University of Connecticut, and collaborative researchers from other universities comprising a team of national experts in the fields of mathematics, mathematics education, and gifted education. The team created 12 curriculum units of advanced mathematics. Using a project-based approach, Project M^3 offers depth and complexity of math concepts taught across grade levels to high-ability students. The program was field-tested over the last several years and includes advanced math curriculum with projects and investigations to foster creativity, critical thinking, and problem-solving skills that lead to higher math and problem scores than comparison group students (Gavin et al., 2009). For example, in place value, students move beyond using tens, hundreds, and thousands and take part in a simulated archaeological dig, where they will discover unusual calculations carved into rock. Using creative problem-solving skills, students are asked to determine which place value system was used by these people.

Hartford schools' math standards were integrated into classroom preparation time each day and compacted for students as part of this process. Flexible cluster grouping was also initially used across the three grade levels to place students in a nongraded mathematics to participate in the open-ended problem solving opportunities that are inherent in Project M^3.

Reading/Language Arts/Writing

The Schoolwide Enrichment Model in Reading (SEM-R; Reis & Fogarty, 2006) also has been integrated into the Renzulli Academy as the core of the reading/language arts program. This approach, developed by Dr. Sally Reis and a team of reading and gifted education specialists, focuses on reading acceleration and enrichment for talented readers through engagement in challenging, self-selected reading. The SEM-R has been the focus of several previous research studies and found to be beneficial for urban students (Reis, Eckert, McCoach, Jacobs, & Coyne, 2008; Reis et al., 2007; Reis & Housand, 2009). The SEM-R incorporates differentiation of reading content and strategies, coupled with more challenging reading experiences and advanced opportunities for meta-cognition and self-regulated reading. In other words, the SEM-R program challenges and prepares students who are talented in reading to begin reading more challenging books in school and to continue this reading at home (Reis et al., 2008; Reis et al., 2007; Reis & Housand, 2009). The goals of the SEM-R approach are to encourage children to begin to enjoy the reading process by giving them access to high-interest, self-selected books that they can read for periods of time at school and at home; to develop independence and self-regulation in reading through the selection of these books, as well as the opportunity to have individualized reading instruction; and, finally, to enable all students to improve in reading fluency and comprehension through the use of reading comprehension strategies. Based on almost a decade of research, the SEM-R has been proven to be effective at increasing achievement in reading and encouraging talented readers to read more challenging material for longer periods of time. Results of randomized studies suggest it is even more effective for urban talented students (Reis et al., 2008; Reis et al., 2007; Reis & Housand, 2009) and for students who speak English as a second language (Reis & Housand, 2009).

Phase 1. At the academy, the SEM-R intervention included three phases. During Phase 1, the "exposure" phase, teachers presented short read-alouds from high-quality, engaging literature to introduce students to a wide variety of titles, genres, authors, and topics. Along with these read-alouds, teachers provided instruction through modeling and discussion, demonstrating reading strategies and self-regulation skills, and using higher order questions to guide discussion. Early in the SEM-R at the Renzulli Academy, these Phase 1 activities lasted about 20 minutes per day; Phase 1 decreased in length over the course of the year when students could spend more time on Phase 2. Currently, all students read for about 50–60 minutes each day.

Phase 2. Phase 2 of the SEM-R emphasized the development of the students' ability to engage in supported independent reading (SIR) of self-selected, appropriately challenging books, with differentiated instructional support provided through conferences with the teacher or another adult. During Phase 2, students selected books that were at least 1 to 1.5 grade levels above their current reading levels. Students learned strategies for recognizing appropriately challenging books, and they were guided and encouraged to select challenging books in areas of their interest to promote engagement. Over the course of the intervention, students initially read for 5–15 minutes a day during Phase 2; over time they extended SIR to 20–25 minutes, and finally to almost an hour each day. During this in-class reading time, students participated in individualized reading conferences with their teachers; on average, each student participated in one to two conferences per week, and conferences usually lasted about 5–7 minutes. In these conferences, teachers and instructional aides assessed reading fluency and comprehension and provided individualized instruction in strategy use, including predicting, using inferences, and making connections. For more advanced readers, conferences focused less on specific reading strategies and more on higher order questions and critical concepts.

Phase 3. In Phase 3, students were encouraged to move from teacher-directed opportunities to self-choice activities over the course of the intervention. Activities included (but were not limited to) opportunities to explore new technology, discussion groups, practice with advanced questioning and thinking skills, creativity training in language arts, learning centers, interest-based projects, free reading, and book chats. These experiences provided time for students to pursue areas of personal interest through the use of interest development centers and the Internet to learn to read critically and to locate other reading materials, especially high-quality, challenging literature. Options for independent study using RLS also were made available for students during Phase 3. The length of Phase 3 varied with the length of the other phases, with more or less time devoted to Phase 3 on particular days based on progress in independent reading and needs for time to be devoted to independent projects and activities. All students in the academy had one period each day for an independent study/Type III block connected to SEM-R that also incorporated the enrichment philosophy of the school.

All teachers received approximately 350 high-interest books across several reading levels to support their SEM-R implementation, and the teachers augmented their collections as needed, choosing literature based on students' interests and experiences. Teachers also used sets of bookmarks with higher order questions that were free and available for download at http://www.gifted.uconn.edu/semr. Each bookmark included about 3–5 questions addressing a particular literary element, theme, genre, or other area of study and was tied to advanced reading strategies as well as state standards. Teachers used the bookmarks in both Phase 1 discussions and Phase 2 conferences to promote higher order thinking. Using the SEM-R, students also completed advanced writing selections on a weekly basis.

Science

The Renzulli Academy science curriculum was based upon challenging standards and big ideas, applied to units of study across the grade levels. Using both the Multiple Menu approach (Renzulli et al., 2000) and Kaplan's (2009) work, a curriculum map was created with essential questions and big ideas across content area units such as habitats and the water cycle. Science units also introduced project-based work that employed the scientific method. Students began by studying key concepts and principles in science based on grade-level standards, and then depth and complexity was added to enable students to work actively on science projects by forming a hypotheses and applying the scientific method to project-based learning and inquiry experiences in science. Enrichment was scaffolded across each of these units, with Type I, II, and III opportunities in science. The goal each year was for students to complete an advanced science project in an area of interest using data collection methods and the scientific method.

Social Studies

Social studies was taught by adding depth and complexity (Kaplan, 2009) to the grade-level standards, infusing enrichment into the content area using the Enrichment Triad Model, and requiring a project based on advanced content acquisition, primary sources, and interests each year. A curriculum map was developed for each grade level, with the goal of enabling these academically talented students to demonstrate and/or acquire knowledge of the grade-level social studies curriculum, as well as to engage in authentic historical research. Units of study on the curriculum map included the following, among others: explorations about Native Americans, Connecticut history, geography and map skills, and government. A focus on big ideas was integrated into these units that also introduced students to critical thinking and problem-solving skills. A social studies project was required each year during the second semester, culminating with a History Day project during sixth grade. In fourth grade, for example, students are required to complete a research project about a significant person or place in Connecticut history incorporating the use of primary sources and at least one big idea introduced during one of the years. The products were expressed in the students' areas of strength and choice, such as dramatic, written, display, technological, auditory, or in any combination of student preferences, and were completed during the last marking period of fourth grade. In sixth grade, advanced themes from the National History Day Competition have been integrated with standards-based instruction and all students completed a historical project of sufficient quality that it could be submitted to the regional competition.

Enrichment Clusters

Enrichment clusters, another component of the Schoolwide Enrichment Model, are nongraded groups of students who share common interests, and who are grouped together during specially designated time blocks to work with an adult who shares their interests and who has some degree of advanced knowledge and expertise in the area. Research has suggested that the use of enrichment clusters results in higher use of advanced thinking and research skills in gifted and in other students as well (Reis, Gentry, & Maxfield, 1998).

Early in the school year, at a before-school professional development session for all teachers in the school, the idea for the Renzulli Academy was discussed and the notion of enrichment clusters was introduced to all teachers as a way to introduce and include other faculty in the mission of the academy. A series of clusters was planned and implemented for all students in the school every Friday afternoon from late September through December as a way to introduce some enrichment for all students. Students completed an interest inventory developed to assess their interests, and an enrichment coordinator, one of the academy teachers, tallied all of the major families of interests and then recruited teachers and other professionals in the school to facilitate enrichment clusters based on these interests, such as drama, history, creative writing, drawing, music, archaeology, and other areas. Training was provided to the facilitators who agreed to offer the clusters, and a brochure was developed and sent to all parents and students with descriptions of enrichment clusters. Students selected their top three choices for the clusters and scheduling was completed to place all children into their first, or in some cases, second choice. Like extracurricular activities and programs such as 4-H and Junior Achievement, the main rationale for participation in one or more clusters was that students and teachers wanted to be there. All teachers (including music, art, and physical education) were involved in facilitating the clusters, and their involvement in any particular cluster was based on the same type of interest assessment that was used for students in selecting clusters of choice.

Strategies That Worked

In reflecting on our efforts to date, the teachers' efforts to challenge these academically talented students by focusing on their strengths and interests have worked well. The ability of teachers to compact students' curriculum—finding out what they already have mastered in the core, basic skills curriculum, eliminating work that they know already, and replacing it with a combination of more challenging and engaging work, as well as some interest-based opportunities, also has been successful. The cluster grouping of students during math enabled some tiering of assignments that also extended to some open-ended, more challenging assignments in reading, social studies, and science. These have enabled students to pursue some of these assignments in more depth, adding writing options to reading and project options to science and social studies. The ability to find some students' interests, learning styles, and product/expression styles using the Renzulli Learning System has helped to identify students' primary areas of interest, learning styles, and product styles, and has matched them with an individualized, differentiated set of enrichment opportunities. Although RLS can be used for all students, these teachers used the advanced materials for more talented students that are a part of the program.

The use of above-grade-level reading content for the most advanced readers also has been successful. Using the SEM-R, teachers have used challenging fiction and nonfiction books related to students' interests as the focus of their reading and language arts program. Our most advanced students now have the chance to encounter words and ideas that are new to them. Integrating creative and critical thinking activities into all content areas has enabled our students to integrate these higher level thinking strategies into all content areas. Enabling all of the students to explore their interests through a daily period of project and independent study time has worked well. Some students did need more scaffolding than others. Posing questions enabled them to consider doing work that might make a difference in their community such as solving problems that relate to children who need shelter or clothing in the cold weather or those among them who do not have enough food. The success of the whole-school enrichment clusters enabled the academy teachers to create an additional weekly cluster time period for academy students in writing, the arts, and social studies. We also have integrated counseling into the academy, recruiting graduate students in school counseling to mentor students who are at most risk for underachievement and whose self-regulation has continued to be limited. This one-on-one counseling approach, given after parent permission was attained, has resulted in some improvement on the parts of some students.

Changes and Modifications

As with any new endeavor, reflecting on what we have put in place enables us to make appropriate modifications and adjustments to improve our Renzulli Academy. In the future, the identification process will be revised, modified, and fine-tuned. Teacher nomination must be more closely supervised. We want to ensure that the students selected to participate in the Renzulli Academy bring with them the potential and motivation to learn, a commitment to fulfill the expectations of the academy, and the willingness to integrate self-regulation and effort to overcome the challenges that may impede their learning.

For the next school year, we are working on developing a School Compact, which clearly defines the respective responsibilities of the students, parents, and staff in order to ensure success of the highest academic and personal goals. Students, parents, and staff will meet, discuss, and adopt the School Compact. The signatures of all parties will validate the expectations of this living document to provide an effective framework for student achievement.

However, as with any new venture, we sometimes focus on what we still need to do instead of focusing on what we have accomplished. We have been successful, we believe, for after just one academic year, most students are working diligently at advanced levels, engaging in higher level thinking and problem solving, and completing advanced products on a regular basis. Student behavior is improving steadily, and we are encouraged that participation in the academy will decrease underachievement, increase achievement, and help to create more highly motivated and engaged students who will achieve at the highest levels, have a successful high school experience, gain acceptance to competitive colleges, and as adults, realize their career aspirations and their dreams for a successful, satisfying, and productive future.

References

Field, G. B. (2009). The effects of using Renzulli Learning on student achievement in reading comprehension, reading fluency, social studies, and science. *International Journal of Emerging Technology, 4,* 29–39.

Ford, D. Y., & Harris, J. J. (2002). *Multicultural gifted education.* New York, NY: Teachers College Press.

Garcia, T., & Pintrich, P. R. (1994). Regulating motivation and cognition in the classroom: The role of self-schemas and self-regulatory strategies. In D. H. Schunk & B. J. Zimmerman, (Eds.), *Self-regulation of learning and performance: Issues and educational applications* (pp. 127–154). Hillsdale, NJ: Lawrence Erlbaum.

Gavin, M. K., Casa, T. M., Adelson, J. L., Carroll, S. R., & Sheffield, L. J. (2009). The impact of advanced curriculum on the achievement of mathematically promising elementary students. *Gifted Child Quarterly, 53,* 188–202.

Gavin, M. K., Casa, T. M., Adelson, J. L., Carroll, S. R., Sheffield, L. J., & Spinelli, A. M. (2007). Project M^3: Mentoring Mathematical Minds: Challenging curriculum for talented elementary students. *Journal of Advanced Academics, 18,* 566–585.

Hébert, T. P., & Reis, S. M. (1999). Culturally diverse high-achieving students in an urban high school. *Urban Education, 34,* 428–457.

Kaplan, S. N. (2009). The grid: A model to construct differentiated curriculum for the gifted. In J. S. Renzulli, E. J. Gubbins, K. S. McMillen, R. D. Eckert, & C. A. Little (Eds.), *Systems and models for developing programs for the gifted and talented* (pp. 235–252). Waco, TX: Prufrock Press.

Neihart, M., Reis, S. M., Robinson, N., & Moon, S. M. (Eds.). (2001). *The social and emotional development of gifted children. What do we know?* Waco, TX: Prufrock Press.

Pintrich, P. R., & De Groot, E. (1990). Motivational and self-regulated components of classroom academic performance. *Journal of Educational Psychology, 82,* 33–40.

Reis, S. M., Burns, D. E., & Renzulli, J. S. (1992). *Curriculum compacting: The complete guide to modifying the regular curriculum for high ability students.* Waco, TX: Prufrock Press.

Reis, S. M., & Colbert, R. D. (2005). Understanding resilience in diverse, talented students in an urban school. *Roeper Review, 27,* 110–120.

Reis, S. M., Eckert, R. D., McCoach, D. B. Jacobs, J. K., & Coyne, M. (2008). Using enrichment reading practices to increase reading fluency, comprehension, and attitudes. *Journal of Educational Research, 101,* 299–314.

Reis, S. M., & Fogarty, E. (2006). Savoring reading schoolwide. *Educational Leadership, 64*(2), 32–36.

Reis, S. M., Gentry, M., & Maxfield, L. R. (1998). The application of enrichment clusters to teachers' classroom practices. *Journal for Education of the Gifted, 21,* 310–324.

Reis, S. M., Hébert, T. P., Díaz, E. I., Maxfield, L. R., & Ratley, M. E. (1995). *Case studies of talented students who achieve and underachieve in an urban high school* (Research Monograph No. 95120). Storrs: University of Connecticut, The National Research Center on the Gifted and Talented.

Reis, S. M., & Housand, A. (2009). The impact of gifted education pedagogy and enriched reading practices on reading achievement for urban students in bilingual and English-speaking classes. *Journal of Urban Education, 6,* 72–86.

Reis, S. M., & McCoach, D. B. (2000). The underachievement of gifted students: What do we know and where do we go? *Gifted Child Quarterly, 44,* 152–170.

Reis, S. M., McCoach, D. B., Coyne, M., Schreiber, F. J., Eckert, R. D., & Gubbins, E. J. (2007). Using planned enrichment strategies with direct instruction to improve reading fluency, comprehension, and attitude toward reading: An evidence-based study. *The Elementary School Journal, 108,* 3–24.

Reis, S. M., & Purcell, J. H. (1993). An analysis of content elimination and strategies used by elementary classroom teachers in the curriculum compacting process. *Journal for the Education of the Gifted, 16,* 147–170.

Reis, S. M. & Renzulli, J. S. (2003). Research related to the Schoolwide Enrichment Triad Model. *Gifted Education International, 18,* 15–40.

Reis, S. M., Westberg, K. L., Kulikowich, J. M., & Purcell, J. H. (1998). Curriculum compacting and achievement test scores: What does the research say? *Gifted Child Quarterly, 42,* 123–129.

Renzulli, J. S. (1977). *The Enrichment Triad Model: A guide for developing defensible programs for the gifted and talented.* Mansfield Center, CT: Creative Learning Press.

Renzulli, J. S., Leppien, J., Hayes, T. (2000). *The Multiple Menu Model.* Waco, TX: Prufrock Press.

Renzulli, J. S., & Reis, S. M. (1985). *The Schoolwide Enrichment Model: A comprehensive plan for educational excellence.* Mansfield Center, CT: Creative Learning Press.

Renzulli, J. S., & Reis, S. M. (1994). Research related to the Schoolwide Enrichment Triad Model. *Gifted Child Quarterly, 38,* 7–20.

Renzulli, J. S., & Reis, S. M. (1997). *The Schoolwide Enrichment Model: A how-to guide for educational excellence* (2nd ed.). Waco, TX: Prufrock Press.

Resnick, L. B., & Hall, M. W. (with the Fellows of the Institute for Learning). (2005). *Principles of learning for effort-based education.* Pittsburgh, PA: University of Pittsburgh, Institute for Learning, Learning Research & Development Center.

Van Tassel-Baska, J., & Brown, E. F. (2007). Toward best practice: An analysis of the efficacy of curriculum models in gifted education. *Gifted Child Quarterly, 51,* 342–358.

Zimmerman, B. J. (1989). A social cognitive view of self-regulated academic learning. *Journal of Educational Psychology, 81,* 329–339.

Zimmerman, B. J. (1990). Self-regulated academic learning and achievement: The emergence of a social cognitive perspective. *Educational Psychology Review, 2,* 173–201.

CHAPTER 19

An Infusion-Based Approach to Enriching the Standards-Driven Curriculum

Joseph S. Renzulli and Nicole Waicunas
University of Connecticut

The goal is excellence, always. And engagement in the task is the means to achieve it. —Nancie Atwell, 2015 Global Teacher of the Year

Introduction From Joe

One of the biggest challenges facing gifted education is how to balance the need to provide students with enrichment opportunities within the context of an overly prescribed or required curriculum. The emergence of standards in individual states and the new Common Core State Standards coupled with the almost overpowering influence of standardized testing has had the effect of squeezing highly engaging enrichment activities out of the curriculum. Many teachers have become so accustomed to requirements for "teaching-the-text" and overusing worksheets to grind up standardized test scores that they no longer have the opportunity or, in some cases, the know-how to deviate from prescribed material. Few would argue that standards-driven curriculum is not important; however, research has clearly and unequivocally shown that high-engagement enrichment experiences do in fact, contribute to higher achievement scores and they also make school more meaningful and enjoyable for students (Dotterer & Lowe, 2011; Greenwood, 1991; Reyes, Brackett, Rivers, White, & Salovey, 2012; Wang & Holcombe, 2010).

In this chapter we present a strategy that teachers can use for achieving some balance between the required curriculum and a way of infusing enrichment activities into standards driven material. Teachers who have used this technique have commented about how it has made them feel more creative about their teaching and more like professionals rather than mere purveyors of other people's material. Examples of exciting ideas developed by teachers are provided to illustrate how the technique has been used.

Q: How do bakers get the jelly in the jelly doughnut?
A: If you don't know the answer to this question, then take a look at the picture on page 426.

The Schoolwide Enrichment Model (SEM) uses an infusion-based approach to make prescribed curricular content more interesting and engaging. We do not criticize nor recommend "throwing out" basic curriculum, current practices, programs, or projects if they are currently producing positive results in both achievement and joyful learning. Rather, the SEM strikes a balance between traditional approaches to learning and approaches that promote thinking skills, hands-on learning, and creative productivity on the parts of all students. Our goals are to minimize boredom and "school turn-offs" and to improve achievement and creative productivity by infusing what we call the Three Es (Enjoyment, Engagement, and Enthusiasm for Learning, see Figure 10.2) into the culture and atmosphere of a school. We can do this by placing an easy-to-use teaching strategy into the tool bags of teachers.

Selection, Injection, and Extension

An infusion-based approach simply means that teachers will:
- review and select highly engaging enrichment-based activities related to particular topics,
- inject them into the curriculum to make the topics more interesting, and

- provide support and encouragement for individuals and small groups who would like to extend their pursuit of the enrichment activities.

Examples of Infusion Related to Prescribed Curricular Standards

Two early childhood teachers in North Carolina collaborated to design a unit steeped in experiential learning that clearly meets the demands of numerous state and national standards.[27] They discovered that infusing the Three Es into the classroom allowed them to select highly engaging enrichment activities related to particular topics, inject them into the curriculum to make them more interesting, and provide support and encouragement for individuals and small groups who would like to extend their pursuit of the enrichment activities. The teachers in this particular unit of study for kindergarten social studies students in general education classes discovered that the Enrichment Triad Model (see Chapter 8) could be infused into their unit of study entitled Global Explorations: A Multisensory, Multicultural Experience while meeting the North Carolina Essential Standards, the North Carolina Foundations for Early Learning, as well as the 2014 National Core Arts Standards, all listed below.

North Carolina Essential Standards—Kindergarten Social Studies

- K.C.1 Understand how individuals are similar and different.
- K.C.1.1 Explain similarities in self and others.
- K.C.1.2 Explain the elements of culture (how people speak, how people dress, foods they eat, etc.).

North Carolina Foundations for Early Learning

Developing a Sense of Self With Others
- Recognize, respect, and accept similarities and differences among people, including people with disabilities and those from varying cultures.

---

[27] We extend our thanks to Kelly Smith and her colleagues at Providence Day School and Gina Terry for sharing this example with us. We also thank Dr. Cindy Gilson for bringing it to our attention.

Social Connections
- Identify, value, and respect similarities and differences between themselves and others (gender, race, special needs, culture, language, history, and family structures).
- Demonstrate awareness of different cultures through exploration of customs and traditions, past and present.

Creative Expression
- Participate in art, music, drama, movement, dance, and other creative experiences.
- Use a variety of materials and activities for sensory experiences, exploration, creative expression, and representation.
- Develop awareness of different musical instruments, rhythms, and tonal patterns.
- Imitate and recall tonal patterns, songs, rhythms, and rhymes.
- Respond through movement and dance to various patterns of beat and rhythm.

Motor Control
- Develop small muscle control and coordination.
- Experiment with hand-held tools that develop strength, control, and dexterity of small muscles (e.g., spoons, paintbrushes, crayons, markers, safety scissors, and a variety of technological tools, with adaptations as needed).
- Increase the ability to move their bodies in space (running, jumping, spinning).

2014 National Core Arts Standards

- MU:Cr.1.1PreKa With substantial guidance, explore and experience a variety of music.
- MU:Cr2.1.PREKa With substantial guidance, explore favorite musical ideas (such as movements, vocalizations, or instrumental accompaniments).
- Visual Standards: Relate artistic ideas and works with societal, cultural and historical context to deepen understanding.
- VA:Cn11.1.1a Understand that people from different places and times have made art for a variety of reasons.
- Dance DA:Cn11.1.1:a Watch and/or perform a dance from a different culture and discuss or demonstrate the types of movement danced.

The SEM, and in particular, the Enrichment Triad Model, provided these teachers with the tools that they needed in order to master each of the standards that North Carolina set forth. The students became engaged in the opportunity to explore three different countries during an integrated, month-long unit of study. Three separate classrooms were dedicated to this unit, each focusing on one of three countries—Greece, Brazil, and Japan—and the students spent one week in each. The exploration in each classroom was rich in details of the culture of each country, with a focus on arts, language, traditions, music, movement, and food. Each classroom had a combination of small-group learning centers where students could explore individual and small-group interests, as well as whole-class lessons. In addition, prior to their journeys, the children created their own "passports" and "suitcases" and then spent their final days preparing to present what they had learned and discovered, based on their interests, to their parents during a Global Day celebration.

Type I Enrichment

The teachers planned ahead by preparing many Type I activities including: websites and DVDs showing images, customs, and traditional celebrations (dances) from each country, as well as children's books (both fictional and reference) for students to explore including individual countries, travel, world, global citizenship, among others. Speakers were invited into classrooms, including the music teacher, dance teacher, travel agents, and presenters who had visited or lived in one of the countries. Globes and maps, instruments and recordings of traditional music, artifacts from countries for display and student exploration were located in each room. In addition, each classroom had Interest Development Centers that held a wide variety of materials and activities that engaged the students and stimulated their individual curiosities. Students toured these "countries" and carried "I Wonder" charts upon which they could write down their questions and ideas. At the end of each opportunity to be in a "country" classroom, the students gathered together with their charts to talk about what they had experienced during the day's "tour." The teacher would follow up with the students by asking:

- What did you learn about today?
- What did you find exciting or interesting?
- Do you have anything to add to the "I Wonder" chart today?

As the teachers moved from these Type I activities into Type II methodology, they had some important questions to ask themselves, and they needed to keep the standards in mind. During the Type I activities, the students had the opportunity to see and question the differences between themselves and other cultures and begin to dig more deeply into what they had discovered. To engage in Type II Enrichment, the students became active thinkers and the teachers became the trainers, facilitators, and discussion leaders (Maker & Schiever, 2005), what we sometimes refer to as the "guide-on-the-side."

There were some important questions that would help to guide the teachers in this enrichment effort and enable them to continue to meet the standards. Infusion of Type II Enrichment allowed for the teacher to meet the standards and keep students engaged in the work.

Type II Enrichment

Type II Enrichment includes both materials and methods that promote the development of thinking and feeling processes. Some Type II training is general and some is specific. Type II Enrichment is usually conducted in classrooms and enrichment programs and includes the development of: (1) creative thinking and problem solving, critical thinking, and affective processes; (2) a wide variety of specific learning how-to-learn skills; (3) skills in the appropriate use of advanced-level reference materials; and (4) written, oral, and visual communication skills. Other Type II Enrichment is specific, as it cannot be planned in advance and usually involves advanced methodological instruction in an area of interest selected by the student. The unit creators thought about the following as they developed the Type II Enrichment:

What prior knowledge should students have to complete this lesson?
- Students will have introductory information about the three countries from Type I activities.
- Students will complete a brainstorming activity with the "I Wonder" chart.

What content or skills will students learn?
- Students will develop skills in the following domains: social, fine motor, gross motor, visual art, musical, aural, spatial awareness, language, writing, emergent reading, creative problem solving, and mathematical.
- Students will gain information in the following content areas: social studies (history, geography, cultural awareness), technology, music, visual art, dance, culinary arts, and foreign language.

How will you model the Type II Enrichment content or skills?
- The teacher will model the appropriate thinking and feeling processes during interactions with students by brainstorming, hypothesizing,

making observations, and offering interpretations of data . . . in a minimal, but guiding way.

Describe any activities related to guided and independent practice.
- Each learning center will have activities with guided practice and completed examples where appropriate.

List at least 3 examples of open-ended questions that you will ask students during the Type II Enrichment experience.
- Analysis—Compare and contrast elements of each culture: How are the dances similar? How are the languages and alphabet different?
- Evaluation—Assess experiences: What were your favorite/least favorite food samples? What art project did you enjoy the most/least?
- Interpretation—What part of the culture is most like your own?
- Hypothesizing—How do you think your life would be different if you were growing up in one of the other countries?

How will you assess student mastery of the Type II content or skills?
- Students will complete a follow up to the group's "I Wonder" chart entitled "Now I Know" through the process of a brief individual interview.

How will you add closure to your lessons?
- Have students identify and share which Type II process skills were learned and utilized at the end of each day.
- "Global Day" will showcase products and activities from learning centers.

Once the teachers took the time to infuse Type II Enrichment into the monthlong integrated unit on different cultures, which would culminate in Global Day, showcasing their accomplishments for an authentic audience, they could see how many standards had been mastered through Type I and Type II activities and how they could utilize Type III Enrichment in order to enable students to finish their projects and complete the list of standards that remained.

Type III Enrichment

In Type III, the students assume the role of the problem finder, data gatherer, producer, and inquirer and the teacher took on the role of the manager and became a resource for students. The unit creators asked themselves:

- What will students do at this stage? Where will they work on their projects?
- What will your role be during this stage?
- How will you assess students' Type III Enrichment?
- How will students share their Type III Enrichment with a real-world audience?

As the students dove into Type III Enrichment, the teacher's role turned to helping to "identify and refine student interests, to find an appropriate outlet for their products, to develop a laboratory environment, and to provide pedagogical assistance (Maker & Schiever, 2005).

As the students geared up to work on refining their interests and discovering the best way to showcase their work, there were specific goals and resources that had to be identified:
- General interests of students must be refined and focused.
- Students must identify a real problem that can be solved.
- Students must apply proper investigative strategies.
- Students must be allowed to make their own decisions.

In addition, the unit creators asked themselves, "Where will students work on their projects?":
- In the classroom
- In the outdoor classroom (particularly if the investigation is related to nature)
- Research can be conducted in the music room if the investigation is related to music
- In the art room, if more resources are necessary
- *It all depends on where student interests lead and what type of research is necessary* (Smith & Terry, 2014).

Based on areas of interest, possible Type III projects included: presentations; designing a brochure; taking a poll of a favorite food or place; creating an advertisement or TV show; creating an interpretive dance or song; creating a short story or skit from the perspective of a child living in said country; sharing a library or personally owned book about one of the countries; expanding learning stations to include an area not part of the lesson (such as indigenous animals, unique consumer products, popular sports, famous figures); creating a photo scrapbook of the classmates' experiences as they visit each room; and constructing a diorama of a landmark or other scene from a country.

Students were assessed on their "level of readiness and interest in presenting to visitors on Global Day" (Smith & Terry, 2014). In addition, they had opportunities to prepare to showcase their findings to their fellow classmates and teachers prior to Global Day. On the final day of presentations, those students who participated in Type III Enrichment presented their problem (what they researched), the solution (what they discovered), and their product (what they created) to their audience. Those students who did not complete a Type III product were stationed at various learning centers to provide information about what was located at each. In this manner, all students, from those who were able to complete a Type III investigation to those who were not, had the opportunity to present, even if at different levels of understanding.

The following less formal but equally demonstrative examples show how an infusion-based enrichment approach works in various subject areas.

- An elementary teacher was required to have her students memorize all the states and capitals of U.S. cities. To make the assignment more interesting, she gave them an opportunity to select a project that had something to do with this topic and that was related to a personal interest. One group of students interested in music decided to develop a rap song for their state's official anthem. Another group interested in history decided to develop historic site maps, posters, and travel brochures for a state they had visited or would like to visit some day. A third group used state-shaped cookie cutters to make an edible map of the U.S. using chocolate bits to designate the locations of each state's capital. This group of students was so enthusiastic that they extended their work by visiting other classrooms, sharing their cookies with other classes, and providing brief historical facts about some of the states.

- A middle-grade math teacher had her students develop fictional fantasy baseball cards and analyze the players' statistics to draft and trade players while building their own teams. They drew caricatures of their players and a "Player Wheel" with geometric representations of players' strengths and weaknesses was created and used to play against other students' teams. A regular season schedule was set for the class, ending with a World Series game to decide the classroom champion.

- A high school AP Physics teacher assigned a yearlong project that encouraged students to use all of the concepts they covered in his course for addressing a practical problem. The project asked students to apply everything they had learned in physics. One group decided to study the topography of their area by launching a weather balloon carrying a video camera, a GPS tracking device, and various weather data-gathering instruments high above the Earth's surface. They recorded the journey, prepared topographical maps, and analyzed data about temperature, air pressure, and humidity. At the end

of each unit of study, the teacher asked students how the principles and concepts they studied in the unit applied to their project, making learning more relevant and meaningful.
- A middle school social studies teacher covering Ancient Egypt used the GoQuest database (see Chapter 14) to find a site that enabled students to conduct a virtual dissection and preservation of their own mummies. Tools for removing organs, labeling them, placing them in jars, and glueing, wrapping, and preserving their mummies enabled them to have hands-on experiences that made this topic more meaningful. Material in hypertext familiarized the students with Egyptian language and culture. The excitement of this activity created far-reaching affects on interest and motivation that extended beyond simply covering the material in a textbook.

The Role of Technology in Finding Resources for Infusion

This engagement and infusion approach works because teachers have the tools to implant highly engaging material into the standards based curriculum and to use technology to locate what we call Just-In-Time (J-I-T) knowledge that is relevant to their projects—exactly what adult researchers do as they go about the investigative and creative processes. The advent and easy access to the larger world of knowledge has provided opportunities to make formal learning a different process than it was a decade or two ago. Today's young people are digital learners and emerging masters of interactive media technology using cell phones and handheld devices regularly to access J-I-T information (e.g., movie, bus, and TV schedules, sports scores, restaurants, etc.). Traditional ways of learning, even under the best of circumstances, cannot compete with students who find texting under their desks more engaging than listening to their teachers and professors or memorizing factual material for a forthcoming test.

Another development in technology that will aid infusion is the unlimited amount of information now available through the Internet. Thousands of free course-related materials are easily accessible through organizations such as the Khan Academy, which has produced more than 4,000 videos on topics across all grade levels and several curricular areas. The Massive Open Online Courses sponsored by some of the best-known universities in the country, including MIT's OpenCourseWare program and Coursera, have produced thousands of courses that can be widely accessed without cost.

Changing the learning process has become a reality due to the unlimited access to the knowledge sources mentioned above. Teachers, however, can also become creative contributors to the resource stockpile and the producers of their own televised lectures, course-related material, and media events. Free or inexpensive software now enables teachers to prepare and upload their own lectures and assignments for student use anytime and anywhere through the application of easy-to-use screen casting software (e.g., Camtasia Studio 8, Screenflow Software).

A program called Juno (http://gofrontrow.com/en/juno) enables easy recording of high-quality audio/video clips without adding any extra work to a teacher's day. The program automatically adds titles and prepares files for uploading that can then be accessed by computers, tablets, smartphones, or interactive white boards. In addition, as mentioned above, content recorded by others is readily available in all subject areas. These resources enable teachers to easily turn their lectures and related lesson planning tools into audio and video podcasts and printed course and video materials that can then be uploaded for student access. We can capitalize on students' fascination and skills with technology and the availability of vast amounts of online material by giving teachers the license and ability to infuse creativity and thinking skills activities into standards driven curriculum.

Although it is not practical to use infusion for every topic or course, this approach makes learning more engaging and creates an enthusiasm for learning that seldom results from covering curricular material in traditional ways. The guidelines for infusion are easy to follow:
- Select an activity that does not always have a single, predetermined correct answer.
- Find things that students do rather than sit and listen to.
- Give students choices that they will enjoy pursuing.
- Select activities that have various levels of challenge to which interested students can escalate.

Finding activities for infusion is now easier than ever. Internet-based search engines (see Chapter 14) allow teachers to enter topics, subtopics, and sub-subtopics by subject area, grade level, and difficulty level. Thousands of high-engagement activities that enable teachers to locate and infuse an almost endless array of exciting enrichment activities can be found with this new technology.

Preparing for the Infusion Process

In the example mentioned above related to learning the names of U.S. states and capitals, teachers used infusion activities in order to engage students' enthusiasm for learning. A traditional brainstorming technique[28] and the Creative Idea Generator presented in Figure 19.1 were infused into the lesson in order to engage students to come up with as many ideas as possible for making the teaching of this topic more interesting. Guidelines for brainstorming were briefly discussed (see Appendix 19.A) and teachers were asked to apply as many of the following criteria as possible to the brainstorming process.

1. The activity has a relationship to one or more regular curriculum topics.
2. There is not a single, predetermined correct answer or solution to the problem raised in the activity.
3. The activity consists of something students do rather than sit and listen to.
4. The activity is fun for most students.
5. The activity should lead to some form of product development on the parts of students.
6. The activity has various levels of challenge to which interested students can escalate if they would like to creatively extend the interest through follow-up activity.

Students were then given an opportunity to select an activity that they would like to pursue based on their individual interests and learning styles. Most students chose to work in groups, however a few students preferred to work on their own. Infusion activities cannot only make a traditional, memory-oriented topic more interesting, they can also present opportunities for developing creative, analytic, and investigative learning skills. Students learn cooperative, collaborative, and other executive function skills, strategies for acquiring J-I-T information, and most importantly, that learning is, in and of itself, an enjoyable process.

---

28 Brainstorming is a group or individual creativity technique by which efforts are made to spontaneously list many ideas for addressing a particular problem. A brief list of brainstorming tips is presented in Appendix 19.A.

Infusion-Based Approach to Enrichment

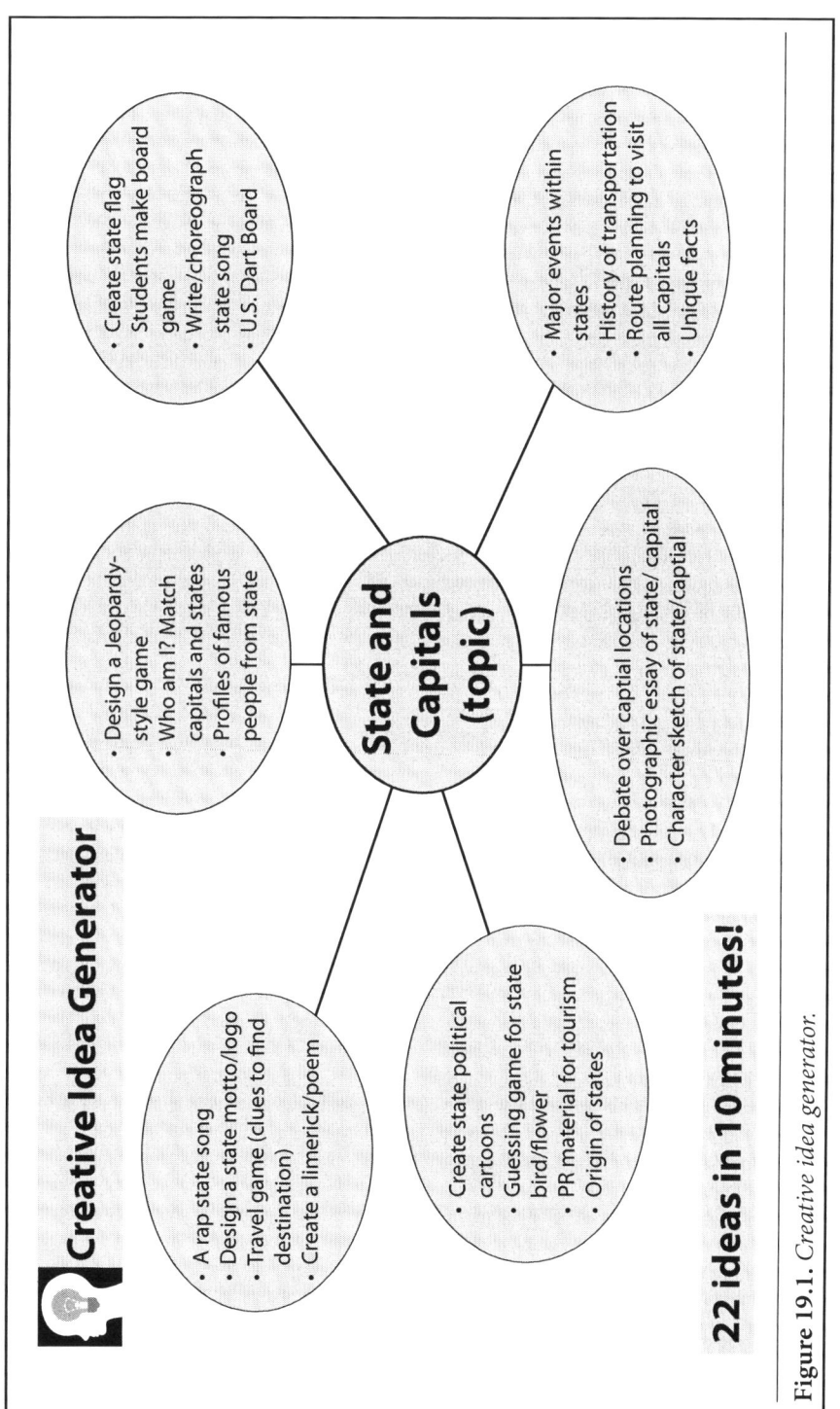

Figure 19.1. *Creative idea generator.*

A Note on Problem-Based Learning

Problem-based learning (PBL) has gained a good deal of attention for making the curriculum for students more engaging. We are a strong supporters of this approach to enhancing learning material in the regular (prescribed) curriculum. We do not, however, view it as creating the same experience as is the case with Type III Enrichment in the Triad Model. Generally speaking—and we know there are many variations on the use of PBL—teachers can use it to cover a standard curricular topic (e.g., Westward Expansion in U.S. history or social studies). There are expected outcomes that will probably show up on an end-of-unit test and perhaps even on a standardized achievement test. If the PBL approach makes the work more interesting and engaging, then such an approach has merit.

Type III Enrichment, however, is different because of the four requirements that make the problem more relevant to student interests and the investigative methods that students choose to select and pursue a topic of their own interest and methodology that further personalizes this approach to advanced level investigations or creative endeavors. The four requirements of a bona fide Type III Enrichment project are as follows:

1. personalization of interest (the student(s) selects the topic)
2. use of authentic methodology (involves some kind of original data gathering or creative expression)
3. no existing solution or "right" answer
4. designed to have an impact on an audience other than or in addition to the teacher

Summary

Someone once asked us what is the "value" of infusing these activities into the curriculum? We answered, "High engagement and involvement activities are remembered long after the facts, or dates, or formulas you learned in fourth period math or social studies are forgotten." An infusion-based approach to education and learning allows teachers to find resources within the school, community, classroom, and in the people who reside within the community that will enable them to select highly engaging enrichment-based activities related to particular topics, inject them into the curriculum to make the topics more interesting, and provide support and encouragement for individuals and small groups who would like to extend their pursuit of enrichment activities.

The Schoolwide Enrichment Model provides a framework to enrich the learning opportunities for students within a classroom where state standards or the CCSS are present and must be addressed and incorporated into the lessons. By infusing prescribed standards with the richness of what lies beyond the standards or textbook, the academic and creative experiences of students become three-dimensional, as they recognize that the world is much bigger, and much more exciting than they could have ever imagined.

We began this chapter with a quote by Nancie Atwell, the winner of the Global Teacher of the Year Award, considered by many to be the Nobel Prize for educators. We end with her comment at the award ceremony about the importance of infusion.

> Teachers are people who can't imagine doing anything else; it's their passion. If there's nothing else you can ever imagine yourself doing, be a teacher. If you're passionate about making a difference in this world, be a teacher. A passionate teacher will find ways to infuse creativity and fun into learning, even amid the demands of testing and curriculum. But if the thought of teaching doesn't light you up—if you think it's just a job—don't go into education. There are more than enough teachers like that already. Am I trying to discourage my students from becoming educators? No. But I don't want to encourage someone to pursue a teaching career if the thought of working with children, teaching from the heart and the intellect, and making a difference in the lives of others doesn't light them up. No matter how bright a student is, no matter the GPA, we don't need people entering the field who aren't on fire. Because frankly, it's that fire that often lights our way when the horizon grows dark and ominous.

References

Dotterer, A. M., & Lowe, K. (2011). Classroom context, school engagement, and academic achievement in early adolescence. *Journal of Youth and Adolescence, 40,* 1649–1660.

Greenwood, C. R. (1991). Longitudinal analysis of time, engagement, and achievement in at-risk versus non-risk students. *Exceptional Children, 57,* 521–535.

Maker, C. J., & Schiever, S. W. (2005). *Teaching models in education of the gifted* (3rd ed.). Austin, TX: Pro-Ed.

Reyes, M. R., Brackett, M. A., Rivers, S. E., White, M., & Salovey, P. (2012). Classroom emotional climate, student engagement, and academic achievement. *Journal of Educational Psychology, 104,* 700–712.

Smith, K., & Terry, G. (2014). *Global explorations–A multisensory, multicultural experience* (Unpublished curriculum unit). Charlotte, NC: University of North Carolina at Charlotte.

Wang, M.-T., & Holcombe, R. (2010). Adolescents' perceptions of school environment, engagement, and academic achievement in middle school. *American Educational Research Journal, 47,* 633–662.

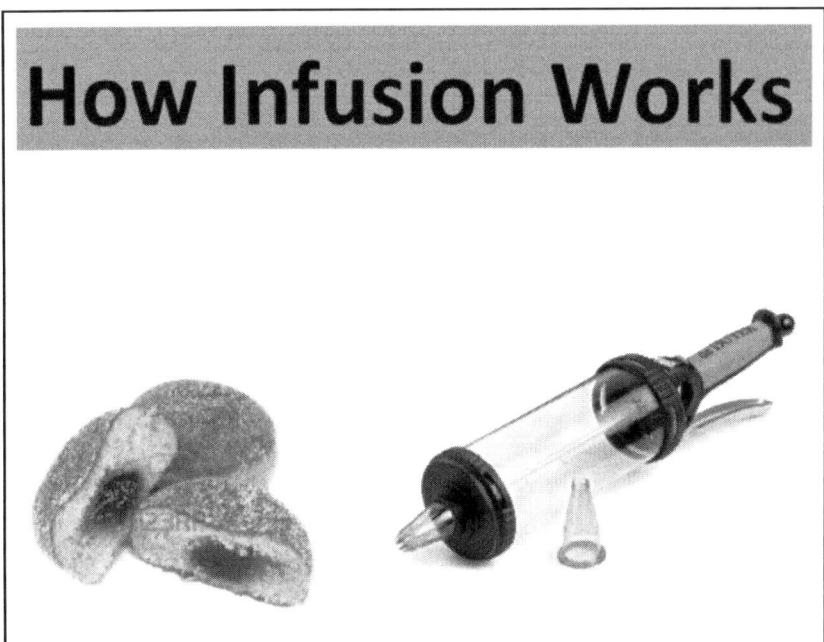

Appendix A
Guidelines for Brainstorming

1. Introduce the question to be brainstormed and review the rules of brainstorming:
   - All ideas are welcome.
   - No comments, criticism, or evaluation during the brainstorm.
   - The more ideas, the better.
   - Don't worry about duplicate ideas at this point.
   - Piggybacking on each other's ideas is encouraged.

2. Explain what will be done with the brainstormed ideas. Write the question to be brainstormed at the top of the first page of flipchart paper.
3. If you wish, offer a one-minute "quiet period" before the brainstorm for people to think about the question and jot down a few idea.
4. Begin the brainstorming.
   - Guide the brainstorm by recording ideas on a flipchart or whiteboard as they come. You may wish to designate a recorder. Stop any comments that evaluate ideas. Invite new ideas, and encourage the group to share their ideas freely. Help generate energy and free-thinking through encouragement.
   - As the responses slow down, offer last chances for additional ideas, then stop the brainstorm. Ask the recorder for his or her ideas. Thank people for participating.

5. Ask for clarification of any ideas that are not clear to you or others.
6. Discuss ways that the ideas can be presented to students in appealing ways (e.g., dramatizations, role playing, artistic or pictorial representations, debates, games, friendly competitions, storytelling, digital graphics, 3-D printing, filmmaking, Facebook or Twitter exchanges, community service projects, entrepreneurial endeavors, etc.).

CHAPTER 20

Reversing Underachievement Through Enrichment[29]

Joseph S. Renzulli,
University of Connecticut,

Susan M. Baum,
Bridges Academy,

Thomas P. Hébert,
University of South Carolina,

and Ken W. McCluskey
University of Winnipeg

Introduction From Joe

The vast majority of letters, phone calls, and e-mails that we collectively have received over the years are from parents of high-ability students who are

---

[29] Renzulli, J. S., Baum, S. M., Hébert, T. P., & McCluskey, K. W. (1999). Reversing underachievement through enrichment. *Reclaiming Children and Youth, 7,* 217–223. Reprinted with permission.

underachieving. Similar frustration has been expressed by teachers and other school personnel, all of whom are seeking solutions to this major challenge in our field. Although a great deal has been written about the underachievement dilemma, there has been surprisingly little research upon which to make recommendations about turning around underachievement. This chapter describes one of the few intervention studies conducted on underachievement and is the basis for most of the recommendations that we make to parents and teachers seeking research-based approaches for dealing with this problem.

Concern with the problem of underachievement, especially among potentially high-ability students, has increased substantially in recent years (Reid, 1991). Professionals have agreed for decades that the phenomenon of underachievement is complex, baffling, and challenging (Rimm, 1986; Whitmore, 1980), yet there is much we still do not know about this topic.

Betts and Neihart (1988) attempted to classify gifted young people who are at risk for substance abuse, delinquency, and dropping out. Many highly capable adolescents simply will not conform to the system—they often behave in a recalcitrant fashion, challenge the teacher, and question authority. Because they receive very little positive attention and affirmation for their unique interests that fall outside the general education curriculum, these troubled, talented students may rebel or withdraw from educational settings that to them seem hostile and irrelevant. They perceive schools to be uncaring, with rigid discipline and attendance policies that more or less push them out the door (Radwanski, 1987). If a student is seen as an underachiever, he or she may be regarded with disdain and disliked by teachers and, consequently, may develop behaviors conforming to the adults' perceptions (Mukhopadyay & Chugh, 1979).

For the most part, there has been little widespread success in reversing the underachievement pattern, perhaps because most typically used approaches are too general and focus predominantly on negative behavior. Some of these efforts include enrolling underachievers in study skills courses (Crittenden, Kaplan, & Helm, 1984; Hastings, 1982), providing full-time special classes (Butler-Por, 1987; Whitmore, 1980), or using behavior management techniques (Rimm, 1986). The "learn-how-to-get-organized-and-you-will-do-well" or "work-hard-and-you-will-be-rewarded" philosophies imply that underachievers consciously want to improve and are willing to become self-disciplined in order to reverse problem behavior patterns. According to Kaufman (1991), this is usually not the case. She defined these learners as discouraged and argued that they need encouragement, not discipline or more time on task, to overcome their failure mode.

The few studies that have examined various curricular approaches that are effective with underachieving students with high academic potential (Baum, 1988; Fehrenbach, 1993; Karnes, McCoy, Zerbach, Wollensheim, & Clarizio, 1962; Tannenbaum & Baldwin, 1983; Whitmore, 1980) have significant points in common. Unlike the "we'll-cure-what-ails-you" strategies, successful methods tend to be child-centered, accentuate strengths, and value student interests. These approaches stress the active nature of the process—students become involved and choose to learn, instead of merely taking notes passively and being tested. Several studies reported that when underachieving students complete a meaningful project, positive gains result in self-esteem, academic self-efficacy, and overall motivation (Baum & Owen, 1988; Emerick, 1992; Whitmore, 1980). Likewise, in general, gifted and talented research has indicated that the highest levels of productivity occur when students are engaged in self-selected investigations. In other words, allowing them to pursue topics of strong—sometimes even passionate—interest often results in meaningful engagement and achievement.

Type III Enrichment

Much has been discovered about applying the self-directed learning experience to bright youngsters and providing them with the guidance necessary for carrying out advanced-level projects. This technology has been incorporated into a major dimension of the Enrichment Triad Model (Renzulli, 1977; Renzulli & Reis, 1985) entitled "Type III Enrichment." The Enrichment Triad Model was designed to transform students from lesson learners and consumers of facts to producers of new knowledge. To help students become creative producers, the model offers three categories of experiences. Type I Enrichment consists of general exploratory activities designed to expose students to new and exciting ideas not covered in the regular curriculum. Type II Enrichment involves group training activities in specific skills and processes.

The goal of Type III Enrichment is to provide opportunities for students to become actual investigators of real problems through suitable means of inquiry and to bring their findings to bear on real-world audiences. In Type III Enrichment, students become producers of creative products through the collection of raw data, use of higher order problem-solving techniques, and the application of research strategies or artistic procedures that are used by frontline people within various fields of study.

Process, Intervention, and Results

The first three authors have explored the possibility of using Type III Enrichment activities to reverse underachievement in talented children and youth (Baum, Renzulli, & Hébert, 1995). In their study, 12 teachers who had received training in the Enrichment Triad Model selected 17 students, each identified as gifted, who were performing below potential in school. The students ranged in age from 8 years to 13 and included 5 girls and 12 boys. Each was guided through a Type III experience by the referring teacher.

Teachers who guide students through the Type III process play the role of researcher. Rather than assuming control of the learning process, they become facilitators—helping students to focus on problems, secure necessary materials, review and revise their work, and overcome obstacles within the context of pursuing a problem that has great personal meaning. Teachers also assume the roles of mentor and confidant to the students and, as such, discover much about the personal lives, frustrations, and dreams of their young charges. These teachers act as participant observers, systematically recording their observations, reflecting upon their entries, and documenting effective strategies.

The Baum et al. (1995) study was carried out during at least 1 academic year and, in three cases, for 2 years. It involved four phases:

- *Phase I* involved identifying underachieving students with high academic potential through scores on ability and achievement tests, grades, classroom records, work samples, and anecdotal information gathered from teachers' and permanent records.
- In *Phase II*, further information about the students' lives and preferences was obtained through the use of interest surveys, personal essays about school, and informal interviews.
- During *Phase III*, teachers worked closely with students on their Type III investigations. Steps included focusing the problem to be examined, setting up a management plan, providing necessary resources and strategies, and helping students share the completed investigation with interested audiences.
- In *Phase IV*, the researchers conducted in-depth interviews with the teachers to get some sense for their feelings about the treatment, the overall experience, and the effect on the students.

A complete discussion of the data collection, analysis, and results can be found in Baum et al. (1995). Positive gains were made by almost all of the students through their involvement in the Type III intervention. Various ambitious projects were undertaken, including:

- Designing a prototype environment for birds for a NASA experiment,

- Building a rocket for actual launch,
- Teaching a computer class,
- Doing set designs for drama club,
- Conducting a comparative study of brain functioning in humans and rats,
- Creating a series of relief and topographic maps,
- Designing and constructing a school planetarium,
- Writing a "choose your own adventure" book,
- Developing a prototype for a solar car,
- Drawing a cartoon strip for publication, and
- Starting a successful campaign to change the school lunch/milk policy.

In most cases, during the course of the year or in the year following the intervention, there was marked improvement in student achievement, attitude, or behavior.

Sample Case Studies

This study's main objective was to understand the achievement phenomenon by collapsing information across cases. This approach, however, does not allow the reader to experience individual case scenarios upon which the cross-case analysis was based. Therefore, we thought it appropriate to provide a few vignettes of individual students who participated in the study.

Jamison

Jamison came from a dysfunctional family struggling with divorce, alcohol problems, and accusations of child abuse. His teacher claimed he was neglected at home: "He never has a haircut, nor does he comb his hair or brush his teeth. He is frequently alone and has been seen riding his bicycle all over town with no adult supervision." Even his mother mentioned "that school is his escape from our rocky home life. . . . His older brother, a high school dropout, is currently in trouble with the law." Jamison was also described by his teacher as "constantly in motion." Diagnosed as hyperactive, he was placed on Ritalin. This 10-year-old boy had no positive role models in his family, and his time after school was totally unsupervised. One afternoon, he was caught spending money on himself that he had collected door to door, ostensibly for a local baseball team.

Jamison's social worker described him as a very bright youngster (who tested in the superior range on an individual intelligence test). And this lad truly connected with his enrichment teacher in school. Over the years, Jamison had been told that he was related to Abraham Lincoln, but he did not have the resources to trace his family's lineage. The enrichment teacher assisted him in pursuing his quest for information and suggested he write a letter to the state archivist. After a year and a half, Jamison succeeded in obtaining conclusive material that confirmed his heritage. He then completed his family tree and prepared a narrated slide show entitled "Jamison and Abe: Ninth Cousins" (which he presented to numerous audiences). Three newspapers carried articles about Jamison. At the conclusion of his Lincoln research, his teacher commented:

> This child has so many strikes against him that I can't predict whether or not he'll be a dropout like his brother, but right now I know that this project was important to him. He finally followed through on something. But most important, he and I have formed a bond that will hopefully give him needed support and encouragement.

Mara

She wore pasty white makeup and shredded jeans, and her eighth-grade wardrobe consisted of only black clothing. A petite blond, Mara was associating with a group of youngsters suspected of being involved with drugs who prided themselves on their dislike of school. Mara's negative attitude and flippant remarks antagonized her teachers. Her counselor discovered her making arrangements for a limousine joyride through her community for herself and a group of younger boys in her junior high school. Mara had difficulty understanding her intelligence. Since she could figure out math problems without having to do computations (the answers just seemed "to pop into her head"), she assumed she had to be a witch! The academic record of this confused young woman had been declining markedly—her grades reflected her lack of interest in schoolwork.

Following her thwarted attempt at the joyride, her classroom teachers, counselor, and enrichment teacher agreed that Mara needed to spend more time pursuing her own interests in the school's enrichment resource room. She became involved in a group project with some girls who, concerned about environmental issues, were conducting research for an Earth Day celebration. As Mara socialized more and more with these young ladies, her peer group associations gradually shifted. Through her involvement in the research study, she began to think of herself as a leader and a producer rather than a follower. Mara moved on to an individual project in which she designed a photographic essay on emotions expressed in junior high. After photographing students throughout the building to capture the emotional trials and tribulations of school life, she created a display with her photography and became recognized for her talent. Impressed with her efforts and her perceptions of the junior high experience, the principal asked Mara to serve as an orientation guide for incoming students the following September. Mara's grades improved, her peer group changed, and, eventually, her appearance evolved—the white makeup, black clothing, and shredded jeans disappeared.

Bryan

Bryan was described by teachers as a serious behavior problem, a young man who was always in trouble. He was identified as having an emotional and behavioral disorder (and had been tested but did not qualify as having a learning disability). As an eighth grader, Bryan was earning only C and D grades, even though his scores on an individual intelligence test were in the very superior range. His progress report included comments by teachers such as "insufficient effort" and "missing or late work," which reflected his general dislike of school subjects.

This lad arrived in the enrichment teacher's classroom complaining about his social studies curriculum. His eighth-grade class was pursuing a mock trial, and Bryan found himself frustrated. He argued that he could write a new and better court case: "I don't like the old one; it's got some stupid character like Candy Cane in it, and I think I can do a better job." Bryan began working toward this end, and was able to convince his social studies teacher to compact his curriculum to provide additional time in the enrichment resource room to work on his court drama. He kept polishing the trial script for an entire academic year.

Bryan discovered that he was better able to concentrate on his writing when "plugged into" his music. He spent marathon sessions on his computer while wearing his headphones. Adapting to his own style provided him with rock-and-roll music and a way of focusing on his work. His teacher commented, "The minute that you took the music away, everything in the room distracted him; the minute you took the computer away, he was abysmal."

Halfway through the project, Bryan expanded his interests to include writing his own novel. His enrichment teacher reported:

He came into my room, threw it on my desk and said, "Here's a new novel and it's on Norad." This was a kid who was tested as not being spatially perceptive yet he had a complete diagram of this Norad underwater installation. It was a visually perfect graphic. It came to him on a 14-hour stint on the computer. What we found was if you had Bryan in front of the computer and you plugged music into him, he could focus.

In English class, Bryan—like many others who have attention deficits—found the writing workshop approach problematic. The noise and movement were simply too distracting. He negotiated with his teacher, who allowed him to leave the room to complete his writing in the computer lab. Bryan met with success by employing his own learning style, and his grades began to improve. By year's end, his grade in English had gone from a D to a B, and this young scriptwriter was feeling positive about the progress on his original novel and the upcoming performance of his mock trial.

Factors Contributing to Underachievement

In reviewing the just-described cases, one can see that four main factors contributed to their underachievement:

1. *Emotional issues*, including dysfunctional families, depression, perfectionism, and the students' extraordinary need for attention.
2. *Social and behavioral concerns.* Included in this category were the influence of an inappropriate peer group, questioning of accepted values, and lack of internal controls and social skills.
3. *Inappropriate curriculum.* Many of the students simply were not motivated by their regular schoolwork. Some believed that the material presented no challenge; others preferred different styles of learning.
4. *Learning disabilities and poor self-regulation.* The presence (or suspicion of the presence) of a learning disability contributed to underachievement in many cases. Poor reading, handwriting, or spelling were common. Other typical complaints included disorganization, failure to complete assignments, forgetfulness, and lack of time-management or attentional skills.

Strategies That Promote Success

Several teacher strategies influenced the degree to which positive change occurred in the students:

1. *Knowing the students.* Successful teachers would explore the student's interests, concerns, and hobbies (by discussing relevant books or articles, accompanying them on visits to local experts, arranging phone interviews, and the like). However, if a teacher tried to identify an interest too quickly and force immediate productivity, the student never seemed to get into the process.
2. *Focusing on the students' positive qualities.* Successful teachers often ignored the fact that their student was an underachiever and focused instead on the development of the Type III investigation. In cases where the enrichment teacher spent time "running interference" with the classroom teachers or trying to make sure that regular assignments were completed, the student was resistant to the intervention.
3. *Viewing their roles as facilitators.* Successful teachers focused their energies on providing resources and ongoing support for their students. Most met with the students several times a week; some managed to see them daily. Instead of acting as if they had climbed the mountain and seen the Ten Commandments, these teachers made suggestions when the project seemed to be at a standstill, without assuming control.
4. *Understanding the Type III process.* Successful teachers recognized that students were acting as practicing professionals—using methods of inquiry and tools of the discipline. They understood that the investigation should have real-world purposes and authentic audiences rather than simply being something to be graded and taken home.
5. *Applying their role as researchers.* Successful teachers were able to see the dynamic nature of the underachievement problem and provide strategies as needed. Their logs were filled with emerging hypotheses about the students. Even though these logs primarily were kept for research purposes, they also helped the teachers capture the complex dynamics of achievement patterns and evaluate which strategies were appropriate in helping each student succeed.
6. *Believing in the student's ability.* Successful teachers consistently had faith in the student! When a day went poorly and things seemed to be moving backward, they continually demonstrated their belief in the students and their patience in allowing the process to unfold. They shared in the excitement of the students' achievement and provided support during periods of discouragement and anger.

Extending the Concept

Of course, there are many other examples of how talented but troubled children and youth—"lost prizes," as it were—have been reclaimed through enrichment opportunities such as mentoring, high-level project work, and learning about effective problem-solving strategies (McCluskey, Baker, O'Hagan, & Treffinger, 1995; McCluskey, O'Hagan, Baker, & Treffinger, 1998; McCluskey & Treffinger, 1998). We know of some instances where the concept of enrichment was broadened to include students who were highly unlikely to be identified as gifted or talented.

Sylvia

One example was Sylvia, who clearly had limited intellectual potential. By junior-high age, she still hadn't learned to read, recognize colors, or manage many basic self-help skills. Frustrated at her inability to handle rudimentary activities and fit in at school, she began to act out in an aggressive and belligerent fashion. When an attempt was made to move her from a segregated special class to a regular junior high setting, some teachers resisted. After the first few weeks of the experiment, they complained, "She doesn't belong in this situation," "She can't make it here," "She isn't even able to find her way to school," and "It's dangerous; she doesn't know her colors and makes mistakes at traffic lights." Instead of dwelling on the negatives, however, resource personnel decided to look for relative talents and strengths and build on those. The home economics teacher noted that Sylvia behaved well in her class, and she volunteered to take Sylvia for double periods in that subject. An educational assistant was hired to accompany Sylvia to school and teach her some landmarks; in a short time, Sylvia was navigating on her own. Through the support of town personnel, a traffic light was set up in the resource room. Although Sylvia couldn't learn all her colors, by focusing on a few—and using position cues—she managed to master green, red, and yellow and to grasp their meaning for traffic patterns. Acquiring added confidence, this evolving young lady even went on to learn a few "survival reading" words. Obviously, Sylvia was never identified as gifted—quite the opposite. Nonetheless, she turned out to have much more potential than anyone would have credited her with at first sight. By picking up on relative strengths and using flexible, innovative activities, educators stretched potential to its maximum, and Sylvia ended up obtaining a job in a restaurant and becoming an independent, self-supporting adult.

Brent

In Brent's case, every bad thing that can be done to someone in school was done to Brent. As a child, he had been identified as severely learning disabled, was placed in a special education class, and was segregated from virtually all of his nondisabled peers. Not surprisingly, by high school he had become rebellious, disconnected, and singularly unproductive. It was the "doing nothing, going nowhere" scenario. Finally, in his early 20s, Brent got his first "enrichment opportunity." As part of a program for young adults with learning disabilities, he was placed as a "teacher assistant" in a special needs classroom. Brent was incredibly empathic and effective with the children because he had "been there." This once-angry young man suddenly became reliable, conscientious, and motivated. Teachers couldn't help but notice that he was beating them during coffee-break games of Trivial Pursuit™ and that he could write excellent poetry. Brent had a definite problem with math—he couldn't do simple operations, count money, or tell time on a standard watch; however, he learned a variety of compensatory strategies (e.g., using a calculator and a digital watch). Reenergized and enthusiastic, Brent applied to take a meat-cutting course at community college. He was turned down, but he persevered and finally was admitted—as a mature student—into a psychology course at a university. He did well. The young man who couldn't be a butcher showed promise as a psychologist (which tells you something!). Brent eventually completed a youth worker program at college and now has moved into a productive career working with intellectually challenged individuals. Again, by providing hitherto denied opportunities, flexible caregivers found and harnessed hidden talent.

The Prism Metaphor

The research we have reviewed in this article suggests that a new perspective and method should be considered for reversing the complex dynamics of underachievement. Metaphorically speaking, previous interventions have used the wrong type of lens to "focus" the problem. This route targeted traditional steps to achievement—study hard, do your homework, get good grades, and please your teachers. The new approach instead uses a prism to redirect the focus. Just as a prism takes in nondescript light and transforms it into colors, so does the Type III experience unleash the hidden potential of underachieving students with high academic ability. This is accomplished by capitalizing on the potential for positive interactions among student abilities, interests, learning styles, and supportive student-teacher relationships. Our

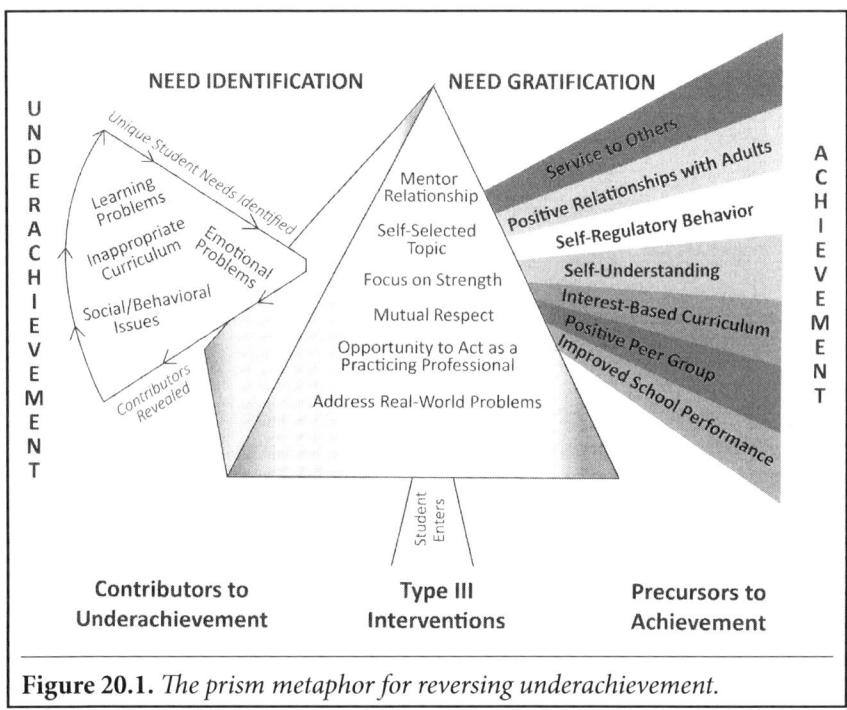

Figure 20.1. *The prism metaphor for reversing underachievement.*

metaphor, pictured in Figure 20.1, illustrates the transformation from underachievement to achievement.

As seen in the figure, underachievement is based on the interrelationship of a variety of contributing factors: emotional issues, social and behavioral problems, inappropriate curricula, and learning deficits. (It was interesting to observe that precipitating factors for some of the underachievers in this study were not apparent until the students were well into the intervention process, and then they only came to light as a result of the close student-teacher interaction.) In this metaphor, the majority of teacher time, energy, and resources is allocated to enabling the underachieving student to experience success and overcome personal obstacles to productivity. In effect, the flexible Type III process satisfies individual student needs, resulting in one or more of the following: positive relationships with adults, acquisition of self-regulation strategies, an understanding of the personal issues of underachievement, an interest-based curriculum, and/or the influence of a positive peer group.

Whereas real images are formed when rays of light are reflected in a mirror, something quite different happens when light is passed through a prism. Not only does the light ray change direction, but it takes on qualitative differences that result in a spectrum of color critically different from the light energy that originally entered this special environment. Only to a certain extent do scientists understand and are able to explain what happens within a prism. Similarly, a "mysterious phenomenon" happens when students pursue Type III Enrichment experiences: They also change their direction and behavior patterns. We can only speculate about the combination of "ingredients" that causes a turnaround within the enriched educational environment. Due to the idiosyncratic nature of Type III activities, the uniqueness of each learner, and the equally unique interaction between teacher and student, certain parts of the explanation for the positive changes may remain a mystery. No formula or prescription can be written that is appropriate for all underachieving students; however, we believe that the prism metaphor provides a grounded and positive signpost for reversing the pattern of underachievement through enrichment.

References

Baum, S. M. (1988). An enrichment program of gifted learning disabled students. *Gifted Child Quarterly, 32,* 226–230.

Baum, S. M., & Owen, S. V. (1988). High ability learning disabled students: How are they different? *Gifted Child Quarterly, 32,* 321–326.

Baum, S. M., Renzulli, J. S., & Hébert, T. (1995). *The prism metaphor: A new paradigm for reversing achievement.* Storrs: University of Connecticut, The National Research Center on the Gifted and Talented.

Betts, G., & Neihart, M. (1988). Profiles of the gifted and talented. *Gifted Child Quarterly, 32,* 248–253.

Butler-Por, N. (1987). *Underachievers in school: Issues and intervention.* New York, NY: John Wiley and Sons.

Crittenden, M. R., Kaplan, M. H., & Helm, J. K. (1984). Developing effective study skills and self-confidence in academically able young adolescents. *Gifted Child Quarterly, 28,* 25–30.

Emerick, L. J. (1992). Academic underachievement among the gifted: Students' perceptions of factors that reverse the pattern. *Gifted Child Quarterly, 36,* 140–146.

Fehrenbach, C. R. (1993). Underachieving gifted students: Programs that work. *Roeper Review, 16,* 88–90.

Hastings, J. M. (1982). A program for gifted underachievers. *Roeper Review, 4,* 42.

Karnes, M. B., McCoy, R. R., Zerbach, R. R., Wollensheim, J. P., & Clarizio, H. F. (1962). *The efficacy of two organizational plans for underachieving intellectually gifted children.* Champaign, IL: Campaign Community Schools, Department of Special Services.

Kaufman, F. (1991). *The courage to succeed: A new look at underachievement.* Keynote address at Fourth Annual AEGUS (Association for the Education of Gifted Underachieving Students) Conference, Tuscaloosa, AL: University of Alabama.

McCluskey, K. W., Baker, P. A., O'Hagan, S. C., & Treffinger, D. J. (Eds.). (1995). *Lost prizes: Talent development and problem-solving with at-risk students.* Sarasota, FL: Center for Creative Learning.

McCluskey, K. W., O'Hagan, S. C., Baker, P. A., & Treffinger, D. J. (1998). Recapturing at-risk, talented high-school dropouts: A summary of the three-year lost prizes project. *Gifted and Talented International, 13,* 73–78.

McCluskey, K. W., & Treffinger, D. J. (1998). Nurturing talented but troubled children and youth. *Reclaiming Children and Youth: Journal of Emotional and Behavioral Problems, 6,* 215–219, 226.

Mukhopadyay, S., & Chugh, A. (1979). *Developing a strategy for minimizing underachievement through teacher classroom behavior.* Bhopal, India: Regional College of Education. (ERIC Document Reproduction Service, No. ED 207725.)

Radwanski, G. (1987). Ontario study of the relevance of education and the issue of dropouts. Toronto, ON: Ministry of Education.

Reid, B. D. (1991). *Research needs in gifted education: A study of practitioners' perceptions* (Unpublished doctoral dissertation). University of Connecticut, Storrs.

Renzulli, J. S. (1977). *The Enrichment Triad Model: A guide for developing defensible programs for the gifted.* Mansfield Center, CT: Creative Learning Press.

Renzulli, J. S., & Reis, S. M. (1985). *The Schoolwide Enrichment Model: A comprehensive plan for educational excellence.* Mansfield Center, CT: Creative Learning Press.

Rimm, S. B. (1986). *Underachievement syndrome: Causes and cures.* Watertown, WI: Apple Publishing.

Tannenbaum, A. E., & Baldwin, L. (1983). Giftedness and learning disability: A paradoxical combination. In L. Fox, L. Brody, & D. Tobin (Eds.), *Learning-disabled/gifted children: Identification and programming* (pp. 11–36). Boston, MA: Allyn & Bacon.

Whitmore, J. R. (1980). *Giftedness, conflict and underachievement.* Boston, MA: Allyn & Bacon.

CHAPTER 21

Commentary on Contemporary Issues

Joseph S. Renzulli
University of Connecticut

Introduction From Joe

Over the years I have written a number of short pieces for the Commentary section of *Education Week,* the nation's most widely read education newspaper. Although this publication has a strict policy limiting articles to 1,200 words, it is extensively read by education leaders and administrators. My purpose for writing these articles is to promote advocacy about issues that are important to the field of gifted education by bringing them to the attention of leaders who are more likely to have decision making power over program and service opportunities in their schools. Editors at *Ed Week* have been somewhat reserved about having too many articles focusing on "the gifted" and therefore I have attempted to pitch our message with titles that would be more appealing to their editorial proclivities and to readers who might routinely skip over articles with "gifted" in the title. I have selected the four of my Commentary articles that follow because they are topics that deal with issues our field has struggled with over the years and that will continue to be relevant in the years ahead.

A Quiet Crisis Clouding the Future R & D People[30]

Those who own the rights to inventions own the world.—From the political platform of the Japanese Democratic Party, June 6, 2000

"Why," I asked the three visitors from the Japanese Ministry of Education "are you interested in the work we are doing?" They had come to our research center to learn about the work we do to promote the development of creative productivity in American schools. I reminded then that our education leaders regularly remind us to look east. "You have the highest scores in the world on international achievement comparisons," I said.

I'll never forget the reply! "Very simple dear professor. We have no Noble prizewinners. Your schools have produced a continuous flow of inventors, designers, entrepreneurs, and innovative leaders. We can make anything you invent faster, cheaper, and, in most cases, better. But we want to learn what role this 'creative productivity' focus plays in the production of creative and inventive people." This experience caused me to think about what might be the one great asset of the American education system—an asset that we may be unwittingly losing as attention is turned more and more to cranking up our achievement test scores.

How much are new ideas worth? What are we willing to pay for the persistence, creativity, and task commitment that research scientists or industrial designers devote to following through on innovative ideas with potential high stakes payoff? Can we calculate the economic value, job opportunities, and contributions to social and political stability that result from investments in young people whose potential for creativity and innovation will develop new products, find solutions to unsolved problems, and even develop entire new industries?

Innovation resulting from research and development is widely recognized as a key ingredient to productivity, but the United States may be losing its edge in the culture of innovation. A quiet crisis is building that could jeopardize our nation's pre-eminence and well being, and this crisis could reverse the global leadership Americans currently enjoy. U.S. productivity growth has slowed significantly since 1973 and continues to grow at a slower rate than our major trading partners. And patent data, one of the best indicators of R & D produc-

---

30 Renzulli, J. (2005). A quiet crisis clouding the future R&D people. *Education Week, 24*(38), 40, 52–53. As first appeared in *Education Week* May 24, 2005. Copyright 2005 *Education Week*. Reprinted with permission.

tivity, also raises concerns about future U.S. competitiveness. Approximately 45 percent of new U.S. patents are now granted to foreigners and the quality of these patents is strong, especially in the high technology areas.

Although many factors contribute to a nation's overall productivity, the education system in any country is a prime source for producing the R & D people of the future. In a recent report the National Science Board pointed out that the United States faces a major shortage of scientists because too few Americans are entering these fields. We are already experiencing a decline in the indicators that track international comparisons in academic achievement. The recently reported PISA study ranked the United States 24th out of 29 countries in the Organization for Economic Cooperation and Development, a Paris-based group that represents the world's richest countries. Our most talented American students rank near the bottom of industrialized nations in mathematics and science comparisons, and only 39 percent of recent American university doctorates in engineering were granted to American students. Thirty-eight percent of all the nation's scientists and engineers with doctorates are now foreign born, however a recent report from the Institute of International Higher Education announced a 2.5 percent decrease in foreign enrollment. The Council of Graduate Schools reported a 28 percent decline in international graduate applications between 2003 to 2004 and a 9 percent decline in the enrollment of first-time international graduate students at the top U.S. universities. The largest drop in applications was in engineering with a decline of 36 percent. International students are turning in greater numbers to the higher education systems of our global competitors and are more likely to remain and seek employment in those countries following graduation. Although our capacity to attract top college and graduate students from abroad remains high, employment opportunities in other countries for our most talented foreign students are increasingly luring these students to return home, and tightening immigration and security regulations threaten to restrict the inflow of foreign students. Even if our net flow of intellectual capital from foreign countries remains high, our domestic development of high-level scientific talent is lagging, and we are relying on inflow, which is increasingly regulated.

In spite of these concerns about our declining reservoir of top foreign and domestic talent, massive investments in the American education system are currently directed toward improving the basic skills of struggling learners. No one can argue against this worthy goal, nor is there any attempt here to suggest that we should deviate from our course that attempts to improve the educational opportunities of all students. This investment will pay off in the form of a more qualified workforce, which is unquestionably an important factor for better preparing the nation's youth for the more demanding jobs required in a knowledge driven economy. Our $350 billion annual investment in public education, however, has shifted quite dramatically, not only to the detriment of in-depth curriculum at the highest levels in areas such as the sciences and social studies, but also to the detriment of physical well being (i.e., physical and health education) and creative and artistic development, which are now considered peripheral curricular components. Many states test only math and reading, and base school and student accountability on these two areas alone.

But what about support for the highly gifted, creative and innovative young people whose ideas will create the products and the jobs that start the wheels of productivity turning? The federal government provides only $11.2 million for research and model programs that serve gifted and talented students. Current estimates of federal education spending indicate that only two cents of every $100 is dedicated to the education of gifted and talented students. And there has been a slow but steady decrease in state level expenditures for this segment of our school population. In the last few years expenditures for services to gifted and talented students have been severely cut by many state departments of education, and states which formerly were shining examples of high quality programs for the gifted—Connecticut, Illinois, Michigan, New York, and Oregon to name a few—have completely eliminated all funding. Pressure on school budgets has also resulted in a decline in allocations for special programs at the local level. Almost weekly I receive yet another phone call or email saying "our program has been cut." Based on the 2002 U.S. Census survey of local government finances, it appears that of state money allocated to schools, less than one-half of one percent was targeted as categorical funding to gifted education programs (on average, across regular K–12 school districts). Only 2,424 of 10,549 public K–12 school districts (reporting) received categorical grants for gifted education from their states. Only about 1,800 K–12 districts received more than $100 per 5% of their enrollment in categorical aid (this excludes states that flow gifted program funds through general funds).

Growth economists believe that improvements in productivity can be linked to a faster pace of innovation and extra investments in human capital, but are we turning our backs on the R & D people of the new century when we fail to support this segment of our school population? Is our education system's current emphasis on just ratcheting up test scores at the expense of promoting creativity and innovative thinking the way to insure our future as a leading nation in the business of generating original ideas, new knowledge, and even entire new industries?

I refer to this neglect of America's most gifted and talented youth as a "quiet crisis" because by the time the damage is done it will be too late to reverse a trend that may place our country in jeopardy. Unchecked, this trend will leave a dearth of scientists, engineers, inventors, entrepreneurs, and cre-

Commentary From Education Week

ative contributors to all areas of the arts and sciences. These kinds of contributions are precisely the things that made America a prosperous and powerful nation through the twentieth century. Our innovation stimulated a powerful knowledge driven economy and shaped a country that made its fame and fortune by creating things rather than merely making them. Neglect of our most gifted and talented students, including those who come from limited economic circumstances, will make it impossible for America to compete in a global economy that is driven by new ideas. Improving the achievement of all students is obviously an important national goal. But let us not turn our back on the one aspect of the American education system that has contributed to our prosperity. Dr. Leon Lederman, the Nobel Prize winning physicist, said in 1990, "Once upon a time, America sheltered an Einstein, went to the Moon, and gave the world the laser, electronic computer, nylons, television, and the cure for polio. Today, we are in the process, albeit unwittingly, of abandoning this leadership role" (Berger, 1994).

Berger, J. (1994). *The young scientist: America's future and the winning of the Westinghouse*. Reading, MA: Addison-Wesley.

Engagement Is the Answer[31]

Closing the achievement gaps between advantaged and disadvantaged students constitutes the biggest challenge facing today's schools. We all know the statistics on test scores and dropout rates. But a sadder commentary may be the resulting collateral damage that has dragged down good instruction, de-skilled many teachers, squeezed subjects other than math and reading out of the curriculum, and produced data juggling and test falsification by desperate administrators trying to avoid having their schools branded as "failing."

How did this mess happen? Why hasn't the estimated $3 trillion spent on school reform since the 1960s made a difference? We've tried just about everything: smaller schools, year-round schools, single-sex classes, after-school mentoring, school uniforms, charter and magnet schools, school-business partnerships, merit pay for teachers, payments to students for performance, private management companies and for-profit schools, takeovers by mayors and state departments of education, site-based management, data-based deci-

---

31 Renzulli, J. (2008). Engagement is the answer. *Education Week, 27*(43), 30–31. As first appeared in *Education Week* July 14, 2008. Copyright 2008 *Education Week*. Reprinted with permission.

sion making, and just about every idea containing the words "standards" and "accountability." All of these suggested silver bullets promised results, but little has changed. Most are built on structural changes and calculated to have an impact on entire school districts or states. But these structural changes have focused too much on low-level, highly prescriptive pedagogy intended to improve standardized-test scores.

The mainstream school diet for many poor and struggling learners is dominated by a remedial pedagogy that has failed to lessen achievement gaps. I believe it has actually contributed to their perpetuation. The instruction these children receive is often designed to determine what they can't do, don't like to do, and see no reason for doing. Then their teachers are told to focus on beating them to death with it.

Evidence of this failed pedagogy is apparent in one national report after another, and yet we continue to search for quick-fix structural solutions rather than alternative methods. The solutions, by whatever new names we give them, are always reiterations of the same pedagogy—the same drill-and-practice model for learning. And our universal criterion for accountability remains the same, with new names given to the same old achievement tests of decades past.

The singular reliance on tests for accountability forces the pedagogy of prescription and hamstrings good instructors in the process. Is it any wonder that some excellent teachers leave the profession, or flee urban schools where prescription is almost universally practiced?

Isn't it time to explore a counter, perhaps even counterintuitive, approach based on pedagogy radically different from what Pavlov used to train his dogs? Accountability for truly educated minds in today's knowledge-driven economy should consider high-end learning skills—those that include the ability to do the following:

- Plan a task and consider alternatives;
- Monitor understanding and the need for additional information;
- Identify patterns, relationships, and discrepancies;
- Generate reasonable arguments, explanations, hypotheses, and ideas;
- Draw comparisons to other problems;
- Formulate meaningful questions;
- Transform factual information into usable knowledge;
- Rapidly and efficiently access information;
- Extend one's thinking;
- Detect bias, make comparisons, draw conclusions, and predict outcomes;
- Apply knowledge and problem-solving strategies to real-world problems;
- Work and communicate effectively with others;

- Derive enjoyment from active engagement in learning; and
- Creatively solve problems and produce new ideas.

These learner-centered skills help develop young minds and promote genuine student engagement, thus increasing achievement. Focusing on these kinds of outcomes may be counterintuitive to the "more practice is better" pedagogy, but our track record with compensatory learning models should help us realize that we need more-creative approaches. We also need an infusion of motivationally rich experiences into the curriculum that will promote engagement, increase enjoyment, and produce a genuine enthusiasm for learning.

Common sense and our own experience tell us that everyone does a better job when working on something that is personally engaging. Extracurricular activities are based, for example, on instruction that is the opposite of drill and practice. How many unengaged students have you seen on the school newspaper staff or the debate team? In the chess club or the concert choir? Engagement occurs when students have choices in what they participate in and how, when they can interact in a goal-oriented environment with like-minded students, and when they are able to use authentic problem-solving, interpersonal skills, and creative learning strategies. Engagement comes when they have the opportunity to produce a product, service, or performance, or to develop work for intended audiences. The enthusiasm and interest that result from such experiences exemplify a learning environment that differs completely from prescriptive pedagogy.

All learning, from diapers to doctorate, exists on a continuum that spans the deductive, didactic, and prescriptive on the one hand, and the inductive, investigative, and inquiry-based on the other. Students with lower achievement are subjected to endless didactic activities, and when their scores don't improve, they receive double the drill-and-kill work. This has turned many schools into joyless places that generate mind-numbing boredom, a lack of genuine student and teacher engagement, absenteeism, and increased dropout rates. Proponents of popular but highly prescriptive programs may boast of test-score increases, but does the endless practice simply prepare students for more test-taking or help them learn to enjoy the act of learning?

Student engagement has been defined in many ways, but I view it as the infectious enthusiasm students display when working on something of personal interest pursued inductively. This and other highly engaging approaches motivate students to improve basic skills and complete higher-level work. True engagement comes from learning activities that challenge young people to stretch above their current comfort level. Such activities are based on resources and methods of inquiry that are qualitatively different from repetitive practice. The guiding principle in this kind of learning can be stated simply: No Child Left Bored.

Research in this area is clear and unequivocal: High engagement results in higher achievement, improved self-concept and self-efficacy, and more-favorable attitudes toward school and learning.

It will not be easy to turn around an education establishment that has made massive financial and policy investments in one particular brand of learning. Nor will it be easy to circumvent the powerful influence of the textbook- and test-publishing industries that thrive on prescriptive curricula and test-driven approaches to accountability.

But change is possible if we take advantage of the remarkable advances in information technologies that have given teachers the equivalent of a dozen teaching assistants in their classrooms. These technologies make it possible to quickly and easily assess students' interests, learning styles, and preferred modes of expression. What formerly took teachers weeks or even months to learn about students' strengths can now be determined electronically. Powerful search engines can then match engaging learning resources to individualized student profiles.

When technology does some of the hard work, true differentiation can occur. Yet while every other field of study has made imaginative uses of technology, educators have too often settled simply for electronic worksheets and encyclopedias online.

We need the courage to explore bolder, more innovative alternatives, so that we can provide all students with highly engaging experiences—the kind of instruction available in the nation's best public and private schools. A more engaging pedagogy, combined with greater and more innovative uses of technology, can deliver the resources to make these alternatives possible.

Going Beyond Gutenberg and Skinner: Fighting the Enemies of Personalized Learning[32]

There are conferences for just about everything these days, but because of my interest in personalized learning, it appeared that this one on redesign-

---

[32] Renzulli, J. (2012). Going beyond Gutenberg and Skinner: Fighting the enemies of personalized learning. *Education Week, 31*(22), 21. As first appeared in *Education Week* February 28, 2012. Copyright 2012 *Education Week*. Reprinted with permission.

ing personalized learning would be just the ticket for gaining new insights into how learning can be more responsive to the divergent needs and diverse populations in today's schools. Most educators agree that the one-size-fits-all curriculum needs addressing, and this by-invitation-only "summit" showed so much promise that I wangled an invite. Resplendent with all the buzzwords of the personalization and differentiation mystique ("flexible," "student-driven," "authentic," "everywhere learning," "systemic redesign"—to mention a few), the event would be staffed by the gurus of school reform and attended by education power brokers and CEOs from the public and private sectors.

Wow! What could be more appealing and hopeful for a change from the harmful direction that education has taken since the No Child Left Behind Act turned the learning process into a gigantic text-consumption and weakness-based test-prep industry? And the expectation that technology was a major answer to this promise of a revolution in personalizing learning made the conference even more appealing.

The emergence of technology in education has certainly created a renewed interest in personalizing learning and providing teachers with the tools necessary for differentiating curriculum. Early efforts to use technology to personalize learning can be traced back to B.F. Skinner's teaching machines, which were designed to use rote-and-drill to automate the task of programmed instruction. Get the correct answer and you moved on to the next question. A wrong answer recycled the student through more practice material until he or she answered the question correctly.

Teaching machines were another failure in the long history of so-called "innovations" in education, but when computers and the Internet came along we seemed poised to capitalize on technology that placed vast amounts of the world's knowledge at students' fingertips. Just as Gutenberg revolutionized access to knowledge, at least for the restricted number of scholars of his time, we now have the capacity to make knowledge public for anyone who can read and log in.

It soon became clear that the general focus of the conference was on basic curriculum competencies and more-efficient procedures for mastery and improved achievement-test scores. Now, rather than covering material in a lock-step fashion for all students at the same time, teachers can direct content at different levels to students according to their varied achievement levels. Although this use of technology extends (by a giant step) the traditional one-size-fits-all instructional model, it only accounts for varying competency levels rather than examining at least three other categories of learner characteristics that define true personalization. This restricted focus led me to conclude that we are using today's technology for what might be called "Gutenberg-online"—the electronic shuffling of worksheets and standard-text material—

and that, pedagogically, we haven't progressed much beyond the type of learning that Skinner advocated with his teaching machines.

A similar case can be made for the explosion of online courses currently available to school-age students. These courses have great value when not available locally, but they almost always follow a linear, sequential instructional model rather than a more inductive and investigative model of learning. To paraphrase Gertrude Stein, a course is a course is a course, or in education-speak: Standards-driven prescriptive material is geared toward answering the questions at the end of the chapter and taking another achievement test. Skinner's teaching-machine movement failed because we were treating students like Pavlov's dogs. We could face the same consequences with today's technology unless we expand our vision about what personalization could be and how technology can help make it happen.

True personalization requires more than just looking at achievement levels and trying to compensate for deficiencies. At least three other characteristics of the learner and differentiation of content and process are necessary to give us a more comprehensive profile of student potentials and point us in the direction of making modifications in the learning process. In addition to achievement levels, information about student interests, learning styles, and preferred modes of expression allow us to make decisions about personalization that take multiple dimensions of the learner into account.

This information can easily be gathered and analyzed through the use of computer-generated profiles and from search engines that match multiple categorized resources from databanks containing vast quantities of highly interactive online material. Teachers can use this technology to infuse into any and all standards-driven curriculum highly engaging enrichment materials that can make any lesson or unit of study more exciting, engaging, and enjoyable. Math concepts improve and become more relevant when students use technology to design and build their own roller coaster. Students can gain a greater appreciation and understanding of ancient Egyptian culture when they do a virtual dissection and preservation of their own mummy.

The differentiation of content requires adding more depth and complexity to the curriculum rather than transmitting more or easier factual material. By focusing on structures of knowledge, basic principles, functional concepts, and methods of inquiry in particular disciplines, students are prepared to assume roles as firsthand inquirers rather than mere consumers of information. The differentiation of process requires the use of a variety of instructional strategies that differ from the traditional deductive, didactic, prescriptive approach used in most classrooms. Respect for learning-style variations can be achieved by using instructional strategies such as simulations, Socratic inquiry, problem-based learning, dramatizations, and individual and small-group investigations of real problems. Expression-style preferences can be accommodated by giving students opportunities to communicate visually, graphically, artistically, and through animatronics, multimedia, and various community-service involvements.

The biggest enemies of differentiation are time and the overprescription of learning. Before the availability of computers and the Internet, teachers simply did not have the time to find and direct customized resources to individual students.

Our obsession with content mastery and Skinner's behavioral theory of learning are slowly but surely giving way to an interest in personalization and differentiation. While it is understandable that our early use of technology was mainly an adaptation of Gutenberg-online and a teaching-machine mentality of what learning is all about, we now have both the pedagogical rationale and technological capability to use the many dimensions of student characteristics that clearly and unequivocally result in higher engagement, enjoyment, and enthusiasm for learning.

Amazon and Netflix know what we like to read and view, and they make use of this information to "differentiate" the material they send us. We can do the same thing to enrich the entire learning environment by capitalizing on a broader spectrum of learner characteristics, creating comprehensive computer-generated student profiles, and using the interactive capabilities of today's technology to revitalize learning. By so doing, we can minimize boredom and make learning the challenging, enjoyable, and relevant process that it should be.

Dealing With the Differentiation Debacle[33]

The two recent Commentaries in *Education Week* on differentiation (Delisle, 2015; Tomlinson, 2015) have accurately described the criticisms and potential of an important concept that has captured unprecedented attention among American educators. Both commentaries, however, have overlooked the one thing that can make differentiation successful without burying teachers under a mountain of time-consuming resource acquisition and classroom management demands that would place unreasonable and perhaps even impossible demands on their time. This argument is truly a "baby and the

---

[33] This piece was written in response to two *Education Week* pieces and submitted for publication.

bathwater" issue; however, there is a way of dealing with differentiating that makes it both feasible and an effective way for adding an element of personalization to all aspects of the curriculum.

So picture this. Students sit down at their computers or pick up their handheld devices and respond to a series of questions that document their academic achievement levels, interests, learning styles, and preferred modes of expression. A search engine then scans through various categorical databases containing thousands of both basic skill builders and highly engaging enrichment activities that are classified by common core standards, achievement levels, interests, learning styles, and preferred modes of expression styles. The search engine next matches these resources to each student's individual profile and sends the resources directly to the student's computer.

Teachers can use the same technology to find topics, subtopics, and sub-subtopics within any general curricular area, unit of study, or preselected standard. Using their class lists and categorized student profile data, teachers can then identify and send differentiated resources at various grade and achievement levels to their students. They can use their knowledge about various student needs and interests to create and name computer-generated achievement level groups and/or interest groups on their classroom dashboard and they can send differentiated resources to individuals, small groups, or their entire classes. The ability to differentiate using this technology is now available and as one teacher who has used it said, "It's like having a dozen teaching assistants in my classroom, every day, all day."

The unfortunate reality of today's standards-driven curriculum and the demands on most teachers to improve standardized test scores at all costs has left little time or motivation for teachers to accommodate the many differences that exist in today's demographically diverse classrooms. Our research on reading, for example, has shown that as many as 12 reading levels exist in some heterogeneously grouped middle grade classrooms (Reis et al., 2011) and in most cases when differentiation strategies are applied, the only changes taking place are content-level adjustments (i.e., more drill and practice for low-performing students and more advanced content for high achievers). True differentiation must also deal with variations in instructional strategies and classroom organization and management as well as simple adjustment to content levels. Some students learn best through group work and some by working alone. Some students learn more effectively by doing projects, while others learn best by discussion, simulations, computer-assisted instruction, or by tracking down on the web Just-In-Time information and resources needed for a project they are pursuing.

Teachers can also differentiate the learning environment and how they manage it by *infusing* differentiated activities into the standard curriculum.

Students can be given opportunities to work individually, in groups with other students who share similar interests or learning styles, or in groups in which every student has a chance to demonstrate his or her own unique style of learning. Students also have preferences for the ways in which they like to express themselves—orally, visually, graphically, dramatically, through construction, through digital media, or through various written genres. In basic skill areas, there is an almost unlimited amount of material that covers math and reading/language arts concepts at various levels. These materials can easily be directed to individuals or small achievement-level groups electronically by letting the computer do the heavy lifting, making the very valuable concept of differentiation a workable reality.

Many of the resources available from the web incorporate opportunities for addressing the kinds of student differences mentioned above and they extend differentiation beyond mere content modifications. A board game called *Escape to Freedom* allows students to learn about the Fugitive Slave Act through a competitive simulation that capitalizes on students who prefer an interactive style of learning about the Civil War. A virtual dissection and mummy preservation activity called Fun With Mummies allows students to study Ancient Egypt through a highly engaging and hands-on experience that incorporates anatomy, Egyptian history, language, and culture into the activity. Students interested in STEM applications can build their own roller coaster or underwater Remotely Operated Vehicles. Existing software makes thousands of resources such as these easy to locate, download, and direct to individuals or groups. In places where this approach to differentiation has been used, we have witnessed remarkable turnarounds and improved achievement test scores on the parts of struggling or turned-off learners (Field, 2009). In addition, high-achieving students have had opportunities to engage in challenging problem-based enrichment projects that extend their thinking skills and creative productivity far beyond what is typically covered in the standards driven curriculum.

As is almost always the case, education is usually slower than other professions to adapt to changes in technology. Conversely, the entire field of health care is now driven by "personalized medicine" literally "differentiated" for patients' needs. Amazon and Netflix know our preferences and only send us selections in which they know we have an interest. And what about the pop-up ads that appear in almost every document downloaded from the Internet? They are always posted by companies from which previous purchases have been made. Differentiation or personalization (my preferred term) in education is a powerful concept, and I agree with critics who say that implementation is challenging. But we need to figure out how to make it work and the use of technology that is now available is one approach that will enable teachers to easily access the almost unlimited resources that will not only improve achievement, but also make learning the enjoyable, engaging, and exciting process that it should be. Although the previous commentaries on this topic present what appear to be opposing points of view, they serve a very useful purpose of calling our attention to the powerful potential of an instructional strategy that can increase at least a part of the personalized learning process for all students.

Delisle, J. R. (2015). Differentiation doesn't work. *Education Week, 34*(15), 28, 36.
Field, G. B. (2009). The effects of the use of Renzulli Learning on student achievement in reading comprehension, reading fluency, social studies, and science. *International Journal of Emerging Technologies in Learning, 4*(1), 23–28.
Reis, S. M., McCoach, D. B., Little, C. M., Muller, L. M., & Kaniskan, R. B. (2011). The effects of differentiated instruction and enrichment pedagogy on reading achievement in five elementary schools. *American Educational Research Journal, 48*, 462–501.
Tomlinson, C. A. (2015). To the contrary: Differentiation does work. *Education Week, 34*(19), 26, 32.

CHAPTER 22

A Biographical Portrait of Joseph S. Renzulli

Scholar, Gifted Educator, and Visionary Leader[34]

Thomas P. Hébert
University of South Carolina

Introduction From Sally

It is amazing how often I am asked about Joe's background and the early influences on his highly productive life. His life story is a fascinating one with difficulties, such as the early death of his father and later, a beloved brother. He was also influenced by an amazing and dedicated mother, who spoke English as a second language and worked as a housekeeper to support her three young boys at home after their father passed away. Joe's early life is characterized by working hard to help his mother maintain the family home and his work

---

[34] Hébert, T. P. (2013). A biographical portrait of Joseph S. Renzulli: Scholar, gifted educator, and visionary leader. In E. A. Romey (Ed.), *Finding John Galt: People, politics, and practice in gifted education* (pp. 99–113). Charlotte, NC: Information Age. Copyright 2013 Information Age. Reprinted with permission.

ethic continued throughout his life. He worked as a caddy, selling vegetables, in an icehouse, and pursued a multitude of jobs to attend college. He became a teacher, pursued a master's degree in school psychology, and worked as a psychologist before heading to the University of Virginia where he studied with the fascinating Virgil Ward. His early interests were creativity and evaluation, both of which led to his subsequent decades of scholarship. Perhaps because of his time as a teacher in New Jersey, Joe has never been satisfied to simply develop ideas at his desk at UConn, but rather, he wants to see and understand how these ideas can be implemented in schools and then make them easier to implement if educators encounter challenges. His work is never done, it is a constant process of evolution.

Rather than write his biography here, we decided to reprint a chapter written by Tom Hébert, a dear friend and former graduate student who completed a case study of Joe's life for a recent book. In introducing this chapter, I will just say that Joe is dedicated in his life as husband, as father to our two daughters, Sara and Liza, and to the rest of our extended family.

Introduction

It was a crisp sunny morning in May, 2008 when I joined Joe Renzulli for a cup of coffee. We were enjoying the Connecticut sunshine and the sounds of birds chirping from the woods surrounding the Reuzullis' beautifully landscaped backyard. As we got situated at a table on the back patio, I realized that I was fortunate to have the opportunity to interview my doctoral mentor about his life. I knew the conversation would enable me to capture details of his significant life experiences and his contributions to gifted education. I also realized that I faced a challenge. I knew the humility of this man and realized that such a personal conversation centered on his experiences might be something he would not necessarily enjoy. As we sipped our coffee and began with casual conversation, I arranged my tape recorder on the table and proceeded with the interview. We engaged in that conversation for two hours before it was time for us to hop in Joe's sporty BMW to travel across the state of Connecticut for an important meeting. Following lunch at Rein's Deli, our conversation continued in the car. As Joe drove, I continued the interview with my trusty cassette recorder capturing his reflections. The stories he shared brought us both some great laughs and even a few tears. My memory of that backyard conversation and our ride across Connecticut is one I cherish today.

Several weeks after the interview, Joe's wife Sally provided me with a copy of a family history that had been written for the Renzullis by Joe's beloved Uncle Ferrar. This significant manuscript served me well in writing this chapter. In addition to the family history, I enjoyed the interview with Joe conducted by Dr. Abbey Block Cash and Dr. Stuart Omdal at the 2008 annual meeting of the National Association for Gifted Children (NAGC, 2009) in Tampa, Florida. This videotaped event at the convention was sponsored by the Conceptual Foundations Network as part of the "Portraits in Gifted Education: The Legacy Series." This dedicated network of NAGC educators is committed to documenting and preserving the theories of the most influential scholars in the field of gifted education in order to honor them and their contributions for future generations.

I have merged these three sources of data in compiling this chapter on the life of Dr. Renzulli. My objective in writing this chapter is to describe his significant contributions to gifted and talented education and shed some light on how Dr. Joseph Renzulli's life experiences shaped his thinking and his influential contributions to his field.

Early Family History

The Renzulli family history begins in Castelnuozo, Italy in the province of Froggia, in the region of Apalia. Joe's grandfather Salvatore and grandmother Angelina Martinelli Renzulli maintained a large farm. Grandfather Renzulli was a devout socialist and became very disenchanted with the rise of fascism. A courageous man, he spoke out against the Mussolini regime and was jailed. His crops were burned and his animals were killed. Eventually he emigrated to the United States. Salvatore and Angelina had eight children and settled in Landisville, New Jersey, a community of approximately 300 people, mostly newly arrived immigrants from Italy. Salvatore had worked in the wine industry in Italy, had acquired a passion for all that was involved in making wine, and dreamed of owning a vineyard. His dream materialized when a farm that included a vineyard became available for sale. The farm included forty acres of land with about ten acres of grapes. With Salvatore Renzulli's hard work and dedication to his family, the vineyard prospered and returned a good profit. In 1918, when Congress passed an amendment to the Constitution that prohibited the manufacture and sale of alcoholic beverages, this forced Salvatore and his sons to shift to raising vegetables and poultry. Salvatore Renzulli lived to be 87 after his beloved wife Angelina passed away of a heart attack at the age of 39. In the Renzullis' family story, entitled *La Famiglia*, the family historian,

Joe's Uncle Ferrar, described how his grandparents' greatest satisfactions in life were the many friends they made. He wrote: "Friends in all walks of life, from the little to the great. Among them were lawyers, judges, doctors, professionals and pasesanos from the old country; all were welcome." He explained the significance of these friendships: "We, their children profited most as we gained a much broader view of life and learned to mingle with all types of people." The family historian also described Salvatore and Angelina's approach to parenting:

> Both parents were great readers. We remember them on many evenings sitting by the kerosene lamp that lighted our kitchen reading the daily newspaper, a magazine or book. We were constantly prodded to study and do well in school. From them we developed a desire to improve ourselves, get the best education and do the best to improve life for our children and grandchildren. (Renzulli, 1999, p. 9)

Joe's father, Marx Libero Renzulli, suffered from rheumatic heart disease as a child. As a result he could not work on the family farm. He was employed by the railroad industry and served as a strong union activist. His employment with the railroads took him to Atlantic Highlands, New Jersey. He met and married Edith Santagelo, and they had three sons, Marx Jr., Joseph, and Walter. They bought a small home in Atlantic Highlands with a mortgage of $17.00 a month.

Marx Libero Renzulli died in 1944 at the age of 40. Joe was eight years old. His father had worked for the railroad company for 19 years and nine months. Railroad company policy required 20 years of service before an employee could acquire a pension. Edith Renzulli was left to raise three young sons. The three young Renzulli boys came to know the "welfare lady" quite well. When the welfare lady explained that they would have to give up their home and move into "lovely garden apartments," Joe and his older brother quickly managed to earn bus fare by recycling soda pop bottles and took the bus into the city to investigate the apartments. They were appalled by the housing and the decrepit neighborhood the welfare agency was suggesting. Upon returning home, they described the horrible conditions, the boarded up windows in many of the buildings, and the derelict characters that lingered in the hallways of the apartments. Edith Renzulli agreed with her young sons that they could not live there. Determined to hold onto the small, modest family home, she cleaned houses for wealthy families in the community in order to provide for her children. There were times when the family experienced the electricity and water being cut off because they could not pay the bills; however, they managed to pay the monthly mortgage of seventeen dollars in order to stay together as a family.

Joe's father's younger brother Ferrar, known as "Uncle Fatty," intervened. He quit his teaching job, and with Mary, his new bride, moved 70 miles to join Edith and her three young sons. He found a new position teaching in Ocean Township and moved in with Joe's family for a year to help them get back on their feet financially. Joe explained, "We might not have made it if it were not for Uncle Fatty. We might have been taken away for adoption." Edith Renzulli, an intelligent woman, had been educated in schools in Italy but spoke no English. Her three young sons became her English teachers. With limited means she raised her three sons to become successful. Joe's older brother Marx earned a doctorate in history and became a successful history professor at Tufts University. Walter, the youngest son, became a barber. Walter suffered from a kidney disease that eventually took his life at age 32.

Childhood on the Jersey Shore

Joe's childhood took place within his community in Oakhurst, New Jersey. He reflected fondly on his first trip outside the state of New Jersey when he was twelve. His school friend Johnny Marcotte's father Joe was a "jack of all trades kind of a guy" who was originally from New Hampshire. All Mr. Marcotte ever talked about were the scenic mountains, rivers, and lakes of his home state. When he was provided an opportunity to transport high quality lumber down from New Hampshire for boat building along the Jersey shore he invited Joe to join him and his son on several trips to transport the lumber. Joe reminisced, "I'll always remember those trips fondly. I had never been out of New Jersey. I may have gone to Brooklyn, New York a couple times, but that was it. I remember traveling through the beautiful mountains." He reflected, "We stayed in a rather primitive camp and washed up in the nearby brook. It was the first time I saw the world beyond the little area I grew up in. It was a real pleasure."

Joe and his neighborhood buddies spent their days involved in adventures that involved a number of get rich quick schemes. They formed a group called "the Explorers Club," investigating abandoned homes along the Jersey shore. They spent their time searching for creative ways to make some extra money. Several small-scale businesses evolved from one summer to the next. He described one business that proved to be quite profitable:

> There were a number of very large estates along the Jersey shore that had been abandoned after the Depression. They had these green-

houses that were broken down. There was one estate where ivy had grown wild and it was covering everything. Behind the greenhouse, my friends and I discovered, were a thousand clay pots and a large overgrown hedge. We got my little wagon, got these clay pots, and filled them with soil. Then we cleaned out an ivy plant and we would cut a stalk out of the hedge. We'd tie the ivy to the stalk in the pots. We'd go around the neighborhood selling these plants. The cost to us was nothing, so that was one of the successful businesses we ran.

During World War II, families were encouraged to produce "victory gardens" in honor of the efforts of the military. The Renzulli family joined this effort, and nine-year-old Joe began a small business selling vegetables in his neighborhood. Joe's garden was quite small and did not yield what he needed. He found that once it was dark outside, he could "borrow" a few vegetables from other people's gardens. He built up his little wagon with three tiers of shelves and went door-to-door selling his produce. On Roosevelt Avenue was a stern, portly widow named Mrs. Hutchinson who called the vegetable seller from her front porch, "Boy! Can you come over here?" The young vegetable salesman approached the porch with trepidation. "Those potatoes you sold me several days ago were so good. Can you get me some more?" The young vegetable salesman was relieved that Mrs. Hutchinson didn't realize she was buying potatoes from her own garden!

As dedicated members of the Explorers Club, Joe and his two brothers discovered an entire basement room in one of the abandoned mansions filled from wall to wall and floor to ceiling with old newspapers. Although his older brother was becoming somewhat of a history buff who reveled in these old newspapers, Joe and his younger brother had another plan. They spent days bundling these papers, piling them onto Joe's little wagon and selling them to the local "rag man'" in the community. To the three young Renzulli boys, this room of old newsprint was a tremendous find, which lead to a substantial fortune in the eyes of these young businessmen. Joe explained that adolescent boys growing up along the Jersey shore could always find little summer jobs in the ice cream stands or fast food places on the boardwalk. He pointed out that he and his brothers applied their personal creativity to address their situation: "We didn't have any money, so you always had to figure, 'You want something? What can I do to get it?' I think that's where my present-day entrepreneurial spirit comes from."

Joe Renzulli, the Student

As a student, Joe Renzulli did well all through school. He earned good grades yet was a "scrappy kid" who got into plenty of schoolyard fights and spent time on the detention bench outside the principal's office. He explained, "I was considered to be a hell raiser." School was pretty routine for him until Miss Elise Kent, his seventh and eighth grade language arts teacher, managed to get him directed. He reflected,

> I was in trouble once, and she sat me down and said, "I really like your writing." She got me to start the school newspaper. Eventually she got two or three other kids involved, but in the beginning I was doing all the writing. I had to use two or three pen names. That was a turning point in terms of doing something that I really liked that was a bit more creative. I was a good lesson learner, but that really changed my attitude. When I went to high school, I was on the school newspaper staff and in the press club. Our high school published a series called "Words and Pictures"—artwork and stories written by kids. I had a few pieces published, and I got a tremendous sense of pleasure doing that. I actually had aspirations of being a journalist and writer.

Joe appreciated the significant influence Miss Kent had on his life. His involvement in the school newspaper became an important outlet for him and also helped him work to channel his energy in positive directions. He explained,

> I understood that my involvement in the school newspaper would be taken away from me if I continued to get in trouble. We were the only Italian family in the neighborhood, and there were a lot of cracks made about Italians, "Wop! Guinea!" My mother always used to put little vegetables wrapped in waxed paper in our lunches. At lunch, this kid would pass my desk every day and say, "Show me a guinea, and I'll show you a garden." After the fifth time he said that, I stood up and pummeled him. I often ended up in trouble—on the detention bench one more time because I started a fight. As result, I developed a reputation.

Joe had a miserable experience with Miss Vogel, his high school guidance counselor, who recognized that his family came from limited means. As a result, she had directed Joe's older brother, Marx, to enroll in the non-college track of courses throughout high school. He eventually went on to earn a doctoral degree in history from the University of Virginia. Joe was determined to pursue a college preparatory track. As a result of his success as a writer in junior and senior high school, he had aspirations of becoming a journalist and eventually "writing the great American novel." Years later the teachers who had sent Joe Renzulli to spend time on the detention bench were rather shocked when they heard that he was going to become a teacher.

During his senior year at Asbury Park High School, he took the city bus and went to his "College Night" at the high school. He knew that his family could not afford to send him to school. He reflected on the experience of that evening:

> I'll never forget that night. You went from room to room, and you got the pitch about each school and all the paperwork. You asked about scholarships. The only scholarships were for athletics. While I was on the high school football team, I wasn't scholarship material. I can remember, I got back on the bus to go home that evening, and I was literally in tears. At that time we were at war with Korea, the draft was on. So many young men simply worked construction and waited to be drafted. We had an expression for anybody not going to college: "You have a career in Korea."

Shortly after that "College Night" experience, Joe's Uncle Fatty interceded once again. Uncle Fatty had earned a degree from Glassboro State Normal School. He assured his nephew, "Teaching has been good to me." He worked his way up through the ranks and had developed an adult education program for returning veterans. He had attended Glassboro with a woman named Grace Bagg, who was then serving as director of admissions and scholarships at what had become Glassboro State Teachers College. With strong SAT scores and good grades, Joe believed that he could gain admission, but he simply needed funding. When Uncle Fatty checked with Grace Bagg on the possibilities of financial aid, she was able to provide a tuition scholarship and a small work-study job. Uncle Fatty also found him a job pumping gas in a gas station on weekends and a 1946 four-door Dodge to commute back and forth to the gas station. When a new grocery store opened up in his neighborhood, he got a job stocking shelves at night. With his extra jobs Joe was able to cover his room and board and living expenses. Living in an apartment house with other college students, he often negotiated loans from Vin Damski, the apartment house moneylender. Joe explained, "He'd give you 15 dollars and in two weeks you owed him 20."

During the summer months, Joe worked in an ice house in Ocean City, New Jersey, seven days a week for 12 hours a day, often earning overtime money for even longer days. With a promotion to foreman of the landing dock at the icehouse, he was able to help his mother financially and pay his car insurance policy. The summers spent working at the icehouse were memorable. Joe pointed out that Ocean City, New Jersey was a great place for young adults to be in the summer. Thousands of young women arrived every summer to work as waitresses. The area was known for great nightclubs and bands and several summer romances resulted in weddings. Joe noted, "We had great times. We worked hard, but it was a fun time."

Early Teaching Career

Joe Renzulli graduated from Glassboro State Teachers College in 1958 with a Bachelor of Arts degree in science education with a minor in math education. His first year of teaching was in Ocean Township, New Jersey in a sixth grade self-contained classroom. His beginning salary was $3,600.00. Following that year, he taught seventh and eighth grade mathematics and science. During his early career years as a teacher, he continued his work at the ice house in Ocean City, as he indicated, "I made as much in one week at the ice house as I did in two weeks teaching."

Joe taught math and science in junior high school for six years. During that time, the Russians had launched Sputnik, and Americans were concerned that we were losing our competitive edge. American schools responded by paying more attention to the teaching of math and science, particularly with gifted students. Edward German, the superintendent of schools in Joe's school district, approached him with an offer. He asked Joe to begin a science program for highly able learners. He paid him an extra $300.00 in salary. When Joe requested a curriculum from the superintendent, he replied, "There isn't one." Years later Joe reflected, "That was the best thing that could have happened. Had there been one—science for the gifted—I would have taught it."

Instead he incorporated guest speakers from nearby science and industry labs in New Jersey. He infused more investigatory experiences and provided opportunities for the students to pursue their own self-selected areas of interest. This science program undoubtedly served as the early field test for what would later become Renzulli's Enrichment Triad Model.

During his first year of teaching Joe enrolled in a master's degree program in school psychology at Rutgers University. As a full-time teacher, he enrolled in evening classes and summer and weekend courses. Psychology intrigued him, and he had no desire to pursue the traditional route to upward mobility through a degree in educational administration. During the 1960s, men in education were destined to become building principals, but Joe had a different view. He explained,

> All the men then had aspirations of becoming administrators because that was the only upwardly mobile path to financial advancement at that time and few women were doing that. I never had any fondness for administration. Going to meetings and pushing paper across the desk did not appeal to me. I really loved the psychology courses I had taken as an undergraduate, and I especially loved the tests and measurement courses.

The Rutgers school psychology program required a practicum experience, and Joe was fortunate to have Bob McKee, a school psychologist, in the junior high school where he was teaching. As part of Joe's training in individual intelligence testing and personality testing, McKee agreed to supervise him. Joe spent many hours testing students and made thoughtful observations of what he was seeing in children during those sessions. He became intrigued with the students like those in his science and math classes, who had a much more conceptual and insightful understanding. Those experiences testing young adolescents and working with highly intelligent seventh and eighth grade students proved to be significant. He indicated, "I had kids in science asking me questions I couldn't answer. That was very intimidating but a very good experience for anyone training to be a doctoral advisor." He enjoyed his work in school psychology and appreciated the strong background he acquired in tests and measurements.

During his time at Rutgers, one of his personality assessment teachers, Jane Beasley Rath, handed him a manuscript to review and provide her with "talking points." He was happy to take on the extra challenge. The manuscript was the earliest version of the Getzels and Jackson (1962) text on creativity and intelligence that would later become the seminal contribution entitled *Creativity and Intelligence*. He began reading it one evening and later reported, "The sun was coming up when I finished it, and I was hooked!" Fascinated with the notion of creativity, he eventually switched his major to educational psychology so he could enroll in courses such as theories of learning, conceptual foundations of thought, and theoretical psychology. He completed the school psychology coursework to become certified as an examiner, and never regretted the work he did in this field since he acquired a good perspective on assessment and would later apply those skills in other professional venues. He graduated from Rutgers University in 1962 with a master's degree in educational psychology.

Doctoral Program at the University of Virginia

Jane Beasely Rath had been a graduate student under Abe Tannenbaum, Miriam Goldberg and A. Harry Passow at Columbia University, significant leaders in gifted education. When he expressed interest in gifted students, she provided Joe with several published manuscripts by Virgil Ward of the University of Virginia. Joe found Ward's work impressive. His older brother Marx was in graduate school in Charlottesville, so Joe decided to travel there for a visit. While in Charlottesville, he made an appointment to meet with Dr. Ward at the University of Virginia. He was able to arrange for Joe to receive a graduate assistantship in special education in order to pursue his doctoral studies. He studied under Virgil Ward for three years and graduated with his doctoral degree in educational psychology in 1966. His dissertation, entitled "Diagnostic and Evaluative Scales for Differential Education of the Gifted," involved developing a paradigm for evaluating programs for the gifted. It was later published and became the leading resource on program evaluation in gifted education.

His relationship with his doctoral mentor had a powerful influence on him as a scholar. He described Dr. Ward as "tough" and "a man of unbelievably high standards." Ward demanded precision in thinking and writing. "Split an infinitive and you would hear about it six times. Later he'd hand you a paper, and he'd say, 'I see you didn't split any infinitives.'" Joe described his intellectual discipline:

> I'd arrive in the office and say "Good morning." And Virgil would respond with "Mr. Renzulli, what do you mean by good? And what do you mean by morning?" You had to defend everything, and you had to defend it logically. You couldn't just say "Research says . . ." He'd say, "What does that research say? And where did they get their data?" He'd ask all the tough questions. But he taught me how to think, and he taught me how to write. My writing improved 300 fold, but my early papers for him were bloody with red ink when he returned them.

Joe indicated that he enjoyed strong intellectual debates with his mentor until the day he died. Dr. Ward was a strong conservative who believed that "the measure of a man was his IQ." He remained committed to high-IQ cut-off scores for entry into gifted education programs, while Joe challenged conventional wisdom and opened up gifted education programs to many more children. Joe reflected, "Virgil and I were on opposite points of the compass in our views of what makes giftedness, but as far as I was concerned, his mentoring was the kind of discipline I needed."

Early Career Years at the University of Connecticut

Following graduation from the University of Virginia, Joe interviewed in several prestigious universities for positions in educational psychology programs. These interviews provided him with the first opportunity in his life to travel on a plane. At that time, the Renzulli family knew that Joe's younger brother Walter did not have much longer to live as he battled the kidney disease that eventually took his life. During that period, Joe wanted to live closer to his family and was interested in schools that would enable him to travel home to New Jersey within a few hours. The University of Connecticut was only three hours from home. When the opportunity to join the faculty at the University of Connecticut was offered in 1966, Joe was delighted to accept the offer and has remained on the faculty at UConn since.

Initially he was intrigued with research that was being conducted by Ellis Paige, who had received a substantial federal research grant to explore the scoring of children's written essays by computer. Project Essay Grading (PEG) took on the challenge of scoring the Torrance Test of Creative Thinking (TTCT). Joe joined Paige in this work, and together they developed an understanding of the creative thinking skills that could be developed through curricular activities, which led to the publication of *New Directions in Creativity*, a series of five volumes of creativity training activities for elementary and middle school students.

When the state of Connecticut passed legislation in 1967 that helped fund gifted education programs at a level equal to special education funding, there was suddenly a need for teachers to be trained in gifted education. Joe approached his dean to teach a graduate course in gifted education. The dean was supportive; however, he would have to teach the course as an overload, as the dean could not pay him anything extra. Within a short time, Joe was teaching an auditorium size class: Introduction to Gifted Education. He went on to design courses in creativity and program and curriculum development for gifted students. Randy Nelson, a faculty member in counseling and a student of Marshall Sanborn, joined him and taught courses in counseling gifted students. Eventually Joe was joined by Vincent Rogers, who became an official faculty member in the gifted education program teaching curriculum courses that were philosophically compatible with gifted education.

Major Contributions to His Field

Today Joseph Renzulli is the Neag Professor of Gifted Education and Talent Development at the University of Connecticut where he also served as the director of the National Research Center on the Gifted and Talented (NRC/GT). His 40-year career in higher education has focused on the identification and development of creativity and giftedness in young people and the use of gifted education pedagogy to increase engagement and achievement in all children. An internationally renowned scholar, he is considered by many to be the world's leading expert in this area. His books and articles have been translated into over 15 languages, and he has lectured in approximately 30 countries.

One highlight of his career is the article he wrote in 1978 entitled, "What Makes Giftedness: Reexamining a Definition," and published in *Phi Delta Kappan*. Prior to its appearance in the *Kappan*, this manuscript had been rejected by every major journal in the field of gifted education. According to the Social Science Citation Index, it is still the most frequently cited publication in the field. In this article, Joe presented his Three-Ring Conception of Giftedness, the foundation of a more flexible approach to identifying and developing gifted behaviors or high levels of potential in young people. Prior to Joe's work on this definition, most professional educators equated giftedness strictly with high IQ scores. Renzulli's definition challenged this antiquated approach and enabled gifted education programs to be open to children of poverty, children from bilingual backgrounds, and children of color.

Joe Renzulli has worked on the development of organizational models and curricular strategies for differentiated learning environments that contribute to total school improvement. His Enrichment Triad Model (Renzulli, 1977) was one of the first efforts on problem-based learning and has been recognized as the most widely used approach for special programs for the gifted and talented. The Enrichment Triad Model served as the foundation for what later became the Schoolwide Enrichment Model (Renzulli & Reis, 1997), which he developed with Dr. Sally Reis. This programming model has been credited as the most widely used approach by schools throughout the world that serve gifted and talented students and seek to enrich and engage all students in enrichment opportunities that are both interest-based and intellectually challenging.

In addition to the development of programming models in gifted education, Dr. Renzulli has engaged in work to support the efforts of educators interested in designing effective curricula. Renzulli created the Multiple Menu Model (Renzulli, Leppien, & Hays, 2000) to help curriculum writers use the information on how knowledge develops to design interesting, rigorous, and authentic units of instruction. His design of the Multiple Menu Model for developing differentiated curriculum provided a management plan that enables curriculum developers to select content and strategies from a number of options or "menus" that are driven by theories of knowledge, curricular design, and instruction. He also joined colleagues in the field in the development of the Parallel Curriculum Model (Tomlinson et al., 2009), an instructional framework for developing the abilities of all students and extending those of students who perform at advanced levels. Through this model Renzulli and his colleagues promote educational equity and excellence by ensuring that all students are appropriately challenged and supported through high quality curriculum.

In the later years of his career, Joe Renzulli has turned his attention again to his Three-Ring Conception of Giftedness and has begun to examine what causes some individuals to mobilize their interpersonal, political, ethical and moral senses in ways that they place human concerns and the common good above all else. He proposed the Houndstooth Theory of Social Capital (Renzulli, 2003). In this theory, the word houndstooth refers to the background pattern of interwoven factors that influence gifted behaviors. Renzulli (2003) defined social capital as "a set of intangible assets that address the collective needs and problems of other individuals and communities at large" (p. 77). In pursuing research on the houndstooth factors that influence the development of social capital, Renzulli looks to expand the definition of giftedness to include several traits that characterize individuals who have a profound impact on the improvement of society.

In his 40-year career in education, Joseph Renzulli has contributed hundreds of books, book chapters, articles, and monographs to the professional literature. He has also generated millions of dollars in research and training grants. However, he maintains that his proudest professional accomplishment is the Confratute Program, a training institute on enriched teaching and learning held every summer at the University of Connecticut. Renzulli founded Confratute in 1978, and it has served more than 30,000 teachers and administrators from around the world, exposing them to enrichment and engagement for all children.

Joe Renzulli's professional awards and honors are extensive. The following are provided as significant highlights of his numerous achievements. Dr. Renzulli was named a board of trustees distinguished professor at the University of Connecticut in 2000, an honor limited to only three professors each year. He has served on numerous editorial boards in the fields of gifted education, educational psychology and research, and law and education. He has also served as a senior research associate for the White House Task Force on Education of the Gifted and Talented. Dr. Renzulli is a fellow in the American Psychological Association and has received numerous distinguished research awards from the National Association for Gifted Children and the University of Connecticut. He was awarded an honorary doctor of law degree from McGill University in Montreal, Canada in 2003 and the 2009 Harold W. McGraw, Jr. Prize for Innovation in Education.

His Greatest Joys With His UConn Family

As professor emeritus in the College of Education, Joe Renzulli's love of family is evident in his pride for the family of graduate students who have graduated from the gifted education and talent development program at the University of Connecticut. In explaining his approach to a successful program of mentoring graduate students, he reflected,

> The kinds of selections we made in getting people to the program made a difference. There are a variety of strengths among the doctoral students—some are prolific, others are more political, and others have been phenomenal teachers. What they see happen here in practice is what makes a good scholar—there is an appreciation of different styles.

Joe pointed out that when doctoral students graduated from the program he made a point to hold an individual conversation with each student. His overarching question during that conversation was: "What are some of the things you learned here that have absolutely nothing to do with courses and content?" He indicated that some were initially taken aback, however:

> They get around to what I consider to be important values—appreciating differences in other people, that secretaries are as valuable members or the team as anybody else, respect for the fact that people are going to bring their own agendas to the table in scholarship. Everybody is different in his or her beliefs about things, and you have to respect that. That to me is what has contributed to the success. I am who I am, and I live that. I try to be kind to others. And of course, having something like Confratute when we come to be back together is kind of glue that holds us together.

In discussing his greatest professional joys, he reported, "I love seeing the successful work of kids using stuff that I've developed. All of those Type

III studies that children have pursued over the years. It verifies the fact that these are the kinds of things that change kids lives." He also highlighted how Confratute: The Summer Institute on Enrichment Teaching and Learning at the University of Connecticut every year is one of his proudest achievements. He noted: "It's something that brings people together under optimal conditions. When you reach 100 teachers, you reach a 1,000 kids." Joe is also proud of his graduate students and their professional accomplishments. "It's nice to open up one of the gifted journals and of the seven articles two or three are UConn graduates." He pointed out that several presidents of the National Association for Gifted Children (NAGC) and editors of leading journals in the field were his former students. He is also proud of others who, as administrators and state department consultants, have contributed to bringing about significant in school districts throughout the country. He also noted that the international interest in the work from the University of Connecticut has been rewarding. "It's very satisfying to see other countries wanting what we have because of our focus on creative productivity. It verifies the fact that we are doing something worthwhile."

Summary

Today Joe Renzulli continues to thrive in his work as the Neag Professor of Gifted Education. His creative productivity continues at a pace that would overwhelm most. His days are spent collaborating with his most trusted colleague, partner, and wife, Dr. Sally Reis, and together they celebrate a life filled with joyful days centered around their families, including their children and grandchildren. Today their work and travels take them to many corners of the globe, yet they are always happy to return to their seaside home in Mystic, Connecticut.

References

Getzels, J. W., & Jackson, P. W. (1962). *Creativity and intelligence*. New York, NY: John Wiley.
Hébert, T. P. (2008, May). *Interview with Joseph S. Renzulli*. Mansfield Center, CT.
National Association for Gifted Children. (2009). *Portraits in gifted education: The legacy series—A conversation with Joe Renzulli*. Washington, DC: Author.
Renzulli, B. F. (1999). *La famiglia*. Unpublished family manuscript.

Renzulli, J. S. (1977). *The Enrichment Triad Model: A guide for developing defensible programs for the gifted and talented.* Mansfield Center, CT: Creative Learning Press.

Renzulli, J. S. (1978). What makes giftedness: Reexamining a definition. *Phi Delta Kappan, 60,* 180–184.

Renzulli, J. S. (2003). Conception of giftedness and its relationship to the development of social capital. In N. Colangelo & G. A. Davis (Eds.), *Handbook of gifted education* (3rd ed., pp. 75–87). Boston, MA: Allyn & Bacon.

Renzulli, J. S., Leppien, J., & Hays, T. (2000). *The Multiple Menu Model.* Waco, TX: Prufrock Press.

Renzulli, J. S., & Reis, S. M. (1997). *The Schoolwide Enrichment Model: A how-to guide for educational excellence* (2nd ed.). Waco, TX: Prufrock Press.

Tomlinson, C. A., Kaplan, S. N., Renzulli, J. S., Purcell, J. H., Leppien, J. H., Burns, D. E., . . . Imbeau, M. B. (2009). *The parallel curriculum: A design to develop learner potential and challenge advanced learners* (2nd ed.). Thousand Oaks, CA: Corwin Press.

About the Editor

Sally M. Reis, Ph.D., is the Vice Provost for Academic Affairs and a Board of Trustees Distinguished Professor at the University of Connecticut. She was previously a department head of the educational psychology department, where she also serves as a Principal Investigator for the National Research Center on the Gifted and Talented. She was a public school teacher for 15 years, 11 of which were spent working with gifted students on the elementary, junior high, and high school levels. She has authored or coauthored more than 250 articles, books, book chapters, monographs, and technical reports.

Her research interests are related to special populations of gifted and talented students, including students with learning disabilities, gifted females, and diverse groups of talented students. She is also interested in extensions of the Schoolwide Enrichment Model for both gifted and talented students and as a way to expand offerings and provide general enrichment to identify talents and potentials in students who have not been previously identified as gifted. She is the Co-Director of Confratute, the longest running summer institute in the development of gifts and talents. She has been a consultant to numerous schools and ministries of education throughout the U.S., and abroad and her work has been translated into several languages and is widely used around the world.

She is coauthor of *The Schoolwide Enrichment Model, The Secondary Triad Model, Dilemmas in Talent Development in the Middle Years*, and a book published in 1998 about women's talent development entitled *Work Left Undone: Choices and Compromises of Talented Females*. Sally serves on several editorial boards, including *Gifted Child Quarterly*, and is a past President of the National Association for Gifted Children. She has been honored with the highest award in her field as the Distinguished Scholar of the National Association for Gifted Children and named a fellow of the American Psychological Association.